PE EXAM PREPARATION

CIVIL ENGINEERING
LICENSE REVIEW

Sixteenth Edition

Donald G. Newnan, PhD, PE Civil Eng., Editor

James H. Banks, PhD, PE, San Diego State University

Braja M. Das, PhD, PE, California State University, Sacramento

Bruce E. Larock, PhD, PE, University of California, Davis

Robert W. Stokes, PhD, Kansas State University

Alan Williams, PhD, SE, Chartered Eng., California Department of Transportation

Kenneth J. Williamson, PhD, PE, Oregon State University

President: Roy Lipner
Vice-President of Product Development and Publishing: Evan M. Butterfield
Editorial Project Manager: Laurie McGuire
Director of Production: Daniel Frey
Creative Director: Lucy Jenkins

Published by Kaplan® AEC Education,
a division of Dearborn Financial Publishing, Inc.®,
a Kaplan Professional Company®

30 South Wacker Drive
Chicago, IL 60606-7481
(312) 836-4400
www.kaplanaecengineering.com

C O N T E N T S

CHAPTER 1

Introduction 1
HOW TO USE THIS BOOK 1
BECOMING A PROFESSIONAL ENGINEER 2
CIVIL ENGINEERING PROFESSIONAL ENGINEER EXAM 2

CHAPTER 2

Building Structures 9
REINFORCED CONCRETE DESIGN 9
PRESTRESSED CONCRETE DESIGN 37
STRUCTURAL STEEL DESIGN 49
DESIGN OF WOOD STRUCTURES 81
REINFORCED MASONRY DESIGN 98
REFERENCES 105

CHAPTER 3

Bridge Structures 107
HIGHWAY BRIDGE LOADS 108
SEISMIC DESIGN 130
REINFORCED CONCRETE DESIGN 140
PRESTRESSED CONCRETE DESIGN 149
STRUCTURAL STEEL DESIGN 173
TIMBER STRUCTURES 185
REFERENCES 187

CHAPTER 4

Foundations and Retaining Structures 189
FOOTING DESIGN 189
RETAINING WALL 211
PILE FOUNDATIONS 224
SELECTED SYMBOLS AND ABBREVIATIONS 233
REFERENCES 234

CHAPTER 5

Seismic Design 235

EARTHQUAKE PHENOMENA 236

STRUCTURAL DYNAMICS 242

RESPONSE SPECTRA 252

MULTISTORY STRUCTURE 264

SIMPLIFIED LATERAL FORCE PROCEDURE 273

REDUNDANCY COEFFICIENT 275

LATERAL-FORCE-RESISTANT SYSTEM 278

STRUCTURAL ELEMENTS AND COMPONENTS 286

TORSION AND RIGIDITY 293

CONFIGURATION REQUIREMENTS 303

DYNAMIC LATERAL FORCE ANALYSIS 307

SEISMICALLY ISOLATED BUILDINGS 312

REFERENCES 316

CHAPTER 6

Hydraulics 319

INTRODUCTION 319

CONSERVATION LAWS 322

PUMPS AND TURBINES 329

OPEN CHANNEL FLOW 334

SELECTED SYMBOLS AND ABBREVIATIONS 342

REFERENCES 342

CHAPTER 7

Engineering Hydrology 343

INTRODUCTION 343

HYDROLOGIC ELEMENTS 343

WATERSHED HYDROGRAPHS 346

PEAK DISCHARGE ESTIMATION 352

HYDROLOGIC ROUTING 355

WELL HYDRAULICS 359

REFERENCES 366

CHAPTER 8

Water Quality, Treatment, and Distribution 367

WATER DISTRIBUTION 367

WATER QUALITY 371

DISSOLVED OXYGEN RELATIONSHIPS IN STREAMS   375

WATER TREATMENT   378

SELECTED SYMBOLS AND ABBREVIATIONS   388

BIBLIOGRAPHY   388

CHAPTER 9

Wastewater Treatment   391

WASTEWATER FLOWS   391

SEWER DESIGN   392

WASTEWATER CHARACTERISTICS   393

WASTEWATER TREATMENT   395

SLUDGE TREATMENT AND DISPOSAL   409

SELECTED SYMBOLS AND ABBREVIATIONS   413

BIBLIOGRAPHY   413

CHAPTER 10

Geotechnical Engineering   415

PARTICLE SIZE   416

SPECIFIC GRAVITY OF SOIL SOLIDS, G_s 417

WEIGHT-VOLUME RELATIONSHIPS   417

RELATIVE DENSITY   419

CONSISTENCY OF CLAYEY SOILS   420

PERMEABILITY   421

FLOW NETS   422

EFFECTIVE STRESS   423

VERTICAL STRESS UNDER A FOUNDATION   425

CONSOLIDATION   427

SHEAR STRENGTH   432

LATERAL EARTH PRESSURE   432

BEARING CAPACITY OF SHALLOW FOUNDATIONS   437

DEEP (PILE) FOUNDATIONS   440

SELECTED SYMBOLS AND ABBREVIATIONS   443

REFERENCES   445

CHAPTER 11

Transportation Engineering   447

TRANSPORTATION PLANNING   449

HIGHWAY SYSTEM CHARACTERISTICS AND DESIGN CONTROLS   452

STATISTICAL METHODS   470

TRAFFIC ENGINEERING STUDIES   477

HIGHWAY ROUTE SURVEYING   484

AASHTO GEOMETRIC DESIGN GUIDELINES   499

HIGHWAY CAPACITY MANUAL   505

TRAFFIC CONTROL DEVICES   529

TRAFFIC SIGNALS TIMING   532

PAVEMENT DESIGN   538

NOTES ON SELECTED SPECIAL TOPICS   548

REFERENCES   551

APPENDIX A

Engineering Economics   555

CASH FLOW   556

TIME VALUE OF MONEY   558

EQUIVALENCE   558

COMPOUND INTEREST   559

NOMINAL AND EFFECTIVE INTEREST   566

SOLVING ENGINEERING ECONOMICS PROBLEMS   568

PRESENT WORTH   568

FUTURE WORTH OR VALUE   571

ANNUAL COST   572

RATE OF RETURN ANALYSIS   573

BENEFIT-COST ANALYSIS   578

BREAKEVEN ANALYSIS   579

OPTIMIZATION   579

VALUATION AND DEPRECIATION   581

TAX CONSEQUENCES   586

INFLATION   587

RISK ANALYSIS   589

REFERENCE   591

INTEREST TABLES   592

Index   603

PERMISSIONS

Figure 6.2 reprinted by permission of ASME.
Source: Moody, L., F, *Transactions of the ASME*, Volume 66: pp. 671-684. 1944.

Table 6.2 reprinted with permission from: Larock, Bruce E., Roland W. Jeppson, and Gary Z. Watters, *Hydraulics of Pipeline Systems*, 2000. Copyright CRC Press, Boca Raton, Florida.

Table 6.3 reprinted by permission of Victor L. Streeter.
Source: Streeter, Victor L., *Handbook of Fluid Dynamics*, McGraw-Hill Education. 1961.

Table 6.4 reprinted by permission of Lora S. Chow Wang.
Source: Chow, V.T., *Open-Channel Hydraulics*, Copyright 1959, Estate of V.T. Chow.

Table 7.1 reprinted with permission of the publisher, ASCE.
Source: *Design and Construction of Sanitary and Storm Sewers, Manual No. 37, 1986*. ASCE (American Society of Civil Engineers).

Table 7.2 reprinted by permission of Pearson Education, Inc., Upper Saddle River, NJ.
Source: Bedient, Philip B. and Wayne C. Huber, *Hydrology and Floodplain Analysis*, 3rd edition, copyright 2002.

Figures 11.3, 11.6 reprinted by permission of AASHTO.
Source: *A Policy on Geometric Design of Highways and Streets, 4th Edition*, 2001. American Association of State Highway and Transportation Officials.

Tables 11.10a-b, 11.11a-b, 11.12a-b, 11.13a-b, 11.14a-b, 11.15a-d, 11.16a-b, 11.17, 11.18; and Figures 11.15a-b, 11.17 reprinted with permission of the Transportation Research Board.
Source: *Highway Capacity Manual 2000, U.S. Customary and Metric Units;* Exhibits 16-1 and 16-2, p. 16-2; Exhibit 16-3, p. 16-3; Exhibit 17-2, p. 17-2; Exhibit 21-2, p. 21-3; Exhibit 21-3, p. 21-4; Exhibit 23-2, p. 23-4; Exhibit 24-2, p. 24-3; Exhibit 24-6, p. 24-6; Exhibit 24-7, p. 24-8; Exhibit 25-4, p. 25-5; Exhibit 25-7, p. 25-8; and Exhibit 25-14, p. 25-14. Copyright National Academy of Sciences, Washington, D.C.

CHAPTER 1

Introduction

Donald G. Newnan

OUTLINE

HOW TO USE THIS BOOK 1

BECOMING A PROFESSIONAL ENGINEER 2
Education ■ Fundamentals of Engineering (FE/EIT)
Exam ■ Experience ■ Professional Engineer Exam

CIVIL ENGINEERING PROFESSIONAL ENGINEER EXAM 2
Examination Development ■ Examination Structure ■ Exam
Dates ■ Exam Procedure ■ Preparing For and Taking
the Exam ■ Exam Day Preparations ■ What to Take to the Exam

HOW TO USE THIS BOOK

Civil Engineering: License Review and its companion text, *Civil Engineering: Problems and Solutions*, form a two-part approach to preparing for the Principles and Practice of Civil Engineering exam:

■ *Civil Engineering: License Review* contains the conceptual review of civil engineering topics for the exam, including key terms, equations, analytical methods and reference data. Because it does not contain problems and solutions, the book can be brought into the open-book PE exam as one of your references.

■ *Civil Engineering: Problems & Solutions* provides problems for you to solve in order to test your understanding of concepts and techniques. Ideally, you should solve these problems after completing your conceptual review. Then, compare your answers to the detailed solutions provided, to get a sense of how well you have mastered the content and what topics you may want to review further. This book also includes a sample exam with solutions, so that you can simulate the experience of taking the PE test within its actual time constraints and with questions that match the test format. Take the sample exam after you're satisfied with your review of concepts and problem-solving techniques, to test your readiness for the real exam.

BECOMING A PROFESSIONAL ENGINEER

To achieve registration as a professional engineer there are four distinct steps: (1) education, (2) the Fundamentals of Engineering/Engineer-In-Training (FE/EIT) exam, (3) professional experience, and (4) the professional engineer (PE) exam, more formally known as the Principles and Practice of Engineering Exam. These steps are described in the following sections.

Education

The obvious appropriate education is a B.S. degree in civil engineering from an accredited college or university. This is not an absolute requirement. Alternative, but less acceptable, education is a B.S. degree in something other than civil engineering, or a degree from a non-accredited institution, or four years of education but no degree.

Fundamentals of Engineering (FE/EIT) Exam

Most people are required to take and pass this eight-hour multiple-choice examination. Different states call it by different names (Fundamentals of Engineering, E.I.T., or Intern Engineer), but the exam is the same in all states. It is prepared and graded by the National Council of Examiners for Engineering and Surveying (NCEES). Review materials for this exam are found in other Engineering Press books such as *Fundamentals of Engineering: FE Exam Preparation*.

Experience

Typically one must have four years of acceptable experience before being permitted to take the Professional Engineer exam (California requires only two years). Both the length and character of the experience will be examined. It may, of course, take more than four years to acquire four years of acceptable experience.

Professional Engineer Exam

The second national exam is called Principles and Practice of Engineering by NCEES, but just about everyone else calls it the Professional Engineer or P.E. exam. All states, plus Guam, the District of Columbia, and Puerto Rico, use the same NCEES exam.

CIVIL ENGINEERING PROFESSIONAL ENGINEER EXAM

The reason for passing laws regulating the practice of civil engineering is to protect the public from incompetent practitioners. Beginning about 1907 the individual states began passing *title* acts regulating who could call themselves civil engineers. As the laws were strengthened, the *practice* of civil engineering was limited to those who were registered civil engineers, or working under the supervision of a registered civil engineer. There is no national registration law; registration is based on individual state laws and is administered by boards of registration in each of the states. A listing of the state boards is in Table 1.1.

Table 1.1 State boards of registration for engineers

State/Territory	Web Site	Telephone
AK	www.dccd.state.ak.us/occ/pael.htm	(907) 465-1676
AL	www.bels.state.al.us	(334) 242-5568
AR	www.state.ar.us/pels	(501) 682-2824
AZ	www.btr.state.az.us	(602) 364-4930
CA	dca.ca.gov/pels/contacts/htm	(916) 263-2230
CO	dova.state.co.us/engineers _surveyors	(303) 894-7788
CT	state.ct.us/dcp	(806) 713-6145
DC		(202) 442-4320
DE	www.dape.org	(302) 368-6708
FL	www.fbpe.org	(850) 521-0500
GA	www.sos.state.ga.us/plb/pels/	(478) 207-1450
GU	www.guam-peals.org	(671) 646-3138
HI	www.hawaii.gov/dcca/pbl	(808) 586-2702
IA	www.ia.us/government/com	(515) 281-4126
ID	www.state.id.us/ipels/index.htm	(208) 334-3860
IL	www.kpr.state.il.us	(217) 785-0877
IN	www.in.gov/pla/bandc/engineers	(317) 232-2980
KS	www.accesskansas.org/ksbtp	(785) 296-3053
KY	www.kybocls.state.ky.us	(502) 573-2680
LA	www.lapels.com	(225) 925-6291
MA	www.state.ma.us/reg	(617) 727-9957
MD	www.dllr.state.md.us	(410) 230-6322
ME	www.professionals.maincusa.com	(207) 287-3236
MI	www.michigan.gov/cis/0,1607,%207-154-10557_12992_14016-41928--,00.html	(517) 241-9253
MN	www.aclslagid.state.mn.us	(651) 296-2388
MO	www.pr.mo.gov/apelsla.asp	(573) 751-0047
MP		(011)-(670) 234-5897
MS	www.pepls.state.ms.us	(601) 359-6160
MT	www.discoveringmontana.com/dli/bsb/license/bsd_board/pel_board/board_page.htm	(406) 841-2367
NC	www.ncbels.org	(919) 881-4000
ND	www.ndpelsboard.org/	(701) 258-0786
NE	www.ea.state.ne.us	(402) 471-2021
NH	www.state.nh.us/jtboard/home.htm	(603) 271-2219
NJ	www.state.nj.us	(973) 504-6460
NM	www.state.nm.us/pepsboard	(518) 827-7561
NV	www.boe.state.nv.us	(775) 688-1231
NY	www.op.nysed.gov	(518) 474-3846 3817×140
OH	www.ohiopeps.org	(614) 466-3651
OK	www.pels.state.ok.us/	(405) 521-2874
OR	www.osbeels.org	(503) 362-2666
PA	www.dos.state.pa.us/eng	(717) 783-7049
PR	P.O. Box 3271, San Juan 00904	(787) 722-2122
RI	www.bdp.state.ri.us	(401) 222-2565
SC	www.lln.state.sc.us/POL/Engineers	(803) 896-4422

(Continued)

Table 1.1 State boards of registration for engineers *(Continued)*

State/Territory	Web Site	Telephone
SD	www.state.sd.us/dol/boards/engineer	(605) 394-2510
TN	www.state.tn.us/commerce/boards/ae	(615) 741-3221
TX	www.tbpe.state.tx.us	(512) 440-7723
UT	www.dopl.utah.gov	(801) 530-6632
VA	www.state.va.us/dopr	(804) 367-8514
VI	www.dlca.gov.vi/pro-aels.html	(340) 773-2226
VT	www.vtprofessionals.org	(802) 828-3256
WA	www.dol.wa.gov/engineers/engfront.htm	(360) 664-1595
WI	www.drl.state.wi.us	(608) 261-7096
WV	www.wvpebd.org	(304) 558-3554
WY	www.wrds.uwyo.edu/wrds/borpe/borpe.html	(307) 777-6155

Examination Development

Initially the states wrote their own examinations, but beginning in 1966 the NCEES took over the task for some of the states. Now the NCEES exams are used by all states. This greatly eases the ability of a civil engineer to move from one state to another and achieve registration in the new state. Ten thousand civil engineers take the exam each year. As a result, about 44 percent of all civil engineers are registered professional engineers.

The development of the civil engineering exam is the responsibility of the NCEES Committee on Examinations for Professional Engineers. The committee is composed of people from industry, consulting, and education, plus consultants and subject matter experts. The starting point for the exam is a civil engineering task analysis survey, which NCEES does at roughly 5- to 10-year intervals. People in industry, consulting, and education are surveyed to determine what civil engineers do and what knowledge is needed. From this NCEES develops what it calls a "matrix of knowledge" that forms the basis for the civil engineering exam structure described in the next section.

The actual exam questions are prepared by the NCEES committee members, subject matter experts, and other volunteers. All people participating must hold professional registration. Using workshop meetings and correspondence by mail, the questions are written and circulated for review. The problems relate to current professional situations. They are structured to quickly orient one to the requirements, so that the examinee can judge whether he or she can successfully solve it. Although based on an understanding of engineering fundamentals, the problems require the application of practical professional judgment and insight.

Examination Structure

The exam is organized into breadth and depth sections.

The morning breadth exam consists of 40 multiple-choice questions covering the following five areas of civil engineering; environmental, geotechnical, structural, transportation, and water resources. Each topic area represents 20 percent of the exam questions. You will have four hours to complete the breadth exam.

The afternoon depth portion is actually five exams, each one focusing on one of the five breadth areas. For each depth exam, the topic of focus makes up 65 percent of the questions, with the balance being related topics. You can choose the depth exam you wish to take; the obvious choice is whichever one best matches your training and professional practice. You will have four hours to answer the 40 multiple-choice questions that make up the depth exam.

Both the breadth and depth questions include four possible answers (A, B, C, D) and are objectively scored by computer.

For more information on the topics and subtopics and their relative weights on the breadth and depth portions, visit the NCEES Web site at www.ncees.org.

Exam Dates

The National Council of Examiners for Engineering and Surveying (NCEES) prepares Civil Engineering Professional Engineer exams for use on a Friday in April and October of each year. Some state boards administer the exam twice a year in their state, whereas others offer the exam once a year. The scheduled exam dates are:

	April	October
2005	15	28
2006	21	27
2007	20	26
2008	11	24

People seeking to take a particular exam must apply to the state board several months in advance.

Exam Procedure

Before the morning four-hour session begins, the proctors pass out an exam booklet and solutions pamphlet to each examinee.

The solution pamphlet contains grid sheets on right-hand pages. Only the work on these grid sheets will be graded. The left-hand pages are blank and are to be used for scratch paper. The scratchwork will not be considered in the scoring.

If you finish more than 30 minutes early, you may turn in the booklets and leave. In the last 30 minutes, however, you must remain to the end to ensure a quiet environment for all those still working and the orderly collection of materials.

The afternoon session will begin following a one-hour lunch break. The afternoon exam booklet will be distributed along with an answer sheet.

Preparing For and Taking the Exam

Give yourself time to prepare for the exam in a calm and unhurried way. Many candidates like to begin several months before the actual exam. Target a number of hours per day or week that you will study, and reserve blocks of time for doing so. Creating a review schedule on a topic-by-topic basis is a good idea. Remember to allow time for both reviewing concepts and solving practice problems. You may want to prioritize the time you spend reviewing specific topics according to their relative weight on the exam, as identified by NCEES, or by your areas of strength and weakness.

In addition to reviewing material your own, you may want to join a study group or take a review course. A group study environment might help you stay committed to a study plan and schedule. Group members can create additional practice problems for one another and share tips and tricks.

People familiar with the psychology of exam taking have several suggestions for people as they prepare to take an exam.

1. Exam taking really involves two skills. One is the skill of illustrating knowledge that you know. The other is the skill of exam taking. The first may be enhanced by a systematic review of the technical material. Exam-taking skills, on the other hand, may be improved by practice with similar problems presented in the exam format.

2. Since there is no deduction for guessing on the multiple choice problems, answers should be given for all of them. Even when one is going to guess, a logical approach is to attempt to first eliminate one or two of the four alternatives. If this can be done, the chance of selecting a correct answer obviously improves from 1 in 4 to 1 in 3 or 1 in 2.

3. Plan ahead with a strategy. Which is your strongest area? Can you expect to see one or two problems in this area? What about your second strongest area? What will you do if you still must find problems in other areas?

4. Plan ahead with a time allocation. Compute how much time you will allow for each of the five subject areas in the breadth exam and the relevant topics in the depth exam. You might allocate a little less time per problem for those areas in which you are most proficient, leaving a little more time in subjects that are difficult for you. Your time plan should include a reserve block for especially difficult problems, for checking your scoring sheet, and to make last-minute guesses on problems you did not work. Your strategy might also include time allotments for two passes through the exam—the first to work all problems for which answers are obvious to you, and the second to return to the more complex, time-consuming problems and the ones at which you might need to guess. A time plan is very important. It gives you the confidence of being in control, and at the same time keeps you from making the serious mistake of misallocation of time in the exam.

5. Read all four multiple-choice answers before making a selection. An answer in a multiple-choice question is sometimes a plausible decoy—not the best answer.

6. Do not change an answer unless you are absolutely certain you have made a mistake. Your first reaction is likely to be correct.

7. Do not sit next to a friend, a window, or other potential distractions.

Exam Day Preparations

The exam day will be a stressful and tiring one. This will be no day to have unpleasant surprises. For this reason we suggest that an advance visit be made to the examination site. Try to determine such items as

1. How much time should I allow for travel to the exam on that day? Plan to arrive about 15 minutes early. That way you will have ample time, but not too much time. Arriving too early, and mingling with others who also are anxious, will increase your anxiety and nervousness.

2. Where will I park?

3. How does the exam site look? Will I have ample workspace? Where will I stack my reference materials? Will it be overly bright (sunglasses), cold (sweater), or noisy (earplugs)? Would a cushion make the chair more comfortable?

4. Where are the drinking fountain, lavatory facilities, pay phone?

5. What about food? Should I take something along for energy in the exam? A bag lunch during the break probably makes sense.

What to Take to the Exam

The NCEES guidelines say you may bring only the following reference materials and aids into the examination room for your personal use:

1. Handbooks and textbooks, including the applicable design standards.

2. Bound reference materials, provided the materials remain bound during the entire examination. The NCEES defines "bound" as books or materials fastened securely in their covers by fasteners that penetrate all papers. Examples are ring binders, spiral binders and notebooks, plastic snap binders, brads, screw posts, and so on.

3. Battery-operated, silent, nonprinting, noncommunicating calculators. Beginning with the April 2004 exam, NCEES has implemented a more stringent policy regarding permitted calculators. For more details, see the NCEES website (www.ncees.org), which includes the updated policy and a list of frequently asked questions about permitted calculators. You also need to determine whether or not your state permits preprogrammed calculators. Bring extra batteries for your calculator just in case; many people feel that bringing a second calculator is also a very good idea.

At one time NCEES had a rule barring "review publications directed principally toward sample questions and their solutions" in the exam room. This set the stage for restricting some kinds of publications from the exam. *State boards may adopt the NCEES guidelines, or adopt either more or less restrictive rules*. Thus an important step in preparing for the exam is to know what will—and will not—be permitted. We suggest that if possible you obtain a written copy of your state's policy for the specific exam you will be taking. Occasionally there has been confusion at individual examination sites, so a copy of the exact applicable policy will not only allow you to carefully and correctly prepare your materials, but will also ensure that the exam proctors will allow all proper materials that you bring to the exam.

As a general rule we recommend that you plan well in advance what books and materials you want to take to the exam. Then they should be obtained promptly so you use the same materials in your review that you will have in the exam.

License Review Books

The review books you use to prepare for the exam are good choices to bring to the exam itself. After weeks or months of studying, you will be very familiar with their organization and content, so you'll be able to quickly locate the material you want to reference during the exam. Keep in mind the caveat just discussed—some state boards will not permit you to bring in review books that consist largely of sample questions and answers.

Textbooks

If you still have your university textbooks, they are the ones you should use in the exam, unless they are too out of date. To a great extent the books will be like old friends with familiar notation.

Bound Reference Materials

The NCEES guidelines suggest that you can take any reference materials you wish, so long as you prepare them properly. You could, for example, prepare several volumes of bound reference materials, with each volume intended to cover a particular category of problem. Maybe the most efficient way to use this book would be to cut it up and insert portions of it in your individually prepared bound materials. Use tabs so that specific material can be located quickly. If you do a careful and systematic review of civil engineering, and prepare a lot of well-organized materials, you just may find that you are so well prepared that you will not have left anything of value at home.

Other Items

In addition to the reference materials just mentioned, you should consider bringing the following to the exam:

- *Clock*—You must have a time plan and a clock or wristwatch.

- *Exam assignment paperwork*—Take along the letter assigning you to the exam at the specified location. To prove you are the correct person, also bring something with your name and picture.

- *Items suggested by advance visit*—If you visit the exam site, you probably will discover an item or two that you need to add to your list.

- *Clothes*—Plan to wear comfortable clothes. You probably will do better if you are slightly cool.

- *Box for everything*—You need to be able to carry all your materials to the exam and have them conveniently organized at your side. Probably a cardboard box is the answer.

Building Structures

Alan Williams

OUTLINE

REINFORCED CONCRETE DESIGN 9
Mix Proportions ■ Control of Concrete Quality ■ Strength Design
Principles ■ Flexure of Reinforced Concrete Beams ■ Serviceability
Requirements ■ Shear and Torsion in Reinforced Concrete
Members ■ Bond and Anchorage in Reinforced
Concrete ■ Reinforced Concrete Columns

PRESTRESSED CONCRETE DESIGN 37
General Design Criteria ■ The Transfer Limit Stage ■ The Serviceability
Limit Stage ■ The Ultimate Limit Stage ■ Loss of Prestress ■ Shear
in Prestressed Concrete Members ■ Load Balancing Technique

STRUCTURAL STEEL DESIGN 49
Elastic Design of Steel Beams ■ Plate Girder Design ■ Composite
Beams ■ Compression Members ■ Combined Compression
and Flexure ■ Bolted Connections ■ Welded Connections

DESIGN OF WOOD STRUCTURES 81
Allowable Stresses ■ Wood Beams ■ Wood Columns ■ Plywood
Diaphragms ■ Plywood Shear Walls ■ Connections in Wood Members

REINFORCED MASONRY DESIGN 98
Quality Control ■ Allowable Stresses ■ Reinforced Masonry
Beams ■ Masonry Columns ■ Masonry Shear Walls

REFERENCES 105

REINFORCED CONCRETE DESIGN

Mix Proportions

Mix proportions may be specified either by weight or by volume in terms of the
ratios of fine aggregate and coarse aggregate to cement. For example, a 1:3:5 concrete
mix consist of three cubic feet (or pounds) of fine aggregate and five cubic feet (or
pounds) of coarse aggregate for each cubic foot (or pound) of cement used.

The water-cement ratio of the mix may be specified in terms of either weight or volume. One sack of cement measures one cubic foot and weighs 94 pounds. One gallon of water weighs 8.34 pounds, and one cubic foot of water contains 7.48 gallons. The water–cement ratio is based on the use of saturated surface dry aggregates, and any deficiency or excess of moisture from this value must be allowed for. The free moisture content of the aggregate is given by

$$m = (\gamma - \gamma_s)/\gamma_s$$

where γ = wet bulk density, γ_s = saturated surface dry bulk density, and $\gamma = \gamma_s(1 + m)$.

Fine aggregate, or sand, passes a Number 4 sieve whereas coarse aggregate, or stone, is retained on a Number 4 sieve. Typical properties of the materials used are

Material	Specific Gravity	Bulk Density
Cement	3.1	94
Sand	2.6	100
Stone	2.6	95
Water	1.0	62.4

The **yield** of a mix is the volume of concrete produced from one sack of cement and is calculated assuming that all the voids in the sand and stone are filled with cement, water, and entrained air. The ratio of entrained air to the total volume of air plus liquid and solids is

$$e = (V_e - V_s)/V_e$$

where V_s = volume of all solids, V_e = total volume solids plus entrained air, and $V_e = V_s/(1 - e)$. The yield of a mix without voids (that is, the solid volume) is given by the absolute volume method as

$$V_s = \Sigma(\gamma_s V/G\gamma_w)$$

where V = volume of the saturated surface dry constituent, G = specific gravity of the constituent, and γ_w = density of water. The **cement factor** is defined as the number of sacks of cement required to produce one cubic yard of concrete.

Example **2.1**

The required proportions of a concrete mix are 1:2.5:3.5 by weight with 5.5 gallons of water per sack and 5 percent air entrainment. The sand contains 4 percent excess moisture, and the stone 2 percent deficiency. Determine: (a) the yield of the mix, (b) the cement factor, and (c) the quantities of water and aggregate required to provide one cubic yard of concrete.

Solution

The solid volumes of the constituents for a one sack mix are

$$\begin{aligned}
\text{cement} &= 94 \times 1/(3.1 \times 62.4) &= 0.486 \text{ cubic feet} \\
\text{sand} &= 94 \times 2.5/(2.6 \times 62.4) &= 1.448 \text{ cubic feet} \\
\text{stone} &= 94 \times 3.5/(2.6 \times 62.4) &= 2.028 \text{ cubic feet} \\
\text{water} &= 5.5 \times 8.34/(1 \times 62.4) &= 0.734 \text{ cubic feet}
\end{aligned}$$

The total solid volume of all constituents is

$$V_s = 0.486 + 1.448 + 2.028 + 0.734 = 4.696 \text{ cubic feet}$$

Using 5 percent air entrainment, the yield is

$$V_e = V_s/(1 - e) = 4.696/(1 - 0.05) = 4.943 \text{ cubic feet per sack}$$

The cement factor is given by

$$c = 1 \times 27/4.943 = 5.46 \text{ sacks per cubic yard}$$

The weight of saturated surface dry sand required for each cubic yard of concrete is

$$W_s = 94 \times 2.5c = 94 \times 2.5 \times 5.46 = 1283 \text{ pounds}$$

Allowing for the 4 percent of excess moisture, the actual weight of sand required is

$$W = W_s(1 + m) = 1283(1 + 0.04) = 1334 \text{ pounds}$$

The weight of excess water in the sand is given by

$$W_f = W - W_s = 1334 - 1283 = 51 \text{ pounds}$$

The weight of saturated surface dry stone required for each cubic yard of concrete is

$$W_s = 94 \times 3.5c = 94 \times 3.5 \times 5.46 = 1796 \text{ pounds}$$

Allowing for the 2 percent moisture deficiency, the actual weight of stone required is

$$W = W_s(1 - m) = 1796(1 - 0.02) = 1760 \text{ pounds}$$

The water deficiency in the stone is

$$W_c = W_s - W = 1796 - 1760 = 36 \text{ pounds}$$

Hence, the total amount of water needed for each cubic yard of concrete is

$$W_w = 5.5c + (W_c - W_f)/8.34 = 5.5 \times 5.46 + (36 - 51)/8.34 = 28.23 \text{ gallons}$$

Thus, to produce one cubic yard of concrete, the constituents required are 5.46 sacks of cement, 1334 pounds of sand, 1760 pounds of stone, and 28.23 gallons of water.

Control of Concrete Quality

All concrete design and references are based upon the following publication[1]: *Building Code Requirements for Structural Concrete (ACI 318-02) and Commentary (ACI 318R-02)* as published by the American Concrete Institute.

To allow for variation in quality control at the concrete plant, the concrete mix must be designed for a target strength in excess of the specified design strength. ACI[1] Section 5.3 provides a statistical method of control based on the past test records of the concrete plant. When the records of at least 30 consecutive strength tests are available, based on similar materials and for a specified strength within 1000 pounds per square inch of the proposed specified strength, the required target strength, for $f_c \le 5000$ pounds per square inch, is given by the larger of ACI Equations (5-1) or (5-2) as

$$f'_{cr} = f'_c + 1.34s$$
$$f'_{cr} = f'_c + 2.33s - 500$$

where f'_{cr} = required target strength, f'_c = proposed specified design strength, and s = standard deviation of the strength tests.

ACI Equation (5-1) provides a probability that 1 in 100 of the average of three consecutive tests may be below f'_c. ACI Equation (5-2) provides a probability that 1 in 100 of the individual tests may be more than 500 pounds per square inch below f'_c. For a specified strengh of $f'_c > 5000$ pounds per square inch, the required target mean strength is given by the larger of ACI Equations (5-1) or (5-3) as

$$f'_{cr} = f'_c + 1.34s$$
$$f'_{cr} = 0.9f'_c + 2.33s$$

ACI Equation (5-3) provides a probability that 1 in 100 of the individual tests may be less than $0.9f'_c$. When the records of 15 to 29 consecutive strength tests only are available, the calculated standard deviation must be increased by a factor obtained from ACI Table 5.3.1.2.

Example **2.2**

A concrete plant is to provide a concrete mix with a specified design strength of 3000 pounds per square inch. The records of 15 consecutive strength tests are: 3050, 3100, 3150, 3250, 3300, 3350, 3480, 3500, 3520, 3650, 3700, 3750, 3850, 3900, 3950. What is the required target strength of the mix?

Solution

The mean strength is $\bar{u} = 3500$ pounds per square inch.
The standard deviation is $s = 295$ pounds per square inch.
From ACI Table 5.3.1.2, the modification factor for 15 records is 1.16.
Applying ACI Equation (5-2), the required target strength is given by

$$f'_{cr} = f'_c + 2.33 \times 1.16s - 500 = 3000 + 2.33 \times 1.16 \times 295 - 500$$
$$= 3297 \text{ pounds per square inch}$$

Applying ACI Equation (5-1), the required target strength is given by

$$f'_{cr} = f'_c + 1.34 \times 1.16s = 3000 + 1.34 \times 1.16 \times 295$$
$$= 3459 \text{ pounds per square inch, which governs}$$

Strength Design Principles

The basic requirement of designing for strength is to ensure that the design strength of a member is not less than the required ultimate strength. The latter consists of the service-level loads multiplied by appropriate load factors, and this is defined in ACI Equations (9-1) through (9-7), which now conform to ASCE[2] Section 2.3.2 Equations 1 through 7.

$$U = 1.4(D + F) \tag{9-1}$$
$$U = 1.2(D + F + T) + 1.6(L + H) + 0.5(L_r \text{ or } S \text{ or } R) \tag{9-2}$$
$$U = 1.2D + 1.6(L_r \text{ or } S \text{ or } R) + (1.0L \text{ or } 0.8W) \tag{9-3}$$
$$U = 1.2D + 1.6W + 1.0L + (0.5)(L_r \text{ or } S \text{ or } R) \tag{9-4}$$
$$U = 1.2D + 1.0E + 1.0L + 0.2S \tag{9-5}$$
$$U = 0.9D + 1.6W + 1.6H \tag{9-6}$$
$$U = 0.9D + 1.0E + 1.6H \tag{9-7}$$

where
- D = dead load
- E = earthquake load
- F = load due to fluids with well defined pressures and heights
- H = load due to lateral earth pressure or bulk materials
- L = live loads
- L_r = roof live load
- R = rain load
- S = snow load
- T = self-straining forces
- U = required strength
- W = wind load

Replace $1.0L$ by $0.5L$ in Equations (9-3) to (9-5) except for garages, places of public assembly, and all areas where $L > 100$ pounds per square foot.

 The design strength of a member consists of the theoretical ultimate strength of the member—the nominal strength—multiplied by the appropriate strength reduction factor, ϕ. Thus,

$$\phi \text{ (nominal strength)} \geq U$$

ACI Section 9.3 defines the reduction factor as $\phi = 0.90$ for flexure of tension-controlled sections, $\phi = 0.75$ for shear and torsion, $\phi = 0.70$ for compression members with spiral reinforcement, $\phi = 0.65$ for compression members with lateral ties, and $\phi = 0.65$ for bearing on concrete, except for post-tensioned anchorage zones where $\phi = 0.85$ and "strut-and-tie" models where $\phi = 0.75$.

Flexure of Reinforced Concrete Beams

The nominal strength of a rectangular beam, with tension reinforcement only, is derived from the assumed ultimate conditions shown in Figure 2.1. ACI Section 10.2.7.1 specifies an equivalent rectangular stress block in the concrete of $0.85f_c'$ with a depth of

$$a = A_s f_y / 0.85 f_c' b = \beta_1 c$$

where c = depth to neutral axis and β_1 = compression zone factor given in ACI Section 10.2.7.3. β_1 shall be taken as 0.85 for concrete strengths up to and including 4000 psi. For strengths above 4000 pounds per square inch, β_1 shall be reduced continuously at the rate of 0.05 for each 1000 pounds per square inch

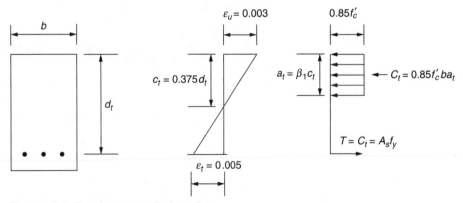

Figure 2.1 Tension-controlled section

of strength in excess of 4000 pounds per square inch, but β_1 shall not be taken less than 0.65. From Figure 2.1, the nominal strength of the member is derived as

$$M_n = A_s f_y d (1 - 0.59 \rho f_y / f_c')$$

where $\rho = A_s / bd$ = reinforcement ratio, $\phi M_n = 0.9 M_n$ = design strength, and M_u = applied factored moment $\leq \phi M_n$. This expression may also be rearranged to give the reinforcement ratio required to provide a given factored moment, M_u, as

$$\rho = 0.85 f_c' \left[1 - \sqrt{1 - 2K/0.9 \times 0.85 f_c'} \right] / f_y$$

where $K = M_u / bd^2$.

These expressions may be readily applied using standard calculator programs[3] and tables.[4,5]

Nominal strength of a member or cross-section subject to flexure (or combined flexure and axial load) must be based upon equilibrium of forces and strain compatibility. The maximum usable strain at extreme concrete compression fiber is assumed equal to 0.003 in accordance with ACI Section 10.2.3.

As specified in ACI Section 10.3.4, sections are tension-controlled when the net tensile strain in the extreme tension steel is equal to or greater than 0.005 just as the concrete reaches its assumed strain limit of 0.003. For nonprestressed flexural members and nonprestressed members with axial load less than $0.10 f_c' A_g$, the net tensile strain shall be not less than 0.004.

$$\text{when } \varepsilon_s \leq 0.005 \quad \text{then} \quad A_s f_s = A_s E_s \varepsilon_s \quad \text{and} \quad \phi \leq 0.9$$
$$\text{when } \varepsilon_s \geq 0.005 \quad \text{then} \quad A_s f_s = A_s f_y \quad \text{and} \quad \phi = 0.9 \text{ for flexure}$$

For a tension-controlled section the following expressions may be derived:

$$c_t = 0.375 d_t$$
$$a_t = \beta_1 c_t = 0.375 \beta_1 d_t$$
$$C_t = 0.85 f_c' b a_t = 0.319 \beta_1 f_c' b d_t$$
$$T = A_s f_y = C_t$$
$$A_s = 0.319 \beta_1 f_c' b d_t / f_y$$
$$\rho_t = A_s / (b d_t) = 0.319 \beta_1 f_c' / f_y$$
$$\omega_t = \rho_t f_y / f_c' = 0.319 \beta_1$$
$$M_{nt} = \omega_t (1 - 0.59 \omega_t) f_c' b d_t^2$$
$$R_{nt} = M_{nt} / b d_t^2 = \omega_t (1 - 0.59 \omega_t) f_c'$$

These parameters are tabulated in Table 2.1.

Table 2.1 Moment factors and reinforcement ratios for tension-controlled sections

f_c'	β_1	$f_y = 40,000$			$f_y = 60,000$		
		ρ_t	ϕR_{nt}	ω_t	ρ_t	ϕR_{nt}	ω_t
3000	0.85	0.0203	615	0.271	0.0136	615	0.271
3500	0.85	0.0237	718	0.271	0.0158	718	0.271
4000	0.85	0.0271	820	0.271	0.0181	820	0.271
4500	0.83	0.0298	906	0.265	0.0199	906	0.265
5000	0.80	0.0319	975	0.255	0.0213	975	0.255

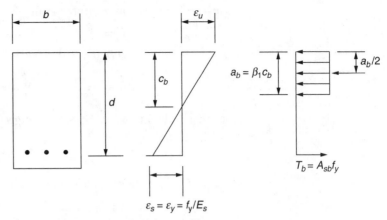

Figure 2.2 Balanced strain condition

The minimum area of steel for flexural members is given by ACI Equation (10-3) as

$$A_{s_{min}} = 3\sqrt{f_c'}\, b_w d/f_y \text{ but not less than } 200 b_w d/f_y'$$

In accordance with ACI Section 10.5.3, the required minimum area of steel need not be applied if at every section the area of tensile reinforcement provided is at least one-third greater than that required by analysis.

A balanced strain condition, as shown in Figure 2.2, occurs when extreme compression fiber of the concrete reaches ε_u simultaneously with first yield strain of steel $\varepsilon_s = \varepsilon_y = f_y/E_s$. Note for Grade 60 steel ε_y may be rounded to $\varepsilon_y = 0.002$.

$$\frac{c_b}{d} = \frac{\varepsilon_u}{\varepsilon_u + \varepsilon_y} = \frac{0.003}{0.003 + f_y/29,000,000} = \frac{0.003}{0.003 + \varepsilon_y}$$

ACI Section 10.3.5 limits the maximum amount of reinforcement in terms of a minimum net tensile strain of $\varepsilon_t = 0.004$. At net tensile strain or $\varepsilon_t = 0.004$, the ϕ factor is reduced to 0.812.

When the applied factored moment exceeds the maximum design strength of a singly reinforced member that has the maximum allowable reinforcement ratio, compression reinforcement and additional tensile reinforcement must be provided, as shown in Figure 2.3. The difference between the applied factored moment and the maximum design moment strength of a singly reinforced section is

$$M_r = M_u - M_{max} = \text{residual moment}$$

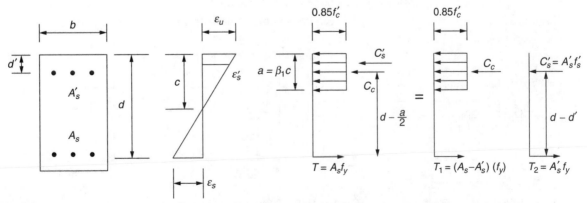

Figure 2.3 Rectangular section with compression reinforcement

Case 1: Compression reinforcement A'_s yields:

$$f'_s = f_y$$

$$a = (A_s - A'_s)(f_y)/(0.85f'_c b)$$

$$M_n = (A_s - A'_s)(f_y)\left(d - \frac{a}{2}\right) + A'_s f_y(d - d')$$

Note that A'_s yields when the following (for Grade 60 reinforcement, with $\varepsilon_y = 0.00207$) is satisfied:

$$d'/c < 0.31 \quad \text{where} \quad c = a/\beta_1$$

Case 2: Compression reinforcement does not yield:

$$f'_s = E_s \varepsilon'_s = E_s \varepsilon_u \left(\frac{c - d'}{c}\right) < f_y$$

Determine location of neutral axis from

$$c^2 - \frac{(A_s f_y - 87 A'_s)c}{0.85 \beta_1 f'_c b} - \frac{87 A'_s d'}{0.85 \beta_1 f'_c b} = 0$$

where f'_c and f_y have units of ksi.

$$M_n = 0.85 f'_c ab\left(d - \frac{a}{2}\right) + A'_s f'_s(d - d')$$

where
$$a = \beta_1 c$$

The conditions at ultimate load in a flanged member, when the depth of the equivalent rectangular stress block exceeds the flange thickness, are shown in Figure 2.4. The nominal moment of resistance is

$$M_n = (A_s - A_{sf})(f_y)\left(d - \frac{a}{2}\right) + (A_{sf})\left(d - \frac{h_f}{2}\right)$$

where A_{sf} is the area of reinforcement required to equilibrate compressive strength of overhanging flanges, and

$$A_{sf} = (0.85f'_c)(b - b_w)(h_f/f_y)$$
$$a = (A_s - A_{sf})(f_y)/(0.85f'_c b_w)$$
$$b = \text{effective flange width from ACI Section 8.10}$$

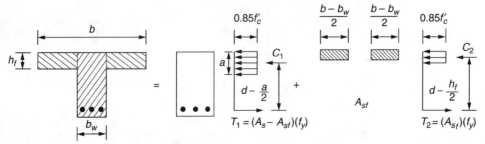

Figure 2.4   Flanged section with tension reinforcement only

Example **2.3**

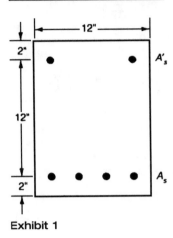

Exhibit 1

The reinforced concrete beam shown in Exhibit 1 is reinforced with Grade 60 bars at the positions indicated and has a concrete cylinder strength of 3000 pounds per square inch. The beam carries a superimposed load of 2 kips per foot run over an effective span of 20 feet. Determine the areas of tension and compression steel required.

Solution

The weight of the beam is $w_D = 16 \times 12 \times 0.15/144 = 0.20$ kips per foot.
The dead load moment is given by $M_D = w_D l^2/8 = 0.2 \times 20^2/8 = 10$ kip-feet.
The live load moment is given by $M_L = w_L l^2/8 = 2 \times 20^2/8 = 100$ kip-feet.
The factored moment at midspan is obtained from ACI Equation (9-2) as

$$M_u = 1.2M_D + 1.6M_L = 1.2 \times 10 + 1.6 \times 100 = 172 \text{ kip-feet}$$

The compression zone factor is given by ACI Section 10.2.7.3 as $\beta_1 = 0.85$.

$$
\begin{aligned}
c_t &= 0.375 d_t \\
&= 0.375 \times 14 = 5.25 \text{ inches} \\
a_t &= \beta_1 c_t \\
&= 0.375 \beta_1 d_t = 0.375 \times 0.85 \times 14 = 4.46 \text{ inches} \\
C_t &= 0.85 f'_c b' a_t \\
&= 0.319 \times 0.85 \times 3 \times 12 \times 14 = 136.7 \text{ kips} \\
T &= C_t = A_s f_y
\end{aligned}
$$

Therefore

$$A_m = C_t/f_y = 136.7/60 = 2.27 \text{ square inches}$$

Alternatively, from Table 2.1,

$$
\begin{aligned}
A_m &= \rho_t bd \\
&= 0.01355 \times 12 \times 14 \\
&= 2.27 \text{ square inches} \\
M_n &= A_m f_y (d_t - a_t/2) \\
&= 2.27 \times 60 \times 11.77/12 = 133.6 \text{ kip-feet} \\
\phi M_n &= 0.9 \times 133.6 \\
&= 120.2 \text{ kip-feet}
\end{aligned}
$$

Alternately, from Table 2.1,

$$
\begin{aligned}
\phi M_n &= \phi R_{nt} bd^2 \\
&= 615 \times 12 \times 14^2/12,000 \\
&= 120.2 \text{ kip-feet}
\end{aligned}
$$

Residual moment:

$$
\begin{aligned}
M_r &= M_u - dM_n \\
&= 172 - 120.2 \\
&= 51.8 \text{ kip-feet}
\end{aligned}
$$

Check to determine whether compression steel yields:

$$d'/c = 2/5.25 = 0.38 > 0.31$$

Therefore, compression steel does not yield.

$$f'_s = E_s \varepsilon_s = E_s \varepsilon_u \left(\frac{c - d'}{c} \right) < f_y$$

$$f'_s = (29,000)(0.003)\left(\frac{5.25 - 2}{5.25} \right) = 53.86 \text{ kips per square inch} < f_y$$

The force in the compression steel is

$$C'_s = M_r/(d - d')\phi$$
$$= (51.8)(12)/(14 - 2)(0.9) = 57.56 \text{ kips}$$

The required area of compression steel is

$$A'_s = C'_s/f'_s$$
$$= 57.56/53.86 = 1.07 \text{ square inches}$$

The total required area of tension steel is

$$A_s = A_m + A'_s f'_s/f_y$$
$$= 2.27 + 1.07 \times 53.86/60 = 3.23 \text{ square inches}$$

Serviceability Requirements

To provide protection from corrosion of the reinforcement, ACI Section 10.6 specifies limitations on reinforcement distribution to control flexural cracking. This is achieved by limiting the spacing of tension reinforcement to the value given by ACI Equation (10-4) as

$$s = 540/f_s - 2.5c_c$$
$$\leq 12(36/f_s)$$

where s = center-to-center spacing, in inches, of the tension reinforcement nearest to the extreme tension face

c_c = clear cover, in inches, from the nearest surface in tension to the surface of the nearest flexural reinforcement

f_s = stress in reinforcement at service load determined by the straight-line, elastic theory

$\approx 0.6f_y$

f_y = specified yield strength of the reinforcement

In addition, in accordance with ACI Section 10.6.7, to control cracking in the webs of beams with an effective depth exceeding 3 feet, skin reinforcement must be provided in the lower half of each face of the web. The total area of steel in both faces does not have to exceed one-half the required flexural tensile reinforcement. The spacing of the bars or wires shall not exceed the least of $d/6$, 12 inches, or $1000A_b/(d - 30)$.

Example **2.4**

The reinforced concrete T-beam shown in Exhibit 2 is reinforced with Grade 60 bars at the positions indicated. Determine the required skin reinforcement and check that the spacing of the tension reinforcement complies with ACI Section 10.6.

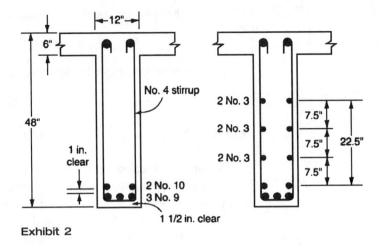

Exhibit 2

Solution

The total area of tensile reinforcement provided is

$$A_s = 3 \times 1 + 2 \times 1.27 = 5.54 \text{ square inches}$$

Concrete cover to the bottom layer of reinforcement is

$$c_c = 1.5 + 0.5 = 2 \text{ inches}$$

Height of the centroid of the bottom layer of tensile reinforcement is

$$y_1 = c_c + 1.128/2 = 2.56 \text{ inches}$$

Height of the centroid of the top layer of tensile reinforcement is

$$y_2 = y_1 + 1.128/2 + 1 + 1.27/2 = 4.76 \text{ inches}$$

Height of the centroid of the total tensile reinforcement is

$$\bar{y} = (1 \times 3y_1 + 1.27 \times 2y_2)/A_s = (1 \times 3 \times 2.56 + 1.27 \times 2 \times 4.76)/5.54 = 3.57 \text{ inches}$$

The effective depth of the tensile reinforcement is

$$d = h - \bar{y} = 48 - 3.57 = 44.43 \text{ inches}$$

Since the effective depth exceeds 3 feet, skin reinforcement must be provided in each face.

The required bars must be placed within a distance from the tensile reinforcement of

$$d/2 = 22.22 \text{ inches}$$

The maximum allowable spacing is the least of

$$s_{sk} = 12 \text{ inches}$$
$$s_{sk} = d/6 = 44.43/6 = 7.41 \text{ inches} \dots \text{ governs}$$
$$s_{sk} = 1000A_b/(d - 30)$$
$$= (1000)(0.11)/(44.43 - 30) = 7.62 \text{ inches}$$

Using No. 3 bars at 7.5-inch spacing, as shown in Exhibit 2, is satisfactory.

Stress in the reinforcement at service load may be taken as

$$f_s = 0.6f_y = 0.6 \times 60 = 36 \text{ kips per square inch}$$

The maximum allowable bar spacing is given by ACI Equation (10-4) as

$$s = 540/f_s - 2.5c_c = 540/36 - 2.5 \times 2 = 10 \text{ inches}$$

Hence, the bar spacing is satisfactory.

Allowable deflections are given in ACI Table 9.5(b). For reinforced concrete members not supporting deflection-sensitive construction, the allowable deflection may be deemed satisfied if the minimum thickness requirements of ACI Tables 9.5(a) and 9.5(c) are adopted.

For other conditions, the short-term deflection may be computed from the effective moment of inertia given by ACI Equation (9-8) and indicated in Figure 2.5 as

$$I_e = (M_{cr}/M_a)^3 I_g + [1 - (M_{cr}/M_a)^3] I_{cr}$$

where I_g = moment of inertia of gross concrete section, neglecting reinforcement
$$= bh^3/12$$
    I_{cr} = moment of inertia of the cracked transformed section
$$= b(kd)^3/3 + nA_s(d - kd)^2$$
    $B = b/nA_s$
$$kd = \frac{\sqrt{2Bd + 1} - 1}{B}$$
    $n = E_s/E_c$ = modular ratio
    $\rho = A_s/bd$ = reinforcement ratio
    M_a = maximum moment in the member
    M_{cr} = cracking moment of the section = $f_r I_g/y_t$ ... ACI Equation (9-9)
    $f_r = 7.5\sqrt{f_c'}$ = modules of rupture of normal-weight concrete... ACI Equation (9-10)
    y_t = Distance from centroidal axis of gross section, neglecting reinforcement, to extreme fiber in tension, inches

When subjected to long-term loads, creep and shrinkage of the member produces additional deflection, which can be determined by multiplying the short-term deflection by the factor

$$\lambda = \xi/(1 + 50\rho') \ldots \text{ACI Equation (9-11)}$$

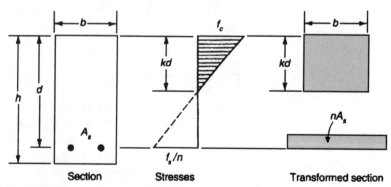

Figure 2.5   Reinforced member at service load

where ξ = time-dependent factor for sustained loads given in ACI
 Section 9.5.2.5
$\rho' = A_s'/b_w d$ = reinforcement ratio for compression reinforcement
$\xi = 2.0$ for duration ≥ 5 years
   $= 1.4$ for duration = 12 months
   $= 1.2$ for duration = 6 months
   $= 1.0$ for duration = 3 months

Shear and Torsion in Reinforced Concrete Members

The factored shear force acting on a member, in accordance with ACI
Equations (11-1) and (11-2), is resisted by the combined design shear strength of
the concrete and shear reinforcement. Thus, the factored applied shear is given by

$$V_u = \phi V_c + \phi V_s$$

where $\phi = 0.75$ = strength reduction factor for shear given by ACI Section 9.3.2.3
$V_c = 2\sqrt{f_c'}b_w d$ = nominal shear strength of normal-weight concrete from ACI
 Equation (11-3), with $\sqrt{f_c'} \leq 100$
$V_s = A_v f_y d/s$ = nominal shear strength of shear reinforcement from ACI Equation
 (11-15)
A_v = area of shear reinforcement
 s = spacing of shear reinforcement specified in ACI Section 11.5.4 as
  $\leq d/2$ or 24 inches when $V_s \leq 4\sqrt{f_c'}b_w d$...ACI Section 11.5.4.1
  $\leq d/4$ or 12 inches when $4\sqrt{f_c'}b_w d < V_s \leq 8\sqrt{f_c'}b_w d$...ACI Section 11.5.4.3

The dimensions of the section or the strength of the concrete must be increased,
in accordance with ACI Section 11.5.6.9, to ensure that $V_s \not> 8\sqrt{f_c'}b_w d$.
 As specified in ACI Section 11.5.5.1, a minimum area of shear reinforcement
is required when

$$V_u > \phi V_c/2 = V_{u(min)}$$

and the minimum area of shear reinforcement is given by ACI Equation (11-13) as

$$A_v = 0.75\sqrt{f_c'}\frac{b_w s}{f_y}, \text{ but not less than } A_{v(min)} = 50 b_w s/f_y$$

When the support reaction produces a compressive stress in the member, ACI
Section 11.1.3.1 specifies that the critical factored shear force is that which is
acting at a distance equal to the effective depth from the face of the support.
Figure 2.6 summarizes the shear provisions of the Code, and Figure 2.7 illustrates
the design principles involved.
 It is assumed, in ACI Section R11.6, that, after cracking, all torsion is resisted
by torsion reinforcement and the concrete is ineffective. In addition, it is assumed
that the shear strength of the concrete V_c is unaffected by the torsion. When both
shear and torsion reinforcements are required, the sum of the individual areas
must be provided in accordance with ACI Section 11.6.3.8. The spacing of the
reinforcement is governed by the minimum required spacing of either the shear
or the torsion reinforcement.

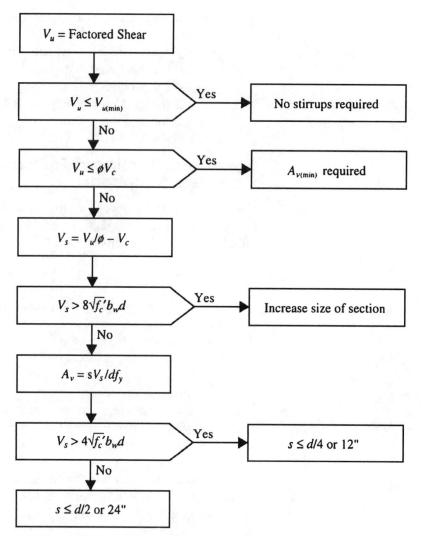

Figure 2.6 Flowchart of design for shear

In an indeterminate structure, redistribution of internal forces is possible by reducing torsional strength while providing a compensating increase in flexural and shear strength. This condition is referred to as **compatibility torsion.** For this condition, in accordance with ACI Section 11.6.2.2, the member may be designed for the factored torque causing cracking, which is given by

$$T_u = 4\phi\sqrt{f_c'}\left(A_{cp}^2/p_{cp}\right)$$

where A_{cp} = area enclosed by the outside perimeter of the concrete cross section
   p_{cp} = outside perimeter of the concrete cross section
   ϕ = strength reduction factor
   = 0.75...from ACI Section 9.3.2.3

ACI Section 11.6.1 specifies that torsional effects may be neglected and closed stirrups are not required when the factored torque is given by

$$T_u \leq \phi\sqrt{f_c'}\left(A_{cp}^2/p_{cp}\right)$$

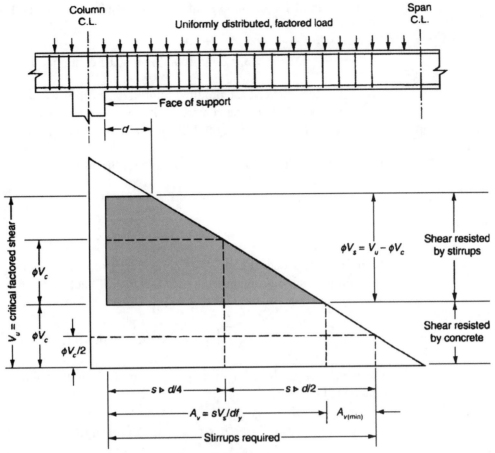

Figure 2.7 Shear in a reinforced concrete beam

When the factored shear exceeds this value, reinforcement shall be provided to resist the full torsion.

ACI Section 11.6.2.4 specifies that the **critical factored torsion** is that acting at a distance equal to the effective depth from the face of the support. If a concentrated torque occurs within this distance, the critical section shall be taken at the face of the support.

ACI Section R11.6.3.6 specifies that the resistance to torsion is provided mainly by closed stirrups, longitudinal bars, and concrete compression diagonals. The concrete outside the closed stirrups is relatively ineffective.

The area of **closed stirrups** required is specified in ACI Section 11.6.3.6 as

$$T_n = (2A_o A_t f_{yv}/s)(\cot\theta) \ldots \text{ACI Equation (11-21)}$$

where A_t = area of one leg of a closed stirrup
   f_{yv} = yield strength of the closed stirrups
   s = spacing of closed stirrups
   $A_o = 0.85A_{oh}$
   A_{oh} = area enclosed by the centerline of the closed stirrups
   θ = angle of compression diagonals with horizontal

In accordance with ACI Section 11.6.3.6 it is permitted to take $\cot\theta = 1$.

The area of longitudinal reinforcement required is specified in ACI Section 11.6.3.7 and is given by

$$A_l = (A_t p_h f_{yv} / f_{yl} s)(\cot^2 \theta) \dots \text{ACI Equation (11-22)}$$

where A_l = total area of longitudinal reinforcement to resist torsion
p_h = perimeter of the centerline of the closed stirrups
f_{yl} = yield strength of the longitudinal reinforcement

To prevent buckling of the longitudinal bars, the **minimum diameter** specified by ACI Section 11.6.6.2 is

$$d_{bl} = 0.042s$$
$$\geq \text{No. 3 bar}$$

To ensure that sudden failure does not occur at torsional cracking, a **minimum area** of torsional reinforcement is specified in ACI Sections 11.6.5.2 and 11.6.5.3 when the factored torsion exceeds

$$T_u = \phi \sqrt{f_c'} \left(A_{cp}^2 / p_{cp} \right) \dots \text{ACI Section 11.6.1(a)}$$

The minimum combined area of stirrups for shear and torsion is given by ACI Equation (11-23) as

$$(A_v + 2A_t) = 0.75 \sqrt{f_c'} b_w s / f_{yv} \text{ but not less than } (A_v + 2A_t) = 50 b_w s / f_{yv}$$

where A_v = area of two legs of a closed stirrups for shear resistance
A_t = area of one leg of a closed stirrup for torsion resistance

The total **minimum** area of longitudinal reinforcement for torsion is given by ACI Equation (11-24) as

$$A_{l(\min)} = 5 A_{cp} \sqrt{f_c'} / f_{yl} - A_t p_h f_{yv} / f_{yl} s$$

where $A_t / s \geq 25 b_w / f_{yv}$.

To control crack widths, ACI Section 11.6.6.1 specifies a maximum spacing of the closed stirrups of

$$s = p_h / 8$$
$$\leq 12 \text{ inches}$$

Example 2.5

The reinforced concrete flanged section shown in Exhibit 3 has an applied, factored shear force of 40 kips and an applied, factored torsional moment of 30 kip-feet. Determine if the shear and torsion reinforcement is adequate if no redistribution of internal forces can occur; the concrete strength is 4000 pounds per square inch, and all reinforcement consists of Grade 60 bars. The area of flexural reinforcement required in the bottom of the web is 1.8 square inches.

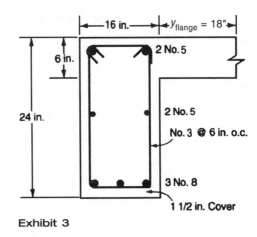

Exhibit 3

Solution

In accordance with ACI Section 11.6.1.1 and 13.2.4, the overhanging flange width to be included in the section properties is given by

$$y_{\text{flange}} = h_w = 18 \text{ inches}$$

The area enclosed by the outside perimeter of the concrete cross section is

$$A_{cp} = 24 \times 16 + 6 \times 18 = 492 \text{ square inches}$$

The length of the outside perimeter of the concrete cross section is

$$p_{cp} = 2(24 + 16) + 2 \times 18 = 116 \text{ inches}$$

Torsional effects may be neglected and closed stirrups are not required when the factored torque does not exceed

$$T_u = \phi \sqrt{f_c'}\left(A_{cp}^2/p_{cp}\right)\ldots \text{ACI Section 11.6.1(a)}$$

where ϕ = strength reduction factor
  = 0.75…from ACI Section 9.3.2.3
$T_u = 0.75\sqrt{4000}\ (492^2/116)/12{,}000 = 8.24$ kip-feet $< T_u$

Hence, torsional effects must be considered.

The area of closed stirrups required for torsional effects is given by ACI Equation (11-21) as

$$A_t/s = T_u/2A_o f_{yv}\cot\theta$$

where $A_o = 0.85\, A_{oh}$
  $= 0.85 x_o y_o \ldots$ since closed stirrups are not provided in the slab.
A_{oh} = area enclosed by the centerline of the closed stirrups
  x_o = distance between centerlines of vertical legs of closed stirrups
    $= b_w - d_b - 2(\text{clear cover}) = 16 - 0.375 - 2 \times 1.5 = 12.625$ inches
  y_o = distance between centerlines of horizontal legs of closed stirrups
    $= h - d_b - 2(\text{clear cover}) = 24 - 0.375 - 2 \times 1.5 = 20.625$ inches
  $\cot\theta = 1$
Then $A_t/s = 12 \times 30 \times 12/(2 \times 0.85 \times 12.625 \times 20.625 \times 60)$
    $= 0.163$ square inches/foot/leg

The design shear strength provided by the concrete is obtained from ACI Section 9.3 and ACI Equation (11-3) as

$$\phi V_c = 2\phi b_w d \sqrt{f'_c}$$

where d = effective depth

$$= 24 - 1.5 - 0.375 - 1.0/2 = 21.63 \text{ inches}$$

$$\phi V_c = 2 \times 0.75 \times 16 \times 21.63\sqrt{4000}/1000 = 32.83 \text{ kips}$$

The design shear strength required from the shear reinforcement is given by ACI Equations (11-1) and (11-2) as

$$\phi V_s = V_u - \phi V_c$$
$$= 40 - 32.83 = 7.17 \text{ kips}$$

The area of shear reinforcement required is given by ACI Equation (11-15) as

$$A_v/s = \phi V_s/\phi d f_y$$
$$= 7.17 \times 12/(0.75 \times 21.63 \times 60) = 0.088 \text{ square inches/foot}$$

The total area of shear and torsional stirrups required, in accordance with ACI Section 11.6.3.8, is given by

$$A/s = A_v/s + 2A_t/s$$
$$= 0.088 + 2 \times 0.163 = 0.414 \text{ square inches/foot}$$

Closed stirrups consisting of No. 3 bars at a spacing of 6 inches provide an area of $A/s = 0.44$, which is satisfactory.

The minimum area of torsion and shear reinforcement that may be provided is given by ACI Equation (11-23) as

$$A/s = 50 b_w/f_{yv}$$
$$= 12 \times 50 \times 16/60,000 = 0.160 \text{ square inches/foot}$$
$$< 0.44 \ldots \text{ satisfactory}$$

The maximum spacing of torsion reinforcement is defined in ACI Section 11.6.6.1 as

$$s = p_h/8$$

where p_h = perimeter of the centerline of the closed stirrups

$$= 2(x_o + y_o)$$
$$= 2(12.625 + 20.625) = 66.50 \text{ inches}$$
$$s = 66.5/8 = 8.3 > 6$$

Hence, closed stirrups consisting of No. 3 bars at a spacing of 6 inches is adequate.

The longitudinal torsional reinforcement required is given by ACI Equation (11-22) as

$$A_l = (A_t p_h f_{yv}/f_{yl} s) \cot^2\theta$$
$$= 0.163 \times 66.5/12 = 0.903 \text{ square inches}$$

The longitudinal torsional reinforcement shall not be less than the value given by ACI Equation (11-24) as

$$A_{l(\min)} = 5A_{cp}\sqrt{f_c'}/f_{yl} - A_t p_h f_{yv}/f_{yl}s$$
$$= 5 \times 492 \times \sqrt{4000}/60{,}000 - 0.163 \times 66.5/12$$
$$= 2.59 - 0.90 = 1.69 \ldots \text{and this value governs}$$

Hence, the required area of longitudinal reinforcement is $A_l = 1.69$ square inches.

The longitudinal torsion reinforcement should be distributed evenly around the inside perimeter of the stirrups, in accordance with ACI Section 11.6.6.2, with no more than 12 inches between bars. At least four bars, one in each corner of the closed stirrups, should be used. The longitudinal torsion reinforcement is additional to any required tension or compression flexural reinforcement and may be provided at the level of the flexural reinforcement by using larger bars than those required for bending alone. Using two No. 5 bars in the top corners and two No. 5 bars in the sides provides an area of

$$A_l' = 1.24 \text{ square inches}$$

The remaining area required at the bottom is $A_l - A_l' = 1.69 - 1.24 = 0.45$ square inches. Combining this with the required area of tension reinforcement gives a total required area in the bottom of the web of

$$A = 1.8 + 0.45 = 2.25 \text{ square inches}$$

Three No. 8 bars are provided to give a total area of

$$A' = 2.37 \text{ square inches}, > 2.25 \text{ square inches}$$

Hence, the longitudinal reinforcement provided is adequate.

Bond and Anchorage in Reinforced Concrete

The length of reinforcement required to develop the maximum stress in the reinforcement is called the **development** or **anchorage length.** The basic development length of tension reinforcement is given by ACI Equation (12-1) as

$$l_d/d_b = 0.075 f_y \alpha\beta\gamma\lambda / \left[\sqrt{f_c'}(c + K_{tr})/d_b \right]$$

where l_d = development length
$\quad d_b$ = bar diameter
$\quad \alpha$ = reinforcement location factor … ACI Section 12.2.4
$\qquad$ = 1.3 for horizontal bars with more than 12 inches of concrete below
$\qquad$ = 1.0 for other bars
$\quad \beta$ = coating factor
$\qquad$ = 1.5 for epoxy-coated bars with cover $<3d_b$ or clear spacing $<6d_b$
$\qquad$ = 1.2 for all other epoxy-coated bars
$\qquad$ = 1.0 for uncoated reinforcement
$\quad \alpha\beta \leq 1.7$ … the product of $(\alpha)(\beta)$ need not exceed 1.7
$\quad \gamma$ = reinforcement size factor
$\qquad$ = 0.8 for No. 6 and smaller bars
$\qquad$ = 1.0 for No. 7 and larger bars
$\quad \lambda$ = lightweight aggregate factor
$\qquad$ = 1.3 for lightweight aggregate concrete
$\qquad$ = $6.7\sqrt{f_c'/f_{ct}} \geq 1.0$ when f_{ct} is specified
$\qquad$ = 1.0 for normal-weight concrete

c = spacing or cover dimension

= distance from center of bar to nearest concrete surface

≤ one-half the center-to-center spacing of the bars being developed

$K_{tr} = A_{tr} f_{yt} / 1500 sn$

A_{tr} = cross-sectional area of transverse reinforcement crossing a potential plane of splitting

f_{yt} = yield strength of the transverse reinforcement

s = spacing the transverse reinforcement

n = number of bars being developed along a potential plane of splitting and $(c + K_{tr})/d_b \leq 2.5$

In addition, as specified by ACI Section 12.2.1, the minimum value of the development length is

$$l_d = 12 \text{ inches}$$

Experimental data for high-strength concrete is not available and for this reason ACI Section 12.1.2 specifies that

$$\sqrt{f_c'} \leq 100 \text{ pounds per square inch}$$

When excess reinforcement is provided in a member, the tensile stress in the reinforcement is less than the design value and development lengths are correspondingly lower. According to ACI Section 12.2.5, the development length may then be reduced by the factor

$$\varepsilon = A_{s(\text{reqd})} / A_{s(\text{provided})} \ldots \text{ACI Section 12.2.5}$$

This reduction factor may not be applied where anchorage is required for the full yield strength of the reinforcement. This occurs for shrinkage and temperature reinforcement as specified in ACI Section 7.12.2.3, for integrity reinforcement as specified in ACI Section 7.13, for positive moment at a support as specified in ACI Section 12.11.2, and for tension lap splices as specified in ACI Sections 12.15.1 and 13.3.8.5.

The strength reduction factor ϕ is not applied in the determination of development length since the specified lengths already include an allowance for understrength. (See ACI Commentary, Section 12.0.)

For commonly occurring design situations, ACI Equation (12-1) may be simplified, as specified in ACI Section 12.2.2, by assuming an estimated value for the factor $(c + K_{tr})/d_b$.

■ Using the minimum clear spacing d_b specified in ACI Section 7.6.1, the minimum clear cover d_b to primary reinforcement specified in ACI Section 7.7, and in the absence of stirrups,

$$c = d_b$$
$$K_{tr} = 0$$
$$(c + K_{tr})/d_b = 1.0$$

Then, for No. 7 and larger bars $\gamma = 1.0$ and

$$l_d/d_b = 0.075 f_y \alpha\beta\lambda/\sqrt{f_c'}$$

For No. 6 and smaller bars $\gamma = 0.8$ and

$$l_d/d_b = 0.06 f_y \alpha \beta \lambda / \sqrt{f_c'}$$

■ Using the minimum clear spacing d_b specified in ACI Section 7.6.1, the minimum clear cover d_b to primary reinforcement specified in ACI Section 7.7, and minimum stirrups specified in ACI Equation (11-13),

$$c = d_b$$
$$K_{tr} = 50 b_w / 1500 n$$
$$\approx 0.5 d_b$$
$$(c + K_{tr})/d_b = 1.5$$

Then, for No. 7 and larger bars $\gamma = 1.0$ and

$$l_d/d_b = 0.05 f_y \alpha \beta \lambda / \sqrt{f_c'} \ldots \text{ACI Section 12.2.2}$$

For No. 6 and smaller bars $\gamma = 0.8$ and

$$l_d/d_b = 0.04 f_y \alpha \beta \lambda / \sqrt{f_c'} \ldots \text{ACI Section 12.2.2}$$

■ Using a minimum clear spacing of $2d_b$, the minimum clear cover d_b to primary reinforcement specified in ACI Section 7.7, and in the absence of stirrups

$$c = 1.5 d_b$$
$$K_{tr} = 0$$
$$(c + K_{tr})/d_b = 1.5$$

Then, for No. 7 and larger bars $\gamma = 1.0$ and

$$l_d/d_b = 0.05 f_y \alpha \beta \lambda / \sqrt{f_c'} \ldots \text{ACI Section 12.2.2}$$

For No. 6 and smaller bars $\gamma = 0.8$ and

$$l_d/d_b = 0.04 f_y \alpha \beta \lambda / \sqrt{f_c'} \ldots \text{ACI Section 12.2.2}$$

The requirements for determining the development length of compression reinforcement are given in ACI Section 12.3.

For bundled bars, ACI Section 12.4 specifies that the development length of an individual bar in the bundle shall be increased 20 percent for a three-bar bundle and 33 percent for a four-bar bundle.

The basic development length for tension reinforcement, with a yield strength of 60,000 pounds per square inch, terminating in a standard hook is given by ACI Section 12.5.2 as

$$l_{hb} = 1200 d_b / \sqrt{f_c'}$$

The required development or anchorage length is obtained by multiplying the basic development length by the modifiers defined in ACI Sections 12.5.3–12.5.4 and is summarized in Figure 2.8. The modifiers are cumulative with the following

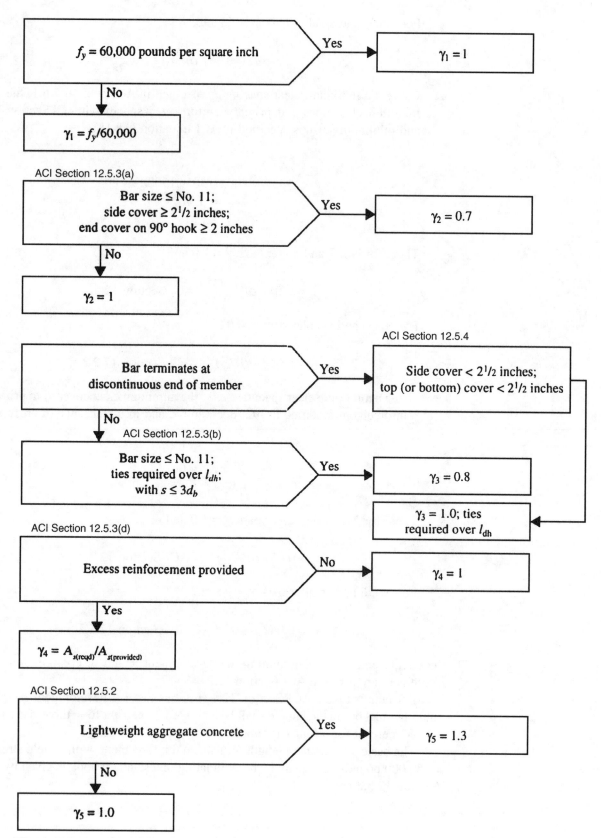

Figure 2.8 Modifiers for standard hooked bars

restrictions imposed: $l_{dh} = \gamma_1 \gamma_2 \gamma_3 \gamma_4 \gamma_5 l_{hb}$ = development or anchorage length, which is $\geq 8d_b$ and ≥ 6 inches. In addition, in accordance with ACI Section 12.5.2, a modifier of 1.2 is applied to epoxy-coated reinforcement.

Tension reinforcement may be curtailed along the length of a flexural member, and the actual cutoff point may not be less than the appropriate anchorage length from the last point at which it is assumed to be fully stressed. The point at which, in theory, a bar is no longer required to resist flexure is the theoretical cutoff point, and it is that point where the design strength of the section, considering only the continuing bars, is equal to the required ultimate strength. Reinforcement must be continued beyond the theoretical cutoff point to account for inaccuracies in the analysis, misplacement of the bars, and the presence of diagonal shear cracks which cause the calculated tensile stress to occur an effective depth beyond the theoretical cutoff point. In accordance with ACI Sections 12.10.3 and 12.10.4, reinforcement shall extend beyond the theoretical cutoff point for a distance at least equal to the greater of the effective depth of the member or 12 times the bar diameter, except at end supports and at the free end of cantilevers. These requirements are illustrated in Figure 2.9.

To prevent excessive flexural and diagonal shear cracking at cutoff points and a local reduction in shear strength, additional precautions are required for the curtailment of tension reinforcement. In accordance with ACI Section 12.10.5, one of the following conditions must be satisfied at the physical cutoff point:

(i) The factored applied shear force does not exceed two-thirds the shear capacity of the section (ACI Section 12.10.5.1).

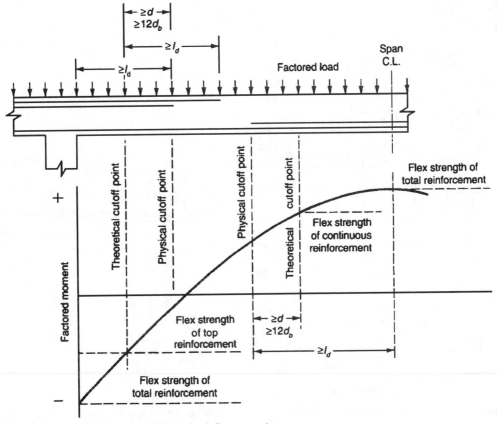

Figure 2.9 Curtailment of flexural reinforcement

(ii) Additional stirrups with an area of $60b_w s/f_y$ are provided along the curtailed reinforcement for a distance equal to three-quarters of the effective depth at a maximum spacing of $d/8\beta_b$, where β_b is the ratio of the area of terminated reinforcement to total reinforcement (ACI Section 12.10.5.2).

(iii) For No. 11 bars and smaller, the continuing reinforcement provides twice the flexural capacity required, and the applied shear force does not exceed three-quarters the shear capacity of the section (ACI Section 12.10.5.3).

ACI Sections 12.11 and 7.13 impose requirements on the amount of positive flexural reinforcement which must be carried into the support. In addition, in order to control local bond stresses, unless anchorage is provided by means of a standard hook, a limitation is placed on the size of the reinforcement by specifying a maximum value for the development length. These requirements are illustrated in Figure 2.10.

ACI Sections 12.12 and 7.13 impose requirements on the amount of negative flexural reinforcement which must be carried into the span. These requirements are illustrated in Figure 2.11.

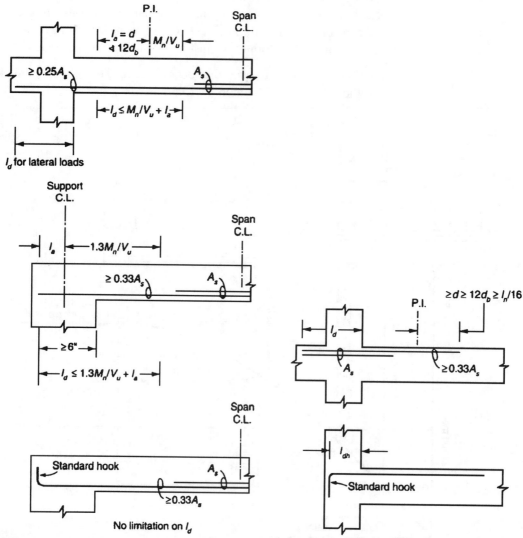

Figure 2.10 Positive flexural reinforcement detailing requirements

Figure 2.11 Negative flexural reinforcement detailing requirements

The requirements for reinforcement splices are covered in ACI Sections 12.14 to 12.19. In accordance with Section 12.14, lap splices shall not be used for bars larger than No. 11 or for bundled bars. Spliced bars shall not be spaced farther apart than one-fifth the lap length, or 6 inches. For bundled bars, the lap length required for the individual bars must be increased 20 percent for a three-bar bundle and 33 percent for a four-bar bundle, and the splices must be staggered.

In accordance with ACI Section 12.15, the required length of lap for tension reinforcement depends on the splice classification and is given by:

Class A splice, lap length = $1.0 l_d$ ... ACI Section 12.15.1
Class B splice, lap length = $1.3 l_d$ ... ACI Section 12.15.1

A Class A splice may be used only when both of the following conditions are satisfied:

 (i) The reinforcement area provided at the splice is not less than twice that required by analysis (ACI Section 12.15.2(a)).

(ii) Not more than half of the total reinforcement may be spliced within the required lap length (ACI Section 12.15.2(b)).

In determining the lap length, all applicable modifiers must be used in calculating the development length, with the exception of the modifier for excess reinforcement. The lap length may not be less than 12 inches (ACI Section 12.15.1).

Reinforced Concrete Columns

Reinforced concrete columns may be classified as either short columns or long columns. Slenderness effects must be considered in the design of long columns, and the secondary moments from the $P - \Delta$ effects must be added to the primary moments. Classification as a short column depends on the slenderness ratio of the column, which is given by

$$kl_u/r$$

where k = effective length factor determined from the alignment charts in ACI Section R10.12.1
l_u = unsupported column length
r = radius of gyration of the column, which is given in ACI Section 10.11.2 as $r = 0.3 \times$ *rectangular* column width or $r = 0.25 \times$ *circular* column diameter

Then, in an unbraced frame (sidesway permitted), slenderness effects may be neglected, in accordance with ACI Section 10.13.2, when the slenderness ratio is given by

$$kl_u/r < 22 ... \text{ACI Section 10.13.2}$$

For a braced frame (sidesway prevented), slenderness effects may be neglected in accordance with ACI Section 10.12.2 when the slenderness ratio as given by

$$kl_u/r \leq 34 - 12M_1/M_2 ... \text{ACI Equation (10-7)}$$

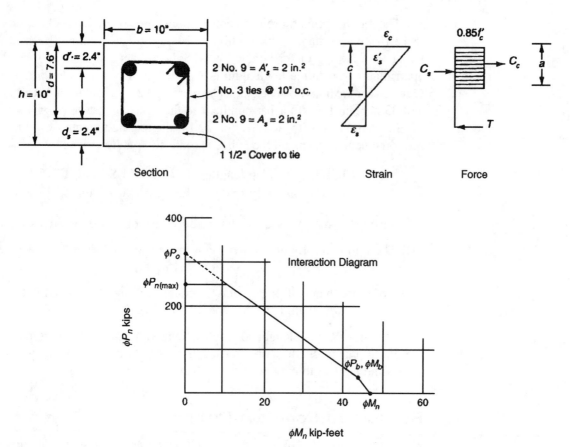

Figure 2.12 Flexure and compression in a short tied column

where M_2 = larger factored moment at end of column, and M_1 = smaller factored moment at end of column (negative if the column is bent in double curvature).

For a short column, the axial load-carrying capacity decreases as the moment applied to the column increases, and design may be facilitated by means of tables and charts.[4,6] To illustrate the principles involved, the derivation of the interaction diagram for the column shown in Figure 2.12 is as follows: The theoretical design axial load strength at zero eccentricity is given by ACI Section R10.3.6. as

$$\phi P_o = \phi[0.85 f_c'(A_g - A_{st}) + A_{st} f_y]$$

where ϕ = strength reduction factor specified in Section 9.3.2.2
     = 0.70 for compression members with spiral reinforcement and
     = 0.65 for compression members with lateral ties
f_c' = concrete cylinder strength = 3.0 kips per square inch
f_y = reinforcement yield strength = 60 kips per square inch
A_g = gross area of the section = 100 square inches
A_{st} = reinforcement area = 4 square inches

Then, $\phi P_o = 0.65[0.85 \times 3(100 - 4) + 4 \times 60] = 315$ kips. This is plotted on the interaction diagram in Figure 2.13.

To account for accidental eccentricity, ACI Section 10.3.6 requires a spirally reinforced column to be designed for a minimum eccentricity of approximately

$0.05h$, which gives a maximum design axial load strength at zero eccentricity, in accordance with ACI Equation (10-1), of

$$\phi P_{n(max)} = 0.85\phi P_o$$

In the case of a column with lateral ties, a minimum eccentricity of approximately $0.10h$ is specified, which gives a maximum design axial load strength at zero eccentricity, in accordance with ACI Equation (10-2), of

$$\phi P_{n(max)} = 0.80\phi P_o = 0.80 \times 315 = 252 \text{ kips}$$

and this is plotted on the interaction diagram.

As increasing moment is applied to the column, a balanced strain is produced when the strain in the concrete and in the tension reinforcement simultaneously reach the values specified in ACI Section 10.3.2 as $\varepsilon_c = 0.003$ and $\varepsilon_s = f_y/E_s = 60/29,000$.

From the strain diagram in Figure 2.12, the depth to the neutral axis and the stress in the compression reinforcement may be derived as

$$c = d\varepsilon_c/(\varepsilon_c + \varepsilon_s) = 87d/(87 + f_y) = 87 \times 7.6/(87 + 60) = 4.5 \text{ inches}$$
$$f'_s = E_s\varepsilon_c(c - d')/c = 87(1 - d'/c) = 87(1 - 2.4/4.5) = 40.58 \text{ kips per square inch} < f_y$$

In accordance with ACI Section 10.2.7.1, the depth of the equivalent rectangular stress block is given by

$$a = c\beta_1$$

where $\beta_1 = 0.85$ as defined in ACI Section 10.2.7.3. Hence, $a = 4.5 \times 0.85 = 3.83$ inches.

Then the forces in the concrete, compression reinforcement, and tensile reinforcement are as indicated in the force diagram in Figure 2.12 and are given by

$$C_c = 0.85f'_c(ab - A'_s) = 0.85 \times 3(3.83 \times 10 - 2) = 92.57 \text{ kips}$$
$$C_s = f'_s A'_s = 40.58 \times 2 = 81.16 \text{ kips}$$
$$T = f_y A_s = 60 \times 2 = 120 \text{ kips}$$

Hence, the nominal axial load capacity at balanced strain is given by

$$P_b = C_c + C_s - T = 92.57 + 81.16 - 120 = 53.73 \text{ kips}$$

The design axial load capacity at balanced strain is given by

$$\phi P_b = 0.65 \times 53.73 = 34.9 \text{ kips}$$

The nominal moment capacity at the balanced strain condition is obtained by summing moments about the mid-depth of the section and is given by

$$\begin{aligned} M_b &= C_c(h/2 - a/2) + C_s(h/2 - d') + T(h/2 - d_s) \\ &= 92.57(5 - 1.92) + 81.16(5 - 2.4) + 120(5 - 2.4) = 808 \text{ kip-inches} \end{aligned}$$

The design moment capacity at balanced strain is

$$\phi M_b = 0.65 \times 808/12 = 43.8 \text{ kip-feet}$$

and the point corresponding to the balanced strain is plotted on the interaction diagram.

Neglecting compression reinforcement, the design moment strength of the section without applied axial load is obtained from

$$
\begin{aligned}
\phi M_n &= \phi A_s f_y d (1 - 0.59 \rho f_y / f_c')/12 \\
&= 0.9 \times 2 \times 60 \times 7.6 (1 - 0.59 \times 0.0263 \times 60/3)/12 = 47.16 \text{ kip-feet}
\end{aligned}
$$

The value of ϕM_n is plotted on the interaction diagram, which may be constructed as shown. All combinations of axial load and moment which lie within the interaction diagram are valid.

If the slenderness ratio of a long column does not exceed 100, ACI Sections 10.12.3 and 10.13.3 permit slenderness effects to the allowed for by means of the approximate moment magnifier method. Design of the column is then based on a magnified factored moment for the non-sway case given by ACI Equation (10-8) as

$$M_c = \delta_{ns} M_2$$

where M_2 = larger factored moment attributable to gravity or transverse loads

$\delta_{ns} = C_m/(1 - P_u/0.75P_c)$ from ACI Equation (10-9)

$C_m = 0.6 + 0.4 M_1/M_2$ from ACI Equation (10-13)

$P_c = \pi^2 EI/(kl_u)^2$ = Euler critical load from ACI Equation (10-10)

For the sway case, the magnified factored moments given by ACI Equations (10-15) and (10-16) are

$$M_1 = M_{1ns} + \delta_s M_{1s}$$

$$M_2 = M_{2ns} + \delta_s M_{2s}$$

where M_1 = smaller factored moment at end of column

M_2 = larger factored moment at end of column

M_{1ns} = factored moment at the end of the column at which M_1 acts, due to loads that cause no appreciable sidesway, calculated using a first-order elastic frame analysis

M_{2ns} = factored moment at the end of the column at which M_2 acts, due to loads that cause no appreciable sidesway, calculated using a first-order elastic frame analysis

M_{1s} = factored moment at the end of the column at which M_1 acts, due to loads that cause appreciable sidesway, calculated using a first-order elastic frame analysis

M_{2s} = factored moment at the end of the column at which M_2 acts, due to loads that cause appreciable sidesway, calculated using a first-order elastic frame analysis

δ_s = moment magnification factor for sway frames

$= 1/[1 - \sum P_u/(0.75 \sum P_c)]$ ... from ACI Equation (10-18), where the summations extend over all the columns in a story

≤ 2.5 ... from ACI Section 10.13.6

PRESTRESSED CONCRETE DESIGN

General Design Criteria

Prestressed concrete members must be designed to ensure an adequate degree of safety and serviceability at the three main construction stages. These stages are:

(i) The transfer limit stage, when the prestressing force is applied to the concrete section. The immediate prestress losses from friction, elastic deformation of the concrete, and anchor set have occurred, giving an initial prestressing force of P_i. Since the initial prestress causes the concrete member to arch, the self-weight of the member produces the bending moment M_G.

(ii) The serviceability limit stage, when all long-term prestress losses from creep, shrinkage, and relaxation have occurred, giving a final effective prestressing force of P_e. The superimposed dead and live loads produce bending moments of M_D and M_L, respectively.

(iii) The ultimate limit stage, when the design strength of the member is sufficient to support the factored loads.

The Transfer Limit Stage

Figure 2.13 illustrates stress conditions at transfer. The limiting concrete stresses at transfer are specified in ACI Section 18.4.1 as:

■ Compressive stress, $0.06 f'_{ci}$

■ Tensile stress (at ends of simply supported beams), $6\sqrt{f'_{ci}}$

■ Tensile stress (at other locations), $3\sqrt{f'_{ci}}$

Where these tensile stresses are exceeded, auxiliary reinforcement—at a stress of $0.6f_y$—must be provided to resist the total tensile force in the concrete. In accordance with ACI Section 18.5.1, the stress in the prestressing tendon immediately after transfer must not exceed the lesser of $0.82f_{py}$ or $0.74f_{pu}$.

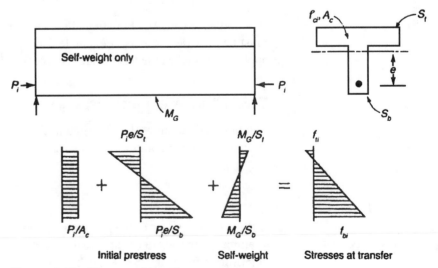

Figure 2.13   Stresses at transfer

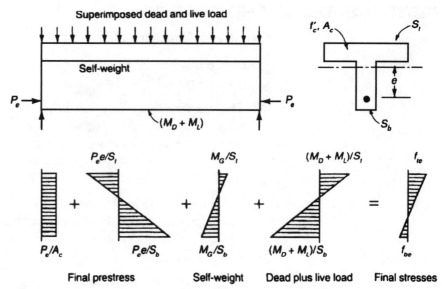

Figure 2.14   Final stresses at working load

The Serviceability Limit Stage

Figure 2.14 illustrates the stress conditions at working load after all prestressing losses have occurred. The limiting concrete stresses at working load are specified in ACI Section 18.4.2.

Compressive stress, $0.45\sqrt{f_c'}$ ... sustained loads, or $0.60\sqrt{f_c'}$ ... total loads

In accordance with ACI Section 18.3.3, prestressed flexural members are classified into three categories based on the computed extreme fiber stress f_t at service loads in the precompressed tensile zone. These categories are:

Class U: $f_t \le 7.5\sqrt{f_c'}$

Class T: $7.5\sqrt{f_c'} < f_t \le 12\sqrt{f_c'}$

Class C: $f_t > 12\sqrt{f_c'}$

In accordance with ACI Equation (18-7), auxiliary reinforcement, at a stress of $0.5f_y$, must be provided to resist the tensile force that is produced in the concrete by the applied loads when the tensile stress exceeds $2\sqrt{f_c'}$.

The Ultimate Limit Stage

The nominal strength of a rectangular fully prestressed beam is derived from the assumed ultimate conditions shown in Figure 2.15 and is given by

$$M_n = A_{ps}f_{ps}(d_p - 0.59A_{ps}f_{ps}/bf_c')$$

If the effective stress in the prestressing tendons f_{se} is not less than half the tensile strength f_{pu}, the value of the stress in the tendons at nominal strength f_{ps} may be determined from ACI Section 18.7.2 as

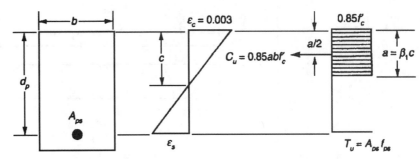

Figure 2.15 Member with prestressing tendon

(i) For unbonded tendons and a span-to-depth ratio not greater than 35:

$$f_{ps} = f_{se} + 10,000 + f_c'/100\rho_p \le f_{py} \quad \text{and} \quad \le f_{se} + 60,000 \ldots \text{ACI Equation}$$
(18-4)

(ii) For unbonded tendons and a span-to-depth ratio greater than 35:

$$f_{ps} = f_{se} + 10,000 + f_c'/300\rho_p \le f_{py} \quad \text{and} \quad \le f_{se} + 30,000 \ldots \text{ACI Equation}$$
(18-5)

(iii) For fully prestressed members with bonded tendons:

$$f_{ps} = f_{pu}\left[1 - \frac{\gamma_p}{\beta_1}\left[\rho_p \frac{f_{pu}}{f_c'} + \frac{d}{d_p}(\omega - \omega')\right]\right] \ldots \text{ACI Equation (18-3)}$$

where $\gamma_p = 0.55$ for $f_{py}/f_{pu} \ge 0.80$ (deformed bars)
       $\gamma_p = 0.40$ for $f_{py}/f_{pu} \ge 0.85$ (stress-relieved wire, strand and plain bars)
       $\gamma_p = 0.28$ for $f_{py}/f_{pu} \ge 0.90$ (low-relaxation wire and strands)

In order to ensure that adequate warning is given of impending failure, ACI Section 18.8.2 stipulates that

$$\phi M_n \ge 1.2 M_{cr}$$

where M_{cr}, the cracking moment strength, is computed by elastic theory using a modulus of rupture given by ACI Equation (9-10) as $f_r = 7.5\sqrt{f_c'}$.

Example 2.6

The pretensioned flanged beam shown in Exhibit 4 has a concrete strength of 4500 pounds per square inch at transfer and 6000 pounds per square inch at 28 days. (a) Determine the magnitude and position of the initial prestressing force required to produce satisfactory stresses immediately after transfer, at midspan, without using auxiliary reinforcement. (b) Using these values, and assuming a total long-term loss in prestress of 25 percent, determine the maximum uniformly distributed live load that the beam can carry over an effective span of 20 feet. The total uniformly distributed live load may be considered nonsustained. Normal concrete cover is provided to the prestressing tendons, and auxiliary reinforcement may not be used.

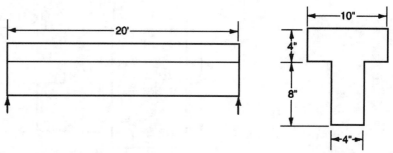

Exhibit 4   Flanged section for Example 6

Solution

The properties of the section may be determined from a standard calculator program[3] or from charts.[4] The relevant properties are:

A_c = area of section = 72 square inches
I_c = moment of inertia of section = 863 inches[4]
$\bar{y}$ = height of centriod = 7.33 inches
S_t = section modulus about top fiber = 185 inches[3]
S_b = section modulus about bottom fiber = 118 inches[3]

(a) The total weight of the beam is

$$W_G = 150\, lA_c/144 = 150 \times 20 \times 72/144 = 1500 \text{ pounds}$$

The self-weight moment of the beam is

$$M_G = W_G l/8 = 1500 \times 20 \times 12/8 = 45,000 \text{ pound-inches}$$

The allowable tensile stress at midspan in the top fiber at transfer is given by ACI Section 18.4.1(b) as

$$\begin{aligned}
f_{ti} &= -3\sqrt{f'_{ci}} = -3\sqrt{4500} = -201 \text{ pounds per square inch}\\
&= P_i/A_c - P_i e/S_t + M_G/S_t\\
&= P_i/72 - P_i e/185 + 45,000/185 = 0.0139 P_i - 0.00541 P_i e + 243
\end{aligned}$$

Hence, $0.0139 P_i - 0.00541 P_i e = -444$.

The allowable compressive stress at midspan in the bottom fiber at transfer is given by ACI Section 18.4.1(a) as

$$\begin{aligned}
f_{bi} &= 0.6 f'_{ci} = 0.6 \times 4500 = 2700 \text{ pounds per square inch}\\
&= P_i/A_c + P_i e/S_b - M_G/S_b\\
&= P_i/72 + P_i e/118 - 45,000/118 = 0.0139 P_i + 0.00847 P_i e - 381
\end{aligned}$$

Hence, $0.0139 P_i + 0.00847 P_i e = 3081$.

Solving these two expressions simultaneously gives

$$P_i = \text{initial prestressing force} = 66{,}934 \text{ pounds}$$
$$e = \text{tendon eccentricity} = 3.79 \text{ inches}$$

Hence, the centroid of the tendon must be positioned $\bar{y} - e = 7.33 - 3.79 = 3.54$ inches from the bottom of the beam, at midspan, and this may be readily accommodated.

(b) The allowable compressive stress at midspan, due to the total load, in the top fiber after all losses have occurred is given by ACI Section 18.4.2 as

$$f_{te} = 0.60 f_c' = 0.60 \times 6000 = 3600 \text{ pounds per square inch}$$
$$= P_e/A_c - P_e e/S_t + M_G/S_t + M_L/S_t$$
$$= 0.75 \times (-444) + 243 + M_L/185$$

Hence, $M_L = 682{,}650$ pound-inches.

The allowable tensile stress at midspan in the bottom fiber after all losses have occurred, and without using auxiliary reinforcement, is given by ACI Section 18.9.3.2 as

$$f_{be} = -2\sqrt{f_c'} = -2\sqrt{6000} = -155 \text{ pounds per square inch}$$
$$= P_e/A_c + P_e e/S_b - M_G/S_b - M_L/S_b$$
$$= 0.75 \times 3081 - 381 - M_L/118$$

Hence, $M_L = 246{,}000$ pound-inches, which is <682,650. Then, the maximum distributed live load is given by

$$W_L = 8M_L/l = 8 \times 246{,}000/(20 \times 12) = 8200 \text{ pounds}$$

Loss of Prestress

For determining loss of prestress, ACI Section R18.6.1 recommends the methods proposed by Zia.[7]

Friction losses occur in post-tensioned tendons from curvature of the duct profile and unintentional out-of-straightness, or wobble, of the duct. The relationship between the prestressing force at the jack and at a distance l_x from the jack is given by ACI Equation (18-1) as

$$P_s = P_x \exp(Kl_x + \mu\alpha)$$

When $(Kl_x + \mu\alpha)$ does not exceed 0.3, this reduces to

$$P_x = P_s(1 - Kl_x - \mu\alpha)$$

where K = wobble coefficient given in ACI Table R18.6.2
μ = friction coefficient given in ACI Table R18.6.2
α = angle turned through in radians $\approx l_x/R$ ($\approx 2y/x$ from Figure 2.16)

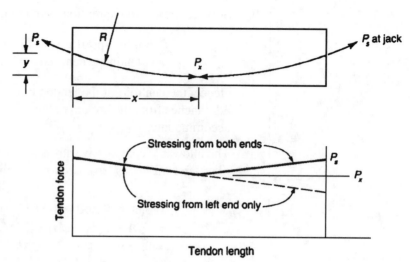

Figure 2.16   Prestress loss from friction

Anchor set losses occur in post-tensioned tendons from the pull-in that occurs in the wedges when the prestressing force is transferred from the jack to the anchor device. Assuming a frictionless tendon, the loss in prestressing force over the whole length of the tendon from a pull-in of Δ inches is

$$P_\Delta = A_{ps} E_{ps} \Delta / 12l$$

where A_{ps} = area of tendon
$\quad E_{ps}$ = modulus of elasticity of tendon
$\quad l$ = length of tendon in feet

In practice, friction resists the inward movement of the tendon and reduces the length over which the loss occurs, as shown in Figure 2.17, and this condition is retained with early grouting of the tendon. For this situation, the pull-in is given by

$$\Delta = 12mx_s^2 / A_{ps} E_{ps}$$

where m = force loss per foot, and x_s = length affected by wedge pull-in, in feet. Hence, x_s may be determined and the maximum force in the tendon is given by

$$P_{max} = P_s - x_s m$$

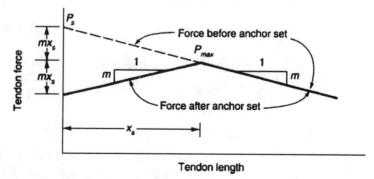

Figure 2.17   Prestress loss from anchor set stressing from left end only

Losses occur in a prestressed beam at transfer because of the elastic shortening of the concrete at the level of the centroid of the prestressing tendons.

In a post-tensioned member with only one tendon, there is no loss from elastic shortening. When several tendons are used and stressed sequentially to the same force, the maximum loss occurs in the first tendon that is stressed and decreases linearly to zero for the last. The total loss in prestress is then

$$P_{el} = A_{ps} n_i f_{pp}/2$$

where $f_{pp} = P_p(1/A_c + e^2/I_c) - M_G e/I_c$
= compressive stress at level of tendon centroid before elastic losses
$P_p = P_i + P_{el}$ = prestressing force in the tendon before elastic losses
P_i = prestressing force in the tendon after elastic losses
$n_i = E_{ps}/E_{ci}$
E_{ci} = modulus of elasticity of concrete at transfer
I_c = moment of inertia of section

In a pretensioned member, where transfer occurs simultaneously in all tendons, the loss of prestress from elastic shortening of the concrete is given by

$$P_{el} = A_{ps} n_i f_{pi}$$

where $f_{pi} = P_i(1/A_c + e^2/I_c) - M_G e/I_c$
= compressive stress at level of tendon centroid after elastic losses

Assuming a 10 percent elastic loss, the compressive stress at the tendon is

$$f_{pi} = 0.9 P_p(1/A_c + e^2/I_c) - M_G e/I_c$$

where P_p = initial force in the tendons immediately after stressing and before transfer. Further iterations may be used if the elastic loss differs considerably from 10 percent.

The immediate prestress loss may, to some extent, be recovered by an initial overstress in the tendons. However, ACI Section 18.5.1 limits the stress in the tendon at jacking to

$$f_{pi} = 0.94 f_{py} \leq 0.80 f_{pu} \quad \text{or} \leq \text{manufacturer's recommended value}$$

Concrete that is subjected to a sustained compressive stress undergoes an increasing compressive strain with time, which is termed creep. Creep causes a prestress loss that is proportional to the initial stress in the concrete and inversely proportional to the modulus of elasticity of the concrete at 28 days. It also increases the earlier the age at which the stress is applied to the concrete. For post-tensioned members, the creep loss is given by

$$P_{cr} = 1.6 A_{ps} n f_{ps}$$

where f_{ps} = compressive stress from self-weight and sustained dead load at the level of the tendon centroid at transfer
= $P_i(1/A_c + e^2/I_c) - (M_G + M_D)e/I_c$
$n = E_{ps}/E_c$
E_c = modulus of elasticity of concrete at 28 days

For pretensioned members creep loss is given by

$$P_{cr} = 2A_{ps}nf_{ps}$$

It may be assumed that half the total creep takes place in the first month and three-quarters of the total creep takes place in the first six months after transfer.

Concrete shrinks with time; consequently there is a corresponding prestress loss. The basic shrinkage strain is taken as

$$\varepsilon_{sh} = 8.2 \times 10^{-6} \text{ inches/inch}$$

This value must be adjusted to allow for the ambient relative humidity, the ratio of the member's surface area to volume, and, in the case of post-tensioned members, the effective time between the completion of curing and the transfer of the prestress force. The prestress loss in pretensioned members is caused by the total shrinkage strain. In post-tensioned members, only the shrinkage strain that occurs after transfer is relevant. For pretensioned members, the shrinkage loss is given by

$$P_{sh} = A_{ps}\varepsilon_{sh}E_s(1 - 0.06A_c/l_p)(100 - R)$$

where l_p = perimeter of section
R = ambient relative humidity[7,8]
   = 45 percent for indoor exposure

For post-tensioned members, the shrinkage loss is given by

$$P_{sh} = K_{sh}A_{ps}E_{sh}E_s(1 - 0.06A_c/l_p)(100 - R)$$

where K_{sh} is a factor[7,8] that accounts for the elapsed time between the completion of curing and the transfer of the prestress force.

A prestressing tendon which is subjected to a sustained tensile strain undergoes decreasing tensile force with time, which is termed relaxation. The amount of loss depends on the initial force in the tendon and the tendon properties and must allow for the effects of strain reductions from creep and shrinkage of the concrete as well as the elastic deformation of the concrete at transfer in the case pretensioning. In pretensioning the initial force is the value immediately after stressing; in the case of post-tensioning, it is the value immediately after transfer. The relaxation loss is given by

$$P_{re} = [A_{ps}K_{re} - J(P_{cr} + P_{sh} + P_{el})]C$$

where K_{re}, J, and C are factors[7,8] that allow for the initial stress in the tendon and the tendon properties.

Example 2.7

The pretensioned flanged beam shown in Exhibit 4 (repeated below) and analyzed in Example 2.6 is manufactured and exposed in San Diego, California, which averages 65 percent ambient relative humidity annually. The prestressing tendons are Grade 270, low-relaxation strand, and the initial stress immediately after transfer is 0.7 × the specified tensile strength, giving relaxation loss factors of K_{re} = 5000 pounds per square inch, $J = 0.04$, $C = 0.95$. Determine the elastic, shrinkage, creep, and relaxation losses.

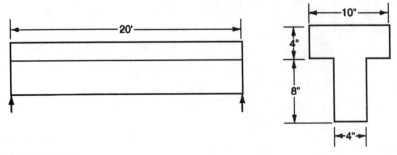

Exhibit 4

Solution

From Example 2.6, the prestressing force immediately after transfer and prior to long-term losses occurring is $P_i = 66.93$ kips, and the eccentricity is $e = 3.79$ inches. From ACI Section 8.5, the moduli of elasticity of the concrete at transfer and at 28 days are given by

$$E_{ci} = 57\sqrt{f'_{ci}} = 57\sqrt{4500} = 3824 \text{ kips per square inch}$$

$$E_c = 57\sqrt{6000} = 4415 \text{ kips per square inch}$$

The perimeter of the section is $l_p = 44$ inches.

The required tendon area is $A_{ps} = P_i/(0.7 \times 270) = 0.354$ square inches. Using two $^1/_4$-inch and two $^1/_2$-inch strands provides $A_{ps} = 0.360$ square inches. The compressive stress in the concrete at the level of the tendon centroid after elastic losses immediately after transfer is

$$f_{pi} = P_i(1/A_c + e^2/I_c) - M_G e/I_c = 66.93(1/72 + 3.79^2/863) - 45 \times 3.79/863$$
$$= 1.85 \text{ kips per square inch}$$

The loss of prestress from elastic shortening of the concrete is then

$$P_{el} = A_{ps} n_i f_{pi}$$
$$= 0.36 \times 1.85 \times 28,000/3824 = 4.87 \text{ kips}$$

Hence, the required force in the tendons immediately before transfer is

$$P_p = P_i + P_{el}$$
$$= 66.93 + 4.87 = 71.8 \text{ kips} = 71.8 P_u/(0.36 \times 270) = 0.74 P_u$$

which is $< 0.80 P_u$, as required by ACI Section 18.5.1.

Since no additional dead load is superimposed on the beam, the compressive stress from self-weight and sustained dead load at the level of the tendon centroid at transfer is

$$f_{ps} = f_{pi} = 1.85 \text{ kips per square inch}$$

Hence, the loss of prestress from creep of the concrete is

$$P_{cr} = 2A_{ps} n f_{ps} = 2 \times 0.36 \times 1.85 \times 28,000/4415 = 8.45 \text{ kips}$$

The loss of prestress from shrinkage is

$$
\begin{aligned}
P_{sh} &= A_{ps}\varepsilon_{sh}E_s(1 - 0.06A_c/l_p)(100 - R) \\
&= 0.36 \times 8.2 \times 10^{-6} \times 28,000(1 - 0.06 \times 72/44)(100 - 65) = 2.61 \text{ kips}
\end{aligned}
$$

The tendon relaxation loss is given by

$$
\begin{aligned}
P_{re} &= [A_{ps}K_{re} - J(P_{cr} + P_{sh} + P_{el})]C \\
&= [0.36 \times 5 - 0.04(8.45 + 2.61 + 4.87)]0.95 = 1.11 \text{ kips}
\end{aligned}
$$

Hence, the total long-term prestress loss is $P_{cr} + P_{sh} + P_{re} = 12.17$ kips $= 0.18\ P_i$.

Shear in Prestressed Concrete Members

The factored shear force acting on a member, in accordance with ACI Equations (11-1) and (11-2), is resisted by the combined shear strength of the concrete and shear reinforcement. Thus, the factored applied shear is given by

$$
V_u = \phi V_c + \phi V_s
$$

where $\phi = 0.75$ = strength reduction factor for shear given by ACI Section 9.3.2.3 and—if the effective prestress is not less than 40 percent of the tensile strength of the flexural reinforcement—the nominal shear strength of normal-weight concrete is given by ACI Equation (11-9) as

$$
V_c = (0.6\sqrt{f_c'} + 700 V_u d/M_u)b_w d
$$

which is $\geq 2\sqrt{f_c'}b_w d$ and $\leq 5\sqrt{f_c'}b_w d$, and $V_u d/M_u \leq 1.0$, with d in the term $V_u d/M_u$ being the distance from the extreme compression fiber to the centroid of the prestressing tendons.

$V_s = A_v f_y d/s$
= nominal shear strength of shear reinforcement from ACI Equation (11-15)
A_v = area of shear reinforcement
s = spacing of shear reinforcement specified in ACI Section 11.5.4 as
   $\leq 0.75h$ or 24 inches when $V_s \leq 4\sqrt{f_c'}b_w d$
   $\leq 0.375h$ or 12 inches when $4\sqrt{f_c'}b_w d < V_s \leq 8\sqrt{f_c'}b_w d$

The dimensions of the section or the strength of the concrete must be increased, in accordance with Section 11.5.6.9, to ensure that $V_s \leq 8\sqrt{f_c'}b_w d$.

As specified in Section 11.5.5, a minimum area of shear reinforcement is required when

$$
V_u > \phi V_c/2 = V_{u(min)}
$$

and the minimum area of shear reinforcement is given by the lesser of ACI Equations (11-13) and (11-14) as

$$
A_{v(min)} = 0.75b_w s\sqrt{f_c'}/f_y
$$

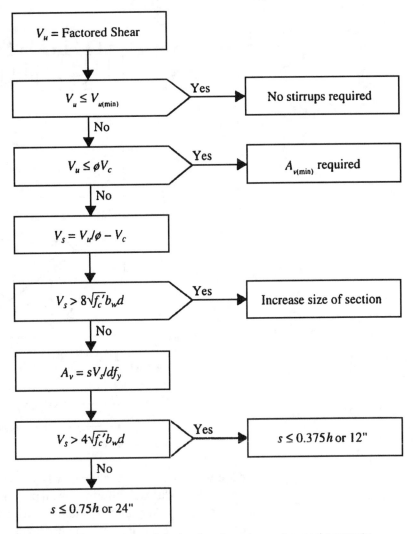

Figure 2.18 Flow chart of design for shear in prestressed concrete

or

$$A_{v(min)} = 50b_w s/f_y \quad \text{or} \quad A_{v(min)} = A_{ps}f_{pu}s\sqrt{d/b_w}\,/(80f_y d)\ldots\text{for } f_{se} > 0.4f_{pu}$$

When the support reaction produces a compressive stress in the member, ACI Section 11.1.3.2 specifies that the critical factored shear force is that which is acting at a distance equal to half the overall depth of the member from the face of the support. Figure 2.18 summarizes the shear provisions of the Code, and Figure 2.19 illustrates the design principles involved.

Load Balancing Technique

The aim of prestressed concrete design is to determine the minimum prestressing force that will produce resultant concrete stresses within the permitted range. This is facilitated, particularly for continuous beams, by the load balancing method,[9] which represents the moment produced by the tendon eccentricity as balancing a portion of the moment produced by the applied loads. The balancing load, for a

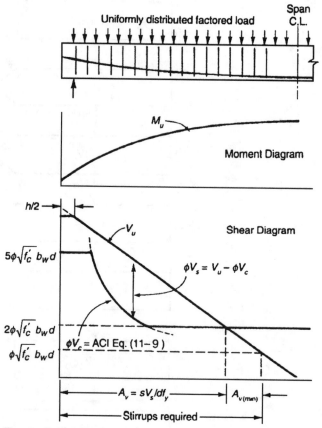

Figure 2.19 Shear in prestressed concrete beam

tendon with a parabolic profile, may be derived as shown in Figure 2.20. The drape of the cable produces a uniform upward pressure on the beam and, equating moments in the free-body diagram, the internal couple is $Pa = w_B L^2/8$. The balancing load is then $w_B = 8P_a/L^2$. If the total applied load on the beam equals w_B, the net lateral load on the beam is zero and the uniform stress produced on the section by the tendon compressive force is $f_c = P/A_c$. In general, it is unnecessary to completely balance the total applied load, giving an out-of-balance load of

$$w_O = w_W - w_B$$

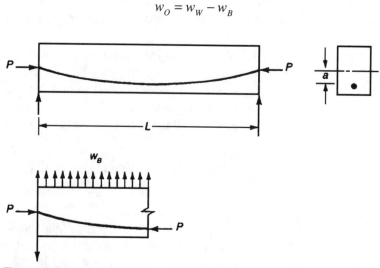

Figure 2.20 Load balancing principles

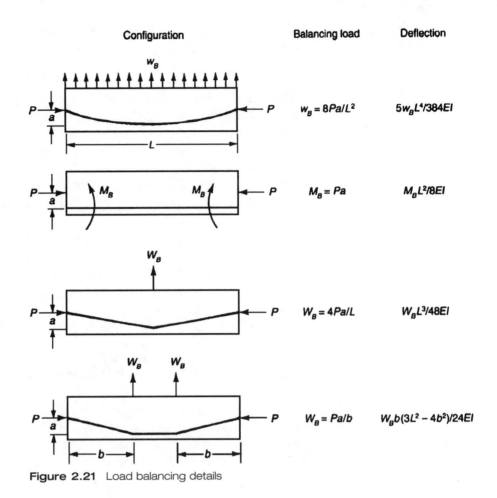

Figure 2.21 Load balancing details

where w_W = total applied load. Then, the stresses produced on the section are

$$f_c = P/A_c \pm M_O/S$$

where M_O = out-of-balance moment due to w_O
$\qquad = M_W - M_B$

where M_W = applied-load moment due to w_W
$\qquad M_B$ = balancing-load moment due to w_B

Typical examples of the load balancing technique are shown in Figure 2.21. More extensive lists of applications are also available.[10,11]

STRUCTURAL STEEL DESIGN

Elastic Design of Steel Beams

The allowable stress on flexural members depends on the shape of the section and the bracing used to prevent lateral instability. Sections are classified as compact, noncompact, and slender in accordance with the criteria given in AISC[12] Table B5.1. Most rolled W shapes qualify as compact sections. The exceptions are indicated in the AISC Tables of Properties by denoting the value of the yield stress F'_y and F'''_y at which a particular shape becomes noncompact. The allowable bending stress for compact symmetrical shapes is given by AISC Equation (F1-1) as

$$F_b = 0.66F_y$$

when the maximum unbraced length of the compression flange does not exceed the smaller value given in AISC Equation (F1-2) of

$$L_c = 76b_f/\sqrt{F_y} \quad \text{or} \quad 20{,}000/(dF_y/A_f)$$

where b_f = flange width and A_f = compression flange area. When the unbraced length of a compact shape exceeds L_c but is less than the greater of

$$L_u = r_T\sqrt{102{,}000C_b/F_y} \quad \text{or} \quad 20{,}000C_b/(dF_y/A_f)$$

The allowable bending stress is given by AISC Section F1.3 as

$$F_b = 0.60F_y$$

where r_T = radius of gyration of the compression flange plus one-third of the web area

C_b = bending coefficient defined in Section F1.3 and Part 5, Table 6
$= 1.75 + 1.05M_1/M_2 + 0.3(M_1/M_2)^2$, but not more than 2.3.

The value of C_b conservatively may be taken as unity. Examples of the derivation of C_b are illustrated in Figure 2.22. Values of L_c and L_u are tabulated in the AISC Beam Tables, assuming a value for C_b of unity.

In general, the allowable bending stress for noncompact symmetrical shapes is given by AISC Equation (F1-5) as

$$F_b = 0.60F_y$$

when the maximum unbraced length of the compression flange does not exceed L_c.

The AISC Selection Tables and Beam Tables tabulate the allowable beam resisting moments and uniformly distributed loads for W, M, S, C and MC shapes that are braced at the appropriate value of L_c or L_u. Adequate bracing is assumed to be provided by a restraint with a capacity of 1 percent of the force in the compression flange in accordance with AISC Section G4.

When the unbraced length of the compression flange exceeds L_u, the allowable bending stress for both compact and noncompact shapes is given by the larger value from AISC Equations (F1-6), (F1-7), and (F1-8) but may not exceed $0.60F_y$. When the unbraced length is less than

$$l = r_T\sqrt{510{,}000C_b/F_y} = L_1$$

the applicable equation is (F1-6) and the allowable stress is

$$F_b = F_y(0.667 - F_y l^2/1{,}530{,}000r_T^2 C_b).$$

When the unbraced length equals or exceeds L_1, the applicable AISC equation is (F1-7) and the allowable stress is

$$F_b = 170{,}000C_b r_T^2/l^2$$

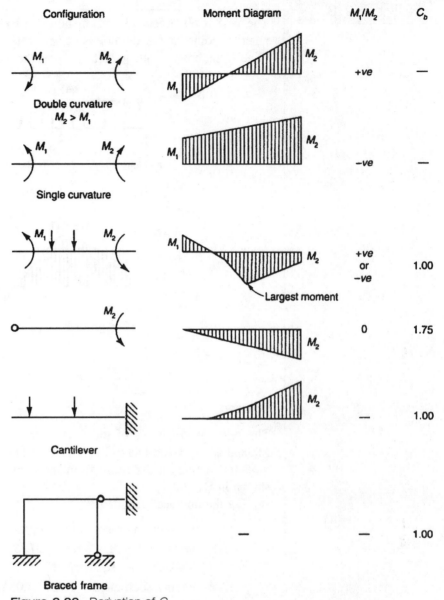

Figure 2.22 Derivation of C_b

Equation (F1-8) is independent of l/r_T and gives an allowable stress of

$$F_b = 12,000 C_b A_f / l d$$

These expressions may be solved by calculator program,[2] or the allowable beam resisting moment may be obtained from AISC Moment Charts, which are based on a value of unity for C_b and are conservative for larger values for C_b.

Compact sections and solid rectangular sections bent about their weak axes, and solid round or square bars have an allowable stress given by AISC Equation (F2-1) of

$$F_b = 0.75 F_y$$

Noncompact sections bent about their weak axes have an allowable stress given by AISC Equation (F2-2) of

$$F_b = 0.60 F_y$$

| Example **2.8** |

The W18 × 60 Grade A36 beam shown in Exhibit 5 is laterally supported at the reaction points and at the points of application of the concentrated loads. Determine if the beam is adequate to support the applied loads indicated.

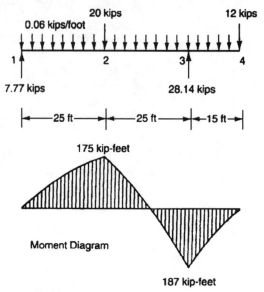

Exhibit 5

Solution

The relevant properties of the W18 × 60 section are obtained from the AISC Manual as $S_x = 108$ inches^3, $r_T = 1.96$ inches, $d/A_f = 3.47$ inches^{-1}. The bending moments acting on the beam from the applied loads and beam self-weight are shown in Exhibit 5.

For the unbraced length 12:

$$M_x = \text{maximum moment} = 175 \text{ kip-feet}$$
$$f_b = \text{maximum bending stress} = M_x/S_x = 175 \times 12/108$$
$$= 19.44 \text{ kips per square inch}$$
$$C_b = \text{bending coefficient} = 1.75 + 1.05M_1/M_2 + 0.3(M_1/M_2)^2 = 1.75$$
$$l/r_T = 153, \text{ which is } <L_1/r_T$$

Hence, AISC Equation (F1-6) is applicable and the allowable stress is

$$F_b = 12.67 \text{ kips per square inch}$$

Applying AISC Equation (F1-8) gives the allowable stress as

$$F_b = 20.17 \text{ kips per square inch}$$

which governs and is $>f_b$. Hence, the W18 × 60 is adequate over the length 12.

For the unbraced length 23:

$$M_x = 187 \text{ kip-feet}$$
$$f_b = 20.78 \text{ kips per square inch}$$
$$C_b = 1.75 + 1.05(175/187) + 0.3(175/187)^2 = 3.0$$

Use the maximum value of $C_b = 2.3$.

$$l/r_T = 153 < L_1/r_T$$

Hence, AISC Equation (F1-6) is applicable, and the allowable stress is

$$F_b = 15.38 \text{ kips per square inch}$$

Applying AISC Equation (F1-8) gives the allowable stress as $F_b = 26.51$ kips per square inch; use the maximum value of $F_b = 0.60F_y = 21.60$ kips per square inch, which governs and is $> f_b$.

Hence, the W18 × 60 is adequate over the length 23.

For the unbraced length 34:

$$M_x = 187 \text{ kip-feet}$$
$$f_b = 20.78 \text{ kips per square inch}$$
$$C_b = 1 \text{ (for a cantilever)}$$
$$l/r_T = 92, \text{ which is } < L_1/r_T$$

Hence, AISC Equation (F1-6) is applicable, and the allowable stress is

$$F_b = 16.87 \text{ kips per square inch}$$

Applying Equation (F1-8) gives the allowable stress as $F_b = 19.21$ kips per square inch, which governs and is $< f_b$.

Hence, the W18 × 60 is in adequate over the length 34.

The allowable shear stress, based on the overall beam depth, is given by AISC Equation (F4-1) as

$$F_v = 0.40F_y$$

provided $h/t_w \leq 380/\sqrt{F_y}$, and the actual shear stress is determined by

$$f_v = V/dt_w$$

where h = clear distance between the flanges, t_w = web thickness, d = overall depth of beam, and V = applied shear force.

When the end of the beam is coped, failure occurs by block shear or web tear-out, which is a combination of shear along a vertical plane and tension along a horizontal plane. The resistance to block shear is given by

$$V_B = A_v F_v + A_t F_t$$

where A_v = net shear area

A_t = net tension area

F_v = allowable shear stress = $0.30F_u$ from AISC Equation (J4-1)

F_t = allowable tensile stress = $0.50F_u$ from AISC Equation (J4-2)

In calculating the area resisting block shear, the diameter of a hole is defined in AISC Part 4, Table I-G as

$$d_h = d_b + \frac{1}{16} \text{ inch}$$

where d_b = diameter of bolt. The resistance to block shear is determined as shown in Figure 2.23.

$$A_v = t_w(l_v + 2s - 2.5d_h) = 0.31[1.5 + 6 - 2.5(0.75 + 0.0625)] = 1.70 \text{ square inches}$$
$$A_t = t_w(l_h - 0.5d_h) = 0.31(1.5 - 0.5 \times 0.8125) = 0.34 \text{ square inches}$$

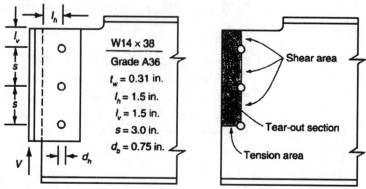

Figure 2.23   Block shear in a coped beam

The resistance to block shear is then

$$V_B = A_v F_v + A_t F_t = 1.7 \times 0.30 \times 58 + 0.34 \times 0.50 \times 58 = 39.44 \text{ kips}$$

When a concentrated load is applied to a beam, the section must be checked for web yielding, web crippling, and side sway web buckling. When the appropriate limits are exceeded, stiffeners must be provided.

To prevent web yielding, bearing stiffeners are used when the compressive stress at the toe of the web fillets exceeds the local capacity of the web specified in AISC Section K1.3 as $F_c = 0.66F_y$.

The concentrated load may be assumed to be distributed over the length of the bearing plate and at 21.8 degrees through the flange and toe of the web fillet, as shown in Figure 2.24. If required, the bearing stiffeners need not extend more than one-half the depth of the web. When the concentrated load is applied at a distance from the end of the beam not less than the depth of the beam, the local compressive stress in the web is given by AISC Equation (K1-2) as

$$f_c = R/t_w (N + 5k)$$

For loads applied closer to the end of the beam, the local web stress is given by AISC Equation (K1-3) as

$$f_c = R/t_w (N + 2.5k)$$

where R = applied load, t_w = web thickness, N = bearing plate length, and k = distance from flange face to toe of web fillet. When stiffeners are provided, AISC Equations (K1-2) and (K1-3) need not be checked.

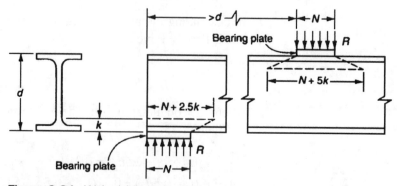

Figure 2.24   Web yielding criteria

To prevent local instability, or crippling of the web, load-carrying stiffeners are used when the concentrated load is applied at a distance from the end of the beam that is not less than one-half the depth of the beam and the load exceeds the value given by AISC Equation (K1-4) as

$$R = 67.5t_w^2[1 + 3(N/d)(t_w/t_f)^{1.5}]\sqrt{F_Y t_f/t_w}$$

For loads applied closer to the end of the beam, the value of the concentrated load is given by AISC Equation (K1-5) as

$$R = 34t_w^2[1 + 3(N/d)(t_w/t_f)^{1.5}]\sqrt{F_Y t_f/t_w}$$

where d = overall depth of the beam, and t_f = flange thickness.

When load-carrying stiffeners are required, AISC Section K1.8 specifies that these shall extend for the full height of the web and provide close bearing on, or be welded to, the loaded flanges. Where a concentrated load is directly over a support, this requirement applies to both top and bottom flanges. The stiffener is designed as an axially loaded cruciform column with a length of the web contributing to the section properties of the column (Figure 2.25). The column is assumed to buckle out of the plane of the web and to have an effective length of $0.75h$, where h is the clear distance between flanges. Additional requirements for load-carrying stiffeners are:

 (i) The limiting slenderness ratio of the column is given by AISC Section B7 as $Kl/r = 0.75h/r \le 200$.

 (ii) The stiffener plates shall extend, approximately, to the edge of the flanges.

(iii) The limiting width-thickness ratio of the stiffener plates, in accordance with Section B5.1, is $b_s/t_s \le 95/\sqrt{F_y}$.

(iv) The allowable bearing stress on the area of the stiffener plate in contact with the loaded flange is specified by AISC Equation (J8-1) as $F_p = 0.90F_y$.

 (v) Where the stiffener plate is welded to the flange, the weld capacity must equal the applied load.

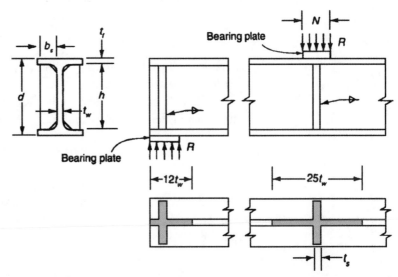

Figure 2.25 Load-carrying stiffener

(vi) The allowable shear stress on the stiffener plate is specified by AISC Equation (F4-1) as $F_v = 0.40F_y$.

(vii) The capacity of the weld between the stiffener plate and the web must not be less than the applied load.

To prevent side sway web buckling when the loaded flange is restrained against rotation, stiffeners are provided when the concentrated load exceeds the value given by AISC Equation (K1-6) as

$$R = R_5\left(1 + 0.4R_6^3\right)$$

When the loaded flange is not restrained against rotation, the value of the concentrated load is given by AISC Equation (K1-7) as

$$R = 0.4R_5R_6^3$$

where $R_5 = 6800t_w^3/h$, $R_6 = d_c b_f/lt_w$, $d_c = d - 2k$ = web depth clear of fillets, b_f = flange width, and l = largest laterally unbraced length along either flange at the point of load.

The stiffeners need not extend more than one-half the depth of the web, and they are not required in accordance with AISC Commentary K1.5 if adequate lateral restraint is provided to both flanges or if, in the case of the loaded flange *restrained* against rotation, $R_6 > 2.3$ or if, in the case of the loaded flange *not restrained* against rotation, $R_6 > 1.7$.

Plate Girder Design

When a hot-rolled section is subjected to combined shear force and bending moment, neither the shear capacity nor the resistance moment is significantly affected. However, in a plate girder, with a web depth-to-thickness ratio of $h/t_w > 970/\sqrt{F_b}$, appreciable interaction may occur, with the web incapable of providing the bending capacity assumed in proportioning the girder on its full moment of inertia, and requiring assistance from the flanges to develop its full-shear capacity. The allowable bending stress in the compression flange is then, in accordance with AISC Equation (G2-1),

$$F_b' = 0.6F_y R_{PG}$$

where $R_{PG} = 1 - 0.0005A_w(h/t_w - 760/\sqrt{F_b})/A_f \le 1$, $A_w = ht_w$ = area of web, and $A_f = b_f t_f$ = area of flange.

The tensile bending stress in the web of a plate girder that has been designed using tension field action is limited by AISC Equation (G5-1) to

$$F_{bw} = F_y(0.825 - 0.375f_v/F_v) \le 0.60F_y$$

where F_v = allowable shear stress from AISC Equation (G3-1) and f_v = calculated shear stress. When the web depth-to-thickness ratio of $h/t_w > 380/\sqrt{F_y}$, the allowable shear stress based on the clear distance between flanges is given by AISC Equation (F4-2) as

$$F_v = F_y C_v/2.89 \le 0.40F_y$$

where $C_v = 45{,}000\ k/F_y(h/t_w)^2$ when $C_v < 0.8$

$\quad C_v = 190\sqrt{k/F_y}/(h/t_w)$ when $C_v > 0.8$

$\quad k = 4.00 + 5.34/(a/h)^2$ when $a/h < 1.0$

$\quad k = 5.34 + 4.00/(a/h)^2$ when $a/h > 1.0$

$\quad a$ = clear distance between transverse stiffeners

Values of F_v in accordance with AISC Equation (F4-2) are given in AISC Part 2, Tables 1-36 and 1-50.

When the actual shear stress is less than the allowable value given by AISC Equation (F4-2) and when the web depth-to-thickness ratio is $h/t_w \leq 260$, no stiffeners are required, in accordance with AISC Section F5, and the allowable shear stress is obtained using a value of infinity for the panel aspect ratio.

When the web depth-to-thickness ratio is, from AISC Equation (G1-1),

$$h/t_w \leq 14{,}000/\sqrt{F_{yf}(F_{yf}+16.5)}$$

the panel aspect ratio, in accordance with AISC Section G1, is given by $a/h > 1.5$. When the web depth-to-thickness ratio is, from AISC Equation (G1-2),

$$h/t_w \leq 2000/\sqrt{F_{yf}}$$

the panel aspect ratio, in accordance with AISC Section G1, is given by $a/h \leq 1.5$.

When stiffeners are required in order to give an actual shear stress less than the allowable value given by AISC Equation (F4-2) or (G3-1), the panel aspect ratio, in accordance with AISC Section F5, is given by

$$a/h \leq (260t_w/h)^2 \text{ and } \leq 3$$

The applied shear stresses along the edges of a length of web plate cause diagonal compressive and tensile membrane stresses as shown in Figure 2.26. Consequently, out-of-plane buckling deformations tend to form along the compression diagonals, and the web develops its maximum strength at the elastic critical load. By providing transverse intermediate stiffeners, when the elastic critical load is reached the web panels can carry no additional load in the direction of the compression diagonals, but they can continue to sustain additional stress in the direction of the tension diagonal. This effect is termed **tensions field action** and the resultant equivalent Pratt truss, shown in Figure 2.26, possesses substantial post-buckling strength. The interior web panels on either side of an intermediate stiffener provide anchorage for the diagonal tension field. No such anchorage is available for the

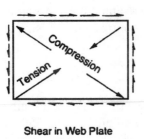

Shear in Web Plate

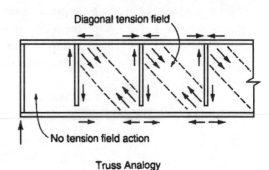

Truss Analogy

Figure 2.26 Tension field action

end panel, which must be reduced in size to prevent tension field action occurring. Similarly, in a web panel with a large hole and in the adjacent panels, tension field action must be prevented. The allowable shear stress in these panels is obtained from AISC Equation (F4-2).

When tension field action is included, the allowable shear stress is given by AISC Equation (G3-1) as

$$F_v = F_y\left[C_v + (1 - C_v)/1.15\sqrt{1 + (a/h)^2}\,\right]/2.89 \le 0.40F_y$$

Values of F_v in accordance with AISC Equation (G3-1) are given in AISC Part 2, Tables 2-36 and 2-50.

The required intermediate stiffeners may consist of pairs of stiffeners on opposite sides of the web or a single stiffener. The minimum moment of inertia of the stiffener is given by AISC Equation (G4-1) as

$$I_{st} = (h/50)^4$$

The minimum required area is given by ASIC Equation (G4-2) as

$$A_{st} = 0.5YDht(1 - C_v)\left[a/h - (a/h)^2/\sqrt{1 + (a/h)^2}\,\right]$$

where Y = ratio of yield stress of web steel to stiffener steel
D = 1.0 for a pair of stiffeners
D = 1.8 for a single angle stiffener
D = 2.4 for a single plate stiffener

The stiffener area may be reduced in the ratio of the actual to allowable shear stress.

The stiffener is connected to the web to resist a shear, in kips per linear inch, given by AISC Equation (G4-3) as

$$f_{vs} = h\sqrt{(F_y/340)^3}$$

It may be stopped short of the tension flange, with welding terminated a distance from the toe of the web-to-flange weld between $4t_w$ and $6t_w$.

Example 2.9

The welded plate girder shown in Exhibit 6 is manufactured with Grade A36 steel using E70XX electrodes. Determine if the girder is capable of supporting the applied loading indicated. It may be assumed that the end-bearing stiffeners and the load-carrying stiffeners under the concentrated loads are adequate and that the compression flange is continuously restrained against lateral displacement throughout its length.

Solution

The relevant section properties may be obtained from a calculator program[2] or from tabulated values[14] and are: I = 53,650 inches^4, $Q = yA_f = 30.625 \times 25 = 766$ inches^3, $S = I/31.25 = 1717$ inches^3, $A_w = 60 \times 0.375 = 22.5$ inches^2, $h/t_w = 60/0.375 = 160$, and $k_c = 4.05/(h/t_w)^{0.46} = 0.39$.

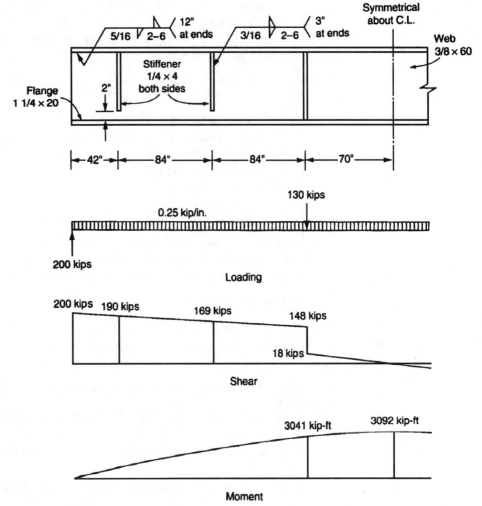

Exhibit 6   Plate girder for Example 9

The maximum allowable flange width-to-thickness ratio, in accordance with AISC Table B5.1, is

$$b/t_f = 95/\sqrt{F_y/k_c} = 95/\sqrt{36/0.39} = 9.91$$

The actual width-to-thickness ratio provided is

$b/t_f = 10/1.25 = 8$, which is < 9.91 and satisfactory.

The maximum allowable web slenderness ratio, for a stiffener spacing exceeding $1.5h$, is given by AISC Equation (G1-1) as

$$h/t_w = 14,000/\sqrt{F_{yf}(F_{yf}+16.5)} = 322$$

For a stiffener spacing of not more than $1.5h$, the limit given by AISC Equation (G1-2) is

$$h/t_w = 2000/\sqrt{F_{yf}} = 333$$

The actual slenderness ratio provided is $h/t_w = 160$, which is < 322 and satisfactory.

In accordance with AISC Section F4, since the web slenderness ratio exceeds $380/\sqrt{F_y} = 63.3$, AISC Equation (F4-1) for the allowable shear stress is not applicable. When stiffeners are required, the maximum allowable panel aspect ratio is given by AISC Equation (F5-1) as

$$a/h = (260t_w/h)^2 = 2.64$$

In the end panel, the panel aspect ratio is $a/h = 42/60 = 0.70$. The Code prohibits the use of tension field action in end panels of girders.

From AISC Part 2, Table 1-36, the maximum allowable shear stress in the web, not including tension field action, is given by $F_v = 9.1$ kips per square inch. The actual shear stress is

$f_v = V/A_w = 200/22.5 = 8.9$ kips per square inch, which is < 9.1 and satisfactory

In the second panel, the panel aspect ratio is $a/h = 84/60 = 1.40$. From AISC Part 2, Table 2-36, the allowable shear stress in the web, including tension field action, is given by $F_v = 8.5$ kips per square inch. The actual shear stress is

$f_v = V/A_w = 190/22.5 = 8.4$ kips per square inch, which is < 8.5 and satisfactory

In the central panel, the panel aspect ratio is $a/h = 140/60 = 2.33$. From AISC Table 1-36, the allowable shear stress in the web, not including tension field action, is given by $F_v = 3.7$ kips per square inch. The actual shear stress is

$f_v = V/A_w = 18/22.5 = 0.80$ kips per square inch, which is < 3.7 and satisfactory

The minimum required area for a pair of stiffener plates on opposite sides of the web, for the second panel designed using tension field action, is given by AISC Equation (G4-2) and may be obtained from Table 2-36 as

$$A_{st} = 0.083A_wf_v/F_v = 0.083 \times 22.5 \times 8.4/8.5 = 1.8 \text{ square inches}$$

The area provided is

$$A_{st} = 2 \times 4 \times 0.25 = 2.0 \text{ square inches, which is } >1.8 \text{ and satisfactory}$$

The minimum required moment of inertia of the pair of stiffeners about the web, in accordance with AISC Equation (G4-1), is

$$I_{st} = (h/50)^4 = (60/50)^4 = 2.07$$

The moment of inertia provided is

$$I_{st} \approx 0.25 \times (8.375)^3/12 = 12.2, \text{ which is } >2.07 \text{ and satisfactory}$$

In accordance with AISC Table B5.1, the maximum allowable width-to-thickness ratio of the stiffener plates is

$$b_{st}/t_{st} = 95/\sqrt{F_y} = 15.83$$

The width-to-thickness ratio provided is $b_{st}/t_{st} = 4/0.25 = 16$, or ≈ 15.83 and satisfactory.

The web thickness is $3/8$ inch and the minimum allowable fillet weld size is given by AISC Table J2.4 as $w = 3/16$ inch. The $3/16$ inch weld indicated is, therefore, satisfactory in this respect.

The capacity of the intermittent E70XX fillet weld is governed by the strength of the weld metal and is obtained from AISC Table J2.5 as

$$q = 4 \times 3 \times 0.928 \times (2/6) = 3.7 \text{ kips per inch}$$

where (2/6) represents two-inch-long welds at six-inch centers.

The shear strength required is given by AISC Equation (G4-3) as

$$f_{vs} = h\sqrt{(F_y/340)^3} = 60\sqrt{(36/340)^3} = 2.07 \text{ kips per inch}$$

which is $< q$ and satisfactory.

From AISC Part 4, Table III, the minimum required web thickness for $3/16$ inch welds on both sides of the web is

$$t_{w/\min} = 0.38 \times 2.07/3.7 = 0.21 \text{ which is } < 0.375 \text{ and satisfactory}$$

In accordance with AISC Section G4, the weld must terminate from the bottom flange a minimum distance of

$$4t_w + (\text{flange weld leg length}) = 4 \times 0.375 + 0.313 = 1.81 \text{ inches}$$

and a maximum distance of

$$6t_w + (\text{flange weld leg length}) = 6 \times 0.375 + 0.313 = 2.56 \text{ inches}$$

The weld provided terminates 2 inches from the bottom flange and is therefore within these limits.

In accordance with Table B5.1, the maximum web slenderness consistent with a compact section is

$$h/t_w = 640/\sqrt{F_y} = 106.7$$

The actual slenderness ratio provided is $h/t_w = 160$, which is >106.7. So the section is not compact, and the allowable bending stress in the flange is given by Equation (F1-5) as

$$F_b = 0.6F_y = 21.6 \text{ kips per square inch}$$

Since the compression flange is laterally restrained throughout its length, no reduction in the bending stress is necessary for lateral instability.

In accordance with AISC Section G2, a reduction in the bending stress is required to account for shear-compressive stress interaction when the web slenderness ratio exceeds

$$h/t_w = 760/\sqrt{F_b} = 760/\sqrt{21.6} = 163.5, \text{ which is } > 160$$

So no reduction to the allowable bending stress is necessary. The maximum bending stress in the flange is

$$M/S = 3092 \times 12/1717 = 21.6 \text{ kips per square inch}$$
$$= F_b \text{ and is satisfactory}$$

In the third panel, the allowable bending tensile stress is reduced because of the tension field action in the panel. The shear stress at the location of the concentrated load is

$$f_v = V/A_w = 148/22.5 = 6.6 \text{ kips per square inch}$$

The allowable bending tensile stress at the location of the concentrated load is given by AISC Equation (G5-1) as

$$F_{bw} = F_y(0.825 - 0.375\,f_v/F_v)$$
$$= 36(0.825 - 0.375 \times 6.6/8.5) = 19.2 \text{ kips per square inch}$$

The actual bending tensile stress is

$$f_{bw} = M/S = 3041 \times 12/1717 = 21.25, \text{ which is } > 19.2$$

So the allowable bending tensile stress is exceeded, and the panel aspect ratio must be reduced by providing an additional stiffener between the support and the concentrated load.

The shear applied to the flange-to-web weld is

$$q = VQ/I = 200 \times 766/53,650 = 2.86 \text{ kips per inch}$$

The flange thickness is 1.25 inches and the minimum allowable fillet weld size is given by AISC Table J2.4 as $t_{wl} = {}^5/_{16}$ inch. The capacity of the intermittent fillet weld indicated is

$$q_a = 2 \times 5 \times 0.928 \times (2/6) = 3.1 \text{ kips per inch, which is } > q \text{ and satisfactory}$$

where (2/6) represents two-inch-long welds at six-inch centers.

Composite Beams

A composite beam, as shown in Figure 2.27, consists of a concrete slab acting compositely with a steel beam to resist the total applied moment. In accordance with AISC Section I1, the effective width of the concrete slab, on either side of the beam centerline, shall not exceed:

(i) one-eighth of the beam span

(ii) one-half of the beam spacing

(iii) the distance to edge of the slab

For deflection calculations, AISC Section I2-2 requires the transformed section properties to be determined using the relevant modular ratio for the strength and weight of the concrete provided for the slab. The concrete modulus is obtained from the ACI Code[1] and the modular ratio is given by

$$n = E/E_c$$

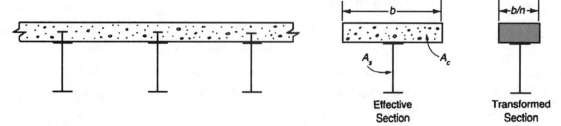

Figure 2.27 Composite beam

where E = modulus of elasticity of steel = 29,000 kips per square inch, from AISC page 5-202

E_c = modulus of elasticity of concrete

= $57,000\sqrt{f_c'}$ pounds per square inch, from ACI Section 8.5.1, for normal-weight concrete

= $33w_c^{1.5}\sqrt{f_c'}$ pounds per square inch, from ACI Section 8.5.1, for light-weight concrete

For stress computations, the modulus of elasticity for both normal-weight and lightweight concrete shall be derived from the expression for normal-weight concrete. For concrete with a compressive strength of 3000 pounds per square inch, it is customary to assume that the value of the modular ratio is $n = 9$. To assist in determining section properties, composite beam selection tables are available from AISC Part 2, Tables 2-259 to 2-291.

Because of stress redistribution, AISC Section I2 stipulates that flexural stress in the steel beam and concrete slab shall be determined from the total load applied to the transformed composite section, for both shored and unshored construction. However, for *unshored construction*, the steel beam alone must support all loads applied before the concrete has attained 75 percent of its required strength. The allowable steel stress is $F_b = 0.66 F_y$, and the combined stress due to the steel beam supporting loads applied before the concrete has hardened plus the transformed composite section supporting the remaining loads may not exceed $f_b = 0.90F_y$.

In *shored construction*, flexural stress in the concrete slab is determined from the total load applied to the transformed composite section. In *unshored construction*, flexural stress shall be determined from the load applied to the transformed composite section after the concrete has attained 75 percent of its required strength. The allowable concrete stress is $F_c = 0.45 f_c'$.

In order to achieve full composite action between the steel section and the concrete slab, shear connectors are provided to transfer the horizontal shear across the interface and prevent vertical separation. The design strength q of different types of shear connectors are given in AISC Table I4.1. Assuming that the connectors are sufficiently flexible and ductile, the required number of connectors may be uniformly distributed between the support and the point of maximum moment, with the total horizontal shear being determined by the lesser value given by AISC Equations (I4-1) and (I4-2) as

$$V_h = 0.85f_c'A_c/2, \quad \text{and} \quad V_h = F_yA_s/2$$

which represent half the compressive force in the concrete and half the tensile force in the steel beam at the limit state, respectively. To provide complete shear connection and full composite action, the required number of connectors on each side of the point of maximum moment is given by

$$N_1 = V_h/q$$

If a smaller number of connectors N_1' is provided, only partial composite action can be achieved, and the effective section modulus is given by AISC Equation (I2-1) as

$$S_{eff} = S_s + (S_{tr} - S_s)\sqrt{qN_1'/V_h}$$

where S_s = section modulus of steel beam referred to its bottom flange
S_{tr} = section modulus of fully composite transformed section referred to its bottom flange

To prevent excessive slip and reduction in stiffness, the minimum number of connectors required is given by AISC Section I4 as

$$N_1' = N_1/4$$

When a concentrated load is applied to the composite section, the number of connectors required between the support and the concentrated load is given by AISC Equation (I4-5) as

$$N_2 = N_1(M\beta/M_{max} - 1)/(\beta - 1)$$

where M = moment at concentrated load point
M_{max} = maximum moment acting on the composite section

$$\beta = S_{tr}/S_s$$

For partial composite action, substitute N_1' for N_1, and S_{eff} for S_{tr} in the above expressions. The requirements for stud spacing, in accordance with AISC Section I4, are illustrated in Figure 2.28.

The requirements for the use of formed steel deck, in accordance with AISC Section I5, are illustrated in Figure 2.29. When the deck ribs are *perpendicular* to the steel beam, the connector design strength given in AISC Table I4.1 is multiplied by the reduction factor given by Equation (I5-1) as

$$\rho = \left(0.85 w_r/h_r \sqrt{N_r}\right)(H_s/h_r - 1.0) \le 1.0$$

where h_r = height of rib
H_s = stud length, $\le (h_r + 3)$ in computations
N_r = number of connectors in one rib, ≤ 3 in computations
w_r = average width of concrete rib

When the deck ribs are *parallel* to the steel beam, the connector design strength given in AISC Table I4.1 is multiplied by the reduction factor given by Equation (I5-2) as

$$\rho = 0.6(w_r/h_r)(H_s/h_r - 1.0) \le 1.0$$

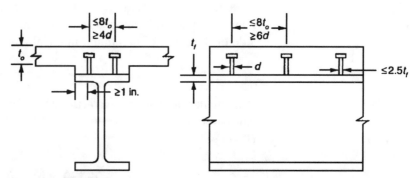

Figure 2.28 Stud spacing requirements

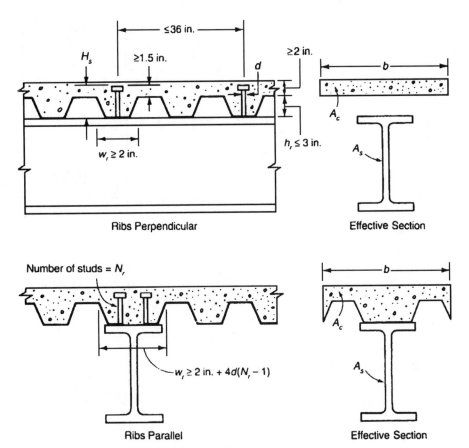

Figure 2.29 Use of formed steel deck

Compression Members

The allowable stress in an axially loaded compression member is dependent on the slenderness ratio, which is defined in AISC Section E2 as Kl/r, where r = the governing radius of gyration, Kl = effective length of the member, K = effective-length factor, and l = unbraced length of the member.

The value of the effective-length factor depends on the restraint conditions at each end of the column. AISC Table C-C2.1 specifies effective-length factors for well-defined, standard conditions of restraint, and these are illustrated in Figure 2.30. Values are indicated for ideal and practical end conditions, allowing for the fact that full fixity may not be realized. These values may be used only in simple cases when the tabulated end conditions are approached in practice.

For compression members in a plane truss, AISC Section C-C2 specifies an effective-length factor of 1.0. For load-bearing web stiffeners on a girder, AISC Section K1.6 specifies an effective-length factor of 0.75. For columns in a rigid frame that is adequately braced, AISC Section C2.1 specifies a conservative value for the effective-length factor of 1.0.

For compression members forming part of a frame with rigid joints, AISC page 3-5 presents alignment charts for determining the effective-length factor for the two conditions of side sway prevented and side sway permitted, and these are illustrated in Figure 2.31. To utilize the alignment charts, the stiffness ratio at the two ends of the column under consideration must be determined, and this is defined by

$$G = \Sigma(I_c/L_c)/\Sigma(I_g/L_g)$$

End Restraints	Ideal *K*	Practical *K*	Shape
Fixed at both ends	0.5	0.65	
Fixed at one end, pinned at the other end	0.7	0.8	
Pinned at both ends	1.0	1.0	

Sidesway prevented

- - - - - - - - - - - -

Sidesway not prevented

End Restraints	Ideal *K*	Practical *K*	Shape
Fixed at one end with the other end fixed in direction but not held in position	1.0	1.2	
Pinned at one end with the other end fixed in direction but not held in position	2.0	2.0*	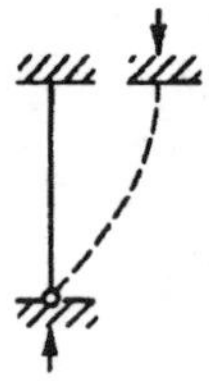
Fixed at one end with the other end free	2.0	2.1	

Note: Practical *k* value used by AISC is different than that used by NDS for wood construction.

Figure 2.30   Effective-length factors

where $\sum(I_c/L_c)$ = the sum of the *I/L* values for all columns meeting at the joint, and $\sum(I_g/L_g)$ = the sum of the *I/L* values for all girders meeting at the joint.

For a braced frame, the critical mode is shown in Figure 2.32. All the columns are assumed to buckle simultaneously, and the beams are bent in single curvature with a stiffness value of 2*EI/L*, provided each end of the beam is connected to a rigid joint in the frame.

For a sway frame, the critical mode is shown in Figure 2.33. All the columns are assumed to buckle simultaneously, and the beams are bent in double curvature with a stiffness value of 6*EI/L*.

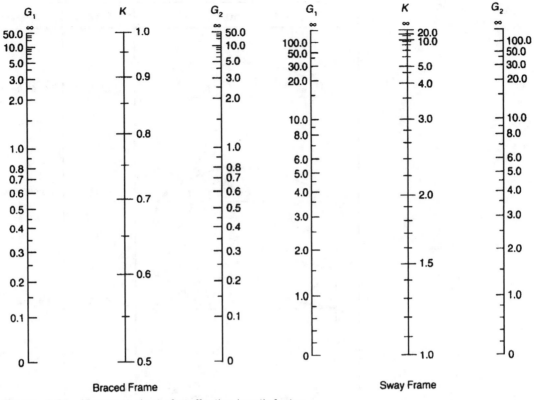

Figure 2.31 Alignment charts for effective-length factor

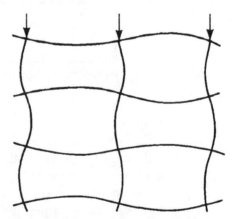

Figure 2.32 Instability of braced frame

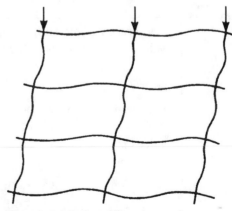

Figure 2.33 Instability of sway frame

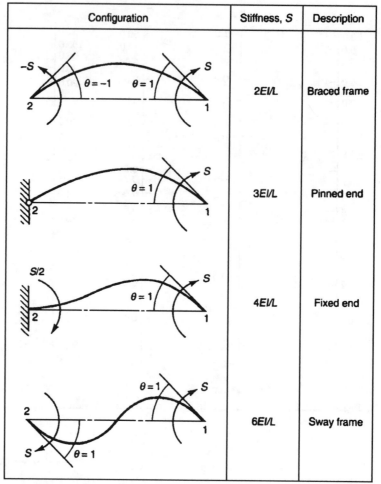

Configuration	Stiffness, S	Description
	$2EI/L$	Braced frame
	$3EI/L$	Pinned end
	$4EI/L$	Fixed end
	$6EI/L$	Sway frame

Figure 2.34   Beam stiffness

As shown in Figure 2.34, if one end of a beam is *pinned*, its stiffness is $3EI/L$, and if one end is *fixed*, its stiffness is $4EI/L$. Hence, for these two cases, adjustments must be made to the (I_g/L_g) values in determining the stiffness ratio G since the charts are based on stiffness values for the beams of $2EI/L$ and $6EI/L$ for braced and sway frames, respectively.

Example 2.10

The braced frame shown in Exhibit 7 consists of members having identical EI values. Determine the effective-lengths of both columns.

Solution

For the pinned connection at joint 5, AISC Section C-C2 specifies a stiffness ratio of $G_1 = 10$. For the two columns connected to joint 2, the sum of the relative stiffness values is

$$\Sigma(I_c/L_c) = I_{25}/L_{25} + I_{24}/L_{24} = I/L + I/L = 2I/L$$

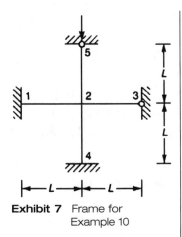

Exhibit 7 Frame for
Example 10

Allowing for the fixed end at joint 1 and the pinned end at joint 3, the sum of the adjusted relative stiffness values for the two beams connected to joint 2 is

$$\Sigma(I_g/L_g) = (4/2)I_{21}/L_{21} + (3/2)I_{23}/L_{23} = 2I/L + 1.5I/L = 3.5I/L$$

So the stiffness ratio at joint 2 is given by

$$G_2 = \Sigma(I_c/L_c)/\Sigma(I_g/L_g) = 2/3.5 = 0.57$$

Consequently, from the alignment chart for a braced frame, the effective-length factor for column 25 is

$$K_{25} = 0.82$$

For the fixed connection at joint 4, AISC Section C-C2 specifies a stiffness ratio of $G_1 = 1$. Hence, from the alignment chart for a braced frame, the effective-length factor for column 24 is

$$K_{24} = 0.74$$

The failure of a short, stocky column occurs at the squash load when the strut yields in direct compression. The allowable stress in the strut is obtained from AISC Equation (E2-1) as

$$F_a = 0.6F_y$$

As the slenderness ratio of the column is increased, the failure load reduces. The Euler elastic critical load is assumed to govern when the column stress equals half the yield stress. The critical slenderness ratio corresponding to this limit is given by AISC Equation (C-E2-1) as

$$C_c = \sqrt{2\pi^2 E/F_y}$$

Once the slenderness ratio of a column is established, the allowable compressive stress may be obtained directly from AISC Part 3, Tables C-36 and C-50 for steel members of Grades A36 and A50, respectively. For steel of any other yield stress, the allowable stress may be obtained from the expression

$$F_a = C_a F_y$$

where C_a = reduction coefficient given in AISC Part 5, Table 3.
In accordance with AISC Section B7, the slenderness ratio should preferably not exceed 200.

Combined Compression and Flexure

The flexural capacity of a member is reduced in the presence of axial load. For small values of the axial load, AISC Equation (H1-3), in order to limit the maximum stress, utilizes the interaction equation

$$f_a/F_a + f_{bx}/F_{bx} + f_{by}/F_{by} \le 1.0$$

This expression is valid if the ratio of computed axial stress to allowable axial stress is given by

$$f_a/F_a \leq 0.15$$

where F_a = axial stress that would be allowed if axial force alone existed
F_b = compressive bending stress that would be permitted if bending moment alone existed
f_a = computed axial stress
f_b = computed compression bending stress at the point considered

For larger values of the ratio (f_a/F_a), it is necessary to consider the secondary bending stresses from the P-Delta effect caused by the eccentricity of the axial force about the displaced centerline of the member. The effect of the secondary stress may be obtained by amplifying the primary bending stress by the factor

$$A_m = 1/(1 - f_a/F'_e)$$

where F'_e = factored Euler critical stress from AISC Part 5, Table 8 = $12\pi^2 E/23(Kl_b/r_b)^2$
l_b = actual unbraced length in the plane of bending
r_b = corresponding radius of gyration
K = corresponding effective-length factor
23/12 = factor safety

This value for the amplification factor is applicable to a member bent in single curvature under uniform bending moment.

For other conditions, AISC Section H1 specifies the use of the reduction factor

$$C_m = 0.6 - 0.4(M_1/M_2)$$

where M_1 = smaller moment at end of member and M_2 = larger moment at end of member. (M_1/M_2) is positive when the member is bent in reverse curvature and negative when it is bent in single curvature. Values of the reduction factor are illustrated in Figure 2.35. The effect of the reduction factor is to transform the maximum bending moment in a member to an equivalent uniform bending moment. Hence, when the member is subjected to biaxial bending, the maximum value of the bending stress about each axis must be used, even if these maximum stresses do not occur at the same point along the length of the member. When the stress ratio $(f_a/F_a) > 0.15$, AISC Equation (H1-1) requires that

$$f_a/F_a + A_{mx} C_{mx} f_{bx}/F_{bx} + A_{my} C_{my} f_{by}/F_{by} \leq 1.0$$

In addition, to control stresses at the ends of the member, AISC Equation (H1-2) requires that

$$f_a/0.6F_y + f_{bx}/F_{bx} + f_{by}/F_{by} \leq 1.0$$

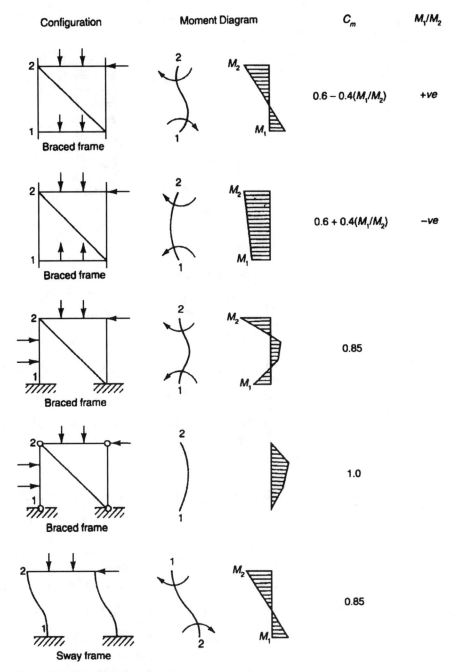

Configuration	Moment Diagram	C_m	M_1/M_2
Braced frame		$0.6 - 0.4(M_1/M_2)$	+ve
Braced frame		$0.6 + 0.4(M_1/M_2)$	−ve
Braced frame		0.85	
Braced frame		1.0	
Sway frame		0.85	

Figure 2.35 Derivation of C_m

Example **2.11**	The W14 × 120 Grade A36 column shown in Exhibit 8 is fixed at the base and unbraced about the *x*-axis. About the *y*-axis, the column is held in position at the top and at midheight, but it is not fixed in direction. Determine if the column is adequate to support an axial load of 100 kips and the indicated moments which are due to dead load, live load, and wind load.

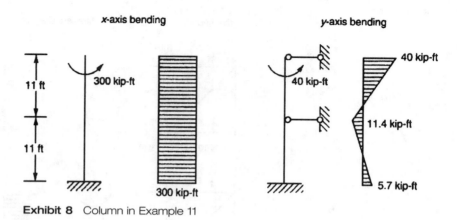

x-axis bending

11 ft

11 ft

300 kip-ft

300 kip-ft

y-axis bending

40 kip-ft

40 kip-ft

11.4 kip-ft

5.7 kip-ft

Exhibit 8 Column in Example 11

Solution

The relevant properties of the W14 × 120 are $S_x = 190$ inches^3, $S_y = 67.5$ inches^3, $A = 35.3$ inches^2, $L_c = 15.5$ feet, $r_x = 6.24$ inches, and $r_y = 3.74$ inches. From Figure 2.31, the slenderness ratio about the y-axis is given by

$$Kl/r_y = 0.8 \times 11 \times 12/3.74 = 28.2$$

The slenderness ratio about the x-axis is given by

$$Kl/r_x = 2.1 \times 22 \times 12/6.24 = 88.8, \text{ which governs}$$

For this value of the slenderness ratio, AISC Part 3, Table C-36 gives an allowable axial stress of

$$F_a = 14.34 \text{ kips per square inch}$$

The axial stress from the imposed loading is

$$f_a = P/A = 100/35.3 = 2.83 \text{ kips per square inch}$$

In accordance with AISC Section A5.2, allowable stresses may be increased by one-third when the applied loading includes wind load. Hence, the ratio of computed axial stress to allowable axial stress is

$$f_a/1.33F_a = 2.83/(1.33 \times 14.34) = 0.148, \text{ which is } <0.15$$

Hence, in accordance with AISC Section H1, Equation (H1-3) is applicable.

For bending about the x-axis, the unbraced length of the compression flange is $l = 11$ feet, which is $<L_c$. Hence, from AISC Equation (F1-1), the allowable bending stress is

$$F_{bx} = 0.66F_y = 0.66 \times 36 = 23.76 \text{ kips per square inch}$$

The bending stress due to the imposed moment about the x-axis is

$$f_{bx} = M_x/S_x = 300 \times 12/190 = 18.95 \text{ kips per square inch}$$

For bending about the y-axis, AISC Equation (F2-1) gives an allowable stress of

$$F_{by} = 0.75F_y = 27 \text{ kips per square inch}$$

The maximum bending stress from the imposed moment about the y-axis is

$$f_{by} = M_y/S_y = 40 \times 12/67.5 = 7.11 \text{ kips per square inch}$$

The left-hand side of AISC interaction Equation (H1-3) is evaluated as

$$f_a/1.33F_a + f_{bx}/1.33F_{bx} + f_{by}/1.33F_{by} = 0.148 + 18.95/(1.33 \times 23.76)$$
$$+ 7.11/(1.33 \times 27) = 0.95$$

which is < 1.0, so the column is satisfactory.

In order to determine whether a trial column section can resist a given combination of biaxial bending and axial load, use may be made of AISC Part 3, Table B. The tabulated values enable the bending moments to be transformed into equivalent axial loads. The required column section may then be selected from the appropriate column load table.

Example 2.12

Select a trial W14 Grade A36 column to support an axial load of 70 kips and the moments indicated in Exhibit 9.

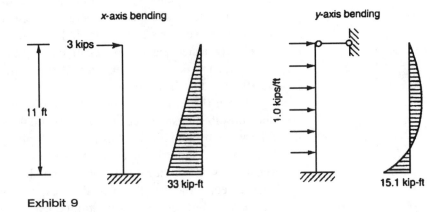

Exhibit 9

Solution

The maximum moments acting on the column are shown in Exhibit 9. The effective length about the *y*-axis, which governs, is obtained from Figure 2.33 as

$$Kl = 0.8 \times 11 = 8.8 \text{ feet}$$

For bending about the *y*-axis, the column acts as a member in a braced frame with applied lateral loading. Hence, the reduction factor is obtained from Figure 2.35 as $C_m = 0.85$, and tabulated values of the factor *m* in AISC Part 3, Table B are directly applicable. (If C_m is other than 0.85, then multiply *m* by $C_m/0.85$.) From Table B, the relevant factors are $m = 1.8$ and $U = 3$. The equivalent axial load is given by

$$P_{eff} = P_0 + M_x m + M_y mU = 70 + 33 \times 1.8 + 15.1 \times 1.8 \times 3 = 211 \text{ kips}$$

From the AISC column load tables, a W14 × 48 may be selected which, for an effective length of 8.8 feet, has an allowable axial load of 252 kips and a value of 4.39 for the factor *U*. The revised value for the equivalent axial load is then

$$P_{eff} = 70 + 33 \times 1.8 + 15.1 \times 1.8 \times 4.39 = 249 \text{ kips, which is} < 252 \text{ kips}$$

Hence, the W14 × 48 may be used as a trial section in applying the accurate design procedure of AISC Section H1.

Bolted Connections

Bolts which are loaded in shear may be classified as either slip-critical or bearing-type. *Slip-critical* bolts are high-strength bolts, Grade A325 or A490, which are pretensioned to the values specified in AISC Table J3.7 so as to produce a clamping force between the parts that prevents slip under service loading. Slip is considered detrimental to the structure in the following situations:

(i) Fatigue loading (Section A-K4.3)

(ii) Oversized holes (Section J3.2)

(iii) Bolts used in conjunction with welds (Section J1.10)

(iv) Impact loading and stress reversal (Section J1.12)

(v) Column splices and girder to column connections in tall structures (J1.12)

Bearing-type connections may be of Grade A307, A325, or A490 and depend upon contact of the bolts against the sides of their holes to resist shear forces. The allowable tensile loads on bolts are tabulated in AISC Part 4, Table I-A, the allowable shear loads are in Part 4, Table I-D, and the allowable bearing capacity of the connected parts is given in Part 4, Table I-E. These values apply if the requirements for bolt spacing and edge distance given in AISC Sections J3.8 and J3.10 and Table J3.5 are met.

When a bearing-type connector is subjected to combined shear and tension, the allowable tensile force is reduced while the allowable shear force is unaffected. The value of the reduced tensile stress is given in AISC Table J3.3.

When a slip-critical connection is subjected to combined shear and direct tension, as shown in Figure 2.36(a), the allowable tensile force in a connector is unaffected, while the allowable shear capacity given in AISC Table I-D, in accordance with Section J3.6, is multiplied by the reduction factor

$$R = (1 - T/T_b)$$

where T = applied tensile force on the bolt and T_b = pretension force on the bolt specified in Table J3.7.

However, when the tensile force in the connector is caused by a bending moment applied in a plane perpendicular to the plane of the connection, as shown in Figure 2.36(b), no reduction is necessary, since the increase in compressive force at the bottom of the connection compensates for the tension produced in the connectors at the top of the connection.

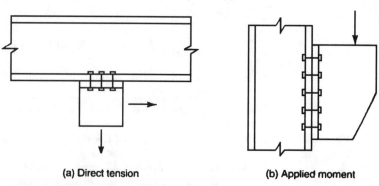

(a) Direct tension   (b) Applied moment

Figure 2.36 Combined shear and tension

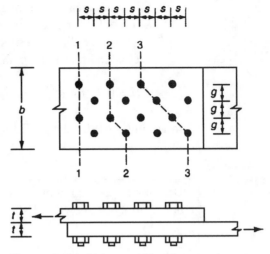

Figure 2.37 Net area of tension member

In determining the capacity of a connection in direct tension, as shown in Figure 2.37, allowance must be made for the effective areas of the members and their method of attachment. To prevent excessive elongation of the members, which may lead to instability of the whole structure, AISC Section D1 limits the maximum tensile force on the connection to

$$P_t = 0.6F_y A_g$$

where A_g = gross area of the member = bt.

To prevent fracture of the member at the section of weakest effective net area, AISC Section D1 limits the maximum tensile force on the connection to

$$P_t = 0.5F_u A_e$$

where A_e = effective net area. The effective net area is defined in AISC Section B2 as

$$A_e = t(b - 2d_h), \text{ for Section 1-1}$$

where d_h = diameter of hole defined in AISC Section B2 and AISC Table J3.1
    = $(d_b + {}^1/_8 \text{ inch})$, where d_b = bolt diameter

$$A_e = t(b - 3d_h + s^2/4g) \text{ for Section 2-2}$$

where s = longitudinal pitch
    g = transverse gage

$$A_e = t(b - 4d_h + 3s^2/4g) \text{ for Section 3-3}$$

The expression $(s^2/4g)$ given by AISC Section B2 is the formula for computing net section through any diagonal or zigzag line of holes.

To account for the effects of eccentricity and shear lag in rolled structural shapes connected through only part of their cross-sectional elements, the effective net area is given by AISC Equation (B3-1) as

$$A_e = UA_n$$

where A_n = net area of the member

    $U = 0.90$ for I-sections with $b_f \geq 2d/3$ and with not less than three bolts in the direction of stress

    $U = 0.85$ for all other shapes with not less than three bolts in the direction of stress

    $U = 0.75$ for all shapes with only two bolts in the direction of stress

In addition, AISC Section B3 specifies that $A_e \leq 0.85A_g$.

Example 2.13

Determine the maximum allowable load that may be applied at position P on the bolted structure shown in Exhibit 10. The structural sections are Grade A36.

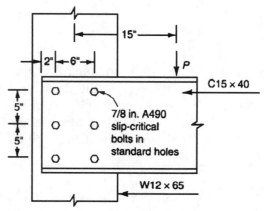

Exhibit 10   Connection for Example 13

Solution

The geometrical properties of the bolt group are obtained by applying the unit area method.

    The inertia about the x-axis is $I_x = 4 \times 5^2 = 100$ inches^4.

    The inertia about the y-axis is $I_y = 6 \times 3^2 = 54$ inches^4.

    The polar inertia about the centroid is $I_o = I_x + I_y = 154$ inches^4.

The top right bolt is the most heavily loaded, and the co-existent forces on this bolt are:

    Vertical force due to vertical load = $P/6 = 0.17P$.

    Vertical force due to moment = $15P_x/I_o = 15P \times 3/154 = 0.29P$.

    Horizontal force due to moment = $15Py/I_o = 15P \times 5/154 = 0.49P$.

    Total vertical force = $P(0.17 + 0.29) = 0.46P$.

    The resultant force is given by $R = P\sqrt{0.49^2 + 0.46^2} = 0.67P$.

From AISC Part 4, Table I-D, the allowable shear force on a $^7/_8$-inch A490 slip-critical bolt in a standard hole in single shear is

$$P_s = 12.6 \text{ kips}$$

The maximum allowable load on the bracket is, then,

$$P = 12.6/0.67 = 18.8 \text{ kips}$$

The connection may slip into bearing, and the bearing capacity is governed by the minimum thickness of the connected parts, which is the channel web thickness $t_w = 0.52$ inches.

From AISC Part 4, Table I-E, the bearing capacity is

$$P_b = 30.5 \times 0.52/0.50 = 31.7 \text{ kips, which is } > 12.6$$

Hence, the maximum allowable load on the bracket is $P = 18.8$ kips

---

Example **2.14**

Determine if the bearing-type bolts shown in Exhibit 11 are adequate to support the indicated wind load. The structural sections are Grade A36.

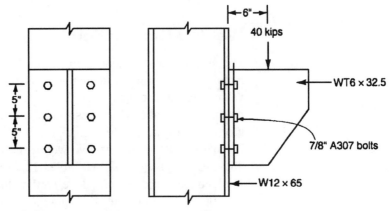

Exhibit 11   Connection for Example 14

Solution

Assuming the neutral axis occurs at the centroid of the bolt group, and applying the unit area method, the inertia about the x-axis is

$$I_x = 4 \times 5^2 = 100 \text{ inches}^4$$

The modulus of the top bolts is

$$S_x = I_x/y = 100/5 = 20 \text{ inches}^3$$

The applied moment on the bolt group is

$$M = P_e = 40 \times 6 = 240 \text{ kip-inches}$$

The tensile force on each of the top bolts due to the moment is

$$P_H = M/2S_x = 240/40 = 6 \text{ kips}$$

The shear force on each bolt due to the vertical load is

$$P_V = P/6 = 40/6 = 6.67 \text{ kips}$$

From AISC Table I-D, the allowable shear force, increased by one-third for wind load, on a $^7/_8$-inch A307 bolt in a standard hole in single shear is

$$P_s = 6.0 \times 1.33 = 8.0 \text{ kips, which is satisfactory because it is} > P_V$$

The shear stress on a top bolt is

$$f_v = P_V / A_b = 6.67/0.60 = 11.12 \text{ kips per square inch}$$

From AISC Table J3.3, the allowable tensile force, increased by one-third for wind load, on a $^7/_8$-inch A307 bolt is

$$P_t = A_b (26 \times 1.33 - 1.8 f_v) = 0.60 (26 \times 1.33 - 1.8 \times 11.12) = 8.76 \text{ kips}$$

which is satisfactory because it is $> P_H$.

Hence, the connection is adequate.

Welded Connections

The strength of a welded connection depends on either the strength of the base metal or the strength of the deposited weld metal, and the relevant allowable stress values are tabulated in AISC Table J2.5. The strength of the weld metal is the product of the allowable stress and the effective area. For a complete-penetration groove weld, the effective thickness is the thickness of the thinner part joined. For partial-penetration groove welds and flare groove welds, the effective throat thickness is given in AISC Tables J2.1 and J2.2. For fillet welds made by the shielded metal arc process, the effective throat thickness in accordance with AISC Section J2.2 is illustrated in Figure 2.38.

The strength of a $^1/_{16}$-inch fillet weld per inch run of Grade E70XX electrodes is given by

$$q = 0.3 F_{u(\text{weld})} \, t_{fw} = 0.3 \times 70 \times 0.707/16 = 0.928 \text{ kips per inch per } ^1/_{16}\text{-inch}$$

The strength of the base metal, in accordance with AISC Section F4, for Grade A36 steel is given by

$$q_{(\text{base})} = 0.4 F_{y(\text{base})} \, t_{(\text{base})} = 0.4 \times 36 \, t_{(\text{base})} = 14.4 \, t_{(\text{base})} \text{ kips per inch}$$

Hence, to develop the full capacity of a $^1/_{16}$-inch weld, the thickness of the base is given by

$$t_{(\text{base})} = 0.928/14.4 = 0.064 \text{ inch} \dots \text{weld on one side of base}$$
$$= 0.128 \text{ inch} \dots \text{weld on both sides of base}$$

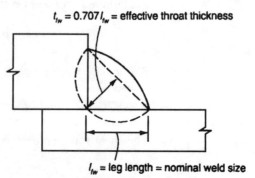

$t_{fw} = 0.707\, l_{fw}$ = effective throat thickness

l_{fw} = leg length = nominal weld size

Figure 2.38   Fillet weld dimensions

Example **2.15**

Determine the size of E70XX fillet weld required for the gusset plate shown in Exhibit 12. All material is Grade A36.

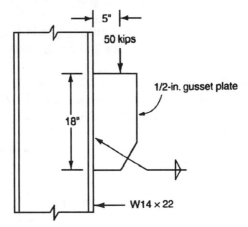

Exhibit 12   Welded gusset plate

Solution

Using the elastic vector analysis technique and assuming unit size of weld, the geometrical properties of the gusset plate weld are

> Length of weld, $L = 2 \times 18 = 36$ inches
> Area, $A = 1 \times L = 36$ inches^2 per inch
> Section modulus, $S = 2 \times 18^2/6 = 108$ inches^3

The moment acting about the centroid of the weld profile is

$$M_o = F_V e = 50 \times 5 = 250 \text{ kip-inches}$$

The co-existent forces acting at the ends of the weld profile in the x-direction and y-direction are

$$f_x = M_o/S = 250/108 = 2.31 \text{ kips per inch}$$
$$f_y = F_V/A = 50/36 = 1.39 \text{ kips per inch}$$

The resultant force at the ends of the weld profile is

$$f_R = \sqrt{f_x^2 + f_y^2} = \sqrt{2.31^2 + 1.39^2} = 2.70 \text{ kips per inch}$$

The required fillet weld size per $^1/_{16}$ inch is

$$l_{fw} = f_R/q = 2.70/0.928 = 2.9$$

Hence, a $^3/_{16}$-inch fillet weld is adequate.

From AISC Table J2.4, the minimum size of fillet weld required for the $^1/_2$-inch-thick gusset plate is $^3/_{16}$ inch, so the $^3/_{16}$-inch weld is satisfactory.

To account for the effects of eccentricity and shear lag in rolled structural shapes connected through only part of their cross-sectional elements, the effective net area is given by AISC Equation (B3-2) as

$$A_e = UA_g$$

where A_g = gross area of member
$U = 1.0$ when $\lambda > 2w$
$U = 0.87$ when $2w = \lambda > 1.5w$
$U = 0.75$ when $1.5w > \lambda > w$

where λ = weld length in inches
      w = plate width (distance between welds) in inches

Example 2.16

Determine the size of the E70XX fillet weld required for the welded bracket shown in Exhibit 13. All material is Grade A36.

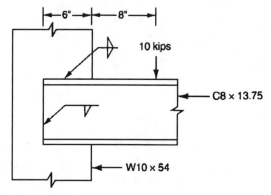

Exhibit 13   Welded connection for Example 16

Solution

Using the elastic vector analysis technique and assuming unit size of weld, the geometrical properties of the weld are:

Length of weld, $L = 8 + 2 \times 6 = 20$ inches,
Area, $A = 1 \times L = 20$ inches^2 per inch,
Centroid location, $\bar{x} = 2 \times 6 \times 3/20 = 1.8$ inches,
Inertia about x-axis, $I_x = 8^3/12 + 2 \times 6 \times 4^2 = 234.7$ inches^4 per inch,
Inertia about y-axis, $I_y = 2 \times 6^3/12 + 2 \times 6 \times 1.2^2 + 8 \times 1.8^2 = 79.2$ inches^4 per inch
Polar inertia, $I_o = I_x + I_y = 234.7 + 79.2 = 313.9$ inches^4 per inch.
The moment acting about the centroid of the weld profile is

$$M_o = F_V e = 10 \, (8 + 6 - \bar{x}) = 10(8 + 6 - 1.8) = 122 \text{ kip-inches}.$$

The top right-hand corner of the weld profile is the most highly stressed, and the co-existent forces acting at this point in the x-direction and y-direction are

$$f_x = M_o y/I_o = 122 \times 4/313.9 = 1.55 \text{ kips per inch},$$
$$f_y = F_V/A + M_o x/I_o = 10/20 + 122 \times 4.2/313.9 = 2.13 \text{ kips per inch}.$$

The resultant force is

$$f_R = \sqrt{f_x^2 + f_y^2} = \sqrt{1.55^2 + 2.13^2} = 2.64 \text{ kips per inch}.$$

The required fillet weld size per $^1/_{16}$ inch is

$$l_{fw} = f_R/q = 2.64/0.928 = 2.8.$$

Hence, a $^3/_{16}$-inch fillet weld is adequate.

The flange thickness of the C8 × 13.75 is $t_f = \frac{3}{8}$ inch. From AISC Table J2.4, the minimum size of fillet weld required is $\frac{3}{16}$ inch. Hence, the $\frac{3}{16}$-inch weld is satisfactory.

The web thickness of the C8 × 13.75 is $t_w = \frac{5}{16}$ inch. From AISC Section J22, the maximum size of weld permitted along the edge of the channel web is $\frac{1}{4}$ inch. Hence, the $\frac{3}{16}$-inch weld is satisfactory.

DESIGN OF WOOD STRUCTURES

Allowable Stresses

For sawn lumber, the allowable stresses depend on the wood species, the size classification, the grade designation, and the method of grading. These items are defined in the NDS.[13] For visually graded sawn lumber, the basic design values are tabulated in the NDS SUPP[14] Table 4A. For machine-stress-rated lumber, the basic design values are tabulated in NDS SUPP Table 4C. For glued-laminated timber, the basic design values are tabulated in NDS SUPP Tables 5A–5D. These tabulated base values are applicable for normal conditions of use and duration of load and for dry conditions of service. NDS Sections 4.1.4 and 5.1.5 define dry conditions of service as moisture content not exceeding 19 percent for sawn lumber and not exceeding 16 percent for glued-laminated timber. For other conditions of use, NDS Section 2.3 specifies the following adjustment factors:

Repetitive Member Factor, C_r

When three or more sawn lumber elements not exceeding 4 inches in thickness and spaced not more than 24 inches apart are joined by a transverse load-distributing element, the bending stress may be increased. NDS Section 4.3.9 specifies that $C_r = 1.15$.

Size Factor, C_F

For visually graded sawn lumber joists exceeding 12 inches in depth and 5 inches in thickness the **size factor,** an adjustment for loss of tensile strength with increasing depth, is applied to the bending stress and is defined in NDS Section 4.3.6 as

$$C_F = (12/d)^{1/9}$$

The size factor for visually graded sawn lumber 2 to 4 inches in thickness may be obtained from NDS SUPP Tables 4A and 4B. The size factor is not applicable to glued-laminated members or machine-stress-rated lumber.

Volume Factor, C_V

The volume factor is applicable to glued-laminated beams only and is given by NDS Section 5.3.6 as

$$C_V = (1291.5/bdL)^{1/x}$$

where L = length of beam between points of zero moment, feet
$\quad b$ = beam width, inches
$\quad d$ = beam depth, inches
$\quad x$ = 20 ... for Southern Pine
$\quad\quad$ = 10 ... for all other species

The volume factor is not cumulative with the **lateral-stability-of-beams factor,** which is an adjustment for loss of compressive strength with increasing slenderness.

The lower allowable bending stress considering either size factor or lateral stability factor governs.

Load Duration Factor, C_D

With the exception of compression-perpendicular-to-the-grain and modulus of elasticity, the load duration factor is applicable to all base values, including those for connectors, with the exception of impact. Values of the load duration factor are provided in NDS Table 2.3.2 and are

Load Duration	C_D
Permanent, >10 years	0.90
Normal, ≤10 years	1.00
Snow load, 2 months	1.15
Construction load, 7 days	1.25
Wind or earthquake	1.60
Impact	2.00 (not applicable to connectors).

Wet Service Factor, C_M

When the moisture content of sawn lumber exceeds 19 percent, and that of glued-laminated timber exceeds 16 percent, wet service factors apply. Values of the wet service factor are provided in the NDS Supplement and are

Basic Design Value	Lumber $b \leq 4"$	Lumber $b \geq 5"$	Glu-lam
Bending stress, F_b	0.85*	1.00	0.80
Tensile stress, F_t	1.00	1.00	0.80
Shear, F_v	0.97	1.00	0.875
Compression perpendicular to grain, $F_{c\perp}$	0.67	0.67	0.53
Compression parallel to grain, F_c	0.80**	0.91	0.73
Modulus of elasticity, E	0.90	1.00	0.833

*When $(F_b)(C_F) \leq 1150$ psi, $C_M = 1.0$.
**When $(F_c)(C_F) \leq 750$ psi, $C_M = 1.0$.

The wet service factors for connectors are given in NDS Table 10.3.3.

Flat Use Factor, C_{fu}

When visually graded lumber is loaded flatwise, the following flat use factors given in the NDS Supplement are applicable to the bending stress:

Thickness	$b = 2"$ or $3"$	$b = 4"$	$b = 5"$	$b = 6"$ or $8"$	$b \geq 10"$
$d = 2"$ or $3"$	1.0	1.1	1.1	1.15	1.2
$d = 4"$	—	1.0	1.05	1.05	1.1

For machine-stress-rated lumber, the flat use factors are

Width, $b =$	2" or 3"	4"	5"	6"	8"	10" or wider
$d = 2"$	1.00	1.10	1.10	1.15	1.15	1.20

Fire-Retardant Treatment

The effects of fire-retardant treatment on strength shall be obtained from the company providing the treatment.

Bearing Area Factor, C_b

For bearings not exceeding 6 inches long, and not nearer than 3 inches to the end of a member, NDS Section 3.10.4 specifies the adjustment factor as

$$C_b = (l_b + 0.375)/l_b$$

where l_b = length of bearing, in inches, along the grain of the wood.

Values of C_b corresponding to various values of l_b are provided in NDS Table 3.10.4.

Curvature Factor, C_c

To account for residual stresses in curved, glued-laminated beams, NDS Section 5.3.8 specifies the adjustment factor as

$$C_c = 1 - 2000(t/R)^2$$

where t = thickness of lamination in inches
R = radius of curvature of inside face of lamination in inches

Form Factor, C_f

The form factor, specified in NDS Section 3.3.4, is applicable to circular beams and square beams loaded on a diagonal. It is given by $C_f = 1.18$ for a circular member and $C_f = 1.414$ for a square member with diagonal vertical.

Applicability of Adjustment Factors

The following matrix indicates the use of each adjustment factor:

Application of adjustment factors

Adjustment Factor	F_b	F_t	F_v	$F_{c\perp}$	F_c	E
C_D, load duration factor	×	×	×	—	×	—
C_M, wet service factor	×	×	×	×	×	×
C_b, bearing area factor	—	—	—	×	—	—
C_L, beam stability factor[1]	×	—	—	—	—	—
C_P, column stability factor	—	—	—	—	×	—
C_t, temperature factor	×	×	×	×	×	×
C_i, incising factor[2]	×	×	×	×	×	×
C_f, form factor[3]	×	—	—	—	—	—
C_F, size factor[4]	×	×	—	—	×	—
C_r, repetitive member factor[5]	×	—	—	—	—	—
C_{fu}, flat use factor[6]	×	—	—	—	—	—
C_V, volume factor[1,7]	×	—	—	—	—	—
C_c, curvature factor[8]	×	—	—	—	—	—

Notes:
1. For glued-laminated members, only the lesser value of C_L or C_V is applicable.
2. Applies only to incised sawn lumber.
3. Applies only to sawn lumber with circular or square section loaded on a diagonal.
4. Applies only to visually graded sawn lumber and round timber members.
5. Applies only to dimension lumber bending members 2" to 4" thick.
6. Applies only to dimension lumber and glued laminated bending members.
7. Applies only to glued laminated bending members.
8. Applies only to curved glued laminated bending members.

Example **2.17**

A glued-laminated, simply supported, curved beam of combination 24F–V4 (24F–1.8E) western species with 1.5-inch-thick laminations has a curvature radius of 40 feet, a width of 6.75 inches, and a depth of 24 inches. The beam is fully supported laterally and has a moisture content exceeding 16 percent. The governing loading combination is dead load plus snow load and the span is 28 feet. Determine the allowable bending and shear stresses and modulus of elasticity.

Solution

The basic design values for bending, shear, and modulus of elasticity are obtained from NDS SUPP Table 5A and are $F_b = 2400$ pounds per square inch, $F_v = 240$ pounds per square inch, and $E = 1.8 \times 10^6$ pounds per square inch, respectively.
   The applicable adjustment factors for bending stress are

(i) C_V = volume factor = $K_L(1291.5/bdL)^{1/x}$ = $1.0(1291.5/6.75 \times 24 \times 28)^{1/10}$ = 0.88

(ii) C_D = load duration factor = 1.15 for snow load

(iii) C_M = wet service factor = 0.80 for glued-laminated beams

(iv) C_c = curvature factor = $1 - 2000(t/R)^2 = 1 - 2000(1.5/12 \times 40)^2 = 0.98$

 (v) C_L = stability factor = 1 ... volume factor governs

The adjusted bending stress is then

$$F_b' = C_V C_D C_M C_c F_b = 0.88 \times 1.15 \times 0.80 \times 0.98 \times 2400$$
$$= 0.80 \times 2400 = 1908 \text{ pounds per square inch}$$

   The applicable adjustment factors for shear stress are

(i) C_D = load duration factor = 1.15

(ii) C_M = wet service factor = 0.875 for glued-laminated beams

The adjusted shear stress is then

$$F_v' = C_D C_M F_v = 1.15 \times 0.875 \times 240$$
$$= 1.01 \times 240 = 241 \text{ pounds per square inch}$$

The applicable adjustment factor for modulus of elasticity is

C_M = wet service factor = 0.833 for glued-laminated beams

The adjusted modulus of elasticity is then

$$E' = C_M E = 0.833 \times 1.8 \times 10^6 = 1.5 \times 10^6 \text{ pounds per square inch}$$

Wood Beams

For simply supported beams, in accordance with NDS Section 3.2.1, the effective beam span is taken as the clear span plus one-half the required bearing length at each end.
   When the depth of a beam does not exceed its breadth or when continuous lateral restraint is provided to the compression edge of a beam with the ends restrained against rotation, lateral instability does not occur. For all other situations,

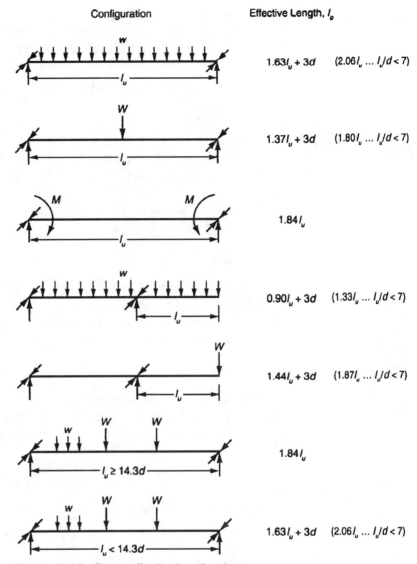

Figure 2.39 Beam effective length values

in accordance with NDS Section 3.3.3, lateral instability must be investigated and a reduction made to the basic design value for the bending stress.

Figure 2.39 illustrates the relationship between the effective length l_e, the unbraced length l_u, and the imposed loading. When lateral restraint is provided at intermediate points along a member, the unbraced length is defined as the distance between such points. The slenderness ratio for the member is then given by NDS Equation (3.3-5) as

$$R_B = \sqrt{l_e d / b^2} \le 50$$

The beam stability factor is given by NDS Section 3.3.3 as

$$C_L = (1.0 + F)/1.9 - \{[(1.0 + F)/1.9]^2 - F/0.95\}^{0.5}$$

where $F = F_{bE}/F_b^*$
  F_b^* = adjusted tabulated bending stress
  F_{bE} = critical buckling design value
    $= K_{bE}E'/R_B^2$

K_{bE} = Euler buckling coefficient

= 0.610… for machine-stress-rated lumber

= 0.439…for visually graded lumber

= 0.561…for machine-evaluated lumber

E' = adjusted tabulated modulus of elasticity

Example **2.18**

A glued-laminated, simply supported beam of western species combination 24F–V5 (24F–1.7E) has its compression edge laterally braced at 8 feet on centers. The beam, which is size $5\,^{1}/_{8} \times 36$ inches, forms part of a roof framing system in an area free from snow and spans 63 feet. Determine the allowable bending stress for the dead plus live load combination.

Solution

The basic design values are obtained from NDS SUPP Table 5A and are $F_b =$ 2400 pounds per square inch and $E = 1.7 \times 10^6$ pounds per square inch.

For a uniformly distributed load and l_u/d ratio less than 7, the effective length between braces is obtained from Figure 2.38 as

$$l_e = 2.06 l_u = 2.06 \times 8 = 16.48 \text{ feet}$$

For roof loading, the load duration factor is $C_D = 1.25$ (7-day construction load). The adjusted bending stress is $F_b^* = 1.25 \times 2400 = 3000$ pounds per square inch. The volume factor applicable to glued-laminated beams is given by

$$C_V = (1291.5/bdL)^{1/x}$$
$$= (1291.5/5.125 \times 36 \times 63)^{1/10} = 0.803$$

The slenderness ratio is given by

$$R_B = (l_e d/b^2)^{0.5} = (12 \times 16.48 \times 36/5.125^2)^{0.5} = 16.46\ldots < 50$$

The Euler buckling coefficient for beams is given by NDS Section 3.3.3.8 as

$$K_{bE} = 0.745 - 1.225 \text{COV}_E$$

where

$\text{COV}_E = 0.10$ for glued-laminated timber

Hence

$$K_{bE} = 0.745 - 1.225 \times 0.10$$
$$= 0.6225\ldots \text{for glued-laminated timber}$$

F_{bE} = critical buckling design value

$$= K_{bE}E'/R_B^2 = 0.6225 \times 1.7 \times 10^6/16.46^2 = 3905 \text{ pounds per square inch.}$$

$$F = F_{bE}/F_b^* = 3905/3000 = 1.30$$

The beam stability factor is given by

$$C_L = (1.0+F)/1.9 - \{[(1.0+F)/1.9]^2 - F/0.95\}^{0.5}$$
$$= 0.899 \quad > C_V = 0.803$$

The volume factor governs and the allowable stress is given by

$$F_b' = C_V F_b^* = 0.803 \times 3000 = 2408 \text{ pounds per square inch}$$

The shear stress in a rectangular beam is defined in NDS Section 3.4.2 as

$$f_v = 1.5 V/bd \leq F_v'$$

where V = shear force on the member, neglecting all loads applied to the top of the beam that are within a distance from either support that equals the depth of the beam. This is illustrated by Figure 2.40, where the shear stress is given by NDS Equation 3.4-1 as

$$f_v = VQ/Ib$$

where Q = statical moment = $bd^2/8$, and I = moment of inertia = $bd^3/12$. So $f_v = 1.5V/bd$.

Notches in a beam introduce stress concentrations that reduce the shear capacity of a beam. NDS Section 3.2.3 imposes restrictions on the size and location of notches in sawn lumber beams as shown in Figure 2.41. Notches are prohibited on the tension side of glued-laminated beams except at the ends for bearing over a support. The notch depth shall not exceed the lesser of $d/10$ or 3 inches. Notches with a maximum depth of $2d/5$ and a maximum length of $l/3$ are permitted on the compression side at the ends of glued-laminated beams. The shear stress at a notch on the tension side of a beam is given by NDS Section 3.4.3.2(a) as

$$f_v = (1.5V/bd_n)(d/d_n)^2 \leq F_v'$$

The shear stress at a notch on the compression side of a beam is given by NDS Equation (3.4-5) as

$$f_v = 1.5V/b[d - e(d - d_n)/d_n] \leq F_v'$$

For a bolted joint less than five times the depth of the member from its end, as shown in Figure 2.41, the shear stress, in accordance with NDS Section 3.4.3.3(a), is given by

$$f_v = (1.5V/bd_e)(d/d_e)^2 \leq F_v'$$

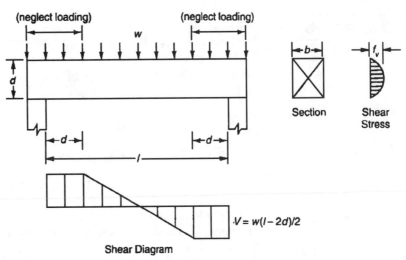

Shear Diagram

Figure 2.40 Shear in a wood beam

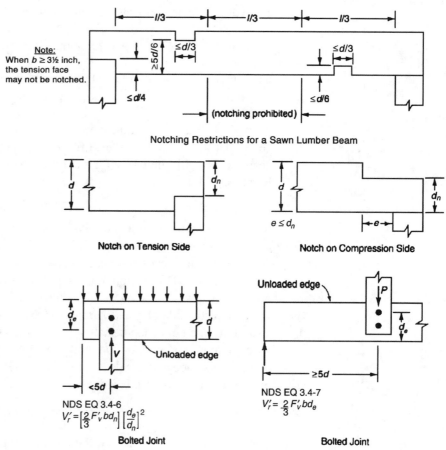

Figure 2.41 Notched beams

When the joint is located not less than five times the depth of the member from its end, the shear stress is given by NDS Equation (3.4-7) as

$$f_v = 1.5V/bd_e \leq 1.5F_v'$$

For joints utilizing connectors, the value of d_e is the depth from the unloaded edge to the farthest edge of the farthest connector.

Example **2.19**

A 2 × 12 Douglas Fir–Larch No. 1 lumber joist is notched 2 inches on the tension side at its end support. The joist forms part of a roof system in an area where snow may be anticipated to be the governing load. Determine the maximum allowable reaction at the support.

Solution

From NDS Section 3.4.3.2(a), the allowable reaction is

$$V = (bd_n C_D F_v/1.5)(d_n/d)^2$$

where $b = 1.5$ inches, $d = 11.25$ inches, $d_n = 11.25 - 2 = 9.25$ inches, $C_D = 1.15$ for snow load, and $F_v = 180$ pounds per square inch from NDS SUPP Table 4A. Then

$$V = (1.5 \times 9.25 \times 1.15 \times 180/1.5)(9.25/11.25)^2 = 1294 \text{ pounds}$$

To facilitate the selection of the appropriate glued-laminated beam section, tables are available[15] that provide shear and bending capacities of sections. For lumber joists, tables are available[16] that assist in the selection of a joist size for various span and live load combinations.

Wood Columns

The allowable stress in an axially loaded simple, solid wood column is dependent on the slenderness ratio, which is defined in NDS Section 3.7.1 as

$$K_e l/d \leq 50$$

where d = least dimension of the cross section

l = unbraced length of the column

$K_e l = l_e$ = effective column length

K_e = buckling factor

The value of the buckling factor depends on the restraint conditions at each end of the column. NDS Appendix G specifies buckling factors for standard conditions of restraint, and these are illustrated in Figure 2.42.

The column stability factor is given by NDS Section 3.7.1 as

$$C_P = (1.0 + F)/2c - \{[(1.0 + F)/2c]^2 - F/c\}^{0.5}$$

where $F = F_{cE}/F_c^*$

F_c^* = tabulated compressive stress multiplied by all applicable adjustment factors except C_P

$= (F_c)(C_D)(C_M)(C_t)(C_F)(C_i)\ldots(C_F$ and C_i apply only to visually graded sawn lumber)

F_c = tabulated compression design value parallel to grain

F_{cE} = critical Euler buckling design value

$= K_{cE}E'/(l_e/d)^2$

K_{cE} = Euler buckling coefficient for columns

$= 0.30\ldots$ for visually graded lumber

$= 0.384\ldots$ for machine-evaluated lumber

$= 0.418\ldots$ for glued-laminated timber and machine-stress-rated lumber

E' = adjusted tabulated modulus of elasticity $= EC_M$

E = tabulated modulus of elasticity

$=$ appropriate value of E_{xx} or E_{yy} for glued-laminated members

c = column parameter

$= 0.8\ldots$ for sawn lumber

$= 0.9\ldots$ for glued-laminated timber

$= 0.85\ldots$ for round timber poles and piles

The allowable compressive stress is given by

$$F_c' = F_c^* C_p$$

The required area of a column is given by

$$A = P/F_c'$$

End Restraints	K_e	Shape
Fixed at both ends	0.65	
Fixed at one end, pinned at the other	0.8	
Pinned at both ends	1.0	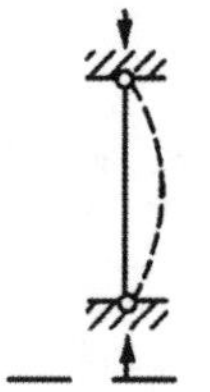
Fixed at one end with the other end fixed in direction but not held in position	1.2*	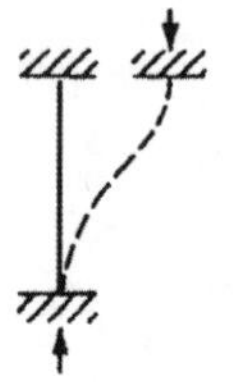
Pinned at one end with the other end fixed in direction but not held in position	2.4*	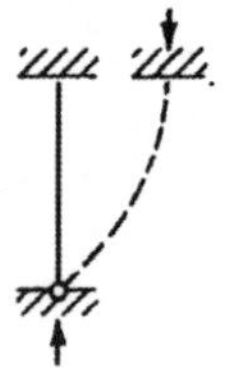
Fixed at one end with the other end free	2.1	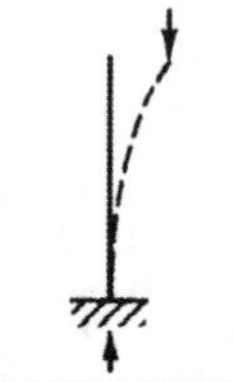

Sidesway prevented

Sidesway not prevented

*Note: K_e value used by NDS is different from that used by AISC for steel construction (see Figure 2.30).

Figure 2.42 Wood column buckling factors

Members subjected to combined compressive and flexural stresses due to vertical and transverse loading must satisfy the interaction equation given in NDS Section 3.9.2 as

$$(f_c/F_c')^2 + f_{b1}/F_{b1}'C_{m1} + f_{b2}/F_{b2}'C_{m2} \leq 1$$

where f_c = compression stress in the member
  f_{b1} = edgewise bending stress in the member
  f_{b2} = wide face bending stress in the member
  F_c' = allowable compression stress in the member
  F_{b_1}' = allowable bending stress for load applied to the narrow face

F'_{b2} = allowable bending stress for load applied to the wide face

C_{m1} = moment magnification factor = $1.0 - f_c/F_{cE1}$

C_{m2} = moment magnification factor = $1.0 - f_c/F_{cE2} - (f_{b1}/F_{bE})^2$

F_{cE1} = critical Euler buckling design value in plane of bending for load applied to the narrow face = $K_{cE}E'/(l_{e1}/d_1)^2$

F_{cE2} = critical Euler buckling design value in plane of bending for load applied to the wide face = $K_{cE}E'/(l_{e2}/d_2)^2$

K_{cE} = Euler buckling coefficient for columns

d_1 = dimension of wide face

d_2 = dimension of narrow face

l_{e1} = effective length between lateral restraints for load applied to narrow face

l_{e2} = effective length between lateral restraints for load applied to wide face

F_{bE} = critical beam buckling design value

For bending load applied to the narrow face of the member and concentric axial compression load, the interaction equation reduces to

$$(f_c/F'_c)^2 + f_{b1}/F'_{b1}C_{m1} \leq 1$$

where, $c_{m4} = -1.0 - f_c/F_{CE1}$. For bending load applied to the wide face for the member and concentric axial compression load, the equation reduces to

$$(f_c/F'_c)^2 + f_{b2}/F'_{b2}C_{m4} \leq 1$$

where $C_{m4} = -1.0 - f_c/F_{cE2}$. For bending loads applied to the narrow and wide faces of the member and no concentric axial load, the equation reduces to

$$f_{b1}/F'_{b1} + f_{b2}/F'_{b2}C_{m2} \leq 1$$

where $C_{m2} = 1.0 - (f_{b1}/F_{bE})^2$.

Example 2.20

An interior load-bearing stud wall (Exhibit 14) consists of 2 × 6 Douglas Fir–Larch No. 1 lumber at 16 inch on centers sheathed on both sides with $^1/_2$-inch plywood. The studs are 13 feet long, and the wall supports a mezzanine floor that applies a vertical load of 500 pounds per linear foot to the top of the wall. Determine if the studs are adequate.

Solution

The relevant properties of one stud are $b = 1.5$ inches, $d = 5.5$ inches, $A = 8.25$ inches^2, $S_x = 7.56$ inches^2, $I_x = 20.8$ inches^4, $F_b = 1000$ pounds per square inch, $F_c = 1500$ pounds per square inch, and $E = 1.7 \times 10^6$ pounds per square inch.

Interior walls, in accordance with IBC[17] Section 1607.13, are designed for a lateral load of $p = 5$ pounds per square foot. Then the lateral load on one stud is

$$w = 16p/12 = 6.67 \text{ pounds per foot}$$

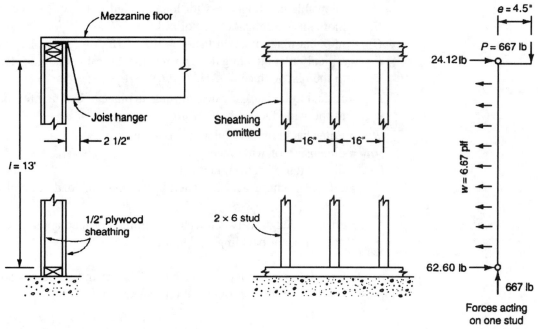

Exhibit 14 Stud wall in Example 20

The horizontal reaction produced at the base of the stud by this lateral load is

$$R_L = wl/2 = 6.67 \times 13/2 = 43.36 \text{ pounds}$$

The vertical force on one stud is

$$P = 500 \times 16/12 = 667 \text{ pounds}$$

The eccentricity of this force is

$$e = d/2 + 2.5/2 + 0.5 = (5.5 + 2.5)/2 + 0.5 = 4.5 \text{ inches}$$

The horizontal reaction produced at the base of the stud by this eccentric force is

$$R_F = Pe/l = 667 \times 4.5/(13 \times 12) = 19.24 \text{ pounds}$$

The total reaction at the base of the stud is

$$R = R_L + R_F = 43.36 + 19.24 = 62.60 \text{ pounds}$$

The bending moment occurring in the stud at a height x from the base is given by

$$M = Rx - wx^2/2 = 62.60x - 6.67x^2/2 = 62.60x - 3.34x^2$$

Differentiating and equating dM/dx to zero gives the location of the maximum moment as

$$\bar{x} = 62.60/6.67 = 9.39 \text{ feet}$$

The maximum moment is then

$$M_{(max)} = 62.60 \times 9.39 - 3.34 \times 9.39^2 = 293 \text{ pound-feet}$$

The bending stress in the stud is

$$f_b = M_{(max)}/S_x = 12 \times 293/7.56 = 466 \text{ pounds per square inch}$$

The stud is provided with continuous lateral bracing giving a beam stability factor of $C_L = 1$. The size factor from NDS SUPP Table 4A is 1.3, the load duration factor for the mezzanine loading is unity, and the repetitive member factor is 1.15, giving an allowable bending stress of

$$F_b' = F_b^* = 1.15 \times 1.3 F_b = 1495 \text{ pounds per square inch, which is } > f_b \text{ and}$$

satisfactory.

The axial stress on one stud is

$$f_c = P/A = 667/8.25 = 81 \text{ pounds per square inch}$$

The relevant column parameters may be obtained from a calculator program[2] and are

$$l_e/d = \text{ governing slenderness ratio in the plane of bending } = K_e l/d$$
$$= 1 \times 13 \times 12/5.5 = 28.36, \text{ which is } < 50 \text{ and satisfactory}$$

The size factor for compression is 1.1 from NDS SUPP Table 4A.

$$F_c^* = 1.1 \times 1500 = 1650$$

The Euler buckling value is

$$F_{cE} = 0.3E/(l_e/d)^2 = 0.3 \times 1.7 \times 10^6/28.36^2 = 634 \text{ pounds per square inch}$$
$$F = F_{cE}/F_c^* = 634/1650 = 0.38$$
$$C_p = 1.38/1.6 - [(1.38/1.6)^2 - 0.38/0.8]^{0.5} = 0.34$$

The allowable compressive stress is $F_c' = F_c^* C_p = 561$ pounds per square inch which is $> f_c$ and satisfactory.

The interaction equation for stability effects in the plane of bending is

$$(f_c/F_c')^2 + f_b/F_b'C_m \leq 1$$

where $C_m = 1 - f_c/F_{cE} = 0.87$.

The left-hand side of this equation is evaluated as

$$(81/561)^2 + 466/(1495 \times 0.87) = 0.02 + 0.36 = 0.38, \text{ which is } <1 \text{ and satisfactory}$$

The bending moment in the stud is given by

$$M = EI\,d^2y/dx^2 = 62.60x - 3.34x^2$$

Integrating this expression and substituting the boundary conditions of $y = 0$ at $x = 0$ and $x = l$, in order to determine the constants of integration, gives

$$EI\,dy/dx = 31.30x^2 - 1.11x^3 - 1147$$
$$EIy = 10.43x^3 - 0.28x^4 - 1147x$$

The maximum deflection occurs when $dy/dx = 0$ at $x = 7.0$ feet and is given by

$$y_{(max)} = (3577 - 672 - 8029)/EI = -5124 \times 12^3/(1.7 \times 10^6 \times 20.8)$$
$$= -0.25 \text{ inches} = l/624$$

The maximum specified deflection in IBC Table 1604.3, for a wall with flexible finishes, is $\delta = l/120$, which is $> l/624$, so the studs are adequate.

Plywood Diaphragms

A plywood diaphragm[18,19,20] acts as a flexible horizontal beam to transfer the lateral loads caused by wind or seismic effects to the supporting shear walls or braced frames. The design capacities of plywood diaphragms are given in IBC Table 2306.3.1. Further details of plywood diaphragms are given in Chapter 5 of this text.

Plywood Shear Walls

The function of a shear wall is to transfer the lateral load from the horizontal diaphragm to the foundations. The design capacities of plywood shear walls are given in IBC Table 2306.4.1. Further details of plywood shear walls are given in Chapter 5 of this text.

Connections in Wood Members

The design capacities of the various types of available connections are influenced by a number of factors, including the following:

  (i) Wood species used.

 (ii) Orientation of the applied force with respect to the direction of the wood grain.

(iii) Orientation of the applied force with respect to the axis of the fastener.

 (iv) Depth of penetration of the fastener into the holding member.

  (v) Spacing of the fasteners and number of fasteners used.

 (vi) Distance provided between the fastener and the end and edge of the member.

(vii) Use of metal side plates.

(viii) Duration of the applied force.

 (ix) Moisture content of the member.

  (x) Fire-retardant treatment.

The basic design capacities are given in NDS Parts 10 through 13.

The modification factors C_M for all types of fasteners, for moisture content of the member, are given in NDS Table 10.3.3.

The group action modification factors, C_g, for split ring connectors, shear plate connectors, bolts, and lag screws, for number of fasteners in a row, are given in NDS Tables 10.3.6A and 10.3.6B.

The modification factor for all types of fasteners, for fire-retardant treatment, shall be obtained from the company providing the treatment.

The modification factor, C_D, for duration of load, for all types of fasteners, is given in NDS Section 10.3.2 and 2.3.2.

The group action modification factor C_g, for shear plate connectors with metal side plates is given in NDS Table 10.3.6D.

The modification factor C_g for bolted joints with metal side plates and parallel-to-grain loading is given in NDS Table 10.3.6C.

The modification factor C_{st} for shear plate connectors with metal side plates is given in NDS Table 12.2.4.

For split ring connectors, shear plate connectors, and timber rivets, the allowable load for inclination at an angle to the grain of $\theta°$, in accordance with NDS Equation (J-3), Appendix J, is obtained from **Hankinson's Formula** as

$$N' = P'Q'/(P' \sin^2 \theta + Q' \cos^2 \theta)$$

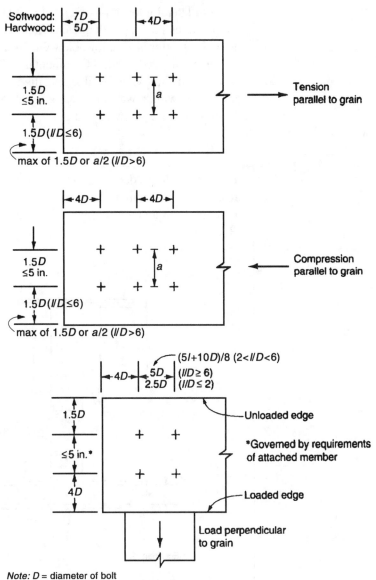

Note: *D* = diameter of bolt
l = lesser of length of bolt in main member or total length of bolt in side members

Figure 2.43 Bolt spacing requirements

where P' = allowable load parallel to grain and Q' = allowable load perpendicular to grain.

For bolts and lag screws, NDS Section 11.5 details the requirements for spacing, and end distance and edge distance, and these are illustrated in Figure 2.43. The indicated end distances, may be reduced by a maximum of 50 percent provided that the applied loads are reduced proportionally.

For laterally loaded nails, NDS Section 11.1.5.6 recommends a spacing and an end or edge distance sufficient to prevent splitting of the wood. The required penetration is specified in NDS Section 11.1.5.5 as being 6 times the diameter. In accordance with NDS Section 11.5.2, the allowable lateral capacity of a nail in end grain is two-thirds the allowable value in side grain, and the allowable lateral capacity of a toenail is five-sixths the allowable value of a nail driven perpendicular to the grain per NDS Section 11.5.4. The allowable withdrawal load for a nail is specified in NDS Table 11.2C. No withdrawal capacity is allowed for a nail driven into end grain.

For laterally loaded wood screws, NDS Section 11.1.4.6 specifies a penetration of six times the shank diameter. The allowable lateral capacity of a screw in end grain is two-thirds the allowable value in side grain. Spacing, edge, and end distances are recommended in NDS Commentary[21] Table C11.4-1. The penetration of a wood screw loaded in withdrawal is specified as the length of the threaded portion of the screw, and withdrawal values are given in NDS Table 11.2B. No withdrawal capacity is allowed for a screw in end grain.

Example **2.21**

Exhibit 15 shows details of a 20-gage steel strap required to transfer a seismic tie force of 3000 pounds between two Douglas Fir–Larch beams. Determine the number of 8-penny common nails required and the minimum dimensions for *A*, *B*, and *C*.

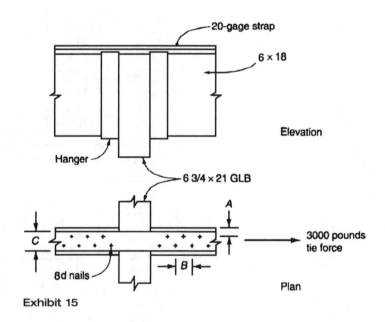

Exhibit 15

Solution

The modified lateral load capacity of one 8-penny common nail with a penetration of $2\frac{1}{2}$ inches is

$$Z' = C_D Z$$

where $Z = 92$ pounds = allowable load from NDS Table 12.3F
$\quad C_D = 1.6$ = load duration factor for seismic loading
$\quad Z' = 92 \times 1.6 = 147$ pounds

The number of 8-penny nails required on each side of the tie is

$$n = T/Z' = 3000/147 = 20 \text{ nails}$$

The minimum dimensions based on NDS COMM[21] Table C12.4-1 are

$$B = p = 10D = 1.31 \text{ inches}$$
$$A = 2.5D = 0.33 \text{ inches}$$

In accordance with AISC[12] Section D1, based on the *gross* area of the strap, the strap width is given by

$$b = T/(1.33 \times 0.6F_y t)$$
$$= 3000/(1.33 \times 0.6 \times 36,000 \times 0.036) = 2.90 \text{ inches}$$

In accordance with AISC Section B3, based on the *net* area of the strap, the strap width is given by

$$b = T/(1.33 \times 0.5F_u \times 0.85t)$$
$$= 3000/(1.33 \times 0.5 \times 58,000 \times 0.85 \times 0.036) = 2.54 \text{ inches}$$

So the required strap width is $C = 3$ inches.

Example **2.22**

A detail is shown in Exhibit 16 of the splice in a 4×6 No. 2 Grade Douglas Fir–Larch chord member to resist lateral wind loading. Determine the maximum chord force that the splice can sustain and the minimum dimensions for *A*, *B*, and *C*.

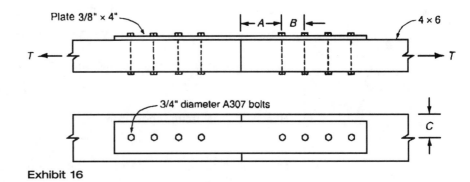

Exhibit 16

Solution

Based on the gross area of the A36 steel side plate, the allowable force is given by AISC Section D1 as

$$T_{p1} = 1.33 \times 0.6\,F_y A_g = 1.33 \times 0.6 \times 36 \times 4 \times 0.375 = 43.09 \text{ kips}$$

In accordance with AISC Section B2, the effective diameter of the bolt holes in the steel side plate is

$$D_h = D_b + {}^1/_8 \text{ inch} = 0.75 + 0.125 = 0.875 \text{ inches}$$

The effective net area of the side plate is

$$A_e = t(b - D_h) = 0.375(4 - 0.875) = 1.17 \text{ square inches, which is} < 0.85A_g$$

Based on the effective net area of the side plate, the allowable force is given by AISC Section D1 as

$$T_{p2} = 1.33 \times 0.5F_u A_e = 1.33 \times 0.5 \times 58 \times 1.17 = 45.13 \text{ kips}$$

The gross areas of the wood member and the side plate are $A_m = 19.25$ square inches and $A_s = 1.5$ square inches. $A_m/A_s = 12.83$, so the group action modification factor for four bolts in a row is obtained from NDS Table 10.3.6C as

$$C_g = 0.93$$

The load duration factor for wind loading, from NDS Section 2.3.2, is

$$C_D = 1.6$$

The basic allowable single shear value for a $^3/_4$-inch-diameter bolt in a $3^1/_2$-inch member, with $^1/_4$-inch side plate, with loading parallel to the grain, is obtained from NDS Table 11B as

$$Z = 1670 \text{ pounds}$$

Hence, the capacity of the four bolts is

$$T_B = 4C_gC_DZ = 4 \times 0.93 \times 1.6 \times 1.67 = 9.94 \text{ kips}$$

The allowable basic tensile stress in the No. 2 Grade Douglas Fir–Larch chord member is obtained from NDS SUPP Table 4A as $F_t = 575$ pounds per square inch. The diameter of the bolt hole in the chord member is obtained from NDS Section 11.1.2 as

$$D_h = D_b + {}^1/_{16} \text{ inch} = 0.75 + 0.0625 = 0.8125 \text{ inches}$$

The net area of the chord member is

$$A_n = A_g - bD_h = 19.25 - 3.5 \times 0.8125 = 16.41 \text{ square inches}$$

The allowable tensile force in the chord member is

$$T_c = C_DF_tA_n = 1.6 \times 575 \times 16.41/1000 = 15.09 \text{ kips}$$

Hence, the maximum chord force is governed by the bolt capacity and is

$$T = T_B = 9.94 \text{ kips}$$

For tension parallel to the grain, the required dimensions are obtained from Figure 2.43 as

$$A = \text{end distance} = 7D = 5.25 \text{ inches}$$
$$B = \text{bolt spacing} = 4D = 3.0 \text{ inches}$$
$$C = \text{edge distance} = 1.5D = 1.125 \text{ inches}$$

REINFORCED MASONRY DESIGN

Quality Control

Section 2105.1 of the IBC requires that, for masonry construction, special inspections shall be provided as prescribed in IBC Section 1704.5. This requires inspecton of the preparation of masonry test prisms, the placing of masonry units and reinforcement, and the inspection of all grouting operations.

Two levels of inspection are specified. Level 1 special inspection is detailed in IBC Table 1704.5.1 and is required for nonessential facilities as listed in IBC Table 1604.5. Level 2 special inspection is detailed in IBC Table 1704.5.3 and is required for essential facilities as listed in IBC Table 1604.5.

To ensure that masonry strength complies with the value specified, IBC Section 2105 permits two alternative methods of quality control, which are

(i) **Prism test method.** A set of three masonry prisms representative of the materials to be used in the project shall be made and tested during construction for each 5000 square feet of wall area. The compressive strength of the masonry shall be taken as the average strength of the three prisms.

(ii) **Unit strength method.** The masonry strength may be based on the strength of the masonry units and the type of mortar used, as indicated in IBC Tables 2105.2.2.1.1 and 2105.2.2.1.2 provided that the strength of the grout in grouted concrete masonry construction is not less than the strength of the units and not less than 2000 pounds per square inch.

Allowable Stresses

Elastic design methods using working stress analysis is specified in BCRMS[22] Section 2.1.1. The modulus of elasticity of masonry is based on the chord modulus of elasticity determined by a compression test.

The modulus of elasticity of steel reinforcement is given by BCRMS Section 1.8.2.1 as

$$E_s = 29,000,000 \text{ pounds per square inch}$$

For Grade 60 reinforcement, the allowable tensile stress and the allowable compressive stress attributable to flexure are given by BCRMS Section 2.3.2.1 as

$$F_s = 24,000 \text{ pounds per square inch}$$

For Grade 50 reinforcement

$$F_s = 20,000 \text{ pounds per square inch}$$

The allowable compressive stress in reinforcement in columns and shear walls confined by lateral ties in accordance with BCRMS Section 2.1.6.5 is given by

$$F_s = 0.4f_y \quad \text{and} \quad \leq 24,000 \text{ pounds per square inch}$$

The allowable compressive stress in masonry due to flexure is given by BCRMS Section 2.3.3.2.2 as

$$F_b = 0.33 f'_m \text{ pounds per square inch}$$

The allowable compressive force in an axially loaded reinforced masonry column is given by BCRMS Section 2.3.3.2.1 as

$$P_a = (0.25 f'_m A_n + 0.65 A_s F_s)R$$

where A_n = net effective column area
$\quad R$ = reduction factor for slenderness effects
$\quad\quad = (70r/h)^2 \dots$ for $h/r > 99$
$\quad\quad = 1 - (h/140r)^2 \dots$ for $h/r \leq 99$
$\quad h$ = effective height
$\quad\quad$ = clear height of columns supported top and bottom
$\quad\quad$ = effective height for unbraced members shall be calculated
$\quad A_s$ = reinforcement area
$\quad r$ = radius of gyration

The allowable shear stress in a flexural member without shear reinforcement is given by BCRMS Equation (2-20) as

$$F_v = 3\sqrt{f'_m} \quad \text{and} \quad \leq 50 \text{ pounds per square inch}$$

The allowable shear stress in a flexural member, with shear reinforcement, at a maximum spacing of half the effective depth, designed to take the entire shear force, is given by BCRMS Equation (2-23) as

$$F_v = 3\sqrt{f'_m} \quad \text{and} \quad \leq 50 \text{ pounds per square inch}$$

IBC Section 2107.1 adopts the working stress design method of BCRMS Chapters 1 and 2 with the exception of Sections 2.1.2.1 and 2.1.3.3.

Reinforced Masonry Beams

For flexural design, the necessary design requirements are given in BCRMS Chapters 1 and 2, and these may be readily programmed on a handheld calculator.[3]

Example 2.23

The reinforced concrete masonry lintel beam shown in Exhibit 17 is constructed of 12-inch block that is solid grouted over a clear span of 10 feet. The specified masonry compressive strength is 1500 pounds per square inch, the modulus of elasticity is 1500 kips per square inch, and reinforcement consists of Grade 60 deformed bars. Applied vertical loading, including self-weight, is 1.5 kips per linear foot. Determine if the beam is satisfactory.

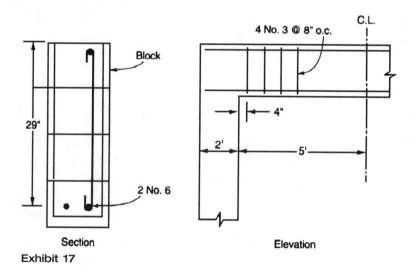

Exhibit 17

Solution

The allowable stresses are

$$F_b = 0.33f'_m = 500 \text{ pounds per square inch}$$
$$F_v = \sqrt{f'_m} = 38.73 \text{ pounds per square inch}$$
$$F_s = 24,000 \text{ pounds per square inch}$$
$$E_m = 1500 \text{ kips per square inch}$$
$$E_s = 29,000 \text{ kips per square inch}$$

The relevant section properties of the intel are

$$b = 11.63 \text{ inches}$$
$$d = 29 \text{ inches}$$
$$A_s = 0.88 \text{ square inches}$$

The effective span is

$$L = 10 + 2 = 12 \text{ feet}$$

The span/width ratio is

$$L/b = 12 \times 12/11.63 = 12.38, \text{ which is} < 32$$

Hence, in accordance with BCRMS Section 2.3.3.4.4, the lateral support of the beam is adequate.

The maximum bending moment produced by the applied load is

$$M = wL^2/8 = 1.5 \times 12^2/8 = 27.0 \text{ kip-feet}$$

In accordance with BCRMS Section 2.3.5.5, the maximum design shear is calculated at a distance of $d/2$ from the face of the support and is given by

$$V = w(L_c - d)/2 = 1.5(10 - 2.42)/2 = 5.69 \text{ kips}$$

Neglecting compression steel, the beam stresses may be obtained from a calculator program[3] and are

$$n = E_s/E_c = 19.33$$
$$\rho = A_s/bd = 0.0026$$
$$k = (n^2\rho^2 + 2n\rho)^{0.5} - np = 0.271$$
$$j = 1 - k/3 = 0.910$$
$$f_b = 24,000 \ M/jkbd^2 = 268 \text{ pounds per square inch}$$
$$< F_b, \text{ which is satisfactory}$$
$$f_s = 12,000 \ M/jdA_s = 13,950 \text{ pounds per square inch}$$
$$< F_s, \text{ which is also satisfactory}$$

The shear stress at the support is given by

$$f_v = V/bjd = 5690/(11.63 \times 0.910 \times 29) = 18.54 \text{ pounds per square inch}$$
$$< F_v$$

Hence, in accordance with BCRMS Section 2.3.5.2.2, shear reinforcement is not required. Hence, the lintel is satisfactory.

Masonry Columns

Limitations are imposed[23] on column dimensions in BCRMS Sections 2.1.6.1 and 2.1.6.2, main reinforcement in BCRMS Section 2.1.6.4, and on lateral ties in BCRMS Section 2.1.6.5. These requirements are

 (i) For the utilization of full design stresses, the minimum nominal column dimension is eight inches. The effective height may not exceed 25 times the least nominal dimension.

 (ii) Main reinforcement is limited to a maximum of 4 percent and a minimum of 0.25 percent, with at least four bars being provided.

 (iii) Lateral ties for the confinement of longitudinal bars shall be not less than $^1/_4$ inch in diameter. Ties shall be spaced a maximum of 16 bar diameters, 48 tie diameters, or the least column dimension.

For uncracked sections, stresses are calculated using transformed section properties.[23] To allow for creep in the masonry, the transformed reinforcement area is taken as $A_s(2n - 1)$. Stress in the reinforcement is taken as $2n$ times the stress in the adjacent mason.

| Example **2.24** |

A nominal 16-inch-square, solid-grouted, concrete column has a specified strength of 1500 pounds per square inch and a modulus of elasticity of 1500 pounds per square inch, and is reinforced with four No. 6, Grade 40 bars. The column, pinned at both ends, is 12 feet in height and supports an axial load, including its own weight, of 60 kips. Neglecting accidental eccentricity, determine if the column is adequate.

Solution

The allowable reinforcement stress is

$$F_s = 0.4 f_y = 16,000 \text{ pounds per square inch}$$

The relevant section properties of the column are

$$b = t = 15.63 \text{ inches}$$
$$d = 13 \text{ inches}$$
$$L = 12 \text{ feet}$$
$$h = 12 \text{ feet}$$
$$A_s = 1.76 \text{ square inches}$$
$$A = t^2 = 244 \text{ square inches}$$

$$r = \sqrt{A/12} = 4.51$$
$$h/r = 144/4.51 = 31.9 < 99$$

The allowable axial load is given by BCRMS Section 2.3.3.2.1(a) as

$$\begin{aligned} P_a &= (0.25 f_m A + 0.65 A_s F_s) R \\ &= (0.25 \times 1.5 \times 244 + 0.65 \times 1.76 \times 16)[1 - (144/140 \times 4.51)^2] \\ &= 104 \text{ kips} > P \text{ and satisfactory} \end{aligned}$$

Masonry Shear Walls

In accordance with IBC Section 2106.5.1, shear walls designed to resist seismic forces, using the working stress method, shall be designed to resist 1.5 times the seismic forces calculated by IBC Chapter 16.

The reinforcement requirements for a shear wall depend on the shear force in the wall and on the seismic design category assigned to the structure.

The minimum nominal reinforcement requirements for a wall assigned to seismic category C are given in BCRMS Sections 1.13.5.2 and 1.13.5.3. In both the horizontal and the vertical directions, reinforcement shall consist of at least one bar spaced at not more than 48 inches.

For seismic design category D, BCRMS Section 1.13.6 requires a minimum reinforcement ratio in either direction of 0.07 percent of the gross cross-sectional area of the masonry, and the sum of the reinforcement ratios in both directions to be at least 0.2 percent of the gross cross-sectional area of the masonry. In addition, the cross-sectional area of the vertical reinforcement shall not be less than one-third of the required shear reinforcement. The spacing of the reinforcement in either direction shall not exceed the lesser of $h/3$, $d_v/3$, or 48 inches.

The minimum reinforcement requirements for a wall assigned to seismic design category E are given in BCRMS Section 1.13.7. Reinforcement shall comply with the requirements of seismic design category D. In addition, for stack bond masonry, the cross-sectional area of the horizontal reinforcement shall not be less than 0.25 percent of the gross cross-sectional area of the masonry spaced at a maximum of 16 inches.

The allowable shear stress in a masonry shear wall is influenced by the ratio M/Vd, where M = moment acting at the location where V is calculated and V = applied shear force.

In a masonry wall without shear reinforcement and with $M/Vd < 1$, the allowable shear stress is given by BCRMS Section 2.3.5.2.2(b) as

$$F_v = 0.333\sqrt{f'_m}(4 - M/Vd) \le 80 - 45M/Vd \text{ pounds per square inch}$$

In a masonry wall without shear reinforcement and with $M/Vd \ge 1$, the allowable shear stress is given by BCRMS Section 2.3.5.2.2(b) as

$$F_v = \sqrt{f'_m} \le 35 \text{ pounds per square inch}$$

In a masonry wall with shear reinforcement designed to carry the entire shear force and with $M/Vd < 1$, the allowable shear stress is given by BCRMS Section 2.3.5.2.3(b) as

$$F_v = 0.5(4 - M/Vd)\sqrt{f'_m} \le 120 - 45M/Vd \text{ pounds per square inch}$$

In a masonry wall with shear reinforcement designed to carry the entire shear force and with $M/Vd \ge 1$, the allowable shear stress is given by BCRMS Section 2.3.5.2.3(b) as

$$F_v = 1.5\sqrt{f'_m} \le 75 \text{ pounds per square inch}$$

The shear stress in the shear wall is determined from BCRMS Section 2.3.5.2.1 as

$$f_v = V/bd_v$$

where d_v = overall depth of wall.

Example **2.25**

A nominal 8-inch, solid-grouted, masonry shear wall, constructed in running bond, with a specified strength of 1500 pounds per square inch and a modulus of elasticity of 1000 kips per square inch is assigned to seismic design category E. The self-weight of the wall and applied vertical loads may be neglected. The lateral in-plane seismic load acting on the wall is shown in Exhibit 18. Using Grade 60 deformed bars, determine the horizontal and vertical reinforcement required in the wall.

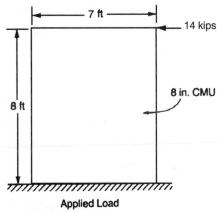

Applied Load

Exhibit 18

Solution

The relevant section properties of the wall for in-plane effects are

$$b = 7.63 \text{ inches}$$
$$d_v = 7 \times 12 = 84 \text{ inches}$$
$$d = L - 4 \text{ inches} = 80 \text{ inches}$$

The allowable stresses, in accordance with BCRMS Section 2.1.2.3

$$F_b = 1.33 \times 0.33 f'_m = 665 \text{ pounds per square inch}$$
$$F_s = 1.33 \times 24{,}000 = 32{,}000$$
$$E_m = 1000 \text{ kips per square inch}$$
$$E_s = 29{,}000 \text{ kips per square inch}$$

In accordance with IBC Section 2106.5.1, when using the working stress design method, the wall is designed to resist the force

$$V' = 1.5V$$
$$= 1.5 \times 1.4$$
$$= 21 \text{ kips}$$

The bending moment at the base of the wall is

$$M = V' \times 8 = 21 \times 8 = 168 \text{ kip-feet}$$

Assuming a lever arm ratio of $j = 0.92$, the required reinforcement area is

$$A_s = M/jdF_s = 168 \times 12/(0.92 \times 80 \times 32) = 0.86 \text{ square inches}$$

Using two No. 6 bars for jamb reinforcement provides a reinforcement area of

$$A_s = 0.88 \text{ square inches}$$

The flexural stresses may now be obtained by the elastic design method and are

$$n = E_s/E_m = 29$$
$$\rho = A_s/bd = (0.88)/(7.63)(80) = 0.144 \text{ percent}$$
$$k = (n^2\rho^2 + 2n\rho)^{0.5} - np = 0.25$$
$$j = 1 - k/3 = 0.92$$

$$f_b = 24{,}000 \; M/jkbd^2 = 360 \text{ pounds per square inch}$$
$$< F_b, \text{ which is satisfactory}$$
$$f_s = 12{,}000 \; M/jdA_s = 31{,}240 \text{ pounds per square inch}$$
$$< F_s, \text{ which is also satisfactory}$$

The shear stress in the wall is given by

$$f_v = V'/bd_v = 21{,}000/(7.63 \times 84) = 32.77 \text{ pounds per square inch}$$
$$M/Vd = 168 \times 12/(21 \times 80) = 1.20 > 1.0$$

The allowable shear stress without shear reinforcement is given by BCRMS Section 2.3.5.2.2(b) as (Eq. 2-22)

$$F_v = 1.33 \times 35 = 46.56 \text{ pounds per square inch}$$
$$> f_v \ldots \text{shear reinforcement is not necessary}$$

To comply with BCRMS Section 1.13.7, the horizontal and vertical reinforcement areas must not be less than

$$0.0007 \times 12b = 0.0007 \times 12 \times 7.63 = 0.064 \text{ square inches per foot}$$

The sum of the horizontal and vertical reinforcement areas must not be less than

$$0.002 \times 12b = 0.002 \times 12 \times 7.63 = 0.183 \text{ square inches per foot}$$

In addition, in accordance with BCRMS Section 1.13.2.2.5, the reinforcement spacing must not exceed $d_v/3 = 28$ inches.

Providing No. 4 horizontal bars at 24 inches on center gives an area of

$$A_{sh} = 0.20 \times 12/24$$
$$= 0.10 \text{ square inches per foot}$$
$$> 0.064 \text{ and satisfactory}$$

Providing two No. 3 vertical bars at 24-inch spacing gives an area of the vertical reinforcement of

$$A_{sv} = (4 \times 0.44 + 2 \times 0.11)/7 = 0.283 \text{ square inches per foot}$$

which is > 0.064 and satisfactory. The sum of the horizontal and vertical reinforcement areas is given by

$$A_{sh} + A_{sv} = 0.10 + 0.283 = 0.383 \text{ square inches per foot}$$

which is > 0.183 and satisfactory. The required reinforcement layout is shown in Exhibit 19.

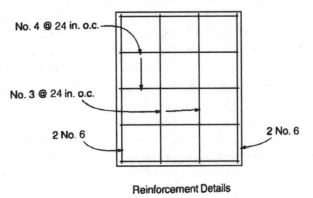

Reinforcement Details

Exhibit 19

REFERENCES

1. American Concrete Institute. *Building Code Requirements and Commentary for Reinforced Concrete* (ACI 318-02). Farmington Hills, MI, 2002.
2. American Society of Civil Engineers. *Minimum Design Loads for Buildings and Other Structures: ASCE 7-02.* New York, 2002.
3. Williams, A. *Structural Engineering License Review: Problems and Solutions,* 5th ed. Dearborn, Chicago, IL, 2004.
4. American Concrete Institute. *ACI Design Handbook.* Detroit, MI, 1997.
5. Ghosh, S. K., and Domel, A. W. *Design of Concrete Buildings for Earthquake and Wind Forces.* Portland Cement Association, Skokie, IL, 1998.

6. Concrete Reinforcing Steel Institute. *CRSI Advanced Column Program.* Schaumburg, IL, 2004.

7. Zia, P., et al. Estimating Prestress Losses. *Concrete International: Design and Construction.* Vol. 1, No. 6, June 1979, pp. 32–38.

8. Portland Cement Association. *Notes on ACI 318-99 Building Code Requirements for Reinforced Concrete.* Skokie, IL, 1999.

9. Lin, T. Y. Load Balancing Method for Design and Analysis of Prestressed Concrete Structure. *Proceedings of the American Concrete Institute.* Vol. 60, 1963, pp. 719–742.

10. Prestressed Concrete Institute. *PCI Design Handbook.* Chicago, IL, 1999.

11. Concrete Society. *Post-Tensioned Flat Slab Design Handbook.* London, 1984.

12. American Institute of Steel Construction. *Manual of Steel Construction, Allowable Stress Design,* 9th ed. Chicago, IL, 1991.

13. American Forest and Paper Association. *National Design Specifications for Wood Construction (ANSI/AF&PA NDS-2001).* Washington, DC, 2001.

14. American Forest and Paper Association. *National Design Specification for Wood Construction: Supplement (ANSI/AF&PA NDS-2001).* Washington, DC, 2001.

15. American Plywood Association. *Glued-Laminated Beam Design Tables.* Tacoma, WA, 2001.

16. Western Wood Products Association. *Western Lumber Span Tables.* Portland, OR, 2001.

17. International Code Council. *International Building Code—2003.* Falls Church, VA, 2003.

18. American Plywood Association. *Diaphragms.* APA Research Report 138. Tacoma, WA, 2000.

19. Brandow, G. E. *UBC Diaphragm Requirements.* Structural Engineering Association of Southern California Design Seminar, Los Angeles, 1992.

20. Coil, J. *Subdiaphragms.* Structural Engineering Association of Southern California Design Seminar. Los Angeles, 1991.

21. American Forest and Paper Association. *Commentary on the National Design Specification for Wood Construction.* Washington, DC, 1993.

22. American Concrete Institute. *Building Code Requirements for Masonry Structures (ACI 530-02).* Farmington Hills, MI, 2002.

23. Concrete Masonry Association of California and Nevada. *1997 Design of Reinforced Masonry Structures.* Citrus Heights, CA, 1997.

Bridge Structures

Alan Williams

OUTLINE

HIGHWAY BRIDGE LOADS 108
Traffic Lanes ■ Vehicle Live Loads ■ Influence Lines ■ Impact Allowance ■ Lateral Load Distribution and Structural Response in Bridge Decks ■ Additional Loads ■ Service Load Design Method ■ Load Factor Design Method ■ Load Combinations

SEISMIC DESIGN 130
Design Procedure ■ Acceleration Coefficient ■ Elastic Seismic Response Coefficient ■ Importance Classification ■ Seismic Performance Category ■ Analysis Procedure ■ Response Modification Factors ■ Combination of Orthogonal Forces ■ Load Combinations ■ Column Plastic Hinges

REINFORCED CONCRETE DESIGN 140
Strength Design Principles ■ Serviceability Requirements

PRESTRESSED CONCRETE DESIGN 149
Transfer Limit State ■ Serviceability Limit State ■ Ultimate Limit State in Flexure ■ Ultimate Limit State in Shear ■ Loss of Prestress ■ Composite Construction ■ Prestressed Continuous Structures

STRUCTURAL STEEL DESIGN 173
Elastic Design of Rolled Steel Girders ■ Elastic Design of Steel Plate Girders ■ Composite Girders ■ Flexural Compression ■ Compression Members ■ Combined Compression and Flexure ■ Connections

TIMBER STRUCTURES 185
Allowable Stresses ■ Timber Beams ■ Timber Columns

REFERENCES 187

HIGHWAY BRIDGE LOADS

Traffic Lanes

Since the number and location of the actual traffic lanes on a bridge deck may be changed during the life of the bridge, design lanes are used to determine the maximum possible loading condition regardless of how the bridge deck width may be demarcated for its initial intended use.

The number of design lanes is defined in AASHTO specifications[1] in Section 3.6. For roadway widths between 20 and 24 feet, two design lanes are adopted, each equal to half the roadway width. For all other roadway widths, the design lanes are specified as being 12 feet wide and the number of design lanes is given by

$$N_L = \mathbb{I}(W/12)$$

where

$\mathbb{I}$ = integer part of the ratio
W = deck width between curbs

The location of the design lanes on the deck shall be such as to produce the maximum load effect on the member under consideration.

The determination of the number of design traffic lanes is illustrated in Figure 3.1.

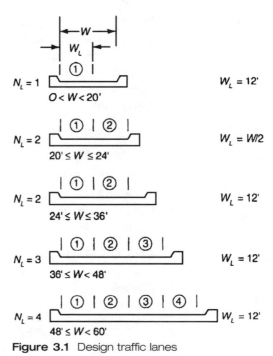

Figure 3.1 Design traffic lanes

Vehicle Live Loads

Vehicular loading is defined in AASHTO Section 3.7. For interstate routes, three load types are specified, and these are the 72-kip HS20-44 standard truck, the equivalent lane load, and the 48-kip alternative tandem loading. These are shown in Figure 3.2. The standard truck load represents a typical heavy tractor truck with semi-trailer and is generally the critical load type for intermediate-span bridges. For long-span bridges, the multiple presence of vehicles in a design lane may be more critical, and the

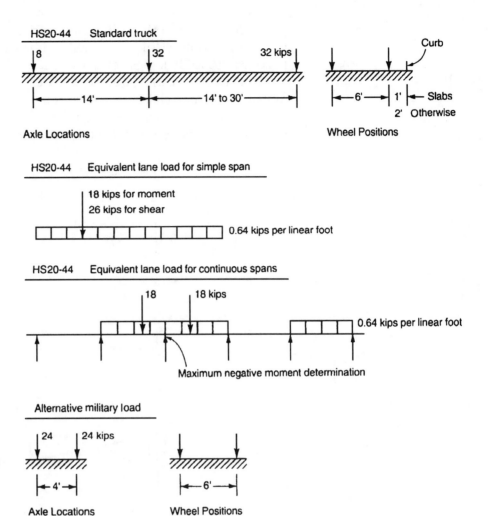

Figure 3.2 Vehicular loadings

equivalent lane load represents a diverse mix of traffic. The alternative loading represents a heavy military vehicle, and this may be the critical load for shorter spans.

All three types of loading are assumed to occupy a width of 10 feet. The design load may be assumed to be located in any position within a design lane, without projecting beyond the lane, and may travel in either direction.

The design load adopted is that which produces the greatest load effect. When more than two design lanes are loaded, to account for the improbability of simultaneous maximum loading, the live loads are multiplied by a factor of 0.9 for three lanes and 0.75 for four or more lanes. The design lanes loaded shall be those which produce the greatest load effect.

Influence Lines

An influence line for a structure is a graphical representation of the variation in shear, moment, member force, or external reaction due to a unit load traversing the structure. Influence lines are used to determine the location of the design load on the structure which will produce the greatest load effect in a particular member. The construction of an influence line may be obtained by the application of Müller-Breslau's principle and Maxwell's reciprocal theorem.

In accordance with Müller-Breslau's principle, the influence line for any restraint in a structure is the elastic curve produced by the corresponding unit virtual displacement applied at the point of application of the restraint. The term *displacement* is used in its general sense, and the displacement corresponding to a moment is a rotation; that corresponding to a force is a linear deflection. The displacement is applied in the same direction as the restraint. To obtain the influence line for reaction in the prop of the propped cantilever shown in Figure 3.3, a unit virtual displacement

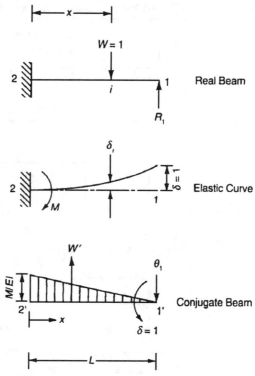

Figure 3.3 Müller-Breslau's principle

is applied in the line of action of R_1. The displacement produced under a unit load at any point i is δ_i. Then, applying the virtual work principle,

$$R_1 \times (\delta = 1) = (W = 1) \times \delta_i$$

that is, $R_1 = \delta_i$, and the elastic curve is the influence line for R_1.

The conjugate beam technique[2] may be applied to determine the actual influence line ordinates. The unit upward displacement applied to end 1 of the real beam produces a moment M at the fixed end 2. This produces the indicated elastic load on the conjugate beam of

$$W' = ML/2EI$$

Taking moments about end 1' of the conjugate beam gives

$$\delta = 1 = 2\ W'L/3$$

Then $M = 3EI/L^2$.

The intensity of loading on the conjugate beam is

$$w' = 3/L^2 - 3x/L^3$$

The shear on the conjugate beam is

$$Q' = \int w' dx = 3x/L^2 - 3x^2/2L^3$$

The moment on the conjugate beam is

$$M' = \int Q' dx = 3x^2/2L^2 - x^3/2L^3$$

and this is the equation of the elastic curve of the real beam and of the influence line for R_1.

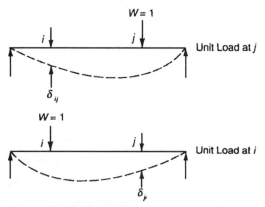

Figure 3.4 Maxwell's reciprocal theorem

In accordance with Maxwell's reciprocal theorem, the displacement produced at any point i in a linear structure due to a force applied at another point j equals the displacement produced at j due to the same force applied at i. The displacement is measured in the line of action of the applied force, and the displacement corresponding to an applied moment is a rotation and to a force is a linear deflection. Referring to Figure 3.4, and applying the virtual work principle, the deflection at point i due to a unit load at point j is

$$\delta_{ij} = \int m_j m_i \, dx/EI$$

where m_i and m_j are the bending moments produced at any section due to a unit load applied at i and j, respectively. Similarly, the deflection at j due to a unit load at i is $\delta_{ji} = dm_i m_j \, dx/EI = \delta_{ij}$. Thus, the influence line for deflection at i is the elastic curve produced by a unit load applied at i.

A general procedure, therefore, for obtaining the influence line for any restraint in a structure is to apply a unit force to the structure in place of and corresponding to the restraint. The elastic curve produced is the influence line for displacement corresponding to the restraint. Dividing the ordinates of this elastic curve by the displacement occurring at the point of application of the unit force gives the influence line for the required restraint. To obtain the influence line for reaction in the prop of the propped cantilever shown in Figure 3.5, the reaction R_1 is replaced by a unit load. This produces the indicated intensity of the elastic load on the conjugate beam of

$$w' = L/EI - x/EI$$

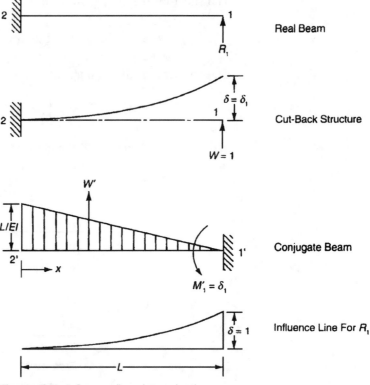

Figure 3.5 Influence line determination

The shear on the conjugate beam is

$$Q' = \int w' \, dx = Lx/EI - x^2/2EI$$

The moment on the conjugate beam is

$$M' = \int Q' \, dx = Lx^2/2EI - x^3/6EI$$

and this is the equation of the elastic curve and of the influence line for deflection of the cut-back structure at end 1. The deflection at end 1 due to the unit applied load is given by the moment at end 1 in the conjugate beam, which is

$$M_1' = L^3/2EI - L^3/6EI$$
$$= L^3/3EI$$
$$= \delta_1$$

Dividing the ordinates of the elastic curve by this displacement gives

$$M'/\delta_1 = 3x^2/2L^2 - x^3/2L^3$$

and this is the equation of the elastic curve for unit displacement at end 1 and of the influence line for R_1.

For statically determinate structures, influence lines are readily determined, and examples for a simple span are shown in Figure 3.6. The maximum bending moment attributable to a train of wheel loads in a simple span occurs under one of the wheels when the center of the span bisects the distance between this wheel and the centroid of the wheel loads. The location of the standard truck load to produce the maximum moment in a simple span exceeding 37 feet is shown in Figure 3.7.

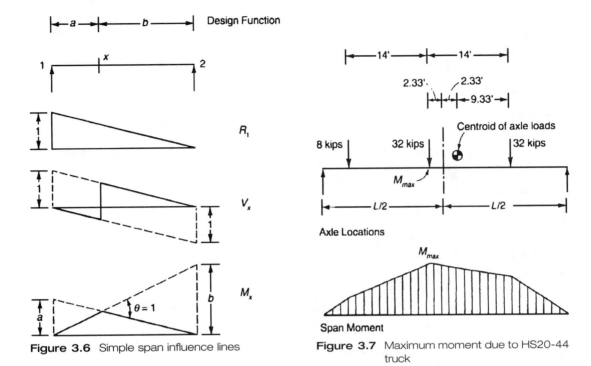

Figure 3.6 Simple span influence lines

Figure 3.7 Maximum moment due to HS20-44 truck

As illustrated in Figure 3.8, the particular load type which produces the maximum moment depends on the span length. For short spans, not exceeding 10.9 feet, a single 32-kip axle of the standard HS20-44 truck controls, and the maximum moment occurs under the axle when this is placed at the center of the span. For longer spans, not exceeding 37.12 feet, the alternative tandem load controls, and the maximum moment occurs under one axle when this is located 1 foot from the center of the span. For longer spans, not exceeding 144.81 feet, the HS20-44 standard truck controls, and the maximum moment occurs under the central axle when this is located 2.33 feet from the center of the span. For longer spans, the equivalent lane load controls, and the maximum moment occurs at the center of the span when the 18-kip concentrated load is located there.

The maximum shear in a simple span occurs at a support and, as shown in Exhibit 1, the particular load type which produces the maximum shear depends on the span length.

For continuous spans, the Müller-Breslau principle allows a rapid determination of the shape of the influence line and of the required location of the live load to produce the maximum effect. In accordance with AASHTO Section 3.11.4.2, only one standard truck per design lane may be considered on the structure. The equivalent lane load, however, is applied to all adverse parts of an influence line to give a patch loading pattern which produces the maximum effect. Examples of typical influence lines and applied loading to produce the maximum effect are shown in Exhibit 2.

Influence line coefficients are available[3] for a limited number of continuous spans and a limited number of span length ratios. For other situations, analytical techniques must be employed, such as matrix methods[4,5] for nonprismatic structures and indeterminate trusses, moment distribution methods[6,7] for nonprismatic spans, the method of angle changes[8] for indeterminate trusses,[9] and the direct distribution of deformation for rigid frames.[10]

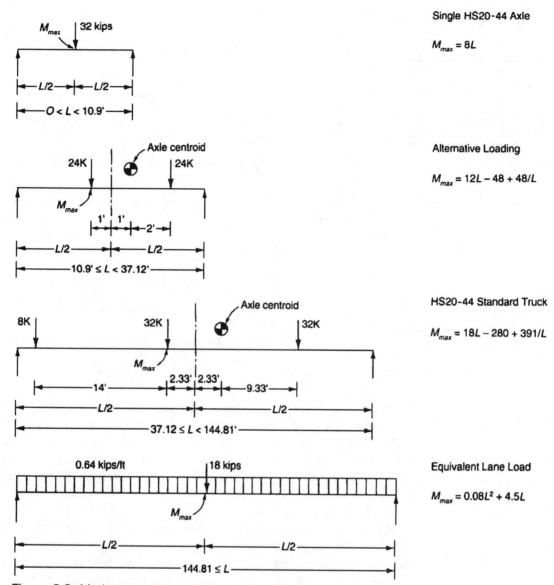

Single HS20-44 Axle

$$M_{max} = 8L$$

Alternative Loading

$$M_{max} = 12L - 48 + 48/L$$

HS20-44 Standard Truck

$$M_{max} = 18L - 280 + 391/L$$

Equivalent Lane Load

$$M_{max} = 0.08L^2 + 4.5L$$

Figure 3.8 Maximum moments due to standard loading

Example 3.1

For the three-span bridge structure shown in Exhibit 3, determine the maximum support reaction R_2, the maximum moment M_2, and the maximum shear V_2 due to the HS20-44 standard truck and the equivalent lane load.

Solution

The deck is statically determinate, and the required influence lines are directly obtained by the application of Müller-Breslau's principle.

The influence line for R_2 is produced by introducing a unit vertical displacement at support 2 as indicated. Placing the standard truck as shown gives the maximum reaction at support 2, which is

$$R_2 = 32(1.2 + 1.06) + 8 \times 1.032$$
$$= 80.58 \text{ kips}$$

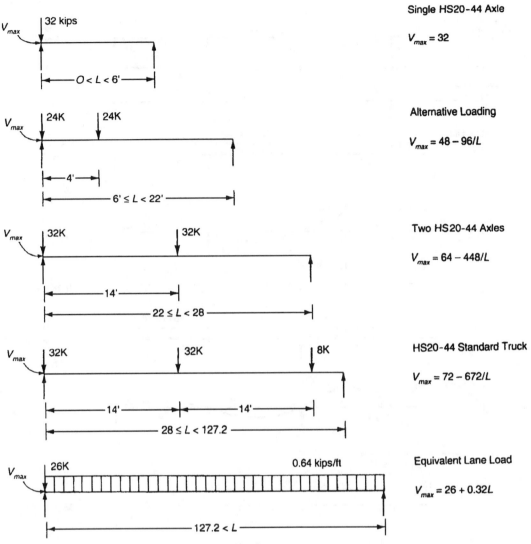

Exhibit 1 Maximum shear due to standard loading

Placing the equivalent lane load as shown gives the maximum reaction at support 2, which is

$$R_2 = 26 \times 1.2 + 0.64 \times 220 \times 1.2/2$$
$$= 115.68 \text{ kips...governs}$$

To obtain the influence line for moment M_2 at support 2, the deck is cut at 2 and a unit virtual rotation imposed at 2. The elastic curve of the structure due to this rotation is, from Müller-Breslau's principle, the influence line for M_2. Placing the equivalent lane load as shown gives the maximum moment at 2, which is

$$M_2 = 18 \times 20 + 0.64 \times 120 \times 20/2$$
$$= 1128 \text{ kip-feet}$$

Placing the standard truck as shown gives the maximum moment at 2, which is

$$M_2 = 32(20 + 17.2) + 8 \times 6$$
$$= 1238.4 \text{ kip-feet...governs}$$

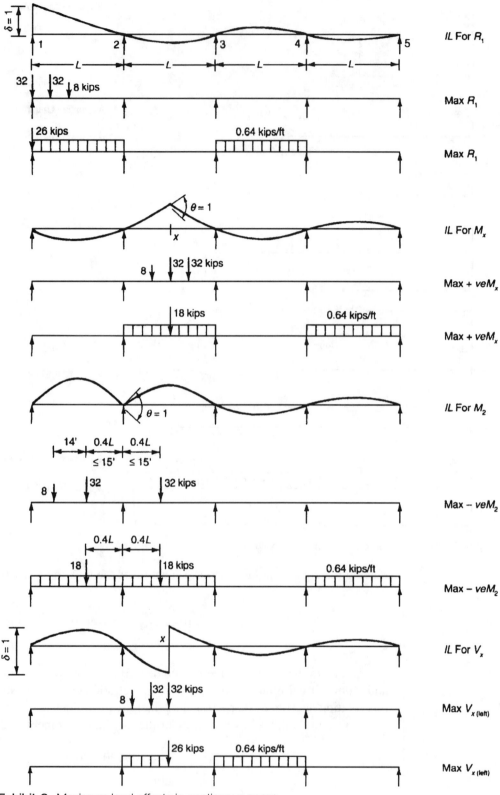

Exhibit 2 Maximum load effects in continuous spans

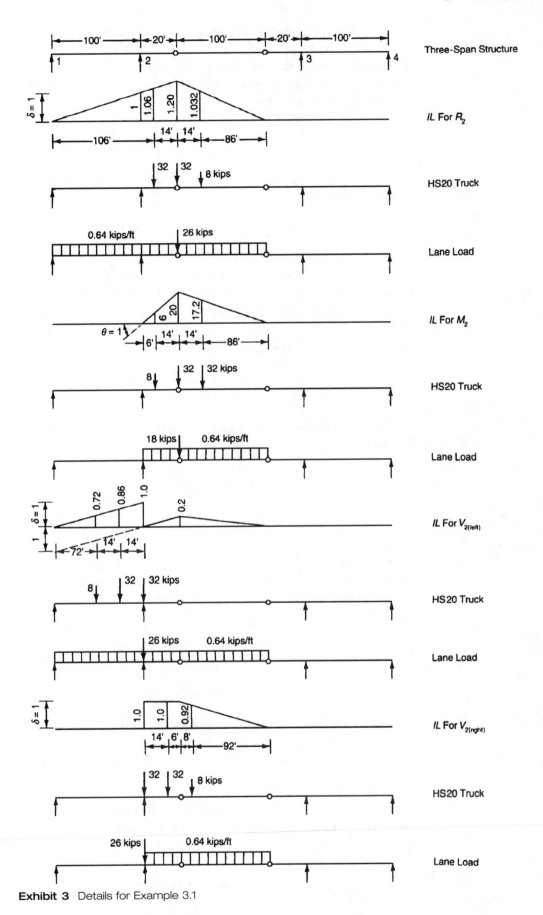

Exhibit 3 Details for Example 3.1

To obtain the influence line for shear V_2 on the left of support 2, the deck is cut at 2 and a unit vertical displacement imposed between the two ends as shown. The elastic curve of the structure is, then, the influence line for V_2 on the left of support 2. Placing the standard truck as shown gives the maximum shear on the left of support 2, which is

$$V_{2(\text{left})} = 32(1 + 0.86) + 8 \times 0.72$$
$$= 65.28 \text{ kips}$$

Placing the equivalent lane load as shown gives the maximum shear on the left of support 2, which is

$$V_{2(\text{left})} = 26 + 0.64(1 \times 100 + 0.2 \times 120)/2$$
$$= 65.68 \text{ kips} \ldots \text{governs}$$

To obtain the influence line for shear V_2 on the right of support 2, the deck is cut at 2 and a unit vertical displacement imposed between the two ends as shown. The elastic curve of the structure is, then, the influence line for V_2 on the right of support 2. Placing the equivalent lane load as shown gives the maximum shear on the right of support 2, which is

$$V_{2(\text{right})} = 26 + 0.64(1 \times 20 + 1 \times 100/2)$$
$$= 70.80 \text{ kips}$$

Placing the standard truck as shown gives the maximum shear on the right of support 2, which is

$$V_{2(\text{right})} = 32 \times 2 + 8 \times 0.92$$
$$= 71.36 \text{ kips} \ldots \text{governs}$$

Example 3.2

Determine the influence line ordinates for the support reaction R_1 for the two-span pin-jointed frame shown in Exhibit 4, as unit load crosses the bottom chord. All members have the same cross-sectional area, modulus of elasticity, and length.

Solution

The change in slope for a member of a rigid structure is given by

$$d\theta = M\,dx/EI$$

and constitutes the load on a small element dx of the conjugate beam.

The change in slope of a pin-jointed frame is concentrated at the pins and is known as the angle change.[8] Thus, the deflections at the panel points of a pin-jointed frame are given by the bending moments at the corresponding points in a conjugate beam loaded with the total angle change at the panel points.

The tensile member forces, P, due to the applied loads in a basic triangle of a pin-jointed frame shown in Exhibit 4 produce positive extensions in the three members of δ_{12}, δ_{23}, and δ_{31}. The angle change at 1 is given by

$$\Delta 1 = \Sigma PuL/AE$$

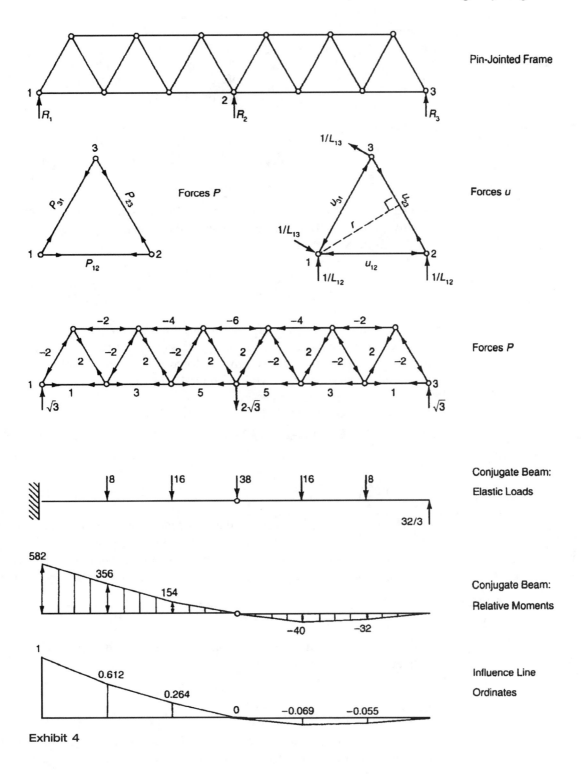

Exhibit 4

where u is the force in a member due to a unit couple applied to node 1 and node 3, as shown in Exhibit 4, with tensile force positive. Thus

$$\Delta 1 = \Sigma PuL/AE$$
$$= \Sigma u\delta$$
$$= u_{12}\delta_{12} + u_{23}\delta_{23} + u_{31}\delta_{31}$$

where

$$u_{12} = -\cot \angle 2/L_{12}$$
$$u_{31} = -\cot \angle 3/L_{31}$$
$$u_{23} = 1/r = (\cot \angle 3 + \cot \angle 2)/L_{23}$$

Hence,

$$\Delta 1 = \cot \angle 2(\delta_{23}/L_{23} - \delta_{12}/L_{12}) + \cot \angle 3(\delta_{23}/L_{23} - \delta_{13}/L_{13})$$
$$= \cot \angle 2(P_{23} - P_{12})/AE + \cot \angle 3(P_{23} - P_{13})/AE$$

where P is the force in a member due to the applied loads with tensile force positive, and A and E are the area and modulus of elasticity, assumed constant for all members. Similarly,

$$\Delta 2 = \cot \angle 3(P_{13} - P_{23})/AE + \cot \angle 1(P_{13} - P_{12})/AE$$
$$\Delta 3 = \cot \angle 1(P_{12} - P_{13})/AE + \cot \angle 2(P_{12} - P_{23})/AE$$

The frame is statically indeterminate, and the required influence line is obtained by the application of Maxwell's reciprocal theorem. The support reaction R_1 is replaced by a vertically upward force of $\sqrt{3}$ units, which produces the resulting member forces shown in Exhibit 4. The total angle changes produced at the bottom chord panel points are

$$\Sigma\Delta 2 = \cot 60°[(-2-1-2-2) + (-2-2-2+2) + (2+2+2-3)]/AE = -8/\left(\sqrt{3}AE\right)$$

$$\Sigma\Delta 3 = \cot 60°([-2-3-2-2) + (-4-2-4+2) + (2+2+2-5)]/AE = -16/\left(\sqrt{3}AE\right)$$

$$\Sigma\Delta 4 = \cot 60°[(-2-5-2-2) + (-6-2-6-2) + (-2-2-2-5)]/AE = -38/\left(\sqrt{3}AE\right)$$

The relative elastic loads on the conjugate beam are as indicated and the bending moments produced in the conjugate beam are shown, and these correspond to the relative deflections at the bottom chord panel points. The maximum moment in the conjugate beam corresponding to the relative deflection at node 1 is

$$M_1' = 582$$

Dividing all the conjugate beam moments by 582 gives the required influence line ordinates for R_1 as shown.

Impact Allowance

In order to account for dynamic wheel load effects in the design of some bridge elements, an allowance for impact loading is added to the vehicular loads. The impact allowance is an equivalent static load, which is a function of the span length, and is expressed as a fraction of the live load to represent the dynamic effects of road surface roughness, vehicle dynamics, and bridge dynamics. The impact allowance is applied to superstructures, piers, and pile bents and is not required for footings, abutments, retaining walls, pedestrian loading, or culverts with more than 3 feet of cover. A reduced impact allowance is applied to culverts with less than 3 feet of cover. The allowance is not applied to wood structures

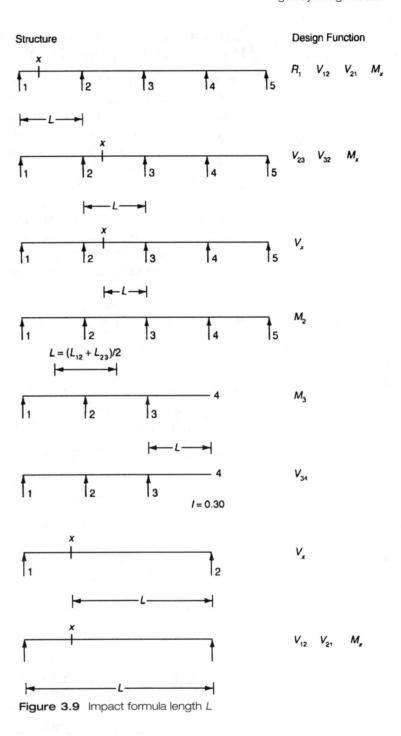

Figure 3.9 Impact formula length L

since these experience reduced dynamic effects due to the damping characteristics of wood and the internal friction between the structural components.

The impact fraction is given by AASHTO Formula (3-1) as

$$I = 50/(L+125) \leq 0.30$$

For simple spans, cantilevers, and continuous spans, the determination of L is illustrated in Figure 3.9.

Lateral Load Distribution and Structural Response in Bridge Decks

Dead loads are distributed to deck members in proportion to the relevant tributary areas. However, curbs, railings, and wearing surfaces, which are placed after the concrete slab has cured, may be distributed uniformly to all beams.

Live loads are distributed to deck members by means of simplified empirical expressions which account for the torsional stiffness of the bridge deck system and which are simpler to apply than the more exact methods of orthotopic plate analysis,[10] grillage analysis,[11] finite strip analysis,[12] and finite element analysis.[13]

The fraction of a wheel line load which is assigned to an interior longitudinal girder, in accordance with AASHTO Section 3.23, depends on the superstructure type, the type of girder, and the girder spacing. A wheel line load is half a standard truck load or half an equivalent lane load. For widely spaced girders, wheel loads are distributed to the girders by the static lever-rule method assuming that the flooring is hinged at each girder.

For closely spaced interior longitudinal girders, the load distribution is determined by means of the girder distribution factor

$$G = S/D$$

where S = girder spacing in feet and D = distribution parameter.

For bridge superstructures with two or more design traffic lanes, the values of D for typical situations are

$D = 3.75$ for $S \leq 6.5$ feet for wood plank floor on wood or steel girders

$D = 4.25$ for $S \leq 6.5$ feet for nail-laminated wood floor, not less than 6 inches thick, on wood or steel girders

$D = 5.0$ for $S \leq 7.5$ feet for glued-laminated wood floor, not less than 6 inches thick, on wood girders

$D = 4.5$ for $S \leq 7.0$ feet for glued-laminated wood floor, not less than 6 inches thick, on steel girders

$D = 5.0$ for $S \leq 10.0$ feet for concrete floor on wood girders

$D = 5.5$ for $S \leq 14.0$ feet for concrete floor on steel or prestressed concrete girders

$D = 6.0$ for $S \leq 10.0$ feet for concrete tee-beam construction

$D = 7.0$ for $S \leq 16.0$ feet for concrete box girder

For exterior longitudinal girders, the load distribution is determined by the lever-rule method. For the load combination of dead load, vehicular live load, impact, and sidewalk live load, allowable stresses may be increased by 25 percent provided the exterior girder has a flexural capacity not less than the capacity of an interior girder. Similarly, in the case of load factor design, the beta factor may be reduced to 1.25 from the usual value of 1.67.

For shear, load distribution is determined in the same manner as for moments, with the exception that for a wheel directly over the support, the load distribution is determined by the lever-rule method.

The fraction of a wheel load that is assigned to transverse girders is determined from the girder distribution factor, and values of D for typical situations are obtained from AASHTO Table 3.23.3.1:

$D = 4.0$ for $S \leq 4.0$ feet for wood plank floor.

$D = 5.0$ for $S \leq 5.0$ feet for nail- or glued-laminated wood floor, not less than 6 inches thick.

$D = 6.0$ for $S \leq 6.0$ feet for concrete floor.

The design of a concrete slab is governed by an individual wheel load, and the simplified design methods adopted in AASHTO Section 3.24 are based on Westergaard's plate theory.[14] For a slab aspect ratio not exceeding 1.5, the slab is considered supported on four sides. For a uniformly distributed load, the proportion of the load carried by the short span is given by AASHTO Equation (3-19) as

$$p = b^4/(a^4 + b^4)$$

where a = effective length of short span, b = effective length of long span, and $b/a \leq 1.5$.

The effective span length is defined in AASHTO Section 3.24.1.2 and is illustrated in Figure 3.10.

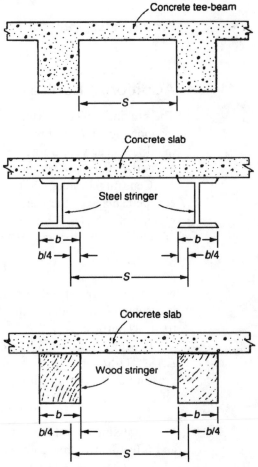

Figure 3.10 Effective span length, S

For a concentrated load at the center of the slab, the proportion of the load carried by the short span is given by AASHTO Equation (3-20) as

$$p = b^3/(a^3 + b^3)$$

In accordance with AASHTO Section 3.24.3.2, when main reinforcement is parallel to traffic, a wheel load is assumed distributed over a width of $E = 4 + 0.06S \leq 7.0$ feet, where S is the effective span length in the relevant direction. Lane loads are distributed over a width of $E = 8 + 0.12S$.

The center half of the slab, in both directions, is designed for 100 percent of the applicable moment, with the outer quarters of the slab designed for 50 percent of this value.

In the case of a simply supported slab spanning perpendicular to the traffic, the design moment for one HS20 wheel load is given by AASHTO Formula (3-15) as

$$M = 0.5(S + 2) \text{ kip-feet per foot width}$$

For slabs continuous over not less than three supports, the positive and negative moments are given by

$$M = 0.4(S + 2) \text{ kip-feet per foot width}$$

For a simply supported slab not exceeding 50 feet span length, spanning in the direction of traffic, the design moment for one HS20 wheel load is given by

$$M = 0.9S \text{ kip-feet per foot width}$$

For span lengths between 50 and 100 feet, the design moment is given by

$$M = (1.3S - 20) \text{ kip-feet per foot width}$$

Additional Loads

The braking effects of vehicular traffic are allowed for in AASHTO Section 3.9 by applying a longitudinal force equal to 5 percent of the equivalent lane live load in all lanes carrying traffic headed in the same direction. The force is assumed to act horizontally at a height of 6 feet above the roadway surface.

Centrifugal force, due to vehicular traffic on a curved structure, is calculated as a percentage of the weight of one standard truck in each design lane since the spacing of vehicles at high speed is assumed to be large, resulting in a low density of vehicles. The applicable percentage is specified in AASHTO Section 3.10 as

$$C = 6.68 \ S^2/R \text{ percent}$$

where S = design speed in miles per hour and R = curve radius in feet. The force is assumed to act radially, in a horizontal direction, at a height of 6 feet above the roadway surface.

In determining wind loads, the base design wind velocity, in accordance with AASHTO Section 3.15, is taken as 100 miles per hour. This produces a wind pressure on a beam or girder structure of

$$WS = 50 \text{ pounds per square foot}$$

Wind pressure on vehicles is represented by a horizontal force acting normal to, and 6 feet above, the roadway surface with a magnitude of

$$WL = 100 \text{ pounds per linear foot}$$

The vertical upward wind pressure, which must be considered when investigating overturning of the structure, is 20 pounds per square foot of deck area when wind on the live load is not included, and 6 pounds per square foot when wind on the live load is included. The force is applied at the windward quarter point of the deck width.

In accordance with AASHTO Section 3.20, lateral earth pressure shall be determined by Rankine's method, with a minimum value for active pressure equivalent to that of a fluid of density 30 pounds per cubic foot. For calculating positive moments in rigid frames, only one-half of the lateral pressure is assumed, and this is reflected in the values specified for the load factors in the relevant load combinations.

A surcharge pressure equivalent to 2 feet of fill is specified in situations when vehicular loads may approach within a horizontal distance from the top of the structure equal to one-half its height.

Other forces which must be considered include water loads; ice loads; seismic loads; thermal, creep, and shrinkage forces; frictional forces; and forces due to vessel collision.

Service Load Design Method

The service load, or allowable stress, design method is based on elastic theory, which assumes elastic material properties and a constant modulus of elasticity to predict the material stresses in the structure under the applied working loads. The allowable stress due to working load is defined as the yield stress or compressive strength divided by a factor of safety. This approach, however, does not ensure a constant factor of safety against failure in different structures. In particular, the margin of safety provided for an increase in the live load decreases as the ratio of live load to dead load increases.

The basic requirement for allowable stress design may be expressed in terms of stresses as

$$D + L + I \leq R$$

where D = stress produced by dead load
  L = stress produced by live load
  I = stress produced by impact
  R = allowable stress

Infrequently occurring overloads are accommodated by permitting a specified increase in the allowable stress, and this may be expressed as

$$D + \text{EQ} \leq 1.33R$$

where EQ = stress produced by seismic effects.

Load Factor Design Method

The load factor design method, also known as the limit state or strength design method, utilizes an ultimate limit state analysis to determine the maximum load-carrying capacity of the structure, and a serviceability limit state analysis to ensure satisfactory behavior at working load conditions. The objective of ultimate limit state design is to ensure a uniform level of reliability for all structures. This is

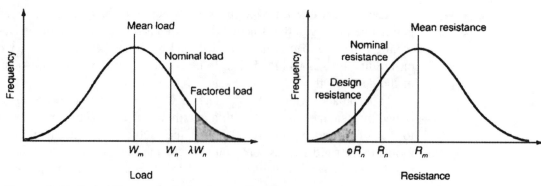

Figure 3.11 Probability curves for loading and resistance capacity

achieved by multiplying the nominal, or service, loads by load factors to obtain an acceptable probability that the factored loads will be exceeded during the life of the structure. In Figure 3.11, the shaded portion of the graph denotes the probability of exceeding the factored loads.

The factored, or ultimate, load is obtained by multiplying the nominal load by a load factor, and this may be expressed as

$$W_u = \lambda W_n$$

where λ = load factor.

The load factor λ is a function of two other partial-load factors denoted by γ and β. The factor γ compensates for the unfavorable deviation of the loading from the nominal value and uncertainties in strength, methods of analysis, and structural behavior. It also represents a control over the stress level developed in the structure. A value of 1.3 for γ enables the use of 77 percent of the ultimate capacity. The factor β reflects the reduced probability of the full nominal loads, in a combination of loads, being present simultaneously.

The total effect on the structure of the factored loads shall not exceed the design, or useable, resistance capacity of the structure, and the basic requirement for load factor design may be expressed in terms of resistance capacity as

$$U \leq \phi R_n$$

where U = total effect on the structure of the factored load, W_u
ϕR_n = design resistance capacity of the structure
R_n = nominal resistance capacity of the structure
ϕ = strength reduction factor

The factor ϕ is also referred to as the confidence factor, performance factor, resistance factor, or capacity reduction factor. This factor allows for the possibility of adverse variations in material strength, workmanship, and dimensional inaccuracies. In Figure 3.11, the shaded portion of the graph denotes the probability of exceeding the design resistance capacity of the structure.

Load Combinations

The different combinations of loads which may act on a structure are represented in AASHTO Section 3.22 by 12 groups. The loading combination for each group is given by AASHTO Equation (3-10) as

$$\text{Group }(N) = \gamma[\beta_D D + \beta_L(L+I) + \beta_C \text{CF} + \beta_E E + \beta_B B + \beta_S \text{SF} + \beta_W \text{WS} + \beta_{WL}\text{WL}$$
$$+ \beta_L \text{LF} + \beta_R(R+S+T) + \beta_{EQ}\text{EQ} + \beta_{ICE}\text{ICE}]$$

where N = group number

γ = load factor

β = coefficient

D = dead load

L = live load

I = live load impact

E = earth pressure

B = buoyancy

WS = wind load on structure

WL = wind load on live load

LF = longitudinal force from live load

CF = centrifugal force

R = rib shortening

S = shrinkage

T = temperature

EQ = earthquake

SF = stream flow pressure

ICE = ice pressure

For service load design, the applicable load factors and the permissible percentage of the basic allowable stresses are summarized in Table 3.1, where

Table 3.1 Service load design coefficients

Load	β Factors for Combination Groups						
	I	**IA**	**IB**	**II**	**III**	**IV**	**VIII**
D	1	1	1	1	1	1	1
$(L+I)_n$	1	2	0	0	1	1	1
$(L+I)_p$	0	0	1	0	0	0	0
CF	1	0	1	0	1	1	1
E	β_E	0	β_E	1	β_E	β_E	1
B	1	0	1	1	1	1	1
SF	1	0	1	1	1	1	1
WS	0	0	0	1	0.3	0	0
WL	0	0	0	0	1	0	0
LF	0	0	0	0	1	0	0
$R+S+T$	0	0	0	0	0	1	0
EQ	0	0	0	0	0	0	0
ICE	0	0	0	0	0	0	1
γ factor	1	1	1	1	1	1	1
% basic stress	100	150	*	125	125	125	140

*As specified by operating agency.

Table 3.2 Load factor design coefficients

Load	β Factors for Combination Froups						
	I	**IA**	**IB**	**II**	**III**	**IV**	**VIII**
D	β_D	β_D	β_D	β_D	β_D	β_D	β_D
$(L+I)_n$	1.67	2.2	0	0	1	1	1
$(L+I)_p$	0	0	1	0	0	0	0
CF	1	0	1	0	1	1	1
E	β_E	0	β_E	β_E	β_E	β_E	β_E
B	1	0	1	1	1	1	1
SF	1	0	1	1	1	1	1
WS	0	0	0	1	0.3	0	0
WL	0	0	0	0	1	0	0
LF	0	0	0	0	1	0	0
$R+S+T$	0	0	0	0	0	1	0
EQ	0	0	0	0	0	0	0
ICE	0	0	0	0	0	0	1
γ factor	1.3	1.3	1.3	1.3	1.3	1.3	1.3

$(L+I)_n$ = live load plus impact for standard truck or equivalent lane loading

$(L+I)_p$ = live load plus impact for agency abnormal load vehicle

β_E = 1.0 or 0.5 for lateral loads on rigid frames

β_E = 1.0 for vertical and lateral loads on all other structures

For load factor design, the applicable load factors are summarized in Table 3.2, where

β_E = 1.3 for lateral earth pressure on retaining walls

β_E = 1.3 or 0.5 for lateral loads on rigid frames

β_E = 1.0 for vertical earth pressure

β_D = 1.0 for flexural and tension members

β_D = 0.75 for columns with minimum axial load and maximum moment

β_D = 1.0 for columns with maximum axial load and minimum moment.

The load combinations may be classified as

Group I: permanent loads plus the primary vehicular loading consisting of the standard truck or equivalent lane load

Group IA: permanent loads plus the maximum design load which may be applied in an emergency

Group IB: permanent loads plus the operating agency's abnormal load vehicle

Group II: permanent loads plus wind load on the structure without vehicular loading

Group III: permanent loads plus primary vehicular loading plus wind load on the live load and reduced wind load on the structure

Group IV: permanent loads plus vehicular loading plus loads originating from rib shortening, shrinkage, and temperature effects

Group VIII: permanent loads plus vehicular loading plus ice pressure

---

| Example **3.3** |

Exhibit 5 shows the cross section of the three-span reinforced concrete tee-beam bridge structure shown in Exhibit 3. For HS20 loading, determine the applicable factored moment for design of the central beam at support 2. The concrete barrier rail has a weight of 0.4 kip per linear foot.

Solution

The dead load acting on the central beam consists of the beam self-weight plus the tributary portion of the deck slab plus, in accordance with AASHTO Section 3.23.2.3.1.1, one-third the weight of the two barrier railings. The applicable dead load is

$$W_D = 0.15(7 \times 16/12 + 10.25 \times 9/12) + 2 \times 0.4/3$$
$$= 2.82 \text{ kips per linear foot}$$

The dead load bending moment at support 2 is

$$M_D = W_D(20 \times 10 + 50 \times 20)$$
$$= 3384 \text{ kip-feet}$$

In accordance with AASHTO Section 3.6.3, the 24-foot-wide roadway width is divided into two lanes each 12 feet wide. From Example 3.1, the maximum moment at support 2 is produced by the standard truck, and for a single truck, the value of the moment is

$$M' = 1238.4 \text{ kip-feet}$$

In accordance with AASHTO Section 3.8.2.2, the loaded length for determining the impact fraction is

$$L = 100 + 20$$
$$= 120 \text{ feet}$$

The impact fraction, as given by Formula (3-1), is

$$I = 50/(L + 125)$$
$$= 50/(120 + 125)$$
$$= 0.204$$

Thus, for a single HS20 standard truck the value of the moment at support 2 due to live load plus impact is

$$M'' = M'(1 + I)$$
$$= 1238.4(1 + 0.204)$$
$$= 1491 \text{ kip-feet}$$

The beam spacing exceeds 10 feet and, in accordance with AASHTO Table 3.23.1, wheel loads from the standard truck are distributed to the beams by the static lever-rule method, assuming that the concrete deck is hinged at each beam. Maximum loading is produced in the central beam by locating one truck in each lane, as shown in Exhibit 5, with one line of wheels a minimum distance of 2 feet from the lane

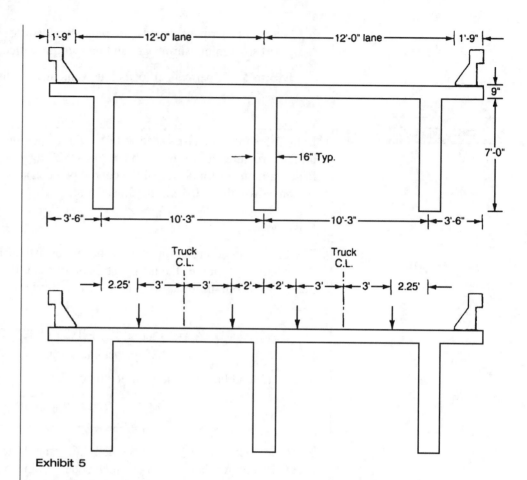

Exhibit 5

edge, as specified in AASHTO Figure 3.7.7A. Since only two lanes are loaded, in accordance with AASHTO Section 3.12.1, no reduction in the intensity of loading is necessary. The total moment distributed to the concrete girders is, then,

$$M_L = 2M'' \times 5.25/10.25$$
$$= 2 \times 1491 \times 5.25/10.25$$
$$= 1527 \text{ kip-feet}$$

The factored design moment for Group I loading is given by AASHTO Table 3.22.1A as

$$M_u = \gamma[\beta_D D + \beta_L (L + I)]$$
$$= 1.3(1 \times M_D + 1.67 \times M_L)$$
$$= 1.3(3384 + 1.67 \times 1527)$$
$$= 7714 \text{ kip-feet}$$

SEISMIC DESIGN

Design Procedure

The objective of a seismic design procedure is to design a structure which may be damaged in an earthquake but will not collapse and which can quickly be put back into service. The analysis procedure to be adopted is specified in AASHTOSD Specifications[17] Section 4.

A detailed seismic analysis is not required for single-span bridges. However, minimum support widths are required, in accordance with AASHTOSD Section 3.10, and the connection of the superstructure to the substructure is designed to resist the product of the dead load reaction, the site coefficient, and the site acceleration coefficient, as specified in Section 3.11.

For multispan regular structures with a maximum of six spans and having no abrupt changes in weight, stiffness, or geometry, the single-mode spectral method may be adopted. The method assumes a predominant single mode of vibration which allows a statical method of analysis to be utilized. The parameters which define a regular bridge are given in AASHTOSD Table 4.2B.

The response spectrum or multimode spectral method is used for complex structures with irregular geometry. Several modes of vibration contribute to the overall response of the structure, and a space frame analysis program with dynamic capabilities is required.

In order to determine the seismic response of the structure, several factors must be considered. These include the acceleration coefficient, importance classification, performance category, site coefficient and response modification factors.

The selection of the design procedure depends on the type of bridge, the magnitude of the accleration coefficient, and the degree of acceptability of loss of operation. The single-mode spectral method is defined as Procedure 2 and the multimode spectral method is defined as Procedure 3, in AASHTOSD Section 4.1.

Acceleration Coefficient

The acceleration coefficient A, given in the contour maps in the Specification, is an estimation of the site-dependent design ground acceleration expressed as a percentage of the gravity constant g. The values of A range from 4 to 80. The acceleration coefficient corresponds to ground acceleration values with a recurrence interval of 475 years, which gives a 10 percent probability of being exceeded in a 50-year period. The acceleration coefficient corresponds to the effective peak acceleration[18] in bedrock, which is based on historical records and geological data, and for sites located near an active fault zone, the coefficient may exceed the 80 percent contour value. Numerical values for A are obtained by dividing contour values by 100.

Elastic Seismic Response Coefficient

The elastic seismic response coefficient, or lateral design force coefficient C_s, is a function of the seismic zone, the fundamental period of the bridge, and the site soil conditions. The value of the lateral design force coefficient is given by AASHTOSD Formula (3-1) as

$$C_s = 1.2AS/T^{2/3} \leq 2.5A$$
$$\leq 2.0A \ldots \text{for soil profile type III or type IV when } A \geq 0.30$$

where S = site coefficient or amplification factor for a specific soil profile
T = fundamental period of the bridge

The specific site soil profile considerably influences the ground motion characteristics, and three profile types and corresponding site coefficients are defined in AASHTOSD Section 3.5. Soil profile type I consists of rock or rock with an overlying layer of stiff soil less than 200 feet deep. The applicable value for the site coefficient is

$$S = 1$$

Soil profile type II consists of a stiff clay layer exceeding 200 feet in depth and has a site coefficient of

$$S = 1.2$$

Soil profile type III consists of a soft to medium clay layer, at least 30 feet deep, and has a site coefficient of

$$S = 1.5$$

Soil profile type IV consists of a soft clay or silt layer, exceeding 40 feet deep, and has a site coefficient of

$$S = 2.0$$

The single-mode spectral procedure assumes that the first mode of vibration predominates during the seismic response of the structure, and this is the case for regular structures. The mode shape may be represented by the elastic curve produced by the application of a uniform unit virtual load to the structure. From consideration of the kinetic and potential energies in the system, values of the fundamental period of vibration and of the generalized seismic force are obtained.[19,20] The analysis for seismic response along the longitudinal axis of the bridge may be reduced to the expression

$$T = 2\pi\sqrt{m/k}$$

where m = mass of the system and k = stiffness of the system.

The analysis for seismic response in the transverse direction requires the use of numerical integration techniques[21] to evaluate the relevant expressions.

The fundamental period T and the equivalent static force are obtained by using the technique detailed in AASHTOSD Section 4.4. This involves the determination of the integrals given in expressions (4-5), (4-6), and (4-7), where the limits of the integrals extend over the whole length of the bridge superstructure. These expressions simplify when the dead weight per unit length of the superstructure and tributary substructure is constant and when the displacement profile is constant, as is the situation in determining longitudinal effects, as shown in Figure 3.12. Hence, for longitudinal seismic force, the expressions for α, β, and γ reduce to

$$\alpha = \int v_s(x)\,dx$$
$$= v_s\int dx$$
$$= v_s L$$

$$\beta = \int w(x)v_s(x)\,dx$$
$$= wv_s\int dx$$
$$= wv_s L$$

$$\gamma = \int w(x)v_s(x)^2\,dx$$
$$= wv_s^2\int dx$$
$$= wv_s^2 L$$

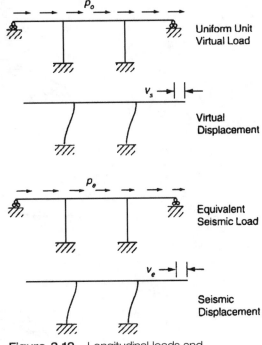

Figure 3.12 Longitudinal loads and displacements

where $v_s(x)$ = displacement profile due to p_o
v_s = total longitudinal displacement of the structure due to p_o
p_o = uniform unit virtual load
$w(x)$ = distribution of dead weight per unit length of the superstructure and tributary substructure
$= w$ for a constant dead weight

The fundamental period is given by expression (4-8) as

$$T = 2\pi\sqrt{\gamma/p_o g \alpha}$$
$$= 2\pi\sqrt{wv_s/p_o g}$$
$$= 0.32\sqrt{Wv_s/P_o}$$
$$= 0.32\sqrt{W/k}$$
$$= 0.32\sqrt{\Delta_W}$$

where $W = wL$ = total weight of superstructure and tributary substructure
$P_o = p_o L$ = total applied virtual load
k = total stiffness of the structure
Δ_W = longitudinal displacement in inches due to the total dead weight acting longitudinally

Hence, the lateral design force coefficient may be obtained from AASHTOSD Formula (3-1), and the equivalent static seismic loading is given by expression (4-9) as

$$p_e(x) = p_e = \beta C_s w(x) v_s(x)/\gamma = w C_s$$

and this produces the longitudinal displacement v_e as shown in Figure 3.12.

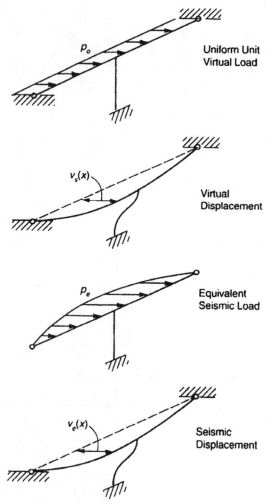

Figure 3.13 Transverse loads and displacements

The total elastic seismic shear is given by

$$V = p_e L = wLC_s = WC_s$$

The procedure for determining the transverse seismic response is shown in Figure 3.13. The abutments are assumed to be rigid and to provide a pinned end restraint at each end of the superstructure. A transverse uniform unit virtual load is applied as shown and is resisted by the lateral stiffness of the superstructure and by the stiffness of the central column bent. As shown in Figure 3.14, the displacements produced are the sum of the displacements in the cut-back structure due to the unit virtual load, plus the displacement in the cut-back structure due to the reaction in the column bent. The value of the reaction in the column bent is obtained by equating the displacements of node 2 in cases (i), (ii), and (iii). The displacement of node 2 in the original structure, as shown at (i), is

$$\delta_2 = k_C R$$

where k_C = stiffness of the column bent
         = $12EI_c/H^3$ for a fixed-end column
    R = reaction in the column bent

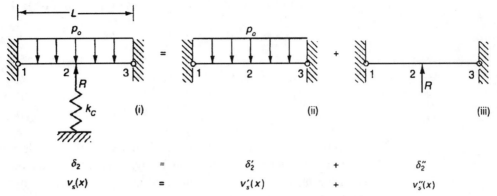

Figure 3.14 Transverse displacements

I_C = moment of inertia of column

H = height of column

The displacement of node 2 in the cut-back structure due to the uniform unit virtual load, as shown at (ii), is

$$\delta_2' = 5L^4/384EI$$

where E = modulus of elasticity of the superstructure

　　　I = lateral stiffness of the superstructure

The displacement of node 2 in the cut-back structure due to the reaction in the column bent, as shown at (iii), is

$$\delta_2'' = -RL^3/48EI$$

Equating these displacements gives

$$\delta_2 = \delta_2' + \delta_2''$$

Hence,

$$R = 5L^4/(8L^3 + 384EIk_C)$$

The displacement profile in the cut-back structure due to the uniform unit virtual load, as shown at (ii), is

$$v_s'(x) = x(L^3 - 2Lx^2 + x^3)/24EI$$

The displacement profile in the cut-back structure due to the reaction in the column bent, as shown at (iii), is

$$v_s''(x) = -Rx(3L^2 - 4x^2)/48EI$$

The displacement profile in the original structure, as shown at (i), is

$$v_s(x) = v_s'(x) + v_s''(x)$$
$$= [2x^4 + 4Rx^3 - 4Lx^2 + (2L - 3R)L^2x]/48EI$$

The values for α, β, and γ are obtained from expressions (4-5), (4-6), and (4-7) as

$$\alpha = \int v_s(x)\,dx$$

$$\beta = \int w(x)v_s(x)\,dx$$

$$\gamma = \int w(x)v_s(x)^2\,dx$$

The limits of integration extend over the whole length of the bridge, and the numerical values of the integrals may be obtained by means of a calculator.[21] Alternatively, values of the integrands may be computed at discrete intervals over the length of the bridge and the numerical integration performed manually.

The fundamental period is obtained from expression (4-8) as

$$T = 2\pi\sqrt{\gamma/p_o g \alpha}$$

The seismic response coefficient is obtained from AASHTOSD Formula (3-1) as

$$C_s = 1.2AS/T^{2/3}$$

The equivalent seismic loading is defined by AASHTOSD Formula (4-9) as

$$p_e(x) = \beta C_s w(x)v_s(x)/\gamma$$

This equivalent static load may now be applied to the structure and the resultant forces calculated.

Importance Classification

The importance classification is defined in AASHTOSD Section 3.3, and two categories are specified. An importance classification of I is assigned to essential bridges which for social or security considerations must remain functional after an earthquake. For this situation a design is required which will ensure the continued operation of the facility. An importance classification of II is assigned to nonessential bridges.

Seismic Performance Category

The seismic performance category is a function of the acceleration coefficient and the importance classification and is defined in AASHTOSD Section 3.4. The four categories are shown in Table 3.3, and these provide flexibility in the specified requirements for selection of the design procedure, minimum support lengths, and substructure design details.

Table 3.3   Seismic performance category

Acceleration Coefficient	Essential Bridges (importance classification I)	Other Bridges (importance classification II)
$A \leq 0.09$	A	A
$0.09 < A \leq 0.19$	B	B
$0.19 < A \leq 0.29$	C	C
$0.29 < A$	D	C

Analysis Procedure

AASTOSD Section 4.1 defines four analysis procedures. Procedure 2 is the single-mode spectral analysis technique, and Procedure 3 is the multimode spectral analysis technique. The procedure selected depends on the seismic performance category and on the bridge classification, and is summarized in Table 3.4. A multispan bridge with a uniform mass distribution, and with the stiffness of adjacent supporting members differing by no more than 25 percent, is classified as a regular structure. In this type of bridge, the fundamental mode of vibration predominates during the seismic response of the structure, and higher modes of vibration do not significantly affect the distribution of seismic forces. An irregular bridge is one that does not satisfy the definition of a regular bridge and, in this type of structure, the higher modes of vibration significantly affect the seismic response.

Table 3.4 Analysis procedure

| SPC | Bridges with Two or More Spans | |
	Regular	Irregular
A	N/A	N/A
B	1 or 2	3
C	1 or 2	3
D	1 or 2	3

A detailed seismic analysis is not required for single-span bridges or for bridges classified as seismic performance category A. However, minimum support widths are required, in accordance with AASHTOSD Sections 3.10 and 5.3, and the connection of the superstructure to the substructure is designed to resist the forces, as specified in AASHTOSD Sections 3.11 and 5.2.

Response Modification Factors

To design a bridge structure to remain within its elastic range during a severe earthquake is uneconomical. Limited structural damage is acceptable provided that total collapse is prevented and public safety is not endangered. Any damage produced in a severe earthquake should be readily detectable, accessible, and reparable. To achieve this end, the response modification factor R is specified in AASHTOSD Section 3.7, and this represents the ratio of the force in a component which would develop in a linearly elastic system to the prescribed design force. The response modification factors are selected to ensure that columns will yield during a severe earthquake, while connections and foundations will undergo little if any damage. The response modification values for substructure components reflect the nonlinear energy dissipation capability, the increase in natural period and damping, and the ductility and redundancy of the component. Thus, the R-factor for a single column is 3 and for a multiple-column bent is 5, which is an indication of the redundancy provided by the multiple-column bent. The R-factor is applied to moments only. Elastic design values are adopted for axial force and shear force unless the values corresponding to plastic hinging of the columns are smaller, in which case the smaller values are used.

The R-factors of 1.0 and 0.8 assigned to connectors require connectors to be designed for 100 percent or 125 percent of the elastic force. This is to ensure enhanced overall integrity of the structure at strategic locations with little increase in construction costs. However, the connector design forces need not exceed the values determined using the maximum probable plastic hinge moment capacities developed in the columns. The maximum probable capacity or overstrength capacity results from the actual material strength exceeding the minimum specified strength.

Table 3.5 Response modification factors

Substructure	R-factor
Wall-type pier	
Strong axis	2
Weak axis	3
Reinforced concrete pile bents	
Vertical piles only	3
One or more batter piles	2
Single columns	3
Steel or composite pile bents	
Vertical piles only	5
One or more batter piles	3
Multiple-column bent	5

Table 3.6 Response modification factors

Connections	R-factor	Design Force
Superstructure to abutment		
Single span	N/A	$A \times DL$
SPC A	N/A	$0.2 \times DL$
SPC B, C, D	0.8	Elastic/R
Expansion joints	0.8	Elastic/R
Pinned columns		
SPC A	N/A	$0.2 \times DL$
SPC B, C, D	1.0	Elastic/R
Fixed column		
SPC A	N/A	$0.2 \times DL$
SPC B	1.0	Elastic/R
SPC C, D	N/A	Plastic hinge forces

Combination of Orthogonal Forces

AASHTOSD Section 3.9 requires the combination of orthogonal seismic forces to account for the directional uncertainty of the earthquake motion and for the possible simultaneous occurrence of earthquake motions in two perpendicular horizontal directions. The combinations specified are

Load case 1: 100 percent of the forces due to a seismic event in the longitudinal direction plus 30 percent of the forces due to a seismic event in the transverse direction

Load case 2: 100 percent of the forces due to a seismic event in the transverse direction plus 30 percent of the forces due to a seismic event in the longitudinal direction

Load Combinations

For superstructure and substructure design down to the base of columns, in accordance with AASHTOSD Sections 6.2 and 7.2, the load combination group for seismic performance categories B, C, and D is given by

$$\text{group load} = \gamma(\beta_D D + \beta_B B + \beta_S \text{SF} + \beta_E E + \beta_{EQ}\text{EQ})$$
$$= 1.0(D + B + \text{SF} + E + \text{EQ})$$

where D = dead load
$\quad B$ = buoyancy
$\quad \text{SF}$ = stream flow pressure
$\quad E$ = earth pressure
$\quad \text{EQ}$ = elastic seismic force for either load case 1 or load case 2, divided by the appropriate R-factor

For service load design, a 50 percent increase is permitted in the allowable stresses for structural steel and a $33^1/_3$ percent increase is permitted for reinforced concrete.

For footings, pile caps, and piles, the same group load is applicable and the appropriate R-factor, for seismic performance category B, is half that of the substructure element to which the footing is attached. For seismic performance categories C and D, an R-factor of unity is applied.

Column Plastic Hinges

The determination of shear and axial forces in column bents due to plastic hinging is shown in Figure 3.15 for transverse seismic loading.

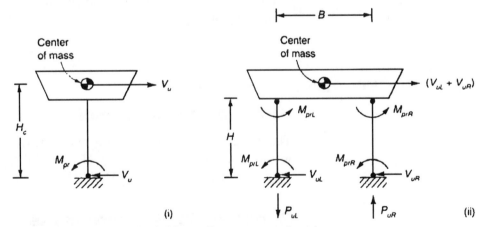

Figure 3.15 Column plastic hinges: Transverse earthquake

For a single column, as shown at (i), the maximum probable or overstrength moment capacity at the foot of the column is

$$M_{pr} = \phi M_n$$

where M_n = nominal moment capacity. The shear developed in the column is given by

$$V_u = M_{pr}/H_C$$

where H_C = height of center of mass.

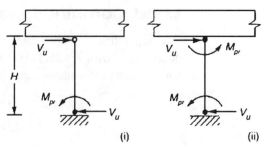

Figure 3.16 Column plastic hinges: Longitudinal earthquake

For a double-column bent with both columns fixed at top and bottom, as shown at (ii), the shears developed in the left and right columns are given by

$$V_{uL} = 2M_{prL}/H$$
$$V_{uR} = 2M_{prR}/H$$

where H = height of column.

The axial force developed in the columns is obtained by equating moments of external forces about the base of one column and is given by

$$P_{uL} = -P_{uR}$$
$$= [H_C(V_{uL} + V_{uR}) - (M_{prL} + M_{prR})]/B$$

Shear and axial forces due to plastic hinging for longitudinal seismic loading are shown in Figure 3.16. For a single column, pinned at the top, as shown at (i), the shear developed in the column is given by

$$V_u = M_{pr}/H$$

For a single column fixed at top and bottom, as shown at (ii), the shear developed in the column is given by

$$V_u = 2M_{pr}/H$$

REINFORCED CONCRETE DESIGN

Strength Design Principles

The strength design procedure adopted in the AASHTO specifications is identical to the procedure adopted in the ACI[23] Building Code, and this is adequately covered in Chapter 2 of this text.

Serviceability Requirements

In order to ensure satisfactory performance under service load conditions, the distribution of reinforcement, fatigue characteristics, and deflection of flexural members is controlled.

Deflections due to service live load plus impact are limited by AASHTO Section 8.9 to

$$\delta_{max} = L/800$$

where L = span length.

To provide additional comfort for pedestrians, the deflections of bridge structures which are also used by pedestrians are limited to

$$\delta_{\max} = L/1000$$

To achieve these limits, AASHTO Table 8.9.2 provides expressions for the determination of minimum superstructure depths. Alternative expressions are given in the ACI Recommendations.[24]

Actual deflections may be calculated in accordance with AASHTO Section 8.13. The modulus of elasticity of normal-weight concrete is given as

$$E_c = 57{,}000\sqrt{f_c'}$$

and the effective moment of inertia may be taken as the moment of inertia of the gross concrete section.

When the yield strength of the reinforcement exceeds 40,000 pounds per square inch, to control flexural cracking of the concrete, the distribution of tension reinforcement shall be in accordance with AASHTO Section 8.16.8. The value of the parameter z, given by AASHTO Equation (8-61), is limited to 170 for moderate exposure conditions and 130 for severe exposure conditions, where z is given by

$$z = f_s (d_c A)^{1/3}$$

where f_s = stress in reinforcement at service load $\leq 0.6 f_y$

d_c = concrete cover measured to center of reinforcement closest to tensile face of concrete

A = effective concrete area in the tension block per equivalent number of bars

In accordance with AASHTO Section 8.17, to prevent sudden tensile failure of a flexural member, a minimum area of tensile reinforcement is required in order to provide a moment capacity of

$$M_{\min} = 1.2 M_{cr}$$

where $M_{cr} = f_r I_g / y_t$ = cracking moment of section

$f_r = 7.5\sqrt{f_c'}$ = modulus of rupture of normal-weight concrete

I_g = moment of inertia of gross concrete section, neglecting reinforcement

y_t = distance of neutral axis from tension face

The minimum reinforcement ratio to satisfy this requirement is given by[24]

$$\rho_{\min} = I_g f_c' (10 + I_g / y_t bd^2) / y_t bd^2 f_y$$

To control cracking in the side faces of members exceeding 3 feet in depth, longitudinal skin reinforcement is provided in the lower half of the effective depth having a total area, in accordance with AASHTO Section 8.17.2, of

$$A_{s(\min)} \geq 0.012(d - 30) \text{ square inches/foot}$$

The spacing of this reinforcement is given by

$$s = d/6$$
$$\leq 12 \text{ inches}$$

Fatigue stress limits are governed by the magnitude of the stress in the reinforcement, the range of stress, and the shape of the deformations on the bar which act as stress raisers. The range between maximum and minimum stress levels, due to dead load and service live load plus impact, must not exceed the value given by AASHTO Equation (8-60) as

$$f_f = 21 - 0.33 f_{min} + 8r/h \text{ kips per square inch}$$

where f_{min} = the algebraic minimum stress, due to dead load and service live load plus impact, with tension positive and compression negative
r = base radius of deformations
h = height of deformations

When the actual dimensions of the deformations are not known, it is adequate to assume that the ratio

$$r/h = 0.3$$

and

$$f_f = 21 - 0.33 f_{min} + 2.4$$
$$= 23.4 - 0.33 f_{min}$$

The actual stress in the reinforcement at service load level is determined by the straight-line elastic theory method.

Spacing limits for reinforcement are specified in AASHTO Section 8.21. For cast-in-place concrete the clear distance between parallel bars in a layer shall be not less than

(i) $1.5 d_b$

(ii) $1.5 \times$ maximum aggregate size

(iii) 1.5 inches

The minimum clear distance required between layers of reinforcement is 1 inch.

For concrete exposed to earth or weather, AASHTO Section 8.22 specifies a minimum concrete cover to primary reinforcement of 2 inches and to secondary reinforcement of 1.5 inches.

Example 3.4

The three-span reinforced concrete tee-beam bridge structure shown in Exhibit 3 and Exhibit 5 and analyzed in Examples 3.1 and 3.3 has a concrete compressive strength of 3250 pounds per square inch and uses Grade 60 reinforcement.

(i) Determine the maximum and minimum service load moment for the central beam, at the center of span 12, for HS20 loading.

(ii) Calculate the corresponding factored design moment.

(iii) Using an effective depth of 88 inches and No. 11 bars, determine the tensile reinforcement required.

(iv) Calculate the maximum live load deflection at the center of span 12.

(v) Determine the minimum moment capacity required to prevent sudden tensile failure.

(vi) Calculate the value of the reinforcement distribution parameter z.

(vii) Determine the amount of longitudinal skin reinforcement required.

(viii) Calculate the range of stress produced by service loading

Solution

(i) To obtain the influence line for moment M_5 at the center of span 12, the deck is cut at 5 and a unit virtual rotation imposed on the two ends. The elastic curve of the structure due to this rotation is the influence line for M_5 as shown in Exhibit 6(ii).

   The standard truck loading governs for both maximum and minimum moments. Placing the standard truck as shown at (iii) gives the maximum service live load at 5, which is

$$M_{L(\text{max})} = 32(25+18)+8 \times 18 = 1520 \text{ kip-feet}$$

Placing the standard truck as shown at (iv) gives the minimum service live load at 5, which is

$$M_{L(\text{min})} = -32(10+8.6)-8 \times 3 = -619 \text{ kip-feet}$$

The dead load moment on the central beam at 5 is obtained as shown at (v) and is given by

$$M_D = 2.82 \times 0.5 \,(25 \times 100 - 10 \times 120) = 1833 \text{ kip-feet}$$

For the maximum live load moment, the loaded length for determining the impact fraction is obtained from AASHTO Section 3.8.2.1 as

$$L = 100 \text{ feet}$$

The impact fraction, as given by AASHTO Formula (3-1), is

$$\begin{aligned} I &= 50/(L+125) \\ &= 50/(100+125) \\ &= 0.222 \end{aligned}$$

The maximum live load plus impact moment due to HS20 loading is

$$\begin{aligned} M'_{L(\text{max})} &= M_{L(\text{max})}(1+I) \\ &= 1520(1+0.222) \\ &= 1857 \text{ kip-feet} \end{aligned}$$

The total moment distributed to the central girder, as determined in Example 3.3, is

$$\begin{aligned} M''_{L(\text{max})} &= 2M'_{L(\text{max})} \times 5.25/10.25 \\ &= 1902 \text{ kip-feet} \end{aligned}$$

The maximum serviceability limit state moment on the central beam at 5 due to dead load and live load plus impact is

$$\begin{aligned} M_{5(\text{max})} &= M_D + M''_{L(\text{max})} \\ &= 1833 + 1902 \\ &= 3735 \text{ kip-feet} \end{aligned}$$

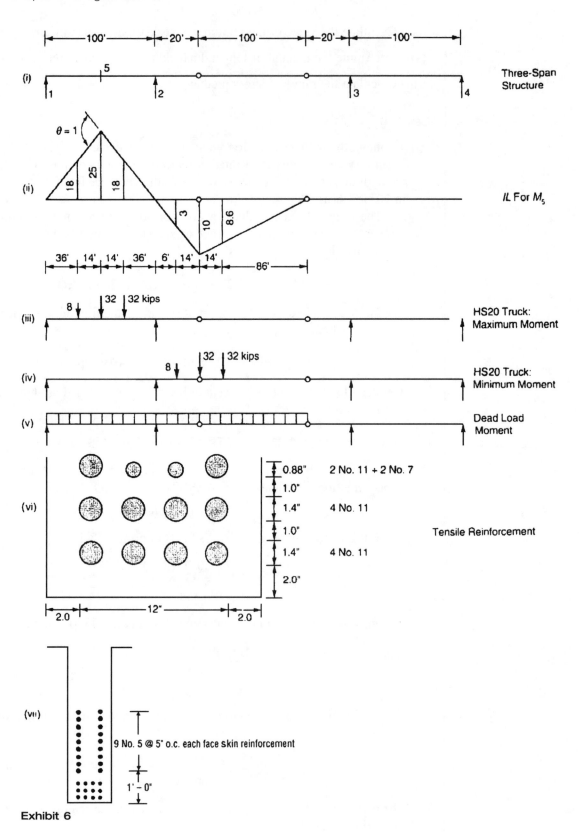

Exhibit 6

For the minimum live load moment, the loaded length for determining the impact fraction is

$$L = 120 \text{ feet}$$

The impact fraction, from AASHTO Formula (3-1), is

$$\begin{aligned}
I &= 50/(L+125) \\
&= 50(120+125) \\
&= 0.204
\end{aligned}$$

The minimum live load plus impact moment due to HS20 loading is

$$\begin{aligned}
M'_{L(\text{min})} &= M_{L(\text{min})}(1+I) \\
&= -619(1+0.204) \\
&= -745 \text{ kip-feet}
\end{aligned}$$

The total moment distributed to the central girder is

$$\begin{aligned}
M''_{L(\text{min})} &= 2M'_{L(\text{min})} \times 5.25/10.25 \\
&= -763 \text{ kip-feet}
\end{aligned}$$

The minimum moment on the central beam at 5 due to dead load and live load plus impact is

$$\begin{aligned}
M_{5(\text{min})} &= M_D + M''_{(\text{min})} \\
&= 1833 - 763 \\
&= 1070 \text{ kip-feet}
\end{aligned}$$

(ii) The factored design moment, at Section 5 of the central beam, for Group I loading is given by AASHTO Table 3.22.1A as

$$\begin{aligned}
M_u &= \gamma[\beta_D D + \beta_L(L+I)] \\
&= 1.3\left(1.0 \times M_D + 1.67 \times M''_{(\text{max})}\right) \\
&= 1.3(1833 + 1.67 \times 1902) \\
&= 6512 \text{ kip-feet}
\end{aligned}$$

(iii) The effective compression flange width is given by AASHTO Section 8.10 as the minimum of

(a)
$$\begin{aligned}
b &= L/4 \\
&= 100/4 \\
&= 25 \text{ feet}
\end{aligned}$$

(b)
$$\begin{aligned}
b &= b_w + 12h_f \\
&= 16 + 12 \times 9 \\
&= 124 \text{ inches}
\end{aligned}$$

(c)
$$\begin{aligned}
b &= S \\
&= 10.25 \times 12 \\
&= 123 \text{ inches} \dots \text{governs}
\end{aligned}$$

Assuming that the stress block lies within the flange, the required tension reinforcement is determined from the principles of AASHTO Section 8.16 as

$$A_s = 0.85bdf'_c\left[1 - \sqrt{1 - 2K/0.765f'_c}\right]/f_y$$

where

$$K = 12M_u/bd^2$$
$$= 12 \times 6512/(123 \times 88^2)$$

Hence

$$A_s = 16.72 \text{ square inches}$$

Provide 10 No. 11 bars and 2 No. 7 bars, as shown at (vi) to give

$$A_s = 16.80 \text{ square inches}$$

The stress block depth is given by

$$a = A_s f_y/0.85b f_c'$$
$$= 16.8 \times 60/(0.85 \times 123 \times 3.25)$$
$$= 3 \text{ inches}$$
$$< h_f \ldots \text{satisfactory}$$

(iv) The recommended minimum depth of the superstructure, in accordance with AASHTO Table 8.9.2, is

$$h_{\min} = 0.07L$$
$$= 0.07 \times 100$$
$$= 7 \text{ feet}$$

The recommended minimum depth of the superstructure, in accordance with ACI[24] Table 8.5.2, is

$$h_{\min} = (L + 9)/18$$
$$= (100 + 9)/18$$
$$= 6.06 \text{ feet}$$

The depth provided is

$$h = 7.75 \text{ feet}$$

Exhibit 7 Member properties for Example 3.4

Part	A	y	I	Ay	Ay^2
Beams	4032	42	790,272		
Flange	2970	88.5	20,047		
Total	7002	—	—	432,189	30,374,230

In calculating live load deflection, AASHTO Section 8.13 requires all traffic lanes to be fully loaded with the moment of inertia based on the full superstructure gross section excluding curbs and railings. The moment of inertia is obtained as shown in Exhibit 7. Hence,

$$y_t = \Sigma Ay/\Sigma A$$
$$= 432,189/7002$$
$$= 61.7 \text{ inches}$$

$$I_g = \Sigma I + \Sigma Ay^2 - y_t^2 \Sigma A$$
$$= 4,508,270 \text{ inches}^4$$

The modulus of elasticity, for short-term loads, is given by AASHTO Section 8.7 as

$$E_c = 57,000\sqrt{f_c'}$$
$$= 57,000\sqrt{3250}/1000$$
$$= 3250 \text{ kips per square inch}$$

The central deflection produced in Span 12 with a standard truck in each lane positioned as indicated at (iii) is given by

$$\delta_s = 2 \times 32L^3/48EI_g + 2 \times 36 \times 12(32+8)(3L^2 - 4 \times 36^2 \times 144)/48EI_g$$
$$= 2304 \times 10^6/EI_g + 2573 \times 10^6/EI_g$$
$$= 0.333 \text{ inches}$$
$$= L/3605$$
$$< L/800 \ldots \text{satisfactory}$$

(v) The modulus of rupture of the concrete is given by AASHTO Section 8.15.2 as

$$f_r = 7.5\sqrt{f_c'}$$
$$= 7.5\sqrt{3250}$$
$$= 428 \text{ pounds per square inch}$$

The cracking moment of the superstructure section is

$$M_{cr} = f_r I_g / y_t$$
$$= 428 \times 4,508,270/(61.7 \times 1000 \times 12)$$
$$= 2606 \text{ kip-feet}$$

In accordance with AASHTO Section 8.17 the minimum required factored design moment capacity is

$$M_{min} = 1.2M_{cr} = 1.2 \times 2606 = 3127 \text{ kip-feet} < M_u \ldots \text{satisfactory}$$

(vi) The height of the centroid of the tensile reinforcement is given by

$$\bar{c} = (4 \times 1.56 \times 2.7 + 4 \times 1.56 \times 5.1 + 2 \times 1.56 \times 7.5 + 2 \times 0.6 \times 7.24)/16.8$$
$$= 4.81 \text{ inches}$$

The total area of the concrete tension block is

$$A_T = 2\bar{c}b_w$$
$$= 2 \times 4.81 \times 16$$
$$= 153.8 \text{ square inches}$$

The equivalent number of No. 11 bars is

$$n = A_s/1.56$$
$$= 16.8/1.56$$
$$= 10.77 \text{ bars}$$

The effective concrete area in the tension block is

$$A = A_T/n$$
$$= 153.8/10.77$$
$$= 14.28 \text{ square inches per bar}$$

The maximum serviceability limit state moment due to dead load and live load plus impact is

$$M_{5(max)} = 3735 \text{ kip-feet}$$

In accordance with AASHTO Section 8.15.3, the modular ratio is taken to the nearest whole number and is given by

$$
\begin{aligned}
n &= E_s/E_c \\
&= 29{,}000/3250 \\
&= 9
\end{aligned}
$$

Assuming the neutral axis, as determined by linear elastic theory, lies within the flange, the tension reinforcement ratio is

$$
\begin{aligned}
\rho &= A_s/bd \\
&= 16.8/(123 \times 88) \\
&= 0.00155
\end{aligned}
$$

The elastic design parameters and the reinforcement stress may be obtained as

$$
\begin{aligned}
k &= \sqrt{(n^2\rho^2 + 2n\rho)} - n\rho \\
&= 0.154 \\
j &= 1 - k/3 \\
&= 0.949 \\
f_s &= 12M_{5(max)}/jdA_s \\
&= 31.954 \text{ kips per square inch}
\end{aligned}
$$

The neutral axis depth is given by

$$
\begin{aligned}
kd &= 0.154 \times 88 \\
&= 13.6 \text{ inches} \\
&> h_f \ldots \text{unsatisfactory}
\end{aligned}
$$

However, an exact analysis[25] indicates a negligible discrepancy, with the steel stress

$$f_s = 31.695 \text{ kips per square inch}$$

Hence, the reinforcement distribution parameter is given by AASHTO Equation (8-61) as

$$
\begin{aligned}
z &= f_s \sqrt[3]{d_c A} \\
&= 31.954 \sqrt[3]{2.7 \times 14.28} \\
&= 108 \text{ kips per square inch} \\
&< 130 \ldots \text{satisfactory}
\end{aligned}
$$

In addition, the steel stress $f_s < 0.6 f_y \ldots$ satisfactory.

(vii) The area of longitudinal skin reinforcement required in each side face of the web is given by AASHTO Section 8.17.2 as

$$
\begin{aligned}
A_{s(min)} &\geq 0.012(d - 30) \\
&= 0.012(88 - 30) \\
&= 0.70 \text{ square inches per foot}
\end{aligned}
$$

The required spacing is 12 inches maximum, and providing nine No. 5 bars in each face, as shown at (vii), gives

$$A_{sl} = 0.74 \text{ square inches per foot}$$
$$> A_{s(\min)} \ldots \text{satisfactory}$$

(viii) The minimum serviceability limit state moment due to dead load and live load plus impact is

$$M_{5(\min)} = 1070 \text{ kip-feet}$$

The minimum reinforcement stress is given by

$$f_{\min} = 12M_{5(\min)} / jdA_s$$
$$= 9.154 \text{ kips per square inch}$$

The actual range between maximum and minimum reinforcement stress due to dead load and service live load plus impact is

$$f_f = f_{\max} - f_{\min}$$
$$= 31.954 - 9.154$$
$$= 22.8 \text{ kips per square inch}$$

The allowable range is given by AASHTO Equation (8-60) as

$$f_{f(\text{all})} = 23.4 - 0.33 f_{\min}$$
$$= 23.4 - 0.33 \times 9.154$$
$$= 20.4 \text{ kips per square inch}$$
$$< f_f \ldots \text{unsatisfactory}$$

PRESTRESSED CONCRETE DESIGN

Transfer Limit State

At the transfer limit state, the prestressing force is applied to the concrete section, and the resultant stresses are obtained as the superposition of the axial stress due to the initial prestressing force, the flexural stresses caused by the bending moment produced by the prestressing force, and the flexural stresses caused by the bending moment produced by the self-weight of the member. The allowable stresses in the concrete and the prestressing steel, at transfer, are specified in AASHTO Section 9.15 and are illustrated in Figure 3.17, where

f'_{ci} = compressive strength of concrete at transfer
≥ 3500 pounds per square inch, post-tensioned member
≥ 4000 pounds per square inch, pretensioned member
f'_s = ultimate strength of prestressing steel
f^*_y = yield stress of prestressing steel

Serviceability Limit State

At the serviceability limit state, all long-term prestress losses due to creep, shrinkage, and relaxation have occurred, to give a final prestressing force of P_e. The resultant stresses in the section are due to the final prestressing force, the self-weight of the member, additional superimposed dead load, and the live load. The allowable

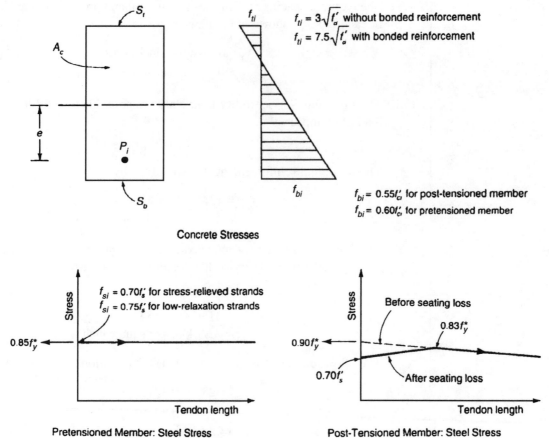

Concrete Stresses

$f_{ti} = 3\sqrt{f_a'}$ without bonded reinforcement

$f_{ti} = 7.5\sqrt{f_a'}$ with bonded reinforcement

$f_{bi} = 0.55f_{ci}'$ for post-tensioned member

$f_{bi} = 0.60f_{ci}'$ for pretensioned member

$f_{si} = 0.70f_s'$ for stress-relieved strands

$f_{si} = 0.75f_s'$ for low-relaxation strands

$0.85f_y^*$

Pretensioned Member: Steel Stress

Before seating loss

$0.83f_y^*$

$0.90f_y^*$

$0.70f_s'$

After seating loss

Post-Tensioned Member: Steel Stress

Figure 3.17 Allowable stresses at transfer

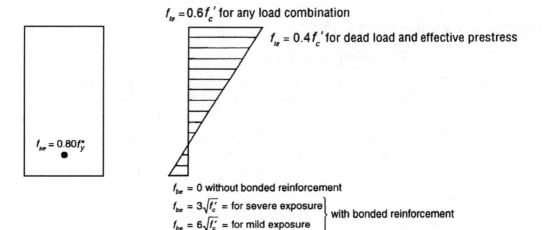

$f_{te} = 0.6f_c'$ for any load combination

$f_{te} = 0.4f_c'$ for dead load and effective prestress

$f_{se} = 0.80f_y^*$

$f_{be} = 0$ without bonded reinforcement

$f_{be} = 3\sqrt{f_c'}$ = for severe exposure

$f_{be} = 6\sqrt{f_c'}$ = for mild exposure

with bonded reinforcement

Figure 3.18 Allowable stresses at working load

stresses in the concrete and the prestressing steel under service loads are specified in AASHTO Section 9.15 and are illustrated in Figure 3.18, where f_{se} = effective steel prestress after losses.

Ultimate Limit State in Flexure

The nominal strength of a prestressed rectangular flexural member is derived in a manner similar to that used for a member that is not prestressed. It is given by

AASHTO Equation (9-13) as

$$M_n = A_s^* f_{su}^* d(1 - 0.60\, p^* f_{su}^* / f_c')$$

where A_s^* = area of prestressing steel
$\quad d$ = depth to centroid of prestressing force
$\quad p^* = A_s^* / bd$ = ratio of prestressing steel
$\quad f_{su}^*$ = average stress in prestressing steel at ultimate load

Provided the effective prestress in the tendons after losses, f_{se}, is not less than half the tensile strength f_s', the stress in bonded tendons at ultimate load is given by AASHTO Equation (9-17a) as

$$f_{su}^* = f_s'\{1 - (\gamma^*/\beta_1)[p^* f_s'/f_c' + (d_t/d)(p f_{sy}/f_c')]\}$$

where β_1 = compression zone factor given in AASHTO Section 8.16.2.7
$\quad \gamma^*$ = prestressing steel factor given in AASHTO Section 9.1.2
$\quad d_t$ = distance to centroid of non-prestressed reinforcement

Similarly, for unbonded tendons, the stress in the tendons at ultimate load is given by AASHTO Equation (9-18) as

$$f_{su}^* = f_{se} + 900(d - y_u) l_e$$

where $l_e = l_i/(1 + 0.5 N_s)$ = effective tendon length
$\quad y_u$ = depth to neutral axis at tendon yielding
$\quad l_i$ = tendon length
$\quad N_s$ = number of support hinges crossed by the tendon

The design flexural capacity is given by

$$\phi M_n \geq M_u$$

where M_u = applied factored moment
$\quad \phi$ = strength reduction factor from AASHTO Section 9.14
$\quad\quad$ = 1.0 for factory-produced precast members
$\quad\quad$ = 0.95 for post-tensioned cast-in-place members

To ensure adequate warning of impending failure, with considerable yielding of the steel before compressive failure of the concrete, the reinforcement index for rectangular sections is given by AASHTO Equation (9-24) as

$$(d_t/d)(p f_{sy}/f_c') + p^* f_{su}^*/f_c' - p' f_y'/f_c' \leq 0.36 \beta_1$$

where $p = A_s/bd_t$ = ratio of non-prestressed tension reinforcement
$\quad d_t$ = depth to centroid of non-prestressed reinforcement
$\quad p^* = A_s^*/bd$ = ratio of prestressing steel
$\quad p' = A_s'/bd$ = ratio of compression steel
$\quad f_y'$ = yield stress in compression of compression reinforcement

The design flexural strength of a prestressed rectangular section with non-prestressed reinforcement is given by AASHTO Equation (9-13a), and the stress in the pre-stressing steel is given by AASHTO Equation (9-17a).

To prevent sudden, premature tensile failure of the steel, AASHTO Section 9.18.2 specifies that

$$\phi M_n \geq 1.2 \; M_{cr}^*$$

where M_{cr}^*, the cracking moment strength, is computed by linear elastic theory using a modulus of rupture given by AASHTO Section 9.15.2 as

$$f_r = 7.5\sqrt{f_c'}$$

Ultimate Limit State in Shear

At the ends of a beam, the critical section for shear is defined in AASHTO Section 9.20.1.4 as being located a distance $h/2$ from the support.

The factored applied shear force acting on a member, in accordance with AASHTO Equation (9-26), is resisted by the combined shear strength of the concrete and the shear reinforcement and is given by

$$V_u = \phi V_c + \phi V_s$$

where $\phi = 0.90$ = strength reduction factor from AASHTO Section 9.14
  V_c = nominal shear capacity provided by the concrete
  V_s = nominal shear capacity provided by the web reinforcement

Shear failure in prestressed concrete beams may occur in two different modes, as shown in Figure 3.19. In a zone which is cracked in flexure, a flexural crack may develop into an inclined crack and eventually cause a shear failure. The position of this crack varies but is usually located at a distance of half the effective depth from the point of maximum moment. In a zone where the bending moment is less than the cracking moment, flexural cracks do not occur and shear failure is caused when the principal tensile stress exceeds the tensile strength of the concrete, thus producing a web shear crack. Since web shear cracks may also occur in a zone cracked in flexure, it is necessary to design for web shear cracking throughout the beam.

The nominal web shear capacity of the concrete is given by AASHTO Equation (9-29) as

$$V_{cw} = b'd\left(3.5\sqrt{f_c'} + 0.3f_{pc}\right) + V_p$$

where b' = web width
  d = depth to centroid of prestressing force $\geq 0.80h$
  f_{pc} = concrete compressive stress at centroid of section due to effective prestress force
  V_p = vertical component of effective prestress force

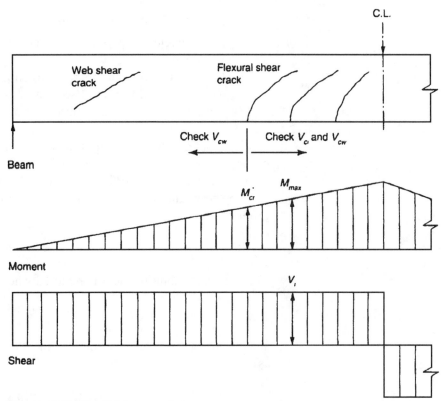

Figure 3.19 Shear failure modes

In a pretensioned member, the prestress force varies linearly from zero at the end of the member to a maximum at the end of the transfer length which is 50 diameters for strand and 100 diameters for wire. Hence, if the critical section at $h/2$ from the support lies within the transfer length, the value of f_{pc} is reduced accordingly.

When the centroid of a flanged section lies within the flange, the value of f_{pc} is determined at the junction of the web and the flange and includes the compressive stresses due to applied dead and live loads.

The nominal flexural shear capacity of the concrete is given by AASHTO Equation (9-27) as

$$V_{ci} = 0.60 \ b'd\sqrt{f_c'} + V_d + V_i M_{cr}/M_{max} \geq 1.70 b'd\sqrt{f_c'}$$

where V_d = shear force due to unfactored dead load

M_{max} = factored moment due to externally applied loads

V_i = factored shear, due to externally applied loads, occurring simultaneously with M_{max}

M_{cr} = the unfactored moment, due to externally applied loads, required to produce cracking

$$= (\phi f_r + f_{pe} - f_d)I/y_t$$
$$= \left(0.8 \times 7.5\sqrt{f_c'} + f_{pe} - f_d\right)I/y_t$$
$$= \left(6.0\sqrt{f_c'} + f_{pe} - f_d\right)I/y_t$$

$\phi = 0.8$ = reduction factor for shrinkage and variable concrete quality

$$f_r = 7.5\sqrt{f'_c} = \text{modulus of rupture}$$

f_{pe} = concrete compressive stress at extreme fiber due to effective prestress force

f_d = stress at extreme fiber due to unfactored dead load

I = moment of inertia of section

y_t = distance of section centroid from extreme fiber

The nominal shear capacity provided by the concrete V_c is taken as the lesser of the values of V_{cw} and V_{ci}. The provision of shear reinforcement is governed by the requirements of AASHTO Section 9.20.1 and Section 9.20.3.

No shear reinforcement is required when the applied factored shear force is given by

$$V_u < \phi V_c/2$$

Nominal shear reinforcement is required when

$$\phi V_c/2 \le V_u \le \phi V_c$$

and the nominal area of shear reinforcement is given by AASHTO Equation (9-31) as

$$A_{v(min)} = 50b's/f_{sy}$$

where f_{sy} = yield strength of shear reinforcement $\le 60,000$ pounds per square inch. Designed shear reinforcement is required when

$$\phi V_c < V_u \le \phi\left(V_c + 8b'd\sqrt{f'_c}\right)$$

and the area of shear reinforcement required is given by AASHTO Equation (9-30) as

$$A_v = sV_s/df_{sy}$$

where s = spacing of shear reinforcement

$V_s = V_u/\phi - V_c$ = nominal capacity of shear reinforcement

When the required nominal capacity is

$$V_s \le 4\,b'd\sqrt{f'_c}$$

the reinforcement spacing is given by

$$0.75d \ge s \le 24 \text{ inches}$$

When the required nominal capacity is

$$4b'd\sqrt{f'_c} < V_s \le 8b'd\sqrt{f'_c}$$

the reinforcement spacing is given by

$$0.375\,d \ge s \le 12 \text{ inches}$$

The dimensions of the section or the concrete strength must be increased to ensure that

$$V_s \leq 8b'd\sqrt{f_c'}$$

Example 3.5

The prestressed concrete cast-in-place tee-beam superstructure shown in Exhibit 8 has a concrete strength of 5000 pounds per square inch. The cable centroid, as shown, is parabolic in shape and the final prestressing force after all losses is 500 kips. At section x-x, which is 26 inches from the support, the unfactored dead load shear and moment are 21 kips and 45 kip-feet, and the unfactored shear and moment due to live load plus impact are 56 kips and 121 kip-feet. Determine the required spacing of No. 3, Grade 60 stirrups.

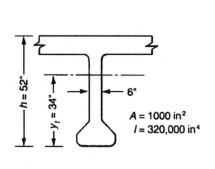

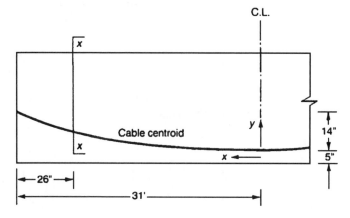

Exhibit 8

Solution

The equation of the parabolic cable profile is

$$y = rx^2/a^2$$

where $r = 14$ inches = cable drape
       a = half-length of cable = 31 feet

The rise of the cable at section x-x is given by

$$y = 14(31 - 26/12)^2/31^2$$
$$= 12 \text{ inches}$$

The cable eccentricity at section x-x is

$$e = y_t - 5 - y$$
$$= 34 - 5 - 12$$
$$= 17 \text{ inches}$$

The effective depth at section x-x is given by

$$d = h - 5 - y$$
$$= 52 - 5 - 12$$
$$= 0.80h \text{ minimum}$$
$$= 41.6 \text{ inches}$$

The equation of the slope of the parabolic cable is

$$dy/dx = 2rx/a^2$$

The slope of the cable at section x-x is given by

$$dy/dx = 2 \times 14(31 - 26/12)/(12 \times 31^2)$$
$$= 0.070$$

The vertical component of the final prestressing force at section x-x is

$$V_p = P_e \, dy/dx$$
$$= 500 \times 0.070$$
$$= 35 \text{ kips}$$

The compressive stress at the centroid of the cross-section, at section x-x, due to the final prestressing force is

$$f_{pc} = P_e/A$$
$$= 500/1000$$
$$= 0.500 \text{ kips per square inch}$$

The nominal web shear capacity of the section is given by AASHTO Equation (9-29) as

$$V_{cw} = b'd \left(3.5 \sqrt{f_c'} + 0.3 f_{pc} \right) + V_p$$
$$= 6 \times 41.6 \left(3.5 \sqrt{5000} + 0.3 \times 500 \right)/1000 + 35$$
$$= 134 \text{ kips}$$

The compressive stress at the bottom face of the cross-section, at section x-x, due to the final prestressing force, is

$$f_{pe} = P_e/A + eP_e y_t/I$$
$$= 500/1000 + 17 \times 500 \times 34/320{,}000$$
$$= 1.403 \text{ kips per square inch}$$

The tensile stress at the bottom face of the cross-section, at section x-x, due to the unfactored dead load is

$$f_d = M_d y_t/I$$
$$= 45 \times 12 \times 34/320{,}000$$
$$= 0.057 \text{ kips per square inch}$$

The unfactored moment, due to externally applied loads, required to produce cracking at section x-x is given by AASHTO Equation (9-28) as

$$M_{cr}' = \left(6.0 \sqrt{f_c'} + f_{pe} - f_d \right) I/y_t$$
$$= \left(6.0 \sqrt{5000} + 1403 - 57 \right) 320{,}000/(12{,}000 \times 34)$$
$$= 1388 \text{ kip-feet}$$

The unfactored live load moment at section x-x is

$$M_L = 121 \text{ kip-feet}$$
$$< M_{cr}'$$

Hence, cracking does not occur at section *x-x* and it is unnecessary to determine the nominal flexural shear capacity. The nominal shear capacity provided by the concrete is, then,

$$V_c = V_{cw}$$
$$= 134 \text{ kips}$$

The factored shear force acting on section *x-x* is given by AASHTO Equation (3-10) as

$$V_u = \gamma[\beta_D D + \beta_L (L + I)]$$
$$= 1.3(1 \times 21 + 1.67 \times 56)$$
$$= 149 \text{ kips}$$

The nominal shear strength required from shear reinforcement is given by AASHTO Equation (9-26) as

$$V_s = V_u/\phi - V_c$$
$$= 149/0.9 - 134$$
$$= 31.6 \text{ kips}$$
$$< 4 \, b'd\sqrt{f_c'}$$

Hence, the stirrup spacing is given by

$$s \leq 0.75d$$
$$\leq 0.75 \times 41.6$$
$$\leq 24 \text{ inches} \ldots \text{governs}$$

The required spacing of No. 3 stirrups is given by AASHTO Equation (9-30) as

$$s = A_v df_{sy}/V_s$$
$$= 0.22 \times 41.6 \times 60/16.6$$
$$= 24 \text{ inches maximum} \ldots \text{governs}$$

To satisfy the minimum area of shear reinforcement given by AASHTO Equation (9-31), the required spacing of No. 3 stirrups is

$$s = A_v f_{sy}/50b'$$
$$= 0.22 \times 60,000/(50 \times 6)$$
$$= 24 \text{ inches maximum} \ldots \text{governs}$$

Loss of Prestress

The determination of friction losses in AASHTO Section 9.16.1 is identical to the method presented in the ACI Code[23] for building structures, and this is covered in Chapter 2 of this text. Values for the wobble and friction coefficients are given in AASHTO Section 9.16.1, and alternative values are proposed in the ACI Code[24] for bridge structures. The effect of friction losses on cable stress, in a post-tensioned member, is illustrated in Figure 2.13.

In a post-tensioned member, allowance is necessary for anchor set, or draw-in, which occurs in the anchorage system when the prestressing force is transferred from the tensioning equipment to the anchorage. The magnitude of this loss depends on the prestressing system employed and is particularly pronounced with short members. The effect of wedge slip on cable stress, in a post-tensioned member, is illustrated in Figure 2.14. Initial over-stressing of the tendon to $0.90f_y^*$, as shown in Figure 3.17, increases the stress in the interior of the member. However, the loss at the stressing, or live, end still occurs.

The remaining loss of prestress, due to all other causes, is summarized in AASHTO Equation (9-3) as

$$\Delta f_s = SH + ES + CR_c + CR_s$$

where

SH = loss due to concrete shrinkage
ES = loss due to elastic shortening
CR_c = loss due to creep of concrete
CR_s = loss due to relaxation of prestressing steel

An approximate estimate of this loss for normal exposure conditions, span length not exceeding 120 feet, and normal-weight concrete may be obtained from AASHTO Table 9.16.2.2. For 5000-pounds-per-square-inch concrete, the value given for pretensioned strand is 45,000 pounds per square inch and for post-tensioned strand is 33,000 pounds per square inch. More accurate estimates may be obtained as detailed in AASHTO Section 9.16.2.

Shrinkage loss is determined by AASHTO Equations (9-4) and (9-5) as

$$SH = 17,000 - 150RH\ldots\text{pretensioned member}$$
$$SH = 0.80(17,000 - 150RH)\ldots\text{post-tensioned member}$$

where RH = percentage mean annual ambient relative humidity. Elastic loss is determined from AASHTO Equations (9-6) and (9-7) as

$$ES = n_i f_{cir}\ldots\text{pretensioned member}$$
$$ES = n_i f_{cir}/2\ldots\text{post-tensioned member}$$

where

$n_i = E_s/E_{ci}$ = modular ratio at transfer
$E_s = 28 \times 10^6$ pounds per square inch = modulus of elasticity of prestressing steel
$E_{ci} = 33\, w^{3/2} \sqrt{f_{ci}'}$ = modulus of elasticity of concrete at transfer
w = density of concrete
f_{ci}' = concrete strength at transfer
f_{cir} = concrete stress at level of tendon centroid immediately after transfer

Creep loss is determined from AASHTO Equation (9-9) as

$$CR_c = 12f_{cir} - 7f_{cds}$$

where f_{cds} = concrete stress at level of tendon centroid due to all sustained dead load except the dead load present at transfer.

Relaxation loss for stress-relieved strand is determined from AASHTO Equations (9-10) and (9-11) as

$$CR_s = 20,000 - 0.4ES - 0.2(SH + CR_c)\ldots\text{pretensioned member}$$
$$CR_s = 20,000 - 0.4ES - 0.2(SH + CR_c) - 0.3FR\ldots\text{post-tensioned member}$$

where FR = friction stress reduction below $0.70\, f_s'$.

| Example **3.6** | Determine the prestressing losses in the post-tensioned member shown in Exhibit 9. The concrete strength at 28 days is 5000 pounds per square inch, and at transfer is 3500 pounds per square inch. The total area of the prestressing tendons is 2.5 square inches, and the stress-relieved strand has a specified tensile strength of 270 kips per square inch, a nominal yield stress of 230 kips per square inch, and an anchor set of 0.125 inches. Stressing is effected from one end of the member only, and the applicable friction coefficient is 0.25 and the wobble coefficient is 0.0015 per foot. The bridge is constructed in an area with an annual average ambient relative humidity of 65 percent. |

Additional superimposed dead load due to diaphragms, surfacing, curbs, and parapets may be neglected.

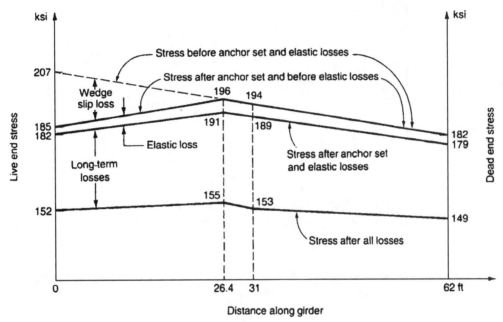

Exhibit 9

Solution

The nominal radius of the cable profile is

$$R = a^2/2r$$
$$= 12 \times 31^2/(2 \times 14)$$
$$= 412 \text{ feet}$$

The cable length, along the curve, from the end of the member to center span is

$$L_c = 2rR/a$$
$$= 2 \times 14 \times 412/(12 \times 31)$$
$$= 31.01 \text{ feet}$$

The friction loss may be determined over the two sections, from the live end to center span and from center span to the dead end.

The maximum allowable jacking stress is given by AASHTO Section 9.15.1 as

$$f_{s0} = 0.90 \, f_y^*$$
$$= 0.90 \times 230$$
$$= 207 \text{ kips per square inch}$$

The combined loss factor due to friction and wobble is

$$c = K + \mu/R$$
$$= 0.0015 + 0.25/412$$
$$= 21 \times 10^{-4} \text{ per foot}$$

The stress at a distance x along the cable is

$$f_{sx} = f_{s0} \, e^{-cx}$$

At center span,

$$x = 31.01 \text{ feet}$$

Hence,

$$f_{s(31.01)} = 207 \times 0.937$$
$$= 194 \text{ kips per square inch}$$

At the dead end,

$$x = 62.02 \text{ feet}$$

Hence,

$$f_{s\,(62.02)} = 207 \times 0.878$$
$$= 182 \text{ kips per square inch}$$

These stress values are plotted in Exhibit 9.

The magnitude of the anchor set is given as

$$\Delta = 0.125 \text{ inches}$$

AASHTO Section 9.16.2 specifies that the modulus of elasticity of prestressing strand is

$$E_s = 28 \times 10^3 \text{ kips per square inch}$$

The stress loss per foot is given by

$$m = (207 - 194)/31$$
$$= 0.419 \text{ kips per square inch per foot}$$

The length of cable at the live end, affected by the wedge pull-in, is derived in Chapter 2 of this text as

$$x_s = \sqrt{\Delta E_s / 12m}$$
$$= \sqrt{0.125 \times 28 \times 10^3 / (12 \times 0.419)}$$
$$= 26.4 \text{ feet}$$

The stress at the end of the pull-in zone is

$$f_{s(26.4)} = f_{s0} - mx_s$$
$$= 207 - 0.419 \times 26.4$$
$$= 196 \text{ kips per square inch}$$

The stress at the live anchorage is

$$f_{s(anc)} = f_{s0} - 2mx_s$$
$$= 185 \text{ kips per square inch}$$

The above stresses, which are fictitious stresses prior to considering elastic losses, are plotted in Exhibit 9.

AASHTO Section 9.16.2. specifies that the modulus of elasticity of the concrete at transfer is

$$E_{ci} = 33 \, w^{3/2} \sqrt{f'_{ci}}$$
$$= 33 \times 150^{3/2} \sqrt{3500}/1000$$
$$= 3590 \text{ kips per square inch}$$

Hence, the modular ratio at transfer is

$$n_i = E_s/E_{ci}$$
$$= 28,000/3590$$
$$= 7.8$$

The total self-weight of the girder is

$$W_G = 0.150LA/144$$
$$= 0.150 \times 62 \times 1000/144$$
$$= 64.58 \text{ kips}$$

The bending moment at midspan due to the self-weight of the girder is

$$M_G = W_G L/8$$
$$= 64.58 \times 62 \times 12/8$$
$$= 6006 \text{ kip-inches}$$

The concrete stress at midspan, at the level of the tendon centroid, due to the girder self-weight is

$$f_{cG} = -eM_G/I$$
$$= -29 \times 6006/320,000$$
$$= -0.544 \text{ kips per square inch}$$

Assuming a 5-kips-per-square-inch loss of prestress in the tendon due to elastic shortening of the concrete section, the initial prestressing force at midspan is

$$P_i = A_s^* f_{si}$$
$$= A_s^* \left(f_{s(31.01)} - 5 \right)$$
$$= 2.5(194 - 5)$$
$$= 473 \text{ kips}$$

The concrete stress at midspan, at the level of the tendon centroid, due to the initial prestressing force is

$$f_{cip} = P_i(1/A + e^2/I)$$
$$= 473(1/1000 + 29^2/320,000)$$
$$= 1.716 \text{ kips per square inch}$$

The concrete stress at midspan, at the level of the tendon centroid, immediately after transfer, and allowing for loss of prestress in the tendon due to elastic shortening of the concrete section, is

$$
\begin{aligned}
f_{cir} &= f_{cip} + f_{cG} \\
&= 1.716 - 0.544 \\
&= 1.172 \text{ kips per square inch}
\end{aligned}
$$

The elastic shortening caused by this stress level produces a loss in prestress in the tendon of

$$
\begin{aligned}
ES &= n_i f_{cir}/2 \\
&= 7.8 \times 1.172/2 \\
&= 4.6 \text{ kips per square inch} \\
&\approx 5 \text{ kips per square inch, assumed\ldots satisfactory}
\end{aligned}
$$

Assuming a 3-kips-per-square-inch loss of prestress in the tendon, due to elastic shortening, at the live anchorage, the initial prestressing force at the live anchor is

$$
\begin{aligned}
P_i &= A_s^* f_{si} \\
&= A_s^* \left(f_{s(anc)} - 3 \right) \\
&= 2.5(185 - 3) \\
&= 455 \text{ kips}
\end{aligned}
$$

The concrete stress at the live anchorage, at the level of the tendon centroid, due to this initial prestressing force is

$$
\begin{aligned}
f_{cip} = f_{cir} &= P_i(1/A + e^2/I) \\
&= 455(1/1000 + 15^2/320{,}000) \\
&= 0.775 \text{ kips per square inch}
\end{aligned}
$$

The elastic shortening caused by this stress level produces a loss in prestress in the tendon of

$$
\begin{aligned}
ES &= n_i f_{cir}/2 \\
&= 7.8 \times 0.775/2 \\
&= 3 \text{ kips per square inch} \\
&= \text{value initially assumed\ldots satisfactory}
\end{aligned}
$$

Hence, immediately after elastic losses have occurred, the stresses in the prestressing tendon are:

at the live anchorage, $f_s = 185 - 3 = 182$ kips per square inch
at midspan, $f_s = 194 - 5 = 189$ kips per square inch
at the dead anchorage, $f_s = 182 - 3 = 179$ kips per square inch
at the end of the pull-in zone, $f_s = 196 - 5 = 191$ kips per square inch

These stress values are plotted in Exhibit 9.

The allowable stress at the live anchorage, immediately after transfer, is given by AASHTO Section 9.15.1 as

$$
\begin{aligned}
f_{s(all)}' &= 0.70\, f_s' \ldots \text{stress-relieved strand} \\
&= 0.70 \times 270 \\
&= 189 \text{ kips per square inch} \\
&> 182 \ldots \text{satisfactory}
\end{aligned}
$$

The allowable stress at the end of the pull-in zone, immediately after transfer, is given by AASHTO Section 9.15.1 as

$$f_{s(all)} = 0.83 f_y^*$$
$$= 0.83 \times 230$$
$$= 191 \text{ kips per square inch}$$
$$= 191, \text{ actual value...satisfactory}$$

The shrinkage loss is determined from AASHTO Equation (9-5) as

$$SH = 0.80(17,000 - 150RH)/1000$$
$$= 0.80(17,0000 - 150 \times 65)/1000$$
$$= 6 \text{ kips per square inch}$$

The creep loss is determined from AASHTO Equation (9-9) as

$$CR_c = 12 f_{cir} - 7 f_{cds} = 12 f_{cir}$$

since additional superimposed dead load may be neglected.

At midspan at transfer, the concrete stress at the level of the tendon, allowing for elastic shortening and self-weight effects, is

$$f_{cir} = 1.172 \text{ kips per square inch}$$

Hence, the creep loss at midspan is

$$CR_c = 12 f_{cir}$$
$$= 12 \times 1.172$$
$$= 14 \text{ kips per square inch}$$

Similarly, at the live anchorage, the creep loss is given by

$$CR_c = 12 f_{cir}$$
$$= 12 \times 0.775$$
$$= 9 \text{ kips per square inch}$$

At midspan, the friction stress reduction below $0.70 f_s'$ is

$$FR = 0.70 f_s' - f_{s(31.01)}$$
$$= 189 - 194$$
$$= -5 \text{ kips per square inch}$$

At the live anchorage, the friction stress reduction below $0.70 f_s'$ is

$$FR = 0.70 f_s' - f_{s(anc)}$$
$$= 189 - 185$$
$$= 4 \text{ kips per square inch}$$

The creep loss, at midspan, is determined from AASHTO Equation (9-11) as

$$CR_s = 20 - 0.4ES - 0.2(SH + CR_c) - 0.3FR$$
$$= 20 - 0.4 \times 5 - 0.2(6 + 14) - 0.3(-5)$$
$$= 16 \text{ kips per square inch}$$

The creep loss, at the live anchorage, is given by

$$CR_s = 20 - 0.4 \times 3 - 0.2(6+9) - 0.3 \times 4$$
$$= 15 \text{ kips per square inch}$$

Hence, the total long-term loss at midspan is

$$\Delta f_c = SH + CR_c + CR_s$$
$$= 6 + 14 + 16$$
$$= 36 \text{ kips per square inch}$$

At the live anchorage, the long-term loss is

$$\Delta f_e = 6 + 9 + 15$$
$$= 30 \text{ kips per square inch}$$

These values are plotted in Exhibit 9.

The maximum allowable stress at service load is given by AASHTO Section 9.15.1 as

$$f_{s(\text{all})} = 0.80\, f_y^*$$
$$= 0.80 \times 230$$
$$= 184$$
$$> 155 \ldots \text{satisfactory}$$

Composite Construction

Composite construction consists of a member in which cast-in-place concrete is added to a precast concrete unit. Provided that measures are employed to prevent excessive slip across the interface between the two concretes, complete interaction may be assumed and the composite member designed as a monolithic member. Typically, the precast concrete unit is prestressed and the cast-in-place concrete is reinforced. In accordance with AASHTO Section 9.20.4, specific values of the horizontal shear resistance at the interface may be assumed if the contact surfaces are roughened and vertical ties are provided over the span length.

Two methods of construction are employed, propped and unpropped. In the unpropped method, the precast unit acts as formwork for, or supports the formwork for, the cast-in-place concrete. For this technique, the precast unit is designed to support its self-weight, formwork if required, and the weight of the cast-in-place concrete. In the propped method, the precast unit is supported during the placing and curing of the cast-in-place concrete.

Requirements at the transfer limit state for the precast section are identical to those for an integral member. Elastic losses occur at this time, together with friction losses if the precast girder is post-tensioned, giving an initial prestressing force of P_i. The self-weight moment of the girder, M_G, also acts on the precasting unit at this time, as shown in Figures 3.20 and 3.21, and the initial stresses are indicated.

Conditions at the serviceability state for unpropped construction are shown in Figure 3.20, and those for propped construction are shown in Figure 3.21.

For unpropped construction, the precast girder supports the weight of the shuttering, which produces a sagging bending moment M_S, and also the weight of the flange concrete, which produces a bending moment M_F, and the resultant stresses are indicated in Figure 3.20. After curing, the flange and precast girder form a composite section, and the effective width of the flange is given by

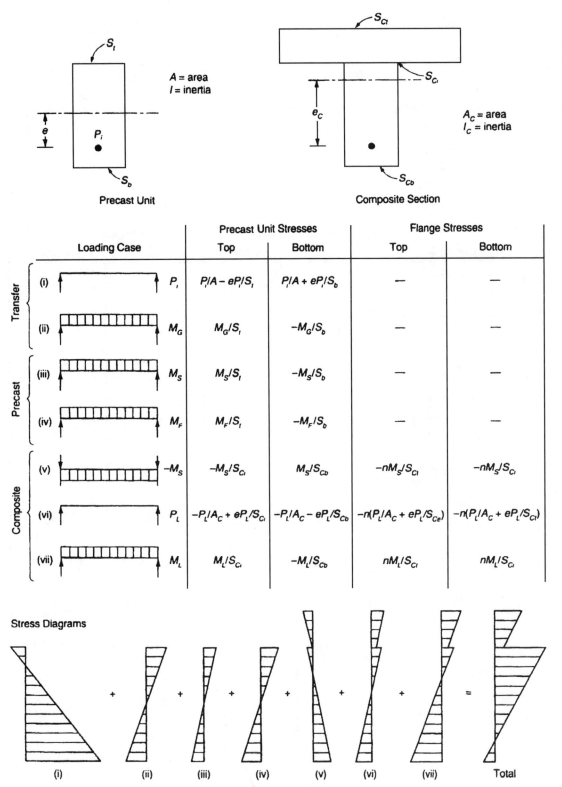

Figure 3.20 Unpropped composite construction

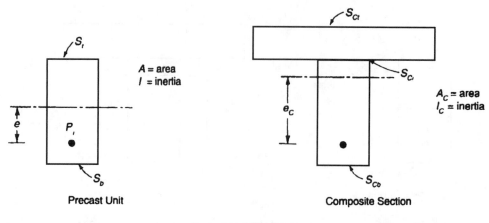

		Precast Unit Stresses		Flange Stresses	
	Loading Case	Top	Bottom	Top	Bottom
Transfer (i)	P_i	$P_i/A - eP_i/S_t$	$P_i/A + eP_i/S_b$	—	—
Transfer (ii)	M_G	M_G/S_t	$-M_G/S_b$	—	—
Precast (iii) Prop		0	0	—	—
Precast (iv) Flange and Shutter		0	0	—	—
Composite (v) −Shuttering		0	0	0	0
Composite (vi)	M_F	M_F/S_{Ci}	$-M_F/S_{Cb}$	nM_F/S_{Ct}	nM_F/S_{Ci}
Composite (vii)	P_L	$-P_L/A_c + eP_L/S_{Ci}$	$-P_L/A_c - eP_L/S_{Cb}$	$-n(P_L/A_C + eP_L/S_{Ct})$	$-n(P_L/A_C + eP_L/S_{Ci})$
Composite (viii)	M_L	M_L/S_{Ci}	$-M_L/S_{Cb}$	nM_L/S_{Ct}	nM_L/S_{Ci}

Stress Diagrams

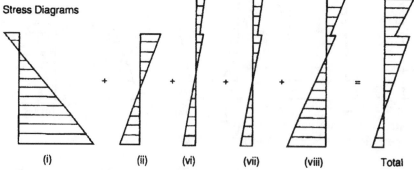

(i)   +   (ii)   +   (vi)   +   (vii)   +   (viii)   =   Total

Figure 3.21   Propped composite construction

AASHTO Section 8.10.1 as the lesser of

    (i) $L/4$

    (ii) $b_w + 6h_f$

    (iii) S

where L = span length
      b_w = web thickness
      h_f = flange depth
      S = rib spacing

In addition, when the 28-day compressive strengths of the precast section and the flange differ, the effective flange width is transformed by dividing by the modular ratio:

$$n = E_f/E_r$$

where E_f = modulus of elasticity of the flange concrete
      E_r = modulus of elasticity of the girder concrete

    Removal of the shuttering produces a hogging moment $-M_s$, which acts on the composite section, giving the stresses indicated.

    Long-term prestressing losses, which cause a loss of prestressing force P_L, now act on the composite section, producing the stresses indicated.

    Additional superimposed dead load, live load, and impact, which produce the bending moment M_L, act on the composite section, producing the stresses indicated.

    In propped construction, the soffit of the precast unit is supported on falsework prior to placing the shuttering and casting the flange. No additional stresses are produced in the precast unit since the weight of the shuttering and the flange are carried by the falsework. Similarly, removal of the shuttering produces no stresses. On removing the falsework, the weight of the flange concrete, which produces a bending moment M_F, acts on the composite section and causes the stresses indicated in Figure 3.21. Long-term prestressing losses, additional superimposed dead load, live load, and impact also act on the composite section, producing the stresses indicated.

    At the serviceability limit state, the effect of differential shrinkage should also be considered. When the flange is cast on the precast unit, much of the shrinkage has already occurred in the unit and the additional shrinkage of the flange is restrained by the precast unit. As shown in Figure 3.22, this produces a force at the center of the flange of

$$F_f = \varepsilon A_f E_f$$

and a moment about the centroid of the composite section of

$$M_f = e_f F_f$$

The resultant stresses in the composite section are reduced[26] due to creep by the creep factor

$$r = [1 - \exp(-E_f c)]/E_f c$$

where ε = differential shrinkage strain
      A_f = actual area of flange
      E_f = modulus of elasticity of flange concrete
      c = unit creep strain

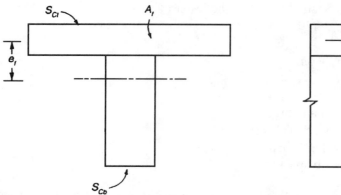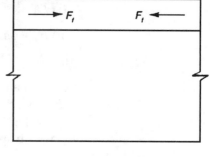

Figure 3.22   Effects of differential shrinkage

Due to these forces, the stress at the top of the composite section is

$$f_{Ct} = r[n(F_f/A_C + M_f/S_{Ct}) - \varepsilon E_f]$$

and at the bottom of the composite section

$$f_{Cb} = r(F_f/A_C - M_f/S_{Cb})$$

where compressive stress is positive.

A multispan bridge composed of simply supported precast units may be made continuous by providing a cast-in-place concrete diaphragm at each support, as shown in Figure 3.23(i). The superstructure is now continuous for live loads and additional superimposed dead load, and continuity reinforcement is provided in the slab to resist the negative moment at the support. In addition, AASHTO Section 9.7.2 requires the provision of reinforcement at the bottom of the connection, in order to provide restraint for positive moment development there.

As shown in Figure 3.23(ii), an unrestrained composite beam tends to hog with time due to differential shrinkage and creep caused by prestressing force and self-weight. When restraint is imposed on the beam ends, a positive moment

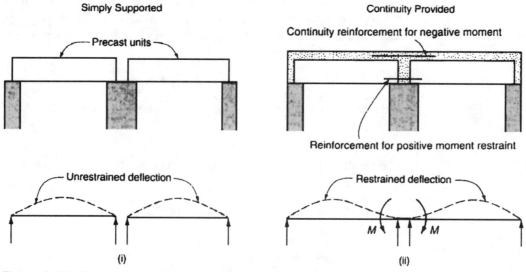

Figure 3.23   Creep and shrinkage effects at connections

is developed as shown. The effects of this may be determined by moment distribution techniques.[27]

The nominal capacity of a composite section, in flexure and shear, is determined at the ultimate limit state, in the same manner as for an integral member. Differential shrinkage effects, which result from restrained deformations, do not affect ultimate limit state conditions.

Prestressed Continuous Structures

Applying a prestressing force P to a statically determinate structure produces a moment Pe at a section, where e is the cable eccentricity at that section. Applying a prestressing force to an indeterminate structure tends to deflect the structure. This produces indeterminate reactions at the redundant supports which cause secondary moments in the structure. By removing the redundant supports, to produce the cut-back structure, and applying the prestressing force P, the primary moments Pe are again produced. The total moment at any section may then be obtained by the superposition of the primary and secondary moments.

The application of the prestressing force P, with an eccentricity e, to the continuous beam shown in Figure 3.24 results, in general, in the production of indeterminate reactions at the supports. The prestressing force tends to deflect the beam, which is restrained against lateral displacement by the supports, and this causes secondary moments. The resultant line of thrust no longer coincides with the cable profile, as is the case with a statically determinate beam. The indeterminate moments M_2 and M_3 at the supports are taken as the redundants and releases introduced at 2 and 3 to produce the cut-back structure.

The application of the prestressing force to the cut-back structure produces the distribution of moment $M = Pe$ shown at (i). Unit values of each redundant applied in turn to the cut-back structure produce the moments m_2 and m_3 shown at (ii) and (iii).

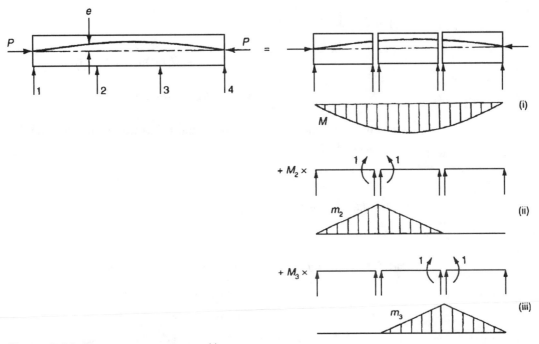

Figure 3.24 Three-span prestressed beam

The discontinuities produced at releases 2 and 3 by the prestressing force applied to the cut-back structure are

$$\theta_2 = \int Pem_2 \, ds/EI$$

$$\theta_3 = \int Pem_3 \, ds/EI$$

The discontinuities produced at release 2 by unit values of M_2 and M_3 applied in turn to the cut-back structure are

$$f_{22} = \int m_2^2 \, ds/EI$$

$$f_{23} = \int m_2 m_3 \, ds/EI$$

The discontinuities produced at release 3 by unit values of M_2 and M_3 applied in turn to the cut-back structure are

$$f_{32} = \int m_2 m_3 \, ds/EI$$

$$f_{33} = \int m_3^2 \, ds/EI$$

Since there are no discontinuities in the original structure at the positions of the releases,

$$\begin{bmatrix} \int m_2^2 \, ds/EI & \int m_2 m_3 \, ds/EI \\ \int m_2 m_3 \, ds/EI & \int m_3^2 \, ds/EI \end{bmatrix} \begin{bmatrix} M_2 \\ M_3 \end{bmatrix} = - \begin{bmatrix} \int Pem_2 \, ds/EI \\ \int Pem_3 \, ds/EI \end{bmatrix}$$

Expanding this expression gives

$$\int (Pe + M_2 m_2 + M_3 m_3) m_2 \, ds/EI = 0$$

$$\int (Pe + M_2 m_2 + M_3 m_3) m_3 \, ds/EI = 0$$

The final distribution of moment in the beam due to the prestressing force and secondary effects is

$$Pe' = Pe + M_2 m_2 + M_3 m_3$$

where the effective cable eccentricity is

$$e' = e + M_2 m_2/P + M_3 m_3/P$$

and the line of thrust has been displaced by an amount

$$M_2 m_2/P + M_3 m_3/P$$
$$Pe = \text{primary moment}$$
$$M_2 m_2 + M_3 m_3 = \text{secondary moment}$$

A cable with an initial eccentricity e' produces discontinuities at releases 2 and 3 of

$$\theta_2 = \int Pe'm_2 \ ds/EI$$
$$= \int (Pe + M_2 m_2 + M_3 m_3) m_2 \ ds/EI$$
$$= 0$$
$$\theta_3 = \int Pe'm_3 \ ds/EI$$
$$= \int (Pe + M_2 m_2 + M_3 m_3) m_3 \ ds/EI$$
$$= 0$$

Thus, no secondary moments are produced on tensioning this cable, and this is the concordant cable. The resultant line of thrust coincides with the cable profile.

Stressing the cable in the two-hinged portal frame shown in Figure 3.25 produces a horizontal thrust H at the supports. The cut-back structure is obtained by introducing

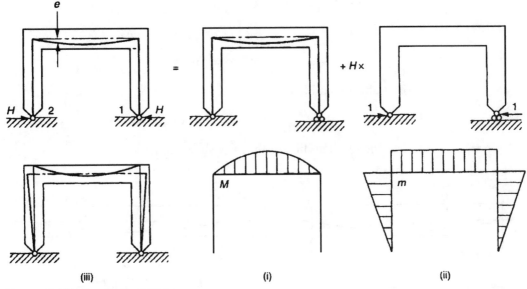

Figure 3.25 Prestressed frame

a release at 1. The application of the prestressing force to the cut-back structure produces the distribution of moment $M = Pe$ shown at (i). Unit value of H applied to the cut-back structure produces the moment m shown at (ii). Equating the discontinuities at the releases to zero gives

$$H \int m^2 ds/EI = -\int Pem \ ds/EI$$

and H may be determined.

The final distribution of moment in the frame due to the prestressing force and secondary effects is

$$Pe' = Pe + Hm$$

where the effective cable eccentricity is

$$e' = e + Hm/P$$

This is the expression for the concordant cable profile which is shown at (iii).

$$Pe = \text{primary moment}$$
$$Hm = \text{secondary moment}$$

Example 3.7

The symmetrical two-span beam shown in Exhibit 10 is prestressed with a cable placed to a parabolic profile with an eccentricity e_0 at the central support. Determine the position of the resultant line of thrust.

Solution

The reaction at the central support V is taken as the redundant and a release introduced at 2 to produce the cut-back structure.

The application of the prestressing force to the cut-back structure produces the distribution of moment $M = Pe$ shown at (i). Unit value of V applied to the cut-back structure produces the moment m shown at (ii). Equating the discontinuities at the release to zero gives

$$V \int m^2 ds/EI = -\int Pem\, ds/EI$$
$$Vl^3/6 = -5l^2 Pe_0/12$$

The effective cable eccentricity is

$$e' = e - 5xe_0/4l$$

and the resultant line of thrust is shown at (iii).

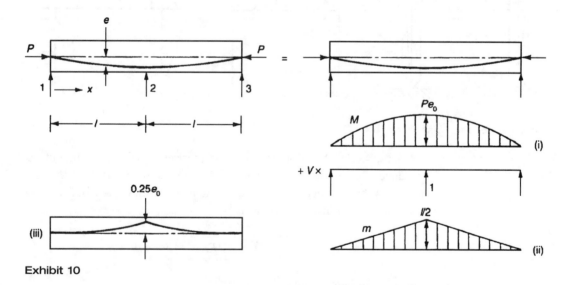

Exhibit 10

When the value of *EI* varies along the length of a member, the integrals involved in the application of the compatibility or flexibility matrix method may be evaluated by Simpson's rule. The member is divided into an even number of segments of equal length, and the integral of the function shown in Figure 3.26 is given by

$$\int g\, dx = s(g_1 + 4g_2 + 2g_3 + 4g_4 + \cdots + 2g_{n-2} + 4g_{n-1} + g_n)/3$$

An alternative design procedure[28,29] is available which utilizes the load balancing technique. The equivalent lateral loads, produced by the cable profile, are obtained from Figure 2.17 of this book and the resultant moments determined by moment distribution.

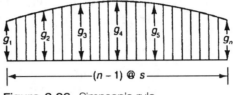

Figure 3.26 Simpson's rule

STRUCTURAL STEEL DESIGN

Elastic Design of Rolled Steel Girders

To ensure satisfactory performance under service load conditions, deflections due to HS20 live load plus impact are limited by AASHTO Section 10.6 to

$$\delta_{max} = L/800$$

where

$$L = \text{span length}$$

To provide additional comfort for pedestrians, the deflections of bridge structures that are also used by pedestrians are limited to

$$\delta_{max} = L/1000$$

To achieve these limits, AASHTO Section 10.5 restricts the depth-to-span ratio of a steel girder to

$$d/L \geq 1/25$$

The same limit applies to the overall depth of a composite section with the steel girder restricted to

$$d/L \geq 1/30$$

The allowable bending stress in adequately braced steel girders is specified by AASHTO Section 10.32 as

$$F_b = 0.55 \ F_y$$

which, for $F_y = 36$ kips per square inch, reduces to

$$F_b = 20 \text{ kips per square inch}$$

Vehicular loading produces stress variations in the structure, which may give rise to premature fatigue failure of the structure. The allowable stress range is specified by AASHTO Section 10.3 and requires an estimate of the total number of stress cycles, the connection details and their location, and the redundancy of the structure. The number of stress cycles is determined from AASHTO Table 10.3.2A and is based on an estimate of the average daily truck traffic. For average daily truck traffic exceeding 2500, the number of stress cycles is given as 2×10^6 for truck loading. Connection details are listed in AASHTO Table 10.3.1B and are illustrated in AASHTO Figure 10.3.1C. A stud shear connector, attached to the flange of a steel girder which is subject to tensile stress, is shown as item 18 in Figure 10.3.1C and is listed as stress category C in Table 10.3.1B. A nonredundant load path structure is one in which a single fatigue failure can cause collapse, as in the case of the failure of one girder of a two-girder bridge.

The bottom flange of the steel girder is subjected to tensile stress, due to dead loads and live load plus impact, and also due to lateral wind load. To control lateral forces, AASHTO Section 10.20 requires the provision of diaphragms at a maximum spacing of 25 feet. In accordance with AASHTO Sections 3.15 and 10.21, a horizontal wind pressure of 50 pounds per square foot is applied to the area of the superstructure in elevation to provide the total lateral force, which shall not be less than 300 pounds per foot. Half of this force is applied to the bottom flange and the resultant stresses are given by AASHTO Equation (10-5) as

$$F = RF_{cb}$$

where $R = (0.2272L - 11)S_d^{-2/3}$ . . . without lateral bracing
$R = (0.059L - 0.64)S_d^{-1/2}$ . . . with lateral bracing
$F_{cb} = 72M_{cb}/t_f b_f^2$ pounds per square inch
$M_{cb} = 0.08\ WS_d^2$ pounds feet
L = span length
S_d = diaphragm spacing
t_f = flange thickness
b_f = flange width
W = wind load per linear foot of bottom flange

In accordance with AASHTO Section 3.22, the stresses due to live load, dead load, and wind load are combined in Group II and Group III as

$$f_D + f_W \leq 1.25F_b$$
$$f_D + f_{(L+I)} + 0.3f_W \leq 1.25F_b$$

where f_D = dead load stress
$f_{(L+I)}$ = stress due to live load plus impact

The allowable shear stress is specified by AASHTO Section 10.32 as

$$F_v = 0.33F_y$$

which for F_y = 36 kips per square inch reduces to

$$F_v = 12 \text{ kips per square inch}$$

The gross web area is assumed to resist the total applied shear force, and the shear stress is given by

$$f_v = V/dt_w$$

where V = applied shear force
d = overall girder depth
t_w = web thickness

When the shear stress in the web at the girder bearings exceeds 75 percent of the allowable shear stress, AASHTO Section 10.33 requires the provision of bearing stiffeners. The stiffeners shall extend for the full height of the web and provide close bearing on, or be groove-welded to, the flange transmitting the reaction. The stiffener plates are placed on both sides of the web and are designed as an axially loaded cruciform column with a length of web, as shown in Figure 3.27, contributing to the section properties of the column. The stiffener plates shall extend approximately to the edge of the flanges, and the limiting thickness of the stiffener plates is given by AASHTO Equation (10-34) as

$$t_s \geq b' \sqrt{F_y}/2600$$

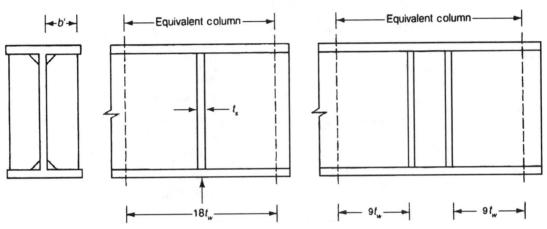

Figure 3.27 Stiffener plate details

where b' = stiffener plate width. The allowable bearing stress on the area of the stiffener plate in contact with the loaded flange is given by AASHTO Section 10.32 as

$$F_p = 0.80F_y$$

which, for F_y = 36 kips per square inch, reduces to F_p = 29 kips per square inch.

Load factor design may also be employed for the design of steel girders, and details of the procedure are given in AASHTO Sections 10.42 to 10.61.

Example 3.8

Exhibit 11 shows part of the cross section of a composite rolled steel girder bridge superstructure. Diaphragms are located at a spacing of 25 feet, and the girder is of Grade A36 steel. Bending stress in the bottom flange due to dead load is 9 kips per square inch, and due to HS20 live load plus impact is 10 kips per square inch. The superstructure is simply supported with a span of 65 feet. Determine if bottom flange lateral bracing is required.

Solution

The height of the superstructure elevation is 5.75 feet and the wind pressure, in accordance with AASHTO Section 3.15, is 50 pounds per square foot. Hence, the total lateral wind force is

$$W_T = 50 \times 5.75/1000$$
$$= 0.29 \text{ kips per foot}$$

The minimum specified wind force is

$$W_{min} = 0.30 \text{ kips per foot} \dots \text{governs}$$

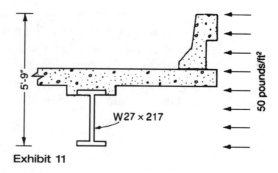

Exhibit 11

Hence, the wind load per linear foot of bottom flange is

$$W = W_{min}/2$$
$$= 0.30/2$$
$$= 0.15 \text{ kips per foot}$$

The bending moment due to this force on the bottom flange is

$$M_{cb} = 0.08WS_d^2$$
$$= 0.08 \times 0.15 \times 25^2$$
$$= 7.5 \text{ kip-feet}$$

The stress in the bottom flange due to this moment is

$$F_{cb} = 72M_{cb}/t_f b_f^2$$
$$= 72 \times 7.5/(0.83 \times 14.12^2)$$
$$= 3.26 \text{ kips per square inch}$$

The factor R is given by AASHTO Equation (10-6), when no bottom lateral bracing is provided, as

$$R = (0.2272L - 11)S_d^{-2/3}$$
$$= (0.2272 \times 65 - 11)\ 25^{-2/3}$$
$$= 0.44$$

Hence, the relevant wind load stress is

$$F = RF_{cb}$$
$$= 0.44 \times 3.26$$
$$= 1.44 \text{ kips per square inch}$$

In accordance with AASHTO Section 3.22, the Group II stress is given by

$$f_{II} = f_D + f_W$$
$$= 9 + 1.44$$
$$= 10.44 \text{ kips per square inch}$$
$$< 1.25\ F_b \ldots \text{satisfactory}$$

The Group III stress is given by

$$f_{III} = f_D + f_{(L+I)} + 0.3f_W$$
$$= 9 + 10 + 0.3 \times 1.44$$
$$= 19.43 \text{ kips per square inch}$$
$$< 1.25F_b \ldots \text{satisfactory}$$

Hence, bottom flange lateral bracing is not required.

Elastic Design of Steel Plate Girders

To prevent instability of the plate girder during fabrication and erection, limiting dimensions are specified. The limiting width-to-thickness ratio of the compression flange is given by AASHTO Equation (10-19) as

$$b/t = 3250/\sqrt{f_b}$$
$$\leq 24$$

where f_b = calculated compressive bending stress in the flange. For $F_y = 36$ kips per square inch and $f_b = 0.55F_y$, this reduces to $b/t = 23$.

The limiting thickness of the web plate without longitudinal stiffeners is given by AASHTO Equation (10-23) as

$$t_w = D\sqrt{f_b}/23{,}000$$
$$\geq D/170$$

where D = depth of web. For $F_y = 36$ kips per square inch and $f_b = 0.55F_y$, this reduces to

$$t_w = D/165$$

Provided that the web thickness is $t_w \geq D/150$ and the calculated shear stress in the web is $f_v \leq 7.33 \times 10^7/(D/t_w)^2 \leq F_y/3$, transverse intermediate stiffeners may be omitted.

For more slender webs, intermediate stiffeners are required in order to produce tension field action, with a spacing, in accordance with AASHTO Section 10.34.4, of

$$d_o \leq 3D$$

and the allowable shear stress is limited to

$$F_v = F_y\left[C + 0.87(1 - C)/\sqrt{1 + (d_o/D)^2}\right]/3$$

where

$$C = 6000\sqrt{k}/\sqrt{F_y}(D/t_w)$$

when $6000\sqrt{k}/\sqrt{F_y} \leq (D/t_w) \leq 7500\sqrt{k}/\sqrt{F_y}$,

$$C = 4.5 \times 10^7 k/F_y(D/t_w)^2$$

when $D/t_w > 7500\sqrt{k}/\sqrt{F_y}$, and

$$C = 1.0$$

when $D/t_w < 6000\sqrt{k}/\sqrt{F_y}$, and

$$k = 5 + 5/(d_o/D)^2$$

When the shear stress exceeds 60 percent of this value of F_v, the bending stress in the web is limited by AASHTO Equation (10-30) to

$$F_s = F_y(0.754 - 0.34f_v/F_v)$$

When, in accordance with AASHTO Section 10.34.4.5,

$$t_w \geq D/78 \ldots \text{ for } F_y = 36 \text{ kips per square inch}$$

and

$$f_v \leq F_v$$

transverse intermediate stiffeners may be omitted.

No tension field action is possible in the end panel adjacent to the simply supported end of a girder, and the length of this panel is limited to

$$d_o \leq 1.5D$$

and the allowable shear stress is given by AASHTO Equation (10-29) as

$$F_v = CF_y/3$$
$$\leq F_y/3$$

Intermediate stiffeners are normally provided on one side of the web only and are welded to the compression flange and stopped short of the tension flange. The minimum moment of inertia of the stiffener is given by AASHTO Equation (10-31) as

$$I_{st} = d_o t_w^3 J$$

where $J = 2.5(D/d_o)^2 - 2$
≥ 0.5

The minimum required area of the stiffener is given by AASHTO Equation (10-32a) as

$$A_{st} = 0.15YBDt_w(1-C)(f_v/F_v) - 18Yt_w^2$$

where Y = ratio of yield stress of web steel to stiffener steel
$B = 1.0$ for a pair of stiffeners
$B = 1.8$ for a single angle stiffener
$B = 2.4$ for a single plate stiffener

The width of the stiffener is given by AASHTO Section 10.34.4.10 as

$$b' \geq d/30 + 2 \text{ inches}$$
$$\geq b_f/4$$

where d = overall depth of girder
b_f = girder flange width

The thickness of the stiffener is

$$t_s \geq b'/16$$

The stiffener welding, in accordance with AASHTO Section 10.34.4.9, shall terminate a distance from the toe of the web-to-flange weld between $4t_w$ and $6t_w$.

Composite Girders

A composite girder, as shown in Figure 3.28, consists of a concrete flange attached to a steel girder with shear connectors. The shear connectors provide a mechanical anchorage between the flange and the girder to transfer the horizontal shear between the two materials, without excessive slip at the interface, to ensure an integral unit. The horizontal shear is caused by dead load, live load, shrinkage of the flange concrete,[30] and differential temperature effects.[30,31]

Vehicular loading on the structure produces a variation of the shear force applied to a connector. Since this may cause premature fatigue failure, the design criterion for a connector consists of the range of shear force applied to the connector.

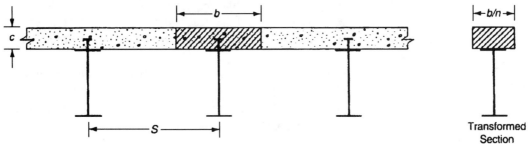

Figure 3.28 Effective flange width

Composite bridges may be constructed either with or without temporary props under the steel girder. In the unpropped method, the steel girder is designed to support its self-weight, the weight of the cast-in-place flange concrete, and the weight of all necessary formwork. Additional superimposed dead load, imposed after the concrete attains 75 percent of its 28-day compressive strength, and live load plus impact are supported by the composite section. In propped construction the steel girder supports only its self-weight, and all additional loads, imposed after the props are removed, are supported by the composite section. The effect of each load is determined using the effective section properties at the stage when each load is applied, and the total effect is obtained by superposition.

Because of the relatively large width of the concrete flange and the effects of shear lag, the resulting stress and strain distribution across the composite section is nonuniform. As shown in Figure 3.28, to compensate for this effect, the actual width of flange S, between girders, is reduced to an effective width b, which is given by AASHTO Section 10.38.3 as the minimum of

(i) $b = L/4$

(ii) $b = S$

(iii) $b = 12c$

For stress computations, the composite section properties are based on the transformed section, as shown in Figure 3.28, which is derived from the relevant modular ratio of the steel and concrete,

$$n = E/E_c$$

where E = modulus of elasticity of steel
E_c = modulus of elasticity of concrete

For short-term loads and a concrete strength of 2900 to 3500 pounds per square inch, AASHTO Section 10.38.1 specifies a modular ratio of

$$n = 9$$

Under sustained load, the modular ratio increases due to creep effects in the concrete flange, and the value specified is three times the short-duration modulus. Hence, in determining stresses in a composite section, two transformed sections are utilized— one for loads of short duration, such as live load plus impact, and one for sustained loads, such as dead loads.

A continuous composite structure may be designed by assuming that negative moments at interior supports are resisted by the steel girder only. Shear connectors are not required for this situation over negative moment regions of the span. Alternatively, it may be assumed that negative moments at supports are resisted by a composite section consisting of the steel girder and steel reinforcement in the concrete flange. Shear connectors are then required over the negative moment regions of the span.

In order to achieve full composite action between the concrete flange and the steel girder, shear connectors must be designed to resist the fluctuation in shear at the interface due to live load plus impact. The range of horizontal shear at the interface is given by AASHTO Equation (10-58) as

$$S_r = V_r Q / I$$

where V_r = range of shear force due to live load plus impact
$\quad\quad Q$ = moment of transformed compressive concrete area about neutral axis
$\quad\quad I$ = moment of inertia of transformed composite section

The allowable range of shear for a welded stud is given by Equation (10-60) as

$$Z_r = \alpha d^2 \ldots \text{for } H/d \geq 4$$

where d = stud diameter
$\quad\quad H$ = stud height
$\quad\quad \alpha = 13{,}000$ for 1×10^5 cycles
$\quad\quad \alpha = 10{,}600$ for 5×10^5 cycles
$\quad\quad \alpha = 7850$ for 2×10^6 cycles
$\quad\quad \alpha = 5500$ for over 2×10^6 cycles

The required connector spacing is

$$p = \Sigma Z_r / S_r$$
$$\leq 24 \text{ inches}$$

where ΣZ_r = total allowable capacity of all connectors at one transverse section.

To ensure integrity of the composite section at ultimate loads, the required number of connectors on each side of the point of maximum moment is given by AASHTO Equation (10-61) as

$$N_1 = P / \phi S_u$$

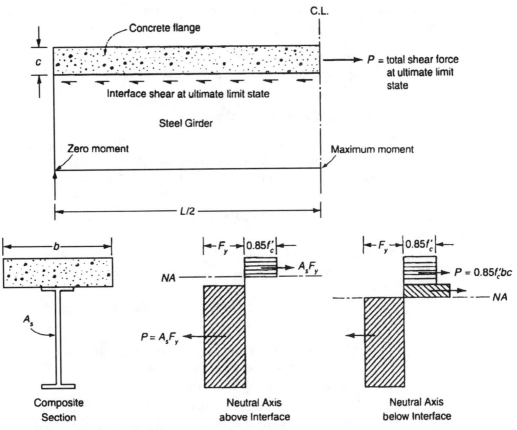

Figure 3.29 Horizontal shear at ultimate limit state

where P = total shear force at interface at ultimate limit state
  ϕ = reduction factor = 0.85
  S_u = ultimate strength of shear connector

As shown in Figure 3.29, the magnitude of the total shear force at the interface depends on the location of the neutral axis at ultimate moment and is given by the lesser of

$$P = A_s F_y \ldots \text{neutral axis below interface}$$

$$P = 0.85 f_c' bc \ldots \text{neutral axis below interface}$$

where A_s = area of steel girder
  F_y = yield stress of steel
  f_c' = 28-day compressive strength of flange concrete
  b = effective flange width
  c = flange depth

The ultimate strength of a welded stud is given by AASHTO Equation (10-67) as

$$S_u = 0.4 d^2 \sqrt{f_c' E_c}$$
$$\leq 60,000 A_{sc}$$

where E_c = modulus of elasticity of concrete

$$= w^{3/2} 33\sqrt{f_c'}$$

w = concrete density

A_{sc} = cross-sectional area of shear connector

Flexural Compression

Due to the lateral instability of the compression flange, as the unsupported length l of the compression flange increases, the allowable flexural compressive stress decreases and is given by AASHTO Table 10.32.1A as

$$F_b = (50 \times 10^6 C_b I_{yc} / l S_{xc})\sqrt{0.772 J / I_{yc} + 9.87(d/l)^2}$$

where d = depth of beam

I_{yc} = moment of inertia of compression flange about a vertical axis through the web

S_{xc} = section modulus with respect to the compression flange

$J = [(bt^3)_c + (bt^3)_t + Dt_w^3]/3$

b = flange width of compression or tension flanges

t = thickness of compression or tension flanges

D = clear distance between flanges

$C_b = 1.75 + 1.05(M_1/M_2) + 0.3(M_1/M_2)^2 \leq 2.3$

M_1 = smaller moment at the end of the unsupported length

M_2 = larger moment at the end of the unsupported length

M_1/M_2 = positive for reverse curvature

When F_y = 36 kips per square inch, the allowable flexural compressive stress is given by

$$F_b \leq 20 \text{ kips per square inch}$$

Compression Members

The allowable stress in an axially loaded compression member is defined in AASHTO Table 10.32.1A in terms of the slenderness ratio

$$KL/r$$

where K = effective length factor

L = unbraced length of the column

r = the governing radius of gyration

Figure 2.26 of this book details the effective length factor applicable to different end conditions. Figure 2.27 of this book presents an alignment chart for a column framing into beams at either end and subjected to side sway.

The failure of a short, stocky strut occurs at the squash load because of yielding in compression. A factor of safety of 2.12 is adopted, and the allowable stress for a slenderness ratio of zero is

$$F_a = F_y/2.12$$

which for $F_y = 36$ kip per square inch reduces to

$$F_a = 17 \text{ kips per square inch}$$

The critical slenderness ratio is

$$C_c = \sqrt{2\pi^2 E/F_y}$$
$$= 126 \text{ for } F_y = 36 \text{ kips per square inch}$$

At this point the allowable stress is

$$F_a = F_y/(2 \times 2.12)$$

which for $F_y = 36$ kips per square inch reduces to

$$F_a = 8.5 \text{ kips per square inch}$$

For larger values of the slenderness ratio, the Euler elastic critical load is assumed to control, and the allowable stress is given by

$$F_a = \pi^2 E/2.12(KL/r)^2$$
$$= 135{,}009/(KL/r)^2 \text{ kips per square inch}$$

For values of the slenderness ratio between zero and the critical slenderness ratio, the allowable stress is given by the parabolic expression

$$F_a = F_y[1 - (KL/r)^2 F_y/4\pi^2 E]/2.12$$

which for $F_y = 36$ kips per square inch reduces to

$$F_a = 17 - 0.53(KL/r)^2/1000 \text{ kips per square inch}$$

Combined Compression and Flexure

The flexural capacity of a member decreases in the presence of axial load, and to limit the stress at the points of support, AASHTO Equation (10-42) utilizes the interaction expression

$$f_a/0.472F_y + f_{bx}/F_{bx} + f_{by}/F_{by} \le 1.0$$

Within the length of a member, the limiting stress is given by AASHTO Equation (10-41) as

$$f_a/F_a + C_{mx}f_{bx}/F_{bx}(1 - f_a/F'_{ex}) + C_{my}f_{by}/F_{by}(1 - f_a/F'_{ey}) \le 1.0$$

where F'_e = factored Euler critical stress divided by a factor of safety 2.12
$$= \pi^2 E/2.12(K_b l_b/r_b)^2$$
l_b = actual unbraced length in the plane of bending
r_b = corresponding radius of gyration
K_b = corresponding effective length factor
C_m = reduction factor defined in Figure 2.31 of this book
2.12 = factor of safety

Connections

Field splices are used in the construction of long-span bridges to enable the girders to be handled and transported in convenient lengths. Because of the difficulties inherent in welding large girders in the field, field splices are usually bolted. In accordance with AASHTO Section 10.32.3, low-carbon steel bolts type A307 may not be used in connections subjected to fatigue, and bearing-type high-strength bolts are undesirable due to the additional deflection produced by slip at the connections. Hence, high-strength slip-critical bolts are preferred.

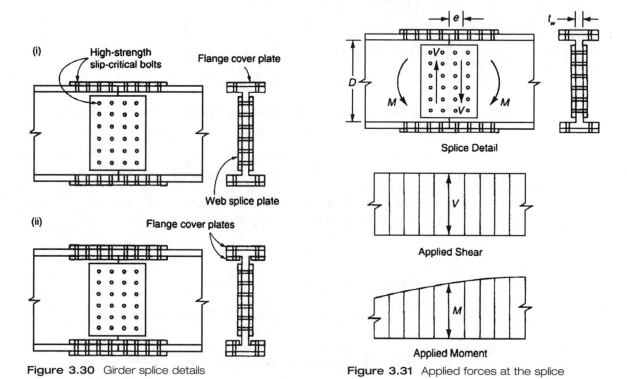

Figure 3.30 Girder splice details

Figure 3.31 Applied forces at the splice

The two types of girder splices utilized are shown in Figure 3.30. The splice may consist of an outer flange cover plate on each flange, plus a web splice plate on each side of the web as shown at (i). Alternatively, one outer flange cover plate plus two inner flange cover plates, on each flange, may be used as shown at (ii). At least two rows of bolts must be provided on each side of the joint in the web splice plate, which must extend the full depth of the girder between flanges.

The splice components must be capable of carrying the applied forces at the joint, as shown in Figure 3.31. The web splice plate is designed for that portion of the bending moment resisted by the girder web, plus the torsional moment induced by the eccentricity of the applied shear force acting at the centroid of the bolt group on each side of the joint. In addition, the web splice plate resists the total applied shear force at the joint. The flange cover plate resists that portion of the applied moment which is not resisted by the web.

Thus, the portion of the applied moment resisted by the girder web is

$$M_{w1} = MS_w/S_G$$

where $S_w = t_w D^2/6$
S_G = total section modulus of the girder

The torsional moment induced by the connector eccentricity is given by

$$M_{w2} = eV$$

The total web splice plate design moment is, then,

$$M_w = M_{w1} + M_{w2}$$
$$= MS_w/S_G + eV$$

The total web splice plate design shear is

$$V_w = V$$

The total flange cover plate design moment is

$$M_f = M - M_{w2}$$
$$= M(1 - S_w/S_G)$$

In accordance with AASHTO Section 10.18.1, the splice components must be designed for the greater value given by

(i) 75 percent of the allowable capacity of the girder section

(ii) The average of the calculated design force in the component and the allowable capacity of the girder section

The allowable shear capacity of the girder web is

$$V_G = F_v A_w$$
$$= 12Dt_w \dots \text{for } F_y = 36 \text{ kips per square inch}$$

The allowable moment capacity of the girder web is

$$M_{Gw} = F_b S_w$$
$$= 3.33 t_w D^2 \dots \text{for } F_y = 36 \text{ kips per square inch}$$

The allowable moment capacity of the girder flange is

$$M_{Gf} = F_b S_G - M_{Gw}$$
$$= 20(S_G - S_w) \dots \text{for } F_y = 36 \text{ kips per square inch}$$

TIMBER STRUCTURES

Allowable Stresses

The allowable stresses for visually graded sawn lumber for normal duration of loading, used under dry conditions, are given in AASHTO Table 13.5.1A. Reduction factors are given for service conditions in which the moisture content exceeds 19 percent. These are identical to the factors given in Chapter 2 of this book.

The allowable stresses for glued-laminated timber are given in AASHTO Tables 13.5.3A and 13.5.3B. Reduction factors are given for service conditions in which the moisture content exceeds 16 percent. These are identical to the factors given in Chapter 2 of this book.

Load duration factors are given in AASHTO Section 13.5.5, and these are similar to the factors given in Chapter 2 of this book.

The bearing area factor specified in AASHTO Section 13.6 is identical to the factor given in Chapter 2.

The size factor is specified in AASHTO Section 13.6.4.2 and is identical to the factor given in Chapter 2.

The beam volume factor specified in AASHTO Section 13.6.4.3 is identical to the factor given in Chapter 2 with $K_L = 1.0$ for all configurations and loading conditions.

Timber Beams

In accordance with AASHTO Section 13.6.4.4, when the depth of a beam does not exceed its breadth or when continuous lateral restraint is provided to the compression edge of a beam, lateral instability does not occur and allowable bending stresses require no reduction for instability effects. For all other situations, lateral instability must be investigated and the applicable reduction made to the bending stress.

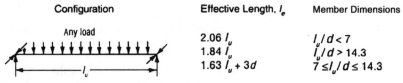

Configuration	Effective Length, l_e	Member Dimensions
Any load	$2.06\,l_u$	$l_u/d < 7$
	$1.84\,l_u$	$l_u/d > 14.3$
	$1.63\,l_u + 3d$	$7 \leq l_u/d \leq 14.3$

Figure 3.32 Beam effective length factors

Figure 3.32 illustrates the relationship between the effective length l_e, the unbraced length l_u, and the applied loading. When lateral restraint is provided at intermediate points along a member, the unbraced length is defined as the distance between such points. The slenderness ratio for the beam is defined by AASHTO Equation (13-6) as

$$R_B = \sqrt{l_e d/b^2} \leq 50$$

The beam stability factor specified in AASHTO Section 13.6.4.4.5 is identical to the factor given in Chapter 2 of this book.

The shear stress in a rectangular beam is given by AASHTO Equation (13-9) as

$$f_v = 1.5V/bd$$

For vehicle live loads, the governing shear force V is defined as the value occurring at a distance from the support given by the minimum of

(i) 3d

(ii) $L/4$

where b = beam width
  d = beam depth
  L = span length

In accordance with AASHTO Section 13.6.5.2, the governing shear force is determined from

$$V_{LL} = (0.60V_{LU} + V_{LD})/2$$

where V_{LU} = shear at $3d$ or $L/4$ due to undistributed wheel loads located over the beam
  V_{LD} = shear at $3d$ or $L/4$ due to wheel loads distributed laterally as specified for moment in AASHTO Section 3.23

As specified in AASHTO Section 3.8, impact is not included in timber structures due to their damping characteristics.

For a beam which is notched, the design limitations and requirements specified in AASHTO Section 13.6.2 are similar to those given in Chapter 2 of this book.

Timber Columns

The design of timber columns specified in AASHTO Section 13.7 is identical to the design method given in Chapter 2 of this book.

REFERENCES

1. American Association of State Highway and Transportation Officials. *Standard Specifications for Highway Bridges,* 17th ed. Washington, DC, 2002.
2. Williams, A. *The Analysis of Indeterminate Structures.* Macmillan, London, 1967.
3. American Institute of Steel Construction. *Moments, Shears and Reactions: Continuous Highway Bridge Tables.* Chicago, 1959.
4. Jenkins, W. M. Influence Line Computations for Structures with Members of Varying Flexural Rigidity Using the Electronic Digital Computer. *Structural Engineer.* Vol. 39, September 1961.
5. Wang, C. K. Matrix Analysis of Statically Indeterminate Trusses. *Proceedings of the American Society of Civil Engineers.* Vol. 85 (ST4), April 1959.
6. Portland Cement Association. *Influence Lines Drawn as Deflection Curves.* Skokie, IL, 1948.
7. Thadani, B. N. Distribution of Deformation Method for the Construction of Influence Lines. *Civil Engineering and Public Works Review.* Vol. 51, June 1956.
8. Lee, S. L., and Patel, P. C. The Bar-Chain Method of Analyzing Truss Deformations. *Proceedings of the American Society of Civil Engineers.* Vol. 86 (ST3), May 1960.
9. Williams, A. The Determination of Influence Lines for Bridge Decks Monolithic with Their Piers. *Structural Engineer.* Vol. 42, May 1964.
10. Morice, P. B., and Little, G. *The Analysis of Right Bridge Decks Subjected to Abnormal Loading.* Cement and Concrete Association, London, 1956.
11. West, R. *Recommendations on the Use of Grillage Analysis for Slab and Pseudo-Slab Bridge Decks.* Cement and Concrete Association, London, 1973.
12. Loo, Y. C., and Cusens, A. R. A Refined Finite Strip Method for the Analysis of Orthotropic Plates. *Proceedings of the Institution of Civil Engineers.* Vol. 48, January 1971.
13. Davis, J. D., Somerville, I. J., and Zienkiewicz, O. C. Analysis of Various Types of Bridges by the Finite Element Method. *Proceedings of the Conference on Developments in Bridge Design and Construction, Cardiff, March 1971.* Crosby Lockwood, London, 1972.
14. Westergaard, H. M. Computation of Stresses in Bridge Slabs Due to Wheel Loads. *Public Roads.* March 1930.
15. Portland Cement Association. *Handbook of Frame Constants.* Skokie, IL, 1948.

16. Lee, S. L. The Conjugate Frame Method and Its Application in the Elastic and Plastic Theory of Structures. *Journal Franklin Institute.* Vol. 266, September 1958.

17. American Association of State Highway and Transportation Officials. *Standard Specifications for Highway Bridges.* 17th ed. *Division I-A Seismic Design.* Washington, DC, 2002.

18. Building Science Safety Council. *NEHRP Recommended Provisions for Seismic Regulations for New Buildings and Other Structures: Part 2, Commentary.* Washington, DC, 2000.

19. Paz, M. *Structural Dynamics.* Van Nostrand Reinhold, New York, 1991.

20. Federal Highway Administration. *Seismic Design and Retrofit Manual for Highway Bridges.* Washington, DC, 1987.

21. Hewlett-Packard Company. *HP-48G Calculator Reference Manual.* Corvallis, OR, 1994.

22. Portland Cement Association. *Notes on ACI 318-99: Building Code Requirements for Reinforced Concrete.* Skokie, IL, 1999.

23. American Concrete Institute. *Building Code Requirements and Commentary for Reinforced Concrete (ACI 318-99).* Detroit, MI, 2000.

24. American Concrete Institute. *Analysis and Design of Reinforced Concrete Bridge Structures (ACI 343R-95).* Detroit, MI, 1995.

25. Reynolds, C. E., and Steedman, J. C. *Reinforced Concrete Designers Handbook.* Cement and Concrete Association, London, 1981.

26. Kajfasz, S., Somerville, G., and Rowe, R. E. *An Investigation of the Behavior of Composite Beams.* Cement and Concrete Association, London, 1963.

27. Freyermuth, C. L. *Design of Continuous Highway Bridges with Precast, Prestressed Concrete Girders.* Portland Cement Association. Skokie, IL, 1969.

28. Freyermuth, C. L., and Shoolbred, R. A. *Post-Tensioned, Prestressed Concrete.* Portland Cement Association, Skokie, IL, 1967.

29. The Concrete Society. *Post-Tensioned Flat-Slab Design Handbook.* London, 1984.

30. Nash, G. F. J. *Steel Bridge Design Guide: Composite Universal Beam Simply Supported Span.* Constructional Steel Research and Development Organization, Croydon, UK, 1984.

31. Knowles, P. R. *Simply Supported Composite Plate Girder Highway Bridge.* Constructional Steel Research and Development Organization, Croydon, UK, 1976.

Foundations and Retaining Structures

Alan Williams

OUTLINE

FOOTING DESIGN   189
Isolated Column Spread Footing ■ Combined Footing ■ Strap Footing ■ Eccentric Footing ■ Footing with Eccentric Load

RETAINING WALL   211
Cantilever Retaining Wall ■ Gravity Retaining Wall ■ Cantilevered Sheetpile Wall   ■ Anchored Sheetpile Retaining Wall

PILE FOUNDATIONS   224
Pile Group with Vertical Piles ■ Pile Group with Inclined Piles ■ Pile Cap Design

SELECTED SYMBOLS AND ABBREVIATIONS   233

REFERENCES   234

FOOTING DESIGN

Isolated Column Spread Footing

An isolated column footing transfers the loads from a single column to the supporting soil. The size of the footing is determined by the allowable soil bearing pressure. The footing is designed for flexure, punching or two-way shear, and flexural or one-way shear. The depth of the footing is generally governed by punching shear.

The ACI Code,[1] in Sections 15.4 and 11.12, specifies the critical sections in the footing for flexure and shear. For a reinforced concrete column the reaction plane is defined in ACI Section 15.4.2 as being located at the face of the column. The location of the critical sections for flexure and shear are specified with respect

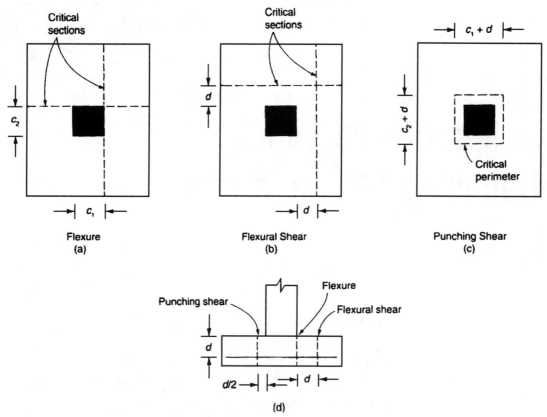

Figure 4.1 (a–d) Critical sections: Footing with reinforced concrete column

to this plane and are illustrated in Figure 4.1 (a–d). The length of the critical perimeter for punching shear is given by

$$b_o = 2(c_1 + c_2) + 4d$$

where

c_1 = short side of column
c_2 = long side of column
d = effective depth of footing reinforcement

The reaction plane for a footing supporting a column with a steel base plate is specified as halfway between the face of the column and the edge of the base plate. The maximum moment is computed at this plane, with the flexural shear at a distance d from this plane and the punching shear at a distance of $d/2$ from this plane, as shown in Figure 4.2.

The reaction plane for a footing supporting a masonry column is specified as halfway between the center and the face of the column. The maximum moment is computed at this plane. The flexural shear is computed at a distance d from the face of the column and the punching shear at a distance of $d/2$ from the face of the column, as shown in Figure 4.3.

Reinforcement is designed for the maximum moment at the reaction plane and is distributed uniformly across the base in the case of a square footing. For a rectangular footing, reinforcement parallel to the shorter side should be concentrated in a central band width equal to the length of the shorter side, as illustrated

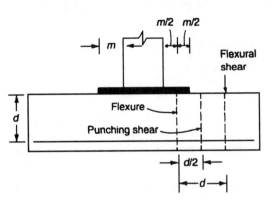

Figure 4.2 Critical sections: Footing with steel base plate

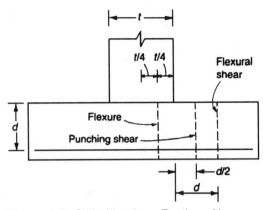

Figure 4.3 Critical sections: Footing with masonry column

in Figure 4.4. The area of reinforcement required in the central band is given by ACI Equation (15-1) as

$$A_b = 2A_s/(\beta + 1)$$

where

A_s = total required reinforcement area in the short direction
$\beta = l_2/l_1$ = ratio of the long side to the shorter side of the footing

The capacity of a footing for flexural shear is given by ACI Equation (11-3) as

$$\phi V_c = 2\phi bd\sqrt{f_c'}$$

where

ϕ = strength reduction factor = 0.75 from ACI Section 9.3
b = width of footing
d = effective depth
f_c' = concrete strength

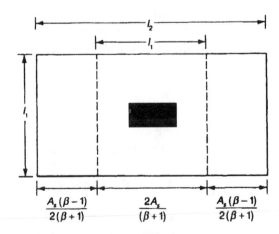

Reinforcement area required

Figure 4.4 Rectangular footing: Reinforcement areas

The capacity of a footing for punching shear is given by ACI Equation (11-33) as

$$\phi V_c = (2 + 4/\beta_c)\phi b_o d\sqrt{f_c'}$$
$$\leq 4\phi b_o d\sqrt{f_c'}$$

where

$\beta_c = c_2/c_1$ = ratio of long side to short side of column

b_o = length of critical perimeter for punching shear = $2(c_1 + c_2) + 4d$

Load transfer between a reinforced concrete column and the footing may be provided by the bearing capacity of the column and the footing. The bearing capacity of the column concrete at the interface is given by ACI Section 10.17.1 as

$$\phi P_n = 0.85\phi f_c' A_1$$

where

ϕ = strength reduction factor = 0.65 from ACI Section 9.3

A_1 = area of column

f_c' = strength of column concrete

The bearing capacity of the footing concrete at the interface is given by ACI Section 10.17.1 as

$$\phi P_n = 0.85\phi f_c' A_1\sqrt{A_2/A_1}$$
$$\leq 0.85\phi f_c' A_1 \times 2$$

where

f_c' = strength of footing concrete

ϕ = strength reduction factor = 0.65 from ACI Section 9.3

A_2 = area of the base of the pyramid, with side slopes of 1:2, formed within the footing by the column base

In accordance with ACI Section 15.8.1.2, when the bearing strength of the concrete is exceeded, reinforcement must be provided at the interface to transfer the excess load. The capacity of this reinforcement is

$$\phi P_s = \phi A_s f_y$$

where

ϕ = strength reduction factor = 0.65 from ACI Section 9.3

f_y = reinforcement yield strength

A_s = reinforcement area

In addition, in accordance with ACI Section 15.8.2.1, a minimum area of reinforcement must be provided across the interface given by

$$A_{s(min)} = 0.005A_1$$

Example **4.1**

Exhibit 1 indicates the loads acting on a steel column with a reinforced concrete footing. Check the adequacy of the footing and determine the required base plate thickness and reinforcement area, using Grade 60 bars, for a concrete strength of 3000 pounds per square inch and a base plate of Grade A36 steel.

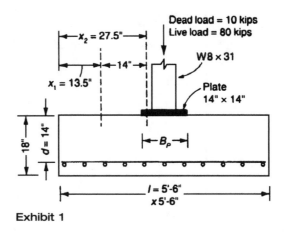

Exhibit 1

Solution

The base plate thickness may be computed by the design method presented in the AISC Manual,[2] page 3-106.

The bearing pressure on the base plate due to the applied service loads is

$$f_p = (P_D + P_L)/A_p$$
$$= (10 + 80)/(14 \times 14)$$
$$= 0.46 \text{ kips per square inch}$$

The relevant design parameters are

$$m = (B_p - 0.95d)/2$$
$$= (14 - 0.95 \times 8)/2$$
$$= 3.2$$
$$n = (B_p - 0.80b_f)/2$$
$$= (14 - 0.80 \times 8)/2$$
$$= 3.8 \dots \text{governs}$$

Hence, the required base plate thickness is given by

$$t_p = 2n\sqrt{f_p/F_y}$$
$$= 2 \times 3.8 \times \sqrt{0.46/36}$$
$$= 0.86 \text{ inches}$$
$$= {}^7/_8 \text{ inch}$$

The factored applied load is given by ACI Equation (9-2) as

$$P_u = 1.2P_D + 1.6P_L$$
$$= 1.2 \times 10 + 1.6 \times 80$$
$$= 140 \text{ kips}$$

The area of the base of the pyramid, with side slopes of 1:2, formed within the footing by the base plate area is

$$A_2 = (B_p + 4d)^2 \\ \leq l^2$$

where

d = effective depth = $18 - 3 - 1 = 14$ inches
l = size of footing = 66 inches

Then

$$A_2 = (14 + 4d)^2 \\ = 4356 \ldots \text{maximum, and}$$

$$\sqrt{A_2/A_p} = \sqrt{4356/14^2} \\ > 2$$

Hence, the bearing capacity of the footing concrete is given by ACI Section 10.17.1 as

$$\phi P_n = 0.85\phi\, f'_c\, A_p \times 2 \\ = 0.85 \times 0.65 \times 3000 \times 196 \times 2/1000 \\ = 650 \text{ kips} \\ > P_u \ldots \text{satisfactory}$$

The net factored pressure acting on the underside of the footing is

$$q_u = P_u/A_f \\ = 140/5.5^2 \\ = 4.63 \text{ kips per square foot}$$

The critical section for flexural shear is located a distance from the edge of the footing which is given by

$$x_1 = l/2 - (B_p + b_f)/4 - d \\ = 5.5/2 - (14 + 8)/48 - 14/12 \\ = 1.125 \text{ feet}$$

The factored applied shear at the critical section is

$$V_u = q_u l x_1 \\ = 4.63 \times 5.5 \times 1.125 \\ = 28.65 \text{ kips}$$

The flexural shear capacity of the footing is given by ACI Equation (11-3) as

$$\phi V_c = 2\phi l d \sqrt{f'_c} \\ = 2 \times 0.75 \times 5.5 \times 12 \times 14 \times \sqrt{3000}/1000 \\ = 75.91 \text{ kips} \\ > V_u \ldots \text{satisfactory}$$

The length of one side of the critical perimeter for punching shear is

$$b_o/4 = (B_p + b_f)/2 + d$$
$$= (14 + 8)/24 + 14/12$$
$$= 2.08 \text{ feet}$$

The factored, applied shear at the critical perimeter is

$$V_u = P_u - q_u(b_o/4)^2$$
$$= 140 - 4.63 \times 2.08^2$$
$$= 106.33 \text{ kips}$$

The ratio of the base plate sides is $\beta_c = 1 < 2$. Then the punching shear capacity of the footing is given by ACI Equation (11-33) as

$$\phi V_c = 4\phi b_o d\sqrt{f_c'}$$
$$= 4 \times 0.75 \times 4 \times 2.08 \times 12 \times 14 \times \sqrt{3000}/1000$$
$$= 230 \text{ kips}$$
$$> V_u \dots \text{satisfactory}$$

The critical section for flexure is located a distance from the edge of the footing which is given by

$$x_2 = l/2 - (B_p + b_f)/4$$
$$= 5.5/2 - (14 + 8)/48$$
$$= 2.29 \text{ feet}$$

The factored, applied moment at this section is

$$M_u = q_u l x_2^2/2$$
$$= 4.63 \times 5.5 \times 2.29^2/2$$
$$= 66.77 \text{ kip-feet}$$

Assuming the section is tension-controlled as defined in ACI Section 10.3.4, the required flexural reinforcement ratio is given by

$$\rho = 0.85 f_c'\left(1 - \sqrt{1 - 2K/0.765 f_c'}\right)/f_y$$

where
$$K = 12M_u/bd^2 = 0.0619$$
$$\rho = 0.116 \text{ percent}$$

The maximum allowable reinforcement ratio for a tension-controlled section is given by[3]

$$\rho_{max} = 1.36 \text{ percent}$$
$$> \rho \dots \text{satisfactory}$$

Hence, the section is tension-controlled with a strength reduction factor of $\phi = 0.90$.

The minimum reinforcement ratio in a footing slab for Grade 60 bars is given by ACI Section 7.12 as

$$\rho_{min} = 0.18 \text{ percent of the gross area...governs}$$
$$> \rho$$

Hence, the required reinforcement area is

$$A_s = lh\rho_{min}$$
$$= 66 \times 18 \times 0.0018$$
$$= 2.14 \text{ square inches}$$

Hence, provide 11 No. 4 bars to give an area of

$$A'_s = 2.20 \text{ square inches}$$

Allowing for an end cover of 3 inches, the available anchorage length for the bars is

$$l_{da} = x_2 - 3$$
$$= (2.29 \times 12) - 3$$
$$= 24.5 \text{ inches}$$

For No. 4 bars in 3000-pound-per-square-inch concrete, the development length of ACI Equation (12-1) governs with

$$2.5 = (c + K_{tr})/d_b$$
$$1 = \alpha = \beta = \lambda$$
$$\gamma = 0.8$$

The required development length is given by

$$l_d = 26.3 \, d_b$$
$$= 26.3 \times 0.5$$
$$= 13.2 \text{ inches}$$
$$< l_{da} \text{...satisfactory}$$

The footing is adequate.

Combined Footing

The rectangular footing shown in Figure 4.5 has one column adjacent to the property line of the building, and this limits the allowable length of the footing. The centroid of the footing is designed to coincide with the centroid of the service loads on the two columns, thus providing a uniform soil bearing pressure for service loads. The factored bearing pressure under factored loads will not, however, be uniform unless the ratio of the factored load to service load for both columns is identical.

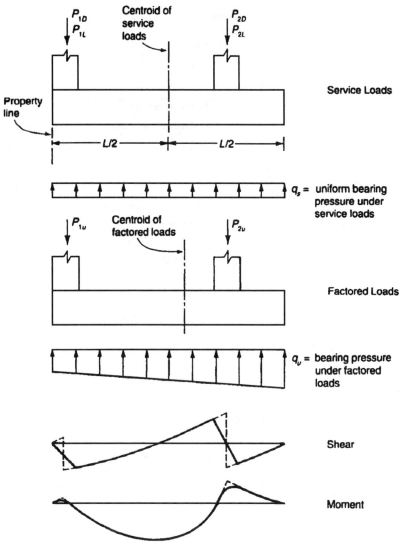

Figure 4.5 Combined footing

Example **4.2**

Exhibit 2 indicates the service loads supported by two 12 inch × 12 inch columns and their location with respect to the property line. The depth of the footing is 24 inches and the concrete strength is 3000 pounds per square inch. Determine the dimensions of a combined footing which will provide an allowable soil bearing pressure of 2000 pounds per square foot. If the ratio of factored load to service load for both columns is 1.5, determine if the Grade 60 reinforcement indicated and the depth of the footing are adequate.

Solution

Allowing for the weight of the footing, the equivalent soil pressure produced by the column service loads is

$$q = q_s - 150h$$
$$= 2000 - (150 \times 2)$$
$$= 1700 \text{ pounds per square foot}$$

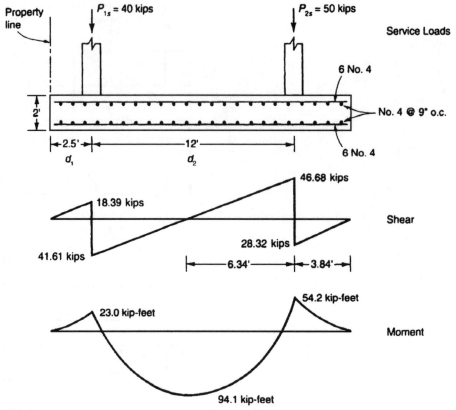

Exhibit 2

The centroid of the service loads is located a distance from the property line given by

$$x_o = (2.5P_{1s} + 14.5P_{2s})/(P_{1s} + P_{2s})$$
$$= (2.5 \times 40 + 14.5 \times 50)/(40 + 50)$$
$$= 9.17 \text{ feet}$$

Then, to produce a uniform pressure under the footing, the length of the footing is

$$L = 2x_o$$
$$= 2 \times 9.17$$
$$= 18.37 \text{ feet}$$

The required width of footing to produce an allowable soil pressure of 2000 pounds per square foot is

$$B = (P_{1s} + P_{2s})/qL$$
$$= (40{,}000 + 50{,}000)/(1700 \times 18.34)$$
$$= 2.89 \text{ feet}$$

Since the ratio of factored load to service load for both columns is 1.5, the net factored pressure acting on the underside of the footing for factored loads is

$$q_u = (P_{1u} + P_{2u})/L$$
$$= 1.5(40 + 50)/18.34$$
$$= 7.36 \text{ kips per linear foot}$$

The shear force and bending moment diagrams for the footing (for factored loading) are shown in Exhibit 2. Allowing for 3 inches of cover for the longitudinal reinforcement, the effective depth is given by

$$d = h - 3 - d_b/2$$
$$= 24 - 3 - 0.5/2$$
$$= 20.75 \text{ inches}$$

The critical section for flexural shear is located a distance equal to the effective depth from column 2. The factored applied shear at this critical section is given by

$$V_u = V_{2u} - q_u(d + c/2)/12$$
$$= 46.68 - 7.36(20.75 + 6)/12$$
$$= 30.27 \text{ kips}$$

The flexural shear capacity of the footing is given by ACI Equation (11-3) as

$$\phi V_c = 2\phi Bd\sqrt{f_c'}$$
$$= 2 \times 0.75 \times 2.89 \times 12 \times 20.75\sqrt{3000}/1000$$
$$= 59.12 \text{ kips}$$
$$> V_u \ldots \text{satisfactory}$$

The length of the critical perimeter for punching shear is given by

$$b_o = 4(c + d)$$
$$= 4(12 + 20.75)$$
$$= 131 \text{ inches}$$

The column side ratio is

$$\beta_c = 1$$
$$< 2$$

Then the punching shear capacity of the footing is

$$\phi V_c = 4\phi b_o d\sqrt{f_c'}$$
$$= 4 \times 0.75 \times 131 \times 20.75 \times \sqrt{3000}/1000$$
$$= 447 \text{ kips}$$
$$> P_{2u} \ldots \text{satisfactory}$$

The minimum reinforcement ratio in a footing slab for Grade 60 bars is given by ACI Section 7.12 as

$$\rho_{\min} = 0.18 \text{ percent of the gross area}$$

The minimum area of reinforcement required is

$$A_{s(\min)} = \rho_{\min} hB$$
$$= 0.18 \times 24 \times 2.89 \times 12/100$$
$$= 1.5 \text{ square inches}$$

The sum of the reinforcement areas in the top and bottom of the footing, which consists of a total of 12 No. 4 bars, is

$$2A_s = 2.4 \text{ square inches}$$
$$> 1.5 \ldots \text{satisfactory}$$

The maximum allowable reinforcement ratio for a tension-controlled section is given by[3]

$$\rho_{max} = 1.36 \text{ percent}$$

The reinforcement ratio provided in the top of the footing is

$$
\begin{aligned}
\rho &= A_s/Bd \\
&= 1.2 \times 100/(2.89 \times 12 \times 20.75) \\
&= 0.17 \text{ percent} \\
&< \rho_{max} \dots \text{satisfactory}
\end{aligned}
$$

Hence, the section is tension-controlled and $\phi = 0.90$.

Neglecting compression reinforcement, the design moment strength of the reinforcement in the top of the footing is

$$
\begin{aligned}
\phi M_n &= 0.9 A_s f_y d (1 - 0.59 \rho f_y/f'_c)/12 \\
&= 109.8 \text{ kip-feet} \\
&> 94.1 \dots \text{satisfactory}
\end{aligned}
$$

The reinforcement provided in the bottom of the footing is clearly adequate.

The critical section for flexure in the transverse direction is at the face of the columns and the factored moment at this section is

$$
\begin{aligned}
M_u &= q_u L (B - c)^2/8 \\
&= 7.36 \times 18.34 \ (2.89 - 1)^2/8 \\
&= 60.3 \text{ kip-feet}
\end{aligned}
$$

The required reinforcement ratio in the bottom of the footing is given by

$$\rho = 0.85 f'_c \left(1 - \sqrt{1 - 2K/0.765 f'_c}\right)/f_y$$

where
$K = 12 M_u/bd^2$
$\rho = 0.0142 \text{ percent}$

Hence, the required reinforcement area is

$$
\begin{aligned}
A_s &= pbd \\
&= 0.0142 \times 18.34 \times 12 \times 20.75/100 \\
&= 0.65 \text{ square inches}
\end{aligned}
$$

The reinforcement area provided at the bottom of the footing in the transverse direction exceeds this, and the combined reinforcement area at the top and bottom of the footing exceeds the requirement for minimum reinforcement of 0.18 percent of gross area, so the footing is satisfactory.

Strap Footing

The strap footing shown in Figure 4.6 consists of two columns on individual pad footings which are connected by a strap beam. The soffit of the strap is not subject to soil pressure because it is poured on a layer of Styrofoam. It is assumed that the strap and footings act as a rigid body with a uniform bearing pressure under the footings. The soil reactions, R_1 and R_2, act at the center of the footings, and the pressure under the footings is given by

$$q_1 = q_2 = q$$

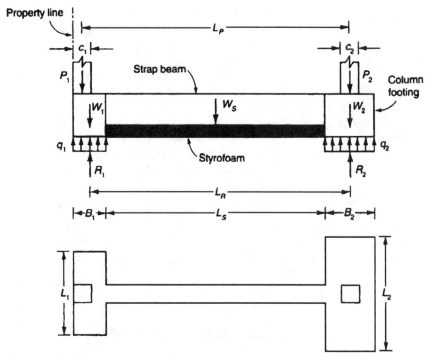

Figure 4.6 Strap footing

The base area of each footing is

$$A_1 = B_1 L_1$$
$$A_2 = B_2 L_2$$

The soil reactions are given by

$$R_1 = qA_1$$
$$R_2 = qA_2$$

By locating the footing under column 2 symmetrical with respect to the center of the column, the lines of action of R_2 and P_2 coincide. Then, from the figure, the distance between R_1 and R_2 is

$$L_R = L_P + c_1/2 - B_1/2$$

The strap length is

$$L_S = L_R - (B_1 + B_2)/2$$

Two equations of statics are available for solving the two unknowns, R_1 and R_2. However, the values of R_1 and R_2 also influence the required dimensions for the members and an iterative technique is required.

Appropriate dimensions are initially selected for B_1 and B_2, the depth of the footings and strap, and the width of the strap. Hence, the weight of the strap, W_S, may be determined. An initial estimate is made of the soil reaction R_1 and the corresponding values of A_1 and W_1 are determined. An estimate is made of W_2. Resolving vertically gives

$$R_2 = P_1 + P_2 - R_1 + W_1 + W_2 + W_S$$

Hence, A_2 may be determined and the initial estimate of W_2 revised. Taking moments about the center of footing 2 gives

$$R_1 = [P_1 L_P + W_1 L_R + W_S (L_S + B_2)/2]/L_R$$

The initial estimate of R_1 may now be revised and the process repeated until convergence is reached.

Example **4.3**

Design the strap beam of the strap footing shown in Exhibit 3. The allowable soil bearing pressure is 3000 pounds per square foot, concrete strength is 3000 pounds per square inch, and all reinforcement is Grade 60.

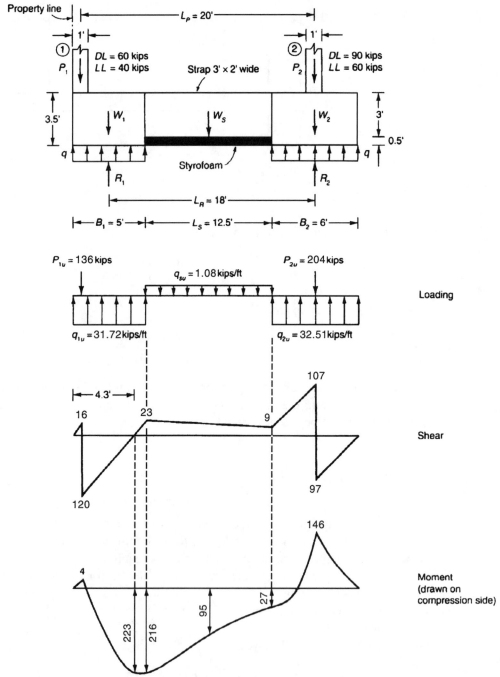

Exhibit 3

Solution

As an initial estimate, assume that the value of the soil reaction under column 1 is given by

$$R_1 = 1.42P_1$$
$$= 1.42(60 + 40)$$
$$= 142 \text{ kips}$$

The area of the footing required for column 1 is

$$A_1 = R_1/q$$
$$= 142/3$$
$$= 47.33 \text{ square feet}$$

The weight of this footing is

$$W_1 = 0.15A_1h_1$$
$$= 0.15 \times 47.33 \times 3.5$$
$$= 24.81 \text{ kips}$$

The weight of the strap beam is

$$W_S = 0.15L_S B_S h_S$$
$$= 0.15 \times 12.5 \times 2 \times 3$$
$$= 11.25 \text{ kips}$$

As an initial estimate, assume that the weight of the footing required for column 2 is

$$W_2 = 30.6 \text{ kips}$$

Then, resolving vertically, the value of the soil reaction under column 2 is

$$R_2 = P_1 + P_2 - R_1 + W_1 + W_2 + W_S$$
$$= 100 + 150 - 142 + 24.81 + 30.6 + 11.25.$$
$$= 174.7 \text{ kips}$$

The area of the footing required for column 2 is

$$A_2 = R_2/q$$
$$= 174.7/3$$
$$= 58.23$$

A revised estimate of the weight of this footing is

$$W_2 = 0.15A_2h_2$$
$$= 0.15 \times 58.23 \times 3.5$$
$$= 30.57 \text{ kips}$$
$$\approx 30.6$$

Hence, the initial estimate of W_2 is sufficiently accurate.
Taking moments about the center of footing 2 gives

$$R_1 = [P_1L_P + W_1L_R + W_S(L_S + B_2)/2]/L_R$$
$$= (100 \times 20 + 24.81 \times 18 + 11.25 \times 18.5/2)/18$$
$$= 141.7 \text{ kips}$$
$$\approx 142$$

Hence, the initial estimate of R_1 is sufficiently accurate.

The factored loading on column 1 is given by ACI Equation (9-1) as

$$
\begin{aligned}
P_{1u} &= 1.2P_D + 1.6P_L \\
&= 1.2 \times 60 + 1.6 \times 40 \\
&= 136 \text{ kips}
\end{aligned}
$$

The ratio of factored load to service load for column 1 is

$$
\begin{aligned}
P_{1u}/P_{1s} &= 136/100 \\
&= 1.36
\end{aligned}
$$

The same ratio is applicable for column 2, which has a factored load of

$$
P_{2u} = 204 \text{ kips}
$$

So, neglecting the effect of the footings' factored dead loads, a uniform factored pressure acts on the underside of both footings under factored loading. The factored weights of the footings are

$$
\begin{aligned}
W_{1u} &= 1.2W_1 \\
&= 29.77 \text{ kips} \\
W_{2u} &= 1.2W_2 \\
&= 36.72 \text{ kips} \\
W_{Su} &= 1.2W_S \\
&= 13.50 \text{ kips}
\end{aligned}
$$

The total factored load is

$$
\begin{aligned}
P_u &= P_{1u} + P_{2u} + W_{1u} + W_{2u} + W_{Su} \\
&= 500 \text{ kips}
\end{aligned}
$$

The uniform factored soil pressure at both footings is

$$
\begin{aligned}
q_u &= P_u/(A_1 + A_2) \\
&= 500/(47.33 + 58.23) \\
&= 3.98 \text{ kips per square foot}
\end{aligned}
$$

The net factored pressures acting on the underside of both footings are

$$
\begin{aligned}
q_{1u} &= (q_u A_1 - W_{1u})/B_1 \\
&= (3.98 \times 47.33 - 29.77)/5 \\
&= 31.72 \text{ kips per linear foot} \\
q_{2u} &= (q_u A_2 - W_{2u})/B_2 \\
&= (3.98 \times 58.23 - 36.72)/6 \\
&= 32.51 \text{ kips per linear foot}
\end{aligned}
$$

The factored self-weight of the strap beam is

$$
\begin{aligned}
q_{Su} &= W_{Su}/L_S \\
&= 13.5/12.5 \\
&= 1.08 \text{ kips per linear foot}
\end{aligned}
$$

The loading, shear and moment diagrams are shown in Exhibit 3.

The maximum negative moment in the strap occurs at the interface with footing 1 and has the value

$$M_u = 216 \text{ kip-feet}$$

The required flexural reinforcement ratio is given by

$$\rho = 0.85 f' \left(1 - \sqrt{1 - 2K/0.765 f_c'} \right) / f_y$$

where
$K = 12M_u/bd^2 = 0.0955$
$d = 33.625$ inches ... using No. 6 bars with 2 inches cover
$\rho = 0.181$ percent

The minimum reinforcement ratio in the strap beam for Grade 60 bars is given by ACI Sections 10.5.1 and 10.5.3 as

$$\rho_{min} = 200/f_y$$
$$= 0.333 \text{ percent}$$
$$\leq 1.333\rho$$
$$= 0.241 \text{ percent} ... \text{governs}$$

The reinforcement area required in the top of the strap beam is given by

$$A_s = bd\rho_{min}$$
$$= 24 \times 33.625 \times 0.00241$$
$$= 1.94 \text{ square inches}$$

Providing five No. 6 bars gives a reinforcement area of

$$A_s' = 2.20 \text{ square inches}$$
$$> A_s ... \text{satisfactory}$$

The maximum shear in the strap occurs at the interface with footing 1 and has the value

$$V_u = 23 \text{ kips}$$

The design shear strength of the concrete section is given by ACI Equation (11-3) as

$$\phi V_c = 2\phi \sqrt{f_c'} b_w d$$
$$= 2 \times 0.85 \times \sqrt{3000} \times 24 \times 33.625/1000$$
$$= 75 \text{ kips}$$
$$> 2V_u$$

So, in accordance with ACI Section 11.5.5, no shear reinforcement is required.

Eccentric Footing

An eccentric footing, as shown in Figure 4.7, may be utilized when the wall of a building must be located on the property line. It is assumed that the footing acts as a rigid body with a uniform soil pressure under the base and that the lateral soil pressures on either side of the footing are balanced. The total gravity load acting on the footing is

$$\Sigma W = W_L + W_F + W_W + W_S + W_B$$

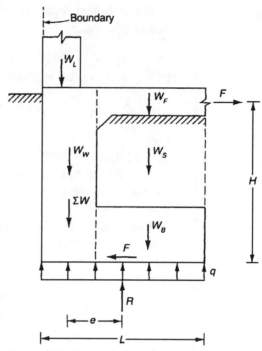

Figure 4.7 Eccentric footing

The soil reaction under the base is

$$R = \Sigma W$$

The required length of the base is

$$L = R/q$$

where, q = allowable soil pressure.

The counterclockwise couple produced by R and ΣW is

$$M_R = Re$$

where e is the eccentricity between R and ΣW.

The frictional force produced at the underside of the base is

$$F = \mu R$$

where μ is the coefficient of friction.

The frictional force is balanced by an equal and opposite tensile force in the top slab, and this produces the clockwise couple $M_F = FH$. Equating the two couples gives

$$M_F = M_R$$
$$FH = Re$$
$$H = Re/F = e/\mu$$

By assuming an initial value for H, W_F, W_S, and W_B, corresponding values of L and e may be determined and a revised value of H computed. The process is repeated until convergence is reached.

Example **4.4**

Design the eccentric footing shown in Exhibit 4 to support a superimposed dead plus live load of 6.2 kips per linear foot. The coefficient of friction is 0.3 and the unit soil weight is 120 pounds per cubic foot. The allowable soil bearing pressure is 2500 pounds per square foot. Concrete strength is 3000 pounds per square inch and all reinforcement is Grade 60.

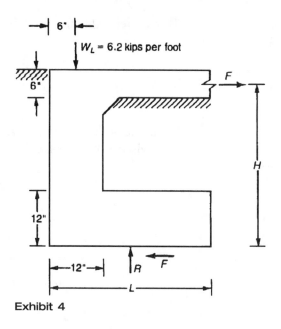

$W_L = 6.2$ kips per foot

Exhibit 4

Solution

As initial estimates, assume that

$$H = 2.75 \text{ feet}$$
$$W_F = 0.15 \text{ kips}$$
$$W_B = 0.30 \text{ kips}$$
$$W_S = 0.36 \text{ kips}$$

Then

$$W_W = 0.15 \times 3 \times 1$$
$$= 0.45 \text{ kips}$$
$$\Sigma W = R = W_L + W_F + W_B + W_S + W_W$$
$$= 6.2 + 0.15 + 0.30 + 0.36 + 0.45$$
$$= 7.46 \text{ kips}$$

The base length required is given by

$$L = R/q$$
$$= 7.46/2.5$$
$$= 2.984 \text{ feet}$$

The eccentricity between the lines of action of ΣW and W_L is

$$x_1 = L(W_F + W_B + W_S)/2\Sigma W$$

The eccentricity between the lines of action of R and W_L is

$$x_2 = L/2 - 0.5$$

The eccentricity between the lines of action of R and ΣW is

$$
\begin{aligned}
e &= x_2 - x_1 \\
&= L[1 - (W_F + W_B + W_S)/\Sigma W]/2 - 0.5 \\
&= 2.984(1 - 0.81/7.46)/2 - 0.5 \\
&= 0.83
\end{aligned}
$$

The required value for H is given by

$$
\begin{aligned}
H &= e/\mu \\
&= 0.83/0.3 \\
&= 2.77 \text{ feet} \\
&\approx 2.75 \text{ feet}
\end{aligned}
$$

Hence, the initial estimate of H is sufficiently accurate. Revised values for the footing and soil weights are

$$
\begin{aligned}
W_F &= 0.15 \times 1.984 \times 0.5 \\
&= 0.149 \\
&\approx 0.150 \\
W_B &= 0.15 \times 1.984 \times 1.0 \\
&= 0.298 \\
&\approx 0.300 \\
W_S &= 0.12 \times 1.984 \times 1.52 \\
&= 0.362 \\
&\approx 0.360 \\
W_W &= 0.15 \times 3.02 \times 1 \\
&= 0.453 \\
&\approx 0.450
\end{aligned}
$$

The net pressure acting on the base of the footing is

$$
\begin{aligned}
q' &= q - (W_F + W_S + W_B)/(L - 1) \\
&= 2.5 - 0.408 \\
&= 2.09 \text{ kips per linear foot}
\end{aligned}
$$

The bending moment at the face of the front wall is

$$
\begin{aligned}
M &= q'(L - 1)^2/2 \\
&= 4.11 \text{ kip-feet}
\end{aligned}
$$

Minimum reinforcement is adequate and is given by ACI Section 7.12.2 as

$$
\begin{aligned}
A_s &= 0.0018bh \\
&= 0.0018 \times 12 \times 12 \\
&= 0.26 \text{ square inches per foot} \\
&= \text{No. 4 bars at 18-inch spacing, top and bottom}
\end{aligned}
$$

Using six No. 3 bars transversely provides a reinforcement ratio of

$$
\begin{aligned}
\rho &= 0.66 \times 100/(12 \times 12) \\
&= 0.20 \text{ percent} \\
&> 0.18 \ldots \text{satisfactory}
\end{aligned}
$$

Minimum reinforcement in the front wall is governed by ACI Section 14.3. Vertical reinforcement consisting of No. 4 bars at 18-inch spacing front and back provides a reinforcement ratio of

$$\rho = 0.4 \times 100/(12 \times 18)$$
$$= 0.19 \text{ percent}$$
$$> 0.12 \ldots \text{satisfactory}$$

Horizontal reinforcement consisting of eight No. 3 bars provides a reinforcement ratio of

$$\rho = 0.88 \times 100/(12 \times 36)$$
$$= 0.204 \text{ percent}$$
$$> 0.20 \ldots \text{satisfactory}$$

The area of tensile reinforcement required in the floor slab is given by

$$A_s = 1.6 F/\phi f_y$$
$$= 1.6 \times 0.3 \times 7.46/(0.9 \times 60)$$
$$= 0.066 \text{ square inches per foot}$$

Using No. 4 bars at 18 inch spacing provides an area

$$A_s' = 0.13 \text{ square inches}$$
$$> 0.066 \ldots \text{satisfactory}$$

The reinforcement layout is shown in Exhibit 5.

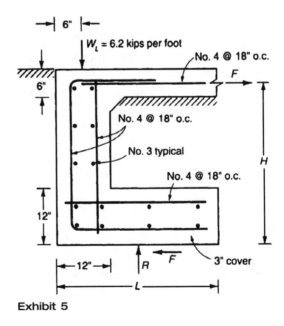

Exhibit 5

Footing with Eccentric Load

An applied load with an eccentricity less than $L/6$ produces the pressure distribution shown in Figure 4.8. The maximum and minimum bearing pressure under the footing is given by

$$q = P/A \pm Pe/S$$
$$= P(1 \pm 6e/L)/BL$$

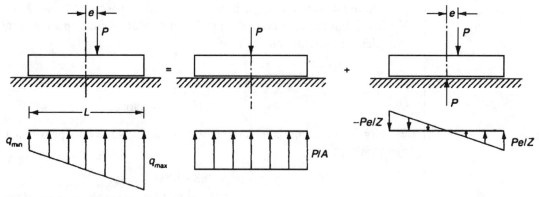

Figure 4.8 Footing with eccentric load

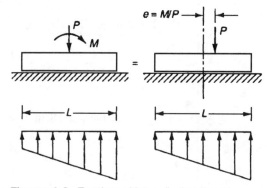

Figure 4.9 Footing with applied moment

where

e = eccentricity of the applied load P
B = width of footing
L = length of footing

An axial load plus bending moment applied to a footing, as shown in Figure 4.9, produces an equivalent eccentricity of $e = M/P$.

The bearing pressure under the footing is similarly obtained as

$$q = P(1 \pm 6e/L)/BL$$

When the magnitude of the eccentricity, as shown in Figure 4.10, is given by

$$e = L/6$$

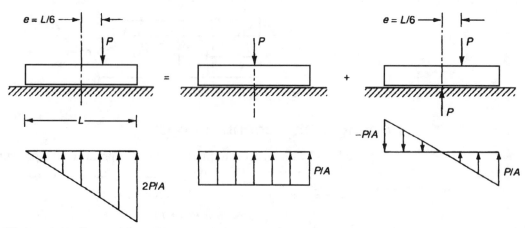

Figure 4.10 Eccentricity = $L/6$

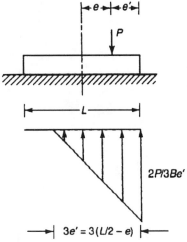

Figure 4.11   Eccentricity $>L/6$

the bearing pressure under the footing is

$$q_{max} = 2P/BL$$
$$q_{min} = 0$$

When the eccentricity exceeds $L/6$, as shown in Figure 4.11, no tension is possible between the soil and the footing, and the bearing pressure under the footing is given by

$$q_{max} = 2P/3Be'$$

where $e' = L/2 - e$

RETAINING WALL

Cantilever Retaining Wall

The forces acting on a reinforced concrete cantilever retaining wall are shown in Figure 4.12. The weight of the stem wall, base, and shear key in pounds per foot length are

$$W_W = 150L_W(H-h)$$
$$W_B = 150hL_B$$
$$W_K = 150L_W(H_K - h)$$

The live load surcharge behind the stem and the weight of the fill supported by the heel are

$$W_L = wL_H$$
$$W_S = \gamma_S L_H(H-h)$$

The active earth pressure behind the wall, acting at a height of $H/3$ above the base, is

$$H_A = p_A H^2/2$$

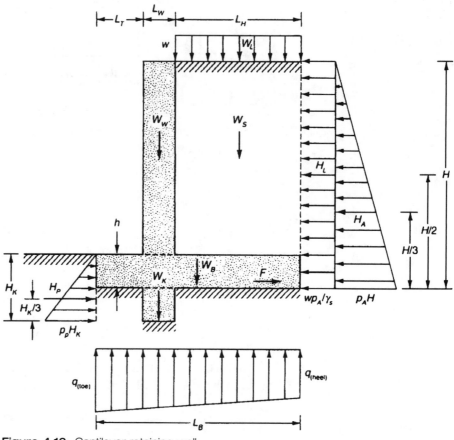

Figure 4.12 Cantilever retaining wall

where

$p_A = K_A\gamma_S$ = lateral pressure equivalent to a fluid of density p_A pounds per cubic foot

γ_S = density of fill

K_A = Rankine coefficient of active earth pressure = $(1 - \sin\phi)/(1 + \sin\phi)$

ϕ = angle of internal friction

Hence, the equivalent fluid pressure for a fill material with a density of 110 pounds per cubic foot and an angle of internal friction of 35° is

$$p_A = 110(1 - \sin 35°)/(1 + \sin 35°)$$
$$= 30 \text{ pounds per square foot per foot}$$

The live load surcharge of w pounds per square foot is equivalent to an additional height of fill which is given by

$$\overline{H} = w/\gamma_S$$

This produces a uniform pressure over the height of the fill of $p_L = \overline{H}p_A$. The total surcharge pressure, acting at a height of $H/2$ above the base, is

$$H_L = p_L H$$
$$= wp_A H/\gamma_S$$

The frictional force produced at the underside of the base is

$$F = \mu\Sigma W$$

where μ = coefficient of friction.

When the frictional force is insufficient to provide an adequate factor of safety against sliding, a shear key is provided to mobilize the passive pressure of the undisturbed soil in front of the wall. The passive earth pressure in front of the wall, acting at a height of $H_K/3$ above the bottom of the key, is

$$H_P = p_P H_K^2/2$$

where

$p_P = K_P \gamma_S = $ lateral pressure equivalent to a fluid of density p_P pounds per cubic foot
$K_P = $ Rankine coefficient of passive earth pressure $= (1 + \sin\phi)/(1 - \sin\phi)$

So, the equivalent fluid pressure for a material with a density of 110 pounds per cubic foot and an angle of internal friction of 35° is

$$P_P = 110 \, (1 + \sin 35°)/(1 - \sin 35°)$$
$$= 400 \text{ pounds per square foot per foot}$$

To provide an adequate factor of safety against sliding, a depth of shear key must be provided to ensue that

$$F + H_P \geq 1.5(H_A + H_L)$$

Similarly, the required factor of safety against overturning about the toe is 1.5.

By determining the eccentricity of the resultant of all forces about the center of the base, the bearing pressure under the base may be obtained.

To design the stem wall and the base, the required strength is determined from ACI Equation (9-4) as

$$U = 1.2D + 1.6L + 1.6H$$

where
$D = $ dead load
$L = $ live load
$H = $ earth pressure

In accordance with ACI Section R11.1.3.1, the governing locations for bending moment and shear in a cantilever retaining wall are the following.

■ The critical section for bending moment and shear in the stem is at the base of the stem.

■ The critical section for bending moment and shear in the toe is at the air face of the stem.

■ The critical section for bending moment and shear in the heel is at the earth face of the stem.

The minimum reinforcement required in the stem wall is specified by ACI Section 14.3. For bars larger than No. 5, the reinforcement ratios, based on the gross concrete area, for vertical and horizontal reinforcement are given by

$$\rho_{\text{vert}} = 0.15 \text{ percent}$$
$$\rho_{\text{hor}} = 0.25 \text{ percent}$$

For bars not larger than No. 5, the corresponding ratios are:

$$\rho_{\text{vert}} = 0.12 \text{ percent}$$
$$\rho_{\text{hor}} = 0.20 \text{ percent}$$

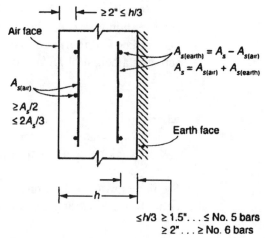

Figure 4.13 Wall reinforcement

For walls exceeding 10 inches thickness, two layers of reinforcement are required, as detailed in Figure 4.13.

Example **4.5**

Determine the bearing pressure and factors of safety for overturning and sliding of the retaining wall shown in Exhibit 6. The wall's backfill weighs 120 pounds per cubic foot, equivalent fluid pressure in the backfill behind the wall is 30 pounds per square foot per foot, and the coefficient of friction at the underside of the base is 0.40. The nominal 8-inch solid grouted concrete masonry stem wall has a specified strength of 1500 pounds per square inch and a modulus of elasticity of 1125 kips per square inch. The base concrete has a compressive strength of

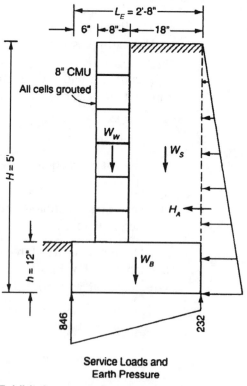

Service Loads and
Earth Pressure

Exhibit 6

3000 pounds per square inch. Using Grade 60 deformed bars, determine the reinforcement required in the stem and base.

Solution

The service loads acting on the retaining wall are given by

$$H_A = \text{lateral pressure from backfill}$$
$$= p_A H^2/2$$
$$= 30 \times 5^2/2$$
$$= 375 \text{ pounds}$$
$$W_W = \text{weight of stem wall}$$
$$= 80(H - h)$$
$$= 80 \times 4$$
$$= 320 \text{ pounds}$$
$$W_B = \text{weight of base}$$
$$= 150 \, hL_B$$
$$= 150 \times 1.0 \times 2.67$$
$$= 400 \text{ pounds}$$
$$W_S = \text{weight of backfill}$$
$$= \gamma_S L_H (H - h)$$
$$= 120 \times 1.5 \times 4$$
$$= 720 \text{ pounds}$$

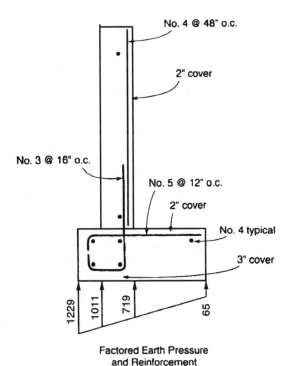

Factored Earth Pressure
and Reinforcement

Exhibit 7

The restoring and overturning moments about the bottom corner of the toe are shown in Exhibit 8.

The factor of safety against overturning is given by

$$\Sigma Wx/\Sigma Hy = 2180/625 = 3.5$$

Exhibit 8

Part	W	x	Wx	H	y	Hy
Backfill	720	1.92	1380	375	1.67	625
Wall	320	0.83	267			
Base	400	1.33	533			
Total	1440		2180	375		625

The frictional force produced at the underside of the base is given by

$$F = \mu \Sigma W$$
$$= 0.40 \times 1440$$
$$= 576 \text{ pounds}$$

The factor of safety against sliding is given by

$$F/\Sigma H = 576/375 = 1.5$$

The eccentricity of the applied loads about the toe is given by

$$e' = (\Sigma Wx - \Sigma Hy)/\Sigma W$$
$$= (2180 - 625)/1440$$
$$= 1.08 \text{ feet}$$

The eccentricity about the base centroid is

$$e = L_B/2 - e'$$
$$= 2.67/2 - 1.08$$
$$= 0.25 \text{ feet}$$
$$< L_B/6 \ldots \text{no tension under the base}$$

The pressure under the toe is

$$q_{(\text{toe})} = \Sigma W(1 + 6e/L_B)/BL_B$$
$$= 1440 \ (1 + 6 \times 0.25/2.67)/(1 \times 2.67)$$
$$= 846 \text{ pounds per square foot}$$

The pressure under the heel is

$$q_{(\text{heel})} = \Sigma W(1 - 6e/L_B)/BL_B$$
$$= 232 \text{ pounds per square foot}$$

The critical section for moment and shear in the stem is at the base of the stem and, due to service loads, these values are

$$V = p_A(H - h)^2/2$$
$$= 30(5 - 1)^2/2$$
$$= 240 \text{ pounds per foot}$$
$$M = V(H - h)/3$$
$$= 240(5 - 1)/3$$
$$= 320 \text{ pounds-feet per foot}$$

The allowable stresses, in accordance with BCRMS[4] Sections 2.3.2, 2.3.3, and 2.3.5, are

$$F_b = 0.33 \ f'_m = 500 \text{ pounds per square inch}$$
$$F_v = \sqrt{f'_m} = 38.73 \text{ pounds per square inch}$$
$$F_s = 24{,}000 \text{ pounds per square inch}$$

$$E_m = 1125 \text{ kips per square inch}$$
$$E_s = 29,000 \text{ kips per square inch}$$

The relevant section properties of the stem are

$$b = 12 \text{ inches}$$
$$d = 7.63 - 2.0 - 0.5/2 = 5.38 \text{ inches}$$

Providing No. 4 bars at 48 inch spacing, the masonry stresses may be obtained from BCRMS Section 2.1.1, and are

$$n = E_s/E_c = 25.8$$
$$p = A_s/bd = 0.049/(12 \times 5.38) = 0.076 \text{ percent}$$

$$k = \sqrt{(np + 2np)} - np = 0.179$$
$$k = (n^2p^2 + 2np)^{0.5} - np = 0.179$$
$$j = 1 - k/3 = 0.940$$
$$f_b = 24M/jkbd^2 = 131 \text{ pounds per square inch}$$
$$< F_b \dots \text{satisfactory}$$
$$f_s = 12M/jdA_s = 15,492 \text{ pounds per square inch}$$
$$< F_s \dots \text{satisfactory.}$$
$$f_v = V/bjd = 4 \text{ pounds per square inch}$$
$$< F_v \dots \text{satisfactory}$$

The reinforcement is indicated in Exhibit 7.

To determine the reinforcement in the base, factored loads must be used. In accordance with ACI[1] Section 9.2.4, the factored total vertical load, restoring moment, and overturning moment about the toe are

$$\Sigma(\gamma W) = 1.2 \times 1440 = 1728 \text{ pounds}$$
$$\Sigma(\gamma W)x = 1.2 \times 2180 = 2616 \text{ pound-feet}$$
$$\Sigma(\gamma H)y = 1.6 \times 625 = 1000 \text{ pound-feet}$$

The eccentricity of the factored loads about the toe is given by

$$e' = [\Sigma(\gamma W)x - \Sigma(\gamma H)y]/\Sigma(\gamma W)$$
$$= (2616 - 1000)/1728$$
$$= 0.94 \text{ feet}$$

The eccentricity about the base centroid is

$$e = L_B/2 - e'$$
$$= 2.67/2 - 0.94$$
$$= 0.40 \text{ feet}$$
$$< L_B/6 \dots \text{no tension under the base}$$

The pressure under the toe is

$$q_{(toe)} = \Sigma(\gamma W)(1 + 6e/L_B)/BL_B$$
$$= 1728 (1 + 6 \times 0.40/2.67)/(1 \times 2.67)$$
$$= 1229 \text{ pounds per square foot}$$

The pressure under the heel is

$$q_{(heel)} = \Sigma(\gamma W)(1 - 6e/L_B)/BL_B$$
$$= 65 \text{ pounds per square foot}$$

The critical section for shear and moment in the heel is at the rear face of the wall and, due to factored loads, these values are

$$V_u = \gamma W_S + 18\gamma W_B/32 - 1.5(719 + 65)/2$$
$$= 1.2 \times 720 + 18 \times 1.2 \times 400/32 - 588$$
$$= 546 \text{ pounds per foot}$$
$$M_u = 0.75(\gamma W_S + 18\gamma W_B/32) - 1.5^2 (829 + 2 \times 164)/6$$
$$= 417 \text{ pounds-feet per foot}$$

The shear capacity of the heel is given by ACI Equation (11-3) as

$$\phi V_c = 2\phi b_w d\sqrt{f_c'}$$
$$= 2 \times 0.85 \times 12 \times 9.5 \times \sqrt{3000}$$
$$= 10{,}615 \text{ pounds}$$
$$> V_u \ldots \text{satisfactory}$$

The required reinforcement ratio is derived from ACI Section 10.2, and is

$$\rho = 0.85 f_c'\left(1 - \sqrt{1 - 2K/0.765 f_c'}\right)/fy$$

where
$$K = 12M_u/bd^2 = 0.0046 \text{ kips per square inch}$$
$$\rho = 0.0085 \text{ percent}$$

The minimum reinforcement ratio in a footing slab for Grade 60 bars is given by ACI Section 7.12 as

$$\rho_{\min} = 0.18 \text{ percent of the gross area}$$
$$> \rho \ldots \text{governs}$$

Hence, the required reinforcement area is

$$A_S = bh\rho_{\min}$$
$$= 12 \times 12 \times 0.18/100$$
$$= 0.26 \text{ square inches per foot}$$

Provide No. 5 bars at 12 inch spacing to give $A'_s = 0.31$ square inches per foot.
   The critical section for shear and moment in the toe is at the front face of the stem and, due to factored loads, these values are

$$V_u = 0.5(1229 + 1011)/2 - 6\gamma W_B/32$$
$$= 470 \text{ pounds per foot}$$
$$< \phi V_c \ldots \text{satisfactory}$$
$$M_u = 0.5^2(1011 + 2 \times 1229)/6 - 0.25 \times 6\gamma W_B/32$$
$$= 122 \text{ pound-feet per foot}$$

The required reinforcement ratio is

$$\rho = 0.85 f_c'\left(1 - \sqrt{1 - 2K/0.765 f_c'}\right)/f_y$$
$$= 0.0025 \text{ percent}$$

Providing No. 3 bars at 16 inch spacing gives a reinforcement ratio of

$$\rho' = 0.083/(12 \times 8.75)$$
$$= 0.079 \text{ percent}$$
$$> 1.33\rho \ldots \text{satisfactory}$$

The required reinforcement layout is shown in Exhibit 7.

Gravity Retaining Wall

In a gravity retaining wall, as shown in Figure 4.14, stability and acceptable earth pressure are provided by the size and mass of the structure. The resultant of the self-weight and applied loads must be adjusted over the full height of the structure to ensure that the allowable tensile stress of the material is not exceeded at any section. When specifications require zero tension at any section, the locus of the resultant thrust must lie within the middle third at any section, as shown in Figure 4.14.

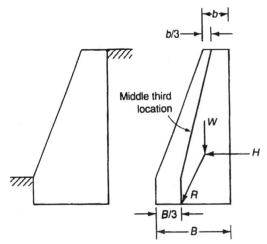

Figure 4.14 Gravity retaining wall

Example **4.6**

The mass concrete gravity dam shown in Exhibit 9 is 18 feet high. Determine the minimum base width if no tensile stresses are allowed in the concrete and the water level is at the top of the dam wall.

Solution

The total weight of the wall is

$$W = 144 \times 18(3 + B)/2$$
$$= 1296(3 + B) \text{ pounds per foot}$$

The total water pressure acting on the wall at a height of 6 feet above the base is

$$H = 62.4 \times 18^2/2$$
$$= 10,108 \text{ pounds per foot}$$

The centroid of the wall mass is located a distance from the heel which is given by

$$\bar{x} = (9 + 3B + B^2)/3(3 + B) \text{ feet}$$

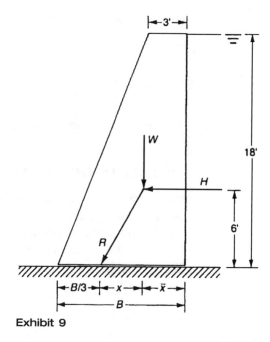

Exhibit 9

The line of action of the resultant thrust cuts the base at a distance from the centroid which is given by

$$x = 6H/W$$
$$= 6 \times 10{,}108/1296(3 + B)$$
$$= 46.80/3(3 + B)$$

To ensure no tensile stress in the base:

$$x + \bar{x} \le 2B/3$$

Hence, the minimum base width is given by

$$46.80/(3 + B) + (9 + 3B + B^2)/3(3 + B) - 2B/3 = 0$$
$$B = 10.81 \text{ feet}$$

The minimum required base width is 10.81 feet.

Cantilevered Sheetpile Wall

The forces acting on a cantilevered sheetpile wall are shown in Figure 4.15. An initial estimate[5] is required of the penetration of the sheetpiling and of the location of the point R about which the sheetpiling rotates. Point O occurs where the passive pressure in front of the sheetpiling equals the active pressure behind the sheetpiling. The forces acting on the wall are

$$H_A = p_A H_1(H_1 + y_1)/2$$
$$H_{P1} = [p_P(H_2 - y_2) - p_A(H_1 + H_2 - y_2)](H_2 - y_1 - y_3)/2$$
$$H_{P2} = [p_P(H_1 + H_2) - p_A H_2]y_3/2$$

where

$$y_1 = p_A H_1/(p_P - p_A)$$
$$y_3 = y_2[p_P(H_1 + H_2) - p_A H_2]/(p_P - p_A)(H_1 + 2H_2 - y_2)$$

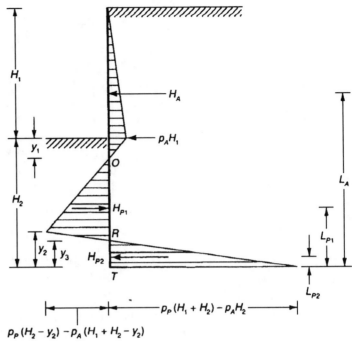

Figure 4.15 Cantilevered sheetpile wall

Resolving horizontally gives

$$H_A - H_{P1} + H_{P2} = 0$$

Taking moments about the toe of the pile at T gives

$$H_A L_A - H_{P1} L_{P1} + H_{P2} L_{P2} = 0$$

Adjustments are made to the initial estimates until the above equations are satisfied. The shear and bending moment in the sheetpiling may then be obtained.

Anchored Sheetpile Retaining Wall

The forces acting on an anchored sheetpile wall are shown in Figure 4.16. An initial estimate[5,6] is required of the penetration of the sheetpiling. The forces acting on the wall are given by

$$H_A = \text{total active pressure behind wall}$$
$$= p_A (H_1 + H_2)^2 / 2$$
$$H_P = \text{total passive pressure in front of wall}$$
$$= p_P H_2^2 / 2$$
$$H_T = \text{force in tie}$$
$$= H_A - H_P$$

Taking moments of all forces about the tie point T gives

$$H_A L_A - H_P L_P = 0$$

Adjustments are made to the initial estimate of the penetration until the above equation is satisfied.

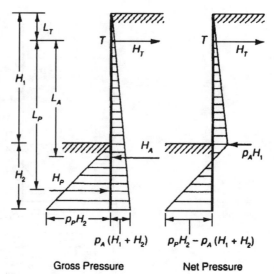

Gross Pressure   Net Pressure

Figure 4.16 Anchored sheetpile wall

The tie my be secured by means of a soil anchor, anchor piles, or a dead-man. Anchor piles are shown in Figure 4.17 and the forces in the piles are given by

$$F_C = \text{force in compression pile}$$
$$= H_T/(\sin\theta_1 + \cos\theta_1\tan\theta_2)$$
$$F_T = \text{force in tension pile}$$
$$= H_T/(\sin\theta_2 + \cos\theta_2\tan\theta_1)$$

A dead-man anchor is shown in Figure 4.18 and may consist of a continuous beam or an isolated anchorage. The resistance of a continuous beam consists of the passive pressure in front of the beam less the active pressure behind the beam. The dead-man must be located a sufficient distance from the wall that the passive wedge in front of the dead-man does not intersect the active wedge behind the wall. Resolving horizontally for a continuous anchor with a tie force per unit length of H_T gives

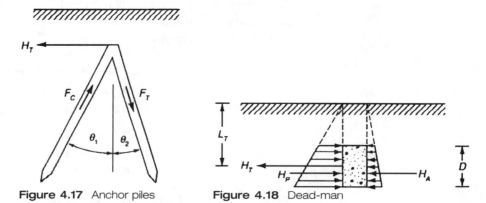

Figure 4.17 Anchor piles   **Figure 4.18** Dead-man

$$H_P - H_A + H_T = 0$$
$$DL_T(p_P - p_A) - H_T = 0$$

Hence, the size of the anchor may be determined.

Example **4.7**

Determine the required penetration of the sheetpile retaining wall shown in Exhibit 10 if active earth pressure may be assumed equivalent to a fluid pressure of 30 pounds per square foot per foot, and passive pressure may be assumed equivalent to a fluid pressure of 400 pounds per square foot per foot. Calculate the force in the tie and the location and magnitude of the maximum shear and the maximum moment in the sheetpiling.

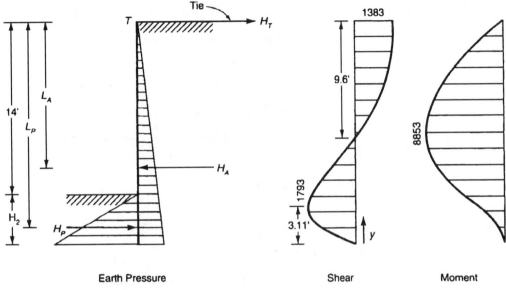

Earth Pressure   Shear   Moment

Exhibit 10

Solution

The total active pressure on the back of the wall is

$$H_A = 30(14 + H_2)^2/2$$
$$= 2940 + 420H_2 + 15H_2^2$$

The total passive pressure on the front of the wall is

$$H_P = 400H_2^2/2$$
$$= 200H_2^2$$

The distance between the line of action of the active pressure and the tie is

$$L_A = 2(14 + H_2)/3$$
$$= 9.33 + 0.67H_2$$

The distance between the line of action of the passive pressure and the tie is

$$L_P = 14 + 0.67H_2$$

Taking moments about the tie point T gives

$$H_A L_A - H_P L_P = 0$$
$$\left(2940 + 420H_2 + 15H_2^2\right)(9.33 + 0.67H_2) - 200H_2^2(14 + 0.67H_2) = 0$$

Solving for H_2 gives the required penetration as

$$H_2 = 4.25 \text{ feet}$$

The force in the tie is

$$H_T = H_A - H_P$$
$$= 4996 - 3613$$
$$= 1383 \text{ pounds per foot}$$

$p_P H_2$ = passive pressure at toe of wall

$$= 400 \times 4.25$$
$$= 1700 \text{ pounds per square foot}$$

$p_A(14 + H_2)$ = active pressure at toe of wall

$$= 30(14 + 4.25)$$
$$= 548 \text{ pounds per square foot}$$

The shear force at a distance y from the toe is

$$V = y(1700 - 200y) - y(548 - 15y)$$
$$= 1152y - 185y^2$$

The maximum shear occurs when

$$dV/dy = 0$$
$$= 1152 - 370y$$

Hence, $y = 3.11$ feet, and

$$V_{max} = 1793 \text{ pounds per foot}$$

The shear force at a distance x from the top of the wall is

$$V = H_T - p_A x^2/2$$
$$= 1383 - 15x^2$$

The maximum moment occurs when

$$V = 0$$

and
$$X = \sqrt{1383/15}$$
$$= 9.6 \text{ feet}$$

The maximum moment is

$$M_{max} = H_T x - P_A x^3/6$$
$$= 1383 \times 9.6 - 30 \times 9.6^3/6$$
$$= 8853 \text{ pound-feet per foot}$$

PILE FOUNDATIONS

Pile Group with Vertical Piles

Using the notation in Figure 4.19, which shows a group of vertical piles with a rigid pile cap with an imposed vertical eccentric load, the location of the pile group centroid is

$$\bar{x} = \Sigma an/\Sigma n$$

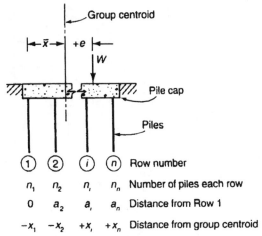

Figure 4.19 Pile group with vertical piles and vertical load

The axial force on each pile in row i, neglecting the self-weight of the pile and the pile cap, is given by

$$P_i = W/\Sigma n + Wex_i/\Sigma nx^2$$

For a symmetrical group, the location of the group centroid is

$$\bar{x} = a_n/2$$

When the applied load coincides with the pile group centroid, the axial force on each pile is given by

$$P = W/\Sigma n$$

When the pile cap is subjected to a bending moment, M, the eccentricity is given by

$$e = M/W$$

When each row in the group has an identical number of piles n_R and the number of piles in each line is n_L, the load applicable to each line is

$$W' = W/n_R$$

The axial force on a pile in row i is

$$P_i = W'/n_L + W'ex_i/\Sigma x^2$$

Figure 4.20 illustrates a group of vertical piles subjected to a horizontal load, as in the case of a pier or wharf. The piles are considered fixed-ended at the pile cap and at a depth of penetration, H, below the bottom of the rigid pile cap, with a point of contraflexure occurring at a depth of $H/2$. The total moment acting on the pile group is

$$M_T = We + FH$$

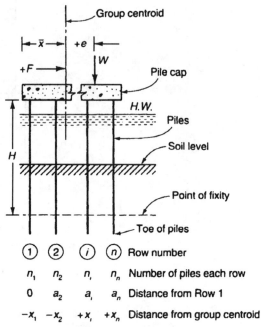

Figure 4.20 Vertical piles with vertical and horizontal loads

The axial force on each pile in row i, neglecting the self-weight of the pile and the pile cap, is given by

$$P_i = W/\Sigma n + M_T x_i / \Sigma n x^2$$

The shearing force on each pile is

$$V = F/\Sigma n$$

The maximum bending moment, at the point of fixity and at the pile cap, in each pile is

$$M_{\max} = VH/2$$

Example **4.8**

Exhibit 11 shows the loading acting on one line of piles supporting a dock. The vertical load indicated includes the self-weight of the rigid pile cap, and the piles may be considered fixed at a depth of 20 feet below the bottom of the cap. Determine the shear force and maximum bending moment in each pile and the maximum axial force produced in a pile.

Solution

The total moment acting on the pile group is

$$M_T = M + FH$$
$$= 200 + 10 \times 20$$
$$= 400 \text{ kip-feet}$$

The pile group is symmetrical with a moment of inertia of

$$\Sigma x^2 = 2(6^2 + 18^2) = 720$$

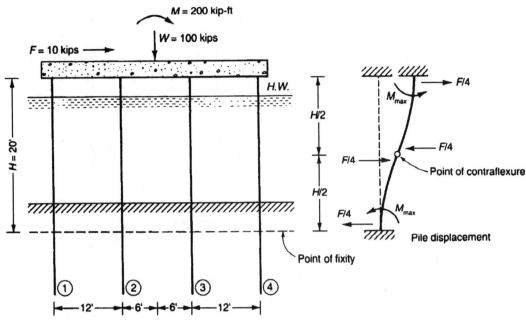

Exhibit 11

The maximum axial force occurs in pile 4 and, neglecting the self-weight, is given by

$$P_4 = W/n_L + M_T x_4 / \Sigma x^2$$
$$= 100/4 + 400 \times 18/720$$
$$= 35 \text{ kips}$$

The shear force in each pile is

$$V = F/\Sigma n$$
$$= 10/4$$
$$= 2.5 \text{ kips}$$

The maximum bending moment in a pile is determined by assuming a point of contraflexure at a depth of $H/2$, as shown in Exhibit 11. The maximum moment is

$$M_{max} = VH/2$$
$$= 2.5 \times 20/2$$
$$= 25 \text{ kip-feet}$$

Pile Group with Inclined Piles

The elastic center method[7,8] may be used to determine the forces in inclined piles. All piles are assumed to be hinged at each end and the rigid pile cap is assumed to rotate about the elastic center, thus producing forces in the piles which balance the moment of the external load about the elastic center. For simple pile arrangements, the location of the elastic center may be determined by inspection, as shown in Figure 4.21.

When the line of action of the external load passes through the elastic center, no rotation of the pile cap occurs and the forces in the piles, due to the translation of the pile cap, may be obtained by resolution.

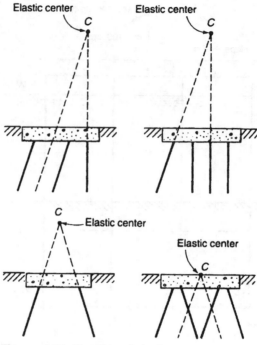

Figure 4.21 Location of elastic center

Example 4.9

Determine the forces, due to the indicated loads, in the raked piles shown in Exhibit 12. The piles have a batter of 1:4, and the line of action of the external loads passes through the elastic center.

Solution

Resolving forces vertically, the vertical component of the axial force in pile 1 is given by

$$V_1 = W/2 - FB/2$$
$$= 100/2 - 10 \times 4/2$$
$$= 30 \text{ kips}$$

The axial force in pile 1 is

$$P_1 = V_1\sqrt{1+B^2}/B$$
$$= 30\sqrt{17}/4$$
$$= 30.92 \text{ kips}$$

The vertical component of the axial force in pile 2 is

$$V_2 = W/2 + FB/2 = 70.00 \text{ kips}$$

The axial force in pile 2 is

$$P_2 = V_2\sqrt{1+B^2}/B = 72.15 \text{ kips}$$

When the line of action of the external loads does not pass through the elastic center, additional axial forces are produced in the piles. As shown in Figure 4.22, the external load, *R*, may be replaced by a force, *R*, through the elastic center plus

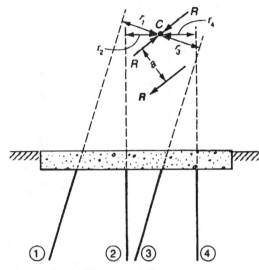

Exhibit 12

Elastic center $\downarrow W = 100$ kips

$F = 10$ kips $\longrightarrow$ C

8'

1   1

$B = 4$ $B = 4$

①   ②

|←2'→|←2'→|

Figure 4.22 Pile cap rotation

① ② ③ ④

a couple of magnitude

$$M = Ra$$

where a is the perpendicular distance from the line of action of R to the elastic center at C. The force, R, through the elastic center produces a translation of the pile cap, and the axial forces in the piles are determined by resolution as previously described.

The couple, M, causes a rotation, θ, of the pile cap which produces an axial deformation in each pile of magnitude

$$\delta = r_i\theta$$

where r_i is the distance from the elastic center perpendicular to each pile. The axial force produced in each pile is

$$P_i = EA\delta/L = EAr_i\theta/L$$

This axial force produces a moment about the elastic center of

$$M_P = P_ir_i = EAr_i^2\theta/L$$

For equilibrium, the sum of the moments of the pile forces about the elastic center must equal the external couple about the elastic center:

$$M = \theta\Sigma EAr^2/L$$
$$\theta = M/\Sigma EAr^2/L$$
$$P_i = (MEAr_i/L)/(\Sigma EAr^2/L) = Mr_i/\Sigma r^2 \ldots \text{for identical piles}$$

Example **4.10**

Determine the forces, due to the indicated loads, in the raked piles shown in Exhibit 13. The piles have a batter of 1:4 and have identical lengths and cross-sectional areas.

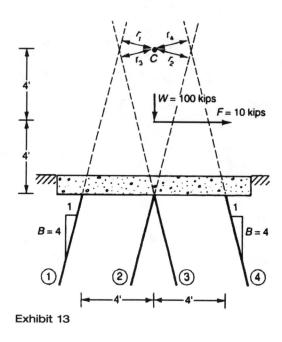

Exhibit 13

Solution

The axial forces due to the translation are obtained from Example 4.9 as

$$P_1 = P_2 = 30.92/2$$
$$= 15.46 \text{ kips}$$
$$P_3 = P_4 = 72.15/2$$
$$= 36.08 \text{ kips}$$

The couple about the elastic center due to the applied load is

$$M = 4F$$
$$= 4 \times 10$$
$$= 40 \text{ kip-feet}$$

The distance from the elastic center perpendicular to each pile is

$$r_1 = r_2 = r_3 = r_4 = 2\cos 14.04°$$
$$= 1.94 \text{ feet}$$
$$\Sigma r^2 = 4(1.94)^2$$
$$= 15.05$$

The axial forces in the piles due to rotation of the pile cap are

$$P_1 = P_3 = + Mr/\Sigma r^2$$
$$= 40 \times 1.94/15.05$$
$$= 5.15 \text{ kips} \dots \text{compression}$$
$$P_2 = P_4 = 5.15 \text{ kips} \dots \text{tension}$$

The final pile forces are given by the sum of the forces due to translation and rotation and are

$$P_1 = 15.46 + 5.15 = 20.61 \text{ kips}$$
$$P_2 = 15.46 - 5.15 = 10.31 \text{ kips}$$
$$P_3 = 36.08 + 5.15 = 41.23 \text{ kips}$$
$$P_4 = 36.08 - 5.15 = 30.93 \text{ kips}$$

Pile Cap Design

When the piles are symmetrically arranged about the column and do not exceed five in number, the truss analogy method[9] may be used, as shown in Figure 4.23. The pile cap is assumed to act as a three-dimensional triangulated space truss. The upper node of the truss is located at the center of the column with the lower nodes at the centers of the piles. The column load is transmitted to the piles by direct thrust on inclined planes through the concrete, with the reinforcement between the piles forming horizontal ties. The reinforcement must be placed within a band width[10] not exceeding three times the width of the piles. Since the reinforcement is fully stressed at the center of the piles, a full anchorage length must be provided beyond this point. By resolving forces at the lower nodes, the tensile force in the reinforcement of a four pile group is given by

$$T = Ws/8d$$

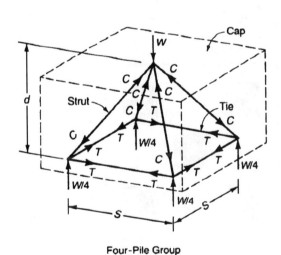
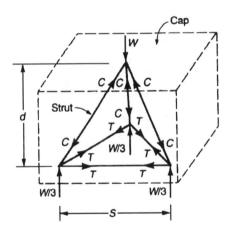

Four-Pile Group   Three-Pile Group

Figure 4.23 Pile cap truss analogy

In a three-pile group the tensile force is

$$T = Ws/9d$$

In a two-pile group the tensile force is

$$T = Ws/4d$$

In a five-pile group the tensile force is

$$T = Ws/10d$$

The area of reinforcement required is

$$A_s = T_u/\phi f_y$$

where

   ϕ = strength reduction factor = 0.90 from ACI Section 9.3. 2.6
   T_u = factored tie force
   f_y = reinforcement yield strength
   W = axial load in column
   s = distance between pile centers

Example **4.11**

Determine the area of Grade 60 reinforcement required in the pile cap shown in Exhibit 14. The concrete strength is 3000 pounds per square inch.

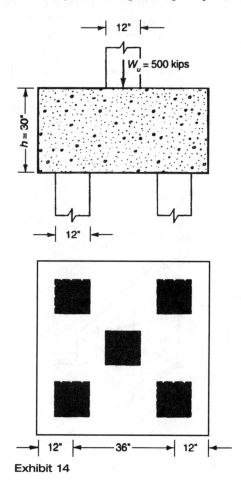

Exhibit 14

Solution

The force in each of the reinforcement ties is

$$T_u = W_u s/8d$$
$$= 500 \times 3/(8 \times 2)$$
$$= 93.75 \text{ kips}$$

The reinforcement area required for each tie is

$$A_s = T_u/\phi f_y$$
$$= 93.75/(0.75 \times 60)$$
$$= 2.08 \text{ square inches}$$

Since there are two ties in each direction, the total reinforcement area in each direction is

$$A_s = 2 \times 2.08$$
$$= 4.16 \text{ square inches}$$

Providing eight No. 7 bars gives an area of

$$A_s' = 4.80 \text{ square inches}$$
$$> A_s \dots \text{satisfactory}$$

This gives a reinforcement ratio based on the gross cross-sectional area of

$$\rho' = A_s'/bh$$
$$= 4.80/(60 \times 30)$$
$$= 0.0027$$

The minimum reinforcement ratio in a pile cap for Grade 60 bars, based on the gross cross-sectional area, is given by ACI Section 7.12 as

$$\rho'_{min} = 0.0018$$
$$< 0.0020 \dots \text{satisfactory}$$

SELECTED SYMBOLS AND ABBREVIATIONS

Symbol or Abbreviation	Description
A_s	Total required reinforcement area
$A_{s(min)}$	Minimum area of reinforcement
B	Width of footing
b	Width of footing
b_0	Length of critical perimeter for punching shear
c_1	Short side of column
c_2	Long side of column
d	Effective depth of footing
f_c'	Concrete strength
f_y	Reinforcement yield strength
f_p	Bearing pressure
H	Earth pressure
H_A	Total active pressure behind wall
H_P	Total passive pressure in front of wall
K	Rankine coefficient
L	Length of footing
M_u	Factored moment at critical section
P_u	Factored applied load
t_p	Base plate thickness
V_u	Factored shear at critical section
W	Weight
$\beta = l_2/l_1$	Ratio of long side to short side of footing
$\beta_c = c_2/c_1$	Ratio of long side to short side of column
μ	Coefficient of friction
ϕ	Strength reduction factor

REFERENCES

1. American Concrete Institute. *Building Code Requirements and Commentary for Reinforced Concrete* (ACI 318-02). Farmington Hills, MI, 2002.
2. American Institute of Steel Construction. *Manual of Steel Construction,* 9th ed. Chicago, 1989.
3. Williams, A. *Design of Reinforced Concrete Structures*, 3rd ed. Dearborn, Chicago, 2005.
4. American Concrete Institute. *Building Code Requirements for Masonry Structures* (ACI 530-02). Farmington Hills, MI, 2002.
5. Construction Industry Research and Information Association. *A Comparison of Quay Wall Design Methods*. CIRIA Technical Note 54. London, 1974.
6. Terzaghi, K. *Anchored Bulkheads*. Transactions, American Society of Civil Engineers, Volume 119. New York, 1954.
7. Westergaard, H. M. *The Resistance of Pile Groups*. Engineering Construction. New York, May 1918.
8. Vetter, C. P. *Design of Pile Foundations*. Transactions, American Society of Civil Engineers, Volume 64. New York, 1938.
9. Allen, A. H. *Reinforced Concrete Design to CP 110*. Cement and Concrete Association, London, 1974.
10. British Standards Institution. *BS 8110: Structural Use of Concrete*. London, 1985.

Seismic Design

OUTLINE

EARTHQUAKE PHENOMENA 236
Basic Seismology ■ Measurement of Earthquake Magnitude
and Intensity ■ Seismic Effects

STRUCTURAL DYNAMICS 242
Undamped Free Vibrations ■ Damped Free Vibrations ■ Multiple-
Degree-of-Freedom System

RESPONSE SPECTRA 252
Dynamic Response of Structures ■ Normalized Design
Spectra ■ Code Requirements ■ Site Classification Characteristics ■ Site
Coefficients ■ Adjusted Response Accelerations ■ Design
Response Accelerations ■ Fundamental Period ■ Building
Performance Criteria ■ Occupancy Categories and Importance
Factors ■ Ductility ■ Response Modification Coefficient ■ Classification
of Structural Systems ■ Combinations of Structural Systems ■ Seismic
Dead Load ■ Seismic Design Category ■ Seismic Response
Coefficient ■ Design Base Shear

MULTISTORY STRUCTURE 264
Vertical Distribution of Base Shear ■ Overturning ■ Story Drift ■ *P*-Delta
Effects ■ Diaphragm Loads

SIMPLIFIED LATERAL FORCE PROCEDURE 273
Base Shear ■ Simplified Vertical Distribution of Base Shear

RELIABILITY FACTOR 275
Design Load ■ Reliability Factor

LATERAL-FORCE-RESISTANT SYSTEM 278
Basic Components ■ Plywood Diaphragms ■ Collector
Elements ■ Wood Shear Wall ■ Braced Frame

STRUCTURAL ELEMENTS AND COMPONENTS 286
Anchorage of Concrete and Masonry Walls ■ Components
and Equipment Supported by Structures ■ Wall Cladding ■ Self-
Supporting Nonbuilding Structures

TORSION AND RIGIDITY 293

Rigid Diaphragm ■ Torsional Moment ■ Center of Mass and Center of Rigidity ■ Torsional Effects ■ Shear Wall Rigidity ■ Braced-Frame Stiffness

CONFIGURATION REQUIREMENTS 303

Structural Irregularities ■ Selection of Lateral Force Procedure

DYNAMIC LATERAL FORCE ANALYSIS 307

Modal Analysis Advantages ■ Modal Analysis Procedure

SEISMICALLY ISOLATED BUILDINGS 312

Advantages of Seismic Isolation ■ General Design Principles ■ Static Lateral Force Procedure

REFERENCES 316

EARTHQUAKE PHENOMENA

Basic Seismology

An earthquake is produced by the sudden rupture or slip of a geological fault.[1,2] Faults occur at the intersection of two segments of the earth's crust, and along the West Coast of the United States where the boundaries of two large tectonic plates, the Pacific plate and the North American plate, are located. The major fault occurring in California is the 600-mile-long San Andreas fault, a nearly vertical right lateral strike-slip fault, readily identified where it intersects the surface of the earth. The Loma Prieta earthquake of October 1989 occurred on the San Andreas fault,[3,4] as shown in Figure 5.1, and the direction of motion[3,5] is shown in Figure 5.2.

The sudden release of energy at the focus or hypocenter of the earthquake causes seismic waves to propagate through the earth's crust and produces vibrations on the earth's surface. The amplitude of the vibrations diminishes with distance from the epicenter, the point on the earth's surface immediately above the hypocenter, and may last for a few seconds or for more than one minute. Typically, a California earthquake is of short duration, with the Loma Prieta earthquake lasting only eight seconds. Two principal types of seismic waves are generated: body waves, which travel from the hypocenter directly through the earth's lithosphere, and surface waves, which travel from the epicenter along the surface of the earth. Body waves consist of the primary or P wave, a compression wave, and the secondary or S wave, a transverse shear wave.[6] Surface waves consist of the Love wave, which produces a sideways motion, and the Rayleigh wave, which produces a rotary wave–like motion.[6] Body waves have a higher frequency range and attenuate more rapidly than surface waves. Hence, structures with longer natural periods, such as high-rise buildings and bridges, are more at risk some distance from the epicenter than low-rise buildings, which have a short natural period.

Measurement of Earthquake Magnitude and Intensity

The Richter magnitude scale is a logarithm-based scale which utilizes the amplitude of seismic vibrations, recorded on a standard seismograph, to determine the strength of an earthquake. A unit increment on the scale represents a 10-fold

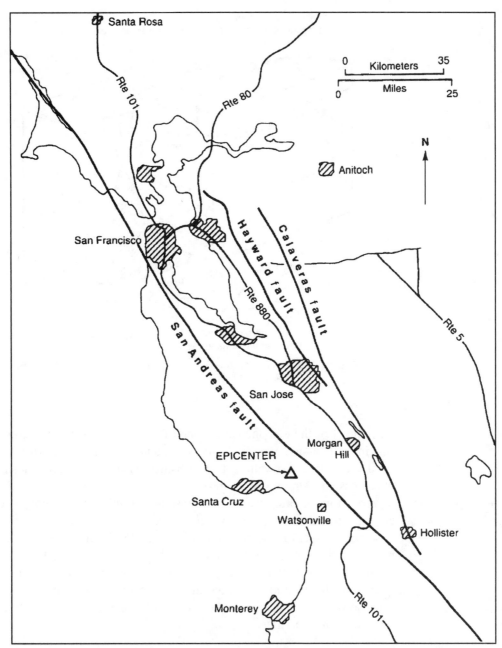

Figure 5.1 Location of Loma Prieta earthquake[4]

increase in amplitude and a 31.6-fold increase in energy released. Earthquakes of Richter magnitude 6, 7, and 8 are categorized respectively as moderate, major, and great earthquakes. Richter magnitude 8.5 is estimated to be the maximum that may be anticipated in California. The Loma Prieta earthquake had a magnitude of 7.1 and was the results of a rupture along a 25-mile-long segment of the San Andreas fault between Los Gatos and Watsonville.[3] The San Francisco earthquake of April 1906 had a magnitude of 8.25 and was the result of a rupture along a 270-mile-long segment of the San Andreas fault.

Earthquake intensity is measured using the modified Mercalli index, which is based on the observed effects of an earthquake at a specific site and a qualitative

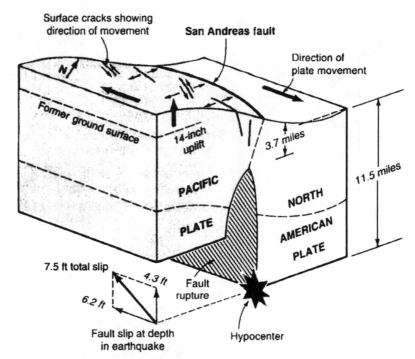

Figure 5.2 Motion on the San Andreas fault during the Loma Prieta earthquake[5]

assessment of the damage caused, and is an indication of the severity of ground shaking at that site. Modified Mercalli intensity values range from a value of I to a value of XII. Index value VII is classified as strong shaking causing damage to older masonry structures, chimneys, and furniture. Index value VIII is classified as very strong shaking causing collapse of unreinforced masonry structures, towers, and monuments. The soil conditions at a particular location affect the observed impact on the surrounding area. This is illustrated by the isoseismal map[3,5] for the Loma Prieta earthquake shown in Figure 5.3. The seismic damage caused at a particular site is influenced by the magnitude, duration, and frequency of the ground vibration, distance from the epicenter, geological conditions between the epicenter and the site, soil properties at the site, and the building type and characteristics.

Seismic Effects

Structural damage during an earthquake is caused by the response of the structure to the ground motion input at its base. The dynamic forces produced in the structure are due to the inertia of its vibrating elements. The magnitude of the effective peak acceleration reached by the ground vibration directly affects the magnitude of the dynamic forces observed in the structure. Accelerograms for the Loma Prieta earthquake[3] obtained at rock sites situated 5 to 20 kilometers from the epicenter are shown in Figure 5.4. Figure 5.5 shows similar accelerograms[3] for rock sites located 76 to 80 kilometers from the epicenter.

The response of the structure exceeds the ground motion, and this dynamic magnification depends on the duration and frequency content of the ground vibration,

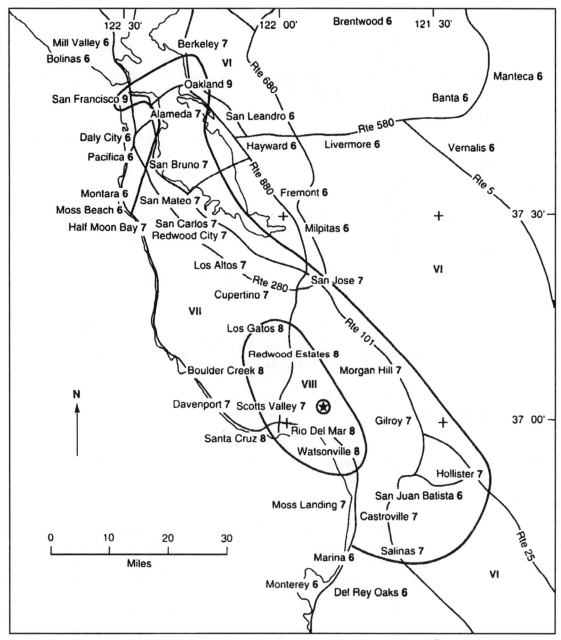

Figure 5.3 Isoseismal map of Mercalli intensities for the Loma Prieta earthquake[5]

the soil properties at the site, distance from the epicenter, and the dynamic characteristics of the structure. The average spectral responses for four different soil types for single-degree-of-freedom systems with 5 percent damping have been determined for the Loma Prieta earthquake[3] and are shown in Figure 5.6. The spectral shapes[3] obtained by normalizing the response curves with respect to the peak ground acceleration are shown in Figure 5.7.

Soil liquefaction is another effect produced by earthquakes. A saturated uniform, fine-grained sand or silt, when subjected to repeated vibration, experiences an increase in pore water pressure because of a redistribution of its particles, with

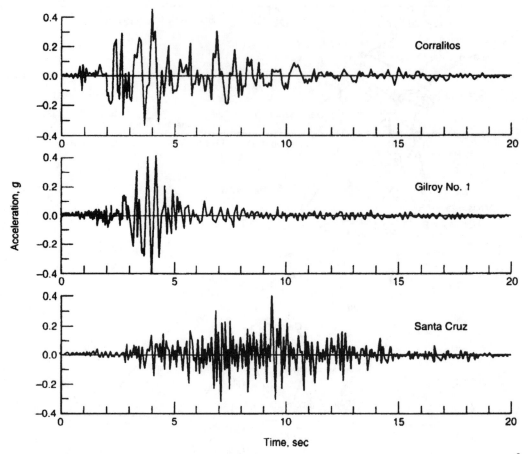

Figure 5.4 Accelerograms of motions recorded at rock sites within 20 kilometers of the source[3]

a consequent reduction in shear strength. This produces a condition similar to quicksand, resulting in a loss of bearing capacity and causing settlement and collapse of structures. In the Loma Prieta earthquake, liquefaction occurred close to the epicenter and in a number of susceptible outlying areas in San Francisco and Oakland.

A number of methods to prevent liquefaction are available. (1) Drainage may be installed to lower the ground water table and remove the pore water. However, the resulting settlement may affect adjacent structures. (2) Preconsolidation of the soil may be achieved by vibroflotation techniques, and this also may affect adjacent structures. (3) Placing a porous overburden over the site will produce preconsolidation and result in increased pore pressures being required before liquefaction can occur. (4) In order to increase the shear strength of the soil, soil grouting or chemical injection may be employed.

Alternatively, all deleterious soil may be removed and replaced with sound material, or pile foundations may be employed with the piles penetrating the unsatisfactory layer to found at a stable level.

When the epicenter of an earthquake is located on a sea bed, a destructive tidal wave, or tsunami, may be produced. The tidal wave may reach a height of 50 feet. Destructive tsunamis occurred in Hawaii in 1946 and in Alaska in 1964.

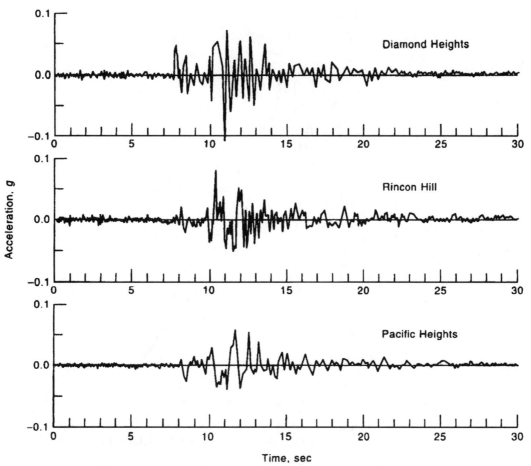

Figure 5.5 Accelerograms of motions recorded at rock sites in San Francisco[3]

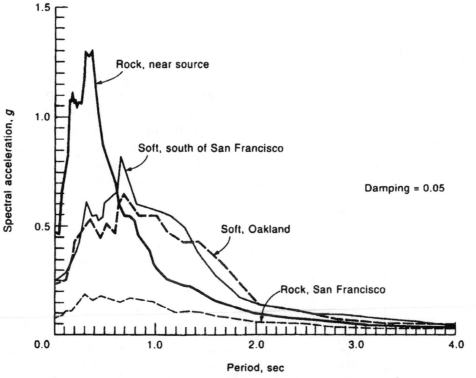

Figure 5.6 Average spectral shapes for motions recorded at various sites[3]

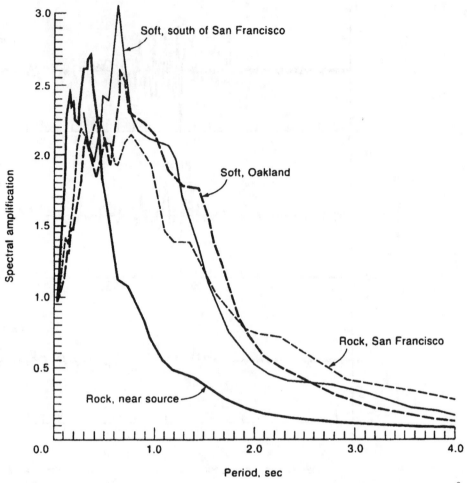

Figure 5.7 Average normalized spectral shapes for motions recorded at various sites[3]

STRUCTURAL DYNAMICS

Undamped Free Vibrations

The single-bay, single-story frame shown in Figure 5.8 is considered to have all of its mass concentrated at the infinitely rigid roof structure. If axial deformation in the columns is neglected, the frame exhibits only one degree of dynamic freedom, which is the lateral or sway displacement indicated. A dynamic model of the structure consists of a single column with stiffness k supporting a mass of magnitude m to give the inverted pendulum or lollipop structure shown. If the mass of this simple oscillator is subjected to an initial displacement and released,

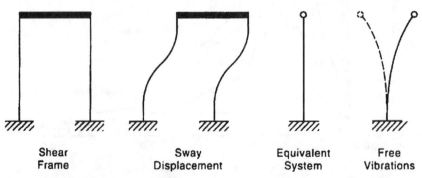

| Shear Frame | Sway Displacement | Equivalent System | Free Vibrations |

Figure 5.8 Simple sway oscillator

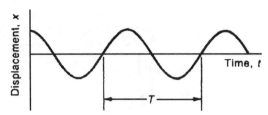

Figure 5.9 Undamped free vibrations

with no external forces acting, free vibrations occur about the static position. The force required to produce a displacement x is

$$P = kx$$

Applying Newton's second law of motion to derive the inertia force produced, and denoting the acceleration of the mass by $\ddot{x}$ gives the expression

$$P = -m\ddot{x}$$

Hence, the time-dependent equation of dynamic equilibrium is

$$0 = -m\ddot{x} + kx$$

This is a second-order, homogeneous, linear differential equation and has the solution

$$x = (\dot{x}_0/\omega)\sin\omega t + x_0 \cos\omega t$$

This expression is a representation of simple harmonic motion, as shown in Figure 5.9, with

$\quad x$ = displacement at time t
$\quad x_0$ = displacement at time $t = 0$
$\quad \dot{x}_0$ = velocity at time $t = 0$
$\quad \omega$ = circular natural frequency or angular velocity
$\qquad = \sqrt{k/m}$
$\qquad = 2\pi/T$
$\qquad = 2\pi f$
where
$\quad T$ = natural period
$\quad f$ = natural frequency of vibration

The form of these expressions indicates that the natural period increases as the mass of the system increases and the stiffness decreases.

Example 5.1

The space grid roof structure of the single-story building shown in Exhibit 1 may be considered infinitely rigid, with a dead load of 20 pounds per square foot. The side sheeting has a dead load, including columns and side rails, of 10 pounds per square foot. All columns are size W10 × 30 and may be considered axially inextensible. If damping may be neglected, determine the dynamic properties of the structure in the east-west direction.

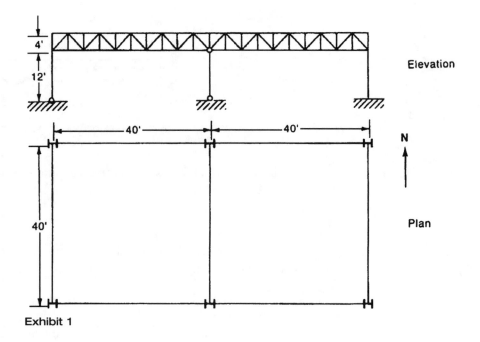

Elevation

N

Plan

Exhibit 1

Solution

The weight tributary to the roof is given by

$$w = 0.02 \times 40 \times 80 + 2 \times 0.01(6 + 4)(40 + 80)$$
$$= 88 \text{ kips}$$

The stiffness of the two east columns is

$$k_E = 12EI/l^3$$
$$= 12 \times 29,000(2 \times 170)/(12 \times 12)^3$$
$$= 39.63 \text{ kips per inch}$$

The stiffness of the center columns is

$$k_C = 0$$

The stiffness of the two west columns is

$$k_W = 3EI/l^3$$
$$= 9.91 \text{ kips per inch}$$

The total stiffness in the east-west direction is

$$k = k_E + k_C + k_W$$
$$= 39.63 + 9.91$$
$$= 49.54 \text{ kips per inch}$$

The circular natural frequency is given by

$$\omega = \sqrt{k/m}$$
$$= \sqrt{kg/w}$$
$$= \sqrt{49.54 \times 386.4/88}$$
$$= 14.75 \text{ radians per second}$$

The natural frequency is given by

$$f = \omega/2\pi$$
$$= 2.35 \text{ hertz}$$

The natural period is given by

$$T = 1/f$$
$$= 0.43 \text{ seconds}$$

Damped Free Vibrations

In practice, the internal frictional resistance in an oscillatory system will cause any induced vibration to die out. The frictional resistance, or damping, dissipates the energy of the system by transforming it into heat. By assuming that the resistance is equivalent to a viscous damping force, which is proportional to the velocity of motion of the system, the dynamic motion may be readily analyzed.[7] Applying a damping coefficient, c, to the simple oscillator of Figure 5.8 provides the differential equation

$$0 = m\ddot{x} + c\dot{x} + kx$$

Substituting the function $x = A \exp(qt)$ in this expression yields the auxiliary equation

$$0 = mq^2 + cq + k$$

which has the roots

$$q_1, q_2 = -c/2m \pm [(c/2m)^2 - \omega^2]^{1/2}$$

Three complementary functions are possible for the system depending on whether the roots of the auxiliary equation are equal, real and distinct, or complex. These three conditions are termed critical damping, overdamping, and underdamping.

Critical Damping
The roots of the auxiliary equation are equal if

$$0 = (c/2m)^2 - w^2$$

Hence, $c = 2m\omega = c_c$, where c_c = critical damping coefficient. The complementary function reduces to

$$x = (A + Bt) \exp(c_c t/2m)$$

where the constants A and B may be determined from the initial conditions. The critical damping coefficient is the minimum value of the damping coefficient sufficient to bring the system to rest exponentially without oscillation.

Overdamping
The roots of the auxiliary equation are real and distinct if

$$(c/2m)^2 > \omega^2$$
$$c > 2m\omega$$
$$c > c_c$$

The complementary function reduces to

$$x = A \exp(q_1 t) + B \exp(q_2 t)$$

The motion of the overdamped system is similar to that of the critically damped system.

Underdamping

For the general condition of an underdamped system with a damping coefficient less than c_c, the roots of the auxiliary equation are complex and may be written in the form

$$q_1, q_2 = -c/2m \pm i\omega_D$$

where $i^2 = -1$. The complementary function reduces to

$$x = (A \sin \omega_D t + B \cos \omega_D t)e^{-ct/2m}$$

which is the equation of oscillatory motion where successive amplitudes form a descending geometrical progression with a common ratio of $\exp(-c\pi/2m\omega_D)$. The damped circular frequency of the system is given by

$$\begin{aligned}
\omega_D &= [\omega^2 - (c/2m)^2]^{1/2} \\
&= \omega[1 - (c/2m\omega)^2]^{1/2} \\
&= \omega[1 - (c/c_c)^2]^{1/2} \\
&= \omega(1 - \xi^2)^{1/2}
\end{aligned}$$

where ξ is defined as the damping ratio and is a measure of the damping capacity of a system. The damped natural period of the system is given by

$$\begin{aligned}
T_D &= 2\pi/\omega_D \\
&= 2\pi/\omega(1 - \xi^2)^{1/2} \\
&= T/(1 - \xi^2)^{1/2}
\end{aligned}$$

Since the amount of viscous damping in buildings is less than 15 percent of the critical value, the damped circular frequency and the undamped circular frequency are almost identical, and the undamped value is customarily used for the damped value in practical applications. Similarly, the amplitude peaks may be assumed to lie on the exponential curve $x = \exp(-ct/2m)$, as shown in Figure 5.10, and the ratio between any two successive amplitude peaks, a time interval T_D

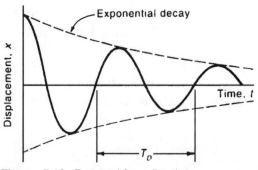

Figure 5.10 Damped free vibrations

apart, is constant. The logarithmic decrement is defined as the natural logarithm of this ratio and is given by

$$\delta = cT_D/2m$$
$$= \xi\omega T_D$$
$$= 2\pi\xi/(1-\xi^2)^{1/2}$$
$$= 2\pi\xi$$

As it is not possible to analytically determine either c or ξ, this latter expression provides a practical means of experimentally obtaining the damping characteristics of a vibrating system. Typical values of the damping coefficient range from 2 percent of the critical damping coefficient for welded steel structures, to 5 percent for concrete framed structures, to 10 percent for masonry shear walls, to 15 percent for wood structures.

Example **5.2**

The frame shown in Exhibit 2 has an infinitely rigid beam and axially inextensible columns. The frame weight of 30 kips may be considered concentrated at the level of the beam, and each column has a flexural rigidity of 1.69×10^6 kip-inches. Sway oscillations are induced in the frame, and it is determined that the amplitude of vibration reduces to 25 percent of its initial value in 10 full cycles of oscillation. Determine the damping characteristics.

Solution

The mass of the frame is given by

$$m = 30/32.2$$
$$= 0.932 \text{ kip-second}^2 \text{ per foot}$$

The stiffness of the frame in the sway mode is given by

$$k = 2 \times 12EI/l^3$$
$$= 2 \times 12 \times 1.69 \times 10^6 \times 12/(240)^3$$
$$= 35.208 \text{ kips per foot}$$

The circular natural frequency of the frame is

$$\omega = \sqrt{k/m}$$
$$= 6.147 \text{ radians per second}$$

The logarithmic decrement is given by

$$10\delta = \ln(100/25)$$
$$\delta = 0.1386$$

The damping ratio is given by

$$\xi = \delta/2\pi$$
$$= 0.02206$$

The damped circular frequency is

$$\omega = \omega(1-\xi^2)^{1/2}$$
$$= 6.1455 \text{ radians per second}$$

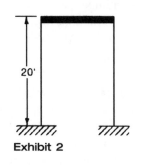

20'

Exhibit 2

The critical damping coefficient is given by

$$c_c = 2m\omega$$
$$= 11.458 \text{ kip-seconds per foot}$$

The damping coefficient is

$$c = \xi c_c$$
$$= 0.2528 \text{ kip-second per foot}$$

The damped natural period of the system is given by

$$T_D = 2\pi/\omega_D$$
$$= 1.0225 \text{ seconds}$$

The natural period is

$$T = 2\pi/\omega$$
$$= 1.0223 \text{ seconds}$$

Multiple-Degree-of-Freedom System

The multistory structure shown in Figure 5.11 may be idealized as a multistory shear building by assuming that the mass is lumped at the floor and roof diaphragms, the diaphragms are infinitely rigid, and the columns are axially inextensible but laterally flexible. The dynamic response of the system is represented by the lateral displacements of the lumped masses, with the number of degrees of dynamic freedom, or modes of vibration, n, being equal to the number of masses. The resultant vibration of the system is given by the superposition of the vibrations of each lumped mass. Each individual mode of vibration has its own period and may be represented by a single-degree-of-freedom system of the same period, and each mode shape, or eigenvector, is of constant relative shape regardless of the amplitude of the displacement. A reference amplitude of a given mode shape may be assigned unit value to give the normal mode shape. The actual amplitudes must be obtained from the initial conditions. Figure 5.11 shows the first three modes of the five-story shear building. The mode of vibration with the longest period (lowest frequency) is termed the first fundamental mode. Modes with shorter periods (higher frequencies) are termed higher modes or harmonics.

A modal analysis procedure may be utilized to determine the dynamic response of a multiple-degree-of-freedom structure.[8] The maximum response for

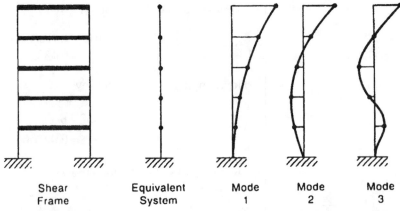

| Shear Frame | Equivalent System | Mode 1 | Mode 2 | Mode 3 |

Figure 5.11 Multistory structure

the separate modes is obtained by modeling each as an individual single-degree-of-freedom oscillator. As the maximum values cannot all occur simultaneously, these values are combined statistically to obtain the total response. The higher modes do not contribute significantly to the total response, and an acceptable procedure is to utilize sufficient modes to ensure that 90 percent of the participating mass of the structure is included in the calculation.

Since each degree of dynamic freedom provides one equation of dynamic equilibrium, the resultant vibration of the system consists of n such equations and may be expressed in matrix form, for undamped free vibrations, as

$$\{0\} = [M]\{\ddot{x}\} + [K]\{x\}$$

For simple harmonic motion, this reduces to

$$\{0\} = ([K] - \omega^2[M])\{x\}$$

This expression is a representation of the eigenvalue equation with

$[K]$ = stiffness matrix of the system
$[M]$ = diagonal mass matrix
$\{x\}$ = eigenvector or mode shape associated with the circular frequency, or eigenvalue, ω

The eigenvalue equation has a nontrivial solution only if the determinant of the coefficient matrix is zero. Thus, the frequency determinant is

$$\left| [K] - \omega^2[M] \right| = 0$$

Expansion of this determinant yields the characteristic polynomial of degree n in (ω^2), the roots of which provide the eigenvalues. Back-substituting the eigenvalues in the eigenvalue equation yields the eigenvectors for each mode.

Example **5.3**

A two-story shear building with the properties shown in Exhibit 3 and with a damping ratio of 5 percent is located on a rock site near the source of the Loma Prieta earthquake. Determine the lateral forces and displacements at each level using the spectral ordinates of Figure 5.6.

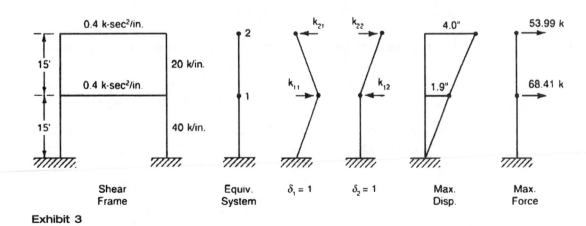

Exhibit 3

Solution

Unit shear displacement is imposed on each node in turn and the coefficient k_{ij}, of the stiffness matrix is obtained as the force produced at node i by a unit displacement at node j. The stiffness matrix is

$$[K] = \begin{bmatrix} k_{11} & k_{12} \\ k_{21} & k_{22} \end{bmatrix}$$

$$= \begin{bmatrix} (40+20) & -20 \\ -20 & 20 \end{bmatrix}$$

$$= \begin{bmatrix} 60 & -20 \\ -20 & 20 \end{bmatrix}$$

The diagonal mass matrix is

$$[M] = \begin{bmatrix} 0.4 & 0 \\ 0 & 0.4 \end{bmatrix}$$

The eigenvalue equation is

$$\begin{Bmatrix} 0 \\ 0 \end{Bmatrix} = \left(\begin{bmatrix} 60 & -20 \\ -20 & 20 \end{bmatrix} - \omega^2 \begin{bmatrix} 0.4 & 0 \\ 0 & 0.4 \end{bmatrix} \right) \begin{Bmatrix} x_1 \\ x_2 \end{Bmatrix}$$

The frequency determinant is

$$T = \begin{vmatrix} (60 - 0.4\omega^2) & -20 \\ -20 & (20 - 0.4\omega^2) \end{vmatrix} = 0.16w^4 - 32w^2 + 800$$

Equating this polynomial in ω to zero provides the circular natural frequencies for the two modes of vibration:

$$\omega_1 = 5.41 \text{ radians per second}$$
$$\omega_2 = 13.07 \text{ radians per second}$$

The corresponding natural periods are

$$T_1 = 1.16 \text{ seconds}$$
$$T_2 = 0.48 \text{ seconds}$$

From the response curves of Figure 5.6, the spectral accelerations are

$$S_{a1} = 0.25g = 96.6 \text{ inches per second}^2$$
$$S_{a2} = 0.85g = 328.4 \text{ inches per second}^2$$

Substituting the values of ω_1 and ω_2 in the eigenvalue equation, and setting the first components of the mode shape factors to unity, provides the modal matrix

$$[x] = \begin{bmatrix} 1 & 1 \\ 2.414 & -0.414 \end{bmatrix}$$

The normalized modal matrix has the orthogonalilty property[7]

$$[I] = [\Phi]^T [M][\Phi]$$

The components of the normalized modal matrix are given by

$$\phi_{ij} = x_{ij} \Big/ \left(\sum_{k=1}^{n} m_{kk} x_{kj}^{2} \right)^{1/2}$$

The normalized modal matrix is

$$[\Phi] = \begin{bmatrix} 0.605 & 1.461 \\ 1.461 & -0.605 \end{bmatrix}$$

The column vector of participation factors[8] is given by

$$\{P\} = [\Phi]^T [M]\{1\}$$
$$= \begin{Bmatrix} 0.826 \\ 0.342 \end{Bmatrix}$$

Assuming the structure remains fully elastic, the matrix of nodal displacements is given by

$$[\delta] = [\Phi]\,[P]\,[S_a]/[\omega^2]$$

where
   $[P]$ = diagonal matrix of participation factors
   $[S_a]$ = diagonal matrix of spectral accelerations
   $[\omega^2]$ = diagonal matrix of squared modal frequencies

Executing the necessary matrix operations gives

$$[\delta] = \begin{bmatrix} 1.648 & 0.961 \\ 3.980 & -0.398 \end{bmatrix}$$

The resultant maximum displacement at each node is obtained from the square root of the sum of the squares of the relevant row vector and is given by the column vector

$$[\delta_c] = \begin{Bmatrix} 1.9 \\ 4.0 \end{Bmatrix}$$

The matrix of lateral forces at each node is given by

$$[F] = [K][\delta]$$
$$= \begin{bmatrix} 19.29 & 65.63 \\ 46.64 & -27.19 \end{bmatrix}$$

Using the square-root-of-the-sum-of-the-squares method, the resultant maximum lateral force at each node is given by

$$[F_c] = \begin{bmatrix} 68.41 \\ 53.99 \end{bmatrix}$$

The row vector of base shears is

$$[V] = ([F]^T \{1\})^T$$
$$= [65.93 \quad 38.44]$$

Taking the square root of the sum of the squares, the resultant base shear is

$$V_c = \sqrt{V_{11}^2 + V_{12}^2}$$
$$= 76.32 \text{ kips}$$

RESPONSE SPECTRA

Dynamic Response of Structures

The member forces produced in a structure by gravity loads are static forces which are time independent. Seismic forces are produced in a structure by a variable ground vibration which causes a time-dependent response in the structure. The response generated depends on the magnitude, duration, and harmonic content of the exciting ground motion; the dynamic properties of the structure; and the characteristics of the soil deposits at the site. A response curve is a graph of the maximum, or spectral, response of a range of single-degree-of-freedom oscillators to a specified ground motion, plotted against the frequency or period of the oscillators. The damping ratio of the oscillator may be varied, and the response recorded may be displacement, velocity, or acceleration. The relationship between these functions is

$$S_a = \omega S_v = \omega^2 S_d$$

where
  S_a = spectral acceleration
  S_v = spectral velocity
  S_d = spectral displacement

Because of this interrelationship, all three spectra may be plotted on the same graph using tripartite axes and logarithmic scales.

Normalized Design Spectra

The response of a simple oscillator to variable seismic ground motions may be determined by the Duhamel integral technique.[7,9] This results in the response curve for a ground motion specific to a particular accelerogram. For design purposes, the response curve must be representative of the characteristics of all seismic events which may be experienced at a particular location. In determining the response of a system, the maximum considered ground acceleration[10] is used. This is defined as a seismic event with a 2 percent probability of being exceeded in 50 years and has a recurrence interval of 2500 years. The selected spectra, which should include both near and distant earthquakes, are averaged and normalized to

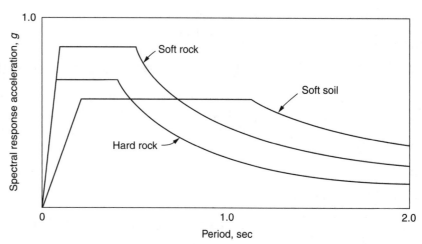

Figure 5.12 Representative response spectra

eliminate irregularities. Since soil conditions at a site substantially affect spectral shapes, separate response curves are required for each representative soil type as shown in Figure 5.12. These spectra are applicable to systems with a 5 percent damping ratio. Values of the ground response coefficients. S_S and S_1 are mapped in the IBC and are also provided on a CD-ROM issued with the code. S_S represents the response acceleration for a period of 0.2 seconds and S_1 represents the response acceleration for a period of 1.0 second.

Code Requirements

The IBC[11] refers to the ASCE[12] standard for many of its code requirements. Complete provisions for the design of simplified structures are contained in IBC Section 1617.5 but, for more complex structures, the provisions of the ASCE standard must be utilized. In accordance with IBC Section 1614.1, the seismic design of all structures may be performed by using the provisions of ASCE Sections 9.1 through 9.6, 9.13 and 9.14 in their entirety. These provisions are applied without modification and are in lieu of IBC Sections 1613 through 1623.

Determination of the importance factor and seismic use group is governed by IBC Sections 1604.5 and 1616.2 which refer to IBC Table 1604.5. Hence, this table, which differs in some details from the ASCE equivalent, must be used to establish the occupancy category and seismic use group of a structure.

Since use of the ASCE provisions provides the simplest approach to seismic design, this text applies the ASCE provisions.

Site Classification Characteristics

ASCE Table 9.4.1.2 specifies six different soil types and requires the use of soil class D when insufficient geotechnical data are available to accurately establish the soil type. Soil classes E and F allow for the large amplifications which occur on sites with very soft soil deposits.

Site Coefficients

Site coefficients are amplification factors applied to the ground response parameters and are a function of the site classification characteristics. F_a is the short-period or acceleration-based amplification factor and is tabulated in

ASCE Table 9.4.1.2.4a. F_v is the long-period or velocity-based amplification factor and is tabulated in ASCE Table 9.4.1.2.4b.

Adjusted Response Accelerations

The maximum considered ground accelerations must be adjusted by the site coefficients to allow for the site classification effects. ASCE Equations (9.4.1.2.4-1) and (9.4.1.2.4-2) define the modified spectral response accelerations at short periods and at a period of 1 second as

$$S_{MS} = F_a S_S$$
$$S_{M1} = F_v S_1$$

Design Response Accelerations

The design objective of the ASCE design method is to provide a margin of safety of 1.5 against collapse under the maximum considered earthquake. This is achieved by designing a structure for two-thirds times the maximum considered earthquake and relying on the overstrength of the structure to prevent collapse under a seismic event with a magnitude 50 percent greater than the design level ground motion. The design response accelerations for a period of 0.2 second and for a period of 1 second are given by ASCE Equations (9.4.1.2.5-1) and (9.4.1.2.5-2) as

$$S_{DS} = 2S_{MS}/3$$
$$S_{D1} = 2S_{M1}/3$$

where

S_{DS} = 5 percent damped design response acceleration, for a period of 0.2 second
S_{D1} = 5 percent damped design response acceleration, for a period of 1 second

The design response spectrum is derived from these parameters as indicated in Figure 5.13, where

T = fundamental period of the structure
$T_S = S_{D1}/S_{DS}$
$T_O = 0.2S_{D1}/S_{DS}$

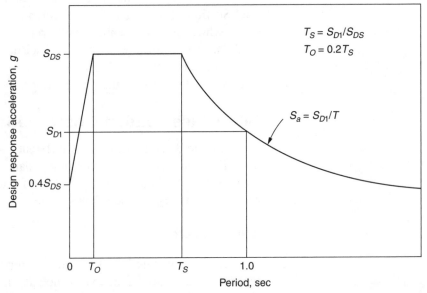

Figure 5.13 Construction of response spectra

For periods greater than or equal to T_O and less than or equal to T_S the design response acceleration is equal to S_{DS}.

For periods greater than T_S the design response acceleration is given by ASCE Equation (9.4.1.2.6-2) as

$$S_a = S_{D1}/T$$

Fundamental Period

Three methods are provided in ASCE Section 9.5.5.3 for determining the natural period of vibration. The *general approximate method* uses ASCE Equation (9.5.5.3.2-1), which is

$T_a = 0.028(h_n)^{0.8}$ for steel moment-resisting frames

$T_a = 0.016(h_n)^{0.9}$ for reinforced concrete moment-resisting frames

$T_a = 0.030(h_n)^{0.75}$ for eccentrically braced steel frames

$T_a = 0.020(h_n)^{0.75}$ for all other structural systems

where

h_n = height in feet of the roof above the base, not including the height of penthouses or parapets

The form of this expression indicates that the natural period increases as the height of the structure increases and is greater for steel frames than for concrete frames.

For *moment-resisting frames* not exceeding 12 stories and having a minimum story height of 10 feet, the approximate period may be determined from ASCE Equation (9.5.5.3.2-1a), which is

$$T_a = 0.1N$$

where N = number of stories.

Alternatively, the *Rayleigh procedure* as given in NEHRP[10] Section 5.4.2 may be used:

$$T = 2\pi \left(\Sigma w_i \delta_i^2 \big/ g \, \Sigma f_i \delta_i \right)^{1/2}$$
$$= (0.32)\left(\Sigma w_i \delta_i^2 \big/ \Sigma f_i \delta_i \right)^{1/2}$$

where

δ_i = elastic deflection at level i

f_i = lateral force at level i

w_i = seismic dead load located at level i

g = acceleration due to gravity

The lateral forces f_i represent any lateral force distribution increasing approximately uniformly with height as shown in Figure 5.14. This distribution, in the form of an inverted triangle, corresponds to the distribution of base shear which is assumed in the NEHRP Commentary and is equivalent to the inertial forces produced in a frame with uniform mass distribution, equal story heights, and acceleration increasing uniformly with height. If the contribution of the nonstructural elements to the stiffness of the structure is underestimated, the calculated

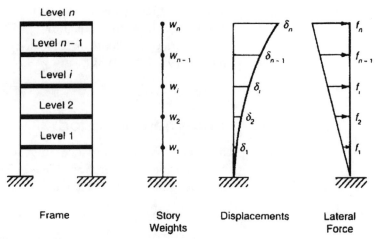

Level n

Level $n-1$

Level i

Level 2

Level 1

Frame

w_n

w_{n-1}

w_i

w_2

w_1

Story
Weights

δ_n

δ_{n-1}

δ_i

δ_2

δ_1

Displacements

f_n

f_{n-1}

f_i

f_2

f_1

Lateral
Force

Figure 5.14 Rayleigh procedure

deflections and natural periods are overestimated, giving a value for the force coefficient which is too low. To reduce the effects of this error, ASCE Section 9.5.5.3 specifies that the value of the natural period determined by the Rayleigh procedure may not exceed the value calculated using the approximate method of ASCE Equation (9.5.5.3.2-1) or (9.5.5.3.2-1a), as appropriate, multiplied by the coefficients in ASCE Table 9.5.5.3.1.

Example 5.4

A three-story, steel, moment-resisting frame with the properties shown in Exhibit 4, with a height of 36 feet and with a damping ratio of 5 percent, is located on a site with a value for S_1 of 0.2. Calculate the fundamental period of vibration using ASCE Equation (9.5.5.3.2-1) and by the Rayleigh method.

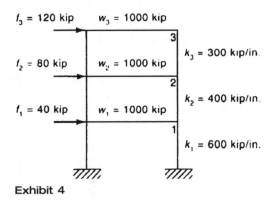

$f_3 = 120$ kip $w_3 = 1000$ kip

3

$k_3 = 300$ kip/in.

$f_2 = 80$ kip $w_2 = 1000$ kip

2

$k_2 = 400$ kip/in.

$f_1 = 40$ kip $w_1 = 1000$ kip

1

$k_1 = 600$ kip/in.

Exhibit 4

Solution

The natural period is given by ASCE Equation (9.5.5.3.2-1) as

$$T_a = 0.028(h_n)^{0.8}$$

where
h_n = roof height = 36 feet

Then the natural period is

$$T_a = (0.028)(36)^{0.8}$$
$$= 0.49 \text{ seconds}$$

Using the Rayleigh method, and applying the force system indicated, the displacements at each level are given by

$$\delta_1 = (f_3 + f_2 + f_1)/k_1$$
$$= (120 + 80 + 40)/600$$
$$= 0.4 \text{ inches}$$

$$\delta_2 = (f_3 + f_2)/k_2 + \delta_1$$
$$= (120 + 80)/400 + 0.4$$
$$= 0.9 \text{ inches}$$

$$\delta_3 = f_3/k_3 + \delta_2$$
$$= 120/300 + 0.9$$
$$= 1.3 \text{ inches}$$

The natural period is given by NEHRP Equation (C5.4.3) as

$$T = 2\pi \left(\sum w_i \delta_i^2 \Big/ g \sum f_i \delta_i \right)^{1/2}$$
$$= 0.32 \left(\sum w_i \delta_i^2 \Big/ \sum f_i \delta_i \right)^{1/2}$$

The relevant values are

Level	w_i	f_i	δ_i	$w_i \delta_i^2$	$f_i \delta_i$
3	1000	120	1.3	1690	156
2	1000	80	0.9	810	72
1	1000	40	0.4	160	16
Total				2660	244

Thus

$$T = 0.32(2660/244)^{1/2}$$
$$= 1.06 \text{ seconds}$$

The natural period obtained by Rayleigh's method, in accordance with ASCE Section 9.5.5.3 and Table 9.5.5.3.1, is limited to $1.5T_a$ for structures with a value of 0.2 for S_{D1}.

$$1.5T_a = (1.5)(0.49)$$
$$= 0.74$$
$$< 1.06 \text{ seconds}$$

Hence the maximum value of $T = 0.74$ seconds.

Building Performance Criteria

Normal building structures designed in accordance with the IBC Code may be expected to resist an upper-level earthquake, with a recurrence interval of 2500 years, without collapse and without endangering life safety.[13] It is anticipated that structural and nonstructural damage will occur, which will necessitate the shutdown of the facility until repairs can be effected. In some circumstances this will be an unacceptable situation, and a design is required which will ensure the continuation of operational capacity.

Occupancy Categories and Importance Factors

Essential facilities and facilities housing hazardous materials are assigned to seismic use group III in IBC Table 1604.5 and in ASCE Tables 1-1 and 9.1.4. Essential facilities are defined in these tables as hospitals, fire and police stations, emergency response centers, and buildings housing equipment for these facilities. Hazardous facilities are defined as structures housing materials which will endanger the safety of the public if released. In order to ensure that essential and hazardous facilities remain functional after an upper-level earthquake, an important factor, I_E, of 1.5 is assigned to these facilities, which are classified as seismic use group III. This has the effect of increasing the prescribed design base shear by 50 percent, raising the level at which inelastic behavior occurs and increasing the level at which the operation of essential facilities is compromised. In the case of some business facilities, the loss of operational capacity following an earthquake may constitute an unacceptable impact on business competitiveness. In addition, downtime costs caused by an earthquake may exceed the costs necessary to increase the seismic safety of the structure. In these circumstances, the building owner may find that improving seismic performance is economically justifiable.

Seismic use group II buildings are facilities with a high occupant load, such as buildings where more than 300 people congregate, schools with a capacity exceeding 250, colleges with a capacity exceeding 500, health care facilities with a capacity of 50 or more that do not have emergency treatment facilities, jails, and power stations. These structures are allocated a seismic importance factor I_E of 1.25.

All other structures are allocated to seismic use group I, with a seismic importance factor I_E of 1.00.

Ductility

Ductility is a measure of the ability of a structural system to deform beyond its elastic load-carrying capacity without collapse. This allows a redundant structure to absorb energy while successive plastic hinges are formed. For applied static loading, collapse of the structure occurs when a sufficient number of hinges have formed to produce a mechanism. In the case of cyclic seismic loading, the structure undergoes successive loading and unloading, and the force-displacement relationship follows a sequence of hysteresis loops. For an idealized elastic-plastic system, this is illustrated in Figure 5.15, where the enclosed area is a measure of the hysteretic energy dissipation.

Response Modification Coefficient

As it is uneconomical to design a structure to remain within its elastic range for a major earthquake, advantage is taken of the nonlinear energy-absorbing capacity of the system to allow limited structural damage without impairing the vertical

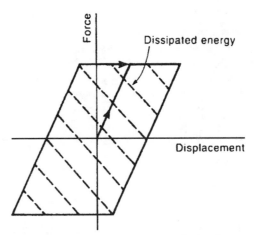

Figure 5.15 Hysteretic energy dissipation

load-carrying capacity and endangering life safety. In addition, as yielding occurs, the natural period and the damping ratio increase, thus reducing the seismic force developed in the structure.

The structure response modification coefficient, R, given in ASCE Table 9.5.2.2, is the ratio of the seismic base shear which would develop in a linearly elastic system to the prescribed design base shear. It is a measure of the ability of the system to absorb energy and sustain cyclic inelastic deformations without collapse. In addition to compensating for the energy dissipation capability, the lateral force system redundancy, and the increase in natural period and damping ratio, the response modification coefficient allows for (1) the provision of secondary lateral support systems, and (2) the observed performance of specific materials and structural systems in past earthquakes.

Classification of Structural Systems

ASCE Table 9.5.2.2 details six general categories of building types, illustrated in Figure 5.16. Fundamental aspects of the determination of the response modification factor are that the detailing provisions for each type of construction material must be strictly adhered to, and the necessary inspection and observation during construction is performed as specified in IBC Sections 1704 and 1709.

In a bearing wall system, shear walls or braced frames provide support for all or most of the gravity loads. In general, a bearing wall system has comparably lower values for R since the system lacks redundancy and the lateral support members also carry gravity loads, and failure of the lateral support members will result in collapse of the gravity load–carrying capacity. In seismic design categories D, E, and F, the concrete and masonry shear walls are required to be specially detailed to satisfy IBC Sections 1910 and 2106, respectively. Steel-braced frames are required to be specially detailed to satisfy IBC Section 2205.

A building frame system has separate systems to provide support for lateral forces and gravity loads. A frame provides support for essentially all gravity loads, with independent shear walls or braced frames resisting all lateral forces. The gravity load–supporting frame does not require special ductile detailing, but it must satisfy the deformation compatibility requirements of ASCE Section 9.5.2.2.4.3, and this imposes a practical limitation on the height of a building frame system.

Moment-resisting frames are specially detailed to provide good ductility and to support both lateral and gravity loads by flexural action. In seismic design

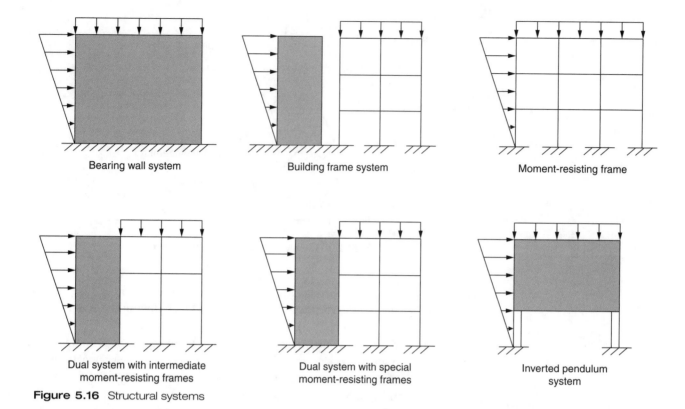

Figure 5.16 Structural systems

categories D, E, and F, the moment-resisting frames are required to be specially detailed to satisfy ACI[14] Sections 21.2 to 21.5 or SEIS[15] Part I, Section 9.

In general, a dual system has a comparably higher value for R since a secondary lateral support system is available to assist the primary nonbearing lateral support system. Nonbearing walls or bracing supply the primary lateral support system with a moment-resisting frame providing primary support for gravity loads and acting as a backup lateral force system. The moment-resisting frame must be designed to independently resist at least 25 percent of the base shear, and in addition, the two systems must be designed to resist the total base shear in proportion to their relative rigidities.

Restrictions on building heights and on the use of the different building types in specific seismic zones are also imposed in ASCE Table 9.5.2.2.

Combinations of Structural Systems

For those cases where different structural systems are employed over the height of the structure, the entire system must be designed using the lowest R value of any story. This requirement is to prevent a concentration of inelastic behavior in the lower stories of a structure, and may be relaxed when the dead load above the particular story is less than 10 percent of the total structure dead load. This effectively permits, without penalty, the construction of a braced-frame penthouse on a moment-resisting frame.

For those designs where a system with R less than 5 is employed along only one axis of a structure, ASCE Section 9.5.2.2.2.1 requires that the same value for R be used in the orthogonal direction in seismic design categories D, E, and F.

Seismic Dead Load

The seismic dead load, W, as specified in ASCE Section 9.5.3, is the total weight of the building and that part of the service load which may be expected to be attached to the building. This consists of

(i) Twenty-five percent of the floor live load for storage and warehouse occupancies

(ii) A minimum allowance of 10 pounds per square foot for movable partitions, or actual weight, whichever is greater

(iii) Twenty percent of flat roof snow loads exceeding 30 pounds per square foot

(iv) The total weight of permanent equipment and fittings

Seismic Design Category

The seismic design category, defined in ASCE Section 9.4.2 and Tables 9.4.2.1a and 9.4.2.1b, establishes the design and detailing requirements necessary in a structure. Six design categories are established based on the design response accelerations and seismic use group. The seismic design category is determined twice, first as a function of S_{DS} using ASCE Table 9.4.2.1a, and then as a function of S_{D1} using ASCE Table 9.4.2.1b. The most severe seismic design category governs. The table below lists the six design categories.

		Seismic Use Group		
S_{DS}	S_{D1}	**I**	**II**	**III**
$S_{DS} < 0.167g$	$S_{D1} < 0.067g$	A	A	A
$0.167g \leq S_{DS} < 0.33g$	$0.067g \leq S_{D1} < 0.133g$	B	B	C
$0.33g \leq S_{DS} < 0.50g$	$0.133g \leq S_{D1} < 0.20g$	C	C	D
$0.50g \leq S_{DS}$	$0.20g \leq S_{D1}$	D	D	D
MCE* acceleration at 1 second period, $S_1 \geq 0.75g$		E	E	F

*MCE = maximum considered earthquake

Seismic Response Coefficient

The seismic response coefficient C_s is given in ASCE Section 9.5.5.2.1 Equation (9.5.5.2.1-2) defines the longer-period, velocity-related region of the spectrum and is given by

$$C_s = S_{D1}I_E/RT$$
$$\geq 0.044S_{DS}I_E$$

where
S_{D1} = design response acceleration at a period of 1 second
I_E = occupancy importance factor
R = response modification factor
T = fundamental period of the structure

The maximum value of the seismic response coefficient, which defines the flat top or acceleration-related region of the spectrum, is given by ASCE Equation (9.5.5.2.1-1) as

$$C_s = S_{DS}I_E/R$$

where S_{DS} = design response acceleration at short periods. This latter expression governs for structures with a fundamental period of less than

$$T_S = S_{D1}/S_{DS}$$

To prevent too low a value of the seismic response coefficient being adopted for long-period structures in seismic design category E or F, the minimum permitted value is given by ASCE Equation (9.5.5.2.1-4) as

$$C_s = 0.5S_1I_E/R$$

where S_1 = maximum considered earthquake spectral response acceleration at a period of 1 second.

For regular structures not exceeding five stories in height and with a fundamental period not exceeding 0.5 seconds, C_s may be calculated using values of $S_S = 1.5g$ and $S_1 = 0.6g$.

Design Base Shear

The prescribed design base shear using the equivalent lateral force procedure is given by ASCE Equation (9.5.5.2-1) as

$$V = C_sW$$

This formula is based on the assumption that the structure will undergo several cycles of inelastic deformation and dissipate energy without collapse. Forces and displacements in the structure are derived assuming linear elastic behavior.[10] The actual forces and displacements produced in the structure are assumed to be greater than these values,[10] as specified for critical elements in ASCE Sections 9.5.2.6.2.4, 9.5.2.6.2.11, 9.5.2.6.3.1 and 9.5.2.6.4.2. The idealized force-displacement relationship is shown in Figure 5.17.

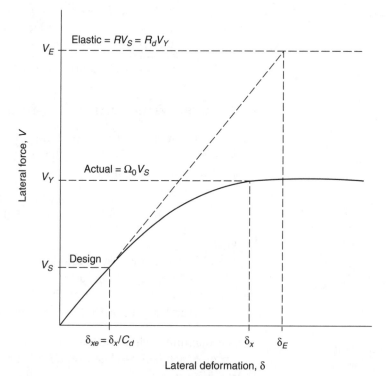

Figure 5.17 Assumed force-displacement curve

The base shear developed in an ideal fully elastic structure is $V_E = RC_sW/I_E$. The design, or strength level value of the base shear, is $V_S = V_EI_E/R$. The calculated displacement for this design value is δ_{xe}, and the actual displacement is given by ASCE Equation (9.5.5.7.1) as $\delta_x = C_d\delta_{xe}/I_E$. The actual base shear developed in the structure at the maximum inelastic displacement is denoted by V_Y.

The response modification factor is $R = V_E/V_S$, and the overstrength factor is $\Omega_0 = V_Y/V_S$.

The ductility reduction factor is $R_d = V_E/V_Y = R/\Omega_0$.

Example **5.5**

The floor plan of a single-story commercial building is shown in Exhibit 5. The 14-foot-high special reinforced masonry shear walls are load bearing and have a weight of 70 pounds per square foot. The weight of the roof is 50 pounds per square foot and all other weights may be neglected. Site classification D may be assumed, and the maximum considered earthquake response accelerations are $S_S = 1.25g$ and $S_1 = 0.5g$. Determine the seismic base shear and the seismic design category.

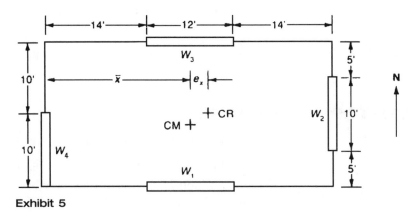

Exhibit 5

Solution

A commerical building is classified as a standard occupancy structure and the applicable seismic use group is obtained from IBC Table 1604.5 as

$$SUG = I$$

The relevant dead loads are given by

$$\text{Roof} = W_R = 0.05 \times 40 \times 20 = 40 \text{ kips}$$
$$\text{North wall} = W_3 = 0.07 \times 12 \times 14 = 11.76 \text{ kips}$$
$$\text{South wall} = W_1 = 11.76 \text{ kips}$$
$$\text{East wall} = W_2 = 0.07 \times 10 \times 14 = 9.80 \text{ kips}$$
$$\text{West wall} = W_4 = 9.80 \text{ kips}$$

Total seismic dead load is then

$$W = W_R + W_1 + W_2 + W_3 + W_4$$
$$= 83.12 \text{ kips}$$

From ASCE Table 9.4.1.2.4a the site coefficient $F_a = 1.0$.
From ASCE Table 9.4.1.2.4b the site coefficient $F_v = 1.5$.
From ASCE Equation (9.4.1.2.4-1) the adjusted response acceleration $S_{MS} = F_aS_S = 1.0 \times 1.25g = 1.25g$.

From ASCE Equation (9.4.1.2.4-2) the adjusted response acceleration $S_{M1} = F_v S_1 = 1.5 \times 0.5g = 0.75g$.

From ASCE Equation (9.4.1.2.5-1) the design response acceleration $S_{DS} = 2S_{MS}/3 = 0.83g$.

From ASCE Equation (9.4.1.2.5-2) the design response acceleration $S_{D1} = 2S_{M1}/3 = 0.5g$.

From ASCE Table 9.4.2.1a the seismic design category is D.

From ASCE Table 9.4.2.1b the seismic design category is D. Hence, seismic design category D governs.

For this type of structure, the maximum value of C_s governs.

The seismic response coefficient is given by ASCE Equation (9.5.5.2.1-1) as

$$C_s = S_{DS}I_E/R$$

$I_E = 1.0$ for a standard occupancy structure as defined in IBC Table 1604.5

$S_{DS} = 0.83g$ as calculated

$R = 5.0$ from ASCE Table 9.5.2.2 for a bearing wall system of special reinforced masonry walls

$W = 83.12$ kips, as calculated

Then the seismic base shear is given by ASCE Equation (9.5.5.2-1) as

$$V = C_s W = 0.83 \times 1.0W/5$$
$$= 0.166W$$
$$= 13.80 \text{ kips}$$

MULTISTORY STRUCTURE

Vertical Distribution of Base Shear

The distribution of base shear over the height of a building is obtained as the superposition of all the modes of vibration of the multiple-degree-of-freedom system. The magnitude of the lateral force at a particular node depends on the mass of that node, the distribution of stiffness over the height of the structure, and the nodal displacements in a given mode and is given by[7]

$$F_x = V' w_x \phi_x / \Sigma w_i \phi_i$$

where

V' = modal base shear

w_i = seismic dead load located at level i

ϕ_i = mode shape component at level i for the given mode

For a structure with a uniform distribution of mass over its height and assuming a linear mode shape, this reduces to the expression

$$F_x = V_1 w_x h_x / \Sigma w_i h_i$$

where h_i = height above the base to level i.

If only the first mode shape is considered, V_1 represents the design base shear for the first mode, and the nodal force distribution is linear, as shown in Figure 5.18. In order to account for higher mode effects when T exceeds 0.5 seconds, ASCE Equation (9.5.5.4-1) combined with Equation (9.5.5.4-2) yields the expression

$$F_x = V w_x h_x^k / \Sigma W_i h_i^k$$

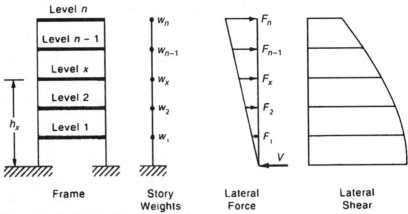

Figure 5.18 Vertical force distribution

where
  $k = 1.0$ for $T \le 0.5$ seconds
  $k = 2.0$ for $T \ge 2.5$ seconds

and for intermediate values of T a linear variation of k may be assumed.

Example 5.6

The two-story bearing wall structure shown in Exhibit 6 has a roof and second floor weighing 20 pounds per square foot, and walls weighing 100 pounds per square foot. The seismic response coefficient may be assumed to be $C_s = 0.183$. Determine the vertical force distribution.

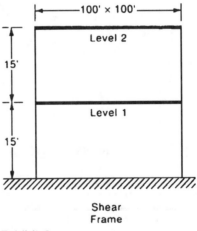

Exhibit 6

Solution

Using ASCE Equation (9.5.5.3.2-1) the natural period is given by
$$T_a = 0.020(h_n)^{0.75}$$

where
  h_n = roof height = 30 feet

Then the natural period is
$$T_a = (0.02)(30)^{0.75}$$
$$= 0.26 \text{ seconds}$$
$$< 0.5 \text{ seconds}$$

Hence $k = 1.0$, and the expression for F_x reduces to

$$F_x = V w_x h_x / \Sigma w_i h_i$$

The seismic dead load located at level 2 is given by

$$\text{Roof} = 0.02 \times 100 \times 100 = 200 \text{ kips}$$
$$\text{Walls} = 4 \times 0.10 \times 100 \times 15/2 = 300 \text{ kips}$$
$$w_2 = 200 + 300$$
$$= 500 \text{ kips}$$

The seismic dead load located at level 1 is given by

$$\text{Second floor} = 0.02 \times 100 \times 100 = 200 \text{ kips}$$
$$\text{Walls} = 4 \times 0.10 \times 100 \times 15 = 600 \text{ kips}$$
$$w_1 = 200 + 600$$
$$= 800 \text{ kips}$$

The relevant values are

Level	W_x	h_x	$w_x h_x$	F_x
2	500	30	15,000	132
1	800	15	12,000	106
Total	1300	15	27,000	238

The base shear is given by

$$V = C_s W$$
$$= 0.183 W$$
$$= 0.183 \times 1300$$
$$= 238 \text{ kips}$$

$$F_x = V w_x h_x / \Sigma_i h_i$$
$$= 238 w_x h_x / 27,000$$
$$= 0.00882 \ w_x h_x.$$

The values of F_x are given in the table and shown in Exhibit 7.

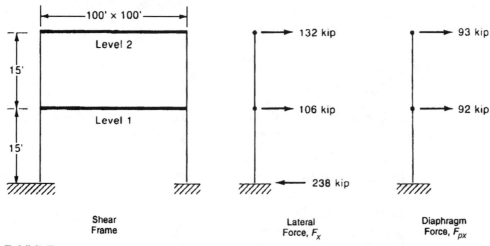

Exhibit 7

Overturning

In accordance with ASCE Section 9.5.5.6, buildings shall be designed to resist seismic overturning. The overturning moment at level x is given by ASCE Equation (9.5.5.6) as

$$M_x = \sum F_i(h_i - h_x)$$

where

F_i = design lateral force at level i
h_i = height above the base to level i
h_x = height above the base to level x
$\sum F_i(h_i - h_x)$ = summation, from level x to the roof, of the product of F_i and $(h_i - h_x)$

In accordance with ASCE Section 9.5.2.1, the allowable stress load factors of 0.6 for dead load and 0.7 for seismic load, given in ASCE Section 2.4.1, may be utilized in evaluating overturning at the soil-structure interface. In ASCE Equations (9.5.2.7-1), (9.5.2.7-2), (9.5.2.7.1-1), and (9.5.2.7.1-2) it is permitted to take $0.2S_{DS}D = 0$.

Example 5.7

Determine the factor of safety against overturning for the structure detailed in Example 5.6.

Solution

For a two-story structure the overturning moment for allowable loads given by ASCE Section 2.4.1 is

$$\begin{aligned} M_O &= 0.7\sum F_x h_x \\ &= 0.7(132 \times 30 + 106 \times 15) \\ &= 3885 \text{ kip-feet} \end{aligned}$$

The restoring moment, allowing for the dead load factor specified in ASCE Section 2.4.1, is given by

$$\begin{aligned} M_R &= 0.6WB/2 \\ &= 0.6 \times 1300 \times 100/2 \\ &= 39{,}000 \text{ kip-feet} \end{aligned}$$

The factor of safety against overturning is

$$\begin{aligned} M_R/M_O &= 39{,}000/3885 \\ &= 10.0 \end{aligned}$$

Story Drift

Story drift is the lateral displacement of one level of a multistory structure relative to the level below. Limitations are imposed on drift to ensure a minimum level of stiffness so as to control inelastic deformation and possible instability. Particularly in taller buildings, large deformations with heavy vertical loads may lead to significant secondary moments and instability.

Since the value of the natural period derived using the Rayleigh expression is a more realistic value than that determined by ASCE Equation (9.5.5.3.2-1) and (9.5.5.3.2-1a), ASCE Section 9.5.5.7.1 allows this value to be used to determine the seismic base shear. The upper bound limitation imposed by ASCE Section 9.5.5.3.1 is not imposed. In addition, ASCE Section 9.5.5.3.1 specifies that *P*-delta effects need not be included in the calculation of drift when the stability coefficient θ does not exceed 0.10.

The maximum allowable story drift Δ_a is given in ASCE Table 9.5.2.8 and shown in the table below.

	Seismic Use Group		
Building Type	**I**	**II**	**III**
One-story buildings with fittings designed to accommodate drift	No limit	No limit	No limit
Buildings, other than masonry shear wall or wall frame buildings, of four stories or less with fittings designed to accommodate drift	$0.025h_{sx}$	$0.020h_{sx}$	$0.015h_{sx}$
Masonry cantilever shear wall buildings	$0.010h_{sx}$	$0.010h_{sx}$	$0.010h_{sx}$
Other masonry shear wall buildings	$0.007h_{sx}$	$0.007h_{sx}$	$0.007h_{sx}$
Masonry wall frame buildings	$0.013h_{sx}$	$0.013h_{sx}$	$0.010h_{sx}$
All other buildings	$0.020h_{sx}$	$0.015h_{sx}$	$0.010h_{sx}$

h_{sx} = story height below level x

To allow for inelastic deformations, drift is determined using the deflection amplification factor C_d given in ASCE Table 9.5.2.2. The amplified deflection at level x is defined by ASCE Equation (9.5.5.7.1) as

$$\delta_x = C_d \delta_{xe}/I_E$$

where
  δ_x = design displacement of the structure
  δ_{xe} = theoretical displacement caused by the Code-prescribed design level forces, as determined by an elastic analysis
  I_E = occupancy importance factor given in ASCE Table 9.1.4

Example 5.8

Determine the value of the story drift, in the top story, for the special moment-resisting steel frame detailed in Exhibit 3 and compare it with the allowable value. The building is assigned to seismic use group I with design response acceleration of $S_{DS} = 0.83g$ and $S_{D1} = 0.36g$. It may be assumed that all fittings are designed to accommodate drift. *P*-delta effects need not be considered.

Solution

The value of the response modification factor for a moment-resisting frame is obtained from ASCE Table 9.5.2.2 as

$$R = 8.0$$

The value of the importance factor for a standard-occupancy structure moment-resisting frame is obtained from and ASCE Table 9.1.4 as

$$I_E = 1.0$$

The fundamental period is given by ASCE Equation (9.5.5.3.2-1) as

$$T_a = 0.028(h_n)^{0.8}$$

where
  h_n = roof height of 30 feet

Then the fundamental period is

$$T_a = 0.028(30)^{0.8}$$
$$= 0.425 \text{ seconds}$$

The value of T_s is given by ASCE Section 9.4.1.2.6 as

$$T_S = S_{D1}/S_{DS}$$
$$= 0.36/0.83$$
$$= 0.434 \text{ seconds}$$
$$> T_a \ldots \text{ ASCE Equation (9.5.5.2.1-1) applies}$$

Hence the seismic response coefficient is given by ASCE Equation (9.5.5.2.1-1) as

$$C_s = S_{DS}I_E/R$$
$$= 0.83 \times 1.0/8$$
$$= 0.10$$

From Exhibit 3, the seismic dead load located at each level is given by

$$w = mg$$
$$= 0.4 \times 386.4$$
$$= 154.6 \text{ kips}$$

The total seismic dead load is given by

$$W = 2w$$
$$= 2 \times 154.6$$
$$= 309.2 \text{ kips}$$

The base shear is given by ASCE Equation (9.5.5.2-1) as

$$V = C_s W$$
$$= 0.10W$$
$$= 30.92 \text{ kips}$$

Since $T_a < 0.5$ seconds, ASCE Equations (9.5.5.4-1) and (9.5.5.4-2) reduce to

$$F_x = V w_x h_x / \sum w_i h_i$$
$$= 30.92 w_x h_x / 6954$$
$$= 0.00445 w_x h_x$$

The relevant values are given in the table:

Level	w_x	h_x	$w_x h_x$	F_x	k	δ
2	154.6	30	4636	20.61	20	1.886
1	154.6	15	2318	10.31	40	0.808
Total	309.2	—	6954	30.92	—	—

The maximum allowable inelastic story drift, for a two-story structure assigned to seismic use group I with fittings designed to accommodate drift, is given by ASCE Section 9.5.2.8 as

$$\Delta_A = 0.25 h_{sx}$$
$$= 0.025 \times 15 \times 12$$
$$= 4.5 \text{ inches}$$

The elastic displacements at each level are given by

$$\delta_1 = (F_2 + F_1)/k_1$$
$$= 30.92/40$$
$$= 0.773 \text{ inches}$$

$$\delta_2 = F_2/k_2 + \delta_1$$
$$= 20.61/20 + 0.773$$
$$= 1.804 \text{ inches}$$

The design level elastic drift in the top story is

$$\delta_{2e} = \delta_2 - \delta_1$$
$$= 1.031 \text{ inches}$$

The amplification factor for a steel moment-resisting frame is given by ASCE Table 9.5.2.2 as

$$C_d = 5.5$$

The anticipated inelastic drift in the top story is derived from ASCE Equation (9.5.5.7.1) as

$$\delta_2 = C_d \delta_{2e}/I_e$$
$$= 5.5 \times 1.031/1.0$$
$$= 5.67 \text{ inches}$$
$$> \Delta_A \ldots \text{unsatisfactory}$$

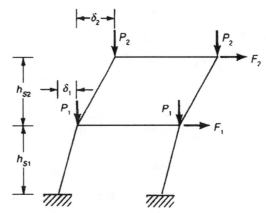

Figure 5.19 *P*-delta effects

P-Delta Effects

The *P*-delta effects in a given story are due to the eccentricity of the gravity load above that story, which produces secondary moments augmenting the sway moments in that story. If the ratio of secondary to primary moment exceeds 0.1, the effects of the secondary moments should be included in the analysis. As shown in Figure 5.19, the primary moment in the second story of the frame is

$$M_P = F_2 h_{S2}$$

and the secondary moment is

$$M_S = 2P_2\delta_2$$

The ratio of the secondary moment to the primary moment is termed the stability coefficient and is given by SEAOC[8] Section C105.1.3 as

$$\theta = M_S/M_P$$

Example 5.9

For the special moment-resisting steel frame detailed in Exhibit 3 and analyzed in Example 5.8, determine the stability coefficient for the top story.

Solution

The secondary *P*-delta moment in the top story is

$$
\begin{aligned}
M_{S2} &= w_2(\delta_2 - \delta_1) \\
&= 154.6(1.804 - 0.773) \\
&= 159.32 \text{ kip-inches}
\end{aligned}
$$

The primary moment in the top story is

$$
\begin{aligned}
M_{P2} &= F_2 hs_2 \\
&= 20.61 \times 15 \times 12 \\
&= 3710 \text{ kip-inches}
\end{aligned}
$$

The stability coefficient is given by ASCE Section 9.5.5.7.2 as

$$\begin{aligned} \theta &= M_{S2}/M_{P2} \\ &= 159.32/3710 \\ &= 0.043 \\ &< 0.1 \end{aligned}$$

Hence in accordance with ASCE Section 9.5.5.7.2, P-delta effects need not be considered in the determination of story drifts and element forces for the structure.

Diaphragm Loads

The load acting on a horizontal diaphragm in seismic design categories B and C is given by ASCE Equation (9.5.2.6.2.7) as

$$F_p = 0.2I_E S_{DS} w_p + V_{px}$$

where

   S_{DS} = design spectral response acceleration coefficient at short periods

   I_E = occupancy importance factor from ASCE Table 9.1.4

   w_p = seismic dead load tributary to the diaphragm, including walls normal to the direction of the seismic load

   V_{px} = force generated by offsets in the vertical lateral-force-resisting elements above and below the diaphragm

The load acting on a horizontal diaphragm in seismic design category D and above is given by ASCE Equation (9.5.2.6.4.4) as

$$\begin{aligned} F_{px} &= w_{px}\Sigma F_i/\Sigma w_i \\ &\geq 0.2S_{DS}I_E w_{px} \\ &\leq 0.4S_{DS}I_E w_{px} \end{aligned}$$

where

   F_i = lateral force at level i

   ΣF_i = total shear force at level i

   w_i = seismic dead load located at level i

   Σw_i = total seismic dead load at level i and above

   w_{px} = seismic dead load tributary to the diaphragm at level x, including walls normal to the direction of the seismic load

For a single-story structure, this reduces to

$$\begin{aligned} F_p &= V w_{px}/W \\ &= C_S w_{px} \end{aligned}$$

Example 5.10

Determine the diaphragm loads for the two-story structure detailed in Example 5.6. The design response acceleration is $S_{DS} = 0.915$ and the seismic design category is D.

Solution

ASCE Equation (9.5.2.6.4.4) is applicable, and the diaphragm loads are given by

$$F_{px} = w_{px} \Sigma F_i / \Sigma w_i$$

The seismic dead load tributary to the diaphragm at level 2 is given by

$$\text{Roof} = 0.02 \times 100 \times 100 = 200 \text{ kips}$$
$$\text{Walls} = 2 \times 0.10 \times 100 \times 15/2 = 150 \text{ kips}$$
$$w_{p2} = 200 + 150$$
$$= 350 \text{ kips}$$

The seismic dead load tributary to the diaphragm at level 1 is given by

$$\text{Second floor} = 0.02 \times 100 \times 100 = 200 \text{ kips}$$
$$\text{Walls} = 2 \times 0.10 \times 100 \times 15 = 300 \text{ kips}$$
$$w_{p1} = 200 + 300$$
$$= 500 \text{ kips}$$

The relevant values are

Level	Σw_i	ΣF_i	$\Sigma F_i/\Sigma w_i$	w_{px}	F_{px}
2	500	132	0.264	350	93
1	1300	238	0.183	500	92

The values of F_{px} are given in the table and shown in Exhibit 7.

The values obtained for F_{px} lie within the stipulated minimum and maximum values, which are

$$F_{px} \not< 0.20 \times 0.915 \times 1.0 \times w_{px} = 0.18 w_{px}$$
$$F_{px} \not> 0.40 \times 0.915 \times 1.0 \times w_{px} = 0.36 w_{px}$$

SIMPLIFIED LATERAL FORCE PROCEDURE

Base Shear

For small structures, ASCE Section 9.5.4 permits an alternative design method. This method provides conservative results by comparison with the other available methods but allows a rapid and simple determination of the seismic base shear. This method is applicable to structures of seismic use group I, of light-frame construction not exceeding three stories in height, or of any construction not exceeding two stories in height with flexible diaphragms. The seismic base shear is given by ASCE Equation (9.5.4.1) as

$$V = (1.2 S_{DS}/R) W$$

| Example **5.11** |

The floor plan is shown, in Exhibit 5, of a single-story commercial building located on a site with an undetermined soil profile. The 14-foot-high special reinforced masonry shear walls are load bearing and have a weight of 70 pounds per square foot. The weight of the roof is 50 pounds per square foot, and all other weights may be neglected. Determine the seismic base shear using the simplified procedure. The maximum considered earthquake response accelerations are $S_S = 1.25g$ and $S_1 = 0.5g$.

Solution

From Example 5.5 the following values are obtained:

$S_{DS} = 0.83g$

$R = 5.0$ from ASCE Table 9.5.2.2 for a masonry bearing wall system of special reinforced masonry walls

$W = 83.12$ kips, as calculated

Then the seismic base shear is given by ASCE Equation (9.5.4.1) as

$$V = (1.2S_{DS}/R)W$$
$$= (1.2 \times 0.83/5.0)W$$
$$= 0.20W$$
$$= 16.62 \text{ kips}$$

Simplified Vertical Distribution of Base Shear

In accordance with ASCE Section 9.5.4.2, when the simplified procedure is used to determine the seismic base shear, the forces at each level may be determined from ASCE Equation (9.5.4.2) as

$$F_x = (1.2S_{DS}/R)w_x$$
$$= w_x V/W$$

where

w_x = seismic dead load located at level x

V = seismic base shear determined using ASCE Equation (9.5.4.1)

W = total seismic dead load

Example 5.12

The two-story bearing wall structure shown in Exhibit 6 has a roof and second floor weighing 20 pounds per square foot and walls weighing 100 pounds per square foot. The design response acceleration is $S_{DS} = 0.915$. Determine the vertical force distribution using the simplified procedure.

Solution

From Example 5.6, the values of the seismic dead loads at each level are obtained and are shown in the table.

The forces at each level are determined from ASCE Equation (9.5.4.2) as

$$F_x = (1.2S_{DS}/R)w_x$$
$$= (1.2 \times 0.915/5)w_x$$
$$= 0.22w_x$$

The values of F_x are given in the table:

Level	w_i	F_x
2	500	110
1	800	176
Total	1300	286

RELIABILITY FACTOR

Design Load

The calculated seismic load E is determined at the strength design level and thus has a load factor of 1 for strength design and a load factor of 0.7 for service load design. The seismic load is a function of both horizontal and vertical earthquake-induced forces and is given by ASCE Equation (9.5.2.7-1) as

$$E = \rho_i Q_E + 0.2 S_{DS} D$$

where
Q_E = effect of horizontal seismic forces
S_{DS} = design response acceleration for a period of 0.2 second
D = dead load
ρ_x = reliability factor
$\quad = 2 - 20/r_{\max x}(A_x)^{0.5}$
$\quad \leq 1.5$
$\quad \geq 1.0$
$r_{\max x}$ = maximum element-story shear ratio
$\quad$ = ratio of the shear in the most heavily loaded lateral-force-resisting element, in any story, to the total shear in that story
A_x = area in square feet of the diaphragm level immediately above the story

Reliability Factor

By providing multiple lateral load-resisting paths in the structure, a degree of redundancy is provided in the system. Yield of one element of the system results in redistribution of the load to the remaining elements, thus controlling displacements and deterioration of the structure and delaying the formation of a collapse mechanism. Thus, to improve the seismic performance of buildings, it is desirable to provide multiple load paths so as to make the lateral resisting system as redundant as possible. To encourage this development, the reliability factor ρ penalizes less redundant structures by increasing the design horizontal force by up to 50 percent. Determination of the reliability factor depends on the values of the element-story shear ratio and the diaphragm areas of the building. In seismic design categories A, B, and C, in calculating drift, the value of the reliability factor shall be assumed equal to 1.

For a *braced frame,* the element-story shear ratio is determined as shown in Figure 5.20. Assuming that each brace resists the seismic shear equally, the maximum element-story shear ratio is

$$r_{\max x} = 0.5$$

The reliability factor is given by ASCE Equation (9.5.2.4.2-1) as

$$\rho_x = 2 - 20/r_{\max x}(A_x)^{0.5}$$
$$= 2 - 20/0.5(30 \times 60)^{0.5}$$
$$= 2 - 0.94$$
$$= 1.06$$

For a *special moment-resisting* frame, the element-story shear ratio is determined as shown in Figure 5.21 for a single-bay, four-bent structure. As specified in ASCE Section 9.5.2.4.2 the element-story shear is the ratio of the sum of the

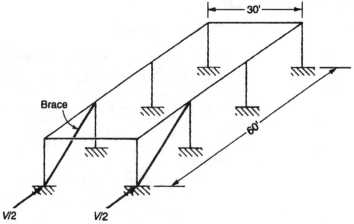

Figure 5.20 Braced frame

shears in two adjacent columns in a bent to the total shear in the story. For a column common to two bays, 70 percent of the shear in that column is used in the summation. Assuming that each bent resists the seismic shear as indicated in Figure 5.21, the maximum element-story shear ratio is

$$r_{\max x} = 0.33$$

The reliability factor is given by ASCE Equation (9.5.2.4.2-1) as

$$
\begin{aligned}
\rho_x &= 2 - 20/r_{\max x}(A_x)^{0.5} \\
&= 2 - 20/0.33(30 \times 60)^{0.5} \\
&= 2 - 1.43 \\
&= 1.0 \ldots \text{minimum}
\end{aligned}
$$

Special moment-resisting frames, except when used in dual systems, must be designed to have a reliability factor not exceeding 1.25 in seismic design category D and 1.1 in seismic design categories E and F.

For a *shear wall,* the element-story shear ratio is determined as shown in Figure 5.22 for a tilt-up concrete structure. As specified in per ASCE Section 9.5.2.4.2, the element-story shear is the ratio of 10 times the unit shear per foot of wall to the shear in the story. Assuming that each shear wall resists half the seismic shear as indicated in Figure 5.22, the maximum element-story shear ratio is

$$
\begin{aligned}
r_{\max x} &= 0.5 \times 10/l_w \\
&= 0.5 \times 10/100 \\
&= 0.05
\end{aligned}
$$

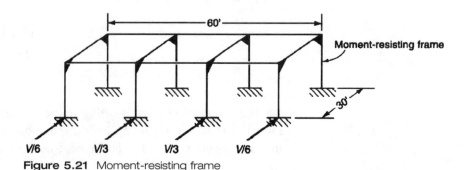

Figure 5.21 Moment-resisting frame

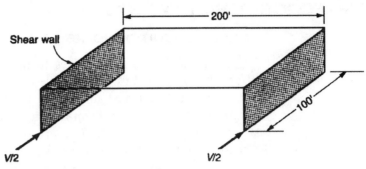

Figure 5.22 Shear wall structure

The reliability factor is given by

$$
\begin{aligned}
\rho_x &= 2 - 20/r_{\max x}(A_x)^{0.5} \\
&= 2 - 20/0.05(100 \times 200)^{0.5} \\
&= 2 - 2.83 \\
&= 1.0 \ldots \text{minimum}
\end{aligned}
$$

For a *dual system,* the element-story shear ratio is determined as shown in Figure 5.23. As specified in ASCE Section 9.5.2.4.2, the element-story shear is the ratio of the shear in the most heavily loaded element to the total shear in the story. The reliability factor is taken as 80 percent of the normally calculated value. Assuming that shear is divided between the elements as indicated in Figure 5.23, the maximum element-story shear ratio is

$$
r_{\max x} = 0.375
$$

The reliability factor for dual systems is given by

$$
\begin{aligned}
\rho_x &= 0.8[2 - 20/r_{\max x}(A_x)^{0.5}] \\
&= 0.8[2 - 20/0.375(100 \times 200)^{0.5}] \\
&= 0.8[2 - 0.38] \\
&= 0.8 \times 1.62 \\
&= 1.3
\end{aligned}
$$

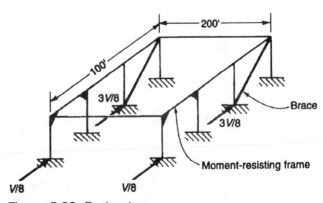

Figure 5.23 Dual system

LATERAL-FORCE-RESISTANT SYSTEM

Basic Components

To transfer the seismic forces to the ground, vertical and horizontal resisting elements must be used to provide a continuous load path from the upper portion of the structure to the foundations.[6] The vertical components consist of shear walls, braced frames, and moment-resisting frames. The horizontal components consist of the roof and floor diaphragms, or horizontal trusses, which distribute lateral forces to the vertical members. A diaphragm is considered flexible, in accordance with ASCE Section 9.5.2.3.1 when the midpoint displacement, under lateral load, exceeds twice the average displacement of the end supports. The diaphragm may then be modeled as a simple beam between end supports, and the distribution of loading to the supports in independent of their relative stiffness. When the midpoint deflection is less than twice the story drift, the diaphragm is considered rigid, and allowance must be made for the additional forces created by torsional effects, with the diaphragm and supports assumed to undergo rigid body rotation.

Plywood Diaphragms

A plywood diaphragm is a flexible diaphragm which acts as a horizontal deep beam, with the plywood sheathing acting as the web to resist shear force and the boundary members, perpendicular to the load, acting as flanges to resist flexural effects.[16] The shear capacity of a plywood diaphragm depends on the sheathing thickness, grade, and orientation; the size of the framing members; the support of the panel edges; and the nail spacing and penetration. This capacity has been determined experimentally,[17,18] and design values are given in IBC Table 2306.3.1. The perpendicular boundary members, or chords, resist the applied moment by developing axial forces which provide a couple equal and opposite to the moment. A limit of 4 to 1 is imposed in IBC Table 2305.2.3 on the diaphragm aspect ratio for blocked diaphragms, in order to control deflection and ensure that the gravity load-carrying capacity of bearing walls perpendicular to the applied load is not impaired. A limit of 3 to 1 is imposed for unblocked diaphragms.

Example **5.13**

Details of a single-story industrial building with a seismic response coefficient of $C_s = 0.28$, are shown in Exhibit 8. The weight of the wood roof is 15 pounds per square foot and the weight of the eight-inch masonry walls is 75 pounds per square foot. The roof sheathing is $^{15}/_{32}$-inch Structural I grade plywood, and the framing member dimensions are indicated on the roof plan. For north-south seismic loads, draw the required nailing diagram and determine the chord reinforcement required. A reliability factor of unity may be assumed.

Solution

The relevant dead load tributary to the roof diaphragm in the north-south direction is due to the north and south wall and the roof dead load, and is given by

$$\text{Roof} = 15 \times 120 = 1800 \text{ pounds per linear foot}$$
$$\text{North wall} = 75 \times 14^2/(2 \times 12.5) = 590 \text{ pounds per linear foot}$$
$$\text{South wall} = 590 \text{ pounds per linear foot}$$

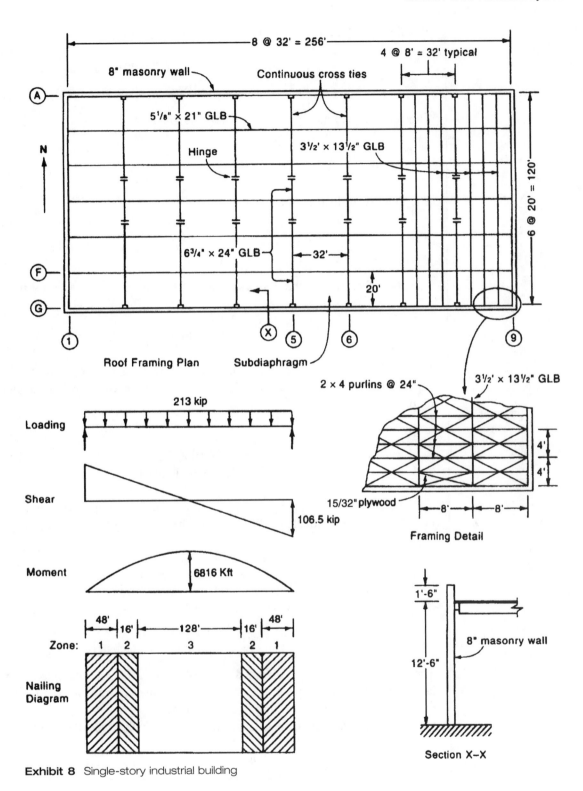

8 @ 32' = 256'

4 @ 8' = 32' typical

8" masonry wall

Continuous cross ties

5¹⁄₈" × 21" GLB

3½' × 13½" GLB

Hinge

6 @ 20' = 120'

N

6¾" × 24" GLB

32'

20'

Roof Framing Plan

Subdiaphragm

213 kip

Loading

Shear

106.5 kip

Moment

6816 Kft

48' | 16' | 128' | 16' | 48'

Zone: 1 2 3 2 1

Nailing Diagram

2 × 4 purlins @ 24"

3½' × 13½" GLB

4'
4'

15/32" plywood

8'   8'

Framing Detail

1'-6"

8" masonry wall

12'-6"

Section X–X

Exhibit 8 Single-story industrial building

The total dead load tributary to the roof diaphragm is

$$w_p = (1800 + 590 + 590)256/1000$$
$$= 762 \text{ kips}$$

The seismic load acting at the roof level is given by

$$V = C_s w_p$$
$$C_s = 0.28$$
$$w_p = 762 \text{ kips, as calculated}$$

The diaphragm load is, then,

$$V = 0.28 \times 762$$
$$= 213 \text{ kips}$$

The shear force along the diaphragm boundaries at grid lines 1 and 9 is

$$Q = V/2$$
$$= 106.5 \text{ kips}$$

For a reliability factor of unity, the service level shear force is given by IBC Equation (16-12) as $E = 0.7Q = 75$ kips. The unit service level shear along the diaphragm boundaries is

$$q_1 = E/B$$
$$= 75 \times 1000/120$$
$$= 625 \text{ pounds per linear foot}$$

The nail spacing may be changed at the beam locations, shown in the figure, and the unit shear a distance 48 feet from the boundary is given by

$$q_2 = q_1 \times 80/128$$
$$= 391 \text{ pounds per linear foot}$$

At 64 feet from the boundary, the unit shear is

$$q_3 = q_1 \times 64/128$$
$$= 313 \text{ pounds per linear foot}$$

The required nail spacing is obtained from IBC Table 2306.3.1 with a case 4 plywood layout applicable, all edges blocked, and with $3\frac{1}{2}$-inch framing at continuous panel edges parallel to the load. Using $\frac{15}{32}$-inch Structural I grade plywood and 10d nails with $1\frac{5}{8}$-inch penetration, the nail spacings required in the three diaphragm zones are

Zone	1	2	3
Diaphragm boundaries	$2\frac{1}{2}$	4"	6"
Continuous panel edges	$2\frac{1}{2}$	4"	6"
Other edges	4"	6"	6"
Intermediate members	12"	12"	12"
Capacity provided, plf	640	425	320
Capacity required, plf	625	391	313

The strength level bending moment at the midpoint of the north and south boundaries due to the north-south seismic force is

$$M = VL/8$$
$$= 213 \times 256/8$$
$$= 6816 \text{ kip-feet}$$

The corresponding chord force is

$$F = M/B$$
$$= 6816/120$$
$$= 56.8 \text{ kips}$$

Using Grade 60 deformed bar reinforcement, the area of reinforcement required is given by ACI Section 9.3 as

$$A_S = F/(\phi \times f_y)$$
$$= 56.8/(0.9 \times 60)$$
$$= 1.05 \text{ square inches}$$

Providing two No. 7 bars gives an area of

$$A'_S = 1.20 \text{ square inches}$$
$$> A_S \ldots \text{satisfactory}$$

Collector Elements

Where shear walls are discontinuous or reentrant corner irregularities are present, collector elements or drag struts are required to ensure deformation compatibility, and to prevent localized tearing of the diaphragm. This is illustrated in Figure 5.24. The drag strut transfers the shear originating in the unsupported portion of the shear wall. Examples of typical drag force calculations involving wood shear walls, where the unit shear is constant in all walls, is shown in Figure 5.25. In the case of masonry or concrete shear walls, the shear resistance of the wall is proportional to its relative rigidity, and this is shown in Figure 5.26.

The design of collectors in seismic design category B and above is covered in ASCE Section 9.5.2.6.3.1. With the exception of light-frame structures, collectors

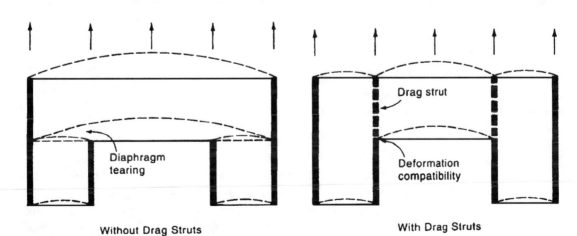

Without Drag Struts   **With Drag Struts**

Figure 5.24 The function of collector elements

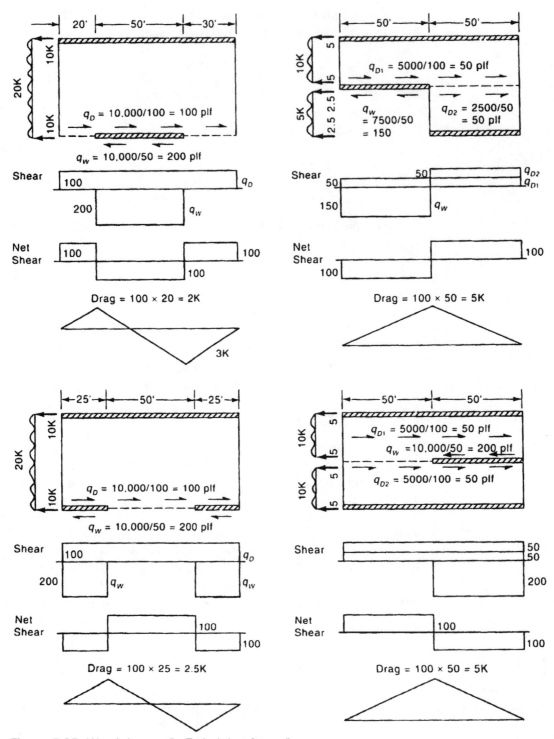

Figure 5.25 Wood shear walls: Typical drag force diagrams

must be designed for the maximum seismic forces specified in IBC Section 1605.4, which requires seismic design forces to be multiplied by the overstrength factor Ω_0 given in ASCE Table 9.5.2.2, For service level design, the allowable stresses may be increased by a factor of 1.7 and, for wood structures, the load duration factor may also be applied.

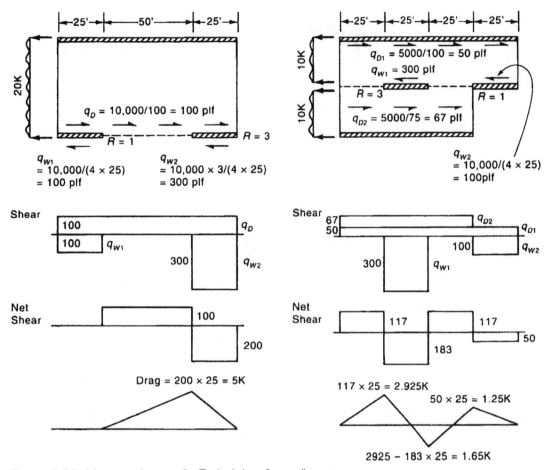

Figure 5.26 Masonry shear walls: Typical drag force diagrams

Light-frame structures may be designed for the basic seismic forces determined from ASCE Equation (9.5.2.6.4.4) and IBC Section 1605.3. However, when plan structural irregularities of type 1, 2, 3, or 4 or vertical structural irregularities of type 4 are present, the basic design forces must be increased by 25 percent.

Example **5.14**

Details of a single-story regular wood structure are shown in Exhibit 9. The weight of the roof is 15 pounds per square foot and the weight of the shear wall is 12 pounds per square foot. The seismic load may be assumed to be given by $V = 0.229w_p$. Determine the drag force at the intersection of grids B and 4.

Solution

For a single-story structure, the lateral force acting at the roof level for north-south seismic loading is given by

$$\text{Roof} = 0.229 \times 15 \times 24 = 82 \text{ pounds per linear foot}$$
$$\text{North wall} = 0.229 \times 12 \times 10/2 = 14 \text{ pounds per linear foot}$$
$$\text{South wall} = 14 \text{ pounds per linear foot}$$

For a flexible diaphragm, the shear wall at line 4 effectively subdivides the roof into two simply supported segments. These are spans 14 and 45. The seismic

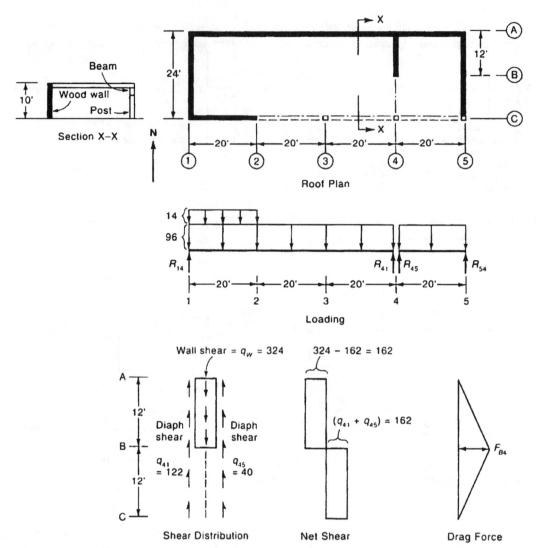

Section X–X

Roof Plan

Loading

Shear Distribution

Net Shear

Drag Force

Exhibit 9

loads acting at the roof diaphragm level are shown in the figure, and the reactions at the shear walls are

$$R_{45} = 96 \times 20/2 = 960 \text{ pounds}$$
$$R_{41} = 96 \times 60/2 + 14 \times 20 \cdot 10/60 = 2927 \text{ pounds}$$

The diaphragm unit shears on either side of the shear wall at grid line 4 are

$$q_{45} = R_{45}/24 = 960/24 = 40 \text{ pounds per linear foot}$$
$$q_{41} = R_{41}/24 = 2927/24 = 122 \text{ pounds per linear foot}$$

The total unit shear in the shear wall at diaphragm level is

$$q_w = (R_{45} + R_{41})/12 = 324 \text{ pounds per linear foot}$$

The shear distribution and net shear at grid line 4 are shown in the figure. For a light-frame structure without irregularities, the drag force at B4 is given by

$$F_{B4} = 12(q_{41} + q_{45}) = 12(122 + 40) = 1944 \text{ pounds}$$

Wood Shear Wall

Vertical walls transmit the lateral load from a horizontal diaphragm to the foundations by means of shear resistance. In the case of plywood shear walls, design values are given in IBC Table 2306.4.1 and the limiting aspect ratio is specified in IBC Table 2305.3.3.

Example 5.15

Determine the nailing requirements for the shear wall on grid line 4 in Example 5.14. The wall consists of $3/8$-inch plywood siding applied on one side of the studs, 16 inches on center. Nailing consists of 8d nails with $1\,3/8$-inch penetration. A reliability factor of unity may be assumed.

Solution

The dead load of the shear wall on grid line 4 is

$$W = 12 \times 10 \times 12 = 1440 \text{ pounds}$$

The seismic unit shear produced by the self-weight of the wall is

$$q_S = 0.229W/L = 0.229 \times 1440/12 = 27 \text{ pounds per linear foot}$$

The total shear at the base of the wall is due to the self-weight of the shear wall plus the seismic force applied at the top of the wall by the diaphragm. The total unit shear in the wall is then

$$\begin{aligned} q &= q_W + q_S \\ &= 324 + 27 \\ &= 351 \text{ pounds per linear foot} \end{aligned}$$

The design service level unit shear is given by IBC Equation (16-10) as $q_E = 0.7q$ = 246 pounds per linear foot.

The aspect ratio of the shear wall is

$$\begin{aligned} h/L &= 10/12 \\ &= 0.83 \\ &< 2.0 \end{aligned}$$

Hence, this conforms to the requirements of IBC Table 2305.3.3 for plywood panels nailed on all edges and full shear values are allowed.

The allowable unit shear, in accordance with IBC Table 2306.4.1, for $3/8$-inch plywood applied to studs at 16 inches on center may be increased to the values shown for $15/32$-inch plywood. The required spacing of 8d nails with $1\,3/8$ inch penetration may be obtained from IBC Table 2306.4.1. With 2-inch nominal Douglas Fir–Larch vertical studs and all panel edges backed with 2-inch nominal blocking, the required nail spacing is

> All panel edges: 6 inches
> Intermediate framing members: 12 inches
> Capacity provided: 260 pounds per linear foot
> Capacity required: 246 pounds per linear foot

Braced Frame

Braced frames are an alternative method of providing resistance to lateral forces. Examples are shown in Figure 5.27.

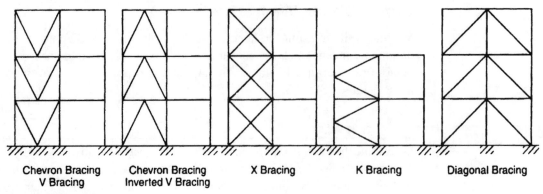

| Chevron Bracing V Bracing | Chevron Bracing Inverted V Bracing | X Bracing | K Bracing | Diagonal Bracing |

Figure 5.27 Braced frames

STRUCTURAL ELEMENTS AND COMPONENTS

Anchorage of Concrete and Masonry Walls

To prevent the separation of concrete and masonry walls from the floor or roof diaphragms, positive anchorage ties must be provided to resist the calculated lateral force.

In seismic design category A, the minimum anchorage force for strength design is given by ASCE Section 9.5.2.6.1.2 as 280 pounds per linear foot. Where the wall anchor spacing exceeds 4 feet, in accordance with ASCE Section 9.5.2.6.2.8 the wall must be designed to span between the anchors.

In seismic design category B, positive anchorage ties must be provided to resist the lateral force specified in ASCE Section 9.5.2.6.2.8, which is

$$F_p = 0.40 I_E S_{DS} W_c$$
$$\geq 0.1 W_c$$

where F_p = design force in an individual anchor
I_E = occupancy importance factor
S_{DS} = design response acceleration, for a period of 0.2 second
W_c = weight of the wall tributary to the anchor

In addition, the minimum anchorage force for strength design may not be less than $400 I_E S_{DS}$ pounds per linear foot of wall. Where the wall anchor spacing exceeds 4 feet, in accordance with ASCE Section 9.5.2.6.2.8, the wall must be designed to span between the anchors.

In seismic design category C and above, anchorage ties for flexible diaphragms must be provided to resist the lateral force calculated from ASCE Equation (9.5.2.6.3.2), which is

$$F_p = 0.80 I_E S_{DS} W_p$$

where

F_p = design force in an individual anchor
I_E = occupancy importance factor
S_{DS} = design response acceleration, for a period of 0.2 second
W_p = weight of the wall tributary to the anchor

In addition, ASCE Section 9.5.2.6.3.2 requires steel elements of the wall anchorage system to resist 1.4 times the values calculated by ASCE Equation (9.5.2.6.3.2). Where the wall anchor spacing exceeds 4 feet, in accordance with ASCE Section 9.5.2.6.2.8, the wall must be designed to span between the anchors.

In seismic design category C and above, anchorages ties for rigid diaphragms must be provided to resist the lateral force calculated from ASCE Equation (9.6.1.3-1), which is

$$F_p = (0.4a_p S_{DS} I_p / R_p)(1 + 2z/h)W_p$$
$$\leq 1.6 S_{DS} I_p W_p$$
$$\geq 0.3 S_{DS} I_p W_p$$

where
F_p = seismic design force on the anchor
I_p = component importance factor given in ASCE Equation (9.6.1.5)
S_{DS} = design response acceleration, for a period of 0.2 second
W_p = weight of wall tributary to the anchor
a_p = component amplification factor from ASCE Table 9.6.2.2
= 1.0
h = height of roof above the base
z = height of anchor above the base
R_p = component response modification factor from ASCE Table 9.6.2.2
= 2.5

In addition, ASCE Section 9.5.2.6.3.2, requires steel elements of the wall anchorage system to resist 1.4 times the values calculated by ASCE Equation (9.6.1.3-1). Where the wall anchor spacing exceeds 4 feet, in accordance with ASCE Section 9.5.2.6.2.8, the wall must be designed to span between the anchors.

To compensate for the poor seismic performance and lack of redundancy of unbraced parapets in seismic design category B and above, ASCE Section 9.6.2.4.1 requires the design force to be determined by ASCE Equation (9.6.1.3-1) with

a_p = component amplification factor from ASCE Table 9.6.2.2
= 2.5
z = height of parapet at point of attachment
= h
R_p = component response modification factor from ASCE Table 9.6.2.2
= 2.5

However, in determining the design moment in a wall with a parapet or the design force in an anchorage, the appropriate design value for the wall shall be taken for the entire wall plus parapet.[8,19]

In order to distribute anchorage forces developed by concrete and masonry walls, in seismic design category C and above, continuous cross ties shall be provided between diaphragm chords, as stipulated in ASCE Section 9.5.2.6.3.2. To reduce the number of continuous full-depth ties required, subdiaphragms may be used to span between the continuous ties.[9,19,20] The subdiaphragm must be designed for all criteria prescribed for the main diaphragm, and provide adequate development length to transfer the wall anchorage force from the anchorage ties to the main diaphragm. A maximum aspect ratio of 2.5 is prescribed for the subdiaphragm.

Example **5.16**

Determine the force developed in wall anchorage ties located at 8 feet on center along the wall on grid line G in Example 5.11. For the subdiaphragm bounded by grid lines F, G, 5, 6, calculate the required nailing, and determine the design force in the continuous cross ties on grid lines 5 and 6. The building is assigned to seismic design category D with a design response acceleration $S_{DS} = 0.98$.

Solution

Weight of the wall is

$$w = 75 \text{ pounds per square foot}$$

The equivalent area of wall tributary to each anchor is

$$A_w = 8 \times 14^2/(2 \times 12.5)$$
$$= 62.72 \text{ square feet}$$

The weight of wall tributary to each anchor is

$$W_p = wA_w$$
$$= 75 \times 62.72/1000$$
$$= 4.70 \text{ kips}$$

For a flexible diaphragm in seismic design category D, the seismic lateral force on an anchor is given by ASCE Equation (9.5.2.6.3.2) as

$$F_p = 0.80 I_E S_{DS} W_p$$
$$= 0.80 \times 1.0 \times 0.98 W_p$$
$$= 0.78 W_p$$
$$= 3.67 \text{ kips}$$

The minimum permissible lateral force on an anchor in given by ASCE Section 9.5.2.6.2.8 as

$$F_{min} = 400 I_E S_{DS}$$
$$= 400 \times 1.0 \times 0.98$$
$$= 392 \text{ pounds per foot}$$

The calculated lateral force on an anchor is

$$p = F_p \times 1000/8$$
$$= 458.75 \text{ pounds per foot}$$
$$> F_{min} \dots \text{satisfactory}$$

The function of the subdiaphragm is to transfer the wall anchorage force into the main diaphragm. The subdiaphragm aspect ratio is

$$b/d = 32/20$$
$$= 1.6$$
$$< 2.5 \dots \text{satisfactory, as specified in ASCE Section 9.5.2.6.3.2}$$

For a reliability factor of unity, the design service level unit shear in the subdiaphragm is

$$q = 0.7pb/2d$$
$$q = 0.7 \times 453 \times 32/40$$
$$= 254 \text{ pounds per linear foot}$$
$$< 320 \dots \text{ the capacity provided}$$

Hence, the capacity of the nailing in the main diaphragm is adequate. The design service level force in the continuous cross ties, at a spacing of 32 feet, is given as

$$P_t = 0.7pb$$
$$= 0.7 \times 453 \times 32$$
$$= 10,147 \text{ pounds}$$

Components and Equipment Supported by Structures

ASCE Section 9.6.1.3 stipulates that the seismic force on components shall be determined by ASCE Equation (9.6.1.3-1). ASCE Section 9.6.1.5 stipulates that a component importance factor of 1.5 shall be used for the design of equipment in essential facilities and for the design of containers enclosing toxic or explosive materials. This is to ensure the continued operation of equipment in essential facilities and to prevent the escape of hazardous materials. In addition, in seismic use group III a value of 1.5 shall be used for components required for continual operation of the facility. A value of 1.5 is also assigned to storage rocks in occupancies open to the public.

The values of a_p listed in ASCE Tables 9.6.2.2 and 9.6.3.2 are dependant on the relative rigidity of the component. Components which have a natural period not exceeding 0.06 seconds and which are considered to be rigid have a value of unity for a_p. Nonrigid components, which may be subjected to resonant behavior, are assigned larger values of a_p. Values assigned to the factor R_p reflect the method of attachment of the component to the structure. Rigidly attached components have smaller values for R_p.

Example **5.17**

An air conditioner located on the roof of a hospital in seismic design category D with a value of $S_{DS} = 0.81g$ weighs 2 kips. Anchorage to the roof is provided by means of a vibration isolated mounting system. Calculate the design seismic force.

Solution

The design seismic force is given by ASCE Equation (9.6.1.3-1)

$$F_p = (0.4a_p S_{DS} I_p/R_p)(1+2z/h)W_p$$
$$\leq 1.6 S_{DS} I_p W_p$$
$$\geq 0.3 S_{DS} I_p W_p$$

where
$$a_p = 2.5 \text{ from ASCE Table 9.6.3.2}$$
$$I_p = 1.5 \text{ from ASCE Section 9.6.1.5}$$
$$S_{DS} = 0.81g, \text{ as given}$$
$$W_p = 2 \text{ kips, as given}$$
$$R_p = 2.5 \text{ from ASCE Table 9.6.3.2}$$
$$z = h$$

The seismic force is then

$$F_p = (0.4 \times 2.5 \times 0.81 \times 1.5/2.5)(1 + 2 \times 1)W_p$$
$$= 2.92 \text{ kips}$$
$$\leq 1.6 S_{DS} I_p W_p$$
$$\geq 0.3 S_{DS} I_p W_p$$

Hence the design force is 2.92 kips.

Wall Cladding

External cladding panels and their connections must be designed, in accordance with ASCE Section 9.6.2.4.1, to accommodate the actual anticipated inelastic deformation specified in ASCE Section 9.6.1.4. To ensure that the connection remains ductile and capable of sustaining the applied loads, all fasteners in the connection must be designed for the forces given by ASCE Equation (9.6.1.3-1) with $R_p = 1$ and $a_p = 1.25$. The panel and the body of the connector must be designed for the forces given by ASCE Equation (9.6.1.3-1) with $R_p = 2.5$ and $a_p = 1$. An additional stipulation in ASCE Section 9.6.1.6.2 is that anchors embedded in concrete or masonry shall be designed for the lesser of the design strength of the connected part, $1.3 \times$ the force in the connected part, or the maximum force that can be transferred by the structural system.

| Example **5.18** |

A wall panel weighing 20 pounds per square foot is externally mounted on an office building in seismic design category D with a value of $S_{DS} = 0.81g$. Calculate the design seismic force on the connectors and fasteners at the top of the building.

Solution

The basic design seismic force on the fasteners is given by ASCE Equation (9.6.1.3-1) as

$$F_p = (0.4 a_p S_{DS} I_p / R_p)(1 + 2z/h)W_p$$
$$\leq 1.6 S_{DS} I_p W_p$$
$$\geq 0.3 S_{DS} I_p W_p$$

where

a_p = 1.25 from ASCE Table 9.6.2.2
I_p = 1.0 from ASCE Section 9.6.1.5
S_{DS} = 0.81g, as given
W_p = 20 pounds per square foot, as given
R_p = 1.0 from ASCE Table 9.6.2.2
$z = h$

The basic design seismic force on the fastener is

$$F_p = (0.4 \times 1.25 \times 0.81 \times 1.0/1.0)(1 + 2 \times 1)W_p$$
$$= 24.30 \text{ pounds per square foot}$$
$$< 1.6 S_{DS} I_p W_p \ldots \text{satisfactory}$$
$$> 0.3 S_{DS} I_p W_p \ldots \text{satisfactory}$$

Hence the design force is 24.30 pounds per square foot.

The design seismic load on the body of the connector using a value of $R_p = 2.5$ and $a_p = 1$ is

$$F_C = 24.3(1.0/2.5)(1.0/1.25)$$
$$< 1.6 S_{DS} I_p W_p \ldots \text{satisfactory}$$
$$> 0.3 S_{DS} I_p W_p \ldots \text{satisfactory}$$

Hence the design force is 7.78 pounds per square foot.

Self-Supporting Nonbuilding Structures

ASCE Section 9.14 governs the seismic design for a number of types of nonbuilding structures. For a rigid structure, which is defined as having a natural period of less than 0.06 seconds, the design lateral force is given by ASCE Equation (9.14.5.2) as

$$V = 0.3 S_{DS} IW$$

where I is the importance factor defined in ASCE Table 9.14.5.1.2. The lateral force must be distributed over the height of the structure in accordance with the distribution of the mass. This method is applicable to equipment mounted directly on a concrete pad foundation at grade level.[21]

For other nonbuilding structures, the design lateral force is given by ASCE Equations (9.5.5.2.1-2), (9.5.5.2.1-1), and (9.14.5.1-1) as

$$V = (S_{D1} I/RT)W \leq (S_{DS} I/R)W \geq 0.14 S_{DS} IW$$

where

R = the lesser response modification factor obtained from ASCE Tables 9.14.5.1.1 or 9.5.2.2
I = importance factor from ASCE Table 9.14.5.1.2

In seismic design category E and F, as specified in ASCE Equation (9.14.5.1.2), the minimum base shear is

$$V \geq (0.8 S_1 I/R) W$$

where S_1 = maximum considered response acceleration at 1-second period.

Example 5.19

A grain bin is supported on braced frames founded on grade in seismic design category D. Determine the seismic lateral force in the north-south direction if the stiffness of the braced frame in this direction is 500 kips per inch and the fully loaded bin weighs 50 kips. The design response accelerations are $S_{DS} = 0.81g$ and $S_{D1} = 0.51g$.

Solution

The natural period is given by

$$T = 2\pi \sqrt{m/k}$$
$$= 0.32 \sqrt{W/k}$$

where
  W = 50 kips, as given
  k = 500 kips per inch, as given

The natural period is then

$$T = 0.32 \sqrt{50/500}$$
$$= 0.10 \text{ seconds}$$
$$> 0.06$$

Hence, the structure is nonrigid, and from ASCE Section 9.5.5 the value of the lateral force is governed by ASCE Equation (9.5.5.2.1-1) as

$$V = (S_{DS} I/R) W$$
$$I = 1.0 \text{ from ASCE Table 9.14.5.1.2}$$
$$S_{DS} = 0.81g$$
$$R = 3 \text{ from ASCE Table 9.14.5.1.1}$$

Then the total lateral force is

$$V = (0.81 \times 1/3)50$$
$$= 13.5 \text{ kips}$$

Example 5.20

The rigid transformer shown in Exhibit 10 weighs 15 kips, and is attached to a concrete foundation pad with four $3/4$-inch diameter A325 anchor bolts. Determine the lateral force on the bolts if the design response accelerations are $S_{DS} = 0.81g$ and $S_{D1} = 0.51g$.

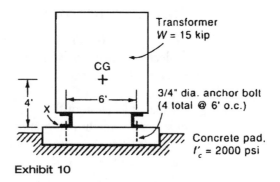

Exhibit 10

Solution

The seismic lateral force for a rigid component mounted at grade is given by ASCE Equation (9.14.5.2) as

$$V = 0.3S_{DS}IW$$

where
$S_{DS} = 0.81g$
$I = 1.0$ from ASCE Table 9.14.5.1.2
$W = 15$ kips, as given

Then the lateral force is given by ASCE Equation (9.14.5.2) as

$$V = 0.3 \times 0.81 \times 1 \times 15$$
$$= 3.65 \text{ kips}$$

The strength-level shear force on each bolt is

$$P_v = 3.65/4$$
$$= 0.91 \text{ kips}$$

Taking moments about axis X, the service-level overturning moment is given by

$$M_O = 0.7 \times 4V = 0.7 \times 4 \times 3.65 = 10.22 \text{ kip-feet}$$

The restoring moment is

$$M_R = 3 \times 0.6W = 3 \times 0.6 \times 15 = 27.0 \text{ kip-feet}$$
$$> M_O$$

Hence, no tension is developed in the bolts.

TORSION AND RIGIDITY

Rigid Diaphragm

As implied by ASCE Section 9.5.2.3.1, a diaphragm may be considered rigid when its midpoint displacement, under lateral load, is less than twice the average displacement at its ends. It is then assumed that the diaphragm and shear walls undergo rigid body rotation, and this produces additional torsional forces in the shear walls.

Torsional Moment

The center of rigidity is that point about which a structure tends to rotate when subjected to an eccentric force. In the case of a seismic force, this acts at the center of mass of the structure, and torsional moment is the product of seismic force and the eccentricity of the center of mass with respect to the center of rigidity. The calculated location of the center of mass may not be exact due to the distribution of structure weight being imprecisely known. Similarly inaccuracies in calculated rigidity of the shear walls, and the neglect of nonstructural components such as partitions and stairs, lead to the inexact location of the center of rigidity.[22] To account for these uncertainties, ASCE Section 9.5.5.5.2 specifies that the center of mass be assumed to be displaced from its calculated position, in each direction, a distance equal to 5 percent of the building dimension perpendicular to the direction of the seismic force. This accidental eccentricity is amplified for structures in seismic design categories C and above where torsional irregularity exists, as defined in ASCE Table 9.5.2.3.2. The amplification factor is given by ASCE Equation (9.5.5.5.2) as

$$A_x = (\delta_{max}/1.2\delta_{avg})^2$$

where
δ_{max} = max displacement at level x
δ_{avg} = average displacement at extreme points of the structure at level x

Figure 5.28 illustrates the analysis required for torsional effects.

Center of Mass and Center of Rigidity

The location of the center of rigidity is obtained by taking statical moments of the wall rigidities about a convenient origin. For seismic loads in the north-south direction, the north-south walls, which have no stiffness in this direction, are omitted and only east and west walls are considered. From Figure 5.28, the center of rigidity is located a distance from the east wall given by

$$
\begin{aligned}
r_E &= \Sigma R_y x / \Sigma R_y \\
&= (R_W \times L + R_E \times 0)/(R_W + R_E) \\
&= R_W L/(R_W + R_E)
\end{aligned}
$$

The center of rigidity is located a distance from the south wall given by

$$
\begin{aligned}
r_S &= \Sigma R_x y / \Sigma R_x \\
&= (R_N \times B + R_S \times 0)/(R_N + R_S) \\
&= R_N B/(R_N + R_S)
\end{aligned}
$$

The polar moment of inertia of the walls is given by

$$
\begin{aligned}
J &= \Sigma r^2 R \\
&= r_N^2 R_N + r_S^2 R_S + r_E^2 R_E + r_W^2 R_W
\end{aligned}
$$

The center of mass is obtained by taking statical moments of the wall weights about a convenient origin. When the lateral seismic force is determined at roof diaphragm level in a single-story building, the force in the north-south direction

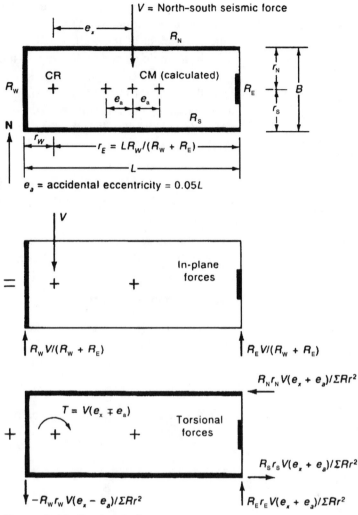

Figure 5.28 Torsional effects

does not include an allowance for the mass of the east and west shear walls. Hence, in locating the center of mass for north-south forces, the east and west walls are omitted. From Figure 5.28, for this situation, the distance of the center of mass from the east wall is given by

$$\bar{x} = \Sigma W_{NS} x / \Sigma W_{NS}$$
$$= (W_R \times L/2 + W_N \times L/2 + W_S \times L/2)(W_R + W_N + W_S)$$

where
W_R = weight of roof
W_N = weight of north wall
W_S = weight of south wall

In this instance, for equal lengths and distribution of mass in the north and south walls and in the roof, the center of mass lies midway between the east and west walls, and

$$\bar{x} = L/2$$

The total shear force at the base of the east and west walls is then given by the sum of the shear due to the in-plane forces, torsional forces, and the force due to the self-weight of the wall.

In a single-story building when the lateral force is determined at base level (i.e., the base shear), and for multistory structures where the lateral force includes an allowance for the mass of all walls, it is appropriate to include all walls in the calculation of the center of mass. From Figure 5.28, for this situation, the center of mass is located a distance from the east wall given by

$$\bar{x} = \Sigma Wx / \Sigma W$$
$$= (W_R \times L/2 + W_N \times L/2 + W_S \times L/2 + W_E \times 0 + W_W \times L)/$$
$$(W_R + W_N + W_S + W_E + W_W)$$

The total shear force at the base of the east and west walls is then given by the sum of the shear due to the in-plane forces and the torsional forces.

Torsional Effects

The eccentricity between the center of mass and the center of rigidity is shown in Figure 5.28 as

$$e_x = r_E - \bar{x}$$

The accidental eccentricity is given by

$$e_a = 0.05L$$

The total eccentricity is

$$e_T = e_x \pm e_a$$

The torsional moment for north-south seismic load is given by

$$T_{NS} = Ve_T$$
$$= V(e_x \pm e_a)$$

The total force in the east wall, when V represents the seismic force at diaphragm level, is given by

$$F = F_S + F_T + F_W$$

where the in-plane shear force is

$$F_S = VR_E/(R_E + R_W)$$

the torsional shear force is

$$F_T = T_{NS}\, r_E R_E / J$$

and the shear force due to the self-weight of the wall is

$$F_W = C_s W_W$$

For the west wall, since torsional forces are of opposite sense to the in-plane forces, the total design force is

$$F = F_S + F_W - F_T$$

When V represents the total base shear, or the lateral force at story level in a multistory structure, the total force in the east wall, for north-south seismic load, is

$$F = F_S + F_T$$

Since the base shear includes an allowance for the mass of all walls, the additional term, F_W, is not required.

For the west wall, allowing for the opposite sense of the torsional forces, the total design force is given by

$$F = F_S - F_T$$

<table><tr><td>Example **5.21**</td></tr></table>

Determine the maximum shear in the east and west shear walls of the building in Example 5.5 for the calculated base shear in the north-south direction. The roof consists of a concrete slab and the relative rigidities of the walls are

$$R_1 = R_3 = 1.0$$
$$R_2 = 0.7$$
$$R_4 = 0.6$$

The effects of torsional irregularity may be neglected.

Solution

The base shear, calculated in Example 5.5, allows for the mass of the roof and all walls. Hence, in locating the center of mass, it is appropriate to include the weight of the roof and all walls. From the symmetry of the structure, for a north-south seismic load, the center of mass is located midway between wall 2 and wall 4, and its distance from wall 4 is

$$\bar{x} = 40/2 = 20 \text{ feet}$$

The position of the center of mass in the orthogonal direction is not relevant to the question.

In locating the center of rigidity for a north-south seismic load, wall 1 and wall 3, which have no stiffness in the north-south direction, are omitted. Taking moments about wall 4, the distance of the center of rigidity from wall 4 is given by

$$r_4 = \Sigma R_y x / \Sigma R_y$$
$$= (0.7 \times 40 + 0.6 \times 0)/(0.7 + 0.6)$$
$$= 21.5 \text{ feet}$$

The distance of the center of rigidity from wall 2 is

$$r_2 = 40 - 21.5$$
$$= 18.5 \text{ feet}$$

In locating the center of rigidity for an east-west seismic load, wall 2 and wall 4, which have no stiffness in the east-west direction, are omitted. Due to the symmetry of the structure, the center of rigidity is located midway between wall 1 and wall 3, and

$$r_1 = r_3 = 10 \text{ feet}$$

The polar moment of inertia of the walls is

$$
\begin{aligned}
J &= \Sigma \, r^2 R \\
&= r_1^2 \times R_1 + r_2^2 \times R_2 + r_3^2 \times R_3 + r_4^2 \times R_4 \\
&= 10^2 \times 1 + 18.5^2 \times 0.7 + 10^2 \times 1 + 21.5^2 \times 0.6 \\
&= 717 \text{ square feet}
\end{aligned}
$$

The sum of the wall rigidities for a seismic load in the north-south direction is

$$
\begin{aligned}
\Sigma R_y &= R_2 + R_4 \\
&= 0.7 + 0.6 \\
&= 1.3
\end{aligned}
$$

For a seismic load in the north-south direction, the eccentricity is

$$
\begin{aligned}
e_x &= r_4 - \overline{x} \\
&= 1.5 \text{ feet}
\end{aligned}
$$

Accidental eccentricity, in accordance with ASCE Section 9.5.5.5.2, is

$$
\begin{aligned}
e_a &= \pm \, 0.05 \times L \\
&= \pm \, 0.05 \times 40 \\
&= \pm \, 2 \text{ feet}
\end{aligned}
$$

The maximum force is produced in wall 4 by an accidental displacement of the center of mass to the west. For an accidental displacement of the center of mass to the west, the total eccentricity is

$$
\begin{aligned}
e_T &= e_x + e_a \\
&= 1.5 + 2.0 \\
&= 3.5 \text{ feet}
\end{aligned}
$$

The counterclockwise torsional moment acting about the center of rigidity is

$$
\begin{aligned}
T &= Ve_T \\
&= 13.80 \times 3.5 \\
&= 48.30 \text{ kip-feet}
\end{aligned}
$$

The force produced in wall 4 by the base shear acting in the north-south direction is the sum of the in-plane shear force and the torsional shear force. The shear force due to the wall self-weight is not required, as this is already included in the value of the base shear. The in-plane shear force is

$$
\begin{aligned}
F_S &= VR_4/\Sigma R_y \\
&= 13.80 \times 0.6/1.3 = 6.37 \text{ kips}
\end{aligned}
$$

The torsional shear force is

$$F_T = Tr_4 R_4 / J$$
$$= 48.30 \times 21.5 \times 0.6/717$$
$$= 0.87 \text{ kips}$$

The total force in wall 4 is

$$F = F_S + F_T$$
$$= 6.37 + 0.87$$
$$= 7.24 \text{ kips}$$

The maximum force is produced in wall 2 for an accidental displacement of the center of the mass to east, and the total eccentricity is then

$$e_T = e_x - e_a$$
$$= 1.5 - 2$$
$$= -0.5 \text{ feet}$$

The clockwise torsional moment acting about the center of rigidity is then

$$T = Ve_T$$
$$= 13.80 \times 0.5$$
$$= 6.90 \text{ kip-feet}$$

The in-plane shear force produced in wall 2 by the base shear acting in the north-south direction is

$$F_S = VR_2 / \Sigma R_y$$
$$= 13.80 \times 0.7/1.3$$
$$= 7.43 \text{ kips}$$

The torsional shear force in wall 2 is

$$F_T = Tr_2 R_2 / J$$
$$= 6.90 \times 18.5 \times 0.7/717$$
$$= 0.13 \text{ kips}$$

The total force in wall 2 is

$$F = F_S + F_T$$
$$= 7.43 + 0.13$$
$$= 7.56 \text{ kips}$$

Shear Wall Rigidity

The rigidity of a concrete or masonry shear wall is the force required to produce unit displacement at the top edge of the wall. This is most readily obtained as the reciprocal of the deflection of the wall due to unit load applied at the top edge. The deflection of a wall or pier due to a unit applied load is given by

$$\delta = \delta_F + \delta_S$$

where

    δ_F = deflection due to flexure

        = $4(H/L)^3/Et$ for a cantilever pier

        = $(H/L)^3/Et$ for a pier fixed at top and bottom

    H = height of pier

    L = length of pier

    E = modulus of elasticity of pier

    t = thickness of pier

    δ_S = deflection due to shear

        = $1.2H/GA$

        = $3(H/L)/Et$

    G = rigidity modulus of pier

        = $0.4E$

    A = cross-sectional area of pier

        = tL

The rigidity, or stiffness, of a pier is given by

$$R = 1/\delta$$

The rigidity of a wall with openings is most accurately determined by the following technique.[23] The deflection of the wall is first obtained as though it is a solid wall. From this is subtracted the deflection of that portion of the wall which contains the opening. The deflection of each pier, formed by the openings, is now added back. The relevant calculations are readily performed by hand or may be obtained from a programmable calculator.[24]

Example 5.22

Determine the rigidity of the masonry wall shown in Exhibit 11. The wall is 8 inches thick with a modulus of elasticity of $E_m = 1,500,000$ pounds per square inch, and may be considered fixed at the top and bottom.

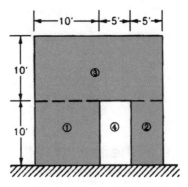

Exhibit 11

Solution

The relevant details are

Pier	H	L	Type	$(H/L)^3$ $= Et\delta_F$	$3H/L$ $= Et\delta_s$	$Et(\delta_F + \delta_s)$ $= Et\delta$	R/Et
Wall	20	20	Fixed	1	3	4.000	—
1 + 2 + 4	10	20	Fixed	−0.125	−1.500	−1.625	—
1	10	10	Fixed	1	3	—	0.250
2	10	5	Fixed	8	6	—	0.071
1 + 2	—	—	—	—	—	3.115	←0.321
Total	—	—	—	—	—	5.490→	0.182

The actual rigidity of the wall is

$$R = 0.182Et$$
$$= 0.182 \times 1500 \times 8$$
$$= 2185 \text{ kips per inch}$$

Braced-Frame Stiffness

The stiffness of a braced frame is the force required to produce unit displacement at the top of the frame. This is obtained as the reciprocal of the deflection of the frame due to a unit horizontal virtual force applied at the top. The horizontal displacement at the point of application of the load is determined by the virtual work method[25,26] by evaluating the expression

$$\delta = \Sigma u^2 L/AE$$

where u is the force in a member due to the unit virtual load, L is the length of the member, A is the sectional area of the member, E is the modulus of elasticity of the member and the summation extends over all the members of the frame. The stiffness is, then,

$$k = 1/\delta = 1/(\Sigma\, u^2 L/AE)$$

For frame A in Figure 5.29, if the elastic shortening of the beam and columns may be neglected, only the diagonal brace contributes to the virtual work summation, and the expression for frame stiffness simplifies to

$$k = \cos^2 \theta(AE/L)$$

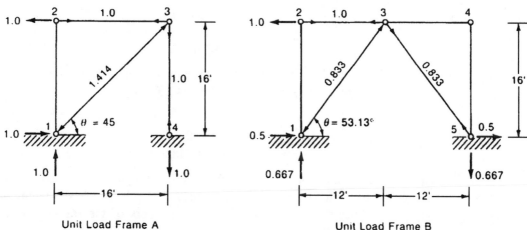

Unit Load Frame A   Unit Load Frame B

Figure 5.29 Braced frames

where L, A, and E are the length, area, and modulus of elasticity of the brace and θ is its angle of inclination to the horizontal.

For frame B in Figure 5.29, there are no forces in the columns due to unit horizontal load. When the elastic shortening of the beam may be neglected, and when both diagonal braces have identical areas, lengths, and moduli of elasticity, the expression for the frame stiffness simplifies to

$$k = \Sigma\cos^2\theta(AE/L)$$

and the summation extends over the diagonal braces only.

Example 5.23

Calculate the stiffness of frame A and frame B in Figure 5.29. The beams in both frames may be considered infinite in area, and the columns are W8 × 31. The diagonal brace in frame A is TS $7 \times 7 \times \frac{1}{4}$, and the braces in frame B are TS $6 \times 6 \times 3/16$.

Solution

The stiffness of frame A is obtained by applying a unit virtual load to the frame, as shown in Figure 5.29. The horizontal displacement at the point of application of the load is determined by the virtual work method, by evaluating the expression

$$\delta = \Sigma u^2 L/AE$$

where u is the force in a member due to the unit virtual load, L is the length of the member, A is the sectional area of the member, and E is the modulus of elasticity. The summation extends over all the members with the exception of the beam, which is considered to have negligible elastic shortening. The relevant values are

Member	L	A	u	u^2L/A
Brace 13	22.62	6.59	−1.414	6.86
Column 34	16.00	9.13	1.000	1.75
Total	—	—	—	8.61

The horizontal displacement of point 2 is given by

$$\begin{aligned} \delta &= \Sigma\, u^2L/AE \\ &= 8.61 \times 12/29{,}000 \\ &= 0.00356 \text{ inches} \end{aligned}$$

The lateral stiffness of frame A, which is defined as the force required to produce unit horizontal displacement, is given by

$$\begin{aligned} k &= 1/\delta \\ &= 1/0.00356 \\ &= 280.7 \text{ kips per inch} \end{aligned}$$

The stiffness of frame B is obtained by applying a unit load at joint 2, which produces the forces shown in Figure 5.29. Since the elastic shortening of the beam may be neglected, only the diagonal members of the frame contribute to the stiffness, which is given by

$$k = \Sigma\, \cos^2\theta(AE/L)$$

where θ is the angle of inclination of the diagonal member to the horizontal, and the summation extends over the diagonal members only.

The stiffness of frame B is

$$k = \Sigma \cos^2\theta(AE/L)$$
$$= 2 \times 4.27 \times 29,000 \times \cos^2(53.13°)/(20 \times 12)$$
$$= 371.5 \text{ kips per inch}$$

CONFIGURATION REQUIREMENTS

Structural Irregularities

The static lateral force procedure is applicable to structures that are of essentially regular construction—that is, structures with uniform distribution of mass and stiffness, and without irregular features that will produce a concentration of torsional stresses. When these conditions are satisfied, the static force procedure provides a reasonable envelope of the forces and deformations due to the actual dynamic response.

ASCE Tables 9.5.2.3.3 and 9.5.2.3.2 define possible vertical and plan structural irregularities,[27] and detail additional requirements that must be satisfied if the irregularities are used. These are illustrated in Figures 5.30 and 5.31.

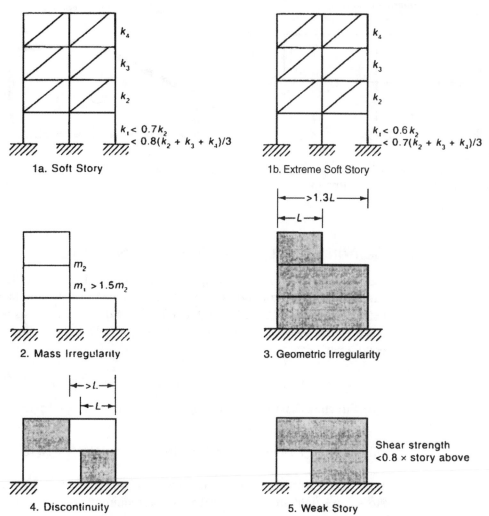

Figure 5.30 Vertical structural irregularities

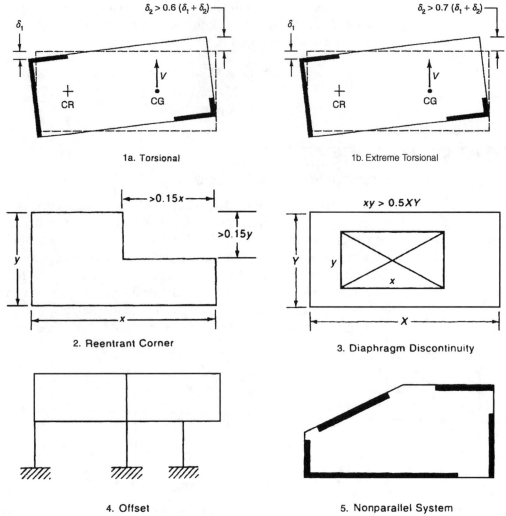

Figure 5.31 Plan structural irregularities

Selection of Lateral Force Procedure

Vertical structural irregularities produce loads at various levels that differ significantly from the distribution of base shear assumed in the static lateral force procedure. As specified in ASCE Table 9.5.2.5.1, a dynamic analysis is necessary for all structures assigned to seismic design categories D, E, and F under the following conditions:

(i) All structures with a fundamental period T not less than $3.5T_S$.

(ii) Structures having vertical irregularities 1a (soft story), 1b (extreme soft story), 2 (mass), or 3 (geometric).

(iii) Structures having plan irregularities 1a (torsional) or 1b (extreme torsional).

Light-framed structures and structures in seismic use group I not exceeding two stories in height are exempted from these requirements.

Example **5.24**

A three-story office building with special moment-resisting frames in the north-south direction and eccentrically braced frames in the east-west direction is assigned to seismic design category D. The dead load, W, at each level and the stiffness, k, and shear strength, v, in the north-south direction, are indicated in Exhibit 12. The fundamental period of the building is $T < 3.5T_S$. Determine the vertical and plan irregularities for the building and indicate additional code requirements and procedures required for each.

Solution

(i) The total stiffness of the second story in the north-south direction is

$$k_2 = 2 \times 200$$
$$= 400 \text{ kips per inch}$$

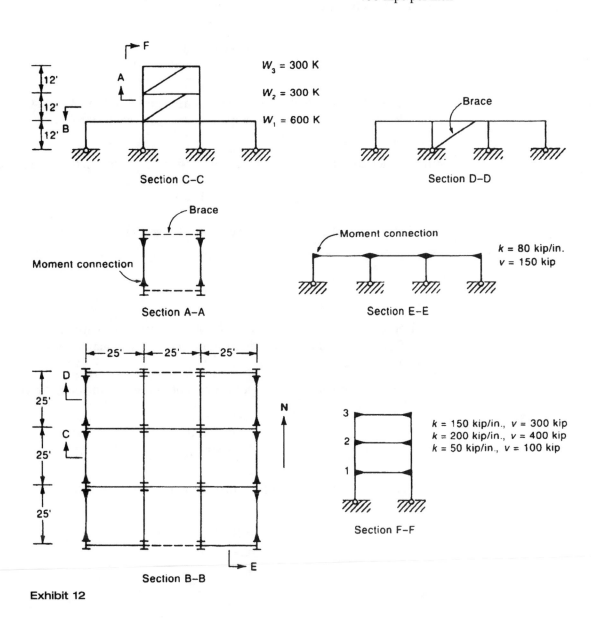

Exhibit 12

The total stiffness of the first story in the north-south direction is

$$k_1 = 2 \times 80 + 2 \times 50$$
$$= 260 \text{ kips per inch}$$
$$= 65\% \times k_2$$
$$> 60\% \times k_2$$
$$< 70\% \times k_2$$

Hence, the first story constitutes a soft story and is considered a vertical irregularity of type 1a in ASCE Table 9.5.2.3.3. ASCE Section 9.5.2.5.1 requires the structure to be designed using the static lateral force procedure.

(ii) The effective weight of the second story is

$$W_2 = 300 \text{ kips}$$

The effective weight of the first story is

$$W_1 = 600 \text{ kips}$$
$$> 150\% \times W_1$$

Hence, this constitutes a vertical mass irregularity of type 2 in ASCE Table 9.5.2.3.3. The additional code requirements are identical to those given for vertical irregularity type 1a.

(iii) The horizontal dimension of the moment-resisting frame in the second story is

$$L_2 = 25 \text{ feet}$$

The horizontal dimension of the moment-resisting frame in the first story is

$$L_1 = 75 \text{ feet}$$
$$> 130\% \times L_2$$

Hence, this constitutes a type 3 vertical geometric irregularity in ASCE Table 9.5.2.3.3. The additional code requirements are identical to those given for vertical irregularity type 1a.

(iv) The total shear strength of the second story in the north-south direction is

$$v_2 = 2 \times 400$$
$$= 800 \text{ kips}$$

The total shear strength of the first story in the north-south direction is

$$v_1 = 2 \times 150 + 2 \times 100$$
$$= 500 \text{ kips}$$
$$= 62.5\% \times v_2$$
$$< 65\% \times v_2$$
$$< 80\% \times v_2$$

Hence, the first story constitutes a weak story and is considered a type 5 vertical irregularity in ASCE Table 9.5.2.3.3.

Since the structure exceeds two stories and is more than 30 feet in height, the first story is required by ASCE Section 9.5.2.6.2.4 to be designed for a lateral force for Ω_0 times the normal design force in the north-south direction.

(v) The lateral-force-resisting system in the east-west direction above the first story consists of braced frames located on the tower section walls. In the first story, the brace lines are on the outer walls of the base. This out-of-plane offset of the vertical elements constitutes a type 4 plan irregularity in ASCE Table 9.5.2.3.2.

ASCE Section 9.5.2.6.4.2 specifies that for this irregularity, connection of diaphragm and collectors to the vertical elements shall be designed for a 25 percent increase in the design forces. In addition, ASCE Section 9.5.2.6.2.11 requires that the first-story columns, under the tower section, which support the discontinuous braced frames in story 2 and above, shall be especially designed and detailed for the load combinations

$$1.2D + f_1L + 1.0E_m \quad \text{and} \quad 0.90 \pm 1.0E_m$$

where
  D = force due to dead load
  L = force due to live load
  E_m = force due to seismic load = $\Omega_0 Q_E \pm 0.2 S_{DS} D$
  f_1 = 1.0 for garages and places of public assembly and for floor loads exceeding 100 psf
    = 0.5 for other live loads
  Q_E = design horizontal earthquake force
  Ω_0 = overstrength factor
  S_{DS} = design response acceleration for a period of 0.2 seconds

DYNAMIC LATERAL FORCE ANALYSIS

Modal Analysis Advantages

The modal analysis procedure is suitable for calculating the response of complex multiple-degree-of-freedom structures to earthquake motion. The structural response is modeled as the maximum response of a number of single-degree-of-freedom oscillators each representing a specific mode of vibration of the actual structure. Combining the responses of the individual modes produces the equivalent external forces and base and story shears, which may then be used in the same manner as in the static lateral force procedure. The modal analysis procedure has the advantage[8] of determining the actual distribution of lateral forces from the actual mass and stiffness distribution over the height of an irregular structure, which may differ appreciably from the simplified linear distribution assumed in the static lateral force method. In addition, it accounts for the effects of the higher modes of response of a structure which may contribute significantly to the overall response of the structure.

Modal Analysis Procedure

The stages necessary in the modal analysis procedure consist of selecting the appropriate ground motion response spectrum, applying a dynamic analysis technique to a mathematical model of the structure, combining the response of a sufficient number of modes to ensure a 90 percent participation of the mass of the structure, and scaling the results to ensure consistency with the static lateral force procedure.

The normalized design spectrum presented in the ASCE standard and shown in Figure 5.13 may be used after applying the appropriate scaling factor to provide the requisite response spectrum envelopes. Alternatively, site-specific design spectra, as illustrated in Figure 5.6, may be utilized after scaling by the factor g to obtain the input spectrum. The design spectrum should be smoothed to eliminate reduced response at specific periods and to correspond to a two percent probability of being exceeded in 50 years and a damping ratio of 5 percent.

Three methods of dynamic analysis are given in ASCE Table 9.5.2.5.1. The response spectrum technique uses an appropriate response spectrum to calculate the peak modal response of all necessary modes. Two time-history techniques, either linear or nonlinear, may be used to determine the structural response through numerical integration over short time increments for a time-dependent seismic input motion.

Since the modal maximums do not all occur simultaneously or act in the same direction, a statistical combination of these values is necessary. The method using the square-root-of-the-sum-of-the-squares is acceptable for a two-dimensional analysis when the ratio of the periods of any higher mode to any lower mode is 0.75 or less. A sufficient number of modes must be combined, as specified in ASCE Section 9.5.6.3, to ensure that 90 percent of the participating mass of the structure is included.

To ensure consistency with the basic design principles adopted in the static lateral force procedure, a minimum value is stipulated in ASCE Section 9.5.6.8 for the base shear derived by dynamic analysis, and all corresponding response parameters must be scaled accordingly. The minimum value is derived from a static lateral force analysis with a value for the fundamental period of $T = C_u T_a$.

In determining the base shear by the static lateral force procedure, the fundamental period assumed is given by ASCE Section 9.5.5.3.1 as

$$T = C_u T_a$$

where

C_u = coefficient for upper limit on the calculated period given in ASCE Table 9.5.5.3.1

T_a = approximate fundamental period of vibration as determined by ASCE Equation (9.5.5.3.2-1)

The equivalent lateral base shear is then obtained from ASCE Equation (9.5.5.2-1) as

$$V = C_s W$$

where

W = seismic dead load

C_s = seismic response coefficient

$\quad = S_{D1} I_E / RT \dots$ ASCE Equation (9.5.5.2.1-2) when $T > T_S$

$\quad = S_{DS} I_E / R \dots$ ASCE Equation (9.5.5.2.1-1) when $T < T_S$

S_{D1} = design response acceleration at a period of 1 second
S_{DS} = 5 percent damped design response acceleration, for a period of 0.2 second
I_E = occupancy importance factor from IBC Table 1604.5
R = response modification factor from ASCE Table 9.5.2.2

Where the modal base shear is less than 85 percent of the base shear determined by the equivalent lateral force procedure, all modal response parameters must be increased by the modification factor given by ASCE Equation (9.5.6.8) as

$$C_m = 0.85\, V/V_t$$

where V_t = modal value of the base shear

When the base shear derived by a modal analysis exceeds the value determined by the equivalent lateral force procedure, no reduction in the modal response parameters is permitted.

Example 5.25

For the two-story building of Example 5.3, determine the number of modes which must be combined to ensure that all significant modes have been included in the analysis, and determine the design base shear and required scaling factors. Use the general design response spectrum with values for the design response accelerations of $S_{DS} = 0.81$ and $S_{D1} = 0.50$.

Solution

From Example 5.3, the values of the structure weights at each node are given by

$$w_1 = 154.5 \text{ kips}$$
$$w_2 = 154.5 \text{ kips}$$

The natural periods are

$$T_1 = 1.16 \text{ seconds}$$
$$T_2 = 0.48 \text{ seconds}$$

The normalized modal matrix is

$$[\Phi] = \begin{bmatrix} 0.605 & 1.461 \\ 1.461 & -0.605 \end{bmatrix}$$

The participation factors are

$$P_1 = 0.826$$
$$P_2 = 0.342$$

The effective modal gravity load for the first mode is given by[8]

$$W_1 = P_1 \Sigma w_i \phi_{i1}$$
$$= 0.826 \times 154.5(0.605 + 1.461)$$
$$= 265 \text{ kips}$$

As a percentage of the total structural weight, the effective modal gravity load for the first mode is

$$100W_1/W = 100 \times 265/309$$
$$= 85.8$$
$$< 90 \text{ percent}$$

Hence, consideration of the second mode is necessary to satisfy ASCE Section 9.5.6.3. The effective modal gravity load for the second mode is given by

$$W_2 = P_2\Sigma w_i\phi_{i2}$$
$$= 0.342 \times 0.856 \times 154.5$$
$$= 45 \text{ kips}$$

As a percentage of the total structural weight, the effective model gravity load for the second mode is

$$100W_2/W = 100 \times 45/309$$
$$= 14.6 \text{ percent}$$

Summing the effective modal gravity loads for both modes gives

$$\Sigma W_m = W_1 + W_2$$
$$= 265 + 45$$
$$= 310 \text{ kips}$$
$$\approx W \dots \text{ satisfactory}$$

For values for the design response accelerations of $S_{DS} = 0.81$ and $S_{D1} = 0.50$,

$$T_S = S_{D1}/S_{DS}$$
$$= 0.617 \text{ seconds}$$
$$T_0 = 0.2T_S$$
$$= 0.123 \text{ seconds}$$

For the first mode of vibration the natural period is

$$T_1 = 1.16 \text{ seconds}$$
$$> T_S \dots \text{ ASCE Equation (9.4.1.2.6-2) is applicable}$$

and

$$S_{a1} = S_{D1}/T_1$$
$$= 0.50/1.16$$
$$= 0.43g$$

Since $T_1 > 0.3$ seconds, the modal seismic response coefficient is given by ASCE Equation (9.5.6.5-3) as

$$C_{s1} = S_{a1}I_E/R$$
$$= 0.43 \times 1.0/8$$
$$= 0.054g$$

The portion of the base shear contributed by the first mode is given by ASCE Equation (9.5.6.5-1) as

$$V_1 = C_{s1}W_1$$
$$= 0.054 \times 265$$
$$= 14.31 \text{ kips}$$

For the second mode of vibration the natural period is

$$T_2 = 0.48 \text{ second}$$
$$> T_0$$
$$> 0.3 \text{ second}$$
$$< T_S \dots \text{ASCE Section 9.4.1.2.6(2) is applicable, and the modal}$$
seismic response coefficient is given by ASCE Equation (9.5.6.5-3) as

$$C_{s2} = S_{a2}I_E/R$$
$$= 0.81 \times 1.0/8$$
$$= 0.10g$$

The portion of the base shear contributed by the second mode is given by ASCE Equation (9.5.6.5-1) as

$$V_2 = C_{s2}W_2$$
$$= 0.10 \times 45$$
$$= 0.45 \text{ kips}$$

The ratio of the period of the second mode of vibration to the fundamental mode is

$$T_2/T_1 = 0.48/1.16$$
$$= 0.41$$
$$< 0.75$$

Hence, the square-root-of-the-sum-of-squares method is an acceptable method of combining the modal values of the base shears, and the design value of the modal base shear is

$$V_t = [(V_1)^2 + (V_2)^2]^{0.5}$$
$$= [(14.31)^2 + (0.45)^2]^{0.5}$$
$$= 14.32 \text{ kips}$$

To determine the scaling factor, the equivalent lateral base shear must be calculated using the amplified fundamental period given by ASCE Section 9.5.6.8.

The approximate fundamental period is given by ASCE Equation (9.5.5.3.2-1) as

$$T_a = C_t(h_n)^{0.8}$$

where
$C_t = 0.028$ for a steel moment-resisting frame
h_n = roof height
    = 30 feet

Then the approximate fundamental period is

$$T_a = 0.028(30)^{0.8}$$
$$= 0.43 \text{ seconds}$$

The value of the coefficient for the upper limit on the calculated period is obtained from ASCE Table 9.5.5.3.1 as

$$C_u = 1.4$$

Hence, the fundamental period, in accordance with ASCE Section 9.5.5.3, is limited to

$$\begin{aligned} T &= C_u T_a \\ &= 1.4 \times 0.43 \\ &= 0.602 \text{ second} \\ &< T_S \end{aligned}$$

Hence, ASCE Equation (9.5.5.2.1-1) is applicable, and the seismic response coefficient is given by

$$\begin{aligned} C_s &= S_{DS} I_E / R \\ &= 0.81 \times 1/8 \\ &= 0.101 \end{aligned}$$

The equivalent lateral base shear is then obtained from ASCE Equation (9.5.5.2-1) as

$$\begin{aligned} V &= C_s W \\ &= 0.101 \times 309 \\ &= 31.21 \text{ kips} \\ &> V_t \end{aligned}$$

Hence, the scaling factor is given by ASCE Equation (9.5.6.8) as

$$\begin{aligned} C_m &= 0.85\, V/V_t \\ &= (0.85)(31.21)/14.32 \\ &= 1.85 \end{aligned}$$

and the scaled modal base shear is

$$\begin{aligned} V &= C_m \times V_t \\ &= 1.85 \times 14.32 \\ &= 26.49 \text{ kips} \end{aligned}$$

SEISMICALLY ISOLATED BUILDINGS

Advantages of Seismic Isolation

Base isolation substantially reduces the transmission of earthquake ground motions to the seismically isolated structure, thus producing a seismic load smaller than in a fixed base structure.[28] This allows the structure to be designed to remain essentially elastic during the design-basis earthquake of $2/3 \times$ maximum considered earthquake ground motion. This provides almost complete protection of the building frame and nonstructural components, and minimum disruption to the business activity. In addition, the isolation system is designed to withstand 100 percent of the maximum considered earthquake with a two percent probability of being exceeded in 50 years, which provides a recurrence interval of 2500 years.

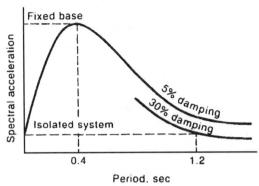

Figure 5.32 Response spectra

General Design Principles

By reducing the stiffness of the system, the natural period is increased, resulting in a reduced response to the earthquake motion. In addition, the provision of increased damping provides increased energy dissipation, thus further reducing the response. This is shown qualitatively in Figure 5.32. In order to ensure essentially elastic response of the structure, the values adopted for the response modification factor, R_1, are $\frac{3}{8}$ times the values of R used for fixed-base structures, but not less than 1.0 or greater than 2.0.

The system may be designed using either a static lateral analysis procedure or a dynamic procedure. The static procedure may be used when the structure is located on a site with $S_1 \leq 0.60g$ and with a site classification of A, B, C, or D. The structure must be of regular configuration, not exceeding four stories or 65 feet in height, and with an isolated period greater than three times the fixed base period but not greater than 3 seconds.

Static Lateral Force Procedure

The ASCE standard presents formulae for determining the effective period and displacement of the isolated structure. Hence, the total design lateral shear on the structure above the isolation system may be calculated. It may not be less than the base shear for a fixed-base structure with the same period as the isolated structure, the factored design wind load, or the force required to activate the isolation system factored by 1.5. The total lateral shear is then distributed over the height of the structure in accordance with ASCE Equation (9.13.3.5).

Example **5.26**

A four-story eccentric braced steel frame with non–moment-resisting connections and of regular configuration is located in an area with $S_S = 1.5g$ and $S_1 = 0.6g$ and on soil profile of site classification D. The structure is 100 feet square in plan, 60 feet high with 15 feet story height, and the seismic dead load at each floor and roof level is 2000 kips. Assume that the effective period of the effective period of the isolated structure T_D is 2 seconds, that the isolation system has an effective damping ratio of 30 percent, that minimum and maximum stiffness values are equal, and that a force of $0.05W$ is required to fully activate the system. Determine the vertical distribution of lateral force on the structure. Wind effects need not be considered.

Solution

The design response accelerations are given by ASCE Equations (9.4.1.2.4-1) and (9.4.1.2.4-2) as

$$S_{DS} = \tfrac{2}{3}F_a S_S = \tfrac{2}{3} \times 1.0 \times 1.5 = 1.0g$$
$$S_{D1} = \tfrac{2}{3}F_v S_1 = \tfrac{2}{3} \times 1.5 \times 0.6 = 0.6g$$
$$T_S = S_{D1}/S_{DS} = 0.6 \text{ seconds}$$

From ASCE Equation (9.5.5.3.2-1), the fundamental period of the fixed-base structure is

$$T_a = C_t(h_n)^x = 0.030(60)^{3/4} = 0.65 \text{ seconds}$$
$$< T_D/3 \ldots \text{satisfies ASCE Section 9.13.2.5.2}$$

The relationship between the effective period of the isolated structure, T_D, and the minimum stiffness of the isolation system is given by ASCE Equation (9.13.3.3.2) as

$$T_D = 2\pi\sqrt{W_I/gk_{D\min}}$$

where
  W_I = total structure weight = 8000 kips
  g = 386.4 inches per second^2
  T_D = 2 seconds as given

Hence, the value of the minimum stiffness is

$$k_{D\min} = (2\pi/2)^2 \times 8000/386.4$$
$$= 204 \text{ kips per inch}$$
$$= k_{D\max} \text{ as given}$$

The design displacement is given by ASCE Equation (9.13.3.3.1) as

$$D_D = (g/4\pi^2)S_{D1}T_D/B_D$$

where
  $S_{D1} = 0.60 \ldots$ as calculated
  $B_D = 1.7$ from ASCE Table 9.13.3.3.1 for a damping ratio of 30 percent

Hence, the design displacement is

$$D_D = (386.4/4 \times 3.142^2) \times 0.60 \times 2/1.7 = 6.91 \text{ inches}$$

The total design lateral force on the structure above the isolation system is given by ASCE Equation (9.13.3.4.2) as

$$V_S = k_{D\max}\, D_D/R_1$$

where $R_1 = \frac{3}{8} \times 7 = 2$ maximum…from ASCE Equation (9.13.3.4.2) for an eccentric braced frame. Then, the design lateral force is

$$V_S = 204 \times 6.91/2 = 705 \text{ kips}$$

The seismic force required to activate the isolation system is given as

$$V_1 = 0.05W_I$$
$$= 0.05 \times 8000 = 400 \text{ kips} < V_S/1.5 \ldots \text{satisfactory}$$

For a fixed-based structure with a fundamental period of 2 seconds $> T_S$, the base shear is given by ASCE Equation (9.5.5.2.1-2) as

$$V = (S_{D1}I_E/RT)W$$

where
  $I_E = 1.0$ for a standard-occupancy structure
  $R = 7$ from ASCE Table 9.5.2.2 for an eccentrically braced frame
  $W = 8000$ kips, as given

Then, the seismic base shear is

$$V = (0.60 \times 1/7 \times 2) \times 8000$$
$$= 342 \text{ kips}$$
$$< V_S \ldots \text{satisfactory}$$

Hence, the governing value for the seismic lateral force, in accordance with ASCE Section 9.13.2.5.2, is $V_S = 705$ kips.

The design lateral force at level x in the structure is given by ASCE Equation (9.13.3.5) as

$$F_x = V_S w_x h_x / \Sigma w_i h_i$$
$$= 705 \times 2000 \times h_x / 300{,}000 = 0.00235 w_x h_x$$

and

$$V_5 = 282 \text{ kips}$$
$$V_4 = 212 \text{ kips}$$
$$V_3 = 141 \text{ kips}$$
$$V_2 = 70 \text{ kips}$$

REFERENCES

1. Harris, J. R. *Overview of Seismic Codes*. BSCES/ASCE Structural Group Lecture Series, Boston, 1991.
2. Smith, S. W. Introduction to Seismological Concepts Related to Earthquake Hazards in the Pacific Northwest. *Societal Implications: Selected Readings*. Building Seismic Safety Council, Washington, DC, 1985.
3. Thiel, C. C., Ed. *Competing Against Time*. Report by the Governor's Board of Inquiry on the 1989 Loma Prieta Earthquake. State of California, Office of Planning and Research, Sacramento, CA, 1990.
4. Shakal, A. M., et al. *CSMPI Strong Motion Records from the Santa Cruz Mountains (Loma Prieta) Earthquake of October 17, 1989*. California Department of Conservation, Division of Mines and Geology, Sacramento, 1989.
5. Plafker, G., and Galloway, J. P. *Lessons Learned from the Loma Prieta, California, Earthquake of October 17, 1989*. U.S. Geological Survey, Washington, DC, 1989.
6. Building Seismic Safety Council. *Improving the Seismic Safety of New Buildings*. Washington, DC, 1986.
7. Paz, M. *Structural Dynamics*. Van Nostrand Reinhold, New York, 1991.
8. Structural Engineering Association of California. *Recommended Lateral Force Requirements and Commentary*. Sacramento, CA, 1999.
9. Federal Highway Administration. *Seismic Design and Retrofit Manual for Highway Bridges*. Washington, DC, 1987.
10. Building Seismic Safety Council. *NEHRP Recommended Provisions for the Development of Seismic Regulations for New Buildings: Part 2, Commentary*. Washington, DC, 2000.
11. International Codes Council. *2003 International Building Code*. Falls Church, VA, 2003.
12. American Society of Civil Engineers. *Minimum Design Loads for Buildings and Other Structures: ASCE 7-02*. New York, 2002.
13. Nester, M. R., and Porusch, A. R. A Rational System for Earthquake Risk Management. *Proceedings of the 1991 Convention of the Structural Engineers Association of California*. Sacramento, 1992.
14. American Concrete Institute. *Building Code Requirements, and Commentary for Reinforced Concrete (ACI 318-02)*. Farmington Hills, MI, 2002.
15. American Institute of Steel Construction. *Seismic Provisions for Structural Steel Buildings*. Chicago, 2002.
16. American Plywood Association. *Diaphragms*. APA Design/Construction Guide, Tacoma, WA, 1989.
17. Tissell, J. R. *Horizontal Plywood Diaphragm Tests*. Laboratory Report 106. American Plywood Association, Tacoma, WA, 1967.
18. Tissell, J. R., and Elliott, J. R. *Plywood Diaphragms*. Research Report 138. American Plywood Association, Tacoma, WA, 2000.
19. Sheedy, P. Anchorage of Concrete and Masonry Walls. *Building Standards*, October 1983 and April 1984. International Conference of Building Officials, Whittier, CA.
20. Coil, J. *Subdiaphragms*. Structural Engineering Association of Southern California Design Seminar. Los Angeles, 1991.

21. Bachman, R. E. C_p and Nonbuilding Structures: 1988 UBC and Blue Book Overview and Perspective. *Proceedings of the 1988 Seminar of the Structural Engineers Association of Southern California*. Los Angeles, November 1988.

22. De la Llera, J. C., and Chopra, A. K. Evaluation of Code-Accidental Torsion Provisions Using Earthquake Records from Three Nominally Symmetric-Plan Buildings. *Proceedings of the SMIP92 Seminar on Seismological and Engineering Implications of Recent Strong-Motion Data*. California Department of Conservation, Division of Mines and Geology, Sacramento, 1992.

23. United States Army Corps of Engineer. *Seismic Design for Buildings*. U.S. Government Printing Office. Washington, DC, 1998.

24. Williams, A. *Structural Engineering License Review: Problems and Solutions*. 5th ed. Dearborn, Chicago, 2004.

25. Tuma, J. J. *Structural Analysis*. McGraw-Hill, New York, 1969.

26. Williams, A. *The Analysis of Indeterminate Structures*. Hart, New York, 1968.

27. Sabol, T. A. *Dynamic Analysis or Not*. Structural Engineers Association of Southern California Design Seminar. Los Angeles, February 1992.

28. Kircher, C. A., and Bachman, R. E. Guidelines for Design Criteria for Base Isolation Retrofit of Existing Buildings. *Proceedings of the 1991 Convention of the Structural Engineers Association of California*. Sacramento, 1992.

Hydraulics

Bruce E. Larock

OUTLINE

INTRODUCTION 319
Hydrostatics

CONSERVATION LAWS 322
Continuity ■ Energy ■ Momentum

PUMPS AND TURBINES 329
Turbomachinery Similitude and Specific Speed ■ Pump Types ■ Net
Positive Suction Head ■ System Performance ■ Turbines

OPEN CHANNEL FLOW 334
Uniform Flow and Manning Equation ■ Hydraulic Jump ■ Efficient
Section ■ Specific Energy ■ Gradually Varied Flow

SELECTED SYMBOLS AND ABBREVIATIONS 342

REFERENCES 342

INTRODUCTION

This chapter will selectively review hydrostatics, the fundamental principles for conservation of fluid mass (continuity), energy and linear momentum, the selection and operation of centrifugal pumps and turbines, and elements of open channel flow. The review focuses primarily on water, assumes it is incompressible, and uses standard values for its properties. (Water density and viscosity depend somewhat on temperature, and these values can be obtained from tables in reference books.) Since entire books have been written on hydraulics, one can augment this review, if desired, by use of the supplementary references following the chapter.

Hydrostatics

The pressure distribution, p, in a motionless body of water is given by

$$\nabla p = \rho g \tag{6.1}$$

Using an (x, y, z) coordinate system, with x and y horizontal and z vertically upward, one obtains

$$\frac{dp}{dz} = -\rho g = -\gamma \qquad (6.2)$$

in which ρ is the density (or mass density) of water (1.94 slugs/ft^3 or 1000 kg/m^3), g is the acceleration of gravity, and γ is the unit weight (or specific weight or weight density) for water (62.4 lb/ft^3 or 9800 N/m^3). The pressure in the horizontal (x, y) plane is uniform, that is, constant. Integration of Equation (6.2) between points 1 and 2 yields

$$p_2 - p_1 = -\gamma(z_2 - z_1) \qquad (6.3)$$

Normally one can use either gage or absolute pressures in a problem so long as they are not mixed. **Gage pressure** registers zero at standard conditions (temperature = 273 K = 0°C; pressure = 1 atm = 760 torr = 760 mm Hg = 101.3 kPa = 14.7 lb/in.). The density or unit weight of other liquids is sometimes given in terms of the ratio $S = \rho/\rho_w = \gamma/\gamma_w$, where S is the specific gravity of the liquid.

Example 6.1

In Exhibit 1, reservoirs A and B are connected by a tube. The specific gravities of the liquids are $S_A = 0.8$, $S_1 = 1.3$, $S_2 = 1.6$, and $S_B = 1.0$. Determine the pressure difference between points A and B.

Solution

The pressures in opposing limbs of the tube at points C and D are equal on the left and right sides of each limb, that is, $p_{CL} = p_{CR}$ and $p_{DL} = p_{DR}$, where L and R indicate "left" and "right."

$$p_{CR} = p_A + (0.3 + 0.2)\gamma_A$$
$$p_{DR} = p_{CL} - 0.2\gamma_1$$
$$p_{DL} = p_B - 0.35\gamma_B - (0.4 + 0.2)\gamma_2.$$

Now algebra is used to eliminate the intermediate pressures:

$$p_B - p_A = 0.5\gamma_A - 0.2\gamma_1 + 0.6\gamma_2 + 0.35\gamma_B.$$

Inserting the specific gravity data, one obtains

$$p_B - p_A = [0.5(0.8) - 0.2(1.3) + 0.6(1.6) + 0.35(1.0)]\gamma_w$$
$$p_B - p_A = 1.45\gamma_w = (1.45\,\text{m})(9800\,\text{N/m}^3) = 14{,}200\ \text{N/m}^2 = 14.2\ \text{kPa}.$$

The **buoyant force** on a floating or fully immersed object is

$$F_B = \gamma(\text{volume}) \qquad (6.4)$$

in which the volume is the amount of fluid of unit weight, γ, displaced.

The fluid pressure distribution on any submerged surface will develop a hydrostatic force on that surface. The overall magnitude and the direction of such a force on a surface of any shape can be computed by first determining the magnitude and direction of the force components in the horizontal and vertical directions; these component results are then combined by direct use of the principles of statics.

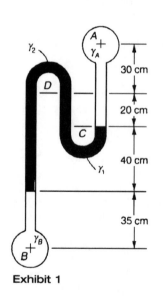

Exhibit 1

The magnitude of the force F on a submerged plane surface is

$$F = \int_A p\,dA = p_C A = \gamma h_C A \tag{6.5}$$

in which A is the surface acted on, and p_C and h_C are the pressure and submerged depth of the centroid of this area.

In Figure 6.1 the two-dimensional curved surface AB is acted upon by fluid above and to the left of it. A free-body diagram of the solid surface and a chunk of fluid above it is labeled ABC, and rectangular component forces F_H and F_{VI} act in the horizontal and vertical directions on the two faces CB and CA, which are each seen on edge. The line of the action of F_{VI} coincides with the centroid of area CA since this area is horizontal. The line of action of F_H lies below the centroid of area CB a distance $I/h_C A$, in which I is the moment of inertia of A about its centroid. The other vertical force component, F_{V2}, is equal to the weight of the fluid within the free body itself and acts through the centroid of this volume of fluid. By direct force summations, the components of the resultant force F_R are

$$(F_R)_h = F_H \quad \text{and} \quad (F_R)_v = F_{VI} + F_{V2}$$

If surface AB is a plane inclined surface, Equation (6.5) may be used directly to find the magnitude of the force normal to it. The method described above for curved surfaces could still be used to find the location of this force, if needed.

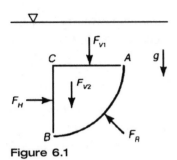

Figure 6.1

Example **6.2**

Exhibit 2 shows two vertical submerged plane areas. Determine the hydrostatic force on each area and the point of application of each equivalent concentrated force.

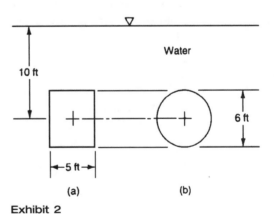

Exhibit 2

Solution

For the rectangle of area $A = (6)(5) = 30$ ft^2 in Exhibit 2(a),

$$F = \gamma h_C A = (62.4)(10)(30) = 18{,}700 \text{ lb}$$

For the circle of area $A = \pi(6)^2/4 = 28.3$ ft^2 in Exhibit 2(b),

$$F = \gamma h_C A = (62.4)(10)(28.3) = 17{,}700 \text{ lb}$$

The moments of inertia of these two shapes about their respective centroids are

$$I = \frac{bh^3}{12} = \frac{(5)(6)^3}{12} = 90.0 \text{ ft}^4 \quad \text{and} \quad I = \frac{\pi}{4}R^4 = \frac{\pi}{4}(3)^4 = 63.6 \text{ ft}^4$$

Thus the distances down from the centroids to the actual point of application of these two forces are $I/(h_C A) = (90)/[(10)(30)] = 0.300$ ft and $I/(h_C A) = (63.6)/[(10)(28.3)] = 0.225$ ft, respectively.

CONSERVATION LAWS

Continuity

The principle of conservation of mass, often called simply **continuity,** can be written for a control volume of fixed volume, V, enclosed by a surface, S, as

$$\frac{\partial}{\partial t}\int_V \rho \, dV + \int_S \rho \mathbf{V} \bullet \mathbf{n} \, dS = 0 \tag{6.6}$$

The two terms express, in turn, the accumulation of mass within the volume and the net outflow of fluid across the boundary, S. The dot product of the velocity vector $\mathbf{V}$ and the unit outer normal $\mathbf{n}$ gives the component of the velocity normal to dS. If the flow is steady, the first term is zero. Applied to a single streamtube in steady incompressible flow, the principle is often written as

$$Q = \int_A V \, dA = \text{Constant} \tag{6.7}$$

or

$$Q = V_1 A_1 = V_2 A_2 \tag{6.8}$$

in which Q is the discharge or volume rate of flow at any cross section of the streamtube, which is also expressible as the product of the mean velocity, V, and cross-sectional area, A. When more than one fluid stream enters or leaves the control volume, additional terms are needed in an overall continuity statement; they come from the evaluation of the second term in Equation (6.6).

Energy

A general statement of mechanical energy conservation between points 1 and 2 in a one-dimensional, steady incompressible flow from 1 to 2 may be written, per unit weight of fluid, as

$$\frac{V_1^2}{2g} + \frac{p_1}{\gamma} + z_1 = \frac{V_2^2}{2g} + \frac{p_2}{\gamma} + z_2 + h_L - E_m \tag{6.9}$$

In Equation (6.9), $V^2/2g$ is the velocity head or kinetic energy per unit weight, p/γ is the pressure head or pressure energy per unit weight, and z is the elevation head or potential energy per unit weight. The head loss, h_L, is the accumulated loss in energy per unit weight occurring between points 1 and 2 caused by local and/or frictional effects. The last term, E_m, is the mechanical energy added to the flow between the two points by the action of hydraulic machinery. A pump adds energy to the flow, so E_m is positive; a turbine removes energy from the flow, and E_m is negative. In the absence of energy losses or gains (that is, h_L and E_m are both zero), one obtains the classic Bernoulli equation for ideal fluid flow.

Fluid power, P, is the product of the energy gained or lost per unit weight, E_m, and the weight rate of flow, $Q\gamma$, or $P = Q\gamma E_m$. If power is to be in horsepower,

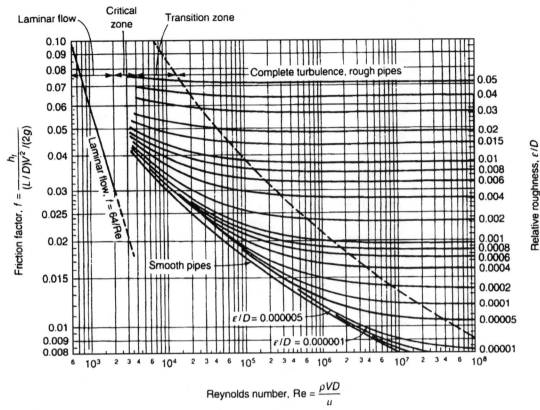

Figure 6.2 (Source: L. F. Moody, *Transactions ASME*, 66, Nov. 1944, pp. 671–684.)

then one should divide this result by the factor 550 ft-lb/sec/horsepower. Depending on the specific application, power should sometimes be multiplied or divided by an efficiency factor η, as some of the problems in this chapter will demonstrate.

In practical pipeflow problems the most important cause of head loss is pipe friction. In a single pipe of length L and diameter D, the Darcy-Weisbach equation for frictional head loss is

$$h_L = h_f \frac{L}{D} \frac{V^2}{2g} \qquad (6.10)$$

The friction factor is $f = f(\text{Re}, \varepsilon/D)$ in which the Reynolds number is $\text{Re} = VD\rho/\mu = VD/v$ and ε/D is called the relative roughness (μ = viscosity, v = kinematic viscosity). The Moody diagram, Figure 6.2, is a plot of the friction factor, f, as a function of Re and ε/D.

Below a transition or critical Reynolds number of approximately 2300, one has laminar flow in a pipe, and the unique relation $f = 64/\text{Re}$ applies. Above a Reynolds number of about 4000, turbulent flow normally occurs, with differing values of f in this regime depending also on ε/D; the lowest of these lines is for a smooth pipe. In the zone of wholly rough turbulent flow (above and to the right of the dashed line), the friction factor effectively depends only on ε/D and not on Re. Values of the absolute roughness, ε, for various pipe materials can be found in Table 6.1.

Although the Darcy-Weisbach equation is the preferred equation to use in determining frictional head losses in pipes, in the United States two primarily empirical formulas are also used for only the turbulent flow of water in pipes.

Table 6.1 Values of absolute roughness ε for new pipes

Material	ε	
	Inches	**Millimeters**
Riveted steel	0.036 to 0.36	0.91 to 9.1
Concrete	0.012 to 0.12	0.3 to 3.0
Wood stave	0.0072 to 0.036	0.18 to 0.9
Cast iron	0.0102	0.26
Galvanized iron	0.006	0.15
Asphalted cast iron	0.0048	0.12
Welded steel pipe	0.0018	0.046
Commercial steel or wrought iron	0.0018	0.046
PVC	0.000084	0.0021
Drawn tubing	0.00006	0.0015
Glass, brass, copper, lead	"Smooth"	"Smooth"

Source: L. F. Moody, *Transactions ASME*, 66, Nov. 1944, pp. 671–684.

They are the Hazen-Williams formula and the Manning formula. The Hazen-Williams formula is

$$Q = 1.318 C_{HW} A R^{0.63} S^{0.54} \quad \text{English units}$$
$$Q = 0.849 C_{HW} A R^{0.63} S^{0.54} \quad \text{SI units}$$

(6.11)

in which C_{HW} is the Hazen-Williams roughness coefficient, $S = h_L/L$ is the slope of the energy line, $R = A/P$ is the hydraulic radius, A = pipe cross-sectional area = $\pi D^2/4$, and P = wetted perimeter. Always $R = D/4$ for pipes flowing full. The Manning equation is introduced later in Equation (6.29). Table 6.2 presents a short table of roughness coefficients for some pipe materials. Investigation would show that use of the Hazen-Williams equation with C_{HW} in the range of 130 to 150 corresponds to the turbulent transitional region of the Moody chart, whereas the use of the Manning formula corresponds to the assumption of a wholly rough flow regime.

All pipe systems are subject to local losses, sometimes called minor losses, of energy in addition to a frictional energy loss. The pipe entrance, exit, and any

Table 6.2

Pipe Material	C_{HW}	n
PVC	150	0.009
Very smooth	140	0.010
Cement-lined ductile iron	140	0.012
New cast iron, welded steel	130	0.014
Wood, concrete	120	0.016
Clay, new riveted steel	110	0.017
Old cast iron, brick	100	0.020
Badly corroded cast iron	80	0.035

Source: Larock et al., *Hydraulics of Pipeline Systems*, CRC Press, 2000.

hardware fittings (valves, etc.) between these points that can change or disrupt the flow in the pipe all cause a local loss in energy. Each loss can be written as

$$h_L = K\frac{V^2}{2g} \tag{6.12}$$

and all such losses are summed as one traverses the pipe from end to end. At the pipe entrance the local loss coefficient depends on the local geometry. For a sharp-edged entrance $K = 0.5$; if the entrance is well rounded, then K is 0.04 to 0.10; if the entrance is reentrant, meaning that the pipe projects into the reservoir, then $K = 0.8$. The appropriate reference velocity, V, is usually, but not always, the mean velocity immediately downstream of the loss-causing device or location. For a sudden expansion from an upstream pipe of area A_1, to a downstream pipe of area A_2 and velocity V_2, the loss coefficient is $K = (A_2/A_1 - 1)^2$ and $V = V_2$. For a sudden contraction between sections 1 and 2, the loss coefficient K is given in Figure 6.3 as a function of A_2/A_1. One exception is the pipe exit to a reservoir, where V must be the upstream velocity and $K = 1.0$ for all exit shapes. A sampling of additional loss coefficients K is given in Table 6.3. More coefficients for other shapes and sizes may be found in textbooks and the references therein.

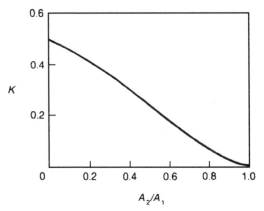

Figure 6.3

Table 6.3 Loss coefficients for a few standard (threaded) pipe fittings

Globe valve, wide open	10.0
Angle valve, wide open	5.0
Gate valve, wide open	0.2
Gate valve, half open	5.6
Return bend	2.2
Tee	1.8
90° elbow	0.9
45° elbow	0.4

Source: Streeter, *Handbook of Fluid Dynamics*, 1961, McGraw-Hill.

The energy equation, Equation (6.9), and the information which follows it can be used to solve a variety of pipeflow problems. However, all of these problems will fit into one of three fundamental problem types:

1. Q and pipeline properties are known, and h_L is to be found.

2. The head difference, H, and the pipeline properties are known, and Q is to be found.

3. Q is prescribed, H is known, and the minimum required pipe diameter, D, is to be found.

The first two problem types are analysis problems, but the third type is typically encountered in a design context. In a Type-1 problem, one can immediately determine ε/D and Re and thus find f. Use of the Darcy-Weisbach expression, Equation (6.10), yields the final result directly. The other two problem types usually require iterative computations, as the next example shows.

Example **6.3**

In Exhibit 3 the head difference between the two reservoirs of water at 10°C is $H = 15$ m. The reservoirs are connected by $L = 300$ m of clean cast-iron pipe. The pipe entrance is sharp edged.

(a) If the pipe diameter is $D = 0.3$ m, find the discharge in the pipe.

(b) Years have passed, and this pipe system is now required to deliver 0.5 m³/s. Is the original pipe diameter adequate, or is a larger pipe diameter now needed?

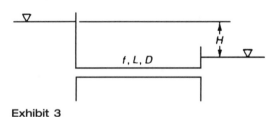

Exhibit 3

Solution

(a) Between the two reservoirs the sum of the entrance, friction, and exit losses is equal to the head difference H,

$$K_{ent}\frac{V^2}{2g} + f\frac{L}{D}\frac{V^2}{2g} + K_{exit}\frac{V^2}{2g} = H$$

or

$$\left[K_{ent} + f\frac{L}{D} + K_{exit}\right]\frac{V^2}{2g} = H$$

For this pipe entrance $K_{ent} = 0.5$, and for all pipe exits $K_{exit} = 1.0$. Hence

$$\left[0.5 + f\frac{300}{0.3} + 1.0\right]\frac{V^2}{2(9.81)} = 15.0 \qquad \textbf{(6.13)}$$

Using Table 6.1, the relative roughness $\varepsilon/D = 0.00026/0.3 = 0.00087$. The Reynolds number is

$$\text{Re} = \frac{VD}{v} = \frac{V(0.3)}{1.3(10^{-6})} = 2.3(10^5)V \tag{6.14}$$

which is not known initially. However, if one assumes that Re is large, then for the computed ε/D one can estimate directly from Figure 6.2 that $f = 0.019$ in the wholly rough flow region. Equation (6.13) can now be solved directly to obtain $V = 3.79$ m/s. Then Equation (6.14) yields Re $= 8.7(10^5)$, and a check of Figure 6.2 suggests that f is between 0.019 and 0.020. If one re-solves Equation (6.13), V changes slightly; the discharge is $Q = VA = (3.79) \times \pi(0.3)^2/4 = 0.268$ m^3/s.

(b) Clearly the original pipe diameter is too small. Rewriting Equation (6.13) to display fully the role of diameter D,

$$\left[0.5 + f\frac{300}{D} + 1.0\right]\frac{1}{2g}\frac{Q^2}{(\pi/4)^2 D^4} = H \tag{6.15}$$

one sees that this equation is highly nonlinear in D. Moreover, the relative roughness and Re also depend on D. A trial solution is required with $Q = 0.5$ m^3/sec. One can begin by estimating that D should be approximately 0.4 m because Q has roughly doubled from part (a), and Q can be expected to vary with A or D^2. For a chosen value of D, ε/D and Re can be computed, yielding $f = 0.018$ from Figure 6.2. Hence $H = 12.1$ m for $D = 0.4$ m. As a next trial, $D = 0.38$ m gave $H = 15.6$ m. Interpolation suggests $D = 0.383$ m will give $H = 15.0$ m, which can be confirmed by calculations. One should select the next larger commercially available pipe size.

Momentum

In steady flow the conservation of linear momentum for a fixed control volume, V, enclosed by a surface S is

$$\mathbf{F}_S + \mathbf{F}_B = \int_S \mathbf{V}(\rho\mathbf{V} \bullet \mathbf{n})\,dS \tag{6.16}$$

In this vector equation the first two terms represent the surface and body forces, respectively, and the integral is the net outward flux of momentum through the surface of the control volume. The first term includes the overall effect of any distributed pressures and any viscous or shear stresses on the surface S. Usually the body force is just the weight of everything within the control volume; it acts in the direction of gravity. For flow in two dimensions with uniform flow across an entrance section 1 and an exit section 2, Equation (6.16) is equivalent to the two scalar component equations

$$\begin{aligned}\Sigma F_x &= \rho Q(V_{2x} - V_{1x})\\ \Sigma F_y &= \rho Q(V_{2y} - V_{1y})\end{aligned} \tag{6.17}$$

in which the volume flow rate is Q.

Example **6.4**

Determine the horizontal component of the force per unit width of the water on the radial gate shown in Exhibit 4.

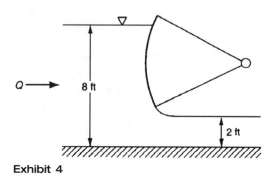

Exhibit 4

Solution

First find the discharge by applying the continuity and energy equations between sections 1 and 2, and then use the x-component of Equation (6.17) to find the force. Between the sections, the discharge per unit width $q = y_1V_1 = y_2V_2$ or $8V_1 = 2V_2$. Now assume as a reasonable approximation that

$$\frac{V_1^2}{2g} + y_1 = \frac{V_2^2}{2g} + y_2$$

or

$$\frac{1}{2g}\left(V_2^2 - V_1^2\right) = \frac{1}{2(32.2)}\left[1 - \left(\frac{2}{8}\right)^2\right]V_2^2 = 8 - 2 = 6$$

by using continuity, so that $V_2 = 20.3$ ft/s, $q = 2V_2 = 40.6$ ft^2/s, and $V_1 = 5.08$ ft/s.

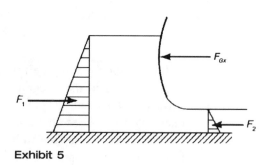

Exhibit 5

Now the horizontal component of Equation (6.16) is specialized to the control volume shown in Exhibit 5 to obtain

$$F_1 - F_2 - F_{Gx} = \rho Q(V_2 - V_1)$$

in which the first two terms are hydrostatic forces, and the third term is the integrated effect of the gate on the water in the x-direction. Thus

$$\frac{1}{2}\rho g\left(y_1^2 - y_2^2\right) - F_{Gx} = \rho q(V_2 - V_1)$$

$$\frac{1}{2}(62.4)(8^2 - 2^2) - F_{Gx} = 1.94(40.6)(20.3 - 5.08)$$

$$1870 - F_{Gx} = 1200$$

and the horizontal force of the water on the gate is equal and opposite this force, or 670 lb per unit width to the right.

PUMPS AND TURBINES

Turbomachinery, which incorporates a central rotating unit or impeller, is reviewed in this section. Positive-displacement pumps also play a significant role in engineering, but they usually operate at relatively lower discharges and will not be reviewed here. After introducing some basic terms, the review will look at non-dimensional pump parameters and their relation to specific speed. The relation of the main centrifugal pump types to specific speed will be mentioned next, followed by a look at pump characteristic curves and their relation to hydraulic system requirements. A review of turbine types concludes the section.

Turbomachinery Similitude and Specific Speed

In the extended energy equation, Equation (6.9), E_m is the mechanical energy per unit weight added to or removed from the fluid stream between two points. For pumps this addition is the net pump head, H, which acts primarily to increase the pressure head. The power delivered to the fluid stream equals the product of H and the weight rate of flow $Q\gamma$ and is called the water power or horsepower, P_w. The mechanical power used in driving the pump is larger and is called brake horsepower, bhp $= \omega T$, in which ω and T are the angular velocity and torque on the rotating shaft that drives the pump. The ratio P_w/bhp is the pump efficiency, η, which may be above 0.8 for large pumps operating near their best efficiency point, but which may be lower, even much lower, for pumps which are small or operating away from best conditions.

Similitude considerations for turbomachinery lead to three nondimensional parameters that can be used to summarize performance:

$$C_H = \frac{gH}{N^2 D^2}; \qquad C_Q = \frac{Q}{ND^3}; \qquad C_P = \frac{P}{\rho N^3 D^5} \qquad \textbf{(6.18)}$$

These coefficients are the head, discharge, and power coefficients, respectively. The length D is to be representative of the size of the unit; usually it is the impeller diameter. The rotative speed parameter, N, should have units of l/time, but rev/s or rev/min is used conventionally. The coefficients in Equation (6.18) are, in principle, all dependent on Reynolds number and relative roughness, but at high Reynolds number this fact is often overlooked. Thus, if pumps 1 and 2 are of similar geometric shape and operate so that internal flow patterns are the same, then the units are called homologous and

$$\left(\frac{H}{N^2 D^2}\right)_1 = \left(\frac{H}{N^2 D^2}\right)_2; \quad \left(\frac{Q}{ND^3}\right)_1 = \left(\frac{Q}{ND^3}\right)_2; \quad \left(\frac{P}{\rho N^3 D^5}\right)_1 = \left(\frac{P}{\rho N^3 D^5}\right)_2 \quad \textbf{(6.19)}$$

These similarity laws are quite versatile. If pumps 1 and 2 have the same diameter, the rules show how H, Q, and P scale with N; or for fixed speed, N, the rules show how these quantities scale with size D. Note also that N may be given in any of the units rad/sec, rev/s, or rev/min in Equation (6.19). In Equation (6.18), however, it is important to know which of these units is being used.

All coefficients so far contain the size of the unit D; a grouping that displays the important variables, Q and H for pumps or P and H for turbines, without D appearing would be a valuable characterization of the performance of the unit. Specific speed is such a grouping; it is a shape parameter and takes on its greatest meaning when defined at the machine's best efficiency point (bep). In the United States, there are two forms that specific speed can take for pumps, and two others for turbines. In each pairing the first form is nondimensional and the second is the U.S. traditional form, which is commonly used but is far from being nondimensional.

Pumps:
$$n_s' = \frac{NQ^{1/2}}{g^{3/4}H^{3/4}} \qquad N_s' = \frac{(\text{rev/min})(\text{gal/min})^{1/2}}{[H(\text{ft})]^{3/4}} \qquad \textbf{(6.20)}$$

Turbines:
$$n_s = \frac{NP^{1/2}}{\gamma^{1/2}g^{3/4}H^{5/4}} \qquad N_s = \frac{(\text{rev/min})(\text{horsepower})^{1/2}}{[H(\text{ft})]^{5/4}} \qquad \textbf{(6.21)}$$

The first forms may be used in any dimensionally consistent set of units.

Pump Types

Specific speed, as a shape parameter, can be used to select the most appropriate kind of pump (or turbine) for a particular application. Pumps are normally classified according to the predominant direction of flow through the pump impeller. Experience has shown when the pump specific speed, N_s', is below roughly 4000 that the most efficient pump type uses a radial-flow impeller; that is, the primary direction of flow through the impeller is normal to the axis of rotation of the impeller. Between specific speeds of 4000 and 10,000, the most efficient pump type uses a mixed-flow impeller, and above a specific speed of 10,000 the efficient pump type uses an axial-flow impeller similar to a propeller. There is some overlap of intervals, however.

Information on pump performance is usually displayed in a set of characteristic curves. Most sets of curves are dimensional, but occasionally they are nondimensionalized. Figure 6.4 presents a set of characteristic curves for a pump operating at 900 rpm. In this case the best efficiency point (bep) is at 80 percent efficiency, corresponding to a head of 13.7 ft, a discharge of 2.5 ft³/s, and a required bhp of 3.5. Thus the computed pump specific speed N_s' is 4230, which is on the lower end of the mixed-flow range.

Net Positive Suction Head

The net positive suction head (NPSH) is the head difference between (1) the energy of the fluid per unit weight at the inlet side of the pump, measured above the inlet elevation, and (2) the vapor-pressure head of the fluid. That is,

$$\text{NPSH} = \frac{p_i}{\gamma} + \frac{V_i^2}{2g} - \frac{p_v}{\gamma} \qquad \textbf{(6.22)}$$

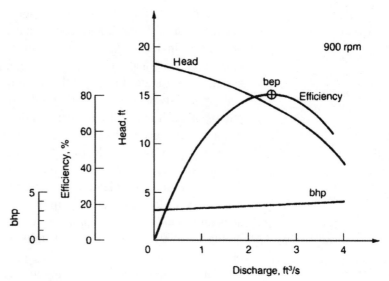

Figure 6.4

In this expression all pressures must be computed as absolute, not gage, pressures. In order to avoid the onset of **cavitation,** which is the local conversion of liquid to vapor due to low pressure, each pump must be located so that the NPSH of the pump is exceeded. Referring to Figure 6.5, if Equation (6.9) is written between the reservoir and the pump inlet i, one obtains

$$R + \frac{p_{atm}}{\gamma} - h_L = \frac{p_i}{\gamma} + \frac{V_i^2}{2g} + R + z_i$$

The resulting relation for NPSH is therefore

$$\text{NPSH} = \frac{p_{atm}}{\gamma} - \frac{p_v}{\gamma} - h_L - z_i \qquad \textbf{(6.23)}$$

This equation clearly shows that the distance z_i that the inlet can be placed above the reservoir surface is limited. Pump manufacturers routinely supply pump characteristic curves and NPSH data to users.

System Performance

Just as Figure 6.4 graphically presents a pump characteristic curve or relation between H and Q, Equation (6.9) describes the head requirement (H or E_m) of the hydraulic system between two points that must be satisfied if the system is to function properly. An inspection of Equation (6.9) shows that the system head

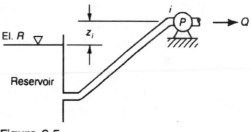

Figure 6.5

requirement consists of two parts: a static lift which is the difference in elevation between points 1 and 2 and a frictional head component that grows in size with an increase in discharge (if f is constant, this part grows as Q^2). Matching the heads, either computationally or by use of a graph, determines the discharge at which the system will operate. If instead the desired discharge is prescribed, then the system head requirement is also fixed, and the problem is to select some pump or set of pumps that can efficiently deliver this discharge at this head. One then inspects the characteristic curves of various pumps until a suitable pump (or pumps) is found.

Complicating this selection process is the fact that, over time, pipes age and the system head increases; the pump ages as well and becomes less efficient. Together these factors lead to a decrease in system discharge. Sets of pumps are sometimes installed in series or in parallel to give system flexibility as the system ages and to aid in pump maintenance. Such arrangements also require additional piping and valving so individual units can be isolated (e.g., for servicing). The primary facts to recall in considering pump combinations are (1) the discharge is constant and heads add for pumps in series, and (2) discharges add whereas the head across a parallel combination is constant.

Turbines

Turbine specific speed, defined in Equation (6.21), can be used to classify the major types of hydropower turbines:

N_s	Type	ϕ
1–10	Impulse (Pelton)	~0.47
15–110	Francis	0.6–0.9
100–250	Propeller (Kaplan)	1.4–2.0

The quantity ϕ is the **peripheral speed factor,** which is the ratio of a typical runner speed to a typical fluid speed for the turbine. The specific speed allows one to identify clearly the different turbine types.

Impulse turbines are low-discharge, high-head devices in which one or more high-speed jets of water at atmospheric pressure act on carefully shaped vanes or "buckets" on the periphery of the rotating turbine wheel. Although its specific speed range is already narrow, it probably should be still narrower because efficiency drops rapidly at both ends of the range; for $N_s \le 2$ the impulse wheel is relatively large and cumbersome with large electrical losses, and at $N_s > 8$ the fluid jet is not handled well by the buckets. The equations for force on a bucket F and for power P are

$$F = \rho Q v_r (1 - \cos\beta) \qquad P = Fu \qquad (6.24)$$

in which the fluid speed relative to the runner is $v_r = V - u$, the speed of the fluid jet is V, the runner speed itself is $u = \omega r$, the angular velocity of the wheel is ω, the midbucket radius from the axis of rotation (the "pitch circle") is r, and β is the angle through which the fluid is turned on impact with the bucket. Normally β is 165° or a bit more.

Both Francis and propeller turbines are reaction turbines. The turbine runner is fully enclosed and acted upon by water under pressure.

Francis turbines are for moderate-head, moderate-discharge applications. At the lower values of N_s the flow through the rotating turbine runner is in the radial direction, whereas at the higher end of the N_s range the flow direction is mixed, being partly radial and partly axial.

For propeller turbines, the predominant flow direction through the runner is axial in order to handle a high discharge at low head. For all reaction turbines, the flow leaves the delivery pipe, called a penstock, and enters the turbine through a scroll case which wraps around the central turbine unit, gradually decreasing its cross section to force the flow toward the rotating impeller through fixed guide vanes and adjustable wicket gates.

The power, torque, and discharge for a reaction turbine are all related to the interaction of the flow with the turbine runner blades. Figure 6.6 depicts a pair of velocity diagrams for flow at the inlet, section 1, and the outlet, section 2, of a typical turbine blade. The runner angular velocity is ω. The absolute velocity, V, of the fluid can be viewed in two ways. It is composed of radial and tangential components V_r and V_t, respectively, but it is also composed of the blade velocity $u = \omega r$ and the fluid velocity w relative to the moving blade. Two angles help to define the velocity diagram: The angle at which the fluid enters the runner region is α, measured from the tangent to the circle surrounding the runner—also $\tan \alpha = V_r / V_t$; the second angle, β, is measured form u to w. The power and torque are

$$P = T\omega \qquad T = \rho Q [V_{t1} r_1 - V_{t2} r_2] \qquad \textbf{(6.25)}$$

The discharge is the product of the radial velocity component and the area through which this velocity flows, or

$$Q = V_r (2\pi r b) \qquad \textbf{(6.26)}$$

in which b is the thickness of the section. Useful velocity relations from Figure 6.6 are $V_r = w \sin \beta$ and $V_t = u + w \cos \beta = u + V_r \cot \beta$.

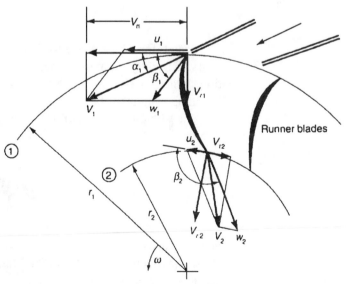

Figure 6.6

OPEN CHANNEL FLOW

Basic elements of open channel flow will be presented here, including descriptions of uniform flow and the use of the Manning equation for discharge determination, the role of the hydraulic jump, efficient section considerations, specific energy, and an introduction to gradually varied flow.

Uniform Flow and Manning Equation

The primary distinguishing feature of open channel flow is the presence of a constant-pressure free surface atop all such flows. If the flow properties at a point or section in a channel are unchanging with time, then the flow is steady; otherwise it is unsteady. If the flow properties in a steady flow are unchanging from one cross section to another in a channel, then the flow is uniform in space. In this case the slopes of the channel bottom, water surface, and energy grade line are all identical, and the shape of the channel section is unchanging with distance along the channel. Then one can select a longitudinal reach of a channel as a control volume and apply the steady linear momentum conservation principle, Equation (6.16), to the reach to find a balance between the force driving the flow, which is the component of the fluid weight down the slope S_o, and the frictional resisting force. The mean shear stress τ on the boundary of the channel cross section turns out to be

$$\tau = \gamma R S_o \tag{6.27}$$

in which $R = A/P$ is called the hydraulic radius of the cross section, and A and P are, respectively, the area and the wetted perimeter of the section. With the aid of a bit of dimensional analysis, one can then develop the discharge equation originated by A. Chézy, which is

$$Q = VA = CA\sqrt{RS_o} \tag{6.28}$$

The search for the best way to characterize or specify C has continued over many years. Currently the most popular approach is to adopt the **Manning** representation, which is $C = R^{1/6}/n$. Table 6.4 lists a variety of typical values for n, the Manning roughness factor.

The Manning equation for discharge determination in uniform, open channel flow is

$$Q = \frac{K}{n} A R^{2/3} S_o^{1/2} \tag{6.29}$$

For SI units use $K = 1.0$; for English units use $K = 1.49$. These choices for K allow one to retain one value of the Manning n for each physical roughness without any need for other unit conversions.

Table 6.4 Values of roughness coefficient n

Type of Channel Surface	Minimum	Normal	Maximum
Brass, smooth	0.009	0.01	0.013
Steel, riveted and spiral	0.013	0.016	0.017
Cast iron, coated	0.01	0.013	0.014
Wrought iron, galvanized	0.013	0.016	0.017
Lucite	0.008	0.009	0.01
Glass	0.009	0.01	0.013
Cement, neat surface	0.01	0.011	0.013
Concrete, finished	0.011	0.012	0.014
Wood, stave	0.01	0.012	0.014
Clay, common drainage tile	0.011	0.013	0.017
Clay, vitrified sewer	0.011	0.014	0.017
Brick work, lined with cement mortar	0.012	0.015	0.017
Rubble masonry, cemented	0.018	0.025	0.03
Smooth steel surface, unpainted	0.011	0.012	0.014
Cement, mortar	0.011	0.013	0.015
Wood, unplaned	0.011	0.013	0.015
Concrete, trowel finish	0.011	0.013	0.015
Concrete, gunite—good section	0.016	0.019	0.023
Gravel bottom with sides of formed concrete	0.017	0.02	0.025
Brick, glazed	0.011	0.013	0.015
Asphalt, smooth	0.013	0.013	—
Asphalt, rough	0.016	0.016	—
Vegetal lining	0.03	—	0.5
Excavated or dredged earth, straight and uniform:			
Clean, recently completed	0.016	0.018	0.02
Clean, after weathering	0.018	0.022	0.025
Gravel, uniform section, clean	0.022	0.025	0.03
With short grass, few weeds	0.022	0.027	0.033
Natural streams:			
Minor streams on plain, top width at flood stage <30 m, clean, straight, full stage, no rifts or deep pools	0.025	0.03	0.033
Mountain streams, no vegetation in channel, banks unusually steep, trees and brush along banks submerged at high stages, bottom with gravels, cobbles, and few boulders	0.03	0.04	0.05

| Example **6.5** |

A gunite concrete trapezoidal channel with 1:2 side slopes, which is shown in Exhibit 6, conveys 200 ft^3/s on a slope $S_o = 0.0005$. Compute the depth of uniform flow.

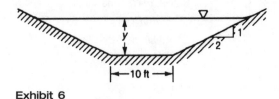

Exhibit 6

Solution

In English units the Manning equation is

$$Q = \frac{1.49}{n} AR^{2/3} S_o^{1/2}$$

From Table 6.4 the appropriate roughness coefficient is $n = 0.019$. Inserting the given information leads to

$$AR^{2/3} = 114 \tag{6.30}$$

in which

$$A = 10y + 2y^2$$
$$P = 10 + 2\sqrt{5}y \quad \text{and} \quad R = A/P$$

Equation (6.30) now must be solved by successive trial. It is convenient to use a table in doing so:

Trial	y	A	P	R	$R^{2/3}$	$AR^{2/3} = 114$?
1	5.0	100.0	32.4	3.09	2.12	212
2	3.5	59.5	25.7	2.32	1.75	104
3	3.7	64.4	26.5	2.43	1.81	116
4	3.66	63.4	26.4	2.40	1.80	114

The normal depth, that is, the depth of uniform flow, is $y = 3.66$ ft.

Hydraulic Jump

When a change from high-speed to low-speed flow occurs in an open channel, a hydraulic jump is observed; over a short distance the depth of flow increases abruptly with a significant energy loss and a very turbulent appearance. The high-speed flow can be caused in a variety of ways, including flow under a gate or down any relatively steep slope. A schematic diagram of this phenomenon for flow on a horizontal channel bottom is given in Figure 6.7. To a good approximation, the flow through the jump can be analyzed directly by applying the linear momentum equation, Equation (6.17), for any shape of cross section. The result is

$$F_1 - F_2 = \rho Q(V_2 - V_1) \tag{6.31}$$

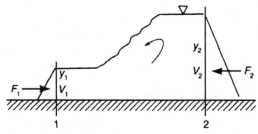

Figure 6.7

in which F and V represent here, respectively, the hydrostatic force and mean velocity at sections 1 and 2. This equation assumes that the overall effect of boundary shear is negligibly small. Specialization of Equation (6.31) to a particular cross-sectional shape will cause the effect of the depths y_1 and y_2 to appear in the equation. As an example, if this equation is specialized to a rectangular channel of width b and the discharge per unit width $q = Q/b$ is introduced, then one can solve Equation (6.31) directly for the depth ratios y_2/y_1 and y_1/y_2 in the forms

$$\frac{y_2}{y_1} = \frac{1}{2}\left[-1 + \left(1 + 8\mathrm{Fr}_1^2\right)^{1/2}\right] \tag{6.32}$$

and

$$\frac{y_1}{y_2} = \frac{1}{2}\left[-1 + \left(1 + 8\mathrm{Fr}_2^2\right)^{1/2}\right] \tag{6.33}$$

In these two equations, the square of the Froude number is $\mathrm{Fr}^2 = q^2/(gy^3)$ and is evaluated at section 1 or 2, as the subscript indicates.

A useful relation for head loss across the jump can be obtained by inserting results from Equation (6.31) into the energy equation, Equation (6.9). If this is done for the rectangular channel, the head loss is found to be

$$h_L = \frac{(y_2 - y_1)^3}{4 y_2 y_1} \tag{6.34}$$

Efficient Section

When one uses the Manning equation, Equation (6.29), it is natural to want to use it efficiently, that is, to want to convey the largest discharge for a given cross-sectional area. So one seeks the largest hydraulic radius, R, for a given A, which means one must minimize the wetted perimeter, P. For both rectangular and trapezoidal cross sections, greatest efficiency is achieved when $R = y/2$. Moreover, the most efficient of all trapezoidal sections has sides that slope at a 60° angle, which means the most efficient trapezoid is a half hexagon. The most efficient section of all is the semicircle.

Specific Energy

Specific energy E is energy per unit weight above a channel bottom, so in general

$$E = y + \frac{V^2}{2g} \tag{6.35}$$

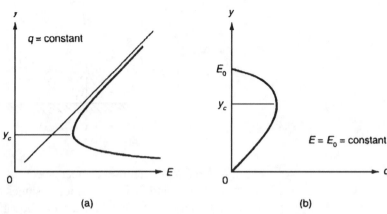

Figure 6.8

For a strictly two-dimensional channel (rectangular or extremely wide) this definition may be rewritten in terms of the discharge per unit width q to give

$$E = y + \frac{q^2}{2g}\frac{1}{y^2} \tag{6.36}$$

Figure 6.8 shows how this expression behaves as a function of y for two situations. In Figure 6.8(a) the specific energy, E, varies with y for a fixed constant value of discharge, and in Figure 6.8(b) the relation between q and y for fixed specific energy $E = E_o$ is displayed. In both cases an extremum is seen to occur at $y = y_c$, which is called the critical flow state. From these diagrams one can see that the **critical flow** state is the point at which minimum specific energy is required to pass a specified q through a channel section, and it is also the state at which the maximum discharge q is passed through a section for a fixed amount of energy E_o. Using differential calculus, one can find the critical depth and corresponding critical specific energy to be

$$y_c = \left(\frac{q^2}{g}\right)^{1/3} \qquad E_c = \frac{3}{2}y_c \tag{6.37}$$

for two-dimensional channels. For any channel of arbitrary cross section $A = A(y)$ with a width at the water surface that is $b = b(y)$, the critical flow state satisfies the relation

$$\frac{Q^2 b}{gA^3} = 1 \tag{6.38}$$

Example **6.6**

Determine the critical depth for the data given in Example 6.5.

Solution

Equation (6.38) must be solved with $A(y)$ given in Example 6.5 and $b = 10 + 4y$. For the given data

$$\frac{A^3}{b} = \frac{Q^2}{g} = \frac{200^2}{32.2} = 1240$$

A small table will aid the search for the solution:

Trial	y	$A(y)$	$b(y)$	$A^3/b = 1240$?
1	3.0	48.0	22.0	5030
2	2.0	28.0	18.0	1220
3	2.1	29.8	18.4	1440
4	2.01	28.2	18.04	1240

Thus $y_c = 2.01$ ft in this case. The last two values of y in the table were simply chosen by estimating an interpolant between the previous values; this is easier than using a formal linear interpolation procedure, which is not strictly accurate when the basic equation is nonlinear.

Gradually Varied Flow

The governing equation for gradually varied flow can be developed by use of either the momentum or the energy principles, but the intermediate steps and the assumptions are not identical. Underlying either approach are the assumptions that the flow is one-dimensional and the pressure distribution is hydrostatic. The resulting equation can be written in either of two ways:

$$\frac{dy}{dx} = \frac{S_o - S}{1 - \mathrm{Fr}^2} \tag{6.39}$$

$$\Delta x = \frac{E_2 - E_1}{S_o - S} \tag{6.40}$$

In Equation (6.39), which applies at one section in the flow, the rate of change of water depth y with respect to distance along the channel x is given as the difference between channel bottom slope S_o and the local slope of the energy line S, divided by 1 minus the square of the local Froude number. Hence $dy/dx = 0$ means the depth of flow is not changing (is uniform), not that the slope of the water surface is horizontal. The energy slope S is found by using the Manning equation, Equation (6.29), with S_o replaced by S. When Q is set, this equation will give $S = S(y)$ through the dependence of A and R on y. The Froude number is also dependent on depth y, since $\mathrm{Fr}^2 = Q^2 b/gA^3$.

Equation (6.40) is a discrete equation and applies between sections 1 and 2, which have different depths of flow. The specific energies at these two sections are E_1 and E_2, respectively. The average energy slope, S, can be determined in several ways. One effective way is to use Equation (6.29) with averaged values for the velocity and hydraulic radius, that is, $V_{avg} = (V_1 + V_2)/2$ and $R_{avg} = (R_1 + R_2)/2$.

From Equation (6.39) one can directly determine the qualitative behavior of the water surface profile. The quickest way to do this is to determine the depth of uniform flow (also called normal depth and denoted as y_o or y_n) by using Equation (6.29) with S_o. Next find the critical depth y_c from Equation (6.38), or Equation (6.37) if it is applicable. Finally consult Table 6.5, which graphically presents all the gradually varied flow profiles that are allowed by Equation (6.39). Use of this table requires only a knowledge of the local flow depth y in relation to y_o and y_c.

Table 6.5 Twelve surface profiles and associated data for gradually varied flow

Slope	Surface Profile	$\dfrac{dy}{dx}$	$\dfrac{d^2y}{dx^2}$	Fr	y_o	Graphic Profile
Mild $S_o < S_c$	M_1	+	+	<1	E x i s t s	
	M_2	−	−	<1		
	M_3	+	+	>1		
Steep $S_o > S_c$	S_1	+	−	<1	E x i s t s	
	S_2	−	+	>1		
	S_3	+	−	>1		
Critical $S_o = S_c$	C_1	+	−	<1	E x i s t s	
	C_3	+	−	>1		
Horizontal $S_o = 0$	H_2	−	−	<1		
	H_3	+	+	>1		
Adverse $S_o < 0$	A_2	−	−	<1	I m a g i n a r y	
	A_3	+	+	>1		

Example 6.7

Two very long open channel reaches convey a discharge of 20 m³/s, as shown in Exhibit 7. Far upstream from the break in slope B the depth of uniform flow is 1.00 m; far downstream from B the uniform flow depth is 2.00 m. The rectangular channel cross section is 4 m wide and is lined with concrete ($n = 0.013$). Determine the flow profile between the regions of uniform flow, and compute approximately the length of the gradually varied flow region.

Solution

The discharge per unit width is $q = Q/b = 20/4 = 5.0$ m²/s. From Equation (6.37) the critical depth is $y_c = (q^2/g)^{1/3} = (5.0^2/9.81)^{1/3} = 1.37$ m. By direct comparison

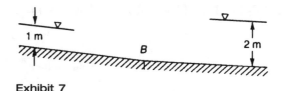

Exhibit 7

of y_c with the uniform flow depths, the flow far upstream is supercritical and far downstream it is subcritical. Since Table 6.5 shows that no gradually varied flow profile can cross critical depth, some other flow event is needed for the flow to cross y_c.

One begins by hypothesizing that the transition between uniform flows is some combination of a hydraulic jump and a gradually varied flow profile. If the jump occurs downstream from B, then an examination of the family of mild profiles in Table 6.5 shows that the jump must end at precisely the depth of downstream uniform flow, since a jump which ends on either side of y_o then moves away from this depth via an M_1 or M_2 profile. Thus, if a jump to $y_2 = 2.0$ m from some depth y_1 occurs, then Equation (6.33) with $\mathrm{Fr}_2^2 = q^2/(gy_2^3) = (5.0)^2/[(9.81)(2.00)^3] = 0.319$ yields $y_1 = 0.88$ m. Since a review of both the steep and mild profiles in Table 6.5 shows that there is no way to move from $y = 1.00$ m to this new depth, the hypothesized jump cannot occur in this way.

The alternative is to assume that the jump is upstream of B and $y_1 = 1.00$ m. Using Equation (6.32) with $\mathrm{Fr}_1^2 = q^2/(gy_1^3) = (5.0)^2/[(9.81)(1.00)^3] = 2.55$ yields $y_2 = 1.81$ m; then Table 6.5 shows that gradually varied flow to a depth of 2.00 m is possible via the S_1 profile. Hence all flow downstream of B is uniform at a depth of 2.00 m.

The length of the S_1 profile will be determined by using Equation (6.40). First the upstream channel-bottom slope, S_o, must be found from the Manning equation, Equation (6.29), with $K = 1$ and a depth of flow $y = 1.00$ m, which yields $S_o = 0.00725$. Now the approximate length of the reach of gradually varied flow will be found by the recommended procedure:

y, m	V, m/sec	R, m	E, m	S	Δx, m
1.81	2.76	1.050	2.20		
				0.00113	8.2
1.90	2.63	1.080	2.25		
				0.000985	11.2
2.00	2.50	1.111	2.32		
					19.4

In summary, a hydraulic jump from 1.00 m to 1.81 m occurs approximately 19.4 m upstream from B and is followed by an S_1 profile to a flow depth of 2.00 m at, and downstream of, B.

SELECTED SYMBOLS AND ABBREVIATIONS

Symbol or Abbreviation	Description
bep	best efficiency point
E	specific energy
η	efficiency factor
Fr	Froude number
f	Darcy friction factor
ϕ	peripheral speed factor
g	gravitational acceleration
γ	unit weight
H	head difference
I	moment of inertia
K	local loss coefficient
μ	viscosity
N	rotative speed
NPSH	net positive suction head
P	power
Q	discharge
Re	Reynolds number
S	specific gravity
τ	mean shear stress
u	runner speed or blade velocity
v	kinematic viscosity
V	velocity
ω	angular velocity

REFERENCES

Chow, V. T. *Open-Channel Hydraulics*. McGraw-Hill, New York, 1959.

Larock, B. E., Jeppson, R. W., and Watters, G. Z. *Hydraulics of Pipeline Systems*. CRC Press, New York, 2000.

Munson, B. R., Young, D. F., and Okiishi, T. H. *Fundamentals of Fluid Mechanics*, 3rd ed., Wiley, New York, 1998.

Sanks, R. L. *Pumping Station Design*. Butterworths, Boston, 1989.

Street, R. L., Watters, G. Z., and Vennard, J. K. *Elementary Fluid Mechanics*, 7th ed., Wiley, New York, 1996.

Sturm, T. W. *Open Channel Hydraulics*. McGraw-Hill, New York, 2001.

White, F. M. *Fluid Mechanics*, 5th ed., McGraw-Hill, New York, 2003.

CHAPTER 7

Engineering Hydrology

Bruce E. Larock

OUTLINE

INTRODUCTION 343

HYDROLOGIC ELEMENTS 343
Precipitation ■ Evapotranspiration ■ Infiltration

WATERSHED HYDROGRAPHS 346
Unit Hydrograph ■ Change of Unitgraph Duration

PEAK DISCHARGE ESTIMATION 352

HYDROLOGIC ROUTING 355
Reservoir Routing ■ River Routing

WELL HYDRAULICS 359
Steady Flow ■ Unsteady Flow

REFERENCES 366

INTRODUCTION

This chapter will focus on selected elements of engineering hydrology that have wide practical application; it cannot really replace the study of any complete volume on the subject. After presenting some introductory matter, this chapter will concentrate primarily on the development and application of watershed hydrographs, peak discharge estimation, hydrologic routing for rivers and reservoirs, and some elements of well hydraulics. Additional information on these and related topics will be found in the references at the end of the chapter.

HYDROLOGIC ELEMENTS

Hydrology is in general a multidisciplinary subject which is the study of water movement and distribution on earth. This movement is a closed loop called the hydrologic cycle in which water is first evaporated primarily from the oceans, then transported as vapor by the atmosphere and, under proper circumstances, precipitated to the earth's surface as rain or snow. The surface water may return to the atmosphere again as evaporation, it may infiltrate into the soil and reach the groundwater or be taken up by plants and transpired back into the air, or it may flow over the land surface and find its way into streams, rivers, or lakes, eventually flowing back into the oceans to complete the cycle.

Precipitation

The most common form of precipitation is liquid rain; when the amounts of other forms, such as snow, must be quantified, they are often melted first, and the amount is reported in terms of its liquid equivalent. The most common precipitation gage in the United States is the Weather Service 8-in.-diameter cylindrical gage, which directs captured rain into a measuring tube which is one tenth the cross-sectional area of the collector, and depths are then measured to 0.01 in. within it. Three types of recording gages are also in common use; they are the tipping-bucket gage, the weighing-type gage, and the float recording gage.

The average precipitation $\bar{p}$ over a region can be obtained from point data in one of three ways, all of which fit the formula

$$\bar{p} = \frac{1}{A_T} \Sigma A_i p_i \qquad A_T = \Sigma A_i \qquad (7.1)$$

in which p_i is a point precipitation value, A_i is a weighting factor, and A_T is the sum of the weighting factors:

 (i) The simple arithmetic mean is appropriate when the individual values are all similar. In this case set each $A_i = 1$, and then A_T is just the number of points.

 (ii) The widely used Thiessen average is a weighted average which in effect assumes that the value p_i best represents the true precipitation at all locations that are closer to gage i than to any other gage. Each A_i is the area surrounding gage i, and A_T is the total gaged area. The boundary of each A_i is formed by lines that are the perpendicular bisectors of lines drawn between the gages themselves.

(iii) The isohyetal method is the only method which allows a knowledge of basin topography to enter the calculation. One begins the computation by drawing contour lines of equal precipitation (isohyets) throughout the region. Then in Equation (7.1) A_i is the area between adjacent isohyets, p_i is the average precipitation between these adjacent isohyets, and A_T is the total gaged area.

Evapotranspiration

The quantification of evaporation or transpiration amounts (or of evapotranspiration, ET, the sum of the two) can become important to engineers who conduct water supply studies. There are several computational approaches and one primary experimental method of estimating evaporation; each approach has its problems and leads to imprecision in the result:

 (i) The water budget or mass conservation method attempts to account for all flows of water to and from the water body under study, including inflow, outflow, direct precipitation, and even seepage to the groundwater.

(ii) The energy budget is like the water budget, except the energy flows rather than mass flows are the basic accounting medium.

(iii) Direct empirical meteorological correlations are used to avoid the uncertainties of the first two methods, but attempts to avoid excessive complexity here usually lead to incomplete, and thus inaccurate, results.

(iv) A combination of the above methods has been relatively successful. For example, the Penman equation, when used with a set of charts, has become popular when all the required data can be obtained or estimated.

(v) The National Weather Service Class A pan is 4 feet in diameter, 10 inches deep, made of unpainted galvanized iron, and used to measure evaporation by direct experiment. Multiplication of this result by a pan coefficient, typically about 0.7, then gives the evaporation from the adjacent larger water body. Difficult correlation studies are needed to ensure that the coefficient is appropriate to a particular application.

Infiltration

Infiltration of water into the soil is important in some studies. Horton's infiltration equation is widely used for this purpose, which is

$$f = f_c + (f_o - f_c)e^{-kt} \tag{7.2}$$

Here f is infiltration rate (in./hr); f_o and f_c are the initial and final infiltration rates, respectively; t is time (hr); and k (1/hr) is an empirically determined constant. Another common way of characterizing infiltration is via the ϕ-index method. In this method one plots the overall precipitation rate versus time; a horizontal line called the ϕ index is drawn on the plot, such that the volume of rainfall excess above this line is equal to the actual volume of observed runoff. Thus the index indicates the average infiltration rate for the storm event.

Example 7.1

Exhibit 1 is a histogram which describes hourly rainfall for a 5-hour storm.

(a) Previous experience has determined that the Horton infiltration parameters for the soil in this region are $f_o = 0.4$ in./hr, $f_c = 0.2$ in./hr, and $k = 0.5$/hr. Determine the volume of rainfall that infiltrates during the 5-hr period.

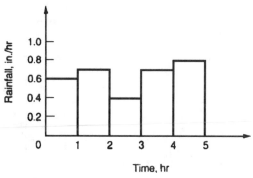

Exhibit 1

(b) If the net runoff from this storm is known to be 1.8 in., compute the ϕ index for this event.

Solution

(a) Using the Horton equation, the infiltrated volume V_I is

$$V_I = \int_0^5 f \, dt = 0.2 \int_0^5 [1 + e^{-0.5t}] \, dt$$

$$V_I = 0.2 \left[t - \frac{1}{0.5} e^{-0.5t} \right]_0^5 = 0.2 \left[5 - \frac{e^{-2.5}}{0.5} + \frac{1}{0.5} \right]$$

$$V_I = 1.37 \text{ in.}$$

(b) The net runoff is the area in Exhibit 1 which lies above the ϕ index. Assuming $\phi < 0.4$ in., then one can write

$$1.8 = \sum_i [p_i - \phi] = (0.6 - \phi) + (0.7 - \phi) + (0.4 - \phi) + (0.7 - \phi) + (0.8 - \phi)$$

$$\phi = 0.28 \text{ in.}$$

WATERSHED HYDROGRAPHS

A watershed or drainage basin is the region drained by a stream or river. When a precipitation event (a storm) occurs over the watershed, it causes several processes within the basin. First is the initial moistening of the land surface and the vegetation, followed by the local filling of small surface indentations (depression storage) and the buildup of some depth of water on the land surface (initial detention storage) before the flow of water over the land begins; at the same time infiltration begins. For the larger storms some, possibly even most, of the precipitation enters a stream and flows out of the basin. The discharge past this outflow point is a time-variant process. A plot of the outflow versus time is called a hydrograph; Figure 7.1 is a definition sketch of a hydrograph.

There are two components to any perennial streamflow, a relatively short-term component which is the storm-induced surfaced water outflow, and a longer-term, slowly varying component called base flow which is the contribution from the

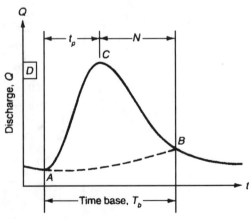

Figure 7.1

groundwater to the flow. In Figure 7.1 the storm hydrograph is caused by an effective storm precipitation of D hr, causing first the increasing discharge on the rising limb of the hydrograph from A to the crest C, and then the recessional limb from C to B when the storm-related discharge ceases. The base flow, below line AB in the figure, can be separated from the storm flow in any of several ways:

(i) From the low point A before the storm outflow begins, simply draw a horizontal line.

(ii) From point A extend the upstream line to a point directly below the crest C. From that point draw a straight line to B, which is located a distance N (days) after point C. The value N is empirically found from

$$N = A^{0.2} \quad A \text{ in sq. miles}$$
$$= 0.8A^{0.2} \quad A \text{ in sq. km} \tag{7.3}$$

The area of the drainage basin is A. Sometimes N is adjusted to the nearest full day.

(iii) Sometimes an attempt is made to mimic near B the character of the flow near A by patching the slope of the recession curve from A into the base-flow separation near B. This method leaves unanswered the choice of the remainder of the separation curve under the rising limb and crest. It must be drawn arbitrarily.

When the base flow has been removed from the original storm hydrograph, the remainder is direct storm runoff.

Unit Hydrograph

A unit hydrograph (unitgraph) has a volume of 1 in. (or 1 cm) of direct runoff over the drainage basin as a result of a storm of D hours' effective duration. Effective duration is the time interval when excess rainfall exists and direct runoff occurs. Any direct storm runoff has a volume

$$V = \int Q\,dt \tag{7.4}$$

which may also be written as $V = xA$, in which x is in inches (cm) and A is the basin area. Determination of the volume V, which is the area ABC in Figure 7.1, can be computed efficiently and accurately by use of the trapezoidal rule. Assume the time base T_b is divided into m intervals $\Delta t = T_b/m$ and the direct runoff ordinates Q_i, $i = 1$ to $m + 1$, are known with $Q_1 = Q_{m+1} = 0$. By the trapezoidal rule,

$$V = \int Q\,dt = (Q_1 + Q_2)\frac{\Delta t}{2} + (Q_2 + Q_3)\frac{\Delta t}{2} + \cdots + (Q_m + Q_{m+1})\frac{\Delta t}{2}$$

or

$$V = \Delta t \sum_{i=2}^{m} Q_i \tag{7.5}$$

Normally x will not be 1.0 in. (cm). The unit hydrograph is simply obtained by dividing each of the ordinates Q_i of the direct storm runoff plot by x. The unitgraph has a variety of application.

The suitability of the unitgraph for these uses, however, depends on the appropriateness of several assumptions, including these:

- Rainfall excesses of one duration D will always produce hydrographs with the same time base, independent of the intensity of the excess.

- The time distribution of the runoff does not change from storm to storm, so long as D is unchanged; thus an increase in runoff volume by P percent increases each hydrograph ordinate Q_i by P percent. Moreover, the distribution is not affected by prior precipitation.

The development of a unit hydrograph that produces reliable results in applications will be enhanced if one follows some experience rules:

- Basin sizes should be between 1000 acres and 1000 sq. miles.

- The direct storm runoff should preferably be within a factor of 2 of 1.0 inch, and the storm structure should be relatively simple.

- The unitgraph should be derived from several storms of the same duration. In other words, compute several unit hydrographs, and then average them.

If one does not have sufficient storm data to derive a unitgraph, then theoretical or empirical methods may be used to develop a "synthetic" unitgraph based on information such as peak flow values and basin characteristics. Numerous such methods have been proposed. Two of the more commonly used synthetic methods are Snyder's method, originally developed for Appalachian watersheds, and the SCS method, developed by the Soil Conservation Service. They must be applied with care for best results; space does not permit an explanation here of these methods in the detail that is needed, so the reader may consult the chapter references for the complete methods.

Change of Unitgraph Duration

Each unit hydrograph is associated with an effective storm duration D. If one wants a unitgraph for some other effective storm duration without developing it directly from storm data, this can be done. (If the new storm duration differs from the existing one by no more than 25 percent, then normal practice is to use the existing one without alteration). Two methods are used:

(i) *Lagging*. This method can be used to construct a new unitgraph for a storm of effective duration nD, given the unitgraph for the storm having effective duration D, where n is an integer only. Simply add together n of the original unit hydrographs, starting each successive unitgraph D hours after the beginning of the preceding one. This step produces a hydrograph associated with an effective duration of nD hours and having a runoff volume of n inches over the basin. Now divide all the hydrograph ordinates Q_i by n to obtain the new unitgraph. The method is easily set up in a table.

(ii) *S-curve*. This method is much more general and can be used to construct a unitgraph for either a shorter or longer effective storm duration than the original. Say the desired new effective storm duration is D_{new}. First one constructs the S-curve (it is a summation curve, that is, a sum of unitgraphs, and it also takes the general shape of an S) by successively lagging by D hours and summing (adding together) the ordinates of a total of T_b/D original unitgraphs. Next draw a second *S*-curve, lagged D_{new} hours after the first *S*-curve. The differences in ordinates of these two *S*-curves, each multiplied by the ratio D/D_{new}, will be the ordinates of the new unitgraph for the storm of effective duration D_{new}.

Example 7.2

Stream runoff from a 1500-acre watershed is plotted in Exhibit 2 for a storm having an effective duration *D* of 2 hours.

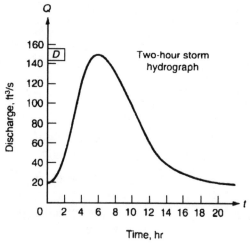

Exhibit 2

(a) Compute the ordinates of, and plot, the 2-hour unit hydrograph.

(b) Use the information for the 2-hour unit hydrograph to construct a 3-hour unit hydrograph.

(c) Construct the composite storm hydrograph caused by 1.5 inches of excess precipitation falling in the first 2 hours, followed immediately by 0.7 inches of excess precipitation in the next 2 hours. Assume a base flow of 10 ft³/s.

Solution

(a) The computations are presented in Exhibit 3. First the amount of the base flow must be identified and separated from the overall runoff. Since little

Exhibit 3

Time, hr (1)	Stream Flow, ft³/s (2)	Storm Flow Q_i, ft³/s (3)	Unitgraph Ord. U_i, ft³/s (4)
0	20	0	0
2	60	40	58
4	113	93	135
6	150	130	188
8	127	107	155
10	96	76	110
12	65	45	65
14	43	23	33
16	27	7	10
18	20	0	0

information is available in this problem and also because the runoff duration is relatively short, it is assumed that the base flow is a constant 20 ft³/s.

The data in column 2 come directly from the hydrograph, Exhibit 2. The storm flow Q_i, column 3, is the stream flow minus the base flow. Selecting a time interval $\Delta t = 2$ hr for use in Equation (7.5), the storm runoff volume is

$$V = \Delta t \sum_{i=2}^{m} Q_i = (2 \text{ hr})(521 \text{ ft}^3/\text{s}) = 1042 \frac{\text{ft}^3}{\text{s}}\text{-hr}$$

$$V = \left[1042 \frac{\text{ft}^3}{\text{s}}\text{-hr}\right]\left[60^2 \frac{\text{s}}{\text{hr}}\right] = 3.75 \times 10^6 \text{ ft}^3$$

This storm runoff volume is equivalent to a depth x of water over the basin of

$$x = \frac{V}{A} = \frac{(3.75 \times 10^6 \text{ ft}^3)(12 \text{ in./ft})}{(1500 \text{ acres})(43,560 \text{ ft}^2/\text{acre})} = 0.69 \text{ in.}$$

The unitgraph ordinates $U_i = Q_i/x$ are tabulated in column 4, and the unit hydrograph is plotted in Exhibit 4.

(b) One constructs the S-curve by repeatedly lagging the 2-hour unitgraph, whose ordinates are listed in column 4 in Exhibit 3, and adding together all the values that are associated with each time instant. The individual ordinates S_i of the S-curve are

$$S_i = \sum_{n=1}^{i} U_n$$

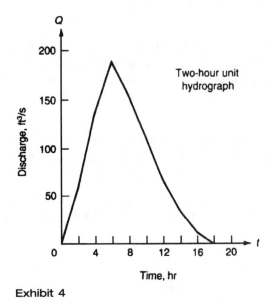

Exhibit 4

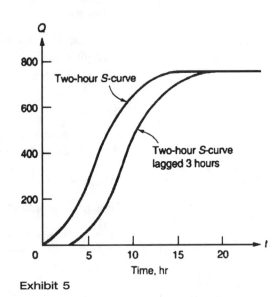

Exhibit 5

The 2-hr S-curve is plotted in Exhibit 5. Also shown is this same S-curve lagged 3 hours; the differences in ordinates of these two S-curves are then multiplied by the ratio $D/D_{\text{new}} = {}^2/_3$ to scale the volume of the new hydrograph properly to end with the 3-hr unitgraph plotted in Exhibit 6.

Scrutiny of this computational sequence shows that the peak discharge in the new unitgraph is slightly smaller than the peak of the 2-hr unitgraph, as one would expect.

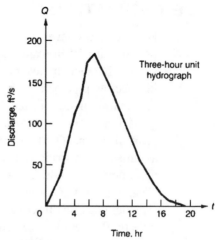

Exhibit 6

(c) Computations are tabulated in Exhibit 7. Time is measured from the start of the storm. The 2-hr unitgraph is multiplied by 1.5 for the first portion of the runoff, followed by a second unitgraph scaled by 0.7. Finally, the base flow is added.

Exhibit 7

Time, hr	Unitgraph Ord., U_i, ft³/s	$1.5 \times U_i$, ft³/s	$0.7 \times U_i$, lag 2 hr, ft³/s	Sum, with BF, ft³/s
0	0	0	—	10
2	58	87	0	97
4	135	203	41	254
6	188	282	95	387
8	155	233	132	375
10	110	165	109	284
12	65	98	77	185
14	33	50	46	106
16	10	15	23	48
18	0	0	7	17
20			0	10

The composite storm hydrograph is plotted in Exhibit 8.

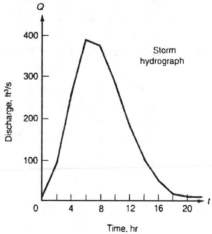

Exhibit 8

PEAK DISCHARGE ESTIMATION

Hydrographs convey a multitude of information. The volume of runoff over a time period is useful in water supply, flood control, and reservoir and detention basin studies. In other studies it is the peak discharge rate that is important—for example, in selecting pipe or culvert sizes or channel dimensions—and the other additional information is not needed.

The rational method is the most widely used method for the estimation of peak discharge Q_p (ft^3/s) from runoff over small surface areas. In using it one assumes that a spatially and temporally uniform rainfall occurs for a time period that allows the entire catchment area to contribute simultaneously to the outflow. Clearly the satisfaction of these limitations becomes more difficult as the basin size increases, so this equation is normally limited to basins that are below 1 square mile (640 acres) in size. The equation is

$$Q_p = CiA \qquad\qquad (7.6)$$

in which C is a nondimensional runoff coefficient that indicates the fraction of the incident rain that runs off the surface, i is the appropriate storm intensity (in./hr), and A is the watershed area (acres). Some add a dimensional conversion factor to this equation, but since 1 ft^3/s = 1.008 acre-in./hr, the conversion factor is usually ignored, as the other factors in the equation are not known with such accuracy. Table 7.1, adapted from Reference 1, gives reasonable ranges for C for various surfaces, as well as some guidance in selecting a value in the range.

The intensity factor must also be chosen carefully. It is normally defined as the intensity of rainfall of a chosen frequency that lasts for a duration equal to the time of concentration t_c for the basin. Sometimes the frequency will be dictated by policy (1-year, 5-year, or 10-year). After the frequency has been chosen, one usually consults an intensity-duration-frequency (IDF) plot to obtain i once the time of concentration has been picked. Conceptually this time is the time required for flow from the most remote point in the basin to reach the outlet, but in some cases it is simply estimated to be in the 5- to 15-minute range. Picking a shorter time usually leads to a higher-intensity i and a larger Q_p; in one sense this is conservative, but it may also be wasteful by causing one to design for an excessively large flow. The IDF plot, if developed properly, reports information that is the result of long-term statistical averages of many individual storms, not just the result of a compilation of relatively few data.

When the basin surface is not homogeneous, one should either subdivide the basin into smaller regions which are (nearly) uniform or compute a weighted average value for C, the weights being the areas.

Several other approaches to the estimation of peak discharge exist, the SCS methods being among the most prominent. If one wants to apply these methods properly, however, a lengthy description of the method and the supporting data and charts are required. One should consult the references at the end of this chapter for an adequate description of the procedures.

Table 7.1 Runoff coefficients, *C*

Description of Area	Runoff Coefficients
Business	
Downtown	0.70 to 0.95
Neighborhood	0.50 to 0.70
Residential	
Single-family	0.30 to 0.50
Multi-units, detached	0.40 to 0.60
Multi-units, attached	0.60 to 0.75
Residential (suburban)	0.25 to 0.40
Apartment	0.50 to 0.70
Industrial	
Light	0.50 to 0.80
Heavy	0.60 to 0.90
Parks, cemeteries	0.10 to 0.25
Playgrounds	0.20 to 0.35
Railroad yard	0.20 to 0.35
Unimproved	0.10 to 0.30

It often is desirable to develop a composite runoff coefficient based on the percentage of different types of surface in the drainage area. This procedure often is applied to typical "sample" blocks as a guide to selection of reasonable values of the coefficient for an entire area. Coefficients with respect to surface type currently in use are:

Character of Surface	Runoff Coefficients
Pavement	
Asphaltic and concrete	0.70 to 0.95
Brick	0.70 to 0.85
Roofs	0.75 to 0.95
Lawns, sandy soil	
Flat, 2 percent	0.05 to 0.10
Average, 2 to 7 percent	0.10 to 0.15
Steep, 7 percent	0.15 to 0.20
Lawns, heavy soil	
Flat, 2 percent	0.13 to 0.17
Average, 2 to 7 percent	0.18 to 0.22
Steep, 7 percent	0.25 to 0.35

The coefficients in these two tabulations are applicable for storms of 5- to 10-yr frequencies. Less frequent, higher-intensity storms require the use of higher coefficients because infiltration and other losses have a proportionally smaller effect on runoff. The coefficients are based on the assumption that the design storm does not occur when the ground surface is frozen.

Source: Design and Construction of Sanitary and Storm Sewers, Manual No. 37, 1986; reproduced by permission of ASCE.

Example 7.3

A storm drain is to be extended to serve two developing areas in a suburb. Exhibit 9 presents the intensity-duration-frequency plot for this region as well as a schematic diagram of the developments. Area *A* consists of 40 acres of mostly single-family residential units, with some multiple-family units; the time of concentration is 15 min.

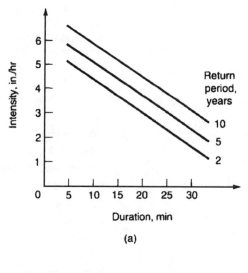

(a)

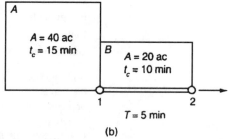

(b)

Exhibit 9

Area *B* drains to inlet 2 and contains several small businesses. The transit time for storm water to move from inlet 1 to inlet 2 is $T = 5$ min. Assuming a 5-year return period, estimate the peak discharges expected at the two inlets.

Solution

For area *A* one assumes a 15-min duration and finds $i = 4.50$ in./hr for a 5-yr return period from Exhibit 9(a). Referring to Table 7.1, it appears that $C = 0.45$ is reasonable for this residential area. For point 1 the peak discharge should be about

$$Q_p = CiA = (0.45)(4.50)(40) = 81 \text{ ft}^3/\text{s}$$

This peak is expected to appear at the second inlet location at $15 + 5 = 20$ min after the storm begins.

If area *B* is considered separately, then a 10-min duration leads, via Exhibit 9(a), to $i = 5.17$ in./hr, the runoff coefficient may be nearly $C = 0.70$, and

$$Q_p = (0.70)(5.17)(20) = 72 \text{ ft}^3/\text{s}$$

at inlet 2 from area *B*. However, the two computed peak discharges do not both arrive at point 2 at the same instant. The peak flow from *B* arrives 10 minutes before the flow from *A* arrives.

To compensate for the fact that the two peak discharges do not coincide in time, the usual approximate procedure is to use an area-weighted coefficient C_w and a time of concentration that applies to the combination of the areas. Here the time of concentration is 20 min. Thus

$$C_w = \Sigma C_i A_i / \Sigma A_i = [0.45(40) + 0.70(20)]/[40 + 20] = 0.53$$

For the 5-yr return period and a 20-min duration Exhibit 9(a) gives $i = 3.83$ in./hr and

$$Q_p = (0.53)(3.83)(60) = 122 \text{ ft}^3/\text{s}$$

which is lower by some 30 ft^3/s than the sum of the individual peak flows.

HYDROLOGIC ROUTING

Routing methods track water masses as a function of time as they course through streams, rivers, and reservoirs. Hydrologic routing is based on conservation of mass, supplemented by a relation between storage and discharge; it is an incomplete, approximate computation since it ignores momentum considerations, but it is often used because it can produce sufficiently accurate results with far less computational effort than is required in hydraulic routing, which does include the momentum equation. In this section the hydrologic routing of flows through reservoirs and rivers will be reviewed.

When the inflow hydrograph to either a reservoir or river reach is compared with the subsequent outflow hydrograph at the other end, two characteristic features are normally present: (1) the peak discharge of the inflow is attenuated—that is, reduced—in the outflow, and (2) the peak outflow occurs later than—that is, lags—the peak inflow. The difference between inflow I and outflow Q at any instant is equal to the rate of change of the storage S of water in the region between the inflow and outflow stations, or

$$I - Q = \frac{dS}{dt} \qquad (7.7)$$

Usually this equation is integrated between two time instants t_n and t_{n+1} and the trapezoidal rule is applied over the interval $\Delta t = t_{n+1} - t_n$ to obtain

$$(I_{n+1} + I_n)\frac{\Delta t}{2} - (Q_{n+1} + Q_n)\frac{\Delta t}{2} = S_{n+1} - S_n \qquad (7.8)$$

The typical routing problem begins with an inflow hydrograph given (a set of values I_n, $n = 1$, N). The value of the initial outflow must also be known. The remaining two unknowns in the equation are Q_{n+1} and S_{n+1}. Once the relation between storage and outflow is specified, the new outflow can be computed, and the computation can progress to the next time increment. This storage relation differs, however, depending on the application.

Reservoir Routing

Reservoir outflow either is controlled by gages and/or valves or is not controlled, owing to their absence. In uncontrolled reservoirs the storage relation is of the form $S = f(Q)$ when the reservoir water surface has no slope, as in short or deep reservoirs, or $S = f(Q, I)$ when the surface does slope, as in shallow reservoirs. For controlled reservoirs the storage representation may again be of either type, with the added problem that a separate storage relation must be determined for each combination of gate/valve settings. When $S = f(Q, I)$ the routing method is similar to river routing.

The storage indication, or Puls, method of hydrologic routing is commonly applied to reservoirs. When storage is assumed to be a function only of outflow, the method uses the following steps:

■ Equation (7.8) is rearranged to give

$$I_n + I_{n+1} + \left(\frac{2}{\Delta t}S_n - Q_n\right) = \left(\frac{2}{\Delta t}S_{n+1} + Q_{n+1}\right) \tag{7.9}$$

■ From whatever data are given, a table or graph of $(2S/\Delta t + Q)$ versus Q is prepared; it is called a storage indication curve.

■ The storage indication curve and inflow data are used in applying Equation (7.9) sequentially over time increments until the outflow has been computed as a function of time.

The Puls method is applied in Example 7.4.

Example **7.4**

Some elevation-discharge and elevation-area data for a small reservoir with an ungated spillway are given below. An inflow sequence to the reservoir for part of a flood is given in a second table.

Elev., ft	0	1	2	3	4	5	6
Area, acres	1000	1020	1040	1050	1060	1080	1100
Outflow, ft³/s	0	525	1490	2730	4200	5880	7660

Date	Hour	Inflow, ft³/s
4/23	12 P.M.	1500
4/24	12 A.M.	1600
	12 P.M.	3100
4/25	12 A.M.	9600

Determine by routing the outflow discharge and reservoir water surface elevation at 12 A.M. on 25 April. Arrange the computations in a tabular form. Use a 12-hour routing period, and assume that the reservoir water level just reaches the spillway crest (elevation 0.0) at 12 P.M. on 23 April.

Solution

Since the outflow Q is given directly as a function of elevation, the first task is to determine the reservoir storage S as a function of elevation also. The given areas are the surface areas of the reservoir water surface; integrating these areas over the incremental elevation changes produces the incremental changes in storage. This computation will be tabulated along with the compilation of data points for the storage indication curve. Elevation values will also be used as the index n in the equations. The equations used in computing the table entries are

$$\bar{A} = \frac{1}{2}(A_n + A_{n+1}) \quad \Delta S = \bar{A}\Delta h \quad S_{AF} = \Sigma\Delta S$$

$$\frac{2}{\Delta t}S + Q = \frac{2S_{AF}(43,560)}{12(60^2)} + Q = 2.02S_{AF} + Q, \text{ ft}^3/\text{s}$$

The resulting storage indication curve is plotted in Exhibit 10.

Elev., n, ft	Area A, acres	Avg. Area, $\bar{A}$, acres	S_{AF}, acre-ft	$\frac{2}{\Delta t}S+Q$, ft^3/s
0	1000		0	0
		1010		
1	1020		1010	2560
		1030		
2	1040		2040	5600
		1045		
3	1050		3085	8950
		1055		
4	1060		4140	12,550
		1070		
5	1080		5210	16,400
		1090		
6	1100		6300	20,400

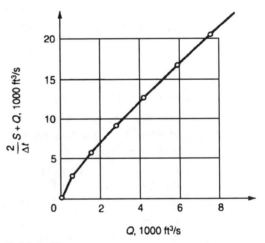

Exhibit 10

Now Equation (7.9) can be applied sequentially in the next table, with all flows in ft^3/s:

n (a)	Time (b)	I (c)	$\frac{2}{\Delta t}S-Q$ (d)	$\frac{2}{\Delta t}S+Q$ (e)	Q (f)
1	4/23 12 P.M.	1500	0	—	0
2	4/24 12 A.M.	1600	1700	3100	700
3	4/24 12 P.M.	3100	2800	6400	1800
4	4/25 12 A.M.	9600		15,500	5500

All inflows were given data. Also $Q_1 = 0$ was given. Thus the value $(2S/\Delta t - Q)_1$ can be computed to be zero. Now all terms on the left side of Equation (7.9) are known for $n = 1$, and this equation gives $2S/\Delta t + Q = 3100$ for $n + 1 = 2$ in column (e). Entering the storage indication curve, Exhibit 10, with this value gives $Q = 700$ ft^3/s [$n = 2$, column (f)]. Since $(2S/\Delta t + Q) - 2Q = 2S/\Delta t - Q$, column (d) with $n = 2$ is $3100 - 2(700) = 1700$. Applying Equation (7.9) with $n = 2$ then yields

$1600 + 3100 + 1700 = 6400$ in column (e) for $n = 3$. And these operations are cyclically repeated until the solution is completed. Thus the outflow from the reservoir at 12 A.M., 25 April, is $Q = 5500$ ft^3/s. Using this discharge and the outflow-discharge data, the water surface elevation E at that time is, using interpolation,

$$E = 4.00 + \left(\frac{5500 - 4200}{5880 - 4200}\right) \times 1.00 = 4.77 \text{ ft}$$

above the spillway crest.

River Routing

All forms of hydrologic river routing begin with the assumption of some relation between storage in the river section and the inflow and outflow at the ends of the section. The most common of these methods is the Muskingum method, which assumes that this relation is a weighted linear relation between storage, inflow, and outflow taking the form

$$S = K[xI + (1 - x)Q] \tag{7.10}$$

in which K is a proportionality factor with units of time, and x is the weighting factor giving the relative importance of the inflow and outflow contributions to storage. For example, for a simple reservoir one expects $S = f(Q)$ only so $x = 0$ could be chosen; if inflow and outflow are of equal importance, then $x = 0.5$ should be selected. For most streams x is between 0.2 and 0.3. The parameters K and x can be determined for a specific routing application if suitable data are available so that $[xI + (1 - x)Q]$ can be plotted versus storage S for several values of x between 0 and 0.5. The value of x that most nearly collapses the plotted data onto a single fitted straight line is used in the routing application, and $1/K$ is the slope of that fitted line.

The final form of the Muskingum routing equation is

$$Q_{n+1} = C_0 I_{n+1} + C_1 I_n + C_2 Q_n \tag{7.11}$$

in which

$$C_0 = (\Delta t/2 - Kx)/D \tag{7.12}$$

$$C_1 = (\Delta t/2 + Kx)/D \tag{7.13}$$

$$C_2 = (K - Kx - \Delta t/2)/D \tag{7.14}$$

and

$$D = K - Kx + \Delta t/2 \tag{7.15}$$

Observe that one must always have $C_0 + C_1 + C_2 = 1$. These equations can be derived by using Equation (7.10) to express S_n and S_{n+1}, inserting the results in Equation (7.9), and rearranging the terms.

Example 7.5

Thirty-six hours of data for stream flow are given in the following table:

Time	6 A.M.	12 A.M.	6 P.M.	12 P.M.	6 A.M.	12 A.M.	6 P.M.
I, ft^3/s	10	30	70	50	40	32	25

The Muskingum parameters have been determined to be $K = 10$ hr, $\Delta t = 6$ hr, and $x = 0.23$. The flow is steady in the reach at 6 A.M. on the first day. Determine the outflow hydrograph from this stream reach.

Solution

Direct computation using first Equation (7.15) and then Equations (7.12)–(7.14) will lead to

$$D = 10.70, \quad C_0 = 0.065, \quad C_1 = 0.495, \quad \text{and} \quad C_2 = 0.440.$$

Use of a table is an aid in organizing the computations:

Time	I_n, ft^3/s	$C_0 I_{n+1}$	$C_1 I_n$	$C_2 Q_n$	Q_{n+1}, ft^3/s
6 A.M.	10				10
12 A.M.	30	2.0	5.0	4.4	11.4
6 P.M.	70	4.6	14.9	5.0	24.5
12 P.M.	50	3.3	34.7	10.8	48.8
6 A.M.	40	2.6	24.8	21.5	48.9
12 A.M.	32	2.1	19.8	21.5	43.4
6 P.M.	25	1.6	15.8	19.1	36.5

The inflow data are reproduced in the first two columns. The next three columns contain the terms that appear on the right side of Equation (7.11); the last column is the sum of the three previous column entries, as Equation (7.11) indicates, and is the outflow hydrograph. According to these computations, the peak outflow is 48.9 ft^3/s and occurs at 6 A.M. on the second day.

WELL HYDRAULICS

The basic equation describing local, steady groundwater movement is Darcy's law, which can be written

$$V = -Ki \tag{7.16}$$

In this equation V is the average velocity of a discharge Q which moves through a soil cross-sectional area A. Darcy's law indicates that V is the product of the local hydraulic conductivity K, which depends on the local soil or rock properties, and the local gradient i of the piezometric head $H = p/\gamma + z$, that is, $i = dH/dL$.

This may also be interpreted as a difference in fluid energy between points, because the kinetic energy associated with groundwater flow is negligible. To obtain the actual fluid velocity, called the seepage velocity, in the subsurface saturated zone, one divides the average velocity by the local porosity. A variety of units are used in describing groundwater parameters, so one should take care to use consistent units in all computations.

Steady Flow

Equations for steady flow from a well in either an unconfined or a confined aquifer can be derived from Darcy's law. These simple equations have meaning and are accurate only when several simplifying assumptions are valid, including the following: (a) The aquifer, which is a geologic formation that contains enough saturated permeable material to yield significant quantities of water, must be large in extent and have uniform hydraulic properties, for example K is constant; (b) the pumping must occur at a constant rate for an extremely long time so that startup transients no longer exist; (c) the well fully penetrates the aquifer; (d) the well depth is much larger than the drawdown near the well; and (e) the estimate of the gradient i is a good one.

An aquifer is called unconfined if the upper edge of the saturated zone (ignoring capillary effects) is at atmospheric pressure; this edge is called the water table. Figure 7.2 is a schematic cross section of a well in an unconfined, horizontal aquifer. A cylindrical coordinate system (x, y) is placed at the base of the well; the drawdown from the undisturbed water table is s; the gradient of the piezometric head is $i = dy/dx$ at the water table and is assumed to apply to the entire water column below it. The radius of the well is $x = r_w$. Applying Darcy's law gives

$$V = \frac{Q}{A} = \frac{Q}{2\pi xy} = -K\frac{dy}{dx} \tag{7.17}$$

Rearranging this expression and integrating it between points (r_1, h_1) and (r_2, h_2) along the water table yields

$$Q = \frac{\pi K\left[h_2^2 - h_1^2\right]}{\ln(r_2/r_1)} \tag{7.18}$$

as the expression for the steady pumping rate, or discharge, for this case.

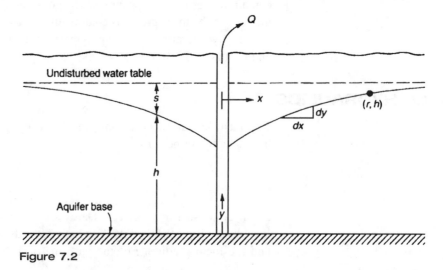

Figure 7.2

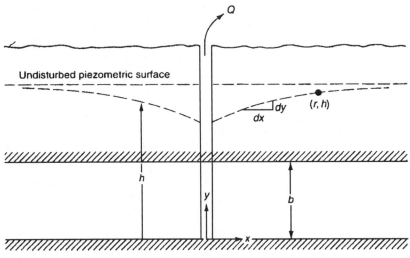

Figure 7.3

The case for steady pumping from a confined, horizontal aquifer of thickness m is similar to the first case, as shown in Figure 7.3. However, the gradient i is determined from the local slope of the piezometric head curve (shown dashed), which is no longer the same as the edge of the saturated zone. Equation (7.17) still applies to this case if the area through which flow occurs is corrected to $A = 2\pi xb$. Now the integration between points (r_1, h_1) and (r_2, h_2) on the piezometric surface results in

$$Q = \frac{2\pi Kb(h_2 - h_1)}{\ln(r_2/r_1)} \tag{7.19}$$

for the discharge. Sometimes the transmissibility $T = Kb$ is introduced into this equation.

Unsteady Flow

The first significant solution for unsteady flow to a well was originally developed by Theis for a confined aquifer. It expresses the drawdown s as

$$s = \frac{Q}{4\pi T} W(u) \tag{7.20}$$

in which

$$u = \frac{r^2 S}{4Tt} \tag{7.21}$$

and

$$W(u) = \int_u^\infty \frac{e^{-u}\,du}{u} = -0.5772 - \ln(u) + u - \frac{u^2}{2\times 2!} + \cdots \tag{7.22}$$

is called the well function of u. Table 7.2 presents tabulated values for this function. The discharge Q is constant over the pumping period, and r is the radius at which s is computed (to find the drawdown at the well, use $r = r_w$) at time t after pumping begins. The solution depends on knowledge of two aquifer properties, the transmissibility T and the storage constant S. The storage constant is the amount of water removed from a unit volume of the aquifer when the piezometric head is lowered one unit. Two methods for the determination of these aquifer properties will be described next.

Table 7.2 Values of the function $W(u)$ for various values of u

u	$W(u)$	u	$W(u)$	u	$W(u)$	u	$W(u)$
1×10^{-10}	22.45	7×10^{-8}	15.90	4×10^{-5}	9.55	1×10^{-2}	4.04
2	21.76	8	15.76	5	9.33	2	3.35
3	21.35	9	15.65	6	9.14	3	2.96
4	21.06	1×10^{-7}	15.54	7	8.99	4	2.68
5	20.84	2	14.85	8	8.86	5	2.47
6	20.66	3	14.44	9	8.74	6	2.30
7	20.50	4	14.15	1×10^{-4}	8.63	7	2.15
8	20.37	5	13.93	2	7.94	8	2.03
9	20.25	6	13.75	3	7.53	9	1.92
1×10^{-9}	20.15	7	13.60	4	7.25	1×10^{-1}	1.823
2	19.45	8	13.46	5	7.02	2	1.223
3	19.05	9	13.34	6	6.84	3	0.906
4	18.76	1×10^{-6}	13.24	7	6.69	4	0.702
5	18.54	2	12.55	8	6.55	5	0.560
6	18.35	3	12.14	9	6.44	6	0.454
7	18.20	4	11.85	1×10^{-3}	6.33	7	0.374
8	18.07	5	11.63	2	5.64	8	0.311
9	17.95	6	11.45	3	5.23	9	0.260
1×10^{-8}	17.84	7	11.29	4	4.95	1×10^{0}	0.219
2	17.15	8	11.16	5	4.73	2	0.049
3	16.74	9	11.04	6	4.54	3	0.013
4	16.46	1×10^{-5}	10.94	7	4.39	4	0.004
5	16.23	2	10.24	8	4.26	5	0.001
6	16.05	3	9.84	9	4.14		

Source: Bedient and Huber, *Hydrology and Floodplain Analysis*, 3rd ed. ©2002 by Addison Wesley Publishing Co. Reprinted by permission.

The first method of determining T and S is by using the original Theis equations. An examination of these equations shows that a plot of $W(u)$ versus u, called a type curve, will have the same shape as a plot of s versus r^2/t on log-log graph paper. The two curves are plotted, and one graph is laid over the other so the curves lie on one another; then a so-called match point, which is a set of data for u, $W(u)$, s, and r^2/t, is taken from the plots, inserted in Equations (7.20) and (7.21), and the resulting relations are solved for S and T. Since the match point is used to establish a connection between one data plot and the other, the match point need not be on the curve itself, although most practitioners do choose the match point atop the superimposed curves.

The second method, called the Cooper-Jacob method, is appropriate when u is small (for example, $u \leq 0.01$ is a common rule). In this method s is plotted against pumping time on semilogarithmic paper; the curve eventually becomes linear. A fitted straight line is then extended to the point $s = 0$, where the value $t = t_0$ is noted. One then solves for the aquifer properties from

$$T = \frac{2.3Q}{4\pi(s_2 - s_1)} \log_{10}\left(\frac{t_2}{t_1}\right) \tag{7.23}$$

and

$$S = \frac{2.25Tt_0}{r^2} \tag{7.24}$$

Use of these equations is simplified if points 1 and 2 are chosen so that $t_2/t_1 = 10$; of course $s_2 - s_1$ is the difference in drawdown over this same time interval. The result in Equation (7.24) must be nondimensional.

Several approaches are possible for unsteady unconfined well flow, but the simplest is to use the Theis method, Equation (7.20), with modified definitions of T and S. Now $T = Kb$ is based on the saturated thickness when pumping commences, and S is the specific yield, the volume of water released when the water table drops one unit. This approach is accurate when the drawdown is small in comparison with the saturated thickness of the acquifer.

Example **7.6**

A well has been pumped at a steady rate for a very long time. The well has a 12-inch diameter and fully penetrates an unconfined aquifer that is 150 ft thick. Two small observation wells are 70 and 150 feet from the well, and the corresponding observed drawdowns are 24 and 20 feet. If the estimated hydraulic conductivity is 10 ft/day (sandstone), what is the discharge?

Solution

The saturated aquifer thicknesses at the observation wells are $h_1 = 150 - 24 = 126$ ft and $h_2 = 150 - 20 = 130$ ft, and the use of Equation (7.18) leads directly to

$$Q = \frac{\pi K \left[h_2^2 - h_1^2 \right]}{\ln(r_2/r_1)} = \frac{\pi(10)[(130)^2 - (126)^2]}{\ln(150/70)} = 42,200 \text{ ft}^3/\text{day}$$

This is equivalent to 0.49 ft^3/s or 220 gal/min.

Example **7.7**

Data on time t since pumping began versus drawdown s were collected from an observation well located 400 ft from a well which fully penetrated a confined aquifer that is 80 ft thick and is pumped at 200 gal/min. The data are presented in Exhibit 11.

Exhibit 11

t, min	s, ft	t, min	s, ft
35	2.82	103	4.43
41	3.12	131	4.60
48	3.25	148	5.00
60	3.60	205	5.35
80	3.98	267	5.80

Determine the aquifer properties T and S.

Solution

The data in Exhibit 11 have been used with $r = 400$ ft to compute s versus r^2/t, which have been plotted in Exhibit 12 on a sheet of log-log paper, and the plot has been placed on top of a log-log plot of $W(u)$ versus u (the type curve). The two plots have been moved around until the closest fit between the curves was found, taking care that the coordinate axes are parallel. If the match point is chosen

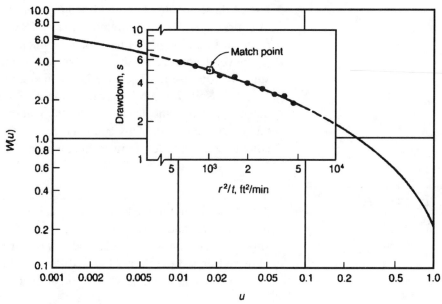

Exhibit 12

as shown in the figure, then $s = 5$ ft, $r^2/t = 10^2$ ft^3/min, $u = 0.0175$, and $W(u) = 3.50$. Rearranging Equation (7.20),

$$T = Q\frac{W(u)}{4\pi s} = \frac{200 \text{ gal/min}}{7.48 \text{ gal/ft}^3}\frac{(3.50)}{4\pi(5 \text{ ft})} = 1.49 \text{ ft}^2/\text{min}$$

Then from Equation (7.21),

$$S = \frac{4Tu}{r^2/t} = \frac{4(1.49)(0.0175)}{10^3} = 1.04\times10^{-4}$$

Example 7.8

Last April pumping began at an 8-inch-diameter well at a steady rate of 300 gal/min while observations were made at a well 100 ft away. Values of elapsed time and drawdown were taken for 16 hours and plotted; see Exhibit 13. Use the plotted data to determine values for the transmissibility and storage constant of this aquifer. In addition, estimate the drawdown in the observation well after four months of steady pumping at 300 gal/min.

Solution

Exhibit 13 is a semilogarithmic plot of data in the form needed to apply the Cooper-Jacob (or modified Theis, as it is also called) method. If one extends the straight-line portion of the plot to $s = 0$, as shown in Exhibit 14, one can read from the plot the value $t_0 = 2$ hr. One also needs a pair of data points (s_1, t_1) and (s_2, t_2) for use in Equation (7.23). For example, at $t_1 = 4.0$ hr, $s_1 = 3.3$ ft, and at $t_2 = 10.0$ hr, $s_2 = 7.4$ ft. Then

$$T = \frac{2.3Q}{4\pi(s_2 - s_1)}\log_{10}\left(\frac{t_2}{t_1}\right) = \frac{2.3(300)}{4\pi(7.4-3.3)}\log_{10}\left(\frac{10.0}{4.0}\right) = 5.33 \text{ gal/min/ft}$$

$$T = \frac{5.33\frac{\text{gal/min}}{\text{ft}}}{7.48\frac{\text{gal}}{\text{ft}^3}}\left(60\frac{\text{min}}{\text{hr}}\right)\left(24\frac{\text{hr}}{\text{day}}\right) = 1026 \text{ ft}^2/\text{day}$$

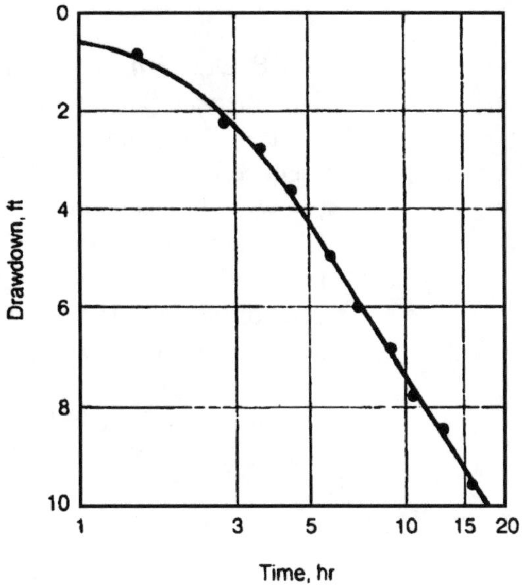

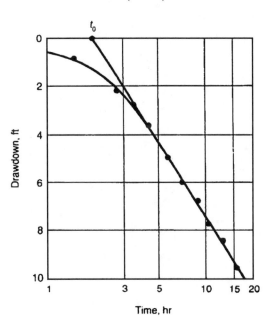

Exhibit 13

The storage constant can then be found as

$$S = \frac{2.25 T t_0}{r^2} = \frac{2.25(1026 \text{ ft}^2/\text{day})\left(\frac{2}{24} \text{ day}\right)}{(100 \text{ ft})^2} = 0.0192$$

Exhibit 14

Equation (7.23) can also be used to find the drawdown after four months. If s_2 is the drawdown after four months, then t_2 is four months or approximately 122 days. If one picks the other point to be $s_1 = 0$ and $t_1 = t_0 = 2.0$ hrs, then

$$s_2 = \frac{2.3 Q}{4 \pi T} \log_{10}\left(\frac{t_2}{t_1}\right) = \frac{2.3(300)}{4 \pi (5.33)} \log_{10}\left(\frac{122(24)}{2}\right) = 32.6 \text{ ft}$$

is the predicted drawdown.

REFERENCES

1. ASCE. *Design and Construction of Sanitary and Storm Sewers*. Manual No. 37. American Society of Civil Engineers, New York, 1986.
2. Bedient, P. B., and Huber, W. C. *Hydrology and Foodplain Analysis*, 3rd ed. Prentice Hall, Upper Saddle River, NJ, 2002.
3. Chow, V. T., Maidment, D. R., and Mays, L. R. *Applied Hydrology*. McGraw-Hill, New York, 1988.
4. Linsley, R. K., Kohler, M. A., and Paulhus, J. L. H. *Hydrology for Engineers*, 2nd ed. McGraw-Hill, New York, 1975.
5. McCuen, R. H. *Hydrologic Analysis and Design*, 2nd ed. Prentice Hall, Englewood Cliffs, NJ, 1998.
6. Viessman, W., Jr., and Lewis, G. L. *Introduction to Hydrology*, 4th ed. HarperCollins, New York, 1996.

CHAPTER 8

Water Quality, Treatment, and Distribution

Kenneth J. Williamson

OUTLINE

WATER DISTRIBUTION 367
Water Source ■ Transmission Line ■ The Distribution Network ■ Water Storage ■ Pumping Requirements ■ Pressure Tests

WATER QUALITY 371
Microbiological Quality and Measurements ■ Ion Balances ■ General Chemistry Concepts

DISSOLVED OXYGEN RELATIONSHIPS IN STREAMS 375
Biochemical Oxygen Demand ■ Oxygen Deficit ■ Mixing ■ Reoxygenation ■ Oxygen Sag Model

WATER TREATMENT 378
Aeration ■ Mixing ■ Coagulation and Flocculation ■ Sedimentation ■ Filtration ■ Softening ■ Chlorination ■ Fluoridation Activated Carbon ■ Chlorination Byproducts ■ Sludge Treatment

SELECTED SYMBOLS AND ABBREVIATIONS 388

BIBLIOGRAPHY 388

WATER DISTRIBUTION

Water distribution systems involve a **water source**, a **transmission line**, the **distribution network**, **pumping**, and **storage**.

Water Source

The engineering significance of the water source is primarily related to the water elevation and the water quality. The water elevation will determine the extent of pumping required to maintain adequate flows in the network. The range of elevations of the water source must be known as a function of flow rates and seasons of the year. Typical water sources include reservoirs, lakes, rivers, and underground aquifers.

Water quality is largely determined by the source. **Surface water** sources typically have low dissolved solids but high suspended solids. As a result, treatment of such sources requires coagulation followed by sedimentation and filtration to remove the suspended solids. **Ground-water** sources are low in suspended solids, but they may be high in dissolved solids and reduced compounds. Ground-water, if high in dissolved solids, requires chemical precipitation or ion exchange processes for the removal of dissolved ions.

Transmission Line

The transmission line is required to convey water from the sources and storage to the distribution of the system. Arterial main lines supply water to the various loops in the distribution system. The main lines should be arranged in loops or in parallel to allow for repairs. Such lines are designed using the Hazen-Williams formula for single pipes [Equation (8.1)], and the equivalent pipe method for single loops. Multiple loops are designed using **Hardy Cross methodology**:

$$v = kCr^{0.63}s^{0.54} \tag{8.1}$$

where v = pipe velocity (fps), k = constant (1.318 fps), C = roughness coefficient (100 for cast iron pipe), r = hydraulic radius (ft), and s = slope of hydraulic grade line (ft/ft).

The **equivalent pipe method** involves two procedures: 1) conversion of pipes of unequal diameters in series into a single pipe, and 2) conversion of pipes in a parallel flow from the same nodes into a single pipe.

The Distribution Network

The distribution network is comprised of the arterial mains, distribution mains, and smaller distribution piping. The mains are spaced in a series of loops to supply redundancy in case of failure. Diameters of mains should be larger than six inches.

Pressure Requirements

The controlling design variable for water distribution networks is the amount of pressure under maximum flow. Typically, a minimum value of 20 to 40 psi is required if pumper fire trucks are used, and 40 to 75 psi if fire flows are taken directly from hydrants. Static pressure should range from 60 to 80 psi. If pressures greater than 100 psi occur in the system, then the system should be separated into levels with separate storage elevations for each level.

Required Flows

Flow from the water distribution network is calculated as the sum of domestic, irrigation, industrial, commercial, and fire requirements. The design flow is the largest of either

$$Q^{\text{design}} = Q^{\text{hourly}} \tag{8.2}$$

where Q^{design} = design flow (cfs) and Q^{hourly} = maximum hourly (cfs), or,

$$Q^{\text{design}} = Q^{\text{daily}} + Q^{\text{fire}} \qquad (8.3)$$

where Q^{daily} = maximum daily flow over the past three years (cfs) and Q^{fire} = fire flow (cfs).

The fire flow is recommended by the National Board of Fire Underwriters as

$$Q^{\text{fire}} = 1020 \sqrt{P}\left(1 - 0.01\sqrt{P}\right) \qquad (8.4)$$

where Q = demand in gpm and P = population in thousands (up to 200,000 persons). Above 200,000 persons, an additional 2000 to 5000 gpm needs to be added to accomodate an additional fire.

Fire flows are dependent upon the type of construction, floor area, height of buildings, fire hazards, and local codes. Fire flows in gpm can also be estimated for specific buildings from Equation (8.5) as

$$Q^{\text{fire}} = 18C(A)^{0.5} \qquad (8.5)$$

where C = construction material constant (1.5 for combustible materials; 0.6 for fire resistant materials), and A = floor area (ft^2).

The various flows for a given community are typically obtained from historical data of water use. Without such data, estimates can be made from the average values listed in Table 8.1. The design flow calculated by Equation (8.2) or Equation (8.3) should be increased by 10 percent to allow for system losses.

Table 8.1 Water flow rates

Flow	Method of Estimation
Average domestic flow	Population served, 100 gal/capita-d, 3000 to 10,000 persons/km^2 (7765 to 25,889 persons/mi^2)
Irrigation flow	Maximum of 0.75 times average daily flow for arid climates
Industrial/commercial flow	Computed from known industries and area of commercial districts
Q^{daily}	2.5 times the sum of yearly average domestic, industrial, and irrigation
Q^{hourly}	1.5 times Q^{daily}
Q^{fire}	Equation (8.5)

Water Storage

Water storage is required to maintain pressure in the system, minimize pumping costs, and meet emergency demands. Typically the storage is placed so that the load center or distribution network is between the water source and the storage, as shown in Figure 8.1.

Storage requirements are calculated based upon variations in hourly flow and fire requirements. If the pumping capacity is set at some value less than the maximum hourly flow, then all flow requirements above that value will have to be provided by storage. Such storage quantities can be estimated by integration of the area in Figure 8.2 above the pumping rate. If pumping rates are set at the average daily flow, the storage requirements can be estimated as about 30 percent of the total daily water requirements.

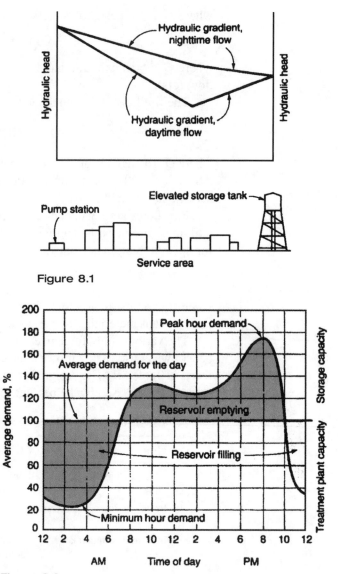

Figure 8.1

Figure 8.2

Storage requirements for fire flows depend upon the required duration. Duration can be estimated as approximately 1 hour for each 1000 gpm of fire flow. The storage requirements for fire are equal to the duration times Q^{fire}. Storage must be supplied to meet the maximum daily requirement, which is equal to the average daily requirement plus the fire flow for the duration of the fire.

Pumping Requirements

The pumping system needs adequate capacity for design flows, taking into account the supply from storage. The required head must be adequate to maintain 20 psi at the load center during maximum flow. Excess pumping capacity is required to account for the possible failure of pumps and storage facilities.

Pressure Tests

The adequacy of the distribution system to maintain required pressure under fire-fighting conditions is tested by measuring pressure drops after opening the valves at a hydrant. For such tests, the fire flow that can be delivered is given by Equation (8.6):

$$\frac{Q^{\text{fire}}}{Q^{\text{test}}} = \frac{(P - P^{\text{fire}})^{0.54}}{(P - P^{\text{test}})^{0.54}}$$

(8.6)

where Q^{fire}, Q^{test} = fire flow and test flow, respectively, and P, P^{fire}, P^{test} = static main pressure, minimum required pressure under fire flow (20 psi), and pressure under hydrant test, respectively.

WATER QUALITY

The design of water treatment facilities requires calculations of both the concentrations and the masses of various constituents in water and chemical additions. Common elements and radicals of various constituents are listed in Table 8.2, and common water-treatment chemicals are listed in Table 8.3. The equivalent weight is equal to the molecular weight divided by the electrical charge.

Table 8.2 Common elements and radicals

Name	Symbol	Atomic Weight	Valence	Equivalent Weight
Aluminum	Al	27.0	+3	9.0
Calcium	Ca	40.1	+2	20.0
Carbon	C	12.0	−4	
Chlorine	Cl	35.5	−1	35.5
Fluorine	F	19.0	−1	19.0
Hydrogen	H	1.0	+1	1.0
Iodine	I	126.9	−1	126.9
Iron	Fe	55.8	+2	27.9
			+3	
Magnesium	Mg	54.9	+2	27.5
			+4	
			+7	
Nitrogen	N	14.0	−3	
			+5	
Oxygen	O	16.0	−2	8.0
Potassium	K	39.1	+1	39.1
Sodium	Na	23.0	+1	23.0
Sulfur	S	32.0	−6	16.0
			−4	
			−2	
			0	
Ammonium	NH_4^+	18	+1	18.0
Hydroxyl	OH^-	17.0	−1	17.0
Bicarbonate	HCO_3^-	61.0	−1	61.0
Carbonate	CO_3^{2-}	60.0	−2	30.0
Nitrate	NO_3^-	62.0	−1	62.0
Hypochlorite	OCl^-	51.5	−1	51.5

Table 8.3 Common inorganic chemicals for water treatment

Name	Formula	Usage	Molecular Weight	Equivalent Weight
Activated carbon	C	Taste and odor	12.0	
Aluminum sulfate	$Al_2(SO_4)_3 \cdot 14.3H_2O$	Coagulation	600	100
Ammonia	NH_3	Chloramines, disinfection	17.0	
Ammonium fluorosilicate	$(NH_4)_2SiF_6$	Fluoridation	178	
Calcium carbonate	$CaCO_3$	Corrosion control	132	66.1
Calcium fluoride	CaF_2	Fluoridation	78.1	
Calcium hydroxide	$Ca(OH)_2$	Softening	74.1	37.0
Calcium hypochlorite	$Ca(ClO)_2 \cdot 2H_2O$	Disinfection	179	
Calcium oxide	CaO	Softening	56.1	28.0
Carbon dioxide	CO_2	Recarbonation	44.0	22.0
Chlorine	Cl_2	Disinfection	71.0	
Chlorine dioxide	ClO_2	Taste and odor	67.0	
Ferric chloride	$FeCl_3$	Coagulation	162	54.1
Ferric hydroxide	$Fe(OH)_3$		107	35.6
Fluorosilicic acid	H_2SiF_6	Fluoridation	144	
Oxygen	O_2	Aeration	32.0	16.0
Sodium bicarbonate	$NaHCO_3$	pH adjustment	84.0	84.0
Sodium carbonate	Na_2CO_3	Softening	106	53.0
Sodium hydroxide	$NaOH$	pH adjustment	40.0	40.0
Sodium hypochlorite	$NaClO$	Disinfection	74.4	
Sodium fluorosilicate	Na_2SiF_6	Fluoridation	188	

Microbiological Quality and Measurements

Treated drinking water is required to avoid spreading diseases to the general population. This is accomplished by removing a variety of pathogenic (disease-causing) organisms by both removal of particulates and chemical disinfection. Such pathogens include bacteria (e.g., salmonella), viruses (e.g., hepatitis), protozoa (e.g., giardia and cryptosporidium), and parasites (e.g., tapeworms).

Measuring for the absence of all pathogens is both difficult and extremely expensive. The tactical approach adopted for drinking water is to measure for the presence of organisms that are indicative of fecal contamination from mammals (either from human or other warm-blooded animals). One type of organism that is always associated with fecal contamination is the fecal coliform, a type of bacteria that grows on a specific type of bacterial media under certain conditions. Fecal bacteria are a subgroup of the larger bacterial group of coliform bacteria (referred to as total coliforms). Testing is typically done by filtering water to remove the bacteria and then growing the bacteria in the specific media until large colonies form that can then be counted.

Testing is done in a sequential manner because it is easier to test for total coliform bacteria than for fecal coliforms. If more than one treated water sample per month (40 samples are required) test positive for total coliforms, then a fecal coliform test is usually conducted to confirm that fecal contamination has occurred. Tests for cryptosporidium and viruses are also conducted, usually on a

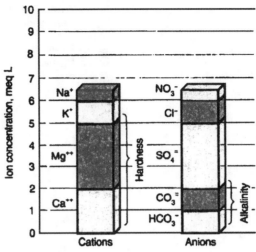

Figure 8.3

monthly basis. Further testing for specific organisms to the genus level can be done if water-borne contamination is suspected.

Ion Balances

Electroneutrality requires that water have an equal number of equivalents of cations and anions. Often bar graphs are used to show this relationship, as shown in Figure 8.3. From such graphs, concentrations of alkalinity, carbonate (calcium and magnesium, both associated with alkalinity), and non-carbonate hardness (calcium and magnesium in other forms) can be easily identified.

General Chemistry Concepts

A number of concepts from general chemistry are required for engineering calculations related to water treatment.

Oxidation-Reduction Reactions

Oxidation-reduction reactions involve the transfer of electrons from an electron donor to an electron acceptor. The easiest method (to construct balanced redox reaction) is through the use of half-reactions. Common half-reactions related to water treatment are listed in Table 8.4.

Henry's Law

Henry's Law states that the weight of any dissolved gas is proportional to the pressure of the gas.

$$C_{equil} = \alpha P_{gas} \tag{8.7}$$

where C_{equil} = equilibrium dissolved gas concentration (mg/L), P_{gas} = partial pressure of gas above liquid (atm), and α = Henry's Law constant (mg/L/atm).

Equilibrium Relationships

For an equilibrium chemical equation expressed as

$$A + B = C + D \tag{8.8}$$

Table 8.4 Common half-reaction for water treatment

Reduced Element	Half-Reaction
Cl	$\frac{1}{2}Cl_2 + e^- = Cl^-$
Cl	$\frac{1}{2}ClO^- + H^+ + e^- = \frac{1}{2}Cl^- + \frac{1}{2}H_2O$
Cl	$\frac{1}{8}ClO_4^- + H^+ + e^- = \frac{1}{8}Cl^- + \frac{1}{2}H_2O$
Fe	$\frac{1}{2}Fe^{2+} + e^- = \frac{1}{2}Fe$
Fe	$Fe^{3+} + e^- = Fe^{2+}$
Fe	$\frac{1}{3}Fe^{3+} + e^- = \frac{1}{3}Fe$
I	$\frac{1}{2}I_2 + e^- = I^-$
N	$\frac{1}{8}NO_3^- + \frac{5}{4}H^+ + e^- = \frac{1}{8}NH_4^+ + \frac{3}{8}H_2O$
N	$\frac{1}{5}NO_3^- + \frac{6}{5}H^+ + e^- = \frac{1}{10}N_2 + \frac{3}{5}H_2O$
O	$\frac{1}{4}O_2 + H^+ + e^- = \frac{1}{2}H_2O$

the relationship of concentrations at equilibrium can be approximated as

$$K_{eq} = \frac{[C][D]}{[A][B]} \tag{8.9}$$

where K_{eq} = equilibrium constant and [ ] = molar concentrations.

Some commonly used equilibrium constants are listed in Table 8.5.

Table 8.5 Common equilibrium constants

Equation	K_{eq}
$H_2CO_3 = H^+ + HCO_3^-$	$10^{-6.4}$
$HCO_3^- = H^+ + CO_3^{2-}$	$10^{-10.3}$
$NH_3 + H_2O = NH_4^+ + OH^-$	$10^{-4.7}$
$CaOH^+ = Ca^{2+} + OH^-$	$10^{-1.5}$
$MgOH^+ = Mg^{2+} + OH^-$	$10^{-2.6}$
$HOCl = H^+ + OCl^-$	$10^{-7.5}$

A common equilibrium relationship is the disassociation of water, which is given as

$$H_2O = H^+ + OH^- \tag{8.10}$$

which has a K_{eq} value of 10^{-14}. The hydrogen ion concentration is typically represented by the pH value or the negative log of its concentration as

$$pH = -\log[H^+] \tag{8.11}$$

Alkalinity

Alkalinity is a measure of the ability of water to consume a strong acid. In the alkalinity test, water is titrated with a strong acid to pH 6.4 and then to pH 4.5. The amount of acid that is used to reach the first pH endpoint is termed the carbonate alkalinity, and the amount to reach the second end point is called the total alkalinity. Alkalinity is expressed as calcium carbonate.

Alkalinity is the sum of the acid neutralization capacity of bicarbonate, carbonate, and hydroxide. For most drinking water sources, alkalinity can be approximated as bicarbonate. Carbonate alkalinity is the predominant species when the pH is above 10.8, and bicarbonate is the predominant species when the pH is between 6.9 and 9.8.

Solubility Relationships

The equilibrium between a compound in its solid crystalline state and its ionic form in solution, where

$$X_{aYb} = aX^{b+} + bY^{a-} \qquad (8.12)$$

is given by

$$K_{sp} = [X^{b+}]^a [Y^{a-}]^b \qquad (8.13)$$

where K_{sp} = solubility product.

Solubility products for common precipitation reactions in water treatment are given in Table 8.6.

Table 8.6 Common solubility products

Compound	K_{sp}
Magnesium carbonate	4×10^{-5}
Magnesium hydroxide	9×10^{-12}
Calcium carbonate	5×10^{-9}
Calcium hydroxide	8×10^{-6}
Aluminum hydroxide	1×10^{-32}
Ferric hydroxide	6×10^{-38}
Ferrous hydroxide	5×10^{-15}
Calcium fluoride	3×10^{-11}

DISSOLVED OXYGEN RELATIONSHIPS IN STREAMS

The **dissolved oxygen concentration** in a stream is determined by the rate of oxygen consumption, commonly caused by the discharge of oxygen demanding substances, and the rate of reoxygenation from the atmosphere.

Biochemical Oxygen Demand

The concentration of oxygen-demanding substances in a river is commonly expressed as the **biochemical oxygen demand**, or BOD. BOD is measured as the oxygen that is removed in a 20°C, five-day test, and is expressed as BOD_5 (mg/L).

This value must be converted to an ultimate BOD (mg/L)—or L value—at the temperature of interest, as

$$L = \frac{BOD_5}{1 - e^{-5k_{20}}} \qquad (8.14)$$

where k_{20} = BOD decay constant at 20 °C (1/d).

Typical k_{20} values for organic wastes range from about 0.10 to 0.30. Higher values are applied to organic wastes that are easily degraded by aerobic bacteria. The k value for the temperature of the river can be estimated as

$$k_{T_1} = k_{T_2} \theta^{(T_1 - T_2)} \qquad (8.15)$$

where θ = temperature correction coefficient, 1.056, and k_{T_1}, k_{T_2} = BOD decay coefficient (1/d) at temperatures T_1 and T_2 (°C), respectively.

The rate of oxygen consumption by the BOD is related to the **ultimate BOD concentration** as

$$r_{BOD} = k_T L \qquad (8.16)$$

where r_{BOD} has units of mg/L/d.

Oxygen Deficit

The dissolved oxygen in water is determined by Henry's Law, based upon a 20 percent partial pressure in the atmosphere. In streams with small levels of natural oxygen-demanding materials, background levels of dissolved oxygen will be from 80 to 100 percent of saturation. The dissolved oxygen in waste-waters with moderate to high BOD levels can be assumed to be zero.

Oxygen saturation values (C_{sat}) are shown in Table 8.7.

Table 8.7 Dissolved oxygen saturation values in river water

Temperature (°C)	Dissolved Oxygen (mg/L)
2	13.84
5	12.80
10	11.33
15	10.15
20	9.17
25	8.38
30	7.63

At a given temperature, the dissolved oxygen deficit is expressed as

$$D = (C_{sat} - C) \qquad (8.17)$$

where C_{sat} and C = saturation and actual dissolved oxygen concentration (mg/L), and D = dissolved oxygen deficit at a given temperature (mg/L).

Mixing

Assuming complete mixing in a river, the concentration of dissolved oxygen and ultimate BOD in a receiving stream are related as

$$C_0 = \frac{Q_r C_r + Q_w C_w}{Q_r + Q_w} \tag{8.18}$$

where C_r, C_w = concentration of constituents in river and waste, respectively, and Q_r, Q_w = flow rate of river and waste, respectively.

Reoxygenation

Reoxygenation occurs through the diffusion of oxygen from the atmosphere to the river. The rate of reoxygenation or reaeration is

$$r_{\text{reoxy}} = k_2 D \tag{8.19}$$

where k_2 = reaeration coefficient (l/d). Typical reaeration coefficients are listed in Table 8.8.

Table 8.8 Reaeration coefficients for water bodies

Water Body	k_2 (1/d)
Small ponds	0.15
Sluggish streams, lake	0.3
Large streams, low velocity	0.4
Large streams, high velocity	0.5
Swift streams	0.8

Reaeration coefficients can be adjusted for temperature as

$$\frac{k_{2,T_1}}{k_{2,T_2}} = 1.024^{T_1 - T_2} \tag{8.20}$$

with T_1 and T_2 expressed in °C.

Oxygen Sag Model

The dissolved-oxygen concentration in a stream after the addition of oxygen-demanding wastes can be expressed in differential form as

$$\frac{dD}{dt_r} = r_{\text{BOD}} - r_{\text{reoxy}} \tag{8.21}$$

where t_r = travel time in the river from the point of waste addition (d).

The resulting dissolved-oxygen profile is shown in Figure 8.4. After addition of the waste, the dissolved oxygen decreases to a maximum deficit (D_c) or minimum dissolved-oxygen level at a distance x_c or travel time t_c. Past this point, the deficit decreases as the river recovers.

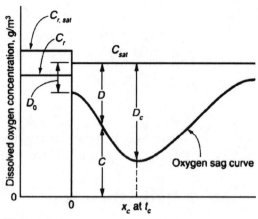

Figure 8.4

Equation (8.21) can be integrated to

$$D = \frac{kL_0}{k_2 - k}\left(e^{-kt_r} - e^{-k_2 t_r}\right) + D_0 e^{-k_2 t_r} \qquad \textbf{(8.22)}$$

where D_0, L_0 = oxygen deficit and the ultimate BOD concentration at the point of waste discharge into the river, respectively.

The **critical deficit** in the river, D_c, from which the minimum dissolved oxygen can be calculated, is given by

$$D_c = \frac{k}{k_2} L_0 e^{-kt_c} \qquad \textbf{(8.23)}$$

and the travel time to the critical deficit, from which the distance down the river to the critical deficit can be calculated, is given by

$$t_c = \frac{1}{k_2 - k}\ln\left[\frac{k_2}{k}\left(1 - \frac{D_0(k_2 - k)}{kL_0}\right)\right] \qquad \textbf{(8.24)}$$

WATER TREATMENT

Water treatment is used to alter the quality of water so that it is chemically and bacteriologically safe for human consumption. Common sources for water are groundwater and surface waters. Groundwater treatment may involve the removal of pathogens, iron and manganese, and hardness (Figure 8.5). Surface water treatment typically involves the simultaneous removal of pathogens, suspended solids, and taste and odor-causing compounds (Figure 8.6). All of these treatment processes are comprised of unit processes. Each unit process and its significant design variables are described below. Often, duplicate unit processes are designed in order to allow for partial operation during maintenance. The design period for water treatment plants is typically 15 to 20 years.

Aeration

Aeration is a unit operation that is used to remove taste- and odor-causing compounds by stripping the water with air and providing dissolved oxygen for the oxidation of reduced compounds.

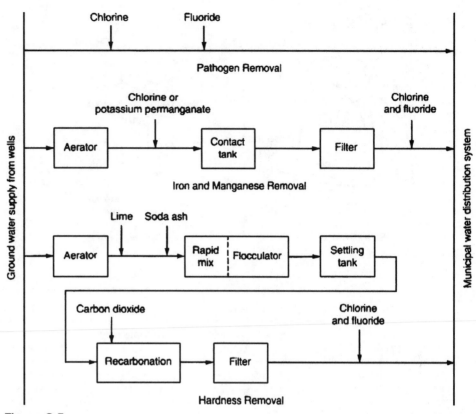

Figure 8.5

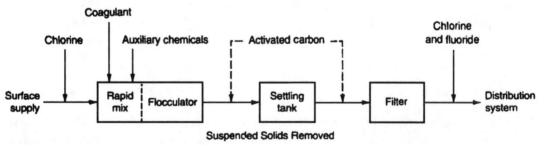

Figure 8.6

Common aerator types in water treatment include **spray, cascade**, and **bubble aerators**. Spray or cascade types break the water into drops or thin films which are passed through a column of air; bubble types force the air into small bubbles that are passed through a column of water (Figure 8.7). Spray- or cascade-type systems are susceptible to precipitation of oxidized compounds and corrosion from reduced compounds.

Stripping

Air stripping can effectively remove volatile compounds including hydrogen sulfide, carbon dioxide, and traces of small-molecular-weight organics. The removal of hydrogen sulfide and carbon dioxide both require pH control to acidic values.

Air stripping with spray aerators involves forcing water through multiple nozzles generally about one inch in diameter. The required areas are from

Stripping

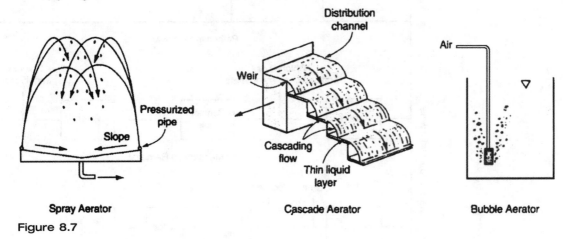

Figure 8.7

Table 8.9 Aeration equipment

Type	Spray Aerators	Multiple-tray Aerators	Cascade Aerators	Bubble Aerators
Stripping	50 to 150 ft^2 per MGD	25 to 50 ft^2 per MGD	40 to 50 ft^2 per MGD	10–30 min detention time 0.1–0.16 ft^3/gal
Oxidation	0.1 to 0.5 kg O_2/kW-h	0.1 to 0.5 kg O_2/kW-h	0.2 to 0.6 kg O_2/kW-h	
Fine bubble (efficiency = 20–45%				1.0 to 2.0 kg O_2/kW-h
Coarse bubble (efficiency = 6–20%)				0.6 to 1.4 kg O_2/kW-h

50 to 150 ft^2 per MGD. Head losses are about 10 psi. Multiple-tray aerators and cascade aerators allow water to flow in thin sheets, exposing it to air. Surface areas of 25 to 50 ft^2 per MGD are required for these (Table 8.9). Head losses are typically less than 10 ft.

Oxidation

For oxidation, the design variable is the mass transfer of oxygen. Oxidation rates are relatively rapid, resulting in detention times of 15 to 30 minutes. Oxygen requirements are estimated from balanced, oxidation-reduction reactions for the compound of interest.

Mixing

Mixing is required to disperse chemicals in the water stream being treated. Common applications include adding coagulants and chlorine. Common types of mixing for water treatment include turbine, propeller, pneumatic, and hydraulic mixing. These are depicted in Figure 8.8.

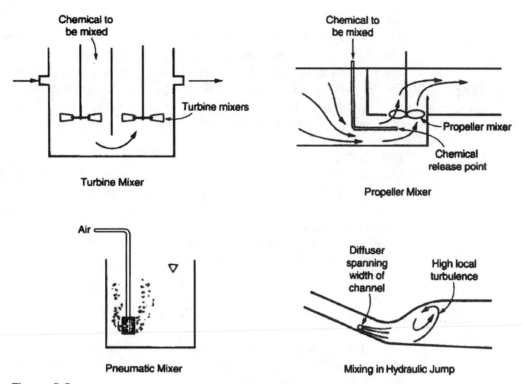

Figure 8.8

Power Requirements

The rapid mixing of chemicals in water treatment plants occurs in the fully turbulent range. For a baffled circular tank with a depth of water equal to the diameter, the following relationship has been developed:

$$P = \Phi \rho n^3 d^5 \qquad (8.25)$$

where P = power input (W), Φ = power function, 6 for fully turbulent conditions; ρ = mass density of water, 1000 kg/m^3; n = rotation of mixer (rps); and d = diameter of mixer (m).

Adequate mixing can be defined by the power per unit volume. Chemical mixing in a water-treatment plant requires a power input from 0.05 to 0.2 kW per m^3. The rapid mixing reactors have a hydraulic detention time from 0.5 to 1 minute.

Coagulation and Flocculation

Many suspended solids in raw water are colloidal (clays, silts, viruses, bacteria, humic acids, and silicates) which cannot be effectively removed by sedimentation or filtration. These small particles are treated by subjecting the water to coagulation and flocculation to increase the particle size. **Coagulation** is the process of reducing the negative charge (called **destabilization**) on the particles to allow attachment. Cationic coagulants such as aluminum sulfate, ferric sulfate, calcium oxide, and organic polymers are used to reduce the charges on the particles. **Flocculation** is the process of mixing the destabilized particles to facilitate attachment or floc formation. Flocculation is controlled by the mixing regime.

Coagulation

The dosage selection of chemicals for coagulation remains an empirical process. The chemicals used and their dosage rates are determined by laboratory testing using jar-test apparatus to determine optimum particle removal. Typically, a reduction in turbidity to less than 1.0 TU (turbidity units) is desired after sand filtration. Coagulation may also result in a significant reduction of color-causing compounds, other organic compounds, and bacteria.

Flocculation

Flocculation in water treatment plants is accomplished by using large flocculation basins with slowly turning flocculation paddles. Hydraulic detention times are from 30 to 60 minutes. Sedimentation basins can be attached directly to the flocculation basins.

Flocculation is controlled by the average **velocity gradient** in the water. Velocity gradient is a function of the power input from the mixing motor as

$$G = \sqrt{\frac{ep}{\mu V}} \qquad (8.26)$$

where G = average velocity gradient (1/s), e = efficiency of energy transfer from motor to paddles, 0.6, p = power input (W), μ = liquid viscosity (kg/m-s), and V = flocculation tank volume (m^3).

Because the flocculation rate increases as the number of particles increases, flocculation basins are designed as plug flow units. Because of this, the tanks are configured to be long and narrow, with the length 5 to 10 times the width or depth. Flocculation units are designed to have G values from 20 to 50/s, with decreasing values as a function of the distance down the tank.

Sedimentation

After flocculation, the larger particles are removed by sedimentation. Settling is also used in water treatment after oxidation of iron or manganese. Flocculated particles have densities of about 1400 to 2000 kg/m^3.

Settling velocities of particles are determined by Stokes' law for Reynolds numbers less than 0.3:

$$V_s = \frac{g(\rho_P - \rho_w)d_p^2}{18\mu} \qquad (8.27)$$

where V_s = terminal settling velocity (m/s), g = gravitational constant (9.8 m/s^2), d_p = particle diameter (m), and μ = water viscosity (0.001 kg/m-s).

Particles enter a sedimentation basin at all depths. A critical settling velocity related to the sedimentation basin can be calculated as

$$V_{sc} = \frac{Q}{A_s} \qquad (8.28)$$

where Q = flow rate into sedimentation basin (m^3/s), and A_s = surface area of sedimentation basin (m^2).

In standard sedimentation theory, if the settling rate (V_s) of the particles to be removed is greater than V_{sc}, then the particles will be 100 percent removed.

For particles with V_s less than V_{sc}, the particles will only be partially removed, with the removal given as

$$R = \frac{V_s}{V_{sc}}$$
(8.29)

where R is the decimal removal fraction.

The critical settling velocities used for design are typically expressed as an overflow rate. Design overflow rates for water-treatment unit processes are approximately 50 m/d (1200 gal/ft^2-d) for alum coagulation particles and 75 m/d (1800 gal/ft^2-d) for lime-softening sludges.

Filtration

Filtration in water treatment is commonly accomplished with granular filters. The **medium** for such filters is comprised of sand, charcoal, and garnet; the filters can utilize one or more different filter media. The water is applied to the top of the filter and is collected through underdrains.

Filtration is a complex process involving entrapment, straining, and absorption. As the filtration process proceeds, the head loss associated with the water flow through the porous medium increases as the filtered material accumulates in the pores. In addition, the number of particles passing through the filter increases with a subsequent increase in effluent turbidity. When either the allowable head loss or effluent quality are exceeded, the filter has to be backwashed to remove the accumulated material. Under backwashing, the filtration bed will expand to about twice its packed depth. The overflow troughs are positioned so that the sand does not wash out of the system during backwashing. Backwashing will require about 20 percent of the treated water flow, with about 10 percent of the filters being backwashed at any given time.

The specifics of sand filtration operations are difficult to model. The head loss through the clean sand bed can be predicted using relationships like the Carmen-Kozeny equation. Such head losses are proportional to the porosity, depth of bed, diameter of the medium, and the flow velocities. Head losses are about 0.5 to 1.0 m for a one-meter bed.

The more important operating parameters of effluent turbidity and head loss near the end of the filter run cannot be predicted. Operating curves must be obtained from historical data or extensive pilot-scale testing.

Design parameters for filtration are listed in Table 8.10.

Softening

The removal of hardness is accomplished by using lime/soda ash softening or ion exchange.

Lime/Soda Ash Softening

Lime/soda ash softening occurs by adding calcium hydroxide and sodium bicarbonate to form a chemical precipitate which is removed by sedimentation and filtration. The calcium hydroxide reacts with carbon dioxide and carbonate hardness as

$$CO_2 + Ca(OH)_2 = CaCO_3 + H_2O$$
$$Ca(HCO_3)_2 + Ca(OH)_2 = 2CaCO_3 + 2H_2O$$
$$Mg(HCO_3)_2 + 2Ca(OH)_2 = 2CaCO_3 + Mg(OH)_2 + 2H_2O$$

In each case, the italicized compounds are precipitates.

Table 8.10 Parameters for filtration

Parameter	Single Medium	Dual Media	Multimedia
Garnet			
Depth (mm)	—	—	100
Size (mm)	—	—	0.25
Anthracite			
Depth (mm)	—	500	500
Size (mm)	—	1.0	1.1
Sand			
Depth (mm)	600	300	300
Size (mm)	0.45	0.5	0.5
Filtration rate,			
$(L/m^2\text{-min})$	160	160	160
Backwash rate,			
$(L/m^2\text{-min})$	500	800	800

$1\ L/m^2\text{-min} = 35.3\ gal/ft^2\text{-d}$

The sodium bicarbonate and calcium hydroxide reacts with the non-carbonate hardness as

$$Ca^{2+} + Na_2CO_3 = CaCO_3 + 2Na^+$$
$$Mg^{2+} + Ca(OH)_2 = Mg(OH)_2 + Ca^{2+}$$

Recarbonation is required after treatment to remove the excess lime, magnesium hydroxide, and carbonate and to reduce the pH to about 8.5 to 9.5.

Based upon these equations, the requirements for lime (L) and soda ash (SA) in meq/L are

$$L = CO_2 + HCO_3^- + Mg^{2+} \tag{8.30}$$

$$SA = Ca^{2+} + Mg^{2+} - \text{Alkalinity} \tag{8.31}$$

The lime requirements need to be increased by about 1 eq/m^3 to raise the pH enough to allow precipitation of the magnesium hydroxide.

Problems involving softening often involve conversions between mass/L, meq/L, and alkalinity (mg CaCO$_3$/L). Some useful conversion factors are shown in Table 8.11.

Table 8.11 Conversion factors for softening calculations

Cation/Anion	MW/Charge (mg/meq)	Alkalinity/Mass (mg CaCO$_3$/mg mass)
Ca^{2+}	20	2.49
Mg^{2+}	12.2	4.12
Na^+	23	4.35
K^+	39	2.658
HCO_3^-	61	1.64
CO_3^{2-}	30	1.67
SO_4^{2-}	48	1.04
Cl^-	35.5	2.82

Solving softening problem can be simplified by reducing the problem to two possible conditions:

Case A:

**Ion Balance
(mg/L as CaCO₃)**

HCO₃⁻		Other	Anions
Ca²⁺	Mg²⁺	Mg²⁺	Cations

Case B:

HCO₃⁻		Other	Anions
Ca²⁺	Ca²⁺	Mg²⁺	Cations

Lime is required to remove carbonate Ca^{2+} (Case A or B) and non-carbonate Mg^{2+} (Case A and B) (1 mole lime/1 mole Ca^{2+} or Mg^{2+}).

Lime is also required to remove carbonate Mg^{2+} (Case A only) (2 moles lime/1 mole Mg^{2+}). Soda ash is added to remove non-carbonate Ca^{2+} (Case B only) (1 mole Na_2CO_3/1 mole Ca^{2+}).

Ion Exchange

Ion exchange processes are used to remove ions of calcium, magnesium, iron, and ammonium. The exchange material is a solid that has functional groups which replace ions in solutions for ions on the exchange material. Ion exchange materials can be made to remove cations or anions. Most materials are regenerated by flushing with solutions having high concentrations of either H^+ or Na^+.

An ion exchange process is controlled by the **exchange capacity** and **selectivity**. The exchange capacity expresses the equivalents of cations or anions that can be exchanged per unit mass. The selectivity for ion B as compared to ion A is expressed as

$$K_{B/A} = \frac{\chi_{R-A}[A^+]}{\chi_{R-B}[B^+]} \tag{8.32}$$

where $K_{B/A}$ = selectivity coefficient for replacing A on resin with χ_{R-A}, χ_{R-B} = mole fractions of A and B for the absorbed species.

Chlorination

Chlorination is the most common form of disinfection in water treatment. Chlorine is a strong oxidation agent which destroys organisms by chemical attack. Chlorine is usually added in the form of chlorine gas at levels of 2 to 5 mg/L such that coliform and fecal coliform bacteria are not detected in the treated water. Other common forms are chlorine dioxide, sodium hypochlorite, and calcium hypochlorite (see Table 8.12).

Table 8.12 Dosage of chorine chemicals for 100,000 gallons of water

Chlorine Conc., mg/L	Liquid Chlorine, lb	Sodium Hypochlorite		Calcium Hypochlorite	
		5% (Gal)	10% (Gal)	15% (Gal)	65% (Gal)
2	1.7	3.9	2.0	1.3	2.6
10	8.3	19.4	9.9	6.7	12.8
50	42.0	97.0	49.6	33.4	64.0

Chlorine in water undergoes an equilibrium reaction to form HOCl and OCl$^-$. The hypochlorite is a weak acid, as listed in Table 8.5. HOCl is a more effective disinfectant than OCl$^-$; as such, the effectiveness is strongly dependent upon pH.

Chlorine will react with all reduced species in solution. Organic compounds, reduced inorganic compounds, and ammonia are common reactants. In treated waters, concentrations of these reactants are typically low, so that less than 1 mg/L of chlorine is required to overcome background chlorine demands.

The effectiveness of chlorination depends upon the time of contact, the chlorine concentration, and the concentration of organisms. The effect of time is modeled as

$$\frac{N_t}{N_0} = e^{-kt^m} \tag{8.33}$$

where N_t, N_0 = number of organisms at time t and time zero, k = decay coefficient (1/d), t = time (d), and m = empirical coefficient (usually near 1).

Disinfection is strongly affected by temperature; the effect is described by the van't Hoff–Arrhenius relationship as

$$\ln \frac{t_1}{t_2} = \frac{E(T_2 - T_1)}{RT_1 T_2} \tag{8.34}$$

where

t_1, t_2 = time for a given bacterial kill at temperature T_1 and T_2 (K), respectively
E = activation energy (J/mole)
R = gas constant (8.3144 J/mole•K)

E varies for chlorine from about 30,000 J/mole at pH 7 to 50,000 J/mole at pH 10.

The effect of chlorine concentration is given as

$$C_1^n t_1 = C_2^n t_2 \tag{8.35}$$

where C = concentration of chlorine, n = coefficient, and t = time.

Fluoridation

Fluoridation of water supplies has been shown to reduce dental caries dramatically. Optimum concentrations are about 1 mg F/L. The most commonly used compounds are sodium fluoride, sodium silicofluoride, and fluorosilicic acid. Fluoride is usually added after coagulation or lime/soda ash softening since high calcium concentrations can result in precipitation.

Activated Carbon

Activated carbon is used in water treatment in a powdered form (5 to 50 μm diameter) added directly to the water or in a granular form (0.1 to 2 mm diameter) in columns or on top of the sand filters. Contaminants in the water are sorbed onto the activated carbon surface at a concentration q_e with an equilibrium water concentration C_e as

$$q_e = K_f C_e^{1/n} \tag{8.36}$$

where

q_e = mass of sorbed material/mass of activated carbon (mg/g)
K_f = Freundlich factor
C_e = Concentration of sorbed material in water (mg/L)
$1/n$ = Freundlich intensity factor

K_f and n vary widely depending upon the compounds removed. Sorption is strongly influenced by mixtures of compounds.

Activated carbon is often added in water treatment to adsorb taste and odor-causing compounds and to remove color. The process usually involves the direct addition of powdered/activated carbon, with its removal in the sedimentation and filtration units or passage of the water through carbon columns. The required carbon in either case is usually determined empirically, using laboratory tests.

Chlorination Byproducts

Chlorine is a strong oxidant that will attack all organic compounds present in water to be treated. The organic compounds that react with chlorine have been termed precursors and the resulting products, disinfection byproducts (DBPs). Many of the DBPs are known or suspected carcinogens to humans. Specific classes of DBPs include trihalomethanes (THMs), haloacetic acids (HAAs), and dihaloacetonitriles (DHANs). The THMs can include bromide if present. Trihalomethanes also include trichloromethane, bromodichloromethane, dibromochloromethane, and thribromomethane. Haloacetic acids include trichloroacetic acid, bromodichloroacetic acid, dibromochloroacetic acid, tribromoacetic acid, dichloroacetic acid, bromochloroacetic acid, dibromoacetic acid, monochloroacetic acid, and monobromoacetic acid. Dihaloacetonitriles include dichloroacetonitrile, bromochloroacetonitrile, and dibromoacetonitrile.

The production of DBPs in drinking water can be avoided by minimizing the contact of high concentrations of chlorine with high concentration of precursors. Known precursors include humic and fulvic acids (degradation products of plant and algal materials). To reduce the concentration of precursors, it is important to use the highest quality of source water as possible. Contact of precursors with chlorine can be reduced through rapid dechlorination if large doses are required in the treatment process. Activated carbon can be used to remove either the precursors or the DBPs. The most common approach, however, is to remove chlorine as the disinfectant in the water treatment process, replacing it with chlorine dioxide or ozone. When ozone is used, chlorine can be added to the treated water (where the precursors have been removed) at less than 1 mg/L to maintain the chlorine residual in the distribution system.

Sludge Treatment

The sources of sludge in water treatment include sand, silt, chemical sludges, and backwash solids. This sludge is typically concentrated in settling basins or lagoons. The sludge can be further concentrated by drying on sand drying beds or by centrifugation.

Sludge Volumes
If the content and specific gravity of the solids are known, the volume of a sludge can be estimated as

$$V = \frac{M_s}{\rho_s \left(\dfrac{S}{100}\right)} \qquad (8.37)$$

where V = sludge volume (m^3), M_s = mass of dry solids (kg), ρ_s = density of sludge solids (kg/m^3), and S = percent solids.

The sludge solids are composed of fixed and volatile solids as

$$\frac{M_s}{S_s} = \frac{M_f}{S_f} + \frac{M_v}{S_v} \qquad (8.38)$$

where M_f, M_v = mass of fixed solids and volatile solids, respectively (kg), and S_s, S_f, S_v = specific gravity of sludge, fixed solids, and volatile solids, respectively.

SELECTED SYMBOLS AND ABBREVIATIONS

Symbol or Abbreviation	Description
C	Roughness coefficient (100 for cast-iron pipe)
C_{sat}	Saturation oxygen concentration
c	Construction material constant
D	Dissolved oxygen deficit
e	Efficiency
G	Average velocity gradient
k	Constant (1.3 h fps)
L	BOD concentration
P, p	Power
P	Pressure
Q	Discharge
s	Slope of hydraulic grade line (ft/ft)
V	Volume, velocity
v	Pipe velocity (fps)
μ	Viscosity

BIBLIOGRAPHY

American Water Works Association. *Introduction to Water Distribution: Principles and Practices of Water Supply Operations*. AWWA, Denver, CO, 1986.

American Water Works Association. *Water Quality and Treatment*. McGraw-Hill, New York, 1990.

American Society of Civil Engineers and the American Water Works Association. *Water Treatment Plant Design*. McGraw-Hill, Inc., New York, 1991.

Hammer, M. *Water and Wastewater Technology*. John Wiley & Sons, New York, 1975.

James M. Montgomery Consulting Engineers. *Water Treatment Principles and Design*. John Wiley & Sons, New York, 1985.

McGhee, T. J. *Water Supply and Sewerage*. McGraw-Hill, New York, 1991.

Sawyer, C. N., and P. L. McCarty. *Chemistry for Environmental Engineers*. McGraw-Hill, New York, 1978.

Steel, E. W., and T. J. McGhee. *Water Supply and Sewerage*. McGraw-Hill, New York, 1979.

Tchobanoglous, G., and E. D. Schroeder. *Water Quality*. Addison-Wesley, Menlo Park, CA, 1985.

Viessman, W., Jr., and M. J. Hammer. *Water Supply and Pollution Control*. Harper & Row, New York, 1985.

CHAPTER 9

Wastewater Treatment

Kenneth J. Williamson

OUTLINE

WASTEWATER FLOWS 391
Domestic Flows ■ Industrial Flows ■ Infiltration ■ Storm Water Flow

SEWER DESIGN 392
Hydraulics of Sewers ■ Minimum and Maximum
Velocities ■ Design Flows ■ Manholes

WASTEWATER CHARACTERISTICS 393
Solids ■ Oxygen Demand

WASTEWATER TREATMENT 395
Process Analysis ■ Physical Treatment Processes ■ Biological
Treatment Processes

SLUDGE TREATMENT AND DISPOSAL 409
Sludge Treatment ■ Disinfection

SELECTED SYMBOLS AND ABBREVIATIONS 413

BIBLIOGRAPHY 413

WASTEWATER FLOWS

Wastewater flows are comprised of domestic and industrial wastewaters, infiltration, inflow, and storm water. Most modern sanitary sewers are separated from storm water systems so these flows are treated separately. Modern sewers are constructed so that inflow rates are assumed to be negligible.

Domestic Flows

Domestic flows are determined from water use rates. Typical values are 150 gallons per day per capita. **Peak daily** and **hourly** rates can be determined from historical data; typical values are 1.8 and 2.7 times the annual average flow, respectively. Peaking factors vary with the size of the area being served such that larger values are used for lateral as compared to interceptor sewers.

Industrial Flows

Industrial flows vary widely. Specific data are required, based upon industry and production rates.

Infiltration

Infiltration rates for new sewers vary from 5 to 20 m^3/ha-d with smaller values for larger areas being served. Infiltration from existing old sewers is estimated from historical data.

Storm Water Flow

Storm water flow rates are estimated by using the rational formula as reviewed in the *Civil Engineering: License Review* hydrology chapter.

SEWER DESIGN

Hydraulics of Sewers

Sewers are designed as open channels, usually with a circular cross section. Flows in sewers are modeled using Manning's Equation, as

$$V = \frac{1.49}{n}(R^{2/3}S^{1/2}) \tag{9.1}$$

where V = velocity (fps), n = Manning coefficient (0.013 is a common design value), R = hydraulic radius (ft), and S = slope of the energy grade line.

The relation between the hydraulic radius and the flow depth for a circular cross section is a complex relationship, and, as a result, flows in partially full sewers are calculated using nomographs, as shown in Figure 9.1. Design calculations usually involve knowing the slope of the sewer, S, and the partially full flow rate, Q. The nomograph is solved by assuming a pipe diameter, D, and solving for the full flow rate, Q_f. From the ratio of Q/Q_f, the ratio of partial depth to pipe diameter, d/D is obtained from the nomograph, from which the depth of flow is calculated.

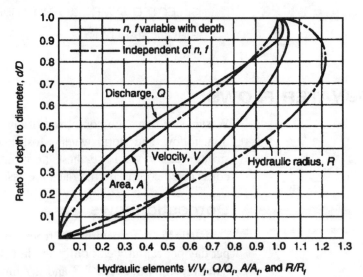

Figure 9.1 Hydraulic elements nomograph for circular sewers

Minimum and Maximum Velocities

Sanitary sewers are designed to maintain a minimum flow velocity of 2 fps at some prescribed flow depth, usually taken as full depth. This velocity is necessary to keep suspended solids in suspension. Since velocity is not strongly dependent upon pipe diameter, design for the minimum flow velocity requires adjustment of the pipe slope.

Maximum velocities in both sanitary and storm sewers are usually taken as 10 fps to control erosion by grit and sand. Excessive flow velocities on steep grades can be controlled by the use of drop manholes.

Design Flows

Sanitary sewers are designed to carry the peak flow, with a depth of flow from one-half to full. Sanitary sewers should not flow full for extensive periods of time because ventilation is necessary to avoid corrosion.

Storm sewers are designed to carry the flow given by the rational formula based upon a given **storm return period.** For storms with less frequent return periods, the flows will exceed the design flow, and the storm sewer will flood the manholes and adjoining streets.

Manholes

Manholes should be spaced no more than about 400 feet apart. Head losses for the flow into manholes can be estimated as about 0.2 feet. Such head losses need to be compensated for by adjustment of the sewer inverts leaving the manhole.

WASTEWATER CHARACTERISTICS

Wastewater can be characterized by a large number of parameters, but only those parameters required for design will be discussed below. Typical concentrations are given in Table 9.1; per capita loading rates for 5-day biochemical oxygen demand [BOD_5, Equation (9.3)] and total suspended solids (TSS) are 100 and 120 g/capita-d, respectively.

Solids

Dissolved solids represent all of the material of a colloid size or smaller. Most of this material consists of small-molecular-weight, organic compounds and dissolved salts. The organic portion is measured as the volatile dissolved solids.

Suspended solids represents those particles with sizes greater than about 10^{-3} mm. The organic portion is reported as volatile, suspended solids.

Table 9.1 Typical composition of domestic wastewater

Constituent	Concentration (mg/L)
Dissolved solids	700
Volatile, dissolved solids	300
Suspended solids	220
Volatile, suspended solids	135
5-day biochemical oxygen demand	200
Organic nitrogen	15
Ammonia nitrogen	25
Total phosphorus	8

Oxygen Demand

Theoretical Oxygen Demand

Theoretical oxygen demand (ThOD) is the calculated amount of oxygen required to convert organic compounds in the wastewater to carbon dioxide and water. To determine the ThOD, the chemical formula of the waste must be known.

Chemical Oxygen Demand

Chemical oxygen demand (COD) is an empirical parameter representing the equivalent amount of oxygen that would be used to oxidize organic compounds under strong, chemical-oxidizing conditions. The COD and the ThOD are approximately equal for most wastes.

Biochemical Oxygen Demand

Biochemical oxygen demand (BOD) is an empirical parameter representing the amount of oxygen that would be used to oxidize organic compounds by aerobic bacteria. The test involves the seeding of diluted wastewater and the measurement of the oxygen depletion after five days in 300 ml glass bottles. For such tests, the BOD_5 is calculated as

$$BOD_5 = \left[(DO_b - DO_i)\left(\frac{100}{\%}\right)\right] - (DO_b - DO_s) \tag{9.2}$$

where BOD_5 = 5-day BOD (mg/L), DO_b = dissolved oxygen in dilution water blank after a five-day incubation, DO_i = dissolved oxygen in a diluted sample after five-day incubation, and DO_s = dissolved oxygen in an undiluted sample, (mg/L); % = v/v percentage of sample in the 300 ml BOD bottle.

The five-day BOD is related to the ultimate BOD as

$$BOD_5 = BOD_L(1 - 10^{-kt}) \tag{9.3}$$

where BOD_L = the maximum BOD exerted after a long period of incubation, (mg/L), and k = the base-10 BOD decay coefficient (d^{-1}).

Equation (9.3) for wastewater calculations is usually expressed in base-10 form. The base-e form of the equation is used for determining oxygen deficits in streams. Care must be taken to ensure that the BOD decay coefficient matches the form of the equation used. The BOD test is conducted at 20°C; the decay coefficient can be converted to other temperatures as

$$k_T = k_{20}\theta^{(T-20)} \tag{9.4}$$

where k_T, k_{20} = BOD decay coefficient at temperature T and 20°C, respectively, and θ = temperature correction coefficient, 1.056 from 20–30°C and 1.135 from 4–20°C. Typical k_{20} values range from about 0.05 to 0.1/d for municipal wastes.

Nitrogenous Oxygen Demand

Nitrogenous oxygen demand results from the oxidation of ammonia to nitrate by nitrifying bacteria. The overall equation is

$$NH_3 + 2O_2 = NO_3^- + H^+ + H_2O \tag{9.5}$$

Nitrification will occur in a BOD test after about seven days of incubation, and it will occur in aerobic biological treatment if the retention time for bacterial cells exceeds 5 to 10 days, depending upon temperature. Nitrogenous oxygen demand is not included in either of the BOD_5 or COD values.

WASTEWATER TREATMENT

Wastewater treatment in the United States is managed under the Federal Water Pollution Control Act Amendments of 1972. This law set the requirements that all publicly-owned treatment facilities must provide secondary treatment; **secondary treatment** is functionally defined as achieving 85 percent removal of BOD and TSS, which for municipial wastes results in an average monthly concentration of BOD_5 and total suspended solids (TSS) of about 30 mg/L each. Individual states can set more restrictive standards. Industrial wastewater must have a treatment level associated with specific, designated treatment technologies termed **Best Available Treatment** (BAT).

The design of wastewater treatment facilities focuses on the two parameters of BOD and TSS. The general approach is to link a series of unit processes to sequentially remove BOD and TSS to meet the discharge requirements. The unit processes are typically chosen to minimize treatment costs.

Process Analysis

Types of Reactions

Most reactions in wastewater treatment are considered to be homogeneous. In homogeneous reactions, the reaction occurs throughout the liquid, and mass transfer effects can be ignored. Chlorination is an example of a homogeneous reaction. In heterogeneous reactions, the reactants must be transferred to a reactive site, and the products must be transferred from the reactive site. Biological reaction in bacterial films is an example of a heterogeneous reaction. Heterogeneous reactions are much more difficult to analyze than homogeneous reactions.

Reaction Rates

Chemical reactions have many different forms, although the most common form is the conversion of a single product to a single reactant as

$$A = B \tag{9.6}$$

If the rate of the reaction is of zero order, then the rate of conversion of A is

$$\frac{dA}{dt} = -k_0 \tag{9.7}$$

where k_0 = the zero-order reaction coefficient (mg/L-d). If the rate of the reaction is first-order, then the rate of conversion of A is

$$\frac{dA}{dt} = -k_1[A] \tag{9.8}$$

where k_1 = first-order reaction coefficient (d^{-1}).

Reactor Types

The three important reactor types are batch, complete-mixed, and plug-flow, as shown in Figure 9.2. **Batch reactors** have no influent or effluent flows and have a hydraulic detention time of t_b, which is the time between filing and emptying. **Complete-mixed reactors** have constant influent and effluent flow rates and are

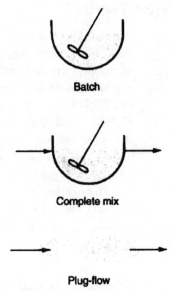

Figure 9.2 Reactor types

mixed so that spatial gradients of concentration are near zero. They have a hydraulic detention time of

$$\theta_h = \frac{V}{Q} \tag{9.9}$$

where θ_h = hydraulic detention time (d), V = reactor volume (L), and Q = influent and effluent flow rate (L/d). **Plug-flow reactors** have constant influent and effluent flow rates but lack internal mixing. The reactors tend to be long and narrow, and the transport of water occurs from one end to the other. Their hydraulic detention time is

$$t_r = \frac{L}{V_e} \tag{9.10}$$

where t_r = hydraulic detention time (d), L = length of reactor (m), and V_e = liquid flow velocity (m/d).

The application of mass balances to the three types of reactors, assuming either zero- or first-order reaction rates, results in the following equations for the effluent concentration of A at steady state:

Batch reactor, zero-order

$$A = A_0 - k_0 t \tag{9.11}$$

Complete-mixed, zero-order

$$A = A_0 - k_0 \theta_h \tag{9.12}$$

Plug-flow, zero-order

$$A = A_0 - k_0 t_r \tag{9.13}$$

Batch reactor, first-order

$$A = A_0 e^{(-k_1 t_b)} \qquad (9.14)$$

Complete-mixed, first-order

$$A = \frac{A_0}{1 + k_1 \theta_h} \qquad (9.15)$$

Plug-flow, first-order

$$A = A_0 e^{-k_1 t_r} \qquad (9.16)$$

Plug-flow reactors will consistently give lower effluent concentrations compared to complete-mixed reactors for all reaction rates greater than zero.

Physical Treatment Processes

Sedimentation

Sedimentation is divided into four types: discrete (Type 1), flocculant (Type 2), zone (Type 3), and compression (Type 4).

In discrete sedimentation, the removal is determined by the terminal settling velocity. Settling velocities for small Reynolds numbers can be estimated by Stokes' Law as

$$V_p = \frac{g(\rho_s - \rho_w)d^2}{18\mu} \qquad (9.17)$$

where V_p = particle settling velocity (m/s), g = gravitational constant (9.8 m/s^2), ρ_p, ρ_w = density of particle and water, respectively (kg/m^3), and μ = water viscosity (N-s/m^2).

For particles with V_p less than the overflow rate of the sedimentation basin, V_c, the removal, R, is

$$R = \frac{V_p}{V_c} \qquad (9.18)$$

where R is 1.0 for all particles with $V_p > V_c$.

Grit chambers are designed to be used with discrete sedimentation. Grit is removed from wastewater to protect mechanical equipment from abrasion, to reduce grit accumulation with precipitates or grease, and to minimize sedimentation in anaerobic digesters.

Three types of grit chambers are utilized: horizontal-flow, vortex, and aerated. Grit in horizontal-flow chambers is removed by gravity sedimentation. In vortex grit chambers, settling is improved by inducing centrifugal acceleration through circular flow. In aerated grit chambers, air is added to the water column to increase grit removal by decreasing the water density. Design parameters for these three forms of grit chambers are listed in Table 9.2.

Aerated grit chambers require an air flow of 2 to 5 ft^3/min-ft of length.

Table 9.2 Design parameters for grit chambers

Type	Detention Time, min
Horizontal-flow	1
Aerated	5
Vortex	0.5

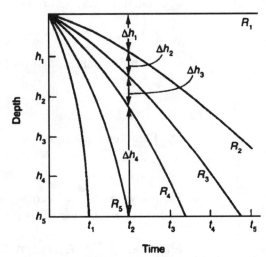

Figure 9.3 Empirical analysis of type 3 setting

Primary sedimentation basins are designed for overflow rates of 800 to 1200 gal/ft²-d (32 to 48 m³/m²-d). Weir loading rates should be less than about 20,000 gal/ft-d (250 m³/m-d). The configuration may be rectangular or circular, with depths ranging from 10 to 15 feet (3 to 6 m). Typical removal rates for domestic wastewaters are 67 percent for TSS and 33 percent for BOD.

Flocculant sedimentation is similar to Type 1 settling except that the particle size increases as the particle settles in the sedimentation reactor. Type 2, or flocculant settling, occurs in coagulation/flocculation treatment for water and at the top of secondary sedimentation basins.

Removal under focculant sedimentation is determined empirically. Data must be collected to give isolines for percent removal as shown in Figure 9.3. Given such data, the total removal is

$$R = \sum_{h=1}^{4} \left(\frac{\Delta h_n}{h_5} \right) \left(\frac{R_n + R_{n+1}}{2} \right) \qquad (9.19)$$

where the symbols are illustrated in Figure 9.3.

Secondary sedimentation basins are designed for overflow rates of 400 to 800 gal/ft²-d (16 to 32 m³/m²-d) and weir loading rates of 20,000 gal/ft-d (250 m³/m-d). Depths are 12 to 20 feet (3 to 6 m). Effluent flows from secondary sedimentation basins for domestic wastewater typically have less than 20 mg/L of suspended solids.

Zone settling occurs at the bottom of secondary sedimentation basins, where the concentration of the solids increases to over 5000 mg/L. A schematic of a sedimentation basin coupled to a biological treatment reactor with cell recycle is shown in Figure 9.4. Under such conditions, the modeling of the zone sedimentation process is based upon the solids flux through the bottom section of the basin. The solids flux results from two components: gravity sedimentation and liquid velocity from the underflow,

$$SF = SF_g + SF_r \qquad (9.20)$$

where SF, SF_g, SF_r = solids flux, solids flux due to gravity, and solids flux due to recycle, respectively (kg/m²-d).

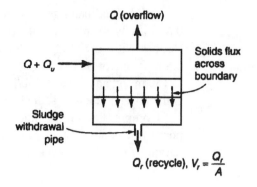

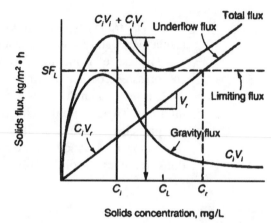

Figure 9.4 Schematic of secondary clarifier and empirical analysis of Type 3 settling

The resulting relationship is

$$SF = C_iV_i + C_iV_r \qquad (9.21)$$

where C_i = concentration of solids at a specified height in the basin (mg/L), V_i = gravity settling velocity of sludge with concentration C_i (m/d), V_r = downward fluid velocity from recycle (m/d) = Q_r/A_H, and A_H = horizontal area of sedimentation basin.

Equation (9.21) is graphed in Figure 9.4. Under a constant recycle flow and a defined sludge, the transport of solids through the bottom of the clarifier becomes limited by the limiting solids flux rate (SF_L) shown in Figure 9.4. Estimates of SF_L are obtained by graphical analysis illustrated in Figure 9.4. The horizontal area of the sedimentation basin is then calculated as

$$A = \frac{(Q + Q_r)(C_{\text{infl}})}{SF_L} \qquad (9.22)$$

or

$$A = \frac{Q_r C_r}{SF_L} \qquad (9.23)$$

where C_{infl} = concentration of TSS in the influent to the sedimentation basin, C_r = concentration of TSS in the recycle from the sedimentation basin, and Q, Q_r = plant influent and recycle flow rates.

Solids flux loadings for design of secondary sedimentation basins range from 0.8 to 1.2 lb/ft^2-hr (4.6 kg/m^2-h). Higher values can be used for systems that produce sludges with low sludge volume indexes (SVI). Typical values would be 0.5 to 0.8 lb/ft^2-hr for SVI values of > 180 mL/g; 0.8 to 1.0 lb/ft^2-hr for SVI values of 180 to 150 mL/g; and 1.0 to 1.2 lb/ft^2-hr for SVI values of 80 to 120 mL/g. The SVI value is the concentration of settled activated sludge after 1 hour in a graduated cylinder.

Compression sedimentation involves the slow movement of water through the pores in a sludge cake. The process is modeled as an exponential decrease in height of the sludge cake as

$$H_t - H_\infty = (H_0 - H_\infty)e^{-i(t-t_0)} \tag{9.24}$$

where H_0, H_t, H_∞ = sludge height initially, after time t, and after a long period, respectively, and i = compression coefficient.

The use of centrifuges, vacuum filters, and filter presses can increase the compression coefficient, which reduces the time required to de-water sludges.

Air or vacuum flotation is a process of inducing small air bubbles into sludge mixtures. The air bubbles attach to the sludge particles and reduce the density of the particles, which then float to the water surface to be removed. Flotation thickening is designed with empirical data relating thickened sludge concentrations to the air-to-solids ratio, A/S. The air-to-solids ratio is given as

$$\frac{A}{S} = \frac{s_a(fP-1)}{S_a} \tag{9.25}$$

where s_a, S_a = air concentration and sludge concentration, respectively, P = atmospheric pressure, and f = efficiency of pressurization, usually 0.5.

The rise velocities of solids are typically in the range of 10 to 150 $\times$ 10^{-3} m/min.

Biological Treatment Processes

Biological treatment involves the conversion of organic and inorganic compounds by bacteria with subsequent growth of the organisms. The common biological treatment processes in wastewater treatment involve the removal of various substrates, including BOD, ammonia, nitrate, and organic sludges.

Description of Homogeneous Processes

The rate of removal of a substrate is given as

$$r_{su} = -\frac{kXs}{(K_s + S)} \tag{9.26}$$

where r_{su} = rate of substrate removal (mg/L-d), k = maximum substrate removal rate (mg/mg-d), X = bacterial concentration, usually expressed as TVSS (mg/L), and S, K_s = substrate and half-velocity coefficient, respectively, (mg/L).

The growth of organisms is given as

$$r_x = -Yr_{su} - k_d X \tag{9.27}$$

where r_x = rate of growth of bacteria (mg/L-d), Y = substrate yield rate (mg/mg), and k_d = bacterial decay coefficient (d^{-1}).

For the complete-mixed reactor without cell recycle [Figure 9.5(a)], the governing equations are

$$X = \frac{Y(S_0 - S)}{(1 + k_d \theta_c)} \tag{9.28}$$

$$S = \frac{K_s(1 + \theta_c k_d)}{\theta_c(Yk - k_d) - 1} \tag{9.29}$$

For the completely-mixed reactor with cell recycle [Figure 9.5(b)], the governing equation is

$$\frac{1}{\theta_c} = Y\left(\frac{kSX}{S + K_s}\right) - k_d \tag{9.30}$$

where θ_c = solids retention time (d). Then,

$$\frac{F}{M} = \frac{S_0}{\theta_h X} \tag{9.31}$$

where F/M = food to microorganism ratio (mg/mg-d), and

$$X = \frac{\theta_c Y(S_0 - S)}{\theta_h(1 + k_d \theta_c)} \tag{9.32}$$

$$S = \frac{K_s(1 + \theta_c k_d)}{\theta_c(Yk - k_d) - 1} \tag{9.33}$$

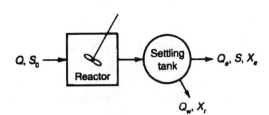

(a) Complete-Mix Without Cell Recycle

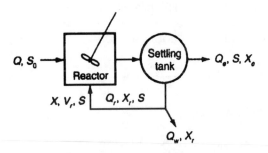

(b) Complete-Mix With Cell Recycle

Figure 9.5 Schematic of complete-mix reactors

The process design proceeds with the selection of a solids retention time (θ_c) as the controlling parameter. The volume of the reactor is determined from Equation (9.32) with $\theta_h = V/Q$. The waste sludge flow rate is computed from

$$\theta_c = \frac{VX}{Q_w X_w + Q_e X_e} \tag{9.34}$$

where Q_w, Q_e = sludge waste and effluent flow rates, respectively (L/d), X_w, X, X_e = sludge waste reactor, recycle, and effluent TSS concentration, respectively (mg/L); X_e is about 20 mg/L.

The cell concentration in a plug-flow reactor can be estimated using Equation (9.32). The effluent substrate concentration can be estimated from

$$\frac{1}{\theta_c} = \frac{Yk(S_0 - S)}{(S_0 - S) + \left(1 + \frac{Q_r}{Q}\right)K_s \ln(S_i/S)} - k_d \tag{9.35}$$

where S_i = the diluted substrate concentration entering the reactor (mg/L).

Description of Heterogeneous Processes

Rock-filled trickling filters are designed by using empirical relationships such as

$$E = \frac{100}{1 + \frac{0.0561}{1 - E_0}\sqrt{\frac{W}{F}}} \tag{9.36}$$

where E, E_0 = efficiency of BOD removal by the stage under consideration and previous stage, respectively, W = BOD loading rate (lb/1000 ft^3-d), $F = (1 + R)/(1 + R/10)^2$ = recirculation factor, and $R = Q_r/Q$ = recirculation ratio.

Plastic-filled trickling filters are designed using an empirical equation such as

$$-\ln\left(\frac{S_{eff}}{S_{infl}}\right) = \frac{-kD}{q^n} \tag{9.37}$$

where S_{eff}, S_{infl} = effluent and influent BOD concentrations (mg/L), k = treatability coefficient [(L/s)^n/m^2], n = packing characteristic, D = depth (m), q = hydraulic loading (L/m^2-s). Typically, n is about 0.5 for plastic media and k vanges from 0.06 to 0.35 depending upon the waste (0.2 for municipal waste water).

Design of Activated Sludge Treatment

Design parameters for common activated sludge processes are shown in Table 9.3. The processes are illustrated in Figure 9.6 and are briefly described below.

Table 9.3 Design parameters for common activated sludge processes

Process	θ_c, d	F/M, mg/mg/d	MLSS, mg/L	θ_h, hr	Q_r/Q
Conventional	5–15	0.2–0.4	1500–3000	4–8	0.25–0.75
Complete-mix	5–15	0.2–0.6	2500–4000	3–5	0.25–1.0
Contact stabilization	5–15	0.2–0.6			0.5–1.5
contact reactor			1000–3000		0.5–1.0
stabilization reactor			4000–10,000	3–6	
Extended aeration	20–30	0.05–0.15	3000–6000	18–36	0.5–1.5
High-purity oxygen	3–10	0.25–1.0	2000–5000	1–3	0.25–0.50

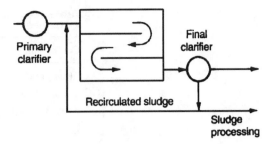

Conventional Aeration

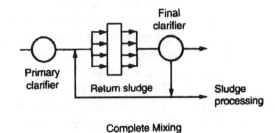

Complete Mixing

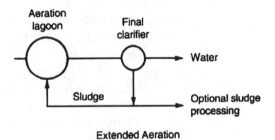

Extended Aeration

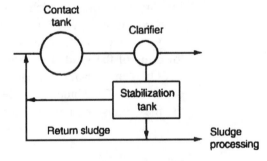

Contact Stabilization

Figure 9.6 Schematics of activated sludge processes

Conventional: Plug-flow configuration.

Complete-Mix: Completely mixed configuration. Used for high-strength wastes.

Contact Stabilization: A two-reactor process in which the first reactor is used for sorption of the soluble substrate followed by concentration of the cells in the secondary clarifier. The second reactor is used for degradation with high solids concentration. The process results in smaller total reactor volumes compared to the conventional process.

Table 9.4 Activated sludge design coefficients for domestic wastewater

Coefficient	Value
k (mg/mg-d)	10
K_s (mg BOD_5/L)	30
Y (mg VSS/mg BOD_5)	0.6
k_d (d^{-1})	0.1

Extended Aeration: Combined activated sludge and aerobic digestion. If sludge is not wasted, then all of the solids will be discharged in the effluent.

High-Purity Oxygen: Completely mixed process with pure oxygen aeration. The process produces sludge with high recycle concentrations, a higher reactor cell concentration, and smaller reactor volumes.

Design coefficients for domestic wastewaters are listed in Table 9.4.

The most common operational problem associated with activated sludge is inadequate sludge settling. One problem is termed **bulking**, which is associated with a high number of filamentous organisms. Bulking results in small solid flux rates for the secondary clarifier, producing problems with sedimentation. Potential causes are inadequate nutrients, high F/M loadings, low dissolved oxygen, and particular characteristics of the wastewater. Bulking can be temporarily controlled by the use of chlorine and hydrogen peroxide, and by switching from complete-mix to a plug-flow operation.

Another common settling problem is **rising sludge**. Rising sludge is caused by denitrification in the secondary clarifier with the subsequent formation of small nitrogen bubbles. The bubbles result in the flotation of the activated sludge. Corrective action is to reduce the sludge holding time in the secondary clarifier and reduce the solids retention time. The latter will stop nitrification and the formation of nitrate, which serves as the substrate for the denitrification reactor.

Growth of the filamentous bacteria *Nocardia* can result in the formation of a brown foam on aeration basins. Numerous corrective actions have been suggested; lowering of the solids retention time is the favored remedy.

Oxygen transfer is a heterogeneous process determined by a mass transfer coefficient, K_{La}. Under non–steady state conditions, as in oxygen transfer tests, the mass transfer coefficient can be estimated from

$$\frac{C_t - C_s}{C_0 - C_s} = e^{-K_{La}^t} \tag{9.38}$$

where C_s, C_0, C_t = dissolved oxygen concentration at saturation, time zero, and at time t (mg/L), and t = time from initiation of the test. K_{La} values are dependent upon temperature, reactor configuration, and wastewater characteristics.

Oxygen is provided to activated sludge processes by various types of aeration devices, including diffuse, non-diffuse, and mechanical. **Diffuse aeration** involves forcing air through small pores to create small bubbles. Diffuse aeration results in high oxygen transfer efficiencies, but it leads to high pressure losses and potential clogging of the diffusers. **Non-diffuse** aeration uses larger bubbles which induce spiral, roll mixing in the activated sludge reactor. Maintenance problems are less, but efficiencies are lower. **Mechanical aeration** uses mechanical devices to mix water and air. Design parameters are listed in Table 9.5.

Table 9.5 Design parameters for aeration types

Aeration Type	Standard Transfer Rate, lb O$_2$/hp-hr	Standard Transfer Efficiencies, %
Diffuse	—	15–40
Non-diffuse	—	10–13
Mechanical	1.5–5	

1.0 lb O$_2$/hp-hr = 0.6 kg O$_2$/ kw-h

Transfer under non-standard conditions is corrected via

$$N = N_0\left(\frac{\beta C_{s,T} - C_L}{C_{s,20}}\right) 1.024^{T-20} \alpha \qquad (9.39)$$

where N, N_0 = oxygen transfer (lb/hp-hr) under field and standard conditions, respectively, β = salinity-surface tension correction factor, near 1 for wastewaters, $C_{s,T}$, $C_{s,20}$ = oxygen concentration at field temperature and 20°C, respectively (mg/L), C_L = oxygen concentration in liquid (mg/L), T = temperature (°C), and α = correction factor for waste (0.8–0.9 for domestic wastewater).

Oxygen requirements can be estimated as the ultimate BOD removed from the wastewater minus the oxygen equivalent of the cells produced. Cells have a COD value of 1.4 mg O$_2$/mg cells.

Trickling Filters

Trickling filters are designed using Equation (9.36) and Equation (9.37). High-rate filters have hydraulic loading rates of 0.1 to 0.7 gal/ft^2-min and depths from 3 to 6 ft. Removal efficiencies per stage range from 65 to 85 percent based upon BOD. Recirculation rates of 1 to 2 times the influent flow rate are commonly used. Several possible configurations for recirculation are shown in Figure 9.7. To achieve high removal rates, the filters are operated in series. For plastic media, the treatability constant, k [Equation (9.37)], ranges from 0.6 to 0.10 gal/min$^{0.5}$-ft.

Rotating Biological Contactors

Rotating biological contactors involve rotating plastic plates on which bacterial films are attached (Figure 9.8). Loading rates are 8 to 20 g BOD$_5$/m^2-d for secondary treatment, and 5 to 16 g BOD$_5$/m^2-d for combined secondary treatment and nitrification. Hydraulic detention times range from 0.1 to 0.16 m^3/m^2-d for secondary treatment, and 1.03 to 0.08 m^3/m^2-d for combined nitrification. BOD removal as a function of hydraulic loading rates is shown in Figure 9.9.

Stabilization Ponds

Stabilization ponds are earth-lined structures used for wastewater treatment. Oxygen is provided by surface reaeration, photosynthesis by algae, or surface aerators. Based upon BOD loading rates and the method of aeration, the ponds may be aerobic, facultative, or anaerobic. Stabilization ponds typically have high TSS and BOD levels in the effluent from growth of algae. Anaerobic ponds are similar to low-rate anaerobic digesters. Aerated stabilization ponds are activated sludge reactors without cell recycling, and they do not depend on algae for aeration. Design parameters are listed in Table 9.6.

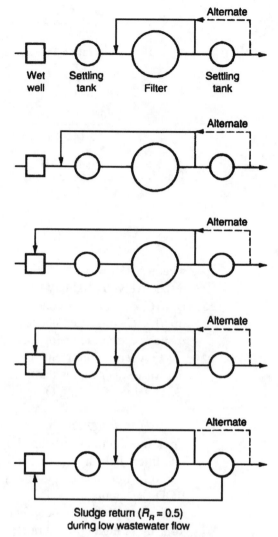

Figure 9.7 Recirculation patterns for trickling filters

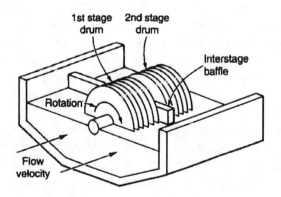

Figure 9.8 Rotating biological contactor

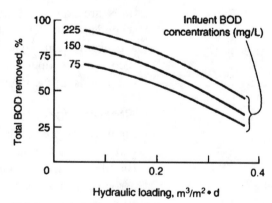

Figure 9.9 BOD removal for RBCs

Table 9.6 Design parameters for stabilization ponds

Parameter	Aerobic	Facultative	Anaerobic	Aerated
Detention time, d	4–40	5–30	20–50	3–10
Depth, ft	1–4	4–8	8–16	6–20
BOD$_5$ Loading, lb/acre-d	60–160	50–180	200–500	
BOD Removal, %	80–95	80–95	50–85	80–95
Effluent TSS, mg/L	80–300	40–60	80–160	80–250

Nitrification

Nitrification is the process of the biological oxidation of ammonia to nitrate [Equation (9.5)]. In biological treatment, the aerobic degradation converts most of the organic nitrogen to ammonia, so nitrification systems are based upon the conversion of both ammonia and organic nitrogen to nitrate. This sum is known as the **total Kjeldahl nitrogen** (TKN).

Nitrification can be achieved in a single-stage system (combined with activated sludge). The single-stage system requires no additional facilities but has limited control and results in increased oxygen utilization. A solids retention time of greater than 5 days is required at 20 °C and greater than 10 days at 10 °C to home effective nitrification.

Nitrification can also be achieved in trickling filters and rotating biological contactors if the organic loading is limited. Organic loadings of less than about 5 lb BOD$_5$/1000 ft^3-d (80 kg/m^3-d) and 8 lb BOD$_5$/1000 ft^3-d (130 kg/m^3-d) for rock and plastic media, respectively, will result in greater than 90 percent nitrification.

The kinetic coefficients are listed in Table 9.7.
Temperature corrections for k are

$$k_T = k_{20} e^{1.053(T-20)} \tag{9.40}$$

where k_T, k_{20} = maximum N utilization rates (mg/mg-d) at temperatures T and 20 °C, respectively.

Nitrification is also strongly affected by pH below 7.2. The overall reaction produces an H$^+$ ion, so adequate alkalinity must be present or added to maintain pH above 7.2.

Biological Denitrification

Biological denitrification is used to reduce nitrate to nitric oxide, nitrous oxide, and nitrogen gas. Coupled with nitrification, it is an integral part of biological nitrogen removal.

Table 9.7 Kinetic coefficients for nitrification reactors

Coefficient	Value for Ammonia-N, 20 °C
k	5 mg/mg-d
K_s	1 mg/L
k_d	0.05/d
Y	0.12 mg/mg-d

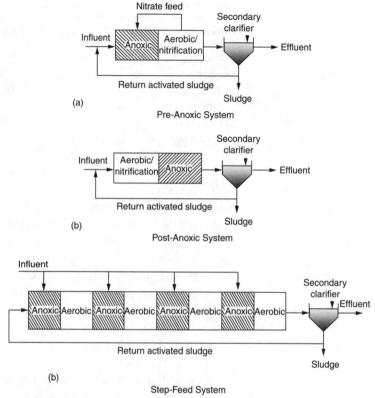

Figure 9.10 Examples of Denitrification Processes

Denitrification occurs in biological treatment under the presence of an organic substrate (BOD) and nitrate, and the near absence of oxygen. A wide range of bacteria can use nitrate in the place of oxygen and are ubiquitious to wastewaters and wastewater treatment processes.

The important parameter in designing denitrification systems is the ratio of BOD needed as an electron donor per NO_3 removed. Typical values range from about 2 to 5 mg BOD/mg NO_3-N.

Several different designs have been used to achieve denitrification for wastewaters. The complexity of the design results from having to provide BOD to reactors or zones of reactors that have high nitrate concentration. The BOD is commonly obtained from the influent flow or from the endogeneous decay of cells. Anoxic conditions can be easily obtained by eliminating aeration. The design of such systems are in Figure 9.10 beyond the scope of this review.

Phosphorus Removal

Phosphorus is removed from wastewater by precipitation with calcium (lime), aluminum (alum), or iron (ferric salt). Alum is the preferred process for a variety of reasons, including minimum sludge volumes and a greater removal at neutral pH. The metal salts can be added before the primary clarifier, aeration basin, or secondary clarifier (Figure 9.11). Required alum dosages (mole Al: mole P) range from 1.2:1 to 1.6:1, 2.3:1, and 2.9:1 for 70, 80, 90, and 95 percent P removal, respectively.

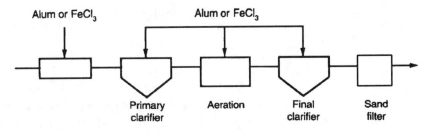

Figure 9.11 Phosphorus removal with alum or chloride

SLUDGE TREATMENT AND DISPOSAL

Wastewater treatment results in a variety of sludge types from primary and secondary sedimentation. Design parameters for these sludges are listed in Tables 9.8 and 9.9:

Table 9.8 Sludge design parameters

	Specific Gravity		Quantities of Dry Solids,
Sludge Type	Solids	Sludge	lb/1000 gal
Primary sedimentation	1.4	1.02	1.25
Activated sludge	1.25	1.005	0.7
Trickling filter	1.45	1.025	0.6
Extended aeration	1.3	1.015	0.8
Aerated lagoon	1.3	1.01	0.8

1 lb/1000 gal = 0.12 kg/m^3

Table 9.9 Sludge concentrations

Sludge Type	Sludge Solids, % Dry Solids
Primary	5.0
Primary and activated sludge	4.0
Primary and trickling filter	5.0
Activated sludge	0.8
Pure-oxygen activated sludge	2.0
Trickling filter	1.5
Rotating biological contactor	1.5
Primary after gravity thickening	8.0
Activated sludge after air flotation	4.0
Activated sludge after centrifugation	5.0
Primary after anaerobic digestion	7.0
Primary and activated sludge after anaerobic digestion	3.5
Primary and trickling filter after anaerobic digestion	4.0
Primary after aerobic digestion	3.5
Primary and trickling filter after aerobic digestion	2.5
Activated sludge after aerobic digestion	1.3

Sludge is comprised primarily of water. The specific gravity of a sludge is given as

$$\frac{W_s}{S_s \rho_w} = \frac{W_f}{S_f \rho_w} + \frac{W_v}{S_v \rho_w} \qquad (9.41)$$

where S_s, S_f, S_v = specific gravity of solids, fixed solids, and volatile solids, respectively; W_s, W_f, W_v = weight of solids, fixed solids, and volatile solids, respectively; and ρ_w = density of water.

The volume of a sludge is given by

$$V = \frac{W_s}{\rho_w S_{sl} P_{sl}} \qquad (9.42)$$

where S_{sl} = specific gravity of sludge, and P_{sl} = solids content of sludge.

Sludge Treatment

Sludge treatment involves the sequential removal of water by thickening, stabilization, conditioning, dewatering, drying, and thermal reduction.

Thickening
Thickening is achieved by gravity, flotation, and mechanically in centrifuges, belt thickeners, and rotary drums. Gravity thickeners are designed based upon Type 3 settling with empirically determined values of settling rates as a function of sludge concentration. Flotation thickeners are designed based upon empirical values of float concentration as a function of air-to-solids ratio. Mechanical thickeners are designed based upon pilot-scale testing with the sludges to be treated.

Stabilization
Stabilization is a process that reduces the ability of sludge to support microbial growth. Stabilization processes include the addition of lime to raise the pH in order to stop microbial growth, heat treatment to sterilize the sludge, and anaerobic and aerobic digestion to remove degradable organic matter.

Lime stabilization requires 250 to 600 lb (110 to 220 kg) $Ca(OH)_2$ per pound of dry solids with two hours of treatment.

Heat treatment requires heating the sludge to 260 °C at a pressure of 400 psi for 30 minutes. In this process, the cells are ruptured, which allows for improved de-watering.

Anaerobic digestion converts the degradable organic matter to a variety of end products including methane and carbon dioxide. The process proceeds from complex, organic molecules to organic acids, to hydrogen and acetate, and, ultimately, to methane. Important environmental variables for successful operation are the absence of oxygen, a neutral pH, elevated temperatures (30 to 38 °C), and a lack of toxic compounds. Kinetic parameters are listed in Table 9.10.

Table 9.10 Kinetic parameters for anaerobic digestion of domestic sludge

Parameter	Value
Y, mg/mg-d	0.05–0.10
k_d, d^{-1}	0.02–0.04
k, mg/mg-d	4

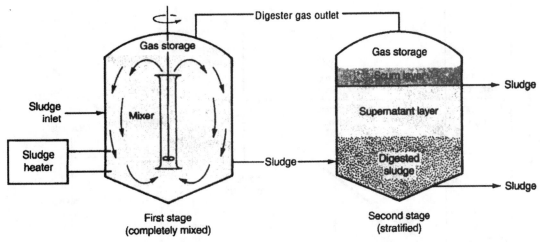

Figure 9.12 Two-stage anaerobic digestion

Long solids retention times (SRT) are required for adequate stabilization. SRTs of 10 to 20 days are necessary for high-rate digesters; those of 30 to 60 days are required for low-rate digesters at 30°C. For every pound of COD removed, about 5.6 ft³ (0.25 m³) of methane is produced. **Low-rate digesters** combine sludge digestion and thickening in a single reactor. No mixing is used. Such digesters are designed for a solids loading of 0.03 to 0.10 lb/ft³-d (0.48 to 1.6 kg/m³-d). Reduction in the volatile suspended solids is about 50 percent.

High-rate digestion involves two reactors, the first operating for biological treatment and the second for thickening (Figure 9.12). The first reactor is mixed and heated, and solids retention-time is about 10 days. In the second reactor, an additional number of days in excess of 10 is needed to allow for sludge storage.

Digesters are designed with a depth of 20 to 45 feet and a diameter approximately equal to the depth. Heating is accomplished by burning the methane gas produced.

Aerobic digestion results in the oxidation of the volatile solids in the sludge under aerobic conditions. Typical loading rates are 0.1 to 0.3 lb VS/ft³-d (0.016 to 0.048 kg/m³-d). Hydraulic detention times range from 10 to 20 days. Oxygen requirements are about 1.6 mg/mg BOD_5 for primary sludge and 2.3 mg/mg cells for secondary sludges. The removal of biodegradable volatile solids is first-order with decay coefficients of about 0.05/d at 15°C to 0.14 at 25°C.

Sludge De-Watering

De-watering is the process of increasing the solids content of sludge to reduce its volume. Common de-watering systems are vacuum filters, centrifuges, and filter presses, sludge drying beds, and sludge lagoons. Vacuum filters, centrifuges, and filter presses often require chemical conditioning of the sludges before treatment. Treated sludges typically have solids contents of 15 to 35 percent.

Sludge drying beds are common for small treatment facilities. Loading rates for digested sludges range from 10 to 30 lb dry solids/ft²-yr.

Disinfection

Disinfection in wastewater treatment is almost universally accomplished by using chlorine gas. The objective of disinfection is to kill bacteria, viruses, and amoebic cysts. Effluent standards for secondary treatment require fecal coliform levels of less than 200 and 400 per 100 mL for 30-day and seven-day averages, respectively.

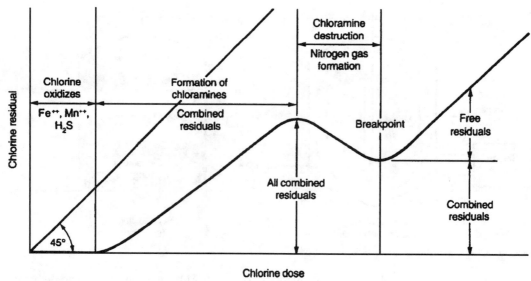

Figure 9.13 Chlorine dosage versus chlorine residual

The modeling of disinfection is described in Chapter 8. The major difference between chlorination of water supplies and wastewater is the reaction of chlorine with ammonia to produce chloroamines:

$$NH_3 + HOCl = NH_2Cl + H_2O$$
$$NH_2Cl + HOCl = NHCl_2 + H_2O$$
$$NHCl_2 + HOCl = NCl_3 + H_2O$$

Chloramines can undergo further oxidation to nitrogen gas with their subsequent removal.

This stepwise oxidation of various compounds is shown in Figure 9.13. As chlorine is initially added, it reacts with easily oxidized compounds such as reduced iron, sulfur, and manganese. Further addition results in the formation of chloramines, collectively termed combined-chlorine residual. This combined-chlorine residual results in the destruction of microorganisms, although much less effectively than with HOCl. Further addition of chlorine results in the destruction of the chloramines and ultimately leads to the formation of free-chlorine residuals such as HOCl and OCl⁻. The development of a free-chlorine residual is termed **breakpoint chlorination.**

The more contaminants present in the wastewater, the greater the chlorine demand before free chlorine is formed. Chlorination requirements vary by state; a typical requirements is a chlorine residual of 0.5 mg/L after 15 minutes of contact time. Typical dosages required to meet such a requirement are listed in Table 9.11.

Table 9.11 Chlorine dosages for wastewaters

Wastewater	Dosage, mg/L
Untreated	6–25
Primary effluent	5–20
Activated sludge effluent	2–8
Trickling filter effluent	3–15
Sand filtered effluent	2–6

SELECTED SYMBOLS AND ABBREVIATIONS

Symbol or Abbreviation	Description
a	correction factor for waste
C	concentration
d	days
DO	dissolved oxygen
d/D	depth-to-diameter ratio
E	efficiency
f	efficiency of pressurization
f	recirculation factor
g	gravitational constant
H	height
ha	hector
i	compression coefficient
K	half velocity coefficient
k	maximum substrate removal rate
k_T	base-10 BOD decay coefficient
N	field transfer rate
n	Manning coefficient
P	pressure
ρ	density
Q	flow rate or discharge
R	hydraulic radius, recirculation ratio
r	rate
S	substrate, solids, slope of energy grade line
S_L	limiting solids flux rate
t	time
V	velocity
W	weight
X	bacterial concentration
Y	substrate yield rate
θ_h	hydraulic detention time
μ	viscosity
β	salinity-surface tension correction factor

BIBLIOGRAPHY

American Society of Civil Engineering. *Design and Construction of Sanitary and Storm Sewers.* ASCE, New York, 1969.

Hammer, M. *Water and Wastewater Technology.* John Wiley & Sons, New York, 1975.

McGhee, T. J. *Water Supply and Sewerage.* McGraw-Hill, New York, 1991.

Metcalf and Eddy, Inc. *Wastewater Engineering: Treatment, Disposal, and Reuse.* McGraw-Hill, New York, 2003.

Sawyer, C. N., and P. L. McCarty. *Chemistry for Environmental Engineers.* McGraw-Hill, New York, 1978.

Steel, E. W., and T. J. McGhee. *Water Supply and Sewerage*. McGraw-Hill, New York, 1979.

Tchobanoglous, G., and E. D. Schroeder. *Water Quality*. Addison-Wesley, Menlo Park, CA, 1985.

Viessman, W., Jr., and M. J. Hammer. *Water Supply and Pollution Control*. Harper & Row, New York, 1985.

Water Environment Federation and American Society of Civil Engineers. *Design of Municipal Waste Water Treatment Plants: Vol 1*. Book Press Inc., Brattleboro, VT, 1991.

Water Environment Federation and American Society of Civil Engineers. *Design of Municipal Waste Water Treatment Plants: Vol 2*. Book Press Inc., Brattleboro, VT, 1991.

Geotechnical Engineering

Braja M. Das

OUTLINE

PARTICLE SIZE   416

SPECIFIC GRAVITY OF SOIL SOLIDS, G_s 417

WEIGHT-VOLUME RELATIONSHIPS   417

RELATIVE DENSITY   419

CONSISTENCY OF CLAYEY SOILS   420

PERMEABILITY   421

FLOW NETS   422

EFFECTIVE STRESS   423

VERTICAL STRESS UNDER A FOUNDATION   425

CONSOLIDATION   427
Calculation of Consolidation Settlement ■ Time Rate of Consolidation

SHEAR STRENGTH   432

LATERAL EARTH PRESSURE   432
At-rest Type ■ Active Type ■ Passive Type

BEARING CAPACITY OF SHALLOW FOUNDATIONS   437

DEEP (PILE) FOUNDATIONS   440

SELECTED SYMBOLS AND ABBREVIATIONS   443

REFERENCES   445

This chapter treats several aspects of geological science as applied to engineering analysis and design. These subjects are sometimes referred to collectively as soil mechanics. The principles, terms, and calculations in this chapter are essential tools for the practicing civil engineer. Many examples, problems, and solutions are included, along with the principles and explanations, to ensure thorough understanding of the material.

PARTICLE SIZE

Soils are assemblages of particles of various sizes and shapes with void spaces in between. They are formed primarily from decomposition of rocks. Based on the size of the particles present, soils can be described as gravel, sand, silt, or clay. Following are two grain size classification systems generally used by geotechnical engineers:

- System of the American Association of State Highway and Transportation Officials (AASHTO)
  Gravel: 75 mm to 2 mm
  Sand: 2 mm to 0.075 mm
  Silt and clay: Less than 0.075 mm

- Unified System
  Gravel: 76.2 mm to 4.75 mm
  Sand: 4.75 mm to 0.075 mm
  Silt and clay: Less than 0.075 mm

The particle size distribution in a given soil is determined in the laboratory by sieve analysis and hydrometer analysis.

A typical particle size distribution curve is shown in Figure 10.1. For classification purposes in coarse-grained soils, the following two parameters can be obtained from a particle size distribution curve:

- Uniformity coefficient:

$$C_c = \frac{D_{60}}{D_{10}} \tag{10.1}$$

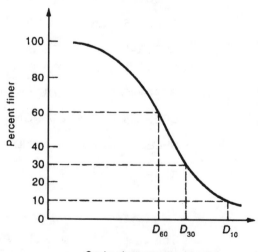

Figure 10.1

■ Coefficient of gradation:

$$C_z = \frac{D_{30}^2}{D_{10} \times D_{60}}$$ **(10.2)**

The coefficient of gradation is also sometimes referred to as the coefficient of curvature. The definitions of D_{10}, D_{30}, and D_{60} are shown in Figure 10.1.

SPECIFIC GRAVITY OF SOIL SOLIDS, G_s

The specific gravity of soil solids is defined as

$$G_s = \frac{\text{unit weight of soil solids only}}{\text{unit weight of water}}$$ **(10.3)**

The general range of G_s for various soils is given in Table 10.1.

Table 10.1 General range of G_s for various soils

Soil Type	Range of G_s
Sand	2.63–2.67
Silt	2.65–2.7
Clay and silty clay	2.67–2.8
Organic soil	Less than 2

WEIGHT-VOLUME RELATIONSHIPS

Soils are three-phase systems containing soil solids, water, and air (Figure 10.2). Referring to Figure 10.2,

$$W = W_s + W_w$$ **(10.4)**

$$V = V_s + V_v = V_s + V_w + V_a$$ **(10.5)**

where W = total weight of the soil specimen, W_s = weight of the solids, W_w = weight of water, V = total volume of the soil, V_s = volume of soil solids, V_v = volume of voids, V_w = volume of water, and V_a = volume of air.

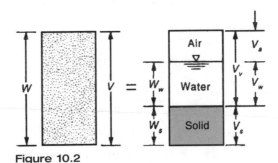

Figure 10.2

The *volume relationships* can then be given as follows:

$$\text{Void ratio} = e = \frac{V_v}{V_s} \tag{10.6}$$

$$\text{Porosity} = n = \frac{V_v}{V} \tag{10.7}$$

$$\text{Degree of saturation} = S = \frac{V_w}{V_v} \tag{10.8}$$

Similarly, the *weight relationships* are

$$\text{Moisture content} = w = \frac{W_w}{W_s} \tag{10.9}$$

$$\text{Moist unit weight} = \gamma = \frac{W}{V} \tag{10.10}$$

$$\text{Dry unit weight} = \gamma_d = \frac{W_s}{V} \tag{10.11}$$

Consider a soil sample with a unit volume of soil solids (Figure 10.3) to derive the following relationships:

1. $e = \dfrac{n}{1-n}$

2. $n = \dfrac{e}{1+e}$

3. $\gamma = \dfrac{G_s \gamma_w + w G_s \gamma_w}{1+e} = \dfrac{G_s \gamma_w (1+w)}{1+e}$

4. $\gamma_d = \dfrac{G_s \gamma_w}{1+e}$

5. $S = \dfrac{w G_s}{e}$

For *saturated soils*, $V_a = 0$ and $V_v = V_w$. Hence,

1. $S = 100\%$

2. $\gamma = \gamma_{\text{sat}} = \dfrac{\gamma_w (G_s + e)}{1+e} = \dfrac{\gamma_w (G_s + w G_s)}{1 + w G_s}$

3. $\gamma_d = \dfrac{G_s \gamma_w}{1+e}$

In the preceding relationships, γ_w = unit weight of water = 62.4 lb/ft^3 (or 9.81 KN/m^3).

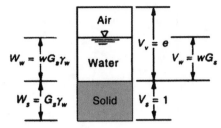

Figure 10.3

Example 10.1

A soil has a volume of 0.3 ft^3 and weighs 36 lb. Given $G_s = 2.67$ and moisture content $(w) = 18$ percent, determine (a) moist unit weight (γ), (b) dry unit weight (γ_d), (c) void ratio (e), (d) porosity (n), and (e) degree of saturation (S).

Solution

(a) $\gamma = \dfrac{W}{V} = \dfrac{36}{0.3} = 120 \text{ lb/ft}^3$

(b) $\gamma_d = \dfrac{W_s}{V} = \dfrac{W}{(1+w)V} = \dfrac{36}{\left(1 + \dfrac{18}{100}\right)0.3} = 101.7 \text{ lb/ft}^3$

(c) $\gamma_d = \dfrac{G_s \gamma_w}{1+e}$

$e = \dfrac{G_s \gamma_w}{\gamma_d} - 1 = \dfrac{(2.67)(62.4)}{101.7} - 1 = 0.64$

(d) $n = \dfrac{e}{1+e} = \dfrac{0.64}{1+0.64} = 0.39$

(e) $S = \dfrac{wG_s}{e} = \dfrac{(0.18)(2.67)}{0.64} = 0.75\,(75\%)$

RELATIVE DENSITY

In granular soils, the degree of compaction is generally expressed by a nondimensional parameter called *relative density, D_r,* or

$$D_r = \frac{e_{max} - e}{e_{max} - e_{min}} \qquad (10.12)$$

where e = actual void ratio in the field
e_{max} = void ratio in the loosest state
e_{min} = void ratio in the densest state

In many practical cases, a granular soil is qualitatively described by its relative density in the following manner.

$D_r(\%)$	Description
0–15	Very loose
15–50	Loose
50–70	Medium
70–85	Dense
85–100	Very dense

Example 10.2

A sand has the following maximum and minimum dry unit weights:

$$\gamma_{d(max)} = 17.29 \text{ kN/m}^3$$
$$\gamma_{d(min)} = 15.41 \text{ kN/m}^3$$

Given $G_s = 2.66$ and dry unit weight in the field = 16.51 kN/m³, determine the relative density in the field.

Solution

$$\gamma_{d(max)} = \frac{G_s \gamma_w}{1 + e_{min}}$$

$$e_{min} = \frac{G_s \gamma_w}{\gamma_{d(max)}} - 1 = \frac{(2.66)(9.81)}{17.29} - 1 = 0.51$$

Similarly,

$$\gamma_{d(min)} = \frac{G_s \gamma_w}{1 + e_{max}}$$

$$e_{max} = \frac{G_s \gamma_w}{\gamma_{d(min)}} - 1 = \frac{(2.66)(9.81)}{15.41} - 1 = 0.69$$

Also,

$$e = \frac{G_s \gamma_w}{\gamma_{d(field)}} - 1 = \frac{(2.66)(9.81)}{16.51} - 1 = 0.58$$

$$D_r = \frac{e_{max} - e}{e_{max} - e_{min}} = \frac{0.69 - 0.58}{0.69 - 0.51} = 0.61 = 61 \text{ percent}$$

CONSISTENCY OF CLAYEY SOILS

When a cohesive soil is mixed with an excessive amount of water, it will be in a somewhat liquid state and flow like a viscous liquid. However, when this viscous liquid is gradually dried, with the loss of moisture it will pass into a plastic state. With further reduction of moisture, the soil will pass into a semisolid and then

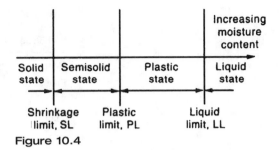

Figure 10.4

into a solid state. This is shown in Figure 10.4. The moisture content, in percent, at which the cohesive soil will pass from a liquid state to a plastic state is called the *liquid limit*. Similarly, the moisture contents at which the soil changes from a plastic state to a semisolid state, and from a semisolid state to a solid state are referred to as the *plastic limit* and the *shrinkage limit*, respectively. These limits are referred to as the *Atterberg limits*.

The liquid limit (LL) is the moisture content, in percent, at which the groove in a Casagrande liquid limit device closes for a distance of 0.5 in. after 25 blows. The plastic limit (PL) is the moisture content, in percent, at which the soil, when rolled into a thread of $1/8$-in. diameter, crumbles. The *plasticity index* (PI) is defined as

$$PI = LL - PL \tag{10.13}$$

The shrinkage limit (SL) is the moisture content, in percent, at or below which the volume of the soil mass no longer changes from drying.

PERMEABILITY

The rate of flow of water through a soil of gross cross-sectional area A can be given by the following relationships (Figure 10.5);

$$v = ki \tag{10.14}$$

where v = discharge velocity
$\quad k$ = coefficient of permeability
$\quad i$ = hydraulic gradient = h/L (see Figure 10.5)

$$q = vA = kiA \tag{10.15}$$

where q = flow through soil in unit time
$\quad A$ = area of cross section of the soil at a right angle to the direction of flow

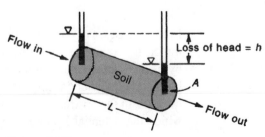

Figure 10.5

Table 10.2 Range of k in various soils

Soil Type	Range of k (cm/sec)
Coarse sand	$1-10^{-2}$
Fine sand	$10^{-2}-10^{-3}$
Silt	$10^{-3}-10^{-5}$
Clay	$<10^{-6}$

Equation (10.14) is known as *Darcy's law.* For granular soils, the coefficient of permeability can be estimated as

$$k \propto e^2 \qquad \qquad \textbf{(10.16)}$$

and

$$k \propto \frac{e^3}{1+e} \qquad \qquad \textbf{(10.17)}$$

where e is the void ratio. The range of the coefficient of permeability in various types of soil is given in Table 10.2.

Example 10.3

A sandy soil has a coefficient of permeability of 0.006 cm/sec at a void ratio of 0.5. Estimate k at a void ratio of 0.7.

Solution

From Equation (10.16),

$$\frac{k_1}{k_2} = \frac{e_1^2}{e_2^2}$$

so

$$\frac{0.006}{k_2} = \frac{(0.5)^2}{(0.7)^2}$$

$$k_2 = \frac{(0.006)(0.7)^2}{(0.5)^2} = 0.0118 \text{ cm/s}$$

FLOW NETS

In many cases, flow of water through soil varies in direction and in magnitude over the cross section. In those cases, calculation of rate of flow of water can be made by using a graph called a *flow net*. A flow net is a combination of a number of flow lines and equipotential lines. A flow line is a line along which a water particle will travel from the upstream to the downstream side. An equipotential line is one along which the potential head at all points is the same. Figure 10.6 shows an example

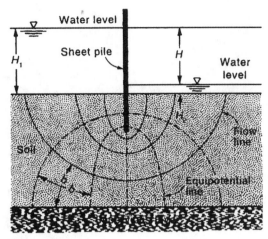

Figure 10.6

of a flow net in which water flows from the upstream to the downstream around a sheet pile. Note that in a flow net the flow lines and equipotential lines cross at right angles. Also, the flow elements constructed are approximately square.

Referring to Figure 10.6, the flow in unit time (q) per unit length normal to the cross section shown is

$$q = k \frac{N_f}{N_d} H \tag{10.18}$$

where N_f = number of flow channels
$\quad N_d$ = number of drops
$\quad H$ = head difference between the upstream and downstream side

(*Note:* In Figure 10.6, $N_f = 4$ and $N_d = 6$.)

Example **10.4**

Refer to the flow net shown in Figure 10.6. Given $k = 0.001$ ft/min, $H_1 = 30$ ft, and $H_2 = 5$ ft, determine the seepage loss per day per foot under the sheet pile structure.

Solution

$$q = k \frac{N_f}{N_d} H = (0.001 \times 60 \times 24 \ \text{ft/day}) \left(\frac{4}{6} \right) (30 - 5) = 24 \ \text{ft}^3/\text{day/ft}$$

EFFECTIVE STRESS

The total stress, σ, at a point in a soil mass is the sum of two components: (a) pore water pressure, u, and (b) effective stress, σ'. Thus

$$\sigma = \sigma' + u \tag{10.19}$$

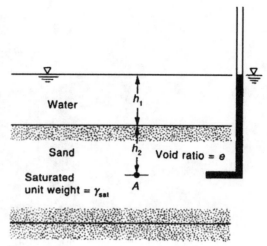

Figure 10.7

The effective stress is the sum of the vertical components of the forces developed at the points of contact of the solid particles per unit cross section of the soil mass. Referring to Figure 10.7, at point A

$$\sigma = h_1 \gamma_w + h_2 \gamma_{sat}$$
$$u = \gamma_w (h_1 + h_2)$$

so

$$\sigma' = \sigma - u = (h_1 \gamma_w + h_2 \gamma_{sat}) - \gamma_w(h_1 + h_2) = h_2(\gamma_{sat} - \gamma_w) = h_2 \gamma'$$

In the preceding relationships, γ_w = unit weight of water, γ_{sat} = saturated unit weight of soil, and $\gamma' = \gamma_{sat} - \gamma_w$ = effective unit weight of soil. From the section on weight-volume relationships,

$$\gamma_{sat} = \frac{\gamma_w(G_s + e)}{1 + e}$$

so

$$\gamma' = \gamma_{sat} - \gamma_w = \frac{\gamma_w(G_s + e)}{1 + e} - \gamma_w = \frac{\gamma_w(G_s - 1)}{1 + e} \qquad (10.20)$$

For a quicksand condition, for example, when the effective stress $\sigma' = 0$, the hydraulic gradient is given as

$$i = i_{cr} = \frac{\gamma'}{\gamma_w} = \frac{G_s - 1}{1 + e} \qquad (10.21)$$

Example **10.5**

Refer to Figure 10.7. For the soil: void ratio $e = 0.5$, $G_s = 2.67$, $h_1 = 1.5$ m, $h_2 = 3.05$ m, determine the effective stress at A.

Solution

$$\gamma' = \frac{\gamma_w(G_s - 1)}{1 + e} = \frac{9.81(2.67 - 1)}{1 + 0.5} = 10.92 \ \text{kN/m}^3$$

So the effective stress is

$$\sigma' = h_2 \gamma' = (3.05)(10.92) = 33.31 \ \text{kN/m}^2$$

Example 10.6

For the sandy soil shown in Figure 10.7, if there is an upward flow of water, what should be the hydraulic gradient for the quicksand condition? Given: $G_s = 2.65$ and $e = 0.7$.

Solution

For the quicksand condition

$$i_{cr} = \frac{\gamma'}{\gamma_w} = \frac{G_s - 1}{1 + e} = \frac{2.65 - 1}{1 + 0.7} = 0.97$$

VERTICAL STRESS UNDER A FOUNDATION

Boussinesq (1883) proposed an equation to determine the increase of vertical stress (Δp) at a point (A) in a soil mass due to a point load (Q) on the surface, which can be expressed as (Figure 10.8)

$$\Delta p = \frac{3Q}{2\pi} \frac{z^3}{(r^2 + z^2)^{5/2}} \tag{10.22}$$

where $r = \sqrt{x^2 + y^2}$.

Equation (10.22) can be used to determine the stress increase below the center of a *flexible* rectangular foundation. In Figure 10.9(a), the plan of a rectangular flexible foundation is shown. The length and the width of the foundation are L and B, respectively. The uniformly distributed load on the foundation is q. Figure 10.9(b) shows the increase of stress (Δp) *below the center of the foundation* [point A in Figure 10.9(a)] due to the distributed load q. In Figure 10.9(b), z is the vertical distance below the foundation.

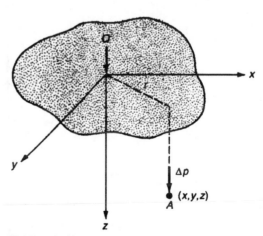

Figure 10.8

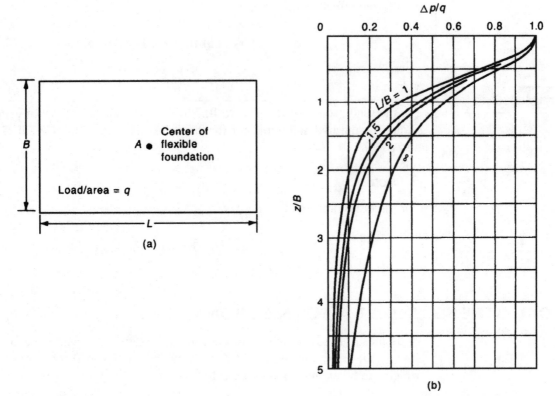

Figure 10.9

Example **10.7**

Exhibit 1 shows a square foundation. The distributed load on the foundation, q, is 4000 lb/ft². Determine the average increase of stress in the clay layer, which has a thickness of 10 ft.

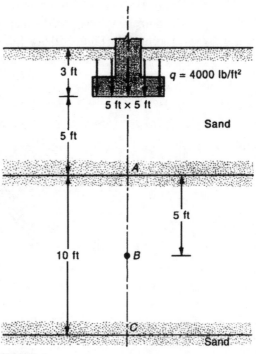

Exhibit 1

Solution

$$\Delta p_{av} = \frac{1}{6}(\Delta p_A + 4\Delta p_B + \Delta p_C)$$

At A, $z/B = 5/5 = 1$. From Figure 10.9(b), for $z/B = 1$, $\Delta p/q \approx 0.325$.

$$\Delta p_A = (0.325)(4000) = 1300 \text{ lb/ft}^2$$

At B, $z/B = 10/5 = 2$. For $z/B = 2$, $\Delta p/q \approx 0.1$.

$$\Delta p_B = (0.1)(4000) = 400 \text{ lb/ft}^2$$

At C, $z/B = 15/5 = 3$. For $z/B = 3$, $\Delta p/q \approx 0.04$.

$$\Delta p_C = (0.04)(4000) = 160 \text{ lb/ft}^2$$

$$\Delta p_{av} = \frac{1}{6}[1300 + (4)(400) + 160] = 510 \text{ lb/ft}^2$$

CONSOLIDATION

Consolidation settlement is the result of volume change in saturated clayey soils due to the expulsion of water occupied in the void spaces. In soft clays, the major portion of the settlement of a foundation may be due to consolidation. Based on the theory of consolidation, a soil can be divided into two major categories:

■ *Normally consolidated clay.* In this case, the *present effective overburden pressure* is the maximum pressure to which the soil has been subjected in the recent geologic past.

■ *Overconsolidated or preconsolidated clay.* In this case, the present effective overburden pressure is less than what the soil has encountered in the past. The past maximum effective overburden pressure is referred to as the *preconsolidation pressure* (p_c). The *overconsolidation ratio* (*OCR*) is defined as

$$OCR = \frac{p_c}{p} \tag{10.23}$$

where p_c is the preconsolidation pressure and p is the effective overburden pressure.

If a normally consolidated soil specimen is collected at a point A as shown in Figure 10.10(a), the nature of variation of void ratio (e) with the effective pressure (p) in the field will be as shown by the curve in Figure 10.10(b). If the soil at A [Figure 10.10(a)] is preconsolidated, the nature of e versus p in the field will be as shown by the curve in Figure 10.10(c). Note the slopes of the lines of the e versus log p plots. The following empirical equations may be used to estimate the slopes C_c and C_s.

$$C_c = \text{compression index} = 0.009(\text{LL} - 10) \tag{10.24}$$

where LL = liquid limit, in percent

$$C_s = \text{swell index} = \frac{1}{5} \text{ to } \frac{1}{6}C_c \tag{10.25}$$

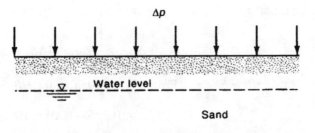

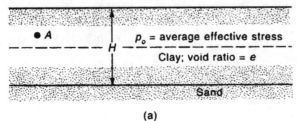

(a)

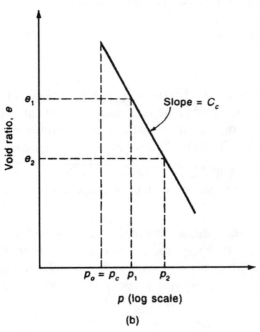

(b)

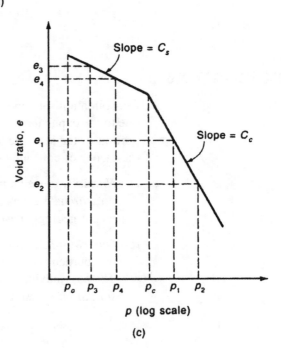

(c)

Figure 10.10

Calculation of Consolidation Settlement

Consolidation settlement of a saturated clay layer of thickness H [Figure 10.10(a)] can be calculated by the following procedure.

1. Calculate the *effective* overburden pressure, p_0, at the middle of the clay layer.

2. Determine the preconsolidation pressure (p_c) of the clay layer.

3. Estimate C_c and C_s by using Equations (10.24) and (10.25), or calculate [Figure 10.10(b) and (c)].

$$C_c = \frac{e_1 - e_2}{\log(p_2/p_1)} \qquad (10.26)$$

$$C_s = \frac{e_3 - e_4}{\log(p_3/p_4)} \qquad (10.27)$$

4. Calculate settlement, S, by using one of the following equations.

$$S = \frac{C_c H}{1 + e_o} \log\left(\frac{p_o + \Delta p}{p_o}\right)$$

(10.28)

(for $p_o = p_c$ for normally consolidated clay)

$$S = \frac{C_s H}{1 + e_o} \log\left(\frac{p_o + \Delta p}{p_o}\right)$$

(10.29)

(for $p_o + \Delta p \leq p_c$)

$$S = \frac{C_s H}{1 + e_o} \log\left(\frac{p_c}{p_o}\right) + \frac{C_c H}{1 + e_o} \log\left(\frac{p_o + \Delta p}{p_c}\right)$$

(10.30)

(for $p_o < p_c < p_o + \Delta p$) where e_o = initial void ratio of the clay and Δp = average increase of pressure in the clay layer.

Time Rate of Consolidation

The average degree of consolidation, U, of a saturated clay layer is a function of the nondimensional time factor, T_v, or

$$U = f(T_v)$$

(10.31)

$$T_v = \frac{c_v t}{H_d^2}$$

(10.32)

where c_v = coefficient of consolidation
$\quad t$ = time
$\quad H_d$ = length of the drainage path

For two-way drainage $H_d = H/2$, and for one-way drainage $H_d = H$ (see Figure 10.11). The coefficient of consolidation is defined as follows:

$$c_v = \frac{k}{\gamma_w\left(\frac{\Delta e / \Delta p}{1 + e_0}\right)}$$

(10.33)

where k = coefficient of permeability of the clay layer
$\quad \Delta e$ = change in void ratio due to an average change of pressure, Δp

The variation of U with T_v is given in Table 10.3.

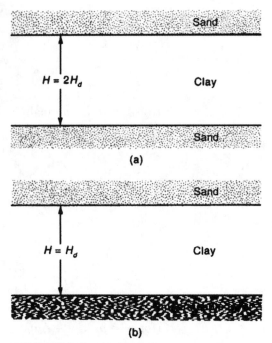

Figure 10.11

Table 10.3 Variation of U with T_v

U (%)	T_v
0	0
10	0.008
20	0.031
30	0.071
40	0.126
50	0.197
60	0.287
70	0.403
80	0.567
90	0.848
100	∞

Example **10.8**

For the shallow foundation shown in Exhibit 2, determine (a) the consolidation settlement and (b) the time for 50 percent consolidation.

Solution

(**a**) For normally consolidated clay

$$S = \frac{C_c H}{1+e_o} \log \frac{p_o + \Delta p}{p_o}.$$

At the middle of the clay layer,

$p_o = (100)(5) + (120 - 62.4)(5) + (108 - 62.4)(10/2)$

$\quad = 500 + 288 + 228 = 1016 \text{ lb/ft}^2$

$e_o = wG_s = (0.28)(2.75) = 0.77$

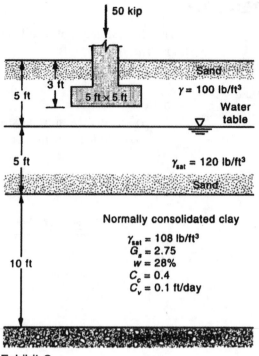

Exhibit 2

Referring to Figure 10.9(b), at the top of the clay layer, $z/B = (10 - 3)/5 = 1.4$.

$$\Delta p_{top} = 0.16q = (0.16)(50,000/25) = 320 \ \text{lb/ft}^2$$

At the middle of the clay layer, $z/B = (7 + 5)/5 = 2.4$.

$$\Delta p_{middle} = 0.07q = (0.07)(2000) = 140 \ \text{lb/ft}^2$$

At the bottom of the clay layer, $z/B = (7 + 10)/5 = 3.4$.

$$\Delta p_{bottom} \approx 0.03q = (0.03)(2000) = 60 \ \text{lb/ft}^2$$

$$\Delta p = \Delta p_{av} = (1/6)[320 + 4(140) + 60] = 156.6 \ \text{lb/ft}^2$$

Hence

$$S = \frac{(0.4)(10)}{1 + 0.77} \ \log\left(\frac{1016 + 156.5}{1016}\right) = 0.14 \ \text{ft} = 1.69 \ \text{in}$$

(b)
$$T_v = \frac{c_v t}{H_d^2}$$

For 50 percent consolidation, $T_v = 0.197$.

$$0.197 = \frac{(0.1 \ \text{ft}^2/\text{day})t}{\left(\frac{10}{2}\right)^2}$$

$$t = \frac{(0.197)\left(\frac{10}{2}\right)^2}{0.1} = 49.25 \ \text{days}$$

SHEAR STRENGTH

The shear strength of a soil (s), in general, is given by the *Mohr-Coulomb failure criteria*, or

$$s = c + \sigma' \tan \phi \qquad (10.34)$$

where c = cohesion
  σ' = effective normal stress
  ϕ = drained friction angle

For sands, $c = 0$, and the magnitude of ϕ varies with the relative density, size, and shape of the soil particles. A general range of the magnitude of ϕ is given in Table 10.4.

Table 10.4   General range of soil friction angle ϕ for sand

Type	Nature of Compaction	ϕ (deg)
Round grained	Loose	28–32
	Medium	30–36
	Dense	35–40
Angular grained	Loose	30–35
	Medium	35–40
	Dense	40–45

For normally consolidated clays, $c = 0$. So $s = \sigma' \tan \phi$. However, for over-consolidated clays, $c \neq 0$; thus $s = c + \sigma' \tan \phi$. An important concept for the shear strength of cohesive soils is the so-called $\phi = 0$ concept. This is the condition where drainage from the soil does not take place during loading. For such a case

$$s = c_u \qquad (10.35)$$

where c_u is the undrained shear strength.

The unconfined compression strength, q_u, of a cohesive soil is (Figure 10.12)

$$q_u = 2c_u \qquad (10.36)$$

A general range of q_u with the consistency of the soil is given in Table 10.5.

LATERAL EARTH PRESSURE

The lateral earth pressure behind a retaining wall can be one of the following three types:

1. At-rest

2. Active

3. Passive

At-Rest Type

In the at-rest type of lateral earth pressure the retaining wall does not move away from or toward the backfill soil (Figure 10.13). Thus

$$\sigma'_h = K_o \sigma'_v \qquad (10.37)$$

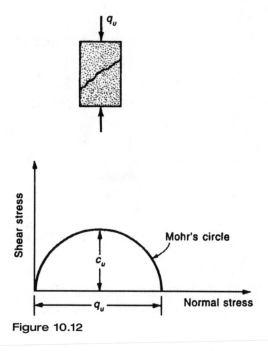

Figure 10.12

Table 10.5 Range of unconfined compression strength of cohesive soils

Consistency	q_u	
	(lb/ft^2)	(kN/m^2)
Very soft	0–500	0–24
Soft	500–1000	24–48
Medium	1000–2000	48–96
Stiff	2000–4000	96–192
Very stiff	4000–8000	192–384

where σ'_h = effective horizontal pressure on the wall
σ'_v = effective vertical pressure at a given depth
K_o = at-rest earth pressure coefficient

$$K_o = 1 - \sin\phi \quad \text{(for granular soil)} \tag{10.38}$$

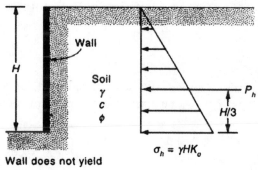

Figure 10.13 At-rest earth pressure

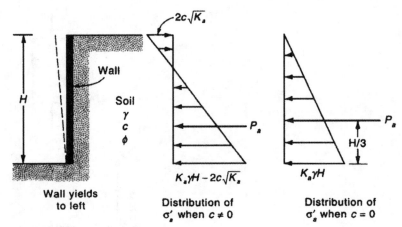

Figure 10.14 Active earth pressure

Thus, the total lateral force, P_h, per unit length of the wall (with dry granular soil as backfill) can be given as

$$P_h = \frac{1}{2} K_o \gamma_d H^2 \tag{10.39}$$

where H is the height of the wall
γ_d = dry unit weight of the soil

Active Type

Figure 10.14 shows the condition where the retaining wall moves away from the soil mass. For a frictionless retaining wall, the *Rankine active pressure* (σ'_a) is given as

$$\sigma'_a = K_a \sigma'_v - 2c\sqrt{K_a} \tag{10.40}$$

where c = cohesion, ϕ = soil friction angle, and

$$K_a = \tan^2(45 - \phi/2) \tag{10.41}$$

For most retaining wall construction, a granular backfill is used for drainage. In that case, $c = 0$. Hence

$$\sigma'_a = K_a \sigma'_v = \tan^2(45 - \phi/2)\sigma'_v$$

Referring to Figure 10.14, for a *dry granular backfill*

$$P_a = \frac{1}{2}\gamma H^2 \tan^2(45 - \phi/2) \tag{10.42}$$

For an inclined granular backfill and *frictionless wall* (Figure 10.15), Rankine's active earth pressure coefficient is

$$K_a = \cos \alpha \left(\frac{\cos \alpha - \sqrt{\cos^2\alpha - \cos^2\phi}}{\cos \alpha + \sqrt{\cos^2\alpha - \cos^2\phi}} \right) \tag{10.43}$$

Table 10.6 Variation of K_a [Equation (10.43)]

$a°$	$\phi°$				
	30	**32**	**34**	**36**	**40**
0	0.361	0.307	0.283	0.260	0.217
5	0.366	0.311	0.286	0.262	0.219
10	0.380	0.321	0.294	0.270	0.225
15	0.409	0.341	0.311	0.283	0.235
20	0.461	0.374	0.338	0.306	0.250
25	0.573	0.434	0.385	0.343	0.275

where α is the angle that the backfill makes with the horizontal, and ϕ is the soil friction angle. The variation of K_a as expressed by Equation (10.43) with α and ϕ is given in Table 10.6. This table is important in the calculation of active earth pressure and the stability check of the retaining wall.

The active force (with dry granular backfill) per unit length of the wall is given as

$$P_a = \frac{1}{2}K_a\gamma H^2 \qquad (10.44)$$

In Figure 10.15, note the direction of the resultant active force.

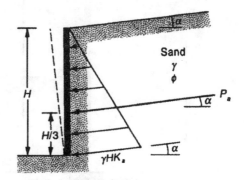

Wall yields to left

Figure 10.15

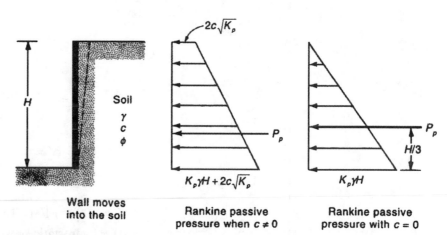

Wall moves into the soil

Rankine passive pressure when $c \neq 0$

Rankine passive pressure with $c = 0$

Figure 10.16 Passive earth pressure

Passive Type

Figure 10.16 illustrates the case where the wall moves into the soil. If the wall is frictionless, the Rankine passive earth pressure at a given depth can be given as

$$\sigma'_p = K_p \sigma'_v + 2c \sqrt{K_p} \qquad (10.45)$$

where σ'_p = passive earth pressure, σ'_v = effective vertical pressure at a certain depth, c = cohesion, and

$$K_p = \text{Rankine passive earth pressure coefficient} = \tan^2(45 + \phi/2) \quad (10.46)$$

Referring to Figure 10.16, for a dry granular backfill, $c = 0$, and

$$P_p = \frac{1}{2}\gamma H^2 \tan^2(45 + \phi/2) \qquad (10.47)$$

where P_p = Rankine passive force per unit length of the wall.

| Example **10.9** |

A retaining wall with a granular backfill is shown in Exhibit 3(a). Determine the Rankine active force per unit length of the wall P_a.

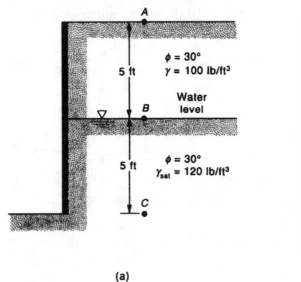

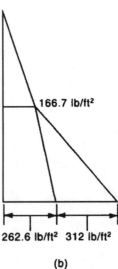

(a)

(b)

Exhibit 3

Solution

$$K_a = \tan^2(45 - \phi/2) = \tan^2(45 - 30/2) = 1/3$$

At level A:

$$\sigma'_a = 0$$

At level B:

$$\sigma'_a = (100)(5)(1/3) = 166.7 \text{ lb/ft}^2$$
$$\sigma_w = \text{hydrostatic pressure} = 0$$

At level C:

$$\sigma_a' = [(100)(5) + (120 - 62.4)(5)](1/3) = 262.6 \text{ lb/ft}^2$$
$$\sigma_w = \text{hydrostatic pressure} = (5)(62.4) = 312 \text{ lb/ft}^2$$
$$P_a = \frac{1}{2}(5)(166.7) + \left(\frac{166.7 + 262.6}{2}\right)(5) + \frac{1}{2}(5)(312)$$
$$= 416.75 + 1073.25 + 780 = 2270 \text{ lb/ft}$$

BEARING CAPACITY OF SHALLOW FOUNDATIONS

Since the original work of Karl Terzaghi (1943), the bearing capacity theories for shallow foundations have gone through extensive study. Figure 10.17 shows a shallow foundation which has a width B and length L. The depth of the foundation is D_f. The ultimate bearing capacity of the foundation can be estimated by the following equation:

$$q_u = cF_{cs}F_{cd}N_c + qF_{qs}F_{qd}N_q + \frac{1}{2}\gamma B F_{\gamma s}F_{\gamma d}N_\gamma \tag{10.48}$$

where

$$c = \text{cohesion}$$
$$\gamma = \text{unit weight of soil}$$
$$B = \text{width of the foundation}$$
$$F_{cs}, F_{qs}, F_{\gamma s} = \text{shape factors}$$
$$F_{cd}, F_{qd}, F_{\gamma d} = \text{depth factors}$$
$$N_c, N_q, N_\gamma = \text{bearing capacity factors}$$
$$q = \gamma D_f$$

The bearing capacity factors (Vesic, 1973) are

$$N_q = e^{\pi \tan \phi} \tan^2(45 + \phi/2) \tag{10.49}$$

$$N_c = (N_q - 1)\cot \phi \tag{10.50}$$

$$N_\gamma = 2(N_q + 1)\tan \phi \tag{10.51}$$

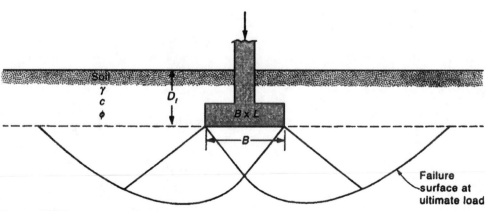

Figure 10.17

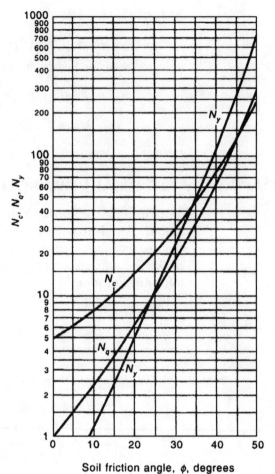

Figure 10.18

The variations of N_q, N_c, and N_γ with soil friction angle ϕ are shown in Figure 10.18. The shape factors for rectangular foundations are as follows (DeBeer, 1970):

$$F_{cs} = 1 + \left(\frac{B}{L}\right)\left(\frac{N_q}{N_c}\right) \qquad (10.52)$$

$$F_{qs} = 1 + \left(\frac{B}{L}\right)\tan\phi \qquad (10.53)$$

$$F_{\gamma s} = 1 - 0.4\left(\frac{B}{L}\right) \qquad (10.54)$$

The depth factors ($D_f \leq B$) are as follows (Hansen, 1970):

$$F_{qd} = 1 + 2\tan\phi(1 - \sin\phi)^2\left(\frac{D_f}{B}\right) \qquad (10.55)$$

$$F_{cd} = F_{qd} - \frac{1 - F_{qd}}{N_q \tan\phi} \qquad (10.56)$$

$$F_{\gamma d} = 1 \qquad (10.57)$$

For the $\phi = 0$ condition,

$$F_{\gamma d} = 1 + 0.4 \left(\frac{D_f}{B} \right) \tag{10.58}$$

A shallow foundation is generally accepted as one in which

$$\frac{D_f}{B} \leq 1 \tag{10.59}$$

In most cases, a factor of safety (F_s) of 3 to 5 is used to estimate the allowable bearing capacity, q_{all},

$$q_{all} = \frac{q_u}{F_s} \tag{10.60}$$

Note that the magnitude of q_{all} obtained by applying a factor of safety to the ultimate bearing capacity may be too high to control the settlement of a foundation as required by the code and designer. For that reason, it is important to check the allowable bearing pressure based on settlement considerations. This bearing capacity for foundations supported on sand can be obtained by the following empirical relationships, as proposed by Meyerhof (1956):

$$q_{all} \ (\text{kip/ft}^2) = \frac{N}{4} \quad (\text{for } B \leq 4 \text{ ft}) \tag{10.61}$$

and

$$q_{all} \ (\text{kip/ft}^2) = \frac{N}{4} \left(\frac{B+1}{B} \right)^2 \quad (\text{for } B > 4 \text{ ft}) \tag{10.62}$$

where q_{all} is the allowable bearing capacity for a 1-inch settlement of the foundation, and N is the standard penetration number obtained during field soil exploration. The design value of N should be estimated by taking into consideration the N values for a depth of $2B$ to $3B$, measured from the bottom of the foundation. Cone penetration resistance values can also be used to estimate q_{all} (for a 1-inch settlement of the foundation). This was also proposed by Meyerhof (1956).

$$q_{all} \ (\text{lb/ft}^2) = \frac{q_c (\text{lb/ft}^2)}{15} \quad (\text{for } B \leq 4 \text{ ft}) \tag{10.63}$$

$$q_{all} \ (\text{lb/ft})^2 = \frac{q_c (\text{lb/ft}^2)}{25} \left(\frac{B+1}{B} \right)^2 \quad (\text{for } B > 4 \text{ ft}) \tag{10.64}$$

where q_c = cone penetration resistance.

Example 10.10

For a shallow foundation, $D_f = 3$ ft, $B = 3$ ft, $L = 6$ ft; for the soil, $\phi = 28°$, $c = 600$ lb/ft^2, $\gamma = 115$ lb/ft^3. Determine the allowable bearing capacity using a factor of safety of 5.

Solution

For $\phi = 28°$, $N_c = 25.8$, $N_q = 14.72$, and $N_\gamma = 16.72$.

$$F_{cs} = 1 + (B/L)(N_q/N_c) = 1 + (3/6)(14.72/25.8) = 1.285$$
$$F_{qs} = 1 + (B/L) \tan \phi = 1 + (3/6) \tan 28 = 1.266$$

$$F_{\gamma s} = 1 - 0.4(B/L) = 1 - 0.4(3/6) = 0.8$$

$$F_{qd} = 1 + 2 \tan\phi (1 - \sin\phi)^2 (D_f/B) = 1.3$$

$$F_{cd} = F_{qd} - \left(\frac{1 - F_{qd}}{N_q \tan\phi} \right) = 1.3 - \left(\frac{1 - 1.3}{14.72 \tan 28} \right) = 1.338$$

$$F_{\gamma d} = 1$$

$$q_u = (600)(1.285)(1.338)(25.8) + (115)(3)(1.266)(1.3)(14.72)$$
$$+ \left(\frac{1}{2} \right)(115)(3)(0.8)(1)(16.72)$$
$$= 26,615 + 8358 + 2307 = 37,280 \text{ lb/ft}^2$$

$$q_{all} = q_u/5 = 37,280/5 = 7456 \text{ lb/ft}^2$$

DEEP (PILE) FOUNDATIONS

Piles and caissons are generally classified as deep foundations. For these, the failure surface in the soil below the tip does not extend to the ground surface. Several methods are now available to estimate the ultimate and allowable bearing capacities of a pile foundation. In any case, the estimated values obtained by different methods vary widely. Hence, extreme caution and judgment should be used in arriving at the design value. Figure 10.19 shows a pile foundation in a saturated clay ($\phi = 0$ condition). The ultimate load-carrying capacity (Q_u) of the pile can be estimated as follows:

$$Q_u = Q_p + Q_s \tag{10.65}$$

where Q_p is the point resistance, and Q_s is the resistance along the pile surface due to adhesion at the pile-clay interface (skin friction).

$$Q_p = 9c_u A_p \tag{10.66}$$

where c_u = the undrained shear strength of the soil under the pile tip
A_p = cross-sectional area of the pile tip

$$Q_s = \alpha c_u pL \tag{10.67}$$

where α = empirical adhesion factor (suggested values given in Figure 10.20)
p = perimeter of the pile cross section
L = length of the pile

Thus, combining Equations (10.65), (10.66), and (10.67),

$$Q_u = 9c_u A_p + \alpha c_u pL \tag{10.68}$$

Figure 10.20(a) shows a pile in a sandy soil ($c = 0$). For this case,

$$Q_u = Q_p + Q_s \tag{10.69}$$

where Q_p = point resistance
Q_s = skin friction

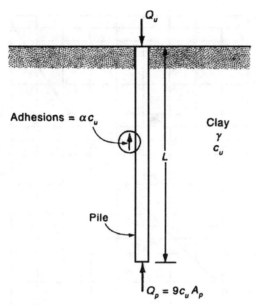

Figure 10.19

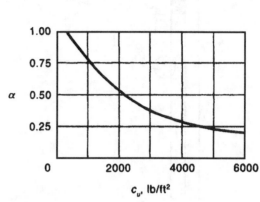

Figure 10.20

For this case (Meyerhof, 1976),

$$Q_p \text{ (lb/ft}^2) = A_p q N_q^* \leq A_p 1000 N_q^* \tan\phi \tag{10.70}$$

where A_p = cross-sectional area of the pile tip
q' = effective overburden pressure at the level of the pile tip
N_q^* = bearing capacity factor [Figure 10.21(b)]
ϕ = soil friction angle

The skin friction, Q_s, can be estimated from the following relationships:

$$Q_s = \Sigma p(\Delta L)f \tag{10.71}$$

where p = perimeter of the pile cross section
f = unit frictional resistance at a depth z

$$f = K\sigma_v' \tan\delta \tag{10.72}$$

where K = earth pressure coefficient
σ_v' = effective vertical stress at a depth z
δ = soil-pile interface friction angle ($\approx$1/3 to 2/3 ϕ)

For bored piles

$$K \approx K_o \approx 1 - \sin\phi \tag{10.73}$$

and for driven piles

$$K = K_o \text{ to } 1.5K_o \tag{10.74}$$

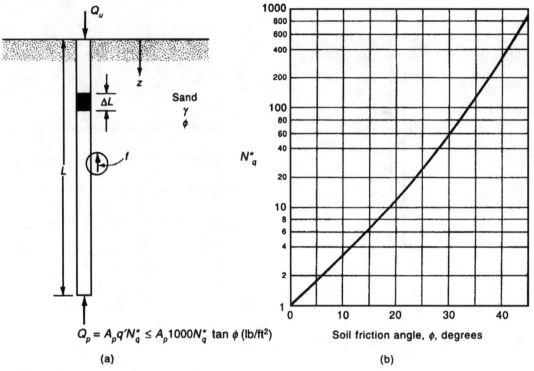

Figure 10.21

Hence, for pile in homogeneous dry sand [Equations (10.71) and (10.72)],

$$Q_s = \frac{1}{2}\gamma L^2 K p \ \tan\delta \qquad (10.75)$$

A large factor of safety (6 to 8) is usually recommended to obtain the allowable load-carrying capacity of a pile.

Example 10.11

A concrete pile having a cross section of 1 ft × 1 ft is shown in Exhibit 4. Determine the load-carrying capacity of the pile.

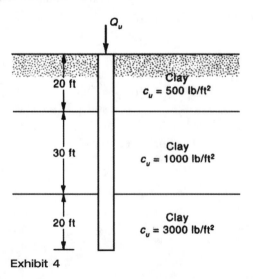

Exhibit 4

Solution

$$Q_p = 9c_u A_p = (9)(3000)(1 \times 1) = 27,000 \text{ lb}$$

$$Q_s = \sum \alpha c_u p \Delta L$$

ΔL (ft)	p (ft)	c_u (lb/ft^2)	α^*	$\alpha c_u p \Delta L$ (lb)
20	4	500	0.925	37,000
30	4	1000	0.775	93,000
20	4	3000	0.375	90,000
				Σ220,000

*From Figure 10.20.

So

$$Q_u = 27,000 + 220,000 = 247,000 \text{ lb} = 247 \text{ kips}$$

SELECTED SYMBOLS AND ABBREVIATIONS

Symbol or Abbreviation	Description
D_{10}	grain size in mm
C_z	coefficient of gradation
G_s	specific gravity of soil solids
W	weight of soil sample
W_s	weight of soil solids
W_w	weight of water in soil sample
V	volume of soil sample
V_s	volume of soil solids
V_v	volume of voids
V_w	volume of water
V_a	volume of air
e	void ratio
n	porosity
S	degree of saturation
w	moisture content
γ	moist unit weight
γ_d	dry unit weight
γ_{sat}	saturated unit weight
γ_w	unit weight of water
D_r	relative density
e_{max}	void ratio in the loosest state
e_{min}	void ratio in the densest state
$\gamma_{d(max)}$	maximum dry unit weight
$\gamma_{d(min)}$	minimum dry unit weight
$\gamma_{d(field)}$	dry unit weight of field sample

Symbol or Abbreviation	Description
LL	liquid limit
PL	plastic limit
PI	plasticity index
SL	shrinkage limit
v	discharge velocity
k	coefficient of permeability
i	hydraulic gradient
L	length of soil sample
h	loss of head
q	flow through sample in unit time
A	area of sample cross section at right angle to direction of flow
N_f	number of flow channels
N_d	number of drops
H	head difference, upstream to downstream
σ	total stress at a point in a soil mass
u	pore water pressure
σ'	effective stress
γ'	effective unit weight
$i_{c\gamma}$	hydraulic gradient for quicksand
Δp	increase of vertical stress
Q	point load on surface
r	$\sqrt{x^2 + y^2}$
L, B	length and width of a rectangular foundation
q	distributed load of foundation
z	vertical distance below foundation
Δp_{av}	average increase of vertical stress
OCR	overconsolidation ratio
p_c	preconsolidation pressure
p	effective overburden pressure
C_c	compression index
C_s	swell index
S	settlement
U	average degree of consolidation
T_v	time factor
c_v	coefficient of consolidation
H_d	length of drainage path
s	shear strength of soil
c	cohesion
ϕ	drained friction angle
c_u	undrained shear strength
q_u	unconfined compression strength
σ'_h	effective horizontal pressure
σ'_v	effective vertical pressure
K_O	at-rest earth pressure coefficient
P_h	total lateral force per unit length of wall
K_a	Rankine active earth pressure coefficient
σ'_a	Rankine active pressure
α	angle between backfill and horizontal
σ'_p	passive earth pressure

Symbol or Abbreviation	Description
K_p	Rankine passive earth pressure coefficient
P_p	Rankine passive force per unit length of wall
P_a	Rankine active force per unit length of wall
σ_w	hydrostatic pressure
$F_{cs}, F_{qs}, F_{\gamma s}$	shape factors
$F_{cd}, F_{qd}, F_{\gamma d}$	depth factors
N_c, N_q, N_γ	bearing capacity factors
D_f	depth of a shallow foundation
F_s	safety factor
q_{all}	allowable bearing capacity
N	standard penetration number
Q_u	ultimate load capacity of pile
Q_p	point resistance of pile
Q_s	pile surface resistance
A_p	cross-sectional area of the pile tip
α	empirical adhesion factor
p	perimeter of pile cross section
L	length of pile
N_q^*	Meyerhof's bearing capacity factor (deep foundation)
f	unit frictional resistance on pile
δ	soil-pile interface friction angle
K	earth pressure coefficient

REFERENCES

Boussinesq, J. *Application des Potentials à L'Etude de L'Equilibre et du Mouvement des Solides Elastiques*. Gauthier-Villars, Paris, 1883.

DeBeer, E. E. Experimental Determination of the Shape Factors and Bearing Capacity Factors of Sand. *Geotechnique*. Vol. 20, No. 4, pp. 387–411, 1970.

Hansen, J. B. A Revised and Extended Formula for Bearing Capacity. Danish Geotechnical Institute, *Bulletin 28*, Copenhagen, 1970.

Meyerhof, G. G. Penetration Tests and Bearing Capacity of Cohesionless Soils. *Journal of the Soil Mechanics and Foundations Division,* American Society of Civil Engineers. Vol. 82, No. SM1, pp. 1–19, 1956.

Meyerhof, G. G. Bearing Capacity and Settlement of Pile Foundations. *Journal of the Geotechnical Engineering Division,* American Society of Civil Engineers. Vol. 102, No. GT3, pp. 197–228, 1976.

Terzaghi, K. *Theoretical Soil Mechanics*. Wiley, New York, 1943.

Vesic, A. S. Analysis of Ultimate Loads of Shallow Foundations. *Journal of the Soil Mechanics and Foundations Division,* American Society of Civil Engineers. Vol. 99, No. SM1, pp. 45–73, 1973.

Recommendations for Further Study

Das, B. M. *Principles of Geotechnical Engineering,* 5th ed. Brooks/Cole, Pacific Grove, CA, 2002.

Das, B. M. *Principles of Foundation Engineering,* 5th ed. Brooks/Cole, Pacific Grove, CA, 2004.

Transportation Engineering

James H. Banks

OUTLINE

TRANSPORTATION PLANNING 449
The Transportation Planning Process ■ Travel Demand Modeling

**HIGHWAY SYSTEM CHARACTERISTICS
AND DESIGN CONTROLS 452**
Driver Performance ■ Vehicle Characteristics ■ Highway Functions
and Design Elements ■ Traffic Flow Characteristics

STATISTICAL METHODS 470
Descriptive Statistics ■ Probability ■ Confidence Bounds ■ Hypothesis
Testing

TRAFFIC ENGINEERING STUDIES 477
Volume Studies ■ Speed Studies ■ Accident Studies ■ Traffic
Impact Studies

HIGHWAY ROUTE SURVEYING 484
Simple Circular Curves ■ Compound Curves ■ Parabolic Vertical
Curves ■ Spiral Curves ■ Slope Staking ■ Earthwork

AASHTO GEOMETRIC DESIGN GUIDELINES 499
Local Roads ■ Collector Roads ■ Rural Arterials ■ Urban
Arterials ■ Freeways ■ At-Grade Intersections ■ Grade Separations
and Interchanges ■ Roadside Design

HIGHWAY CAPACITY MANUAL 505
Basic Concepts ■ Two-Lane Highways ■ Multilane Highways ■ Freeway
Facilities ■ Basic Freeway Segments ■ Weaving Areas ■ Ramps and
Ramp Junctions ■ Urban Streets ■ Signalized Intersections ■ Unsignalized
Intersections ■ Pedestrians ■ Bicycles

TRAFFIC CONTROL DEVICES 529
The MUTCD ■ Traffic Markings ■ Traffic Signs ■ Traffic Signals

TRAFFIC SIGNALS TIMING   532
Elements of Signal Timing ■ Cycle Lengths ■ Change Intervals ■ Signal
Coordination

PAVEMENT DESIGN   538
AASHTO Design Method ■ Asphalt Institute Method ■ Portland Cement
Association Method

NOTES ON SELECTED SPECIAL TOPICS   548
Parking ■ Queueing Models ■ Evaluating Transportation
Alternatives ■ Computer Applications

REFERENCES   551

The Institute of Transportation Engineers (ITE, 1991a) defines transportation engineering as "the application of technology and scientific principles to the planning, functional design, operation, and management of facilities for any mode of transportation in order to provide for the safe, rapid, comfortable, convenient, economical, and environmentally compatible movement of people and goods. Traffic Engineering is that phase of transportation engineering which deals with the planning, geometric design and traffic operations of roads, streets and highways, their networks, terminals, abutting lands, and relationships with other modes of transportation."

While the professional engineer may be involved in the planning, design, operation and/or management of transportation facilities and services, it is typically only the design-related activities which must be supervised and approved by a registered professional engineer. The general focus of this chapter, therefore, is on the design of transportation facilities. Because travel in this country is largely highway oriented, the specific focus of this chapter is the design of streets and highways. This is not to say that the other aspects of transportation engineering (i.e., planning, operations, and management) are any less important than the design function. They are not. The development of a safe, efficient, and economical transportation system requires the incorporation of all of these aspects of transportation engineering in an integrated, systems approach to solving transportation problems. The emphasis of this chapter on the design of transportation facilities reflects the emphasis given this aspect of transportation engineering in most state professional licensing examinations. Given the very special responsibility of the designer with regard to public safety, this emphasis is entirely appropriate.

The material in this chapter is presented under the following major topics: transportation planning; characteristics of the highway system in terms of drivers, vehicles, roadways and traffic flow; statistical methods; traffic studies; route surveying; geometric design guidelines; highway capacity; traffic control devices; signal timing; pavement design; and special topics. Within many of these topics are example problems which illustrate the fundamental principles and concepts outlined in the text. In the case of those design methods which make extensive use of special design charts, such as AASHTO Geometric Design Guidelines, the Highway Capacity Manual, and Pavement Design Methods, the reader is referred to specific references for additional details and example applications.

The chapter includes a list of recommended references for further study and an extensive set of sample problems which illustrate the applications of concepts reviewed in this chapter. In selecting references for additional study and/or to take into the licensing examination, note that there have been considerable changes in several important areas of transportation engineering in recent years, and care should be taken to select current reference materials. The National Council of Examiners for Engineering and Surveying (NCEES) publishes a list of current references for transportation engineering on the Internet at www.ncees.org/exams/professional/pe_design_standards/transportation_design_standards.pdf.

The reader should keep in mind that the intent of this chapter is to provide a review/summary of standard transportation engineering practices. The reader should consult the references cited at the end this chapter for more detailed treatment of specific subject areas.

TRANSPORTATION PLANNING

The design of transportation facilities is often thought of as a very routine matter, consisting primarily of the straightforward application of standard methods. While some design projects are of this type, many are not, and require the cooperative and creative efforts of specialists from a wide range of disciplines. To fully understand and appreciate design as part of a "process" consisting of planning, design, construction, and operation, maintenance, and management, a brief introduction to transportation planning is necessary.

The Transportation Planning Process

The transportation planning process, and the travel demand modeling phase of the process, has been described as more art then science. Because of this, it is extremely difficult to provide more than a brief introduction to the topic in the limited space of this chapter. An introduction to transportation planning, however, is considered essential in understanding the multimodal, interdisciplinary nature of transportation engineering. It is through the transportation planning process that many of the basic decisions concerning the location, size, and timing of transportation improvements are made.

Transportation planning is an ongoing process which seeks to assess the short- and long-range transportation problems of a region and to develop, evaluate, select, and implement plans and strategies for solving those problems. The travel demand modeling phase of the transportation planning process is based on the interaction between two basic systems: the transportation system (origins, destinations, volumes of people and goods) and the activity system (land uses, population, social and economic activities) within which the transportation system operates. Specifically, travel demand modeling is based on the assumption that travel patterns and traffic volumes are a direct and measurable function of the pattern of activities that generate them. The transportation planning process is depicted in Figure 11.1.

Perhaps the single most important event in fostering the near universal adoption and application of the transportation planning process illustrated in Figure 11.1 was the Federal-Aid Highway Act of 1962. As a result of the 1962 Act, the urban transportation planning process has been standardized and institutionalized in the United States and many other nations as the process for the planning of all publicly owned transportation facilities within metropolitan areas. Basically, the Act required all urban areas with populations over 50,000 to develop transportation plans that were coordinated with land use and other plans for the region.

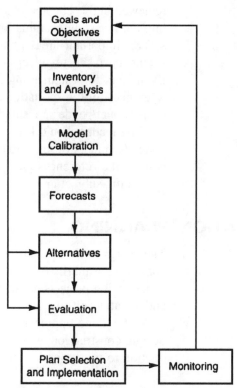

Figure 11.1 Transportation planning process

This planning must be undertaken continuously, so that long-range plans as well as short-term actions and programs can be modified to meet changing needs. As a result of these requirements, the traditional transportation planning process is often referred to as the 3C (comprehensive, coordinated, and continuing) planning process.

As shown in Figure 11.1, the first step in the process consists of the formulation of explicit statements concerning the expected performance of the system. These goals and objectives define the overall direction of the planning process and provide explicit, quantifiable measures against which alternative solutions to the region's transportation problems can be evaluated. The second step of the process involves the compilation of extensive inventories of the existing state of the system, both in terms of existing travel patterns and traffic flows and the activities that give rise to these transportation system demands. These inventories, which make up the database, typically include information concerning the following aspects of the region: (1) population, (2) land use, (3) economic activity, (4) transportation facilities and services, (5) travel patterns and traffic volumes, (6) laws and ordinances, (7) regional financial resources, and (8) community values and expectations. From these inventories, models are developed to quantify the relationships between travel demand and characteristics of the activity system. Once these models have been calibrated to provide reasonably accurate simulations of existing travel demands, they can be used to develop forecasts of future travel demands based on the relationship reflected by the calibrated models. From these forecasts of future conditions, potential problems in the system can be identified and alternative solutions can be designed and evaluated in order to choose a preferred option. Once the preferred alternatives have been designed and implemented, the database (the inventory data) is continually monitored and the system models and resulting plans and programs modified as necessary. [The reader is referred to Meyer and Miller (2001) and Garber and Hoel (1997) for details concerning the transportation planning process and the specific procedures and models employed in the process.]

Travel Demand Modeling

At the heart of the transportation planning process is the development and application of travel demand models which describe the relationships between trip making and the region's pattern of population, land use, and economic activities. In general, travel demand modeling attempts to quantify the amount of travel on the transportation system in terms of the activities which create that demand.

There are many methods available to model and forecast travel demand. Figure 11.2 illustrates what has become known as the "traditional four-step travel demand modeling process." It has been developed over the past fifty years and is the most common approach to regional travel demand modeling. The four basic phases of the traditional approach to travel demand modeling are (1) *trip generation* (the number of trips that will be made), (2) *trip distribution* (where the trips will go), (3) *mode choice* (how the trips will be divided among the available modes of travel), and (4) *traffic assignment* (the routes that the trips will take).

Note that the process shown in Figure 11.2 is sequential. The three activity system models (population, economics, and land use) describe the location and magnitude of activities in the area, and the four travel demand models translate this activity into the corresponding demand on the transportation system. Also, the first three travel demand models (generation, distribution, and mode choice),

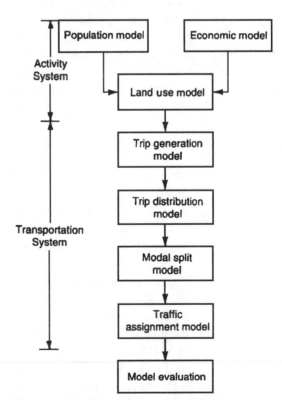

Figure 11.2 Travel demand modeling

though useful in their own right, are in most cases intermediate steps in arriving at the ultimate goal of the process, which is the estimation of travel volumes on individual roadways and transit routes in the study area, as obtained from the trip assignment phase of the process.

Even a very general description of the calibration and application of travel demand models in a regional (systemwide) context is beyond the scope of this manual. However, the preceding discussion provides a useful introduction to a simplified, but very important and widely used, application of travel demand models. The application alluded to is commonly referred to as the "traffic impact study." The basic steps in conducting a traffic impact study are presented later in this chapter. [The reader should consult Meyer and Miller (2001), Garber and Hoel (1997), and/or the U.S. Department of Transportation (USDOT, 1977) for an introduction to travel demand models.]

HIGHWAY SYSTEM CHARACTERISTICS AND DESIGN CONTROLS

The characteristics of traffic flows on the highway system are the results of complex interactions between the following three basic elements: drivers, vehicles, and the roadway itself. Effective transportation engineering requires an understanding of these three elements and the traffic flows resulting from their interactions.

Driver Performance

The perception of, and reaction to, cues and stimuli encountered by the driver of a vehicle involve four distinct actions: perception, identification, emotion or decision (determination of appropriate response), and volition (reaction). The total time taken for this sequence is referred to as PIEV (perception, identification, emotion, and volition) time or perception-reaction time. Perception-reaction time is an important factor in the determination of braking distance, which in turn dictates minimum sight distance and the length of yellow phase at signalized interactions. The distance traveled during this time is calculated from the following equation:

$$d_p = 0.278vt \qquad \textbf{(11.1a)}$$

$$d_p = 1.47vt \qquad \textbf{(11.1b)}$$

where

d_p = perception-reaction distance (m or ft)
v = speed of vehicle (km/hr)
t = perception-reaction time (s)
0.278 = conversion factor (km/hr to m/s)
1.47 = conversion factor (mph to ft/s)

In most situations, a PIEV time of 2.0 to 2.5 seconds is considered realistic. The American Association of State Highway and Transportation Officials (AASHTO) recommends a value of 2.5 seconds for design purposes (AASHTO, 2001). The AASHTO *Policy on Geometric Design of Highways and Streets* (2001) is *the standard reference* in the field of geometric design. It should be one of the reference documents taken to the exam. Key figures and tables from the Green

Book are identified from appropriate points in this chapter. It will be very helpful if these figures and tables are "tagged" in the Green Book prior to the exam.

Example **11.1**

Consider a driver approaching a hazard at 90 km/hr with a PIEV time of 2.5 seconds. The distance traveled during the perception-reaction time is most nearly:

(a) 30 m

(b) 50 m

(c) 63 m

(d) 250 m

(e) 330 m

Solution

From Equation (11.1a), the distance traveled during the PIEV sequence is $d_p =$ 0.278(90)(2.5) = 62.6 m. This represents approximately 11 car lengths traveled while the driver's response is initiated. This does not include the distance to stop the vehicle after the brakes are applied. The answer is (c).

Vehicle Characteristics

The geometric design of streets and highways is based on the static, kinematic, and dynamic characteristics of the vehicles that are expected to use them. Some of the more critical characteristics are summarized below.

Static Characteristics

For the purposes of geometric design, AASHTO (2001) has established a set of 19 "design vehicles." These are vehicles of representative size within each class used for design, and are used to establish highway design controls. Dimensions of the AASHTO design vehicles are shown in Exhibit 2-1 of the Green Book. The most important geometric feature controlled by design vehicle dimensions is the minimum turning radius. Minimum turning paths for each design vehicle are illustrated in Exhibits 2-3 through 2-23 (pp. 21–41) of the Green Book.

Kinematic Characteristics

In the geometric design of highways, the kinematic characteristic of primary concern is the acceleration capabilities of the vehicle. Two cases are of interest in defining the relationships between acceleration, velocity, distance, and time: (1) constant acceleration and (2) acceleration that varies as a function of velocity (nonuniform acceleration). For the *constant acceleration* case, the following relationships hold:

$$v = v_0 + at \tag{11.2}$$

$$d = v_0 t + \frac{1}{2} at^2 \tag{11.3}$$

$$d = \frac{1}{2} a \left(v^2 - v_0^2 \right) \tag{11.4}$$

where

d = distance (m or ft)
v = final velocity (m/s or ft/s)
v_0 = initial velocity (m/s or ft/s)
a = acceleration (m/s^2 or ft/s^2)
t = time (s)

In real-world situations it is often necessary to consider *nonuniform acceleration*. The relationship between acceleration and velocity in this case is

$$a = \alpha - \beta v \qquad (11.5)$$

where α and β are constant. [When $v = 0$, a represents the maximum acceleration attainable (a_{max}). When $a = 0$, α/β is the maximum possible velocity (v_{max}). Given these relationships, Equation (11.5) can be written as $a = a_{max} - (a_{max}/(v_{max})v$.]

Integration of Equation (11.5) between v and v_0 yields the following relationship for velocity as a function of time:

$$v = (\alpha/\beta)(1 - e^{-\beta t}) + v_0 e^{-\beta t}$$
$$= v_{max}(1 - e^{-\beta t}) + v_0 e^{-\beta t} \qquad (11.6)$$

The distance-time relationship is

$$d = (\alpha t/\beta) - (\alpha/\beta^2)(1 - e^{-\beta t}) + (v_0/\beta)(1 - e^{-\beta t}) \qquad (11.7)$$

The acceleration-time equation is

$$a = (\alpha - \beta v_0)e^{-\beta t} \qquad (11.8)$$

Example 11.2

A driver traveling at 45 km/h (66 ft/s) sees a stalled car 120 ft ahead. If the driver applies the brakes immediately (PIEV time = 0) and begins slowing the vehicle at 18 ft/s^2 (emergency deceleration), the distance the vehicle will travel before stopping, most nearly:

(a) 90 ft

(b) 119 ft

(c) 121 ft

(d) 180 ft

(e) 240 ft

Solution

From Equation (11.2), the time required to bring the vehicle to a stop is

$$t = (v - v_0)/a = (0 \text{ m/s} - 66 \text{ ft/s})/-18 \text{ ft/s}^2 = 3.67 \text{ s}$$

From Equation (11.3), the distance traveled in these 3.67 s is

$$d = (66)(3.67) + (0.5)(-18)(3.67)^2 = 121 \text{ ft}$$

The correct answer is (c).

Dynamic Characteristics

The forces acting on the motion of a vehicle include air resistance, rolling resistance, friction resistance, and grade resistance. The fundamental relationship between the net tractive force (F_n) of a vehicle and its acceleration is defined by Newton's second law of motion:

$$F_n = ma \qquad \text{(11.9)}$$

where m = mass (kg), a = acceleration (m/s^2), and F_n is in newtons.

The vehicle's tractive force is the difference between the force supplied by the engine and the various forces opposing its motion. Net tractive force is a function of the vehicle's velocity and the power required at that velocity:

$$F_n = (1000P)/v \qquad \text{(11.10)}$$

where

P = power delivered (kW)

v = speed of vehicle (m/s)

The forces acting on the motion of a vehicle serve as the basis for determining several important parameters related to the dynamic characteristics of vehicles. These include braking distance and radius of curvature requirement. The general equation for braking distance is

$$d_b = \frac{V_0^2 - V^2}{254[(a/9.81) \pm G]} \qquad \text{(11.11a)}$$

$$d_b = \frac{V_0^2 - V^2}{30[(a/32.2) \pm G]} \qquad \text{(11.11b)}$$

where

d_b = braking distance [m in Equation (11.11a) and ft in Equation (11.11b)]

V_0 = initial velocity of the vehicle [km/hr in Equation (11.11a) and mph in Equation (11.11b)]

V = final velocity of the vehicle

a = deceleration rate

G = grade (plus for uphill, minus for downhill), expressed as a decimal

The AASHTO Green Book recommends that 3.4 m/s^2 (11.2 ft/s^2) be used as the deceleration rate for determining stopping sight distance. Where V and G are approximately zero, the braking distance is given by

$$d_b = 0.039 \, V^2/a \qquad \text{(11.12a)}$$
$$d_b = 1.075 \, V^2/a \qquad \text{(11.12b)}$$

where V is now the vehicle's initial speed and Equation (11.12a) is in metric units and Equation (11.12b) is U.S. Customary units.

Equation (11.11) has a number of useful applications, such as determination of safe stopping distance. The total stopping distance (d_s) for a vehicle is

$$d_s = d_p + d_b = 0.278v_t + \frac{V^2}{254[(a/9.81) \pm G]} \qquad \text{(11.13a)}$$

$$d_s = d_p + d_b = 1.47v + \frac{V^2}{30[(a/32.2) \pm G]} \qquad \text{(11.13b)}$$

where d_p is the PIEV distance as previously defined. Equation (11.11) may also be used for estimating vehicle speeds in accident investigations. In this application, the braking distance is given as

$$d_b = \frac{V_0^2 - V^2}{254(f \pm G)} \tag{11.14a}$$

$$d_b = \frac{V_0^2 - V^2}{30(f \pm G)} \tag{11.14b}$$

where f is the coefficient of friction and V is the velocity at the time of collision (normally not zero).

In accident investigations, transportation engineers are often called upon to estimate the speeds of the vehicles involved in the accident. A typical approach to this problem is to assume that skid marks on the roadway represent braking distance and solve the basic braking distance equation for the unknown initial speed (the final speed is assumed to be zero). The speed estimated in this manner will always be lower than the actual speed because any reduction in speed before skidding and any speed at impact (if there is a collision) will not be reflected in the length of the skid marks.

Highway Functions and Design Elements

This section summarizes some basic terminology and concepts concerning highway functions, sight distances, and the horizontal and vertical alignments of roadways. The roadway characteristics reviewed here are those related primarily to the characteristics of the driver and vehicle. Detailed treatment of specific aspects of the geometric design of streets and highways is also presented in this chapter.

Functional Classification

Streets and highways serve two distinct and very different functions: (1) through movement, or mobility, and (2) land access. Functional classification is the identification of streets and highways in terms of the degree to which the competing and conflicting functions of movement and access are to be served. Three general classifications are commonly employed: arterials, collectors, and local streets.

Roadways are classified according to their function or use and then designed to fulfill that function. Hence, the functional classification of roadways is the initial requirement for design. An understanding of the following aspects of the concept of functional classification is essential to effective design:

1. The relationship between the three primary roadway classifications and the type of service provided is a continuous one. Travel involves movement through a hierarchy of facility types. This means that each functional class should intersect with facilities of the next higher and lower classifications. Failure to recognize and to accommodate this hierarchy by appropriate design is the principal cause of inefficiency in the roadway system.

2. Functional classification is a function of movement versus access, ranging from little or no restriction of access to complete control of access. Counted or projected traffic volume is not an element in functional classification.

Roadways are classified according to their function or use then designed to fulfill that function. This emphasis on function rather than traffic volume is a recent and significant philosophical change in the approach to roadway design.

The concept of functional classification and its application in geometric design, capacity analysis, and traffic control is elaborated in this chapter.

Sight Distance

The controlling criteria in the horizontal and vertical alignment of roadways are design speed and sight distance. Design speed is a minimum control on design since all other design elements must accommodate safe operations at or above this speed. Streets and highways must also be designed to provide the driver sufficient sight distance to see an object in the roadway and avoid hitting it while maintaining control of the vehicle. The roadway design engineer must consider four basic aspects of sight distance: (1) stopping sight distance, (2) passing sight distance, (3) decision sight distance, and (4) measurement of sight distance parameters.

Stopping sight distances are calculated using the equation for total stopping distance presented earlier in Equation (11.13). Exhibits 3.57 and 3.58 (pp. 229–231) in the Green Book are design charts showing the required distance to the nearest roadside object to satisfy stopping sight distance requirements for horizontal curves of various radii and design speeds. *These relationships between curve radius, design speed, and distance to roadside object can be used to find the limiting value of any of the variables, given the other two.* Exhibit 3-57 is one of the more frequently used charts in the Green Book, and the reader is urged to become familiar with it. The stopping sight distances in these figures are presented in tabular form in Exhibit 3-1 (p. 112) in the Green Book.

The amount of sight distance at intersections depends to some degree on the type of control used at the intersection. The following general types of control (or cases) are applicable: (a) no control, (b) stop control on the minor road, (c) yield control on the minor road, (d) traffic signal control, (e) all-way stop control, and (f) left turns from the major road.

In all cases, sight distances are specified in terms of clear sight triangles, as illustrated by Figure 11.3 (same as Exhibit 9-50, p. 656 in the Green Book). There are two types of sight triangles, approach sight triangles and departure sight triangles. Approach sight triangles define an area that should be free of obstructions to provide adequate sight distance so that vehicles approaching an intersection can see potentially conflicting vehicles in time to slow or stop without colliding in the intersection. They are particularly applicable to intersections with no control or yield control. Departure sight triangles provide the sight distance for a vehicle stopped on a minor road to enter or cross the major road, and also allow drivers on the major road to see vehicles stopped on the minor road approach.

The dimensions of the sight triangles vary with design speed and the type of control. Details of the different control cases are as follows.

Case A—No control. As a general rule, approach sight triangles, but not departure sight triangles, are used at intersections with no control. Dimensions of the sight triangles are given in Exhibit 9-51 (p. 659) and Exhibit 9-52 (p. 661) of the Green Book.

Case B—Stop control. Three different subcases are involved. Case B1 applies to left turns from the minor road. The intersection sight distance along the major

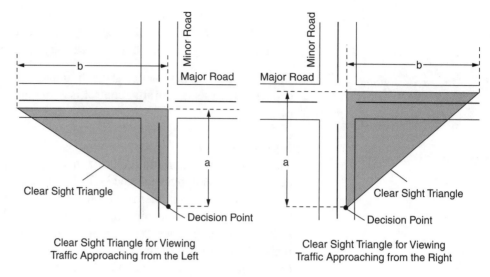

A – Approach Sight Triangles

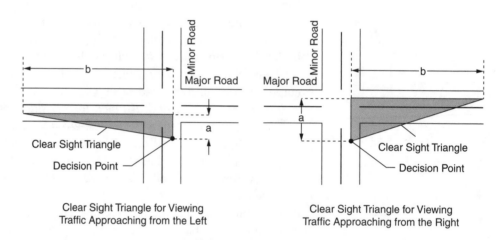

B – Departure Sight Triangles

Figure 11.3 Intersection sight triangles.
[*Source:* AASHTO (2001)]

road is given by

$$\text{ISD} = 2.078 V_{\text{major}}\, t_g \qquad (11.15a)$$

$$\text{ISD} = 1.47 V_{\text{major}}\, t_g \qquad (11.15b)$$

where ISD = intersection sight distance [m in Equation (11.15a) and ft in Equation (11.15b)], V_{major} is the design speed of the major road [km/hr in Equation (11.15a) and mph in Equation (11.15b)], and t_g = time gap for the minor road vehicle to enter the major road (sec). Values of t_g are given in Exhibit 9-54 (p. 664). Exhibits 9-55 (p. 665) and 9-56 (p. 666) give sight distances as a function of design speed.

Case B2 applies to the right turn from the minor road. The sight distance calculation is the same as that for case B1, except that the time gaps are reduced by 1.0 sec. Exhibits 9-57 (p. 668), 9-58 (p. 668), and 9-59 (p. 669) give time gaps and sight distances for this case.

Case B3 applies to the crossing maneuver from the minor road. Where sight distance triangles have been established for cases B1 and B2, these will usually be sufficient for crossing maneuvers as well. Where sight distance triangles have not been established for turning vehicles, those for case B3 will be similar to those for case B2. The calculation is the same as for case B1, but the time gaps for case B2 should be used.

Case C—Yield control. As in the case of stop control, there are separate subcases for crossing maneuvers and turning maneuvers. Case C1 applies to the crossing maneuver from the minor road. Sight distance along the major road is based on time gaps given by

$$t_g = t_a + \frac{w + L_a}{0.167V_{\text{minor}}} \tag{11.16a}$$

$$t_g = t_a + \frac{w + L_a}{0.88V_{\text{minor}}} \tag{11.16b}$$

where

t_g = time gap (s)

t_a = travel time to reach the major road from the decision point (s) [see Exhibit 9-60 (p. 772) in the Green Book]

w = width of the intersection [m in Equation (11.16a) and ft in Equation (11.16b)]

L_a = length of the design vehicle [m in Equation (11.16a) and ft in Equation (11.16b)

V_{minor} = design speed of the minor road [km/hr in Equation (11.16a) and mph in Equation (11.16b)].

Sight distances are calculated using Equation (11.15a) or (11.15b) with the time gap calculated by Equation (11.16a) or (11.16b). The time gaps and dimensions of the approach sight triangle for this case are given by Exhibits 9-60 (p. 672), 9-61 (p. 673), and 9-62 (p. 674).

Case C2 applies to left- and right-turn maneuvers. These use departure sight triangles similar to those in cases B1 and B2. Time gaps and dimensions of sight triangles are given by Exhibits 9-63 (p. 676), 9-64 (p. 676), and 9-65 (p. 677).

Case D—Signal control. In this case, the first vehicle stopped on each approach should be visible to the first vehicle stopped on any other approach. In addition, left-turning vehicles should have sufficient sight distance to select gaps in oncoming traffic and complete left turns. Otherwise, sight triangles are not needed unless the intersection is to be operated on flashing yellow on the major street at certain times of day or right turns on red are permitted. In either of those cases, the appropriate sight triangles for case B should be provided.

Case E—All-way stop control. The first vehicle stopped on each approach should be able to see the first vehicle stopped on all other approaches.

Case F—Left turns from the major road. Vehicles turning left from the major roadway should have sufficient sight distance along the major road to accommodate the maneuver. Exhibits 9-66 (p. 678), 9-67 (p. 679), and 9-68 (p. 680) give time gaps and sight distances.

In design, the passing sight distance is the length needed to allow a single vehicle to safely pass another vehicle in a normal passing maneuver. The *minimum passing sight distance* is the total of the following four distances (AASHTO, 2001):

d_1—distance traversed during perception-reaction time and during the initial acceleration to the point of encroachment on the left lane:

$$d_1 = 0.278t_i \left[v - m + \frac{1}{2}(at_i) \right] \tag{11.17a}$$

$$d_1 = 1.47t_i \left[v - m + \frac{1}{2}(at_i) \right] \tag{11.17b}$$

d_2—distance traveled while the passing vehicle occupies the left lane:

$$d_2 = 0.278vt_2 \qquad \textbf{(11.18a)}$$

$$d_2 = 1.47vt_2 \qquad \textbf{(11.18b)}$$

d_3—distance between the passing vehicle and the opposing vehicle at the end of the maneuver. [This clearance interval (d_3) is assumed to vary from 30 m (100 ft) to 75 m (250 ft).]

d_4—distance traversed by an opposing vehicle for two-thirds of the time the passing vehicle occupies the left lane (two-thirds of d_2):

$$d_4 = 2d_2/3 \qquad \textbf{(11.19)}$$

where
   t_i = time of initial maneuver (s)
   a = average acceleration (km/hr/s or mph/s)
   v = average speed of passing vehicle (km/hr or mph)
   m = difference in speed of passed and passing vehicles (km/hr or mph)
   t_2 = time passing vehicle occupies the left lane (s)

The "average" acceleration results when a linear (constant) relationship between acceleration and velocity is assumed. See Equation (11.2).

The design lengths for passing sight distances for various speeds and the corresponding individual values of d_1, d_2, d_3, and d_4 are shown in Exhibit 3-6 (p. 123) and Exhibit 3-7 (p. 124) in the Green Book.

Stopping sight distances are usually sufficient to allow drivers to safely avoid objects in the roadway. However, there are many "busy" locations where longer sight distances may be desirable. In such cases, *decision sight distance* requirements should be considered to provide the greater sight distances that drivers need. Examples of critical locations where decision sight distance considerations apply are

1. Interchanges, particularly where a "left" exit is located

2. Unusual/complex intersection

3. Changes in cross section, such as those at toll plazas and lane drops

4. Locations where significant "visual noise," such as commercial signs, competes for the driver's attention

5. Locations where unusual or expected maneuvers are required

Exhibit 3-3 (p. 116) in the Green Book contains suggested decision sight distances for various conditions. Because decision sight distance give drivers sufficient length to maneuver their vehicles, process additional information, and adjust their speed, its values are substantially greater than stopping sight distance.

Sight distances can be determined in the design phase by measuring both passing and stopping sight distances on roadway plan and profile sheets. Exhibit 3-8 (p. 129) in the Green Book illustrates this procedure for scaling and recording sight distances on plans.

Sight distance depends on the driver's eye height, the height of the object on the road, and the height of obstructions along the roadside. The 2001 Green Book uses the following sight distance measurement criteria:

Driver eye height = 1080 mm (3.5 ft)

Object height for braking = 600 mm (2.0 ft)

Object height for passing = 1800 mm (3.5 ft) (*Note*: This is also the assumed height of approaching vehicles in at-grade intersection sight distances.)

Horizontal Alignment

The primary element of horizontal alignment is horizontal curvature. The minimum radius of horizontal circular curves is determined by the dynamics of vehicle operation and sight distance requirements.

The forces on a vehicle moving on a horizontal curve are shown in Figure 11.4. The tangent of the angle of inclination of the roadway is known as the rate of superelevation, e. The minimum radius of curve necessary for the vehicle to remain in equilibrium with respect to the incline is given by

$$R = v^2/g(e + f_s) \qquad \text{(11.20)}$$

where
  R = radius of curve
  v = vehicle speed
  g = acceleration due to gravity
  e = superelevation rate
  f_s = coefficient of side friction

If g is taken as 9.8 m/s^2, and v is expressed in km/hr, Equation (11.19) can be restated in the following, more common form:

$$R = v^2/127(e + f_s) \qquad \text{(11.21a)}$$

In U.S. Customary units,

$$R = v^2/15(e + f_s) \qquad \text{(11.21b)}$$

Representative values for e and f_s are presented in Exhibit 3-14 (p. 145) in the Green Book.

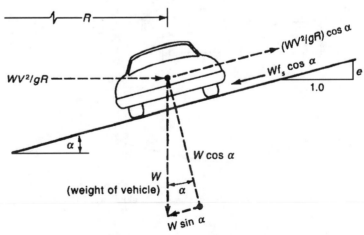

Figure 11.4 Forces on vehicle on horizontal curve

Example **11.3**

A horizontal curve has a radius of 237 m. Determine the maximum permissible speed on the curve (assume $e = 0.08$, and $f_s = 0.14$). If the curve is to be improved to a design speed of 110 km/hr, the minimum radius of curvature is most nearly (assume $e = 0.08$, $f_s = 0.10$):

(a) 50 m

(b) 65 m

(c) 200 m

(d) 525 m

(e) 750 m

Solution

From Equation (11.21),

$$V = [R \times 127(e + f_s)]^{1/2} = [237 \times 127(0.08 + 0.14)]^{1/2} \approx 80 \text{ km/hr}$$

$$R = 110^2/127(0.08 + 0.10) = 530 \text{ m for 110 km/hr design speed.}$$

The answer is (d).

Vertical Alignment

The vertical alignment of the highway refers to its design in the profile view. Vertical curves are parabolic in form to provide a smooth transition between tangent (straight) sections and the curve. when the profile goes from a positive slope to a negative slope, from a positive slope to a flatter positive slope, or from a negative slope to a steeper negative slope, the curve is referred to as a *crest vertical curve*. When the slope goes from a negative slope to a positive slope, from a negative slope to a flatter negative slope, or from a positive slope to a steeper positive slope, the curve is referred to as a *sag vertical curve*. Figure 11.5 illustrates the basic types of vertical curves that exist.

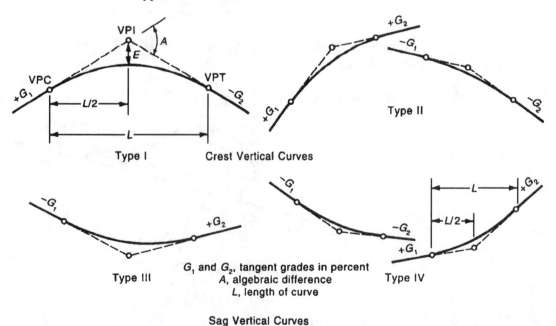

Figure 11.5 Types of vertical curves

The primary design controls for vertical curves are grade and sight distance requirements. Passenger cars, except for some compact and subcompact models, can easily negotiate upgrades as steep as 4 to 5 percent without appreciable speed loss. Trucks and recreational vehicles, on the other hand, cannot negotiate steep upgrades without speed loss, particularly when the length of the grade extends 150 to 300 meters. Exhibits 3-59 through 3-61 (pp. 237–240) in the Green Book illustrate the effect of upgrades on truck and recreational vehicle deceleration and of upgrades and downgrades on truck acceleration. Exhibit 3-63 (p. 245) in the Green Book shows the length of grade that will cause a "representative" truck entering a grade at 110 km/hr (70 mph) to reduce its speed by various amounts below the average running speed of all traffic. Exhibit 3-63 from the Green Book is shown in Figure 11.6. Exhibit 3-64 (p. 246) is a similar set of charts for recreational vehicles.

Consider a 4 percent grade and a 10 km/hr maximum design speed reduction from 110 km/hr to 100 km/hr. Figure 11.6 indicates that the critical (maximum) length of grade would be approximately 230 m. When the length of critical grade is exceeded, the designer should consider adding an uphill lane ("climbing lane") for slow-moving vehicles.

Maximum grades of about 5 percent are appropriate for a 110 km/hr (70 mph) design speed, and steeper grades in the range of 7 to 12 percent are permissible for a design speed of 50 km/hr (30 mph). Maximum grades for the various highway classifications are addressed later in this chapter.

From the motorist's viewpoint, a vertical curve should be pleasing in appearance and comfortable when negotiated at legal highway speed. The rate of change of grade is an important factor that determines the comfort level. This rate of change is equal to the algebraic difference between intersecting grades divided by the length of the curve. The reciprocal of this relationship, K, is the horizontal distance necessary to effect a 1 percent change in grade and is therefore a measure of curvature:

$$K = L/A \qquad\qquad (11.22)$$

where
   K = rate of vertical curvature (m/percent of A or ft/percent of A)
   A = algebraic difference in grades (percent)
   L = length of vertical curve (m or ft).

The value of K is very useful in designing vertical curves. It is used in establishing design criteria and in determining the location of the zero slope on the curve (top-of-crest vertical curves and bottom-of-sag vertical curves). The location of the zero slope of any curve is K times the approach gradient.

The desired minimum length of a crest vertical curve depends on whether stopping sight distance or passing sight distance is selected as the design criterion. As a minimum, the vertical curve length should be sufficient to provide the stopping sight distance required for the design speed. When it is necessary to provide passing opportunities, the vertical curve length should be sufficient to accommodate passing sight distance for the design speed.

The equations for minimum length of vertical curve are based on the properties of the parabola. Two conditions exist for the minimum length of vertical curves: (1) the sight distance is greater than the length of the curve, and (2) the sight distance

Metric

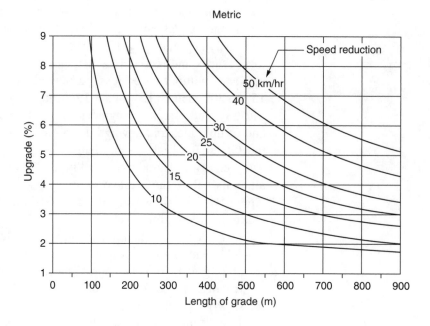

U.S. Customary

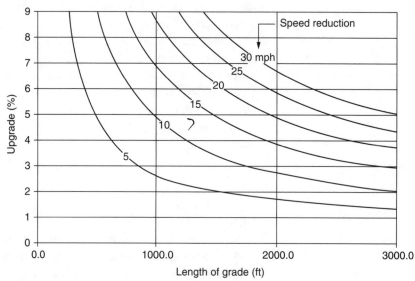

Figure 11.6 Critical lengths of grade for design, assumed typical heavy truck of 120 kg/kW (200 lb/hp), entering speed = 110 km/hr (70 mpm) [*Source:* AASHTO (2001)].

is less than the length of the curve. The equations for determining minimum lengths for various types of vertical curves are

Minimum length of crest vertical curves with $S < L$:

$$L = (AS^2)/658 \quad \text{[for stopping sight distance (m)]} \qquad \textbf{(11.23a)}$$

$$L = (AS^2)/2158 \quad \text{[for stopping sight distance (ft)]} \qquad \textbf{(11.23b)}$$

$$L = (AS^2)/864 \quad \text{[for passing sight distance (m)]} \qquad \textbf{(11.24a)}$$

$$L = (AS^2)/2800 \quad \text{[for passing sight distance (ft)]} \qquad \textbf{(11.24b)}$$

Minimum length of crest vertical curves with $S > L$:

$$L = 2S - 658/A \quad \text{[for stopping sight distance (m)]} \quad \textbf{(11.25a)}$$
$$L = 2S - 2158/A \quad \text{[for stopping sight distance (ft)]} \quad \textbf{(11.25b)}$$
$$L = 2S - 864/A \quad \text{[for passing sight distance (m)]} \quad \textbf{(11.26a)}$$
$$L = 2S - 2800/A \quad \text{[for passing sight distance (ft)]} \quad \textbf{(11.26b)}$$

Minimum length of sag vertical curves with $S < L$:

$$L = AS^2/(120 + 3.5S) \quad \text{(for } L \text{ in m)} \quad \textbf{(11.27a)}$$
$$L = AS^2/(400 + 3.5S) \quad \text{(for } L \text{ in ft)} \quad \textbf{(11.27b)}$$

Minimum length of sag vertical curves with $S > L$:

$$L = 2S - (120 + 3.5S)/A \quad \text{(for } L \text{ in m)} \quad \textbf{(11.28a)}$$
$$L = 2S - (400 + 3.5S)/A \quad \text{(for } L \text{ in ft)} \quad \textbf{(11.28b)}$$

where
  L = minimum length of vertical curve (m or ft)
  A = algebraic difference in grades (percent)
  S = sight distance required (m or ft)

The value of S for sag vertical curves is actually "headlight sight distance," which is assumed to be the same as stopping sight distance.

The Green Book provides various charts and tables of recommended design values for vertical curves based on the expression presented above. [See Exhibits 3-75 through 3-79 (pp. 273–280) in the Green Book.]

Example 11.4

A crest vertical curve joins a +2 percent grade with a −2 percent grade on a section of highway with a 50 mph design speed. If the PIEV time is 2.5 s, the minimum length of vertical curve to provide stopping sight distance is most nearly:

(a) 100 ft

(b) 200 ft

(c) 300 ft

(d) 400 ft

(e) 500 ft

Solution

The average grade through the curve is zero. From Equation (11.13b), the required stopping sight distance is

$$d_s = 1.47vt + \frac{V^2}{30[(a/32.2) \pm G]} = 1.47(50)(2.5) + \frac{50^2}{30[(11.2/32.2) + 0]} = 423 \text{ ft}$$

Assuming $S < L$, from Equation (11.23b), the minimum length of vertical curve is

$$L = AS^2/2158 = 4(423^2)/2158 = 331.66 \text{ ft}$$

Since $423 > 331.66$, we use Equation (11.25b):

$$L = 2S - 2158/A = 2(423) - 2158/4 = 306.5 \text{ ft}$$

The answer is (c).

Traffic Flow Characteristics

The characteristics of traffic flows in the highway system are the result of interactions between drivers, vehicles, the roadway, and traffic control devices. The characteristics of traffic may be described by three general parameters: volume or rate of flow, speed, and density. This section presents a review of basic traffic stream characteristics. An understanding of these basic characteristics is essential in the design, operation, and management of streets and highways.

Traffic volume is the number of vehicles that pass a point on a highway during a specified time interval. Volumes can be expressed in daily or hourly volumes or in terms of subhourly rates of flow. There are four commonly used measures of daily volume:

1. *Average annual daily traffic* (AADT) is the average 24-hour traffic volume at a specific location over a full year (365 days).

2. *Average annual weekday traffic* (AAWT) is the average 24-hour traffic volume occurring on weekdays at a specific location over a full year.

3. *Average daily traffic* (ADT) is basically an estimate of AADT based on a time period less than a full year.

4. *Average weekday traffic* (AWT) is an estimate of AAWT based on a time period less than a full year.

Daily traffic volumes are expressed in terms of vehicles per day (vpd) and generally are not differentiated by direction of travel or lane.

Because traffic volumes vary considerably by time of day, daily volumes are not particularly useful in highway design. A highway designed on the basic of average daily traffic volumes is very likely to be underdesigned in terms of the traffic volumes occurring during rush hours. The traffic volume during the single hour of the day that has the highest hourly volume (the "peak-hour volume") is generally of the greatest interest to engineers in design and operational analysis of highways. The peak-hour volume is generally expressed as a directional volume.

In design, peak hourly volumes are sometimes estimated from daily volumes from the following equation:

$$\text{DDHV} = \text{AADT} \times K \times D \qquad\qquad (11.29)$$

where
   DDHV = directional design hour volume (veh/hr)
   AADT = average annual daily traffic (veh/day)
      K = proportion of daily traffic occurring in the peak hour
      D = proportion of peak hour traffic traveling in the peak direction of travel

Just as a highway designed on the basis of average daily traffic is likely to be underdesigned, one designed on the basis of peak hour traffic is likely to be over-designed in terms of its use during non-peak time periods. For design purposes, K in Equation (11.29) often represents the proportion of AADT occurring during the thirtieth highest hour of the year on rural highways, and the fiftieth highest hour of the year on urban highways. (See Exhibit 2-28 (p. 60) and the accompanying discussion in the Green Book.)

Traffic volumes can also exhibit considerable variation within a given hour. Traffic volumes for periods of time less than one hour (typically measured in 15-minute increments) are expressed as "equivalent hourly rates of flow." The relationship between hourly volume and the maximum 15-minute rate of flow within the hour is defined as the *peak-hour factor* (PHF)

$$\text{PHF} = V_h / (4V_{15}) \tag{11.30}$$

where

V_h = hourly volume (veh/hr)
V_{15} = maximum 15-minute rate of vehicle flow within the hour

Basically, the PHF represents the ratio of observed hourly traffic to what could have been observed had the peak 15-minute flow rate been constant across the entire hour. The PHF is a measure of the uniformity of traffic demand within a one-hour period.

The second major traffic stream parameter is speed. The traffic stream consists of a distribution of individual vehicle speeds from which average or typical values can be calculated to represent the entire traffic stream. Two different measures of average speed are commonly used. *Time mean speed* is the average speed of all vehicles passing a point on the highway over a given time period. *Space mean speed* is the average speed obtained by measuring the instantaneous speeds of all vehicles on a section of roadway. Both of these measures can be calculated from a series of measured travel times over a measured distance from the following equations:

$$\mu_t = [\Sigma(d/t_i)]/n \tag{11.31}$$

$$\mu_s = (nd)/\Sigma t_i \tag{11.32}$$

where

μ_t = time mean speed (m/s or km/hr)
μ_s = space mean speed (m/s or km/hr)
d = distance traversed (m or km)
n = number of travel times observed
t_i = travel time of ith vehicle (s or hr)

Because the space mean speed gives more weight to slower vehicles than time mean speed does, it results in a lower average speed. The relationship between these two mean speeds is approximately

$$\mu_t = \mu_s + \sigma_s^2/\mu_s \tag{11.33}$$

where σ_s^2 = the variance of the space speed distribution.

Example **11.5**

The following travel times were observed for four vehicles traversing a 1.6 km segment of highway.

Vehicle	Time (min)
1	1.6
2	1.2
3	1.5
4	1.7

The space and time mean speeds of these vehicles are approximately:

(a) $\mu_s = 63.8$ mph, $\mu_t = 60.5$ mph

(b) $\mu_s = 64.2$ mph, $\mu_t = 65.4$ mph

(c) $\mu_s = 63.8$ mph, $\mu_t = 69.2$ mph

(d) $\mu_s = 65.4$ mph, $\mu_t = 62.4$ mph

(e) $\mu_s = 61.6$ mph, $\mu_t = 65.4$ mph

Solution

From Equation (11.32), the space mean speed is $\mu_s = (nd)/\Sigma t_i = 4(1.6)/(1.6 + 1.2 + 1.5 + 1.7) = 1.07$ km/min = 64.2 km/hr.

From Equation (11.31), the time mean speed is $\mu_t = \Sigma(d/t_i)/n = [(1.6/1.6) + (1.6/1.2) + (1.6/1.5)] + (1.6/1.7)]/4 = 1.09$ km/min = 65.4 km/hr.

The correct answer is (b).

The third measure of traffic stream conditions, density (sometimes referred to as concentration), is the number of vehicles traveling over a unit length of highway at a given time. Density is generally expressed in vehicles per km (vehicles per mile) or vehicles per km per lane (vehicles per mile per lane).

The general equation relating flow, density, and speed is

$$q = k\mu_s \tag{11.34}$$

where

q = rate of flow (veh/hr)
μ_s = space mean speed (km/hr or mph)
k = density (veh/km or veh/mi)

These three parameters (flow, speed and density) are macroscopic measures in that they apply to the traffic stream as a whole. *Spacing* and *headway*, on the other hand, are microscopic measures because they apply to individual vehicles within the traffic stream. Spacing (or *space headway*) is the distance between vehicles in a traffic stream, and headway (or *time headway*) is the time between successive vehicles as they pass a reference point along the roadway. Some important relationships between these macroscopic and microscopic parameters are shown below:

$$\mu_s = qd \tag{11.35}$$

$$d = (1/k) \tag{11.36}$$

$$k = qt_t \tag{11.37}$$

$$d = \mu_s h \tag{11.38}$$

$$h = t_t d \tag{11.39}$$

where
  d = average space headway
  t_t = average travel time per unit distance
  h = average time headway

The relationship between density and flow is commonly referred to as the "fundamental diagram of traffic flow." This relationship, and the corresponding speed-density and speed-volume relationships, is shown in Figure 11.7. While there is some controversy concerning the exact shapes of the curves, the following theory is generally accepted in support of these relationship (Garber and Hoel, 1997).

1. When density is zero, the flow is also zero.

2. As density increases, the flow also increases up to capacity; as density increases beyond critical density, flow decreases.

3. When density reaches its maximum, referred to as jam density (k_j), the flow is zero.

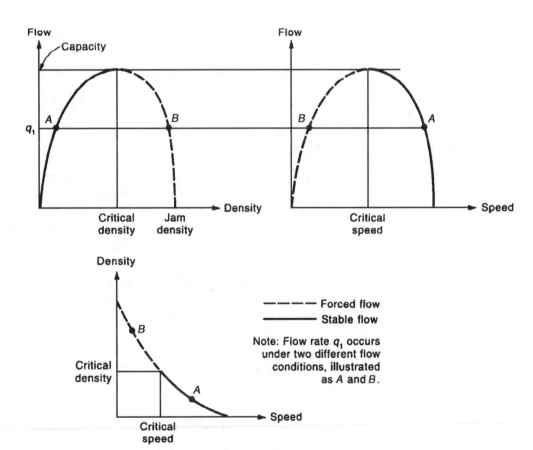

Figure 11.7 Relationships among speed, density and rate of flow

The peak of the speed-flow and density-flow curves represents the maximum possible rate of flow, or capacity. The speed and density at this point are called the critical speed and critical density. At these critical points, flow becomes forced or unstable; any disruption in the traffic stream can result in sudden changes in traffic flow—from relatively free-flow conditions to stop-and-go conditions and back to free-flow conditions again.

Note in Figure 11.7 that flow rates less than capacity can occur under two different conditions: (1) high-speed and low-density or free-flow conditions, and (2) low-speed and high-density or forced-flow conditions. As a result, volume is not a particularly good measure of the state of the traffic stream. Speed and density, on the other hand, both uniquely describe the state of the traffic stream and are good measures of the quality of operations (Roess et al., 2004).

Various macroscopic (flow-density) and microscopic (spacing/headway-speed) approaches have been used to describe traffic flow. The most commonly used macroscopic models are the Greenshields and Greenberg models. The Greenshields model is based on an assumed linear relationship between speed and density, whereas Greenberg theorized a logarithmic speed-density relationship. Greenshields hypothesized the following linear relationship between and density:

$$\mu_s = \mu_f - (\mu_f/k_j)k \tag{11.40}$$

where μ_f = mean free speed (maximum speed as flow tends to zero). The corresponding relationships for speed and flow, and flow and density are

$$\mu_s^2 = \mu_f\mu_s - (\mu_f/k_j)q \tag{11.41}$$

$$q = \mu_f k - (\mu_f/k_j)k^2 \tag{11.42}$$

The maximum flow for the Greenshields model is

$$q_{max} = (k_j\mu_f)/4 \tag{11.43}$$

STATISTICAL METHODS

Many of the processes of interest to the transportation engineer exhibit a great deal of natural variability and uncertainty. The traffic stream, for example, does not have a single characteristic speed but a "distribution" of individual vehicle speeds. The transportation engineer needs a working knowledge of basic statistical procedures to account for the variability inherent in this "distribution of speeds" and to develop average or typical values that may be used to characterize the speed of the traffic stream as a whole. This section presents a review of some key statistical concepts and methods commonly used in transportation engineering. The review focuses on the following aspects of statistics and probability: descriptive statistics, probability, confidence bounds, and hypothesis testing.

The reader should consult a basic statistics textbook for additional background. [The *Handbook of Statistical Methods for Engineers and Scientists* (Wadsworth, 1990) is suggested.]

Descriptive Statistics

Descriptive statistics is concerned with recording and summarizing data. One way of summarizing data is to compute a value about which the data are centered.

Three commonly used *measures of central tendency* are the mean, the mode, and the median. The mean is computed as

$$\bar{x} = (1/n)\Sigma x_i \qquad\qquad (11.44)$$

where n is the sample size (number of observations), x_i are the individual observation of x. The mode is simply the most frequently occurring value in the data set, and the median is the middle number (50th percentile) in an ordered set of numbers.

In addition to summarizing a data set in terms of a representative value such as its mean, median, or mode, we should also be concerned about the amount of variability (or spread) in the data. The dispersion of a set of observations is most often measured in terms of the deviations of the observations from their mean, as calculated from the following equation:

$$s^2 = (1/n-1)\Sigma(x_i - \bar{x})^2 \qquad\qquad (11.45)$$

where s^2 = sample variance of x. The square root of the variance is called the standard deviation. To facilitate calculator computations, Equation (11.45) can be manipulated into the following form:

$$s^2 = (1/n-1)\Sigma(x_i)^2 - (n/n-1)(\bar{x})^2 \qquad\qquad (11.46)$$

The mean is also a random variable with a standard deviation which can be calculated from s according to the following formula

$$s_{\bar{x}} = s/(n)^{1/2} \qquad\qquad (11.47)$$

where $s_{\bar{x}}$ = the standard deviation of the mean (sometimes called the *standard error of the mean*).

At this point, a few comments on notation and terminology are in order. In the vocabulary of the statistician, the terms *population, sample, statistic*, and *parameter* have very important distinctions. Population refers to the largest collection of persons, places, or things—including measurements—in which we have an interest; for example, the ages of all civil engineers in this country. A sample is a part or subset of a population, such as the ages of civil engineers in a particular city or firm. A parameter is a measure that describes a population, such as the population mean or population variance. Population parameters are generally unknown. A statistic is a measure computed from sample data, such as a sample mean. The population variance and mean are denoted by σ^2 and μ, respectively. The corresponding measures of a sample are s^2 and $\bar{x}$. Sample data (statistics) are used to estimate population parameters.

Probability

Probability is a measure that describes the likelihood that an event will occur. Probability is a dimensionless number that ranges from 0 (meaning the event cannot occur) to 1 (meaning the event is certain to occur). The probability of occurrence of an event, A, is simply the number of ways A may occur divided by the total number of possible outcomes of the experiment under consideration.

$$P(A) = n_A/N \qquad\qquad (11.48)$$

where

P(A) = probability event A will occur

n_A = number of ways A can occur

N = total number of possible outcomes

For example, the probability of being dealt an ace from a newly shuffled deck of 52 cards is 4 (number of aces in the deck) divided by 52 (total number of possible outcomes), or 0.08.

In situations involving the probability of the occurrence of multiple events, the following rules apply.

Rule 1. Addition rule for mutually exclusive events (A or B can occur, but not simultaneously):

$$P(A \text{ or } B) = P(A) + P(B) \tag{11.49}$$

Rule 2. Multiplication rule for independent events (two events could both occur, but the occurrence of one does not influence the occurrence of the other):

$$P(A \text{ and } B) = P(A)P(B) \tag{11.50}$$

Rule 3. General addition rule (A or B can occur, but outcomes are not necessarily mutually exclusive):

$$P(A \text{ or } B) = P(A) + P(B) - P(A \text{ and } B) \tag{11.51}$$

Rule 4. General multiplication rule (probability of two events occurring when they are not independent, i.e., the probability of one event occurring differs depending on whether the other has occurred):

$$P(A \text{ and } B) = P(A)P(B|A) \tag{11.52}$$

where $P(B|A)$ is read as "the probability of B given the occurrence of A."

The basic rules of probability outlined above assume that the distribution of the values of the variables in question is known. Usually, this is not the case, and a procedure for computing probabilities when dealing with unknown populations is needed. That is, it would be very useful to be able to write mathematical equations, graphs, or tables to describe the population in question. A number of *theoretical distributions* are often used to describe the possible values of a variable and the probability that each value will occur. The theoretical distributions most commonly used in transportation engineering are (1) the normal distribution, (2) the poisson distribution, (3) the exponential distribution, and (4) the chi-square distribution. [The chi-square distribution is commonly used in statistical tests (goodness-of-fit tests) rather than in traffic models directly. The exponential distribution is used primarily in microscopic traffic flow models. Therefore, the discussion in the section is limited to the normal and Poisson distributions.]

The Normal Distribution

The theoretical distribution most frequently used by engineers and scientists in the normal distribution. Many variables such as heights, test scores, and linear dimensions in general conform to a normal (or approximately normal) distribution. Many non-normal distributions can be transformed to induce normality (for example, by taking the square root or logarithm of the variable). Even if the distribution in the subject population is far from normal, the distribution of sample means tends to become normal in a sufficiently large number of repeated random samples. This is the single most important reason for the use of the normal distribution.

The normal distribution is a symmetric, continuous distribution. The normal "density function" is written as

$$f(x) = \left[1/(\sigma\sqrt{2\pi})\exp{-(x-\mu)^2/(2\sigma^2)} \right] \tag{11.53}$$

where
  σ = standard deviation of x
  π = 3.1416...
  μ = the mean of x

The probability distribution functions for continuous distribution are often referred to as "density functions." Probability functions for discrete distributions are referred to as "mass functions."

The probability of an outcome falling in a specified range is given by the corresponding area under the density function—integrating the density function between the desired limits. As can be seen from Equation (11.53), the normal distribution is actually a family of distributions, with each member having unique values of μ and σ. To facilitate tabulation of areas under the normal curve, that is, probabilities, the "standard" normal curve is used. The standard normal curve has mean = 0, standard deviation = 1.0, and total area = 1.0. Any normal distribution can be transformed to the standard normal distribution of the random variable Z by the following equation:

$$Z = (x-\mu)/\sigma \tag{11.54}$$

where Z is the transformed value of x (Z is a measure of the deviation from the mean in units of standard deviations).

Tabulations of the area under the cumulative standard normal distribution can be found in standard statistics textbooks. Table 11.1 summarizes some important probabilities in the standard normal distribution. For example, approximately 95 percent of the area under the curve lies within ±2.0 standard deviations from the mean. Thus, we could expect a normally distributed variable to be within this range about 95 percent of the time.

Table 11.1 Area under the standard normal curve

Boundaries	Area Between Boundaries
$\mu \pm 0.5\sigma$	0.383
$\mu \pm 1.0\sigma$	0.683
$\mu \pm 1.5\sigma$	0.866
$\mu \pm 2.0\sigma$	0.954
$\mu \pm 2.5\sigma$	0.988
$\mu \pm 3.0\sigma$	0.977
$\mu \pm 3.5\sigma$	0.999

The Poisson Distribution

The second theoretical distribution that has many useful applications in transportation engineering is the Poisson distribution. The Poisson distribution is useful in describing the occurrence of discrete random events, such as vehicle arrivals at an intersection and the occurrence of certain types of accidents. The probability of x events occurring in time t is given by the following expression:

$$P(x) = (e^{-m}m^x)/x! \qquad (11.55)$$

where
  e = base of the natural logarithm
  m = mean frequency of occurrence, or total vehicles observed divided by total observations, or number of time periods
  $!$ = factorial operator (for example, $3! = 3 \times 2 \times 1 = 6$)

The terms of the Poisson distribution may be summed to give the probability of fewer than or more than x events per time period. If, for example, the traffic engineer is interested in the probability of $\leq x$ cars arriving at an intersection, it may be expressed as

$$P(\leq x) = \Sigma\ [(m^i e^{-m})/i!], \quad \text{for } i = 0, 1, \ldots, x \qquad (11.56)$$

For the case of fewer than x,

$$P(<x) = \Sigma\ [(m^i e^{-m})/i!], \quad \text{for } i = 0, 1, \ldots, x-1 \qquad (11.57)$$

For the case of more than x,

$$P(>x) = 1 - \Sigma\ [(m^i e^{-m})/i!, \quad \text{for } i = 0, 1, \ldots, x \qquad (11.58)$$

For the case of x or more,

$$P(\geq x) = 1 - \Sigma\ [(m^i e^{-m})/i!], \quad \text{for } i = 0, 1, \ldots, x-1 \qquad (11.59)$$

or

$$P(\geq x) = \Sigma\ [(m^i e^{-m})/i!], \quad \text{for } i = x, x+1, \ldots, \infty \qquad (11.60)$$

For the case of at least x but not more than y,

$$P(x \leq i \leq y) = \Sigma\ [(m^i e^{-m})/i!], \quad \text{for } i = x, \ldots, y \qquad (11.61)$$

It should be noted that for the Poisson distribution, the mean and variance are equal. Therefore, when the ratio of the variance to the mean is markedly different from 1.0, this is an indication that the observed data do not follow a Poisson distribution.

Tabulated values of the Poisson distribution can be found in most standard statistics textbooks.

Confidence Bounds

Referring to Table 11.1, it can be seen that in a normal distribution there is a probability of approximately 0.95 that an outcome will fall within about two standard deviations of the mean. More precisely, there is a probability of 0.95 that an outcome will lie within 1.96 standard deviations of the mean. That is,

$$P(-1.96 \leq Z \leq +1.96) = 0.95 \tag{11.62}$$

Recall that any variable x can be expressed in "standard form" by changing from x to $(x - \mu)/\sigma$. For $\bar{x}$ (the sample mean), the corresponding expression is

$$Z = (\bar{x} - \mu)/\left(\sigma/\sqrt{n}\right) \tag{11.63}$$

where $\sigma/\sqrt{n}$ is the standard error of the mean.

From Equation (11.61) it follows that

$$P\left[\bar{x} - \left(1.96\sigma/\sqrt{n}\right) \leq \mu \leq \bar{x} + \left(1.96\sigma/\sqrt{n}\right)\right] = 0.95 \tag{11.64}$$

Equation (11.64) can be read as "the probability that the true (population) mean lies in the interval $\bar{x} - (1.96\, \sigma/\sqrt{n})$ and $\bar{x} + (1.96\, \sigma/\sqrt{n})$ is 0.95." This is referred to as a *confidence bound*, or confidence interval, on the estimate of the true mean. Other confidence intervals can be constructed by replacing 1.96 with the Z-score corresponding to the desired confidence probability. The general expression for confidence limits on $\bar{x}$ is

$$\text{CL} = \bar{x} \pm Z\left(s/\sqrt{n}\right) \tag{11.65}$$

The general expression for the probability of a value of x greater, or less, than the mean is

$$x = \bar{x} \pm Zs \tag{11.66}$$

In the preceding discussion, the Z values of the standard normal distribution are—strictly speaking—applicable only when the sample size is "large" ($n > 30$). For small samples ($n < 30$) values from the "t-distribution" should be used in place of Z. Tabulated t values can be found in most standard statistics textbooks.

If the required confidence bound (or tolerable error) is specified, the sample size required to estimate the mean with this confidence can be estimated by solving the following expression for n:

$$1.96\left(\sigma/\sqrt{n}\right) \leq e \tag{11.67}$$

and

$$n = (1.96s)^2/e^2 \tag{11.68}$$

where $e = $ the desired tolerance (error).

Hypothesis Testing

Hypothesis testing belongs to that branch of statistics known as inferential statistics and is the basis for statistical decision making. To test a hypothesis is to make a decision regarding the reasonableness of the results obtained from statistical analyses.

In statistics there are two hypotheses: the *null hypothesis* (H_0), and the *alternative hypothesis* (H_1). The test procedure uses sample data to make one of two statistical decisions: (1) reject the null hypothesis (as false), or (2) *not* reject the null hypothesis. The test is performed on the null hypothesis. When we reject the null hypothesis, we accept the alternative hypothesis as being true. In making this decision, we incur two possible types of error: (1) Type 1 error (concluding the hypothesis is false when it is really true), and (2) Type II error (concluding the hypothesis is true when it is really false). These errors are commonly referred to as α and β, respectively (Daniel, 1978). The basic steps in hypothesis testing are outlined below.

Step 1: State the statistical hypotheses. If the parameters of interest are the means of two populations, the following hypotheses could be considered:

$$H_0 : \mu_1 = \mu_2, \qquad H_1 : \mu_1 \neq \mu_2$$
$$H_0 : \mu_1 \leq \mu_2, \qquad H_1 : \mu_1 > \mu_2$$
$$H_0 : \mu_1 \geq \mu_2, \qquad H_1 : \mu_1 < \mu_2$$

The first case is an example of a "two-sided" or "two-tailed" hypothesis. In this case, we are asking, "Can we conclude that the two populations have different means?" If the issue is which population has the larger mean, then the second or third pair of statements would be appropriate. These represents "one-sided" or "one-tailed" hypotheses. In hypothesis testing, the alternative hypothesis is the statement of what we expect to be able to conclude. If the question is whether population 1 has a larger mean than population 2, then H_0: $\mu_1 \leq \mu_2$ would be tested. If this H_0 can be rejected, we accept H_1: $\mu_1 > \mu_2$ as true.

Step 2: Calculate the test statistics. To test the hypothesis, the analyst selects an appropriate test statistics and specifies its distribution when H_0 is true; that is, the test procedure is based on the underlying distribution of the statistics used to estimate the parameters in question. For example, *testing the significance of the difference between means from two independent samples* may be based on the *t* statistic,

$$t = (\bar{x}_1 - \bar{x}_2) \Big/ \left[s_p^2 (1/n_1 + 1/n_2) \right]^{1/2} \qquad \textbf{(11.69)}$$

where $\bar{x}_1$, $\bar{x}_2$ and n_1, n_2 refer to the means and sample sizes of the two groups, and s_p^2 is obtained by pooling the two sample variances s_1^2 and s_2^2:

$$s_p^2 = \left[(n_1 - 1)s_1^2 + (n_2 - 1)s_2^2 \right] / (n_1 + n_2 - 2) \qquad \textbf{(11.70)}$$

Step 3: State the "decision rule." (The decision rule is usually formulated even prior to stating the statistical hypotheses. Its location in the sequence of steps presented here is largely illustrative.) The issue here is to determine whether the magnitude of the test statistic computed from sample data in step 2 is sufficiently extreme (either too large or too small) to justify rejecting H_0. Two basic approaches are commonly used to formulate the decision rule. In the first, the analyst rejects H_0 if the probability of obtaining a value of the test statistic of a given or more extreme value is equal to or less than some small number α (referred to as the level of significance). Commonly used values for α are 0.10, 0.05, or 0.01. The second approach involves stating the decision rule in terms of critical values of the test statistic. Because critical values are a function of the level of significance, the two approaches are equivalent. Tabulated values for α and the corresponding critical values for commonly used probability distribution can be found in many statistics textbooks.

Step 4: Apply the decision rule. If the probability of obtaining the computed or a larger value of the test statistic is $\leq \alpha$, reject H_0 and conclude that H_1 is true.

Alternatively, if the computed value of the test statistic is greater than the critical value for the stated level of significance, reject H_0 and conclude that H_1 is true.

A summary of test statistics for use in several other important hypothesis testing situations is presented below.

Testing the difference between an observed and a hypothesized mean:

$$Z = (\bar{x} - \mu_0)/\left(\sigma/\sqrt{n}\right) \tag{11.71}$$

$$t = (\bar{x} - \mu_0)/\left(s/\sqrt{n}\right) \tag{11.72}$$

where $\bar{x}$ is the observed mean, and μ_0 is the value of the hypothesized mean, such as a known population mean. The test statistic in this case is compared with values in the standard normal distribution or the t-distribution, depending upon the size of n.

Tests concerning population variances:

$$\chi^2 = (n-1)s^2/\sigma_0^2 \tag{11.73}$$

$$F = s_1^2/s_2^2 \tag{11.74}$$

Equation (11.73) tests the difference between a hypothesized population variance (σ_0^2) and a sample variance (s^2) using the chi-square distribution (χ^2). Equation (11.74) uses values from an F distribution to determine whether two populations have equal variances. Values of the chi-square and F distribution can be found in standard statistics textbooks.

TRAFFIC ENGINEERING STUDIES

Transportation/traffic engineering studies tend to fall into four basic categories (Roess et al., 2004): (1) physical inventories, such as roadway characteristics and conditions, control devices, and parking spaces; (2) population characteristics, such as road-user and vehicle-population data; (3) measurement of operational parameters, such as volume, speed, and density; and (4) special studies such as accident and parking studies, and trip generation/traffic impact studies. The review in this section is limited to the following four principal classes of traffic engineering studies: volume studies, speed studies, accident studies, and traffic impact studies.

Additional information on designing and conducting traffic engineering studies can be found in the ITE *Manual of Transportation Engineering Studies* (Robertson, 2000).

Volume Studies

Traffic volume studies provide information on the number of vehicles that pass a point on the roadway during a specified period of time. As discussed in the section "Traffic Flow Characteristics," this time period can range from as little as 15 minutes for determining the peak-hour factor to as much as a full year (AADT). The data may be collected by direction of movement, by lane, and by vehicle classification, weight, and occupancy levels.

To estimate certain traffic volume parameters, such as AADT, it is necessary to collect volume data on a continuous basis. However, it is not feasible to continuously monitor traffic volumes on all roads because of the high costs involved.

This problem can be overcome by using data from continuous counts conducted at "representative" highway locations as the basis for developing *expansion factors* to adjust periodic count data to represent annual traffic characteristics. Such adjustments are necessary because traffic volumes exhibit hourly, daily, monthly, and seasonal variations. The periodic counts usually conducted are continuous, control, and coverage counts.

Continuous counts are conducted at permanent count stations using mechanical and/or electronic traffic counting devices. Data from these stations are used to develop factors to expand the data from counts carried out for shorter time periods.

Control counts are conducted on representative samples of each type (functional class) of roadway. Data from these samples are used to develop seasonal and monthly adjustment factors to determine year-round average volumes from short counts.

Coverage counts use the expansion factors determined from control counts to estimate ADT. The standard approach is to divide the study area into zones, carry out at least one 24-hour coverage count in each zone, and then expand the coverage count data to represent area-wide traffic characteristics.

The expansion factors commonly used to adjust periodic traffic volume count data are of the following general form (Garber and Hoel, 1997):

$$F_h = v_{24}/v_h \qquad (11.75)$$

$$F_d = v_w/v_d \qquad (11.76)$$

$$F_m = \text{AADT}/\text{ADT}_m \qquad (11.77)$$

where

F_h = hourly expansion factor
v_{24} = total volume for 24-hr period
v_h = volume for a particular hour
F_d = daily expansion factor
v_w = average total volume for week
v_d = average volume for a particular day
F_m = monthly expansion factor
AADT = average annual daily traffic
ADT_m = ADT for a particular month

The hourly expansion factors (F_h) use data from continuous or control stations to expand counts of duration shorter than 24 hours to 24-hour volumes by multiplying hourly volumes for each hour by F_h for that hour. The average of these products represents the adjusted average hourly volume.

The daily adjustment factors are used to estimate weekly volumes from 24-hours counts by multiplying the 24-hours volume by F_d.

The AADT for a given year can be estimated from the ADT for a particular month by multiplying this ADT by F_m.

As mentioned earlier, it is not feasible to continuously monitor traffic volumes on all roadways. Instead, traffic volumes are "sampled" and expanded to represent the traffic volume "populations" of interest. The size of the sample required to estimate traffic volumes depends on the level of accuracy desired in the resulting estimates. If the traffic sampling locations (count stations) are randomly selected, the minimum number of count locations for a given significance level and allowable error (tolerance) is

$$n = [t^2(s^2/d^2)]/[1 + t^2(1/N)(s^2/d^2)]$$ **(11.78)**

where
- n = minimum number of count locations required
- t = value of t-distribution for desired confidence level
- N = total number of highway segments (links) from which the sample is to be drawn
- s = estimate of the spatial standard deviation of the link volumes
- d = allowable range of error

Speed Studies

The speed characteristics of the traffic stream may be used to established speed limits and no-passing zones, to design geometric alignment, to analyze accident data, and to evaluate the effects of physical roadway improvements. The speed of the traffic stream is typically defined in terms of one or more of the following values: (1) mean speed, (2) median speed, (3) modal speed, (4) the ith percentile speed (such as the 85th percentile speed) and (5) pace speed, which is the 10-km/hr interval that has the largest number of observations.

Speed data are frequently presented in classes, with each class consisting of a range of speeds. The mean and variance for grouped data such as these are computed as follows:

$$\mu = (\Sigma f_i \mu_i)/\Sigma f_i$$ **(11.79)**

$$s^2 = \left[\Sigma f_i \mu_i^2 - (\Sigma f_i \mu_i)^2/\Sigma f_i\right]/\Sigma f_i - 1$$ **(11.80)**

where μ = average speed, f_i = observed frequency of ith speed group, and μ_t = midvalue of the ith speed group.

Sample sizes for speed studies can be computed from Equation (11.68).

Tests of the significance of differences in average speeds are conducted using the methods outlined at the end of the section under "Hypothesis Testing." Additional material regarding speed characteristics of the traffic stream is presented at the end of the section "Highway System Characteristics and Design Controls."

Accident Studies

Because highway design can significantly affect traffic safety, the transportation engineer has a very special responsibility to public safety. The following design elements are particularly important in terms of highway safety (Roess et al., 2004): (1) horizontal and vertical alignment, (2) roadside design, (3) median barriers, and (4) gore areas.

Accidents are normally expressed in terms of an accident rate rather than accident frequency because rates account for differences in traffic volume. Accident rates can be calculated on the basis of injuries, deaths, or property damage as shown below.

$$\text{Rate} = (\text{number of accidents})/\text{exposure}$$ **(11.81)**

where "exposure" is a measure of traffic volumes at an intersection or along a segment of roadway. Accident rates for intersections and for roadway sections, or "links," are computed as follows:

$$R_I = (A \times 10^6)/V_I \tag{11.82}$$

$$R_S = (A \times 10^6)/\text{VMT} \tag{11.83}$$

where

R_I = intersection accident rate (accidents per million vehicles entering the intersection annually)

A = annual number of accidents

V_I = annual traffic entering the intersection

R_S = roadway section accident rate (accidents per million veh-km or veh-mi of travel)

VMT = annual veh-km or veh-mi of travel = AADT $\times$ 365 days/year $\times$ section length in km or mi

Other accident measures include the severity index (SI) and equivalent property damage only (EPDO).

$$\text{SI} = \text{number of fatalities/total number of accidents} \tag{11.84}$$

$$\text{EPDO} = \text{PDO} + (\text{INJ} \times w_I) + (\text{FAT} \times w_F) \tag{11.85}$$

where

PDO = number of property-damage-only accidents

INJ = number of injury accidents

w_I = injury accident weight (cost of injury accidents/cost of PDO accidents)

FAT = number of fatal accidents

w_F = cost of fatal accidents/cost of PDO accidents

The traffic engineer is frequently called upon to identify sites with higher-than-normal numbers of accidents and to design and implement accident reduction measures. One approach to identifying high accident locations is expected value analysis (Garber and Hoel, 1997).

$$\text{EV} = \bar{x} \pm Zs \tag{11.86}$$

where

EV = expected range of accident frequency

$\bar{x}$ = average number of accidents per locations

s = estimated standard deviation of accident frequencies

Z = number of standard deviations corresponding to the required confidence level

Locations with accident frequencies higher than the expected value are considered high accident sites for that specific accident type and should be considered candidates for various accident reduction measures.

Once an accident problem site has been identified, and an improvement has been implemented, the engineer must conduct an evaluation to determine whether or not the improvement has been effective in reducing accidents. In such cases, a before-after analysis is conducted. A procedure commonly used in before-after studies is the test of the significance of differences in means from two independent samples, as described in the previous section. In this procedure, if the absolute value of the difference in the average number of accidents before and after the improvement is $>Zs_p$ (where s_p = the pooled standard deviation of the two samples), then it can be concluded that the average accident rates are significantly different at the confidence level corresponding to Z.

Figure 11.8 shows two other statistical tests (chi-square and Poisson) that can be used to evaluate the significance of accident reduction. The graph is entered with the number of "before" accidents on the x-axis and the percentage reduction in accidents in the "after" period on the y-axis. The chi-square test is more stringent than the Poisson test. When the two are used together, the following conclusions may be reached (Roess et al., 2004): (1) if the test point falls above the chi-square curve, the reduction in accidents may be considered to be significant; (2) if the test point falls between the chi-square and Poisson curves, the reduction may be considered to be significant with reservations; (3) if the test point is below the Poisson curve, the reduction is considered to be not significant.

Example 11.6

Accident statistics from data collected at a local unsignalized intersection show an average of 30 accidents per year. Analyses suggest that the installation of a traffic signal would result in a substantial reduction in the number of accidents at this intersection. The maximum number of accidents in the first year after signal installations that is compatible with the hypothesis that there was a statistically significant reduction in accidents is about

(a) 5

(b) 10

(c) 15

(d) 20

(e) 25

Solution

Referring to Figure 11.8, the critical value for accident reduction is 30 percent for those cases with 30 accidents before installation of the signal. Therefore, the maximum number of accidents consistent with the hypothesis that there was a reduction in accidents is $N = 30 - 0.30(30) = 21$. The answer is (d).

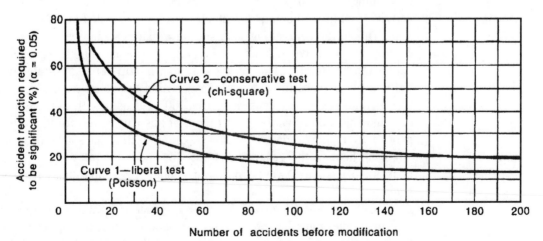

Figure 11.8 Significance tests for accident reduction

Traffic Impact Studies

The days of large-scale, capital-intensive highway construction programs are, in most cases, a thing of the past. The transportation engineer's effort are now focused primarily on managing and improving the efficiency of the existing transportation system. Traffic impact studies are studies that describe, project, and suggest ways of mitigating the traffic and environmental effects from the development of new activities within a geographic area (ITE, 1999). These studies are frequently conducted as part of environmental impact studies (EIS) and/or in response to local ordinances which require such studies as a part of the local site development review process. Traffic impact analyses typically address the following aspects of proposed new developments: (1) roadway operations, (2) site access and on-site circulation, (3) traffic safety, and (4) neighborhood impacts. The major steps in the traffic impact analysis process are described below. The procedure is essentially a scaled-down version of the travel demand modeling process presented earlier in this chapter.

Step 1: Define the analysis period. The year by which the proposed development is to be completed (date of full "build-out") is the most commonly used analysis period.

Step 2: Define the study area. The study area should include all portions of the highway network that may be significantly affected by the proposed development. In general, this includes all major roadways and intersections in the surrounding transportation network.

Step 3: Project description. The project should be described in terms of its potential traffic impacts. The project description should address the following two key elements: (1) the type and intensity of the proposed land use, and (2) the location and number of site access points.

Step 4: Inventory of existing traffic conditions. The following data are generally needed to perform a traffic impact study (ITE, 1999): (1) current traffic volumes, including peak-hour intersection turning movement counts and daily and peak-hour traffic volumes on all streets in the study area, (2) roadway and intersection geometries, (3) traffic signal phasing and timing information, and (4) accident records for study area intersections and major roadway sections.

Step 5: Trip generation. Trip generation analysis consists of estimating the number of trips produced at and attracted to the proposed development. The characteristics of this traffic vary with the type of land use and the intensity of development. The trip generation rates needed in traffic impact studies can be derived from ground counts of vehicular traffic conducted at individual generator sites. This traffic data, along with site information such as floor area, number of employees, and acres of land, can be used to estimate vehicle trips per employee and/or other variables. The principal source of trip generation rates used in site traffic analysis is the Institute of Transportation Engineers' (ITE) *Trip Generation* (2003). The ITE data represent nearly 100 land uses with average vehicles trip rates as a function of various descriptors of intensity of use for the following time periods: average weekday, weekday peak hour of the adjacent street system, weekday peak hour of the generator, twenty-four-hour Saturday trips, Saturday peak hour of the generator, twenty-four-hour Sunday trips, and Sunday peak hour of the generator.

Step 6: Trip distribution. After the site-generated traffic is estimated, the next step is to determine the directional distribution of that traffic. The method used to accomplish this is a function of the size of the development, conditions on the existing street system, and available analytic tools and data. Two common approaches to trip distribution are *market area analysis* and the *gravity model*. The gravity model is commonly used in regional (3C) transportation planning studies to estimate zone-to-zone trip distributions. These are determined on the basis of the distances, in terms of travel time, between traffic zones and the relative attractiveness of each zone in terms of the type and intensity of development. The gravity model is typically one of a set of computerized travel demand models used in the traditional four-step approach to urban transportation planning.

The market area approach to trip distribution is a manual procedure which, though lacking in the appearance of sophistication exhibited by the gravity model, produces reasonable results for most planning applications. The market area is the geographical area from which a high percentage (typically 80 percent) of the site-generated traffic will be drawn. The market area approach consists of the following steps:

Select the appropriate maximum trip length for the proposed development. This average trip length can be obtained from local regional travel demand models or from a number of secondary sources concerning maximum travel times to various land uses. For a regional shopping center, for example, the primary market area is that which is within 30 minutes of the generator; 20 percent of the site's trips will come from a longer distance.

Delineate the market area as a regular geometric shape such as a circle or square with the generator at the center, with a radius of travel time appropriate for the type of development being analyzed.

Divide the market area into zones and determine the amount of activity in each. The zone boundaries should be based on natural or apparent features such as major streets, rivers, or topography. Zonal activities should include population, income, and/or employment. Projections of these variables should be used for the design year.

Calculate the percentage of the total market area activity within each zone.

Determine (by inspection and/or local knowledge) the most logical route(s) from the center (centroid) of each zone to the generator. This information could also be obtained from the regional traffic assignment model, if one exists.

Determine the directional distribution of site traffic on the basis of the percentages of the total market area activity within each zone.

Step 7: Traffic assignment. In this step, the site-generated traffic from each zone to the generator site is assigned to each street segment comprising the minimum-travel-time path between the center of each zone and the generator. The estimated site traffic added to each roadway segment is then calculated by summing the individual zone-to-generator volumes on that segment. In the traditional 3C transportation planning process, this is accomplished with a computerized traffic assignment algorithm. It assigns and sums traffic volumes on those roadway segments which represent the minimum zone-to-zone travel time paths in the street network.

Step 8: Combine site and nonsite traffic. The traffic volumes estimated in step 7 are added to the existing traffic volumes (step 4) to arrive at an estimate of total traffic volumes with the generator in full operation.

Step 9: Capacity analysis. The adequacy of the existing street system to accommodate the traffic volumes estimated in step 8 is assessed using standard capacity analysis techniques. The results of the capacity analysis provide the basis for determining any on- and/or off-site improvements that might be needed to accommodate the projected total traffic volumes. These might include adding lanes to existing roadways, adding turn lanes at key intersections and/or at site access points, installing signals and/or other traffic control devices at key intersections, and redesigning traffic signal phasing and timing plans.

The reader is referred to *Travel Estimation Techniques for Urban Planning* (TRB, 1998) for additional information concerning simplified traffic impact analyses.

Example 11.7

The staff of a local traffic engineering department has estimated that large shopping centers generate an average of 49.64 vehicle trips per day per 1000 sq. ft. of retail floor area. This estimate is based on a sample of 146 shopping center sites. The sample standard deviation is ±22.26 trips. The likelihood that a particular shopping center will generate more than 86 trips per 1000 sq. ft is most nearly:

(a) .01

(b) .05

(c) .10

(d) .25

(e) .50

Solution

From Equation (11.66) the 95 percent confidence interval is

$$\text{CL} = \bar{x} \pm Z\left(s/\sqrt{n}\right) = 49.64 \pm 1.96\left(22.26/\sqrt{146}\right) = 49.64 \pm 3.61$$

Therefore, there is a 95 percent chance that the true mean trip rate for such shopping centers is between 46.0 and 53.3 trips.

Equation (11.66) can be used to assess the likelihood that a shopping center will generate more traffic than 86 trips per 1000 sq. ft (note that this is a "one-tail" situation).

$$x = \bar{x} + Zs = 49.64 + 1.7(22.26) = 86.0$$
$$z = 1.63$$

In this case it can be concluded that there is only a 1 in 20 chance that a shopping center will generate more than about 86 trips per 1000 sq. ft. The correct answer is (b).

HIGHWAY ROUTE SURVEYING

Highway surveys involve measuring and computing horizontal and vertical angles, elevations, and horizontal distances. The results of these surveys are used to prepare detailed plan and profile base maps of proposed roadways. In addition, the elevations determined in the survey serve as the basis for calculation of construction cut and fill quantities, and in determining roadway banking. This section presents a review of basic terminology, concepts, and standard procedures used in highway surveys. The review begins with some basic definitions.

Highway curves can be either circular arcs or spirals. A *simple curve* is a circular arc connecting two straight lines (tangents). A *compound curve* consists of two or more circular arcs of different radii tangent to each other with their centers on the same side of the common tangent. Compound curves where two circular arcs having centers on the same side are connected by a short tangent are called *broken-back curves*. A *reverse curve* is two circular arcs tangent to each other but with their centers on opposite sides of the common tangent. A curve whose radius decreases uniformly from infinity to that of the curve it meets is called a *spiral curve*. Spiral curves with the proper *superelevation* (banking) provide safe and smooth riding qualities. Circular and spiral curves are used for curves in the horizontal plane. Tangents in the vertical plane are joined by *parabolic curves* (also referred to simply as *vertical curves*).

Simple Circular Curves

The location of highway centerlines is initially laid out as a series of straight lines (tangent sections). These tangent sections are then joined by circular curves to allow for smooth vehicle operations at the design speed selected for the roadway. Figure 11.9 shows the basic geometry of a simple circular curve. The point of transition from tangent to circular alignment is called the *point of curve* (PC). The point where the alignment changes from circular back to tangent (straight) is the *point of tangency* (PT). *Stations* are located along the alignment according to the distance from some reference point, commonly the beginning point of the project. Where metric units are used full stations may be set at either 1-km or 100-m intervals. Where U.S. Customary Units are used, stations are set at 100-ft intervals. For example, when kilometer stations are used, station (STA) 5 + 000.000 refers to a point 5000 m from the reference point, which is STA 0 + 000. *Full stations* are located every 1000 m (or 100 m or 100 ft) along the highway alignment. The *forward tangent* is in the direction of increasing station numbers.

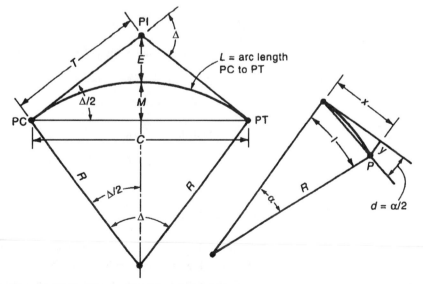

Figure 11.9 Simple circular curve notation

The *back tangent* is in the direction of decreasing station numbers. The intersection of the back and forward tangents is called the *point of intersection* (PI). The angle between the back and forward tangents is called the *tangent deflection angle* (Δ). The angle between T and the long chord (C) is called the *curve deflection angle* and is equal to $\Delta/2$. Because the simple circular curve is symmetrical about the PI, the PC and PT are located a distance T from the PI.

If the two tangents intersecting at PI are laid out, and the angle Δ between them is measured, only one other element of the curve must be known to calculate the remaining elements. The design parameter R is the other element most commonly used. Therefore, given R (which is a function of design speed), and Δ, all other curve elements can be computed as summarized below:

$$T = R \tan(\Delta/2) \tag{11.87}$$

$$C = 2R \sin(\Delta/2) \tag{11.88}$$

$$M = R[1 - \cos(\Delta/2)] \tag{11.89}$$

$$L = 2\pi R(\Delta/360) \tag{11.90}$$

Example **11.8**

The following horizontal curve is laid out in metric units, using kilometer stations.

$$PI = STA\ 7 + 110.000$$
$$\Delta = 41°10'$$
$$T = 114.574\ m$$

The station of the PT is most nearly:

(a) 7 + 990

(b) 6 + 500

(c) 7 + 500

(d) 7 + 000

(e) 7 + 215

Solution

$$PC\ sta = PI\ sta - T = 7110.000 - 114.574 = 6 + 995.426$$

From Equation (11.87),

$$R = T/\tan(\Delta/2) = 114.574/0.3755 = 305.124\ m.$$

From Equation (11.90),

$$L = 2\pi R(\Delta/360) = 2(3.1416)(305.124)(0.1143) = 219.131\ m.$$

$$PT\ sta = PC\ sta + L = 6995.426 + 219.131 = 7 + 214.557$$

The correct answer is (e).

In laying out curve centerlines in the field, stakes should be placed at the PC and PT and at intervals of 50, 20, or 10 m, depending on the complexity of situation. For projects in U.S. Customary units, stakes will be placed at intervals of 100, 50, or 25 ft (Brinker and Minnick, 1995). Circular curves can be laid out by (1) deflection angles and chords, (2) tangent offsets, (3) chord offsets, or

(4) middle ordinates. Layout by deflection angles from the tangents in the most commonly used method.

Deflection Angles

The layout of simple circular curves in the field by the deflection angle method consists of the following steps: (1) set up the instrument at the PC; (2) orient on the PI with the vernier at zero; (3) turn the deflection angle of the first station; (4) set the location of the station on the line established by the instrument person at a distance c from the PC; (5) repeat steps 3 and 4 until all stations have been set (staked). The deflection angles for the individual stations, sometimes called subdeflection angles, are computed as follows:

$$\delta = [(\Delta/2)/l]c_n \qquad \textbf{(11.91)}$$

where δ is the angle between the tangent T and a chord from the PC (or other setup point) to the station being established, and c_n = the nominal chord length.

Nominal chords do not represent arc distance; they are straight lines (sometimes called subchords). To illustrate this, assume that the transit is set up over the PC at STA 6 + 217. Assuming staking is at 50 m intervals, the first point to be marked on the curve should be the next full station, STA 6 + 250. It follows that STA 6 + 250 could be located by placing a stake on the transit line at δ degrees and at distance of 33 m (6250 − 6217) from the PC. This nominal chord length is used to calculate δ but should not be used to determine station locations in the field. True chord lengths should be used to lay out curves in the field. The true length of any subchord can be computed from its deflection angle by

$$c = 2R \sin\delta \qquad \textbf{(11.92)}$$

The curve notes (calculations) necessary to lay out a curve in the field should contain the following information for each station to be located: (1) nominal chord length (to compute δ); (2) true chord length (chord distance used to lay out the curve in the field); and (3) deflection angles, δ, listed in cumulative form. As a check, the deflection angle to the last station, the PT, should equal $\Delta/2$. In addition, the notes should clearly identify the stationing of the PC, PT, and PI and the appropriate value of T, L, Δ, and R.

Tangent Offsets

The layout of curves by the tangent offset method requires determination of the distances x and y in Figure 11.9. The basic formulas for this method are listed below.

$$d = \alpha/2 = (1718.873l)/R \text{ (in minutes)} \qquad \textbf{(11.93)}$$

$$= (28.64789l)/R \text{ (in degrees)} \qquad \textbf{(11.94)}$$

$$y \text{ (for any } x) = R - (R^2 - x^2)^{1/2} \qquad \textbf{(11.95)}$$

$$x \text{ (for any } l) = R \sin\alpha \qquad \textbf{(11.96)}$$

$$y \text{ (for any } l) = R(1 - \cos\alpha) \qquad \textbf{(11.97)}$$

where

R = radius of curve (m or ft)

l = length of arc (m or ft)

α = central angle subtended by l

d = deflection angle for arc length l

x = distance along tangent from PC or PT to set any point P on the curve (m or ft)

y = offset from tangent at distance x to set any point P on the curve (m or ft)

Concentric Circular Curves

The location and full lengths of inner and outer concentric circular arcs relative to the roadway centerline are often required for reference during roadway construction. These indicate the locations of property lines, curb lines, and/or grading reference points.

Referring to Figure 11.10 for the appropriate notation, Hickerson (1964) provides the following basic relationships concerning outer and inner concentric curves:

$$L = R\Delta \tag{11.98}$$

$$L_o = R_o\Delta \tag{11.99}$$

or

$$L_o = L + w\Delta \tag{11.100}$$

or

$$L_o = L + a \tag{11.101}$$

$$L_i = R_i\Delta \tag{11.102}$$

or

$$L_i = L - w\Delta \tag{11.103}$$

or

$$L_i = L - a \quad \text{(Note that } L_o + L_i = 2L, \text{ and } L_o - L_i = 2a\text{)} \tag{11.104}$$

where

Δ = total central angle
L, R = length and radius of the centerline curve
L_o, R_o = corresponding elements of outside curve
L_i, R_i = corresponding elements of inside curve
C = arc (or chord) subtended by θ
C_o, C_i = outside and inside arcs subtended by θ
w = radial distance from center to outer or inner curve
$a = w\Delta = 0.017453w\Delta$ (Δ in degrees)

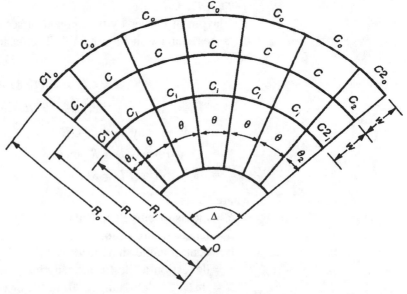

Figure 11.10 Concentric circular curves

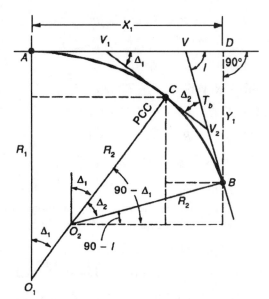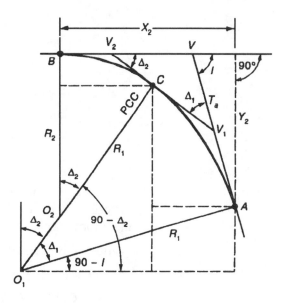

Figure 11.11 Two-centered compound curve

The inner and outer curves may be staked in the field by setting points at the desired radial distance from the centerline curve and at the proper chord length from adjacent points on the concentric curve by the *tangent offset* method, or by *deflection angles* from stations on the outside or inside curves.

Compound Curves

A compound curve consists of two or more circular arcs joined at a point of tangency with the curves on the same side of their common tangent. The radii of the curves are different but in the same direction. The point of tangency is called the *point of compound curvature* (PCC).

Figure 11.11 shows a typical *two-centered compound curve.* The notation in the upper diagram is with reference to A as the origin, and the lower diagram is with reference to B as the origin. There are seven elements of this two-centered compound curve: $I(\Delta_1 + \Delta_2)$, R_1, T_a (the long tangent), Δ_1, R_2, T_b (the short tangent), and Δ_2. If four of these elements, including an angle, are known, the other three can be computed. Typically, Δ_1 and Δ_2, or I, are measured in the field, and R_1 and R_2 are determined based on the design speed of the curve. The two simple curves AC and CB (in Figure 11.11) are laid out in the field as separate circular curves with the PC of the second curve coinciding with the PT of the first curve.

Hickerson (1964) gives the following formulas for computing the basic parameters of two-centered compound curves (see Hickerson for formulas for the long and short tangents of three- and four-centered compound curves):

$$X_1 = R_2 \sin I + (R_1 - R_2)\sin \Delta_1 \qquad (11.105)$$

$$Y_1 = R_1 - R_2 \cos I - (R_1 - R_2)\cos \Delta_1 \qquad (11.106)$$

$$T_b = [R_1 - R_2 \cos I - (R_1 - R_2)\cos \Delta_1]/\sin I \qquad (11.107)$$

$$X_2 = R_1 \sin I - (R_1 - R_2)\sin \Delta_2 \qquad (11.108)$$

$$Y_2 = R_2 - R_1 \cos I + (R_1 - R_2)\cos \Delta_2 \qquad (11.109)$$

$$T_a = [R_2 - R_1 \cos I + (R_1 - R_2) \cos \Delta_2]/\sin I \qquad \textbf{(11.110)}$$

$$\text{vers } \Delta_1 = (T_b \sin I - R_2 \text{ vers } I)/(R_1 - R_2) \qquad \textbf{(11.111)}$$

$$\text{vers } \Delta_2 = (R_1 \text{ vers } I - T_a \sin I)/(R_1 - R_2) \qquad \textbf{(11.112)}$$

$$\tan \Delta_1/2 = (T_b \sin I - R_2 \text{ vers } I)/(T_a + T_b \cos I - R_2 \sin I) \qquad \textbf{(11.113)}$$

$$\tan \Delta_2/2 = (R_1 \text{ vers } I - T_a \sin I)/(R_1 \sin I - T_a \cos I - T_b) \qquad \textbf{(11.114)}$$

$$R_1 = R_2 + [(T_b \sin I - R_2 \text{ vers } I)/\text{vers } \Delta_1] \qquad \textbf{(11.115)}$$

$$R_2 = R_1 - [(R_1 \text{ vers } I - T_a \sin I)/\text{vers } \Delta_2] \qquad \textbf{(11.116)}$$

where vers I = versine $I = 1 - \cos I$.

Hickerson (1964, pp. 126–127) provides the following summary of the use of these formulas in solving seven typical compound curve problems.

Case 1. Given R_1, R_2, Δ_1, and Δ_2, find I, T_a, and T_b.

Solution. $I = \Delta_1 + \Delta_2$. Use Equation (11.110) for T_a, Equation (11.107) for T_b.

Case 2. Given I, T_a, T_b, and R_1 (or R_2), find R_2 (or R_1), Δ_1, and Δ_2.

Solution (R_1 given). Use Equation (11.114) for Δ_2, Equation (11.116) for R_2; $\Delta_1 = I - \Delta_2$.

Solution (R_2 given). Use Equation (11.113) for Δ_1, Equation (11.115) for R_1; $\Delta_2 = I - \Delta_1$.

Case 3. Given R_1, R_2, I, and T_a (or T_b), find Δ_1, Δ_2 and T_b (or T_a).

Solution (T_a given). Use Equation (11.112) for Δ_2, Equation (11.107) for T_b; $\Delta_1 = I - \Delta_2$.

Solution (T_b given). Use Equation (11.111) for Δ_1, Equation (11.110) for T_a; $\Delta_2 = I - \Delta_1$.

Case 4. Given I, Δ_1, R_1, and T_a, find Δ_2, R_2, and T_b.

Solution. $\Delta_2 = I - \Delta_1$; use Equation (11.116) for R_2, Equation (11.107) for T_b.

Case 5. Given I, Δ_2, R_2, and T_b, find Δ_1, R_1, and T_a.

Solution. $\Delta_1 = I - \Delta_2$; use Equation (11.115) for R_1, Equation (11.110) for T_a.

Case 6. Given AB, angles VAB and VBA, and R_1, find T_a, T_b, Δ_2, and R_2.

Solution. $I = VAB + VBA$; solve triangle AVB for T_a and T_b; use Equation (11.114) for Δ_2, Equation (11.116) for R_2; $\Delta_1 = I - \Delta_2$.

Case 7. Given AB, angles VAB and VBA, and R_2, find T_a, T_b, Δ_1, and R_1.

Solution. $I = VAB + VBA$; solve triangle AVB for T_a and T_b; use Equation (11.113) for Δ_1; Equation (11.115) for R_1; $\Delta_2 = I - \Delta_1$.

Parabolic Vertical Curves

The vertical axis parabola (see Figure 11.12) is the geometric curve used in the design of the vertical alignment of roadways. The general equation of the parabola is

$$Y = aX^2 + bX + c \qquad \textbf{(11.117)}$$

With reference to Figure 11.12, the constant a is an indication of the rate of change of slope (see below), b is the slope of the back tangent (g_1), and c is the elevation of the *point of vertical curve* (PVC).

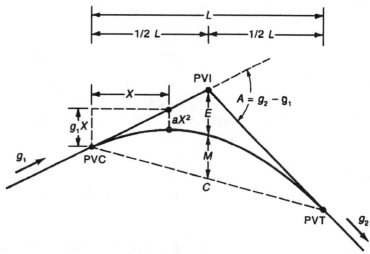

Figure 11.12 Vertical curve notation

The slope of the parabola at any point is

$$dy/dx = 2aX + b \tag{11.118}$$

and the rate of change of the slope is

$$d^2y/dx^2 = 2a \tag{11.119}$$

The rate of change of the slope can also be written as

$$2a = (g_2 - g_1)/L = A/L \tag{11.120}$$

where g_1 = grade (slope) of the back tangent (percent), g_2 = grade of the forward tangent (percent), A = algebraic difference in grade $(g_2 - g_1)$, and L = length of curve in 100 m or 100 ft stations if grades are in percent (L is actually the horizontal projection of the true length of curve). Alternatively, g_1 and g_2 may be given as decimals and L in m or ft.

Recall from the review of vertical alignment earlier in this chapter that the rate of vertical curvature $K = L/A$, which is the inverse of the rate of the change of slope. The value of K—the horizontal distance needed to effect a 1 percent change in grade—is very useful in designing vertical curves. Many of the recommended design values for vertical curves in the AASHTO Green Book, for example, are presented in terms of a range of K values. Therefore, the equations in the following sections are presented in terms of K wherever appropriate.

Presented below are equations that apply to symmetrical or equal-tangent vertical curves [see Hickerson (1964) for comparable equations for non-symmetrical vertical curves].

The *difference in elevation* between the PVC and a point on the g_1 grade line at a distance x from the PVC is

$$\Delta E_x = g_1 x \tag{11.121}$$

Vertical offsets from a tangent to the vertical curve vary as the square of the horizontal distance from the PVC. Therefore, the *tangent offset y between the grade line and the curve* is

$$y = ax^2 = [(g_2 - g_1)/2L]x^2 = (A/2L)x^2 \tag{11.122}$$

where x = horizontal distance from the PVC.

For a *crest vertical curve*, the elevation of the curve at distance x from the PVC is

$$E_x = E_{\text{PVC}} + g_1 x - ax^2 = E_{\text{PVC}} + g_1 x - y \qquad (11.123)$$

For a *sag vertical curve*, the signs are reversed.

The vertical curve lies midway between the PVI and the midpoint of the chord between the PVC and the PVT. The *middle ordinate, M*, and the *offset, d*, at the PVI are equal.

$$M = d = (AL)/8 = (KA^2)/8 \qquad (11.124)$$

The distance x from the PVC to the high or low point on the curve is given by

$$x = (-g_1 L)/A = -g_1 K \qquad (11.125)$$

The elevation of the high or low point can be computed from Equation (11.123).

Kavanagh (1995) suggests the following nine-step procedure for computing a vertical curve.

Step 1. Compute A. $A = g_2 - g_1$.

Step 2. Locate the PVC and PVT. Typically, g_1, g_2, L, and the stationing and elevation of a point on tangent (usually PVI) will be given. If the PVI is known, $L/2$ is simply subtracted and added to the PVI to obtain the PVC and PVT, respectively.

Step 3. Compute the distance from the PVC to the high or low point and determine the station of the high/low point.

$$x = (-g_1 L)/A = -g_1 K \qquad (11.126)$$

Step 4. Compute the tangent grade-line elevation, E, of the PVC and the PVT.

$$E_{\text{PVC}} = E_{\text{PVI}} + g_1(L/2) \qquad (11.127)$$

$$E_{\text{PVT}} = E_{\text{PVI}} + g_2(L/2) \qquad (11.128)$$

Step 5. Compute the tangent grade-line elevation for each station.

$$E_{\text{STA}} = E_{\text{PVC}} + g_1 x \qquad (11.129)$$

$$E_{\text{STA}} = E_{\text{PVT}} + g_2 x \qquad (11.130)$$

where x is the distance from the PVC or the PVT (whichever is closer) to the required station.

Step 6. Compute the elevation of the curve at the PVI (elevation of the midchord).

$$E_{\text{MID}} = (E_{\text{PVC}} + E_{\text{PVT}})/2 \qquad (11.131)$$

Step 7. Compute the tangent offset, d, at the PVI.

$$d = \Delta E/2 \qquad (11.132)$$

where ΔE is the difference in elevation between the PVI and the midpoint of the chord.

Step 8. Compute the tangent offset, y, for each station.

$$y = [x/(L/2)]^2 d \qquad (11.133)$$

where x is the distance from the PVC or PVT (whichever is closer) to the required station.

Step 9. Compute the elevation of the curve at each station by combining the tangent offsets (from step 8) with the appropriate tangent grade-line elevations (from step 5). *Add for sag curves; subtract for crest curves.*

Spiral Curves

Spiral curves are used in highway design to provide a gradual transition from a straight to a circular path. The length of the spiral curve is also used in the transition from normally crowned pavement to fully superelevated pavement.

The spiral is a curve of variable radius in which the radius varies inversely and uniformly with the length of the curve. Figure 11.13 illustrates and defines the basic elements of transition, or spiral, curves. At the beginning of the spiral (TS), the radius of the spiral is infinity. The radius of the spiral decreases at a uniform rate until it equals the radius of the circular curve at the point of tangency with the circular arc (SC).

The following discussion refers to the situation where equal spirals are used to join circular or compound curves to the main tangents [see Hickerson (1964) for more advanced spiral applications].

Kavanagh (1995) suggests the following spiral layout procedure. Refer to Figure 11.13 for notation.

Step 1. Based on design speed, select the length of spiral, L_s. Take note that the stationing of PI and Δ are determined in the field. R is determined based on design considerations that are limited by design speed. Values for various elements of spirals have been published in spiral tables and can be found in route surveying texts [for example, see Table 15 in Hickerson (1964, p. 460)].

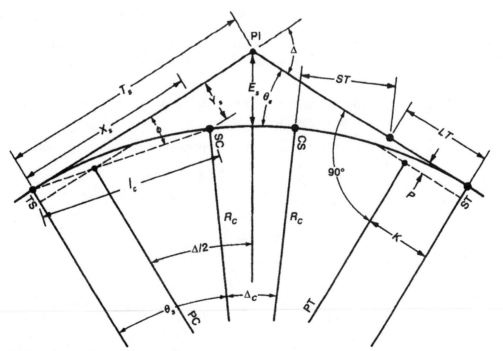

Figure 11.13 Transition (spiral) curve notation

Step 2. From the spiral tables, determine p, k, X_s, Y_s, etc.

Step 3. Compute the spiral tangent (T_s) and the circular tangent (T_c).

$$T_s = (R_c + p) \tan(\Delta/2) + k \tag{11.134}$$

$$T_c = R_c \tan(\Delta/2) \tag{11.135}$$

Step 4. Compute the spiral angle (θ_s).

$$\theta_s = (2p/360)[L_s/(2R_c)] \tag{11.136}$$

Step 5. Prepare a list of relevant layout stations. The list should include all key horizontal alignment points such as TS, SC, CS, and ST and all key vertical alignment points such as grade points, PVC, low point, and PVT.

Step 6. Calculate the deflection angles.

$$\phi = 1/3[(l/L_s)^2 \theta_s] \tag{11.137}$$

where ϕ is the deflection angle at any distance l along the spiral.

Step 7. Locate the TS by measuring the distance T_s from the PI.

$$\text{Stationing of TS} = \text{stationing of PI} - T_s \tag{11.138}$$

Step 8. From the TS, turn the spiral deflection (ϕ_s), measure the long chord (LC), and thus locate the SC.

$$\phi_s = \theta_s/3 - C_s \tag{11.139}$$

where C_s is a correction factor than can be found in tables in many route surveying texts. For angles <10 degrees, the correction is negligible. An approximate value of the spiral deflection angle is $\theta_s/3$.

$$\text{Stationing of SC} = \text{stationing of TS} + L_s \tag{11.140}$$

$$\text{Stationing of CS} = \text{stationing of SC} + R_c(2\pi\Delta/360 - 2\theta_s) \tag{11.141}$$

$$\text{Stationing of ST} = \text{stationing of CS} + L_s \tag{11.142}$$

An alternative approach is to measure the LT (from the TS) to locate the spiral PI. The spiral angle θ_s can then be turned, and the ST distance measured to locate the SC.

Step 9. The PI for the circular curve is established by measuring the circular tangent from the SC.

Step 10. Repeat the procedure to this point, starting at the ST.

Several additional spiral formulas follow.

$$\textit{Total length of curve system:} \quad L = L_c + 2L_s \tag{11.143}$$

$$\textit{Length of circular curve:} \quad L_c = R_c(2\pi/360)(\Delta - 2\theta_s) \tag{11.144}$$

$$\textit{Length of tangent chord:} \quad l_c = 2[R_s \sin(\theta_s/2)] \tag{11.145}$$

where R_s = spiral radius.

$$\textit{Total deflection:} \quad \Delta = \Delta_c + 2\theta_s \tag{11.146}$$

A useful relationship between the radii of spiral (s) and circular (c) curves and their lengths is

$$R_s/R_c = L_s/L_c \tag{11.147}$$

The AASHTO Green Book (2001, p. 180) provides equations for computing the *minimum length of spiral*, L_s, required for gradual transition into a curved section of roadway.

Superelevation

Recall from the section "Vehicle Characteristics" that the centrifugal force acting on vehicles on horizontal curves tends to cause overturning or skidding outward from the center of curvature. To resist these outward (horizontal) forces, it is customary to bank the highway surface. This banking is called superelevation.

The spiral provides a gradual and uniform change in curvature from a straight to a circular path. This property makes the length of spiral, L_s, ideally suited to transition the pavement cross-slope from normal crown to full superelevation. The distance required to accomplish the transition from a normal to a superelevated section, sometimes referred to as the transition runoff, is a function of the design speed, degree of curvature, and the rate of superelevation. The AASHTO Green Book (2001, p. 183) provides a table of recommended minimum lengths of superelevation runoff for various design speeds and superelevation rates.

Four methods of profile design are used to attain superelevation: (1) revolving a crowned pavement about the centerline profile, (2) revolving a crowned pavement about the inside edge profile, (3) revolving a crowned pavement about the outside edge profile, and (4) revolving a straight cross-slope pavement about the outside edge profile. The first method is the most widely used. In this method, the calculated centerline profile is the baseline, and one-half of the required elevation change is made at each edge.

Kavanagh (1995) presents an excellent illustrative superelevation design problem.

Slope Staking

The process of slope staking consists of finding and recording the positions where the side slopes of the graded roadway will intersect the ground surface. Slope stakes mark the limits of excavation and embankment. The basic slope staking method may be used to set stakes to guide roadway grading during construction, and/or to obtain data for calculating cut and fill volumes.

The notation defined below and illustrated in Figure 11.14 is used in the following summary of the basic slope staking method.

> *Grade rod*, R_g, is the reading that would be obtained from the existing height of instrument, HI, if the foot of the rod were at the profile grade. It is equal to the difference in elevation between the HI and the *finished grade*, G_f.

$$R_g = \text{HI} - G_f \qquad (11.148)$$

> *Actual (or ground) rod*, R_a, equals the difference in elevation between HI and the *existing ground* level, G_e.

$$R_a = \text{HI} - G_e \qquad (11.149)$$

$$\textit{Cut (+) or fill (−)} = R_g - R_a \qquad (11.150)$$

$$d_2 = (b/2) + \text{SC}_2 \qquad (11.151)$$

$$d_1 = (b/2) + \text{SC}_1 \qquad (11.152)$$

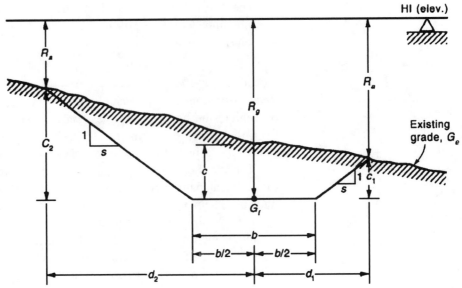

Figure 11.14 Slope staking notation

where

d = horizontal distance from G_f to the slope stake

b = width of roadbed

S = slope ratio = ratio of horizontal to vertical (+ for cut, − for fill)

C = vertical distance from G_f to the existing grade

The procedure for determining slope stake locations in the field is a matter of trial and error based on known values of S and C at the center of the roadbed. The basic procedure is (Ives and Kissam, 1952)

1. Establish HI (by means of differential leveling from the nearest benchmark).

2. Compute the grade rod, R_g = HI − finished (profile) grade.

3. Record the cut or fill at the centerline of the roadbed ($R_g − R_a$).

4. Locate the rod at the estimated offset for the slope stake. The estimated offset from the centerline is computed as if the ground were level [offset = ($b/2$) + S × centerline cut or fill].

5. Take a rod reading at the estimated distance and find the actual cut or fill ($R_g − R_a$). If the actual and estimated values differ by more than about 30 mm (0.10 ft), have the rod held at a greater or lesser offset than for level ground using the following general rule as a guide: On uphill cuts or downhill fills, move the rod away from the centerline; on uphill fills and downhill cuts, move the rod toward the centerline. Repeat the process until $d = (b/2) + SC$.

6. Set and label the slope stakes. The stakes should be marked with the station number, the offset from the centerline, the cut or fill, and the slope ratio.

Earthwork

One of the major objectives in evaluating alternative route locations is to minimize the amount of cut and fill. To determine the amount of earthwork required for a given alignment, cross sections (such as those developed using the slope staking procedure outlined in the previous section) are plotted and the areas of cuts and fills at each cross section are calculated. Cross-sectional areas may be measured with a planimeter, or calculated by either dividing the area into triangles and trapezoids or by applying the following coordinate formula:

$$A = \left| \sum_{i=1}^{n} [X_1(Y_{i+1} - Y_{i-1})]/2 \right| \qquad (11.153)$$

In Equation (11.154), points are numbered consecutively around the cross section. Since the cross section is closed, when $i = n$, $i + 1$ is understood to equal 1; similarly, when $i = 1$, $i - 1$ is understood to equal n.

A common method of determining the volume of earthwork is the *average end area method*. This method is based on the assumption that the volume between two consecutive cross sections is the average of their areas multiplied by the distance between them (Garber and Hoel, 1997):

$$V = (L)[(A_1 + A_2)/2] \qquad (11.154a)$$

where

V = volume (cubic meters)
A_1, A_2 = end areas (m^2)
L = distance between cross sections (m)

or (in U.S. Customary units)

$$V = L[(A_1 + A_2)/54] \qquad (11.154b)$$

where V is in cubic yards, A_1 and A_2 in ft^2, and L in ft.

In situations where there is a significant difference between A_1 and A_2, it may be advisable to calculate the volume as a pyramid:

$$V = (1/3)(\text{area of base})(\text{length}) \qquad (11.155a)$$

where V is in cubic meters, the area of the base is in square meters, and the length is in meters, or

$$V = (1/81)(\text{area of base})(\text{length}) \qquad (11.155b)$$

where V is in cubic yards, area in ft^2, and L in ft.

The average end area and the pyramid methods provide reasonably accurate estimates of volumes of earthwork. When a more precise estimate of volume is desired, the *prismoidal formula* is frequently used (Garber and Hoel, 1997):

$$V = (L/6)(A_1 + 4A_m + A_2) \qquad (11.156a)$$

where

V = volume (m^3)
A_1, A_2 = end areas (m^2)
A_m = middle area, determined by averaging corresponding linear *dimensions* (not the end areas) of the end sections (m^2)

or

$$V = (L/162)(A_1 + 4A_m + A_2) \qquad (11.156b)$$

where V is in cubic yards, the areas in ft^2, and L in ft.

The difference between the volume computed by the average end area method and that computed by the prismoidal formula (in metric units) is

$$C_v = (L/12)(C_1 - C_2)(d_1 - d_2) \qquad \textbf{(11.157)}$$

where

C_v = difference in volume between average end area method and prismoidal method (m^3)

C_1, C_2 = center heights at end points

d_1, d_2 = distance between slope stakes at corresponding end sections

The *prismoidal correction* C_v is algebraically subtracted from the volume obtained from the average end area formula to obtain a more accurate estimate of the volume (Garber and Hoel, 1997).

When materials from cut sections are moved to fill sections, *shrinkage factors*, generally in the range of 1.10 to 1.25, are applied to the fill volumes to determine the quantities of fill required.

The primary reason for calculating earthwork quantities is to estimate the costs for excavating and transporting the excavated materials. Construction contracts generally contain provisions for extra payment for hauling material beyond some maximum *free-haul distance*. In this case, there is one unit price per cubic meter or cubic yard within the free-haul distance and another unit price per station-meter or station-yard for *overhaul*, which is any distance greater than the free-haul distance.

The *mass diagram* is a useful graphical form for summarizing the net amount of cut and fill along the length of a project and for indicating the direction of haul. Figure 11.15 is a schematic representation of a typical mass haul diagram. The mass diagram has the following useful characteristics (Garber and Hoel, 1997):

1. Sections of the curve with steep slopes indicate areas where large amounts of earthwork are required. Flat slopes indicate areas where small amounts of earthwork are required.

2. Rising sections of the curve indicate areas where cut exceeds fill. In falling sections of the curve, fill exceeds cut.

3. The net difference of earthwork between any two points is the difference between the ordinates at these points.

4. Points at which the earthwork changes from cut to fill or from fill to cut are generally indicated by zero slopes.

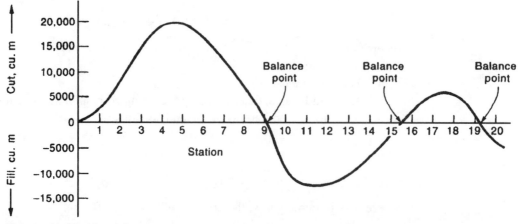

Figure 11.15 Mass diagram

5. Any horizontal line drawn between two points within the same curve indicates a balance of cut and fill quantities between the points.

6. In cases where there is a balance of cut and fill quantities, both ends of the mass diagram will lie on the baseline.

Garber and Hoel (1997) present an excellent step-by-step illustrative application of the mass haul diagram. Also see Banks (2002) for rules for the optimal location of balance lines.

AASHTO GEOMETRIC DESIGN GUIDELINES

Previous sections of this chapter reviewed the basic fundamentals of the geometric design of streets and highways. This section summarizes the guidelines in *A Policy on Geometric Design of Highways and Streets* (AASHTO, 2001), commonly called the Green Book. Throughout this section, any reference to the Green Book will pertain to the 2001 edition unless stated otherwise.

The Green Book is widely accepted as the standard reference for the geometric design of roadways. However, it exceeds 900 pages and is somewhat difficult to use by the uninitiated. The reader is urged to become familiar with the Green Book prior to the exam. This section is intended to help in that effort.

The guidelines summarized in this section are for the design of local, collector, and arterial roadways, including freeways, in both rural and urban areas. A summary of design guidelines for at-grade intersections and for grade separations and interchanges is also presented. The design guidelines are summarized in a series of tables. The tables refer the reader to key tables, figures, and page numbers in the Green Book. This section is more of a quick reference guide than a stand-alone summary of the Green Book, and it concludes with a brief review of roadside-design guidelines.

Local Roads

Table 11.2 AASHTO design guidelines for local roads

Design Elements	Local Rural Roads	Local Urban Roads
Traffic volumes	20-year design volume	n/a residential streets 10–20-year design volume commercial and industrial sites
Design speed	Ex. 5-1, p. 385	30–50 km/hr (20–30 mph)
Sight distance		
Stopping	Ex. 5-2, p. 385	≥30–60 m (100–200 ft)
Passing	Ex. 5-3, p. 386	Seldom applicable
Grades	Ex. 5-4, p. 386	Residential ≤15% Commercial industrial ≤8% max.
Horizontal alignment	No abrupt changes	≥30 m (100 ft) radius; ≥25 m (75 ft) with superelevation @ 30 km/hr (20 mph)
Crown	High-type pavement: 1.5–2%: low-type pavement: 2–6%	High-type pavement 1.5–2%; low-type pavement; 2–6%
Superelevation (See Ch. III)	≤12%; ≤8% if snow; Ice present 12% (aggregate surface)	≥0.04–0.06
Number of Lanes	2 (usually)	≥2

(Continued)

Table 11.2 AASHTO design guidelines for local roads (*Continued*)

Design Elements	Local Rural Roads	Local Urban Roads
Width	Ex. 5-5, p. 388	≥3 m (10 ft) lanes; 3.3 m (11 ft) design; 3.6 m (12 ft) industrial areas With parking: 2.2 m (7 ft) residential, 2.9 m (9 ft) industrial commercial
Median	n/a	≥12 m (40 ft) left turn radius
Curbs	n/a	100–150 mm (4–6 in.) high
Drainage	n/a	≥0.20% grade
Cul-de-sacs	n/a	10 m (30 ft) radius residential, 15 m (50 ft) commercial Ex. 5-8, p. 399
Alleys	n/a	5–6 m (16–20 ft) wide. Ex. 5-9, p. 401
Sidewalks	n/a	1.2 m (4 ft) residential, 2.4 m (8 ft) commercial
Driveways	n/a	1.0 m (3 ft) return radius
Structures		
New	Ex. 5-6, p. 390	Ex. 5-6, p. 390
In-place	Ex. 5-7, p. 390	Ex. 5-7, p. 390
Vertical clearance	4.3 m (14 ft)	4.3 m (14 ft)
Right-of-way	Variable	Sufficient to accommodate ultimate planned roadway
Foreslopes	1:2 max.	n/a
Horizontal clearance	2–3 m (7–10 ft)	≥0.5 m (1.5 ft)
Intersections		
Angle	60–90°	60–90°
Sight distance	Ch. 9, pp. 655–681 (various cases)	Ch. 9, pp. 655–681 (various cases)
Curb radius	Based on design vehicles	7.5 m (25 ft) (residential), 10 m (30 ft) (commercial)
RR crossings	MUTCD* & Ch. 9	MUTCD & Ch. 9
Traffic control	MUTCD	MUTCD
Street lighting	n/a	Ex. 5-11, p. 406
Comments		

See "Highway System Characteristics and Design Controls" for details in this chapter concerning functional classification, sight distances, and horizontal and vertical alignment design controls.
See Table 11.7 in this section for guidelines for at-grade intersections.

Manual on Uniform Traffic Control Devices.

Collector Roads

Table 11.3 AASHTO design guidelines for collector roads

Design Elements	Rural Collectors	Urban Collectors
Traffic volumes	20-year design volume	10–20-year design volume
Design speed	70–80 km/hr (45–50 mph) Ex. 6-1, p. 426	≥50 km/hr (30 mph)
Sight distance		
Stopping	Ex. 6-2, p. 426	Ex. 6-2, p. 426
Passing	Ex. 6-3, p. 427	Ex. 6-3, p. 427
Grades	Ex. 6-4, p. 427	Ex. 6-8, p. 436
Crown	High-type pavements: 1.5–2% Low-type pavement: 3–6%	1.5–3.0%
Superelevation	≤0.12; ≤0.8 if snow/ice present	≤0.06
Number of lanes	2	2 + shoulders (use capacity analysi)
Width	Ex. 6-5, p. 429	Residential 3.0–3.6 m (10–12 ft) Industrial 3.6 m (12 ft) Parking: 2.1–3.3 m (7–11 ft)

(*Continued*)

Table 11.3 AASHTO design guidelines for collector roads (*Continued*)

Design Elements	Rural Collectors	Urban Collectors
Median	n/a	Paint: 0.6–1.2 m (2–4 ft) Curbed: 0.6–1.8 m (2–6 ft) Left turns: 3.0–4.8 m (10–16 ft) "Shielding": 5.4–12.0 m (18–40 ft)
Curbs	n/a	150 mm high (6 in.)
Drainage	n/a	≥0.30
Sidewalks	n/a	1.2 m, (4 ft) residential, 1.2–2.4 m (4–8 ft) commercial
Structures		
In-place	Ex. 6-6, p. 430	n/a
Vertical clearance	4.3 m (14 ft)	4.3 m (14 ft) + allowance for future resurfacing
Right-of-way	As required	12–18 m (40–60 ft)
Foreslopes	1:3 or flatter	n/a
Horizontal clearance	3.0 m (10 ft) min.	≥0.5 m (1.5 ft) from curb
Intersections	See Chap. 9	See Chap. 9
RR crossings	MUTCD* and Chap. 9	MUTCD and Chap. 9
Traffic control	MUTCD	MUTCD
Street lighting	n/a	See Chap. 3
Comments		

See "Highway System Characteristics and Design Controls" in this chapter for details concerning functional
  classification, sight distances, and horizontal and vertical alignment design controls.
See Table 11.7 in this chapter for guidelines for at-grade intersections.

Manual on Uniform Traffic Control Devices.

Rural Arterials

Table 11.4 AASHTO design guidelines for rural arterials

Design Elements	Rural Arterials	Divided Arterials
Traffic volumes	20-year design ADT converted to DHV	20-year DHV
Design speed	60–120 km/hr (40–75 mph)	60–120 km/hr (40–75 mph)
Sight distance	Ex. 7-1, p. 449	Ex. 7-1, p. 449
Grades	Ex. 7-2, p. 450	Ex. 7-2, p. 450
Crown	1.5–2%	1.5–2%
Superelevation	≤12%, ≤8% if snow/ice present	≤12%, ≤8% if snow/ice present. See pp. 463–466 for methods of attaining
Number of lanes	Based on capacity analysis	Based on capacity analysis
Width	Ex. 7-3, p. 452	3.6 m (12 ft) lanes; shoulders ≥2.4 m, (8 ft) Ex. 7-9, p. 469 (frontage road)
Median	See pp. 454–456	See pp. 460–461
Vertical clearance	4.9 m (16 ft)	4.9 m (16 ft)
Right-of-way	As required	Ex. 7-8, p. 468
Intersections	Chap. 9 and 10	Chaps. 9 and 10
RR crossings	MUTCD* and Chap. 9	MUTCD and Chap. 9
Traffic control	MUTCD	MUTCD
Comments		

See "Highway System Characteristics and Design Controls" in this chapter for details concerning
functional classification, sight distances, and horizontal and vertical alignment design controls.
See Tables 11.7 and 11.8 in this chapter for guidelines for at-grade intersections and interchanges.

*ADT, average daily traffic; DHV, design hourly volume; MUTCD, Manual on Uniform Traffic Control Devices.

Urban Arterials

Table 11.5 AASHTO design guidelines for urban arterials

Design Element	Urban Arterials
Traffic volumes	20-yr DHV
Design speed	50–100 km/hr (30–60 mph)
Sight distance	Ex. 7-1, p. 449
Grades	Ex. 7-10, p. 476
Crown	1.5–3%
Superelevation	Generally not used
Number of Lanes	4–8
Width	3.0–3.6 m (10–12 ft) lanes. 3.3 m (11 ft) adequate for through lanes, 3.0 m (10 ft) for left turn lanes. Ex. 7-14, p. 485 for parking
Median	Ex. 7-8, p. 468
Curbs	See Chap. 4, starting on p. 324–327
Drainage	Inlets designed for bikes and pedestrians
Sidewalks	2.4–3.6 m (8–12 ft) border area
Vertical clearance	4.9 m (16 ft)
Right-of-way	As required
Comments	
Access control	By statute, zoning or driveway permits By design (p. 488)
Operating control	pp. 490–498
Frontage roads	p. 498
Bus stops	pp. 500–506. Ex. 7-17, p. 503

See "Highway System Characteristics and Design Controls" in this chapter for details concerning functional classification, sight distances, and horizontal and vertical alignment design controls.
See Tables 11.7 and 11.8 of this section for guidelines for at-grade intersections and interchanges.

Freeways

Table 11.6 AASHTO design guidelines for freeways

Design Elements	General	Urban	Rural
Traffic volumes	20-year design vol.	LOS* C	LOS B
Design speed	Terrain may dictate	80–110 km/h (50–70 mph)	110 km/hr (70 mph)
Grades	Ex. 8-1, p. 510	Ex. 8-1	Ex. 8-1
Crown	1.5–2%	1.5–2%	1.5–2%
Superelevation	≤12%, 6–8% on viaducts	≤12%	≤12%
Number of lanes	≥2, each direction	≥2, each direction	≥2, each direction
Width			
Lanes	3.6 m (12 ft)	3.6 m (12 ft)	3.6 m (12 ft)
Shoulders	3.0–3.6 m (10–12 ft)	3.0–3.6 m (10–12 ft)	3.0–3.6 m (10–12 ft)
Medians		Ex. 8-3 (p. 515)	≥3.0 m (10 ft) (4 lanes) ≥6.6 m (22 ft) (≥6 lanes)
Curbs	No barrier curbs	No barrier curbs	No barrier curbs

* LOS = level of service.

(*Continued*)

Table 11.6 AASHTO design guidelines for freeways (*Continued*)

Design Elements	General	Urban	Rural
Structures	Must carry MS-18 loads	Ex. 8-9 and 8-10 (pp. 528–529)	Ex. 8-9 and 8-10
Vertical clearance	≥4.9 m (16 ft) (5.1 m (17 ft) for signs)	≥4.9 m (16 ft)	≥4.9 m (16 ft)
Right-of-way		Ex. 8-5 to 8-15, pp. 520–534	
Cross sections	Ex. 8-3–18, pp. 515–534	Ex. 8-3–18	Ex. 8-3–18
Horizontal clearance	Clear zone concept, pp. 322–325	Clear zone	Clear zone
Comments			
Special designs	Ex. 8-16 to -18, pp. 535–538 Ex. 8-21, p. 541. Ex. 8-24, p. 546		
Transit	Ex. 8-26 to -33, pp. 548–557		

See "Highway System Characteristics and Design Controls" in this chapter for details concerning functional classification, sight distances, and horizontal and vertical alignment design controls.
See Tables 11.7 and 11.8 in this chapter for guidelines for intersections and interchanges.

* Level of service.

At-Grade Intersections

Table 11.7 AASHTO design guidelines for at-grade intersections

Design Elements	At-Grade Intersections
Traffic volumes	DHV (including traffic composition—trucks—and left-turn volumes). See "Highway Capacity Manual" in this chapter.
Basic types	3-leg ("T"), 4-leg, and multi-leg, each with and without channelization. Ex. 9-4 to 9-14, pp. 563–577; also modern roundabouts, Ex. 9-15, p. 579
Alignment	Flat, 90° approaches with ≤4 legs preferred Ex. 9-15, p. 579. 60°–120° approach angles allowed
Grades	3% or less desired
Left-turn lanes	Ex. 9-75, p. 689 for volume warrants
Channelization	p. 691 for warrants
Curves	9 m (30 ft) radius (simple curve) for passenger car [6 m (20 ft) with 10:1 taper]; 14–37 m (45–125 ft) radius for trucks. Three-centered compound curves preferred for right turns. Ex. 9-19–9-28, pp. 588–612, for recommended minimum radii, offsets, and tapers
Curb radii	4.5–7.5 m (15–25 ft) for cars, 9–12 m (30–40 ft) for trucks. Ex. 9-29 to -31, pp. 616–625 for summary
Parking	Restricted 4.5 m (15 ft) in advance of PC, 9–12 m (30–40 ft) beyond PT. Ex. 9-32, pp. 621–622.
Islands	
Function	Channelization, division, refuge
Size	9 m² (100 ft²) preferred (urban and rural)
Offsets	0.6–2 m (1–6 ft). Ex. 9-37 and -38. pp. 634–635.
Turn lanes	4.2–11.4 m (14–38 ft) wide, depending on destination vehicle and angle of turn. Ex. 9-41, pp. 639–640, Ex. 9-42, p. 642.
Sight distance	Several cases depending on type of control (see Highway System Characteristics and Design Controls," in this chapter)
Superelevation	See pp. 643–653
Median openings	Design speed: 15–25 km/hr (10–15 mph). Length: 12 m (40 ft) or width of cross street, whichever is smaller. See Exhibits, pp. 696–704 and Ex. 9-87, p. 708.
Speed-change lanes	See pp. 692–693 for warrants.
Continuous two-way left turn lanes	Median width required: 3.0–4.8 m (10–16 ft). See Ex. 9-94, p. 717
Auxiliary lanes	Separated (protected) turning lanes and running (access) lanes. Total length = deceleration length + storage + taper. Minimum storage = 2 cars. Left turn storage = 1.5 to 2.0 times average storage per cycle. Taper rate = 8:1 (50 km/h), 15:1 (80 km/hr or 30 mph). See Ex. 9-95, pp. 721–722 for taper design.
Frontage roads	Separation between arterial street and frontage road ≥50 m (150 ft). See Ex. 9-100, p. 731 for typical designs.

(*Continued*)

Table 11.7 AASHTO design guidelines for at-grade intersections *(Continued)*

Design Elements	At-Grade Intersections
Driveways	Should not be within functional boundary of intersection.
Railroad crossings	Two-crossing event cases. See Ex. 9-103 to -105, pp. 738–742 for required sight distances.
Traffic control	MUTCD* and capacity analysis. See "Highway System Characteristics and Design Control" in this chapter.

* MUTCD, Manual on Uniform Traffic Control Devices.

Grade Separations and Interchanges

Table 11.8 AASHTO design guidelines for grade separations and interchanges

Design Elements	Grade Separations
Types	Ex. 10-3 to 10-5, pp. 760–762
Warrants	See p. 763–764
Lateral clearance	Four-lane roadways: 3.0 m (10 ft) median. Six or more lanes: 6.6 m (22 ft) (3.0 m shoulders + median barrier)
Vertical clearance	4.4 m (14.5 ft) min.
Horizontal distance required for grade separation	6.0–8.4 m (20–28 ft) difference in elevation. Horizontal distance between roadways varies with design speed, gradient, and rise and fall required. See Ex. 10-8, pp. 772–773

	Interchanges
Types	Seven basic types. See Ex. 10-1, p. 748. Most common type is the Diamond interchange. (See Ex. 10-16 to -18, pp. 783–784, for examples.)
Warrants	Six basic warrants (design designation, congestion relief, elimination of hazard, topography, user benefits, traffic volume). See pp. 749–750.
Spacing	Urban areas: 1.5 km (1 mi). Rural areas: 3 km (2 mi)
Ramps	
Design speed	≥20 km/hr (15 mph). See Ex. 10-56, p. 830
Grades	3–8%. See pp. 832–833
Superelevation	See pp. 834–836
Cross slopes	1.5–2.0%
Pavement width	3.6–13.6 m (12–45 ft). See Ex. 10-67, p. 843.
Lateral clearance	See pp. 842–844 for eight design values.
Spacing	120–600 m (400–2000 ft) See Ex. 10-68, p. 848.
Design	See Exhibits pp. 849–866 for typical ramp designs.
Comments	

See "Highway System Characteristics and Design Controls" for details concerning functional classification, sight distances, and horizontal and vertical alignment design controls.

Roadside Design

The design of safe and efficient roadways must consider the elements of alignment, grade, traveled way, and the roadside environment. Because accidents involving single vehicles running off the road constitute more than 50 percent of all fatal accidents, the design of the roadside environment is an essential element in the total engineering of the roadway. The guiding philosophy behind roadside design is the provision of a traversable roadside recovery area or *clear zone*, which should be free of obstacles such as unyielding signs and supports, drainage structures, utility poles, and steep slopes. Studies have indicated that on high-speed highways, a relatively level traversable width of 10 m (30 ft) from the edge of the traveled way is sufficient to permit about 80 percent of the vehicles leaving the roadway to stop safely or return to the roadway.

Design options for addressing roadside obstacles have generally been considered in the following order (AASHTO, 2002):

1. Remove the obstacle.

2. Relocate the obstacle.

3. Reduce the severity of impact by using an appropriate breakaway device.

4. Redirect the vehicle by shielding the obstacle with a barrier or crash cushion.

5. Delineate the obstacle if the above alternatives are not appropriate.

The AASHTO guidelines for treatment of roadside obstacles can be found in the Roadside Design Guide (AASHTO, 2002). The AASHTO Green Book and the Roadside Design Guide are companion documents which summarize state-of-the-art practices in highway design.

The Roadside Design Guide addresses benefit-cost issues related to roadside design; the clear zone concept; slope and drainage treatments to reduce run-off-the-road hazards; signs, luminaire supports, etc.; and the design of roadside barriers, median barriers, bridge railings, and crash cushions. The following specific topics are covered:

- Required clear zone distances, as a function of traffic volume, speed, and roadside geometry

- Ditch cross sections

- Warrants for shielding of embankments and provision of median barriers

- Shy line offsets, i.e., the distance from the edge of travel beyond which an object will not be perceived as hazardous by motorists

- Barrier design standards, including recommended length, placement, and layout

- Barrier design parameters based on vehicle dynamics, including bumper height for vehicles traversing embankments and runout lengths

HIGHWAY CAPACITY MANUAL

The standard reference for highway capacity analysis is the *Highway Capacity Manual* (HCM), published by the Transportation Research Board (TRB). The current edition addresses the design, operational analysis and planning of freeways, rural two-lane and multilane highways, intersections, arterial streets, and pedestrian and bicycle facilities. The basic procedures for analyzing these facilities are reviewed in this section. The HCM also contains a chapter on transit facilities, but it is not reviewed in this section.

Application of many of the procedures in the HCM requires extensive use of numerous charts and nomographs. Space limitations preclude the reproduction of these charts and nomographs in this chapter. Therefore, like much of the material in this chapter, the material in this section is in the form of a review of basic procedures with reference to key equations, nomographs, tables, and so on in the HCM. It is recommended that the reader consult the HCM (TRB, 2000) directly for additional background and details. Note that two versions of the HCM are available, one in metric units and the other in U.S. Customary units.

The HCM contains worksheets and numerous sample calculations to aid the analyst in becoming familiar with the procedures. Rather than reproducing those example problems in this section, the reader is referred directly to the HCM.

Basic Concepts

The 2000 HCM defines capacity as "the maximum hourly rate at which persons or vehicles can be expected to traverse a point or uniform section of a lane or roadway under prevailing roadway, traffic, and control conditions." Most analyses in the HCM are based on rates of flow for the peak 15-minute period within the hour of interest, usually the peak hour. Level of service (LOS) is defined as "a quality measure describing operational conditions within a traffic stream," with these conditions generally described by "such service measures as speed and travel time, freedom to maneuver, traffic interruptions, comfort and convenience." The HCM defines six levels of service for each type of facility. They are given letter designations, from A to F, with LOS A representing the best operating conditions and F the worst. Level of service C is typically used for design purposes. Table 11.9 summarizes the measures of effectiveness used to define levels of service in the 2000 HCM.

Table 11.9 Level of service measures in the 2000 HCM

Type of Facility	Measure of Effectiveness
Basic freeway sections	Density (pass. cars/mi/lane or pass. cars/km/lane)
Weaving sections	Density (pass. cars/mi/lane or pass. cars km/lane)
Ramp junctions	Density (pass. cars/mi/lane or pass. cars/km/lane)
Multilane highways	Density (pass. cars/mi/lane or pass. cars/km/lane)
Two-lane rural highways	Percent time delay and speed (mph or km/hr)
Unsignalized intersections	Delay (s/veh)
Signalized intersections	Delay (s/veh)
Arterials	Avg. travel speed (mph or km/hr)
Transit	Service frequency (veh/hr), hours of sevice (hr/day) and load factor (persons/seat)
Pedestrians	Space (sq ft/ped or m^2/ped)

Chapters 7 and 8 of the HCM provide a review of various traffic parameters and traffic characteristics which affect or form the basis of capacity analysis. These include: (1) maximum observed volumes and flow rates; (2) volume characteristics, such as temporal and spatial variations, traffic composition, and weather impacts; (3) speed characteristics; (4) speed-flow-density relationships; (5) spacing and headway characteristics; and (6) saturation headways and lost times. (*Note*: See "Traffic Flow Characteristics" in this chapter for a review of these key topics.)

Two-Lane Highways

Chapter 20 of the HCM deals with two-lane highways. Many of the HCM procedures used to analyze two-lane highways are similar to those used for basic freeway sections, except that procedures for two-lane highways are influenced by the need for vehicles to pass in the face of oncoming traffic. The HCM presents two procedures for analyzing two-lane highways, one applying to two-way segments and the other to directional segments. The procedure for analyzing two-way segments applies only to roads in level or rolling terrain. Two-lane highways in mountainous terrain and those containing grades of 3.0 percent or more with lengths 0.6 mi (1.0 km) or more are analyzed as directional segments.

The HCM gives the capacity of two-lane highways as 1700 passenger cars per hour (pc/hr) for each direction of travel and states that this capacity is nearly independent of the directional distribution of traffic, although capacity will normally not exceed 3200 pc/hr for both directions of travel combined over extended lengths. Levels of service are given by HCM Exhibits 20-2 through 20-4 (pp. 20-3 and 20-4 of the HCM). For Class I highways (highways that serve a high percentage of long trips) levels of service depend on the percent time spent following in platoons and the average highway speed. For Class II highways, level of service depends on the percent time spent following only.

The procedure for analyzing two-way segments begins by determining the free-flow speed. Where actual speed measurements are not available, the free-flow speed may be estimated by

$$\text{FFS} = \text{BFFS} - f_{LS} - f_A \qquad (11.158)$$

where f_{LS} = adjustment for lane and shoulder width and f_A = adjustment for access points.

The adjustments are given in HCM Exhibits 20-5 and 20-6 (p. 20-6 of the HCM).

The peak 15-minute flow rate is given by

$$v_p = V/(\text{PHF} f_G f_{HV}) \qquad (11.159)$$

where PHF is the peak hour factor, f_G is a grade adjustment factor, and f_{HV} is a heavy-vehicle factor. Two different types of grade adjustment factors are used, depending on whether the analysis is intended to determine speeds or percent time spent following. These are given in HCM Exhibits 20-7 and 20-8 (p. 20-7 of the HCM). The heavy-vehicle factor is given by

$$f_{HV} = 1/[1 + P_T(E_T - 1) + P_R(E_R - 1)] \qquad (11.160)$$

where P_T is the proportion of trucks and buses in the traffic stream, P_R is proportion of recreational vehicles in the traffic stream, and E_T and E_R are the passenger car equivalents of trucks and buses and of recreational vehicles, respectively. Passenger car equivalents for determining f_{HV} also depend on whether speed or percent time spent following is being calculated, and are given in HCM Exhibits 20-9 and 20-10 (p. 20-8 of the HCM).

Both f_G and the passenger car equivalents, E_T and E_R, depend on the flow rate v_p; consequently, iterative calculations are required to find v_p. The procedure for calculating v_p is to begin by setting v_p equal to V/PHF. Then, using the appropriate values of f_G, E_T, and E_R, calculate a new value for v_p. If this is outside the flow limits for which f_G, E_T, and E_R where calculated, recalculate v_p with new values of f_G, E_T, and E_R. Continue this process until the value of v_p is consistent with the flow ranges assumed in choosing f_G, E_T, and E_R.

Once v_p is determined, average travel speed is estimated by

$$\text{ATS} = \text{FFS} - 0.0125 v_p - f_{\text{np}} \qquad (11.161)$$

where ATS = average travel speed for both directions of travel combined (km/hr or mph) and f_{np} = adjustment for percentage of no-passing zones, from HCM Exhibit 20-11 (p. 20-10 of the HCM).

Percent time spent following is determined by

$$\text{PTSF} = \text{BPTSF} + f_{\text{d/np}} \qquad (11.162)$$

where PTSF = percent time spent following, BPTSF = base percent time spent following, and $f_{d/np}$ = adjustment for combined effect of the directional distribution of traffic and percent no-passing zones, from HCM Exhibit 20-12 (p. 20-11 of the HCM). The base percent time spent following is given by

$$BPTSF = 100(1 - e^{-0.000879 v_p}) \tag{11.163}$$

The level of service is determined by first comparing v_p with the two-way capacity of 3200 pc/hr. If v_p is greater than capacity, the level of service is F. Furthermore, if the demand flow rate in either direction (v_p times the directional split) is greater than 1700 pc/hr, the level of service is F. For a segment on a Class I facility with demand less than capacity, the level of service is determined by comparing the speed and percent time spent following with the limits given by HCM Exhibit 20-2, with the more restrictive case governing. For a segment on a Class II facility with demand less than capacity, the level of service is determined by comparing the percent time spent following with the times given by HCM Exhibit 20-4.

The HCM also presents a methodology for analyzing directional segments of two-lane highways. This methodology may be applied to extended directional segments, specific upgrades, and specific downgrades. The directional segment method involves calculation of adjusted flow rates for both the direction of travel being analyzed and the opposite direction. These are given by

$$v_d = V/(\text{PHF} f_G f_{HV}) \tag{11.164}$$

and

$$v_o = V_o/(\text{PHF} f_G F_{HV}) \tag{11.165}$$

where v_d = the peak 15-minute passenger-car-equivalent flow rate in the direction analyzed (pc/hr); v_o = the peak 15-minute passenger-car-equivalent flow rate in the opposite direction; and PHF, f_G, and f_{HV} apply to the direction of travel being analyzed or the opposite direction, depending on the equation. As in the case of two-way segments, f_G and the passenger car equivalents for trucks and recreational vehicles that are used to calculate f_{HV} vary depending on whether they are used to estimate average speed or the percent time spent following. Values of f_G for specific upgrades are given in HCM Exhibits 20-13 and 20-14 (pp. 20-15 and 20-16 of the HCM). Passenger car equivalents for trucks and RVs on specific upgrades are given in HCM Exhibits 20-15 through 20-17 (pp. 20-17 to 20-19) of the HCM. In addition, passenger car equivalents for estimating the effect on average travel speed of trucks that operate at crawl speed on long, steep downgrades are given in HCM Exhibit 20-18 (p. 20-20 of the HCM). Where trucks are expected to operate at crawl speeds on specific downgrades, the heavy-vehicle factor is calculated by

$$f_{HV} = 1/[1 + P_{TC}P_T(E_{TC} - 1) + (1 - P_{TC})P_T(E_T - 1) + P_R(E_R - 1)] \tag{11.166}$$

where P_{TC} is the proportion of all trucks that travel at crawl speed and E_{TC} is the passenger car equivalent for trucks at crawl speed. Values of E_T and E_R are those applying to level terrain in HCM Exhibits 20-9 and 20-10 (p. 20-8 of the HCM).

v_d and v_o may need to be determined iteratively. The procedure is similar to that described for two-way segments.

Average travel speed for directional segments is estimated by

$$\text{ATS}_d = \text{FFS}_d - 0.0125(v_d + v_o) - f_{np} \tag{11.167}$$

In this case, the adjustment for the percentage of no-passing zones is given by HCM Exhibit 20-19 (p. 20-22 of the HCM).

The percent time spent following for directional segments is estimated by

$$\text{PTSF}_d = \text{BPTSF}_d - f_{\text{np}} \tag{11.168}$$

where PTSF_d = percent time spent following in the direction analyzed and f_{np} is given by HCM Exhibit 20-20 (p. 20-23 of the HCM). For directional segments, the base percent time spent following is given by

$$\text{BPTSF}_d = 100\left(1 - e^{av_d^b}\right) \tag{11.169}$$

where the coefficients a and b are determined from the flow rate in the opposing direction, as shown in HCM Exhibit 20-21 (p. 20–24 of the HCM).

The level of service is determined by comparing v_d with the directional capacity of 1700 pc/hr. If v_d is greater than capacity, the level of service is F. If not, the level of service is determined from HCM Exhibits 20-2 through 20-4 (pp. 20-3 and 20-4 of the HCM), as in the case of two-way segments. Weighted average values of percent time spent following and average travel speed may be used to determine the level of service of extended directional facilities (see pp. 20-29 and 20-30 of the HCM).

The HCM also contains procedures for analyzing directional segments with passing lanes or climbing lanes (pp. 20-24 through 20-29 of the HCM).

Multilane Highways

Chapter 21 addresses the capacity of multilane highways that cannot be classified as freeways because they are undivided, lack full control of access, or both. The analyses assume uninterrupted flow. A 2-mile (3 km) spacing between signals is assumed for uninterrupted flow to exist. For closer signal spacing, the facility would be classified as an arterial.

The capacity of multilane facilities operating under uninterrupted flow ranges from 1900 to 2200 pc/hr/ln, depending on free-flow speed, when all conditions are ideal. Ideal conditions for multilane highways include level terrain, 12 ft (3.6 m) lane widths, a minimum of 12 ft (3.6 m) of total lateral clearance in the direction of travel (sum of clearances on both sides of the roadway), no direct access points along the roadway, a divided roadway, only passenger cars in the traffic stream, and a free-flow speed of 60 mph (100 km/hr) or more.

Capacities and speed-flow relationships for multilane highways depend on the free-flow speed for the facility. This can either be measured directly or estimated by means of the following equation:

$$\text{FFS} = \text{BFFS}_1 - f_M - f_{LW} - f_{LC} - f_A$$

where FFS is the estimated free-flow speed, BFFS_1 is the estimated free-flow speed for ideal conditions, and the other terms are adjustment for median type, lane width, lateral clearance, and access points. The adjustments are given in HCM Exhibit 21-4 through 21-7 (pp. 21-5–21-7 of the HCM).

Peak 15-minute flow rates in pc/hr/ln are given by

$$v_p = \frac{V}{(N)(\text{PHF})(f_{HV})(f_p)}$$

where v_p is the service flow rate in pc/hr/ln, V is the hourly volume, N is the number of lanes, PHF is the peak hour factor, and f_{HV} is a heavy-vehicle factor. Heavy-vehicle factors may be calculated from information in Exhibits 21-8 through 21-11 (pp. 21-8 through 21-11 of the HCM).

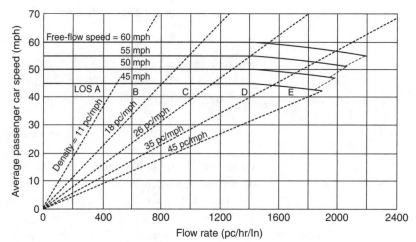

Figure 11.16a   Speed-flow curves with LOS criteria, U.S. Customary units
Source: TRB (2000)

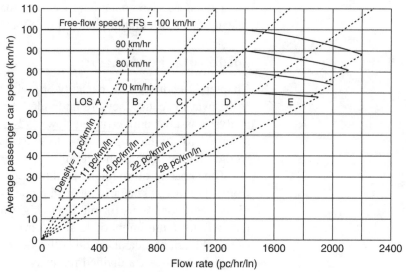

Figure 11.16b   Speed-flow curves with LOS criteria, metric units
Source: TRB (2000)

Level of service may be calculated by first determining the free-flow speed and the flow rate as described above and then using Figure 11.16a or 11.16b to set a speed-flow curve at the appropriate free-flow speed. From this, an estimated speed may be determined, based on the flow rate. Density may be determined from Table 11.10 and the equation $D = v_p/S$, where D is the density and S is the estimated average passenger car travel speed. Level of service may then be determined from Table 11.10a or 11.10b by comparing either the speed or the density with the limiting values listed in the table. HCM Exhibit 21-2 may also be used to determine the maximum service flow rate and maximum v/c ratio for a given level of service.

Freeway Facilities

Chapter 22 of the HCM presents a methodology for analyzing freeway facilities as a whole. This methodology integrates procedures for analyzing basic freeway

Table 11.10a LOS criteria for multilane highways: U.S. customary units

Free-Flow Speed	Criterion	LOS				
		A	B	C	D	E
60 mph	Maximum density (pc/mi/ln)	11	18	26	35	40
	Average speed (mph)	60.0	60.0	59.4	56.7	55.0
	Maximum volume-to-capacity ratio (v/c)	0.30	0.49	0.70	0.90	1.00
	Maximum service flow rate (pc/hr/ln)	660	1080	1550	1980	2200
55 mph	Maximum density (pc/mi/ln)	11	18	26	35	41
	Average speed (ml/hr)	55.0	55.0	54.9	52.9	51.2
	Maximum v/c	0.29	0.47	0.68	0.88	1.00
	Maximum service flow rate (pc/hr/ln)	600	990	1430	1850	2100
50 mph	Maximum density (pc/mi/ln)	11	18	26	35	43
	Average speed	50.0	50.0	50.0	48.9	47.5
	Maximum v/c	0.28	0.45	0.65	0.86	1.00
	Maximum service flow rate (pc/hr/ln)	560	900	1300	1710	2000
45 mph	Maximum density (pc/mi/ln)	11	18	26	35	45
	Average speed (mph)	45.0	45.0	45.0	44.4	42.2
	Maximum v/c	0.26	0.43	0.62	0.82	1.00
	Maximum service flow rate (pc/hr/ln)	490	810	1170	1550	1900

Note: The exact mathematical relationship between density and volume-to-capacity ratio (v/c) has not always been maintained at LOS boundaries because of the use of rounded values. Density is the primary determinant of LOS, LOS F is characterized by highly instable and variable traffic flow. Prediction of accurate flow rate, density, and speed at LOS F is difficult.
Source: TRB (2000).

segments, ramp junctions, and weaving segments. Basic steps in the application of this methodology are as follows.

Step 1. Collect data for the directional facility. Provide guidance on limits of congestion in time and space. Document any demand and capacity adjustments to be used in the analysis. Divided the facility into sections, documenting geometric conditions.

Step 2. Check whether adjustments from counts to estimate demand are needed. This applies especially if the facility is oversaturated.

Step 3. Establish spatial and time analysis unit. Convert sections to segments, calculate the time step for oversaturation, and establish other time units such as time intervals and analysis duration.

Step 4. Make manual adjustments to segment demands, if appropriate. This may encompass the application of overall growth factors to account for projected demands or diverted traffic.

Step 5. Calculate segment capacity by methodologies applying to basic freeway segments, weaving sections, and ramps and ramp junctions.

Step 6. Generate an adjusted demand-to-capacity (d/c) matrix by segment and time interval. Identify whether the facility is undersaturated or has some oversaturated time intervals.

Table 11.10b LOS criteria for multilane highways: metric units

Free-Flow Speed	Criterion	LOS				
		A	B	C	D	E
100 km/hr	Maximum density (pc/kn/ln)	7	11	16	22	25
	Average speed (km/hr)	100.0	100.0	98.4	91.5	88.0
	Maximum volume-to-capacity ratio (*v/c*)	0.32	0.50	0.72	0.92	1.00
	Maximum service flow rate (pc/hr/ln)	700	1100	1575	2015	2200
90 km/hr	Maximum density (pc/km/ln)	7	11	16	22	28
	Average speed (km/hr)	90.0	90.0	89.8	84.7	80.8
	Maximum *v/c*	0.30	0.47	0.68	0.89	1.00
	Maximum service flow rate (pc/hr/ln)	630	990	1435	1860	2100
80 km/hr	Maximum density (pc/km/ln)	7	11	16	22	27
	Average speed (km/hr)	80.0	80.0	80.0	77.6	74.1
	Maximum *v/c*	0.28	0.44	0.64	0.85	1.00
	Maximum service flow rate (pc/hr/ln)	560	880	1280	1705	2000
70 km/hr	Maximum density (pc/km/ln)	7	11	16	22	28
	Average speed (km/hr)	70.0	70.0	70.0	69.6	67.9
	Maximum *v/c*	0.26	0.41	0.59	0.81	1.00
	Maximum service flow rate (pc/hr/ln)	490	770	1120	1530	1900

Note: The exact mathematical relationship between density and volume-to-capacity ratio (*v/c*) has not always been maintained at LOS boundaries because of the use of rounded values. Density is the primary determinant of LOS. LOS F is characterized by highly unstable and variable traffic flow. Prediction of accurate flow rate, density, and speed at LOC F is difficult.
Source: TRB (2000).

Step 7. For the first time interval with d/c > 1.0 for some segment, begin using a reduced time step to carry out computations. Calculate the position of bottlenecks and queues in each time step. Use appropriate flow regimes to estimate speeds and denstities on each segment.

Step 8. Bottleneck analysis. Begin by setting the flow-to-capacity ratio to 1.0 on that segment and transferring unmet demand to the next time interval. Reduced flow rate is propagated upstream in the form of a queue whose density depends on the severity of the bottleneck. When an upstream on-ramp is encountered, its flow rate is calculated on the basis of the level of congestion on the segment immediately downstream and the magnitude of mainline and on-ramp flows. Downstream of the bottleneck, flows are metered at the bottleneck capacity rate.

Step 9. Aggregate individual segment measures of effectiveness (MOEs) into a directional MOE for each time interval.

Basic Freeway Segments

Tables 11.11a and 11.11b show the level-of-service criteria used for basic freeway segments. Levels of service are defined in terms of density (passenger cars/mile/lane). Capacities and levels of service depend on the free-flow speed of the segment. For each free-flow speed, the speed and volume-to-capacity (*v/c*)

Table 11.11a LOS criteria for basic freeway segments: U.S. customary units

Criterion	LOS				
	A	**B**	**C**	**D**	**E**
FFS = 75 mph					
Maximum density (pc/mi/ln)	11	18	26	35	45
Minimum speed (mph)	75.0	74.8	70.6	62.2	53.3
Maximum v/c	0.34	0.56	0.76	0.90	1.00
Maximum service flow rate (pc/hr/ln)	820	1350	1830	2170	2400
FFS = 70 mph					
Maximum density (pc/mi/ln)	11	18	26	35	45
Minimum speed (mph)	70.0	70.0	68.2	61.5	53.3
Maximum v/c	0.32	0.53	0.74	0.90	1.00
Maximum service flow rate (pc/hr/ln)	770	1260	1770	2150	2400
FFS = 65 mph					
Maximum density (pc/mi/ln)	11	18	26	35	45
Minimum speed (mph)	65.0	65.0	64.6	59.7	52.2
Maximum v/c	0.30	0.50	0.71	0.89	1.00
Maximum service flow rate (pc/hr/ln)	710	1170	1680	2090	2350
FFS = 60 mph					
Maximum density (pc/mi/ln)	11	18	26	35	45
Minimum speed (mph)	60.0	60.0	60.0	57.6	51.1
Maximum v/c	0.29	0.47	0.68	0.88	1.00
Maximum service flow rate (pc/hr/ln)	660	1080	1580	2020	2300
FFS = 55 mph					
Maximum density (pc/mi/ln)	11	18	26	35	45
Minimum speed (mph)	55.0	55.0	55.0	54.7	50.0
Maximum v/c	0.27	0.44	0.64	0.85	1.00
Maximum service flow rate (pc/hr/ln)	600	990	1430	1910	2250

Note: The exact mathematical relationship between density and v/c has not always been maintained at LOS boundaries because of the use of rounded values. Density is the primary determinant of LOS. The speed criterion is the maximum density for a given LOS.
Source: TRB (2000).

Table 11.11b LOS criteria for basic freeway segments, metric units

Criterion	LOS				
	A	**B**	**C**	**D**	**E**
FFS = 120 km/hr					
Maximum density (pc/km/ln)	7	11	16	22	28
Minimum speed (km/hr)	120.0	120.0	114.6	99.6	85.7
Maximum v/c	0.35	0.55	0.77	0.92	1.00
Maximum service flow rate (pc/hr/ln)	840	1320	1840	2200	2400
FFS = 110 km/hr					
Maximum density (pc/km/ln)	7	11	16	22	28
Minimum speed (km/hr)	110.0	110.0	108.5	97.2	83.9

(Continued)

Table 11.11b   LOS criteria for basic freeway segments, metric units (*Continued*)

Criterion	LOS				
	A	**B**	**C**	**D**	**E**
Maximum v/c	0.33	0.51	0.74	0.91	1.00
Maximum service flow rate (pc/hr/ln)	770	1210	1740	2135	2350
FFS = 100 km/hr					
Maximum density (pc/km/ln)	7	11	16	22	28
Minimum speed (km/hr)	100.0	100.0	100.0	93.8	82.1
Maximum v/c	0.30	0.48	0.70	0.90	1.00
Maximum service flow rate (pc/hr/ln)	700	1100	1600	2065	2300
FFS = 90 km/hr					
Maximum density (pc/km/ln)	7	11	16	22	28
Minimum speed (km/hr)	90.0	90.0	90.0	89.1	80.4
Maximum v/c	0.28	0.44	0.64	0.87	1.00
Maximum service flow rate (pc/hr/ln)	630	990	1440	1955	2250

Note: The exact mathematical relationship between density and v/c has not always been maintained at LOS boundaries because of the use of rounded values. Density is the primary determinant of LOS. The speed criterion is the speed at maximum density for a given LOS.

Source: TRB (2000).

ratio for each LOS is shown (these values were determined from speed-flow and density-flow relationships similar to those outlined in "Traffic Flow Characteristics and Design Controls" earlier in this chapter). The capacity of basic freeway sections depends on the free-flow speed, with capacities ranging from 2400 passenger cars per hour per lane (pc/hr/ln) for free-flow speeds of 75 mph and 70 mph, down to 2250 pc/hr/ln for free-flow speeds of 55 mph. All values refer to maximum flow rates which can be accommodated in a peak 15-minute period for the given LOS. For each LOS and free-flow speed, the maximum service flow rate (MSF) is computed as capacity times the v/c ratio.

Capacities and maximum service flow rates in Tables 11.11a and 11.11b are expressed in terms of equivalent passenger car flow rates. These are calculated from actual hourly volumes by means of

$$v_p = V/(\text{PHF} \times N \times f_{HV} \times f_p) \tag{11.170}$$

where

$\quad v_p$ = 15-minute passenger-car-equivalent flow rate (pc/hr/ln)

$\quad V$ = hourly volume

PHF = peak hour factor

$\quad N$ = number of lanes

$\quad f_{HV}$ = heavy-vehicle adjustment factor

$\quad f_p$ = driver population factor

The heavy vehicle factor, in turn, is calculated as

$$f_{HV} = 1/[1 + P_T(E_T - 1) + P_R(E_R - 1)] \tag{11.171}$$

where P_T and P_R are the proportions of trucks or buses and recreational vehicles in the traffic stream, and E_T and E_R are passenger car equivalents for trucks or buses and recreational vehicles. Values of f_p, E_T, and E_R are tabulated in Chapter 23 of the HCM.

Free-flow speeds may be either measured directly or estimated by a procedure given in the HCM. If the procedure in the HCM is used, the free-flow speed is calculated as

$$\text{FFS} = \text{BFFS}_i - f_{LW} - f_{LC} - f_N - f_{ID} \qquad (11.172)$$

where

FFS = estimated free-flow speed
BFFS_i = estimated ideal free-flow speed (either 70 or 75 mph or 110 or 120 km/hr)
f_{LW} = adjustment for lane width
f_{LC} = estimated adjustment for right-shoulder lateral clearance
f_N = adjustment for number of lanes
f_{ID} = adjustment for interchange density

Values for these adjustments are tabulated in Chapter 23 of the HCM. Exhibit 23-3 of the HCM shows speed-flow curves for the various free-flow speeds and their relationship to the different levels of service. This figure may be used to interpolate between the levels of free-flow speed given in Tables 11.11a and 11.11b.

Example 11.9

A four-lane urban freeway section currently serves a total of 6000 passenger cars per hour. Assuming a 60-mph free-flow speed, the likely level of service is

(a) A

(b) B

(c) C

(d) D

(e) E

Solution

Assuming a lane volume of 1500 pc/hr/ln (6000/4 lanes), Table 11.11a indicates a LOS of D. The correct answer is (d).

Example 11.10

An urban freeway is to be designed to accommodate an adjusted peak 15-minute flow rate of 6250 pc/hr is the peak direction at level of service C. Free-flow speed is 100 km/hr. The total number of lanes required is:

(a) 4

(b) 6

(c) 7.8

(d) 8

(e) 10

Solution

From Table 11.10b the maximum service flow rate for FFS = 100 at level of service C is 1600. The number of lanes required in the peak direction is 6250/1600 = 3.91. This is rounded up to 4 lanes. Since there will normally be one peak period in each direction per day, and these are assumed to be similar, the total number of lanes is 2 × 4 = 8. The correct answer is (d).

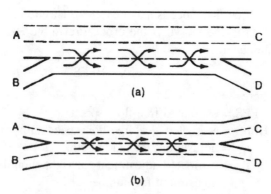

Type A weaving areas: (a) ramp weave/one-sided
weave, and (b) major weave with crown line

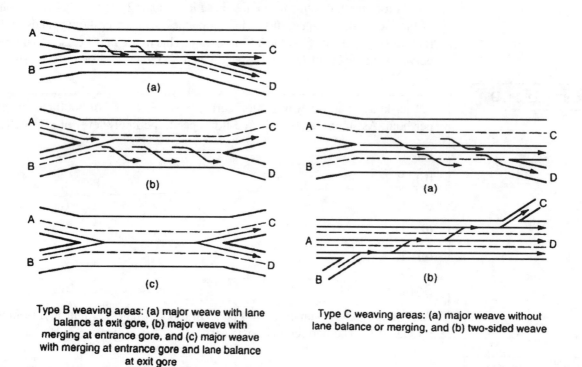

Type B weaving areas: (a) major weave with lane
balance at exit gore, (b) major weave with
merging at entrance gore, and (c) major weave
with merging at entrance gore and lane balance
at exit gore

Type C weaving areas: (a) major weave without
lane balance or merging, and (b) two-sided weave

Figure 11.17   Weaving area configuration types

Weaving Areas

Weaving is defined as the crossing of two or more traffic streams traveling in the same direction. Weaving areas require intense lane changing maneuvers and present special operational and design problems. The weaving area analysis procedure in the HCM addresses three geometric parameters which influence lane changing behavior in a weaving section: length of the weaving section, number of lanes, and configuration. The three basic weaving configurations identified in the HCM are shown in Figure 11.17.

The HCM weaving analysis procedure involves three primary steps:

Step 1. Estimate average travel speed of weaving and nonweaving vehicles assuming unconstrained operations. Weaving and nonweaving speeds are calculated as

$$S_i = S_{min} + [(S_{max} - S_{min})/(1 + W_i)] \tag{11.173}$$

where

S_i = speed of weaving ($i = w$) or nonweaving ($i = nw$) vehicles
S_{min} = minimum speed in the section (mph or km/hr)

S_{max} = maximum speed in the section

W_i = weaving intensity factor

Using assumed maximum and minimum speeds as defined in the Highway Capacity Manual, Equation (11.173) becomes

$$S_i = 15 + [(S_{FF} - 10)/(1 + W_i)] \quad \text{U.S.} \tag{11.174a}$$

$$S_i = 24 + [(S_{FF} - 16)/(1 + W_i)] \quad \text{Metric} \tag{11.174b}$$

where S_{FF} is the average free-flow speed. Equation (11.174a) applies to U.S. Customary units and Equation (11.174b) applies to metric units. The equation for calculating W is shown in Tables 11.12a and 11.12b.

The variables in Table 11.12a and 11.12b are defined below:

Table 11.12a Constants for computation of weaving intensity factors: metric units

General Form

$$W = \frac{a(1 + VR)^b \left(\frac{V}{N}\right)^c}{L_d}$$

	Constants for Weaving Speed, S_w				Constants for Nonweaving Speed, S_{nw}			
	a	*b*	*c*	*d*	*a*	*b*	*c*	*d*
Type A Configuration								
Unconstrained	0.15	2.2	0.97	0.80	0.0035	4.0	1.3	0.75
Constrained	0.35	2.2	0.97	0.80	0.0020	4.0	1.3	0.75
Type B Configuration								
Unconstrained	0.08	2.2	0.70	0.50	0.0020	6.0	1.0	0.50
Constrained	0.15	2.2	0.70	0.50	0.0010	6.0	1.0	0.50
Type C Configuration								
Unconstrained	0.08	2.3	0.80	0.60	0.0020	6.0	1.1	0.60
Constrained	0.14	2.3	0.80	0.60	0.0010	6.0	1.1	0.60

Source: TRB (2000).

a, b, c, d = constants of calibration

VR = ratio of weaving volume to total volume

V = total flow rate in the weaving area (vh/hr)

N = number of lanes in the weaving area

L = length of the weaving area (ft or m)

Table 11.12b Constants for computation of weaving intensity factors: metric units

General form

$$W = \frac{a(1 + VR)^b \left(\frac{V}{N}\right)^c}{(3.28L)^d}$$

	Constants for Weaving Speed, S_w				Constants for Nonweaving Speed, S_{nw}			
	a	*b*	*c*	*d*	*a*	*b*	*c*	*d*
Type A Configuration								
Unconstrained	0.15	2.2	0.97	0.80	0.0035	4.0	1.3	0.75
Constrained	0.35	2.2	0.97	0.80	0.0020	4.0	1.3	0.75

(Continued)

Table 11.12b Constants for computation of weaving intensity factors: metric units *(Continued)*

General form

$$W = \frac{a(1 + VR)^b \left(\frac{v}{N}\right)^c}{(3.28L)^d}$$

	Constants for Weaving Speed, S_W				Constants for Nonweaving Speed, S_{nw}			
	a	*b*	*c*	*d*	*a*	*b*	*c*	*d*
	Type B Configuration							
Unconstrained	0.08	2.2	0.70	0.50	0.0020	6.0	1.0	0.50
Constrained	0.15	2.2	0.70	0.50	0.0010	6.0	1.0	0.50
	Type C Configuration							
Unconstrained	0.08	2.3	0.80	0.60	0.0020	6.0	1.1	0.60
Constrained	0.14	2.3	0.80	0.60	0.0010	6.0	1.1	0.60

Source: TRB (2000).

Step 2. Check unconstrained operations assumption. Table 11.13a and 11.13b show the equations used in this step.

Table 11.13a Criteria for unconstrained versus constrained operation of weaving segments: U.S. customary units

Configuration	Number of Lanes Required for Unconstrained Operation, N_W	N_W (max)
Type A	$0.74(N) \, VR^{0.571} L^{0.234}/S_W^{\,0.438}$	1.4
Type B	$N[0.085 + 0.703VR + (234.8/L) - 0.018 \, (S_{nw} - S_W)]$	3.5
Type C	$N[0.761 + 0.047VR - 0.00011 - 0.005(S_{nw} - S_W)]$	3.0^a

[a] For two-sided weaving segments, all freeway lanes may be used by weaving vehicles.
Source: TRB (2000).

Table 11.13b Criteria for unconstrained versus constrained operation of weaving segments: metric units

Configuration	Number of Lanes Required for Unconstrained Operation, N_W	N_W (max)
Type A	$1.21(N) \, VR^{0.571} L^{0.234}/S_W^{\,0.438}$	1.4
Type B	$N[0.085 + 0.703VR + (71.57/L) - 0.0112 \, (S_{nw} - S_W)]$	3.5
Type C	$N[0.761 + 0.047VR - 0.00036 - 0.0031(S_{nw} - S_W)]$	3.0^a

[a] For two-sided weaving segments, all freeway lanes may be used by weaving vehicles.
Source: TRB (2000).

The variables in Table 11.13a and 11.13b are defined below:

L_H = length of weaving area (ft or m)
N = number of lanes in the weaving area
N_w = number of lanes used by weaving vehicles in the weaving area
v_w = total weaving flow rate in the weaving area in passenger car equivalents per hour (pc/hr)
v = total flow rate in the weaving area (pc/hr)
$VR = v_w/v$

For each type of configuration, N_w (number of lanes required to achieve unconstrained operation) is computed. If $N_w \le N_w$ (max), the operation is unconstrained

Table 11.14a LOS criteria for weaving segments: U.S. customary units

	Density (pc/mi/ln)	
LOS	Freeway Weaving Segment	Multilane and Collector-Distributor Weaving Segments
A	≤10.0	≤12.0
B	>10.0–20.0	>12.0–24.0
C	>20.0–28.0	>24.0–32.0
D	>28.0–35.0	>32.0–36.0
E	>35.0–43.0	>36.0–40.0
F	>43.0	>40.0

Source: TRB (2000).

Table 11.14b LOS criteria for weaving segments: metric units

	Density (pc/mi/ln)	
LOS	Freeway Weaving Segment	Multilane and Collector-Distributor Weaving Segments
A	≤6.0	≤8.0
B	>6.0–12.0	>8.0–15.0
C	>12.0–17.0	>15.0–20.0
D	>17.0–22.0	>20.0–23.0
E	>22.0–27.0	>23.0–25.0
F	>27.0	>25.0

Source: TRB (2000).

and the analysis advances to step 3. If $N_w > N_w$ (max), the speeds must be recomputed using the constrained equations in Table 11.13 (see step 1) before advancing to step 3.

Step 3. Determine level of service for weaving and nonweaving vehicles.
Levels of service are determined using the criteria in Table 11.14a or 11.14b. Density is calculated by

$$D = (v/N)/S \qquad (11.175)$$

where S is the space-mean speed, calculated as follows:

$$S = (v_w + v_{nw})/[(v_w/S_w) + (v_{nw}/S_{nw})] \qquad (11.176)$$

In Equation (11.176), v_{nw} = total nonweaving flow rate in the weaving area (pc/hr).

Ramps and Ramp Junctions

Chapter 25 of the HCM addresses the capacity characteristics of freeway merging and diverging at ramps, as well as the basic characteristics of ramp roadways themselves. The computational procedures for ramp-freeway terminals are intended to find the level of service for an existing or proposed situation. Design is established by a trial-and-error process.

Application of the HCM procedure for ramps and ramp junctions involves five basic steps:

Step 1. Specify geometry and demand volumes. Information required includes all lanes and their configuration, lane widths, ramp volume (V_R), upstream approaching freeway volume (V_F), and information about adjacent upstream or downstream ramps.

Step 2. Convert all demand volumes to flow rates (in passenger cars per hour) under ideal conditions. This is accomplished by means of the following equation:

$$V_{pcph} = \frac{V_{vph}}{PHF f_{HV} f_p} \tag{11.177}$$

where V_{pcph} is the flow rate in passenger cars per hour, V_{vph} is the volume in mixed vehicles, per hour, and the adjustment factors are similar to those for basic freeway segments.

Step 3. Estimate the flow rate of freeway vehicles remaining in the two rightmost lanes immediately upstream of the merge point or the beginning of the deceleration lane (V_{12}). The flow rate V_{12} is critical for determining the level of service for ramp junctions. It is estimated using a two-step process. First, the fraction of freeway traffic remaining in lanes 1 and 2 (P_{FM} or P_{FD}) is determined (in the case of merges) from Exhibits 5-5 and 5-6 (p. 25-6 of the HCM) or (in the case of diverges) from Exhibits 25-12 and 25-13 (pp. 25-12 and 25-13 of the HCM). For six-lane freeways, there are several equations given in Exhibits 25-5 and 25-12. Exhibits 25-6 and 25-13 are guides to selecting the relevant equations for particular ramp configurations. Where more than one equation applies, the selection also depends on the distance between the ramps. HCM Equations (25-2), (25-3), (25-8), and (25-9) (p. 25-7 and p. 25-13 of the HCM) give equilibrium distances to be used in determining the appropriate equation. Once P_{FM} or P_{FD} has been calculated, V_{12} is calculated by means of the equation at the top of Exhibit 25-5 or 25-12.

Step 4. Find checkpoint flow rates. Once the value of V_{12} is known, it is combined with the values of V_F and V_R to find checkpoint flow rates to compare with the maximum desirable flow rates in the ramp influence area. For merge areas the maximum desirable flow check is for $V_{R12} = V_{12} + V_R$; for diverge areas, it is for V_{12}. If these rates are exceeded, but freeway capacity is not, locally high densities are expected but no queuing is expected to occur on the freeway. Values of V_F and V_R are also combined to determine freeway flow upstream and downstream of the ramp junction. For merges, the critical flow is $V_{FO} = V_F + V_R$; for diverges it is V_F. If freeway capacity is exceeded, the level of service is F and the analysis stops. Critical checkpoint volumes, including freeway capacities, are given in Tables 11-15a through 11-15d [Exhibits 25-7 (p. 25-8 of the HCM) and 25-14 (p. 25-14 of the HCM)].

Step 5. Determine level of service. If step 4 has already resulted in level of service F, this step may be eliminated. Otherwise the density in lanes 1 and 2 is calculated. For merges, density is calculated by means of HCM Equation (11.25-5) (p. 25-8 of the HCM); for diverges, it is calculated by means of HCM Equation (11.25-10) (p. 25-14 of the HCM). Calculated densities are compared with limiting values to be found in Tables 11-16a or 11-16b [Exhibit 25-4 (p. 25-5 of the HCM)] to determine the level of service.

Table 11.15a Capacity values for merge areas, U.S. customary units

| Freeway Free-Flow Speed (mph) | Maximum Downstream Freeway Flow, v (pc/hr) | | | | Max Desirable Flow Entering Influence Area, V_{R12} (pc/hr) |
| | Number of Lanes in One Direction | | | | |
	2	3	4	>4	
≥70	4800	7200	9600	2400/in	4600
65	4700	7050	9400	2350/in	4600
60	4600	6900	9200	2300/in	4600
55	4500	6750	9000	2250/in	4600

Source: TRB (2000).

Table 11.15b Capacity values for diverge areas: U.S. customary units

| Freeway Free-Flow Speed (mph) | Maximum Upstream, V_{FI} or Downstream Freeway Flow, V (pc/hr) | | | | Max Flow Entering Influence Area, V_{R12} (pc/hr) |
| | Number of Lanes in One Direction | | | | |
	2	3	4	>4	
≥70	4800	7200	9600	2400/in	4400
65	4700	7050	9400	2350/in	4400
60	4600	6900	9200	2300/in	4400
55	4500	6750	9000	2250/in	4400

Note: For capacity of off-ramp roadways, see Exhibit 25-3 of the HCM.
Source: TRB (2000).

Table 11.15c Capacity values for merge areas: metric units

| Freeway Free-Flow Speed (km/hr) | Maximum Downstream Freeway Flow, V (pc/hr) | | | | Max Desirable Flow Entering Influence Area, V_{R12} (pc/hr) |
| | Number of Lanes in One Direction | | | | |
	2	3	4	>4	
120	4800	7200	9600	2400/in	4600
110	4700	7050	9400	2350/in	4600
100	4600	6900	9200	2300/in	4600
90	4500	6750	9000	2250/in	4600

Source: TRB (2000).

Table 11.15d Capacity values for diverge areas: metric units

| Freeway Free-Flow Speed (km/hr) | Maximum Upstream, V_{FI} or Downstream Freeway Flow, V (pc/hr) | | | | Max Flow Entering Influence Area, V_{12} (pc/hr) |
| | Number of Lanes in One Direction | | | | |
	2	3	4	>4	
120	4800	7200	9600	2400/in	4400
110	4700	7050	9400	2350/in	4400
100	4600	6900	9200	2300/in	4400
90	4500	6750	9000	2250/in	4400

Note: For capacity of off-ramp roadways, see Exhibit 25-3 of the HCM.
Source: TRB (2000).

Table 11.16a LOS criteria for merge and diverge area: U.S. customary units

LOS	Density (pc/mi/ln)
A	≤10
B	>10–20
C	>20–28
D	>28–35
E	>35
F	Demand exceeds capacity

Source: TRB (2000).

Table 11.16b LOS Criteria for merge and diverge area: U.S. metric units

LOS	Density (pc/km/ln)
A	≤6
B	>6–12
C	>12–17
D	>17–22
E	>22
F	Demand exceeds capacity

Source: TRB (2000).

The above procedure applies to single-lane on- and off-ramps. Other situations are discussed in sections on special cases (pp. 25-8 through 25-11 of the HCM for merges and pp. 25-14 through 25-17 of the HCM for diverges). The capacity of ramp roadways is also discussed, and approximate capacities may be found in Exhibit 25-3 (p. 25-4 of the HCM).

Urban Streets

Chapter 15 of the HCM presents a methodology for analyzing urban streets in terms of their travel speeds. This methodology can also be used to analyze suburban streets that have signal spacing of 2 miles (3 km) or less.

Level of service for urban streets is based on the average through-vehicle speed, which in turn depends on running times and control delay at intersections. Urban streets are divided into four classes based on their free-flow speed or, alternatively, their functional and design categories. Within each class, level of service depends on average travel speed, with the limits of the levels of service varying according to the class. Running times are computed based on free-flow speed and segment length. Control delay is computed as in Chapter 16 of the HCM. Travel speeds are then calculated from the segment length, the running time, and the control delay and used to determine the level of service. The HCM also discusses the sensitivity of the results to the input variables, and includes a set of speed-flow curves relating travel speed to peak direction *v/c* ratio (HCM Exhibits 15-8 through 15-11, pp. 15-10 and 15-11 of the HCM).

Signalized Intersections

Signalized intersections are the most complex points in any traffic stream, and the procedures in Chapter 16 of the HCM reflect this complexity. Capacity analysis computations for signalized intersections are reciprocal to signal-timing computations. In capacity analysis, the signal timing is known and the LOS for known roadway conditions is determined. In signal-timing computations, known traffic and roadway conditions are manipulated to find a signal timing which will accommodate a given LOS. Chapter 16 of the HCM presents methods for determining the LOS of intersections. Signal timing is discussed in an appendix to Chapter 10 of the HCM.

The methodology adopted in the HCM is based on critical movement analysis, and focuses on the identification of those movements in particular lanes or lane groups that control the requirements for green signal time allocation. Once critical movements are identified and provided for, all other movements will operate as well or better.

The HCM uses the average control delay per vehicle during a 15-minute analysis period as the measure of signalized intersection level of service. Control delay includes delay from deceleration, queue move-up, and acceleration, as well as time spent stopped. Delay is a very complex measure which depends upon the following five factors: (1) quality of signal progression, (2) cycle length, (3) green signal times, (4) v/c ratios, and (5) queue present at the beginning of the analysis period, if applicable.

Delay is not heavily dependent on the v/c ratio. Low delays can result at intersections with a high v/c ratio if signals are favorably progressed and the timing is efficient. Conversely, high delay can occur with a low v/c ratio where progression is poor and timing is inefficient. Very low v/c ratios and high delays, for example, can result when the green time in the cycle is excessive. The important point here is that it is not necessary to achieve low v/c ratios to have a good level of service based on delay. Analysis of both v/c ratios and delay levels is required to fully evaluate the operation of signalized intersections.

Operational analysis of signalized intersections is complex and time-consuming; particularly if all computations are performed manually. Figure 11.18 illustrates the process.

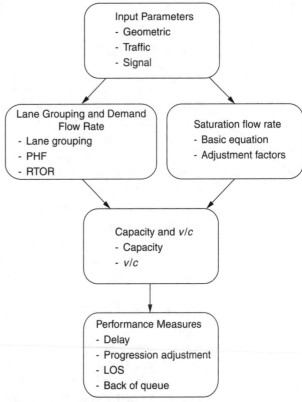

Figure 11.18 Signalized intersection methodology
[*Source:* TRB (2000).]

Table 11.17 Input data needs for each analysis lane group

Type of Condition	Parameter
Geometric conditions	Area type
	Number of lanes, N
	Average lane width, W (ft)
	Grade, G (%)
	Existence of exclusive LT or RT lanes
	Length of storage bay, LT or RT lane, L_s (ft)
	Parking
Traffic conditions	Demand volume by movement, V (veh/hr)
	Base saturation flow rate, s_0 (pc/hr/ln)
	Peak-hour factor, PHF
	Percent heavy vehicles, HV (%)
	Approach pedestrian flow rate, v_{ped} (p/hr)
	Local buses stopping at intersection, N_B (buses/hr)
	Parking activity, N_m (maneuvers/hr)
	Arrival type, AT
	Proportion of vehicles arriving on green, P
	Approach speed, S_A (mph)
Signalization conditions	Cycle length, C (s)
	Green time, G (s)
	Yellow-plus-all-red change-and-clearance interval (intergreen), Y (s)
	Actuated or pretimed operation
	Pedestrian push-button
	Minimum pedestrian green, G_p (s)
	Phase plan
	Analysis period, T (hr)

Source: TRB (2000).

The input module is simply a worksheet for summarizing all of the variables needed for the analyses. The HCM provides a tabulation of default values for many of the input variables which may not be readily available from local data.

In the volume adjustment module, all hourly volumes are converted to peak flow rates by lane groups for analysis. All exclusive turning lanes are considered as separate lane groups. Preliminary steps include summarizing input parameters such as intersection geometry, traffic conditions, and signal features and determining lane groups and demand flows for each lane group. Table 11.17 summarizes information required for the analysis.

A saturation flow rate is calculated for each lane group under prevailing conditions. The saturation flow rate is the capacity of an intersection approach lane if the signal were always green and the flow of vehicles were never stopped. Saturation flow is expressed in terms of vehicles per hour of green signal time. Under ideal conditions, the saturation flow rate for signalized intersection approaches is 1900 pc/hr/ln. Ideal conditions include 12 ft (3.6 m) lane widths, level approach grade, all passenger cars in the traffic stream, no turning vehicles in the traffic stream, intersection located in a non-central business district, and no parking within 250 ft (75 m) of the intersection. The saturation flow for a given lane group under prevailing conditions is computed from the following equation:

$$s = s_0 \times N \times f_w \times f_{HV} \times f_g \times f_p \times f_{bb} \times f_a \times f_{LU} \times f_{LT} \times f_{RT} \times f_{Lpb} \times f_{Rpb} \quad \textbf{(11.178)}$$

where

s = saturation flow rate for a lane group under prevailing conditions (vehicles per hour of green signal time)

s_0 = saturation flow rate per lane group under ideal conditions (1900 passenger) per hour of green signal time per lane

N = number of lanes in the lane group

f_w = adjustment for lane widths

f_{HV} = adjustment factor for heavy vehicles

f_g = adjustment factor for grade

f_p = adjustment factor for parking activity

f_{bb} = adjustment factor for bus blockage

f_a = adjustment factor for area type

f_{LU} = adjustment factor for lane utilization

f_{LT} = adjustment factor for left turns

f_{RT} = adjustment factor for right turns

f_{Lpb} = pedestrian adjustment factor for left turns

f_{Rpb} = pedestrian-bicycle adjustment factor for right turns

Adjustment factors are summarized in HCM Exhibit 16-7 (p. 16-11 of the HCM). Most may be calculated by simple formulas given in this table; however, the factors related to pedestrian-bicycle blockage involve a complicated iterative process. This is also true of left-turn factors where there are permitted left turns.

Capacities and v/c ratios may be calculated for individual lane groups and for the intersection as a whole. The capacity of each lane group is calculated as follows:

$$c_i = s_i \times (g/C)_i \tag{11.179}$$

where

c_i = capacity of lane group or approach i (veh/hr)

s_i = saturation flow rate for lane group or approach i (veh/hr)

$(g/C)_i$ = ratio of green signal time (g) to cycle time (C) for lane group or approach i

The ratio of flow rate to capacity, v/c, is given the symbol X in intersection analysis and is computed by dividing the adjusted flows by the capacities computed above.

$$X_i = v_i/c_i \tag{11.180}$$

where v_i = actual flow rate for lane group or approach i (veh/hr).

The critical v/c ratio for the intersection as a whole is defined in terms of critical lane groups or approaches as shown below:

$$X_c = \Sigma(v/s)_{ci}[C/(C-L)] \tag{11.181}$$

where

X_c = critical v/c ratio for the intersection

$\Sigma(v/s)_{ci}$ = summation of flow ratios for all critical lane groups or approaches

C = cycle length (s)

L = total lost time per cycle (s)

This equation is also useful in estimating signal timings where they are not known.

Level of service is defined in terms of the average control delay per vehicle. Delay is computed for each lane group as follows:

$$d = d_1 PF + d_2 + d_3 \tag{11.182}$$

$$d_1 = [0.50C(1 - g/C)^2/[1 - \text{Min}(1, X)g/C] \tag{11.183}$$

$$PF = [(1 - P)f_{pA}]/[1 - (g/C)] \tag{11.184}$$

$$d_2 = 900T\{(X - 1) + [(X - 1)^2 + (8kIX/cT)]^{1/2}\} \tag{11.185}$$

where

d_1 = uniform control delay component assuming uniform arrivals (s/veh)

PF = uniform delay progression adjustment factor

d_2 = incremental delay component (s/veh)

d_3 = residual delay component to account for queues present at the beginning of the analysis period (s/veh)

C = cycle length (s)

g = green signal time for lane group (s)

X = v/c ratio for lane group

P = proportion of vehicles arriving on green

f_{pA} = supplemental adjustment factor for when the platoon arrives during the green

T = duration of the analysis period (hr)

k = incremental delay factor that is dependent on signal setting

I = upstream filtering/metering adjustment factor

c = lane group capacity (veh/hr).

d_3 = initial queue delay

The progression adjustment factor PF may be calculated or determined from Table 9-13 (p. 9–29 of the HCM). Values of k are given in HCM Exhibits 16-11 and 16-12 (p. 16–20 of the HCM). Values of I may be found in Exhibit 15-7 (p. 15-8 of the HCM).

The determination of the appropriate "arrival type" is one of the most critical factors in the analysis. The HCM defines six arrival types for various signal and lane types, and v/c ratios (see Exhibit 16-11, p. 16–20 of the HCM). The arrival types are a measure of the quality of signal progression and range from the condition where a dense platoon of vehicles arrives at the intersection at the beginning of the red phase (Type 1), to the condition where the platoon arrives at the beginning of a green phase (Type 5). Type 6 is reserved for exceptional progression quality on routes with near ideal progression characteristics.

Levels of service based upon delay estimates and the following criteria are then determined.

Level of Service	Control Delay (s/veh)
A	≤10
B	>10 and ≤20
C	>20 and ≤35
D	>35 and ≤55
E	>55 and ≤80
F	>80

Unsignalized Intersections

Chapter 17 of the HCM provides two separate methodologies. One of these is used to analyze the capacity of two-way-stop–controlled (TWSC) intersections, and the other is to analyze all-way-stop–controlled (AWSC) intersection. Levels of service are based on average control delay in seconds per vehicle and are given in Table 11.18. The TWSC methodology includes the following steps:

1. Define geometric and traffic conditions for the intersection under study.

2. Determine the conflicting traffic through which each minor-street movement, and the major-street left turn, must cross.

3. Determine the size of the gap in the conflicting traffic stream needed by vehicles in each movement.

4. Determine the capacity of the gaps in the major traffic stream to accommodate each minor movement.

Table 11.18 Level-of-service criteria

Level of Service	Delay Range
A	≤10
B	>10 and ≤15
C	>15 and ≤25
D	>25 and ≤35
E	>35 and ≤50
F	>50

5. Adjust the calculated capacities to account for impedance and use of shared lanes.

6. Adjust calculated capacities to account for the effect of upstream signals on the major street headway distribution.

7. Adjust calculated capacities to account for a two-stage gap acceptance process at intersection with medians or two-way left-turn lanes.

8. Adjust the calculated capacities to account for flared minor-street approaches.

9. Estimate the average control delay and queue length for each minor movement and determine the level of service for each movement and for the intersection.

Impedance refers to the fact that vehicles at a TWSC intersection use gaps in a prioritized manner. When traffic becomes congested in a high-priority movement, it can keep lower-priority movements from using gaps and thus reduce the capacity of these movements. Because the methodology is based on the use of gaps in a prioritized manner, it is important that calculations be made in the following order: (1) right turns from the minor street, (2) left turns from the major street, (3) through movements from the minor street, and (4) and left turns from the minor street. The HCM provides worksheets to assist in maintaining the proper order of computations. Delay is calculated by means of Equation 17-38 (p. 17–24 of the HCM).

All drivers at AWSC intersections must stop. When vehicles are present on conflicting approaches, a pattern tends to develop in which the right-of-way passes to each approach in turn. Departure headways on the approaches depend on intersection geometry, vehicle type, and the presence of conflicting vehicles. The HCM method for AWSC intersections involves a complicated capacity model. This model consists of a number of different degree-of-conflict cases, for which there are different saturation headways and probabilities of occurrence. For site with a single lane on each approach, the model involves 5 cases that are based on presence of vehicles on the opposing approach and the conflicting approaches to the left and right. For multilane sites, the model involves 64 cases, based on the presence and number of vehicles on the various approaches. The probability of each case depends on the degree of utilization of each other approach. The degree of utilization of an approach, in turn, depends on its capacity, which depends on the degree of utilization of the other approaches. Consequently, the model involves iterative calculations. It is given by Equations 17-42 through 17-55 on pp. 17-34 through 17-40 of the HCM. Level-of-service definitions are the same as those for TWSC intersections.

Pedestrians

Chapter 18 of the HCM presents a methodology for analyzing pedestrian flows from the point of view of the pedestrian. Effects of pedestrians on vehicular flows are discussed in other chapters, such as those dealing with signalized and unsignalized intersections.

Level-of-service analysis procedures are provided for the following types of pedestrian facilities: walkways and sidewalks, pedestrian queuing areas, shared off-street paths, pedestrian crosswalks, and pedestrian facilities along urban streets. Level-of-service definitions vary according to the type of facility.

The HCM provides estimates of walking speed based on the age distribution of the population and effective walkway width where walkway obstructions such as light poles, fire hydrants, telephone booths, and benches are present (Exhibit 18-2, p. 18-3 of the HCM).

The level of service for uninterrupted pedestrian facilities such as walkways and sidewalks is based on pedestrian space (the reciprocal of density) given in ft^2 or m^2 per pedestrian. Exhibits 18-3 through 18-6 (pp. 18-4 and 18-5 of the HCM) give levels of service for these facilities under various conditions. Levels of service for pedestrian queuing areas are also based on space, and are given by Exhibit 18-7 (p. 18-6 of the HCM). Levels of service for facilities shared with bicycles depend on the number of meeting events between pedestrians and bicycles, which in turn depends of the bicycle flow rate. Levels of service for such facilities are given by Exhibit 18-8 (p. 18-7 of the HCM). The level of service for pedestrians at signalized intersections is based on pedestrian delay in seconds per pedestrian, calculated as

$$d_p = 0.5(C - g)^2/C \qquad (11.186)$$

where
  d_p = average pedestrian delay (s)
  g = effective green time for pedestrians (s)
  C = cycle length (s)

Levels of service are given in Exhibit 18-9 (p. 18-8 of the HCM). The HCM also includes procedures for calculating pedestrian area requirements at street corners of signalized intersections (pp. 18-8 through 18-13 of the HCM). The level of service for pedestrians at unsignalized intersections is based on average delay per pedestrian and is given in Exhibit 18-13 (p. 18-15 of the HCM). Procedures for calculating pedestrian delay at unsignalized intersections are discussed on pages 18-13 through 18-15 of the HCM. The level of service for pedestrian sidewalks on urban streets is defined in terms of pedestrian travel speed, which in turn depends on walking speeds and intersection delays. Levels of service for this case are given in Exhibit 18-14 (p. 18-16 of the HCM).

Bicycles

Chapter 19 of the HCM presents procedures for analyzing bicycle facilities. Procedures are provided for the following types of facilities: exclusive off-street bicycle paths, shared off-street paths, bicycle lanes on streets, interrupted-flow bicycle facilities, and bicycle lanes on urban streets.

The level of service for uninterrupted-flow bicycle facilities, both exclusive and shared, is based on the frequency of meeting events between bicycles or bicycles and other users such as pedestrians. Levels of service are given in Exhibit 19-1 (p. 19-3 of the HCM) for exclusive facilities and Exhibit 19-2 (p. 19-4 of the HCM) for shared facilities. Formulas for calculating the number of meeting events in those two cases are presented on pp. 19-2 through 19-4 of the HCM. Exhibit 19-3 (p. 19-5 of the HCM) presents estimates of the number of meeting events experienced by bicycles in uninterrupted on-street bicycle lanes as a function of the bicycle flow, rate, the mean speed of bicycles, and the standard deviation of bicycle speed. Once the number of events is calculated by means of Exhibit 19-3, Exhibit 19-1 may be used to determine the level of service for on-street bicycle lanes.

The level of service for bicycles at signalized intersections is based on control delay for bicycles and is given in Exhibit 19-4 (p. 19-6 of the HCM). Formulas for calculating control delay for bicycles are given on p. 19-6 of the HCM. The level of service for bicycle lanes on urban streets subject to interrupted flow depends on the average bicycle travel speed and is given in Exhibit 19-5 (p. 19-8 of the HCM). Bicycle travel speed, in turn, is calculated from the sums of bicycle running speed over each segment of the street and the bicycle control delay at each intersection.

TRAFFIC CONTROL DEVICES

Traffic control devices are all signs, signals, markings, and devices placed on, over, or adjacent to a street or highway by authority of a public body or official having jurisdiction to regulate, warn, or guide traffic. The *Manual on Uniform Traffic Control Devices* (MUTCD), issued by the Federal Highway Administration (FHWA), is the standard reference concerning traffic control devices and their use. The federal government is limited to encouraging the adoption of the MUTCD by the states. However, most states have adopted the federal MUTCD without revision, or have at least adopted the minimum requirements of the federal manual. This section provides a review of the basic principles of the MUTCD. The reader should consult both the federal and applicable state MUTCDs for complete details.

The MUTCD

According to the federal MUTCD (USDOT, 2003), "The purpose of traffic control devices, as well as the principles for their use, is to promote highway safety and efficiency by providing for the orderly movement of all road users on streets and highways throughout the nation. Traffic control devices notify road users of regulations and provide warning and guidance needed for the safe, uniform, and efficient operation of all elements of the traffic stream."

To be effective, a traffic control device should meet five basic requirements: (1) fulfill a need, (2) command attention, (3) convey a clear, simple meaning, (4) command respect from road users, and (5) give adequate time for proper response. Four basic considerations are employed to ensure that these requirements are met: (1) design, (2) placement and operation, (3) maintenance, and (4) uniformity.

The federal MUTCD provides mandatory *standards*, denoted by "shall"; *guidance* (recommended but not mandatory), denoted by "should"; and *options*, denoted by "may." The MUTCD also contains *support*, which consists of explanatory material.

Traffic control devices are to be used only where justified or "warranted." The MUTCD contains a detailed set of warrants for each major type of traffic control device.

Traffic Markings

Markings are used to supplement the regulations or warnings of other devices such as signs and signals and are also used alone in some applications. The most common method of placing pavement, curb, and object markings is by painting, though a variety of other suitable materials, including raised pavement markers, is available.

Longitudinal pavement markings are governed by the following basic concepts:

1. Yellow lines delineate the separation of traffic flows in opposing directions, mark the left edge of the pavement of divided highways and one-way highways and ramps, or the separation of two-way left-turn lanes and reversible lanes from other lanes.

2. White lines delineate the separation of traffic flows in the same direction, or mark the right edge of the pavement.

3. Red markings delineate roadways that *shall* not be entered or used.

4. Blue markings indicate parking spaces for persons with disabilities, and the location of fire hydrants along a roadway.

5. Broken lines indicate permissive conditions.

6. Solid lines prohibit or discourage crossing.

7. The width of a line indicates the degree of emphasis.

8. Double lines indicated maximum or special restrictions.

9. Markings which must be visible at night *shall* be reflectorized unless ambient illumination ensures that the markings are adequately visible.

Traffic Signs

The federal MUTCD identifies three basic categories of traffic signs:

1. Regulatory signs give notice of traffic laws or regulations.

2. Warning signs give notice of a situation that might not be readily apparent.

3. Guide signs show route designation, destinations, directions, distances, services, points of interest, and other geographical, recreational, or cultural information.

Regulatory Signs

The basic categories of regulatory signs are: (1) right of way (STOP, YIELD), (2) speed control, (3) movement control, (4) parking, (5) pedestrian, and (6) miscellaneous. With the exception of STOP and YIELD signs, most regulatory signs are rectangular in shape, with a black legend on a white background.

According to the MUTCD (USDOT, 2001), the YIELD sign may be warranted under the following conditions (see MUTCD for specifics):

1. The ability to see all potentially conflicting traffic is sufficient to allow a road user traveling at the posted speed, the 85th-percentile speed, or the statutory speed to pass through the intersection or to stop in a safe manner.

2. Controlling a merge-type movement on the entering roadway where acceleration geometry and/or sight distance is not adequate for merging traffic operation.

3. At the second crossroad of a divided highway, where the median is 9 m (30 ft) or greater, a STOP sign may be installed at the entrance to the first roadway of a divided highway, and a YIELD sign may be installed at the entrance to the second roadway.

4. At an intersection where a special problem exists and where engineering judgment indicates the problem to be amenable to correction by use of a YIELD sign.

A STOP sign may be warranted where one or more of the following conditions exist:

1. Intersection of a less important road with a main road where application of the normal right-of-way rule would not be expected to provide reasonable compliance with the law

2. A street entering a through highway or street

3. An unsignalized intersection in a signalized area

4. High speed, restricted view, or crash records indicate a need for control by a STOP sign

Warning Signs

Warning signs call attention to unexpected conditions on or adjacent to a highway or street that might not be readily apparent to road users. Such locations or conditions include (1) changes in horizontal alignment, (2) changes in vertical alignment, (3) changes in cross section, (4) changes in roadway surface condition, (5) advance warning of traffic control, (6) traffic flow, (7) change in speed, (8) intersections, (9) vehiculared traffic, (10) nonvehicular traffic crossings, and (11) supplemental plaques providing information about distance, speed, arrows, hills, street names, dead-end/no-outlet locations, and sharing the road.

Warning signs are generally diamond-shaped with a black legend on a yellow background.

Guide Signs and Other Signs

The MUTCD states that guide signs "are essential to direct road users along streets and highways, to inform them of intersecting routes, to direct them to cities, towns, villages, or other important destinations, to identify nearby rivers and streams, parks, forests, and historical sites, and generally to give such information as will help them along their way in the most simple, direct manner possible." Major types of guide signs include (1) guide signs for conventional roads, (2) guide signs for freeways and expressways, (3) specific service (logo) signs, (4) tourist-oriented direction signs, (5) recreational and cultural interest area signs, and (6) emergency management signs. Like other traffic control devices, the dimensions, placement, and other features of guide signs and others are described in detail in the MUTCD.

Traffic Signals

Traffic signals can be one of the most effective means of controlling traffic at an intersection. However, it is important that traffic signals be used only when necessary. The MUTCD specifies eight warrants for the installation of traffic signals: (1) eight-hour vehicular volume, (2) four-hour vehicular volume, (3) peak hour, (4) pedestrian volume, (5) school crossing, (6) coordinated signal system, (7) crash experience, and (8) roadway network. The MUCTD advises that traffic signals should not be installed unless one or more of these warrants are satisfied. The MUTCD presents various tables and charts to assist in the evaluation of these warrants.

TRAFFIC SIGNAL TIMING

This section provides a brief review of basic terminology, concepts, and procedures related to the timing of traffic signals, specifically pretimed signal systems.

Elements of Signal Timing

The essential elements that constitute pretimed signal timing are: (1) cycle length, (2) interval length, (3) phase duration, (4) phase sequence, and (5) offset or yield point. Figure 11.19 illustrates these elements, which are discussed below.

The *cycle length* is the amount of time for the signal to complete one complete sequence of signal indications. In a coordinated signal system, the cycle length is constant for all signals during any given control period. This is true whether the individual controllers are pretimed or actuated.

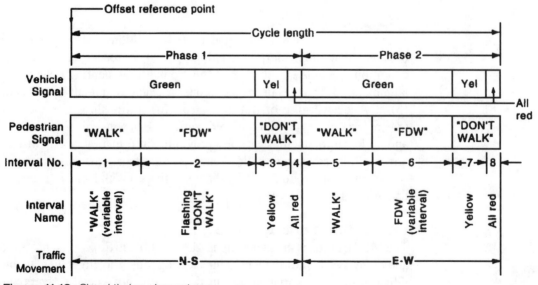

Figure 11.19 Signal timing elements

An *interval* is the smallest unit of measure used in defining a timing plan and is the segment of the cycle when all signal displays remain constant. A *phase* is a combination of two or more intervals during which the traffic movements given the right of way remain unchanged. A phase is part of a cycle allocated to any combination of traffic movements receiving the right of way simultaneously during one or more intervals.

A signal cycle is composed of as few as two or as many as eight phases, depending upon the traffic movements that require protection during their respective green signal times. A two-phase operation is generally preferable in terms of traffic performance because it permits shorter cycle lengths and more green time for through movements. However, heavy turning movements, particularly heavy left-turning movements, necessitate multiphase operation.

There are three left turn *phase sequencing* alternatives. When the protected left turn precedes the accompanying through movement, it is called a *leading left*. When the left turn phase follows the through movement, it is called a *lagging left*. These may be combined so that one left turn leads and the other lags. This is referred to as leadlag phasing.

The *offset* is normally the time from a system reference point to the beginning point of the cycle at each of the signal controllers in the system. It is the time lapse between the beginning of a green signal phase at an intersection and the beginning of a corresponding green signal phase at the next intersection. A *yield point*, when used in lieu of an offset, is referenced to the beginning of any interval other than the first interval in the cycle. The importance of the offset is discussed under the heading "Signal Coordination."

There are two other important concepts concerning traffic signals. The *clearance interval* is the duration of the yellow signal that allows vehicles to clear the intersection after the end of the green signal interval. The all-red signal interval is the display time of a red indication for all approaches. Several additional concepts are introduced at appropriate points in the following discussion.

Cycle Lengths

A number of procedures have been developed to determine the optimal cycle length of traffic signals. This section describes two of these methods: (1) The Highway Capacity Manual (HCM) procedure, and (2) Webster's method. Garber and Hoel (1997) describe several alternative methods and present example applications of those procedures.

The HCM Method

Appendix A of Chapter 10 of the HCM outlines some general guidelines to assist the analyst in estimating a signal design or timing for use in capacity analysis of signalized intersections. The guidelines in the HCM are intended only to assist the analyst in estimating an initial signal design for study, and do not represent recognized standards (TRB, 2000).

The basic design of a traffic signal involves three primary determinations: (1) the type of signal controller to be used, (2) the phase plan to be used, and (3) the allocation of green signal time among the various phases. There are three general types of signal control: (1) *pretimed* control, whereby signal times operate on a fixed, preset sequence of phases in repetitive order; (2) *semiactuated* control, for which the green signal is always on for the major street unless vehicles on the minor street actuate the signal phasing for that street; and (3) *actuated* control, for which all signal phases are controlled by vehicle detector actuations.

As previously discussed, the signal phasing scheme determines which movement or movements are given the right of way at the intersection. A two-phase system is the simplest phasing plan and is generally used when no left-turn phases are required. Multiphase systems are used where right or left turns require protected (separate) phasing. It is generally the left-turn movement that determines the need for partially or fully protected turn movement phasings. Most agencies use threshold volumes in the range of 100 to 200 left-turning vehicles per hour to determine the need for protected phasings. A three-phase system is generally used when only one approach requires a separate left-turn phase, and a four-phase system is typically used when all four approaches require separate left-turn phases. It is also sometimes necessary to provide leading and/or lagging green signal overlapping phases to provide for both protected and permitted left turns.

Once the signal type and phasing plan have been determined, the allocation of green time among the phases can be estimated. This can be accomplished by solving the following equations for the cycle length and green times for a particular phase, respectively.

$$C = LX_c/[X_c - \Sigma(v/s)_{ci}] \tag{11.186}$$

$$g_i = v_i C/s_i X_i = (v/s)_i (C/X_i) \tag{11.187}$$

where

C = cycle length, s
L = lost time per cycle, s
X_c = critical v/c ratio for the intersection
X_i = v/c ratio for lane group
$(v/s)_i$ = flow ratio for lane group i
g_i = effective green time for lane group i

Lost time is the time during which the intersection is not effectively used by any movement and is typically assumed to be 3.5 to 4 seconds per phase. *Effective green time* is the time during which a given phase is effectively used by any movement and is equal to the actual green signal time plus the change interval (yellow and/or all-red intervals) minus the lost time per phase.

The HCM procedure for timing pretimed signals is summarized below.

Step 1: Estimate absolute minimum cycle length. This is accomplished using Equation (11.186) and assuming $X_c = 1.0$.

Step 2: Estimate cycle length for the desired v/c ratio. This is accomplished using Equation (11.186) and the v/c ratio selected by the analyst.

Step 3: Select appropriate cycle length. The results of step 1 and 2 will provide an indication of the range of cycle lengths. Cycle lengths in the range of 30 to 120 seconds are commonly used.

Step 4: Allocate green time. A number of different policies may be used in allocating the available green signal time estimated from Equation (11.187). One common policy is to allocate the green signal time such that the v/c ratios for critical movements in each phase are equal. Another common policy is to allocate the minimum required green signal time to the minor street, and assign all remaining green signal time to the major street (TRB, 2000).

Step 5: Check the results. The timing should be checked to ensure that the sum of green times plus the lost times equals the cycle length.

The *Highway Capacity Manual* also contains a procedure for timing actuated signals, but it is very complicated and is not suitable for hand calculations.

Webster's Method

Webster and Cobbe (1958) have shown that the cycle length which minimizes intersection delay can be computed from the following equation:

$$C_o = (1.5L + 5)/(1 - \Sigma Y_i) \qquad (11.188)$$

where

C_o = optimum cycle length (s)
L = total lost time per cycle (s)
Y_i = maximum value of approach *v/s* ratios for phase *i*

The total effective green signal time available per cycle can now be computed as shown below.

$$g_T = C - L \qquad (11.189)$$

where

C = cycle length (C_o rounded to the nearest 5 s)
g_T = total effective green time per cycle

To minimize overall delay, the total effective green signal time is allocated among the different phases in proportion to their *Y* values.

$$g_i = [Y_i/(Y_1 + Y_2 + \cdots + Y_\phi)] \times g_T \qquad (11.190)$$

where

g_i = effective green time for phase *i*
ϕ = number of phases

Change Intervals

The primary purpose of the yellow signal indication is to alert drivers that the green signal phase is about to end and the red is about to begin, to allow vehicles at the intersection to cross it. If the intent of the yellow signal interval is to allow all vehicles to clear the intersection by the end of the yellow, then each vehicle must either stop prior to entering the intersection, or pass through it without stopping. The Institute of Transportation Engineers recommends the following equation for computing the length of the yellow interval [see Roess et al. (2004, pp. 515–516) for an interesting discussion of the meaning of "clearance interval"]:

$$y = t_{PR} + [V/(2d \pm 2Gg)] \qquad (11.191)$$

where

y = length of yellow signal interval to the nearest 0.1 s
t_{PR} = driver perception-reaction time (recommended as 1.0 s)
V = velocity of approaching vehicle (m/s or ft/s)
d = deceleration rate (recommended as 3 m/s^2 or 10 ft/s^2)
G = acceleration due to gravity (9.8 m/s^2 or 32.2 ft/s^2)
g = approach grade (in decimal; downgrade is negative)

Depending on local policy and site conditions, the all-red (or red clearance interval) may be determined from one of the following equations (Roess et al., 2004):

1. *No pedestrian traffic:*

$$r = (W + L_v)/V \qquad\qquad (11.192)$$

2. *Likelihood of pedestrian crossings:*

$$r = \text{max. of } (W + L_v)/V \text{ or } P/V \qquad\qquad (11.193)$$

3. *Significant pedestrian traffic:*

$$r = (P + L_v)/V \qquad\qquad (11.194)$$

where
r = length of all-red period (s)
W = length of vehicle path from departure stop line to far side of the farthest conflicting traffic lane (m or ft)
P = length of vehicle path from departure stop line to the far side of the farthest conflicting pedestrian crosswalk (m or ft)
L_v = length of vehicle (usually set at 6 m or 20 ft)
V = speed of vehicle through the intersection, m/s or ft/s

The selection of an inappropriate clearance interval can lead to the creation of a dilemma zone (Figure 11.20), an area where a vehicle can neither stop safely prior to the intersection nor clear the intersection without speeding before the onset of the red indication (Garber and Hoel, 1997). The following example illustrates the nature of the dilemma zone problem and its solution.

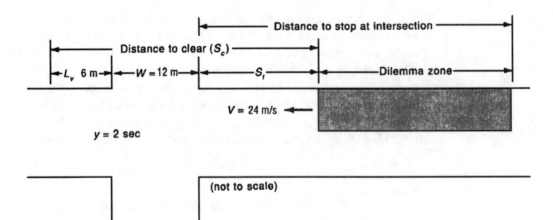

Figure 11.20 Dilemma zone

Example **11.10**	

For the intersection described below, a dilemma zone exists between which pair of distances?

(a) 66 m and 120 m

(b) 50 m and 120 m

(c) 66 m and 120 m

(d) 85 m and 150 m

(e) 70 m and 130 m

L_v = length of vehicle = 6 m (for this example)
W = width of intersection = 12 m
V = 85th percentile approach speed = 86 km/hr = 24 m/s
y = yellow time = 2 s
d = deceleration rate = 3 m/s^2
t_{PR} = perception-reaction time = 1 s

Solution

$$S_t = \text{distance to continue into intersection} = yV \qquad (11.195)$$
$$S_c = \text{distance to clear intersection} = S_t + (L_v + W) \qquad (11.196)$$

$$S_s = \text{distance to stop at intersection} = (V^2/2d) + t_{PR}V \qquad (11.197)$$
$$t_c = \text{time to clear the intersection} = \text{min. yellow signal time} = S_s/V \qquad (11.198)$$

From Equation (11.195): $S_t = 2 \times 24 = 48$ m
From Equation (11.196): $S_c = 48 + 12 + 6 = 66$ m
From Equation (11.197): $S_s = [0.5 \times (24)^2/3] + 24 = 120$ m

Conclusion: Because $S_c < S_s$, a dilemma zone exists. Between 120 m and 66 m from the intersection, a dilemma zone exists where a vehicle could neither stop safely nor continue through the intersection during the 2-second yellow period.
The correct answer is (c).

Signal Coordination

In urban areas, traffic signals should be timed in such a way that the first vehicle in a platoon of vehicles will arrive at successive intersections at the beginning of each intersection's green signal phase. To obtain this coordination, all intersections in the system must have the same cycle length.

The Institute of Transportation Engineers (1999) suggests the use of coupling index analysis as a means for determining whether to try signal coordination. Stated as an equation, the coupling index is

$$I = V/x \qquad (11.199)$$

where
I = coupling index
V = two-way traffic volume (v/hr)
x = signal spacing (ft)

Use of the index has shown that a level of 0.5 or greater indicates that signals should be considered for coordination during the time period examined (ITE, 1999).

The signal timing element used to achieve this coordination is the offset, as defined earlier in this section. The speed at which a platoon of vehicles proceed

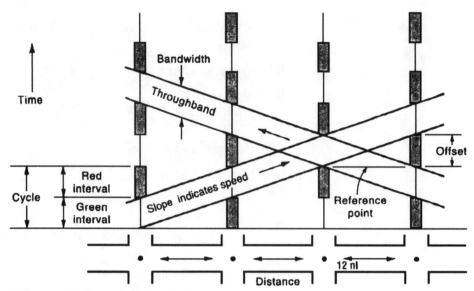

Figure 11.21 Time-space diagram

along an arterial is known as the speed of progression, or band speed. The space delineated by two progressive speed lines on a time-space diagram (see Figure 11.21) is referred to as the throughband, or "green window" of travel. The time-space diagram is a plot of signal indications as a function of time and distance.

The ideal offset, in terms of coordination, is simply (Roess et al., 2004):

$$O_I = x/V \qquad (11.200)$$

where
O_I = ideal offset (s)
x = signal spacing (m or ft)
V = vehicle speed (m/s or ft/s)

The speed of progression of a platoon of vehicles is given by (Banks, 2002):

$$V = nx/C \qquad (11.201)$$

where
V = progression speed (m/s or ft/s)
C = cycle time (s)
n = alternative number (1 = single alternate, etc.)

Prior to the widespread use of computers for signal timing, signal coordination was accomplished using *simultaneous, single alternate*, or *double alternate* methods. Garber and Hoel (1997) and Roess et al. (2004) describe the various methods used to achieve coordination, and provide several examples to illustrate their applications.

PAVEMENT DESIGN

Roadway pavements are divided into two general categories: rigid and flexible. Rigid pavements are usually constructed of portland cement concrete, which behaves much like a beam over any irregularities in the underlying supporting materials. Flexible pavements are usually constructed of bituminous materials which transfer vehicle loadings directly to the underlying support materials.

The damage to roadway pavements caused by passenger cars is very limited compared with that caused by trucks. Therefore, pavements are designed to support a specified number of heavy vehicle loadings over their design life. An equivalent single-axle load (ESAL) is a standard term used in pavement design to describe the damage caused by one pass of an 18,000-pound (18-kip) axle load over the pavement surface (in SI notation, 18,000 pounds = 80 kN). Consequently, in order to design a pavement, it is necessary to express all of the traffic that will use the pavement as an equivalent number of 18,000-pound axle loads. The use of an 18,000-pound standard stems from the maximum legal axle loadings in effect at the time many pavement design methods were developed. This conversion is accomplished by first determining an ESAL factor for each classification of vehicle using the pavement. An ESAL factor is a ratio relating the damage caused by a passing vehicle of specified weight relative to the damage caused by an 18-kip axle load, or

$$\text{ESAL Factor} = D_i/D_{18} \tag{11.202}$$

where
D_i = damage caused by vehicle class i
D_{18} = damage caused by 18-kip axle load

Studies have shown that the ESAL factor for passenger cars is about 0.0008. The ESAL factors for heavy trucks, on the other hand, approach 2.4 when loaded to the legal limit and can be as high as 10 for overloaded trucks.

The truck factor is defined as the number of 18-kip single-load applications caused by a single passage of a vehicle. The load equivalency factor is the number of equivalent 18-kip single-axle load applications contributed by one passage of an axle. An average truck factor (f_i) can be calculated by multiplying the number of axles in each weight class (N_i) by the appropriate load equivalency factor (F_{Ei}) and dividing the sum of the products by the total number of vehicles involved (V_T). This relationship between truck factors and load equivalency factors is as follows:

$$f_i = \Sigma(N_i F_{Ei})/V_T \tag{11.203}$$

The accumulated annual design year ESAL for each category of axle load using *load equivalency factors* is calculated as follows (Garber and Hoel, 1997):

$$\text{ESAL}_i = \text{AADT}_i \times 365 \times F_{Ei} \times N_i \times g_{jt} \times f_d \tag{11.204}$$

where
ESAL_i = equivalent accumulated 18-kip single-axle load for axle category i
AADT_i = base-year annual average daily traffic for axle category i
F_{Ei} = load equivalency factor for axle category i
N_i = number of axles on each vehicle in axle category i
g_{jt} = growth factor for growth rate j and design period t
f_d = design lane factor (directional and lane distribution factor)

The accumulated annual design year ESAL using truck factors for each category of truck is

$$\text{ESAL}_i = \text{AADT}_i \times 365 \times f_i \times g_{jt} \times f_d \tag{11.205}$$

where
> $ESAL_i$ = equivalent accumulated 18-kip axle load for truck category i
> $AADT_i$ = base-year annual average daily traffic for vehicles in truck category i
> f_i = truck factor for vehicles in truck category i

The accumulated ESAL for all categories of axle loads or vehicles is

$$ESAL = \Sigma ESAL_i \tag{11.206}$$

The three most commonly used pavement thickness design methods are the AASHTO (1993) method, the Asphalt Institute (AI) (1991) method, and the Portland Cement Association (PCA) (1984) method. The AASHTO method addresses both flexible and rigid pavements, while the Asphalt Institute method and the Portland Cement Association method are concerned with the design of flexible and rigid pavements, respectively. This section presents a review of these three pavement design methods as they are used to determine pavement thickness.

Because of the complexity of the procedures and their heavy reliance on nomographs and design charts, the reader should consult the individual design manuals for example problems. Garber and Hoel (1997) also provide an excellent overview of the three design methods reviewed in this section. Like much of the material in this chapter, it is not the intent of this section to relieve the reader of the need to consult these three design manuals directly for the details of the individual design methods.

AASHTO Design Method

The AASHTO pavement design method is documented in the *AASHTO Guide for Design of Pavement Structure* (AASHTO, 1993). The AASHTO method is based on results obtained from the "AASHTO Road Test" conducted in the late 1950s and early 1960s in northern Illinois. The method is an empirical method that relates pavement performance measurements (loss of serviceability) directly to traffic loading and volume characteristics, roadbed soil strength, pavement layer material characteristics, and environmental factors. The AASHTO Road Test resulted in many important concepts, including demonstration of the major influences of traffic loads and repetitions on design thickness.

Equally important was the development of the serviceability-performance method of analysis, which provided a quantifiable way of defining "failure" based on a user-defined definition rather than one based primarily on structural failure. This is achieved through an initial serviceability index, p_0, which is the serviceability index immediately after construction; and the terminal serviceability index, p_t, which is the minimum acceptable value before resurfacing or reconstruction is necessary. The AASHTO guide suggests the use of p_0 values of 4.2 for flexible pavements and 4.5 for rigid pavements. A terminal serviceability index (p_t) of 2.5 or higher is suggested for design of major highways, and an index of 2.0 is suggested for highways with lesser traffic volumes.

The AASHTO method also incorporates a reliability design factor (F_R) to account for uncertainty in traffic forecasts and pavement performance.

The 1986 AASHTO Guide considers the following factors in the design process: (1) pavement performance, (2) traffic, (3) roadbed soil, (4) materials of construction, (5) environment, (6) drainage, (7) reliability, (8) life-cycle costs, and (9) shoulder design.

The basic design equations used for flexible and rigid pavements in the 1993 AASHTO Design Guide are as follows:

Flexible pavements:

$$\log_{10}(W_{18}) = Z_R \times S_0 + 9.36 \times \log_{10}(SN + 1) - 0.20$$
$$+ \{\log_{10}(\Delta PSI/2.7)/[0.40 + 1094/(SN + 1)^{5.19}]\}$$
$$+ 2.32 \times \log_{10}(M_R) - 8.07 \qquad \textbf{(11.207)}$$

where

W_{18} = predicted number of 18-kip ESAL applications

Z_R = standard normal deviate

S_0 = combined standard error of the traffic forecast and performance prediction

ΔPSI = difference between the initial design serviceability index, p_0, and the design terminal serviceability index, p_t

M_R = resilient modulus (psi)

SN = structural number (indicative of the total pavement thickness required)

The structural number (SN) is computed as follows:

$$SN = a_1 D_1 + a_2 D_2 m_2 + a_3 D_3 m_3 \qquad \textbf{(11.208)}$$

where

a_1, a_2, a_3 = layer coefficients of surface, base, and subbase course, respectively

D_1, D_2, D_3 = thickness (inches) of surface, base, and subbase courses, respectively

m_i = drainage coefficient for layer i

Rigid pavements:

$$\log_{10}(W_{18}) = Z_R \times S_0 + 7.35 \times \log_{10}(D + 1) - 0.06 + \frac{\log_{10}[\Delta PSI/3.0]}{1+[1.624 \times 10^7/(D+1)^{8.46}]}$$

$$+ (4.22 - 0.32 p_t) \times \log_{10} \left\{ \frac{S_c' \times C_d \times (D^{0.75} - 1.132)}{215.63 J[D^{0.75} - 18.42/(E_c/k)]^{0.25}} \right\} \qquad \textbf{(11.209)}$$

where

D = thickness of pavement slab (in.)

S_c' = modulus of rupture for portland cement concrete used on a specific project (psi)

J = load transfer coefficient used to adjust for load transfer characteristics of a specific design

C_d = drainage coefficient

E_c = modulus of elasticity for portland cement concrete (psi)

k = modulus of subgrade reaction (pci)

The AASHTO Guide provides a series of nomographs to solve these equations for the structural number (SN) for flexible pavements and the thickness of the pavement slab (D) for rigid pavements. The basic procedures are outlined below.

Flexible Pavements

The structural design of flexible pavements involves the determination of the thickness and vertical position of paving materials which can best be combined to provide a serviceable roadway for predicted traffic over the pavement's design life. The pavement structure is designed to use the most economical arrangement and minimum thickness of each material necessary to protect the underlying courses and the roadbed from stresses caused by traffic loads. The objective of the AASHTO design method is to determine a flexible pavement structural number (*SN*) adequate to carry the design ESAL. The basic method is applicable for 18-kip ESALs greater than 50,000 for the design period. Lower ESAL values are considered under the method described in the AASHTO Guide for low-volume roads. The flexible pavement design procedure is described in Section 3.1 (pp. II-31 to II-37) of the AASHTO Guide. Appendix H (pp. H-1 to H-7) of the AASHTO Guide presents a flexible pavement design example.

A summary of the basic steps in the AASHTO method for flexible pavement design is presented below. The section numbers, tables, and figures cited below refer to the AASHTO Guide (AASHTO, 1993).

Step 1: Determine the structural number. Figure 3.1 (p. II-32) of the AASHTO Guide presents the nomograph which can be used to solve Equation (11.207) for *SN* based on the following inputs.

1. Future traffic, W_{18}. Estimated as described in Section 2.1.2 (p. II-7). The basic procedure is similar to Equation (11.202), except the equivalence factors are based on the terminal serviceability index (p_t) and *SN*. The use of an assumed *SN* value of 5 will normally give results that are sufficiently accurate for design purposes. Appendix D of the AASHTO Guide presents tables of axle load equivalency factors for various axle configurations, and a range of values for p_t and *SN*. Appendix D also contains a worksheet to guide the analyst through the computations.
2. Reliability, *R*. Suggested levels of reliability for various functional classes of highways are presented in Table 2-2 (p. II-9) of the AASHTO Guide.
3. Overall standard deviation S_0. A value of 0.45 is recommended for flexible pavements.
4. Effective resilient modulus of roadbed material, M_R. The 1993 AASHTO Guide allows for the conversion of California Bearing Ratio (CBR) and stabilometer *R*-values to an equivalent M_R value through the following conversion factors:

$$M_R \text{ (psi)} = 1500 \times \text{CBR} \qquad \textbf{(11.210)}$$

$$M_R \text{ (psi)} = 1000 + 555 \times (R\text{-value}) \qquad \textbf{(11.211)}$$

5. Design serviceability loss, $\Delta PSI = p_0 - p_t$. Values of $p_0 = 4.2$ and $p_t = 2.0$ to 2.5 are suggested for flexible pavements.

Step 2: Evaluate need for staged construction (optional). If the analysis period (e.g., 20 years) is longer than the service life selected for the initial pavement structure, it will be necessary to consider staged construction and planned rehabilitation alternatives. In such cases, the analyst should consult Part III of the AASHTO Guide to develop design strategies which will last the entire analysis period. The design example in Appendix H of the AASHTO Guide provides an illustration of the application of staged construction alternatives. If staged construction is not a viable or necessary alternative, the analyst should proceed to step 3.

Step 3: Evaluate need to consider roadbed swelling and frost heave (optional).
If the site of the highway construction project is in an area where the roadbed
is subject to swelling and/or frost heave, the effects of these factors on the
rate of serviceability loss must be taken into account. This is accomplished
through the following iterative process. Table 3-1 (p. II-34) of the AASHTO
Guide provides an example of the process.

Step 3.1: Select an appropriate *SN* for the initial pavement. The maximum
initial *SN* recommended is that derived for conditions assuming no swelling
or frost heave.

Step 3.2: Select a trial performance period that might be expected under
the swelling/frost heave conditions anticipated. This number should be less
than the maximum performance period corresponding to the pavement
structural number selected in step 3.1.

Step 3.3: Use the nomograph in AASHTO Guide (Figure 2-2, p. II-11) to
estimate the total serviceability loss due to swelling and frost heave
($\Delta PSI_{SW,FH}$) that can be expected for the trial performance period selected
in step 3.2.

Step 3.4: Calculate the traffic serviceability loss (ΔPSI_{TR}).

$$\Delta PSI_{TR} = \Delta PSI - \Delta PSI_{SW,FH} \qquad\qquad \textbf{(11.212)}$$

Step 3.5: Estimate the allowable cumulative 18-kip ESAL traffic corresponding
to the traffic serviceability loss determined in step 3.4. Figure 3-1 (p. II-32) of
the AASHTO Guide is used in this step.

Step 3.6: Estimate the year at which the cumulative 18-kip ESAL traffic
from step 3.5 will be reached. This is accomplished with the aid of a
cumulative-traffic-versus-time plot. See Figure 2.1 (p. II-8) of the AASHTO
Guide for an example.

Step 3.7: Compare the trial performance period (step 3.2) with that calculated in step 3.6. If the difference is greater than 1 year, calculate the
average of the two and use this average as the trial value for the start of
the next iteration (return to step 3.2). If the difference is less than 1 year,
convergence is achieved and the average is the predicted performance
period of the initial pavement structure for the selected initial *SN*.

Step 4: Calculate layer thicknesses. In this step, a set of pavement layer
thicknesses are determined which, when combined, will provide the load-
carrying capacity corresponding to the design *SN*. Equation (11.208) is used
to convert the *SN* to actual thicknesses of surfacing, base, and subbase courses.
This equation does not have a unique solution; many combinations of layer
thicknesses provide satisfactory solutions. The AASHTO Guide provides some
guidance for determining a practical design. Sections 2.3.5 (p. II-17) and 2.4.1
(p. II-22) of the AASHTO Guide provide guidance concerning the selection
of appropriate layer (a_i) and drainage (m_i) coefficients, respectively, Page II-
35 of the AASHTO Guide suggests minimum practical thicknesses for each
pavement course which should also be considered when determining layer
thicknesses. Figure 3.2 (p. II-36) of the AASHTO Guide outlines a procedure
for determining thicknesses of layers using a layered analysis approach.

The reader is referred to Appendix H of the AASHTO Guide for a comprehensive flexible pavement design example problem. Garber and Hoel (1997) also
present an excellent overview of the AASHTO pavement design methods and
present a number of example problems.

Rigid Pavements

Chapter 3, Section 3.2 (pp. II-37 to II-48) of the AASHTO Guide describes the rigid pavement design procedure. Sections 3.3 and 3.4 of the Guide address joint and reinforcement design, respectively. Appendix I of the AASHTO Guide presents a detailed rigid pavement design example problem. The following review of the basic steps in the AASHTO procedure is limited to the determination of the required slab thickness (*D*). As in the design of flexible pavements, the following procedure is applicable to pavements that are expected to carry traffic levels in excess of 50,000 18-kip ESALs over the design period.

Step 1: Determine effective modulus of subgrade reaction (k). The AASHTO Guide provides a worksheet to facilitate the determination of an appropriate value for *k* (see Table 3.2, p. II-38 of the AASHTO Guide). The determination of *k* involves eight steps and the use of a number of nomographs (see Figure 3-3 to 3-6, pp. II-39 to II-42 of the AASHTO Guide). These are outlined below.

Step 1.1: Determine levels of slab support to be considered in determining *k*. These include (1) subbase types, (2) subbase thicknesses, (3) loss of support due to erosion, and (4) depth to rigid foundation. A separate worksheet and corresponding *k*-value is prepared for each combination of these factors.

Step 1.2: Identify seasonal roadbed soil resilient modulus values (from Section 2.3.1, p. II-12 of the AASHTO Guide).

Step 1.3: Assign subbase elastic (resilient) modulus (E_{SB}) values for each season (from Section 2.3.3, p. II-16 of the AASHTO Guide).

Step 1.4: Estimate the composite *k*-value for each season. This is accomplished with the aid of Figure 3-3 (p. II-39) in the AASHTO Guide.

Step 1.5: Develop the *k*-value which includes effects of a rigid foundation near the surface (disregard if depth to rigid foundation is >10 ft). Figure 3-4 (p. II-40) in the Guide is used to estimate this modified *k*-value for each season.

Step 1.6: Estimate the required slab thickness and use Figure 3-5 (p. II-41) to determine the relative damage, u_r, in each season.

Step 1.7: Sum all the u_r values and divide by the number of seasonal increments (12 to 24) to determine the average relative damage. The effective modulus of subgrade reaction is the value corresponding to the average relative damage and projected slab thickness in Figure 3-5 (p. II-41).

Step 1.8: Adjust the effective modulus of subgrade reaction to account for potential loss of support from subbase erosion. This is accomplished with the aid of Figure 3-6 (p. II-42) in the AASHTO Guide.

Step 2: Determine required slab thickness. Figure 3-7 (pp. II-45 to II-46) is the nomograph used for determining slab thickness for each of the effective *k*-values determined in step 1. In addition to the design *k*-value, the nomograph requires the following inputs (section references refer to the AASHTO Guide):

1. Estimated future traffic, W_{18} (Section 2.1.2)
2. Reliability, *R* (Section 2.1.3)
3. Overall standard deviation, S_0 (Section 2.1.3)
4. Design serviceability loss, $\Delta PSI = p_0 - p_t$ (Section 2.2.1)
5. Concrete elastic modulus, E_c (Section 2.3.3)
6. Concrete modulus of rupture, S_c' (Section 2.3.4)

7. Load transfer coefficient, J (Section 2.4.2)
8. Drainage coefficient, C_d (Section 2.4.1)

If staged construction and roadbed swelling/frost heave are not factors in the analyses, then the thickness design procedure is considered complete at this point.

Step 3: Evaluate need for staged construction (optional). Same as step 2 for the flexible pavement design procedure.

Step 4: Evaluate the need to consider roadbed swelling and frost heave (optional). This step is almost identical to step 3 of the flexible pavement design procedure. For rigid pavements, the iterative process outlined in step 3 of the flexible pavement design procedure would begin with the selection of an appropriate slab thickness, D (instead of *SN*), and Figure 3-7 (pp. II-45 to II-46) is used to estimate the allowable cumulative 18-kip ESAL traffic corresponding to the computed traffic serviceability loss (step 4.5 of the process). As with the flexible pavement design procedure, the AASHTO Guide provides a worksheet to aid in the computations (see Table 3-4, p. II-48).

The reader is referred to Appendix I of the AASHTO Guide for a comprehensive example problem which illustrates the application of the rigid pavement design procedure. Garber and Hoel (1997) also present an excellent overview of the AASHTO (and other) pavement design methods and present a number of example problems.

Asphalt Institute Method

The Asphalt Institute (AI) method for thickness design of asphalt pavements is documented in *Thickness Design: Asphalt Pavements for Streets and Highways* (Manual Series No. 1 (MS-1), Asphalt Institute, Feb. 1991). The procedure is intended to allow the analyst to determine the minimum thickness of the asphalt layer to withstand the critical vertical compressive strains at the surface of the subgrade and the critical horizontal tensile strains at the bottom of the asphalt layer.

The procedures are applicable to the thickness design of pavement structures consisting of asphalt concrete surfaces, emulsified asphalt surfaces with surface treatment, asphalt concrete bases, emulsified asphalt bases, and untreated aggregate bases or subbases. The AI procedure makes extensive use of design charts in determining pavement thicknesses. The procedure consists of five main steps.

Step 1: Select or determine input data. The three basic design inputs are traffic (expressed as the total number of equivalent 18-kip single-axle load applications over the design period), the subgrade resilient modulus (M_r), and the surface and base types to be considered (asphalt concrete; emulsified asphalt mix Type I, II, or III; or untreated base or subbase). Determination of the design year axle loads consists of the following steps.

Step 1.1: Determine the average number of each type of vehicle expected on the design lane during the first year of traffic. In the absence of local traffic count and classification data, Table IV-1 (p. 13 of the AI Manual) can be used to estimate the distribution of trucks on different classes of highways. Table IV-2 (p. 14 of the AI Manual) can be used to estimate the relative proportion of trucks in the design lane, usually the outside lane for multilane roadways.

Step 1.2: Determine from local axle weight data, or select from Table IV-5 (p. 20 of the AI Manual) a truck factor for each vehicle type identified in step 1.1.

Step 1.3: Select a rate to forecast the design period traffic. This may be a single factor for all vehicles, or a separate factor for each vehicle type. Table IV-3 (p. 15 of the AI Manual) is a table of uniform series compound amount factors which can be used in this step.

Step 1.4: Multiply the number of vehicles of each type by the truck factor and the growth factor(s) from steps 1.2 and 1.3.

Step 1.5: Sum the values from step 1.4 to determine the design ESAL.

Step 1.6: The AI Manual suggests the following graphical procedure for determining the design subgrade resilient modulus, M_r. Test six to eight samples of the subgrade material and convert the CBR or R-values using the following relationships:

$$M_r (\text{psi}) = 1500(\text{CBR}) \qquad \textbf{(11.213)}$$

$$M_r (\text{psi}) = 1155 + 555(R\text{-value}) \qquad \textbf{(11.214)}$$

Step 1.7: Arrange the test values in descending numerical order.

Step 1.8: For each test value, compute the percentage of the total number of values that are equal to or greater than the test value.

Step 1.9: Plot the results from step 1.8.

Step 1.10: Fit a smooth curve through the plotted points. (The curve should be *S*-shaped with the 50th percentile close to the average of the sample data.)

Step 1.11: Read the design value of M_r from the curve at the percentile which corresponds to the anticipated traffic volume as indicated below.

ESAL	M_r
$<10^6$	60
10^4 to 10^6	75
$\geq 10^6$	87.5

Step 1.12: Determine the base types to be considered. These include asphalt concrete; emulsified asphalt Type I, II, or III; or untreated base or subbase. Guidelines for selecting the base type are discussed in Chapter II of the AI Manual.

Step 2: Determine design thickness. The design thickness is determined by entering the appropriate design chart in the AI Manual with the ESAL and M_r values previously selected. The design charts are stratified into three sets of temperature conditions (cold, warm, hot) which are typical of conditions throughout most of North America.

Step 3: Evaluate the need for staged construction (optional). The staged construction design method recommended in the AI Manual involves three steps: (1) first stage design, (2) preliminary design of second-stage overlay, and (3) final design of second stage overlay. Basically, the method involves reducing the design ESAL to account for the remaining life in preceding stages of the design. The AI Manual suggests that designs for equivalent axle loads in excess of 3×10^6 should be considered candidates for staged construction. The method is described in detail on pages 41–43 of the AI Manual.

Step 4: Conduct an economic analysis of the design alternatives. The AI Manual recommends the use of present worth analysis to compare the design alternatives.

Step 5: Select final design. The selection of a base type or the decision to use staged construction is often based on the results of an economic analysis of the design alternatives.

Portland Cement Association Method

The Portland Cement Association (PCA) method for the thickness design of rigid pavements is documented in *Thickness Design for Concrete Highway and Street Pavements* (PCA, 1984). The PCA method consists of two parts: fatigue analysis and erosion analysis. The minimum thickness that satisfies both analyses is the design thickness.

The PCA Manual describes two design procedures: one procedure for use when axle load data are available, and a second, simplified procedure which can be used if axle load data are not available. The following review is limited to the first procedure.

Unlike the AASHTO and Asphalt Institute methods reviewed earlier in this section, the PCA method considers only trucks with six or more axles. Like the other two methods, application of the PCA method relies heavily upon design charts, tables, and nomographs. However, the required pavement thickness calculations can be completed on a single worksheet (see p. 47 of the PCA Manual for a blank worksheet).

The application of the PCA method is illustrated through numerous sample problems in the Manual. Garber and Hoel (1997) provide an excellent summary of the PCA method and also present numerous example applications.

The PCA method requires as inputs the following design factors: a trial pavement thickness; type of joint (doweled or undoweled) and shoulder (with or without concrete shoulder); concrete flexural strength (modulus of rupture, *MR*); *k*-value of the subgrade or subgrade and subbase combination; load safety factor (LSF); axle load distribution consisting of weights, frequencies, and types of truck axle loads that the pavement will carry; and the expected number of axle load repetitions during the design period (calculated by multiplying the axle load distribution by the LSF). These design factors are discussed in Chapter 2 of the PCA Manual.

The step-by-step procedure for the fatigue analysis phase of the PCA method is as follows.

Step 1: Determine the equivalent fatigue stress factors. These factors are determined by entering Table 6a (no concrete shoulders) or Table 6b (concrete shoulders) on page 14 of the PCA Manual with the appropriate trial thickness, *k*-value, and axle configuration (single or tandem).

Step 2: Calculate the fatigue stress ratio factors. The stress ratio factors are calculated for each axle configuration by dividing the Equivalent stress factors from step 1 by the concrete modulus of rupture.

Step 3: Determine allowable axle load repetitions. The allowable repetitions are determined from Figure 5 (p. 15 of the PCA Manual) based on the stress ratio factor.

Step 4: Calculate total percent fatigue damage. The percent fatigue damage is computed by dividing the expected repetitions of each axle load class by the allowable repetitions, multiplying by 100 percent, and summing across all load and axle configuration classes.

Step 5: Determine the erosion factors. These factors are a function of shoulder and joint type, the trial thickness, and the *k*-value. Tables 7a, 7b, 8a, and 8b (pp. 16 and 18 in the PCA Manual) are used to determine the erosion factors.

Step 6: Determine allowable repetitions. Figure 6a (without shoulders) and 6b (with shoulders) on pp. 17 and 19 of the PCA Manual are used to determine allowable repetitions based on the erosion factors determined in step 5.

Step 7: Calculate total percent erosion damage. The percent erosion damage is computed by dividing the expected repetitions by the allowable repetitions, multiplying by 100 percent, and summing across all load and axle configuration classes.

Step 8: Assess adequacy of trial thickness. The trial thickness is not adequate if the total for either fatigue damage (step 4) or erosion damage (step 7) is greater than 100 percent. If either is greater than 100 percent, select a greater trial thickness and repeat the analysis. A lesser trial thickness should be selected if the totals are much lower than 100 percent. [The PCA Manual (p. 13) provides some guidance in reducing the number of interactions required to complete the analyses.]

NOTES ON SELECTED SPECIAL TOPICS

The previous sections of this chapter have presented a general outline of the major transportation-related topics which should be reviewed in preparation for the professional engineering licensing examination in civil engineering. This section provides some general commentary and suggestions concerning additional, special topics which the reader may wish to review in preparation for the licensing exam. The intent of this section is to review some basic terminology and to identify data sources and reference materials.

Parking

Some terms commonly used in parking studies include (Garber and Hoel, 1997) *space hour*, which is the use of a single parking space for a period of 1 hr; *parking volume*, the number of vehicles parking in a study area during a period of time, usually 1 day; *parking accumulation*, the number of vehicles parked in a study area at any specified time period; *parking duration*, the length of time a vehicle is parked at a parking space; and *parking frequency*, the rate of use of a parking space.

Graber and Hoel (1997) provide the following useful relationships commonly used in the analysis of parking data.

$$T = V/N \qquad (11.215)$$

$$D = \Sigma(n_i t_i) \qquad (11.216)$$

$$S = f \Sigma t_i \qquad (11.217)$$

$$C = Npf/d \qquad (11.218)$$

where

T = turnover rate

V = number of different vehicles parked

N = number of parking spaces

D = vehicle space hours of demand for a specific time period

n_i = number of vehicles parked for the ith duration range

t_i = midpoint of the ith parking duration class

S = practical number of space hours of supply for a specific time period

f = efficiency factor

C = number of vehicles that can park during time period p (sometimes called practical capacity)

d = average duration

The efficiency factor (f) is used to account for time lost during turnover. Average values for f range from 80 percent for garages, to 85 percent for surface lots, to 90 percent for curb parking (Garber and Hoel, 1997).

Information concerning parking facility layout and design can be found in the AASHTO Green Book (AASHTO, 2001) and the ITE *Traffic Engineering Handbook* (1999). Parking space requirements for various land uses can be found in ITE's *Parking Generation* (1987).

Queueing Models

One of the objectives of traffic engineering should be to minimize the delay experienced by users of transportation facilities. Much of the delay encountered in the transportation system is attributable to the need to wait in line at traffic signals, freeway ramps, and service facilities. Queueing models, which were originally developed early in the twentieth century to study telephone switching problems, use the principles of probability and statistics to analyze waiting lines.

A queueing process is described by a series of symbols and slashes such as $A/B/C$, where A denotes the arrival pattern (more specifically, A indicates the interarrival-time distribution), B represents the service pattern as described by the probability distribution for service time, and C indicates the number of parallel service channels or lanes. This notation is frequently extended to include an indication of any restrictions on system capacity and the queue discipline, such as first in, first out. For example, an $M/M/N$ queueing process indicates random (Poisson) customer arrivals, negative exponential service times, and N parallel service channels. The $M/M/N$ model is frequently used to analyze queues at drive-in service facilities, entrances and exits at large parking facilities, toll booths, and loading/unloading areas.

The basic equations used in the analysis of $M/M/N$ queueing systems are summarized below. The following notation is employed.

n = number of customers (vehicles) in the system

M = number of customers in the queue waiting to be served (number of customers in the system minus the number being served)

$P(n)$ = probability that exactly n customers are in the queueing system

$P(0)$ = probability that zero customers are in the queueing system

N = number of parallel service channels

q = average arrival rate of customers into the system (customers/hr)

Q = average service rate per service position (customers/hr/position)

t = average service time per customer (minutes)

ρ = coefficient of utilization, a measure of the average use of the service facility, also called utilization or traffic intensity factor

$E(m)$ = expected average number of customers waiting in the queue

$E(n)$ = expected average number of customers in the system

$E(t)$ = expected average waiting time in the system, including service time

$E(w)$ = expected (average) waiting time in the queue, excluding service time

Coefficient of utilization

$$\rho = q/(NQ) \tag{11.219}$$

Probability of no customers in the system

$$P(0) = \left\{ \sum_{n=0}^{N=1} [(q/Q)^n/n!] + (q/Q)^N/[N!(1-\rho)] \right\}^{-1} \tag{11.220}$$

Average number in the queue

$$E(m) = \{[\rho(q/Q)^N]/[N!(1-\rho)^2]\}P(0) \tag{11.221}$$

Average number in the system

$$E(n) = E(m) + q/Q \tag{11.222}$$

Average wait time in the queue

$$E(w) = E(m)/q \tag{11.223}$$

Average time in the system

$$E(t) = E(w) + 1/Q \tag{11.224}$$

Proportion of customers who wait

$$P[E(w) > 0] = \{(q/Q)^N/[N!(1-\rho)]\}P(0) \tag{11.225}$$

Probability of a queue exceeding length M

$$P(x > M) = (\rho^{N+1})P[E(w) > 0] \tag{11.226}$$

Queue storage required

$$M = \{[\ln P(x > M) - \ln P(E(w) > 0)]/\ln \rho\} - 1 \tag{11.227}$$

Evaluating Transportation Alternatives

Many transportation improvements, particularly highway-related projects, are public works projects funded by federal, state, and/or local governments. Because of this, the evaluation of transportation improvement projects typically involves the use of standard methods specified by the funding agency. The most frequently used economic analysis methods are the benefit-cost ratio (B/C ratio) and cost-effectiveness analysis.

The benefit-cost ratio is simply the ratio of project benefits to project costs, where all benefits and costs are expressed in terms of their *present worth* or *equivalent uniform annual worth*. A benefit-cost ratio >1, or benefits > costs, indicates an economically viable alternative.

Cost-effectiveness analysis attempts to compensate for some of the shortcomings of traditional economic analysis methods—such as benefit-cost analysis—by incorporating various intangible effects, such as environmental consequences. In this method, the cost effectiveness of the alternatives is expressed in terms of the costs of achieving the goals of the project, where the project costs are determined using standard economic analysis methods, such as present worth or annualized costs.

The use of cost-effectiveness techniques is often required in the alternatives analysis (AA) phase of many federal transit projects. In these situations, the relative attractiveness of the various alternatives may be expressed in terms of total or annualized costs per millions of passengers served or per ton of vehicle pollutants emitted, or annualized costs with respect to some other criteria that represent the goals of the project. The intent of the cost—effectiveness approach in not so much to identify a clearly superior, single alternative but to define more fully the impacts of each course of action and to clarify the issues and trade-offs involved.

The basic economic analysis methods are described in Appendix A of this book. Most standard transportation engineering textbooks provide a description of the application of these and other techniques in evaluating transportation projects.

Computer Applications

There are probably more computer software packages oriented to transportation applications than to any other area of civil engineering. Many of these packages were developed under the sponsorship of state and federal transportation agencies and are, therefore, in the public domain. All of the procedures reviewed in this chapter have been automated and many can be implemented with little or no knowledge of the underlying principles. Because of the complexity of many transportation systems, the variability inherent in these systems, and the relatively crude models and methods currently available to study these systems, "black box" engineering can lead to poor solutions and, worse yet, disastrous results in the real world.

An inventory of currently available transportation engineering software is beyond the scope and purpose of this section. Those readers who are interested in such an inventory should contact the Transportation Centers at the University of Florida (McTRANS Center, 512 Weil Hall, Gainesville, FL 32611–2083) or the University of Kansas (PC-TRANS, 2011 Learned Hall, Lawrence, KS 66045).

REFERENCES

This section provides a listing of the references cited in this chapter. The reader should consult these references for additional details concerning the procedures that have been reviewed. This section also presents recommendations concerning selected key references that the reader may wish to include in the reference materials taken into the exam.

REFERENCES

American Association of State Highway and Transportation Officials (AASHTO). *AASHTO Guide for Design of Pavement Structures*. Washington, DC, 1993.

American Association of State Highway and Transportation Officials (AASHTO). *A Policy on Geometric Design of Highways and Streets*. Washington, DC, 2001.

American Association of State Highway and Transportation Officials (AASHTO). *Roadside Design Guide*. Washington, DC, 2002.

Asphalt Institute. *Thickness Design: Asphalt Pavements for Highways and Streets*. Manual Series No. 1 (MS-1). Asphalt Institute, Lexington, KY, Feb. 1991.

Banks, J. H. *Introduction to Transportation Engineering*, 2nd ed. McGraw-Hill, NY, 2002.

Brinker, R. C., and Minnick, R. *The Surveying Handbook*, 2nd ed. Chapman and Hall, New York, 1995.

Daniel, W. W. *Applied Nonparametric Statistics*. Houghton Mifflin, Boston, 1978.

Drew, D. R. *Traffic Flow Theory and Control*, McGraw-Hill, New York, 1968.

Fambro, D. B., Chang, E. C. P., and Messer, C. J. *Effects of the Quality of Progression on Delay*. National Cooperative Highway Research Program Report No. 339. TRB, Washington, DC, Sept. 1991.

Garber, N. J., and Hoel, L. A. *Traffic and Highway Engineering*, 2nd ed. PWS, Boston, 1997.

Hickerson, T. F. *Route Location and Design*, 5th ed. McGraw-Hill, New York, 1964.

Institute of Transportation Engineers (ITE). *Parking Generation* 2nd ed. Washington, DC, 1987.

Institute of Transportation Engineers (ITE). *1991 Membership Directory*. Washington, DC, 1991.

Institute of Transportation Engineers (ITE). *Traffic Engineering Handbooks*, 5th ed. Washington, DC, 1999.

Institute of Transportation Engineers (ITE). *Trip Generation*, 7th ed. Washington, DC, 2003.

Ives, H. C., and Kissam, P. *Highway Curves*, 4th ed. John Wiley & Sons, New York, 1952.

Kavanagh, B. F. *Surveying Principles and Applications*, 4th ed. Prentice Hall, Englewood Cliffs, NJ, 1995.

Meyer, M. D., and Miller, E. J. *Urban Transportation Planning: A Decision-Oriented Approach*, 2nd ed. McGraw-Hill, New York, 2001.

Portland Cement Association (PCA). *Thickness Design for Concrete Highway and Street Pavements*. PCA, Skokie, IL, 1984.

Robertson, H. D., *Manual of Transportation Engineering Studies*, 1st ed. Prentice Hall, Englewood Cliffs, NJ, 1994.

Roess, R. P., Prassas, E. S., and McShane, W. R. *Traffic Engineering*, 3rd ed. Prentice Hall, Englewood Cliffs, NJ, 2004.

Transportation Research Board (TRB). *Travel Estimation Techniques for Urban Planning*. National Cooperative Highway Research Program Report No. 365. TRB, Washington, DC, 1998.

Transportation Research Board (TRB). *Highway Capacity Manual 2000*. TRB, Washington, DC, 2000.

U.S. Department of Transportation (USDOT), Federal Highway Administration, Federal Transit Administration. *An Introduction to Urban Travel Demand Forecasting: A Self-Instructional Text.* USDOT, Washington, DC, 1977.

U.S. Department of Transportation (USDOT), Federal Highway Administration. *TRANSYT-7F: Traffic Network Study Tool (Version 7F).* Self-study guide. USDOT, Washington, DC, July 1986.

U.S. Department of Transportation (USDOT), Federal Highway Administration. *Manual on Uniform Traffic Control Devices for Streets and Highways,* USDOT, Washington, DC, 2003. (may be downloaded at http://mutcd.fhwa.dot.gov/).

Wadsworth, H. M., Jr. (ed.). *Handbook of Statistical Methods for Engineers and Scientists.* McGraw-Hill, New York, 1990.

Webster, F. V., and Cobbe, B. M. *Traffic Signals.* Road Research Technical Paper No. 39. Her Majesty's Stationery Office, London, 1958.

Recommended References

The licensing examination is open book, and most states do not limit the number of books that the examinee can bring to the exam. However, the exam is very fast-paced and there is generally not enough time to use books with which the examinee is not already thoroughly familiar. Therefore, is it extremely important to be selective in choosing reference materials. With this in mind, the author recommends the following basic references for the reader's consideration. Depending upon the reader's background, additional references should be selected as deemed necessary.

1. **Garber and Hoel, *Traffic and Highway Engineering*, 1997.** This textbook provides an excellent overview of the major topics reviewed in this chapter, and it contains the key design charts and equations for many of the procedures such as highway capacity procedures, AASHTO geometric and pavement design procedures, and the Asphalt Institute and Portland Cement Association pavement design methods. The textbook is particularly strong in its treatment of pavement design procedures. The treatment of the various topics includes numerous example problems with step-by-step solutions.

2. **AASHTO, *A Policy on Geometric Design of Highway and Streets*, 2001.** This is the standard reference on highway design, and the reader should become familiar with the basic organization of this voluminous manual prior to the exam.

3. **Hickerson, *Route Location and Design*, 1964.** This is the classic text on the topic. It provides extensive and detailed treatment of route surveying and related topics, including numerous example problems with step-by-step solutions.

4. **Brinker and Minnick, *The Surveying Handbook*, 1995.** This is a comprehensive, up-to-date reference on surveying practice and includes material on the use of the metric system in surveying.

5. **Roess, Prassas, and McShane. *Traffic Engineering*, 2004.** An excellent overview of the state of the art. The treatment of highway capacity analysis is especially insightful and well documented. Includes most of the key equations, design charts, and tables needed to apply the 2000 HCM procedures. It is extensively illustrated with example problems and solutions.

Engineering Economics

Donald G. Newnan

OUTLINE

CASH FLOW   556

TIME VALUE OF MONEY   558
Simple Interest

EQUIVALENCE   558

COMPOUND INTEREST   559
Symbols and Functional Notation ■ Single-Payment Formulas ■ Uniform Payment Series Formulas ■ Uniform Gradient ■ Continuous Compounding

NOMINAL AND EFFECTIVE INTEREST   566
Non-Annual Compounding ■ Continuous Compounding

SOLVING ENGINEERING ECONOMICS PROBLEMS   568
Criteria

PRESENT WORTH   568
Appropriate Problems ■ Infinite Life and Capitalized Cost

FUTURE WORTH OR VALUE   571

ANNUAL COST   572
Criteria ■ Application of Annual Cost Analysis

RATE OF RETURN ANALYSIS   573
Two Alternatives ■ Three or More Alternatives

BENEFIT-COST ANALYSIS   578

BREAKEVEN ANALYSIS   579

OPTIMIZATION   579
Minima-Maxima ■ Economic Problem—Best Alternative ■ Economic Order Quantity

VALUATION AND DEPRECIATION   581

Notation ■ Straight-Line Depreciation ■ Sum-of-Years'-Digits Depreciation ■ Declining-Balance Depreciation ■ Sinking-Fund Depreciation ■ Modified Accelerated Cost Recovery System Depreciation

TAX CONSEQUENCES   586

INFLATION   587

Effect of Inflation on Rate of Return

RISK ANALYSIS   589

Probability ■ Risk ■ Expected Value

REFERENCE   591

INTEREST TABLES   592

This is a review of the field known variously as *engineering economics, engineering economy*, or *engineering economic analysis*. Since engineering economics is straightforward and logical, even people who have not had a formal course should be able to gain sufficient knowledge from this chapter to successfully solve most engineering economics problems.

There are 35 example problems scattered throughout the chapter. These examples are an integral part of the review and should be examined as you come to them.

The field of engineering economics uses mathematical and economics techniques to systematically analyze situations which pose alternative courses of action. The initial step in engineering economics problems is to resolve a situation, or each alternative in a given situation, into its favorable and unfavorable consequences or factors. These are then measured in some common unit—usually money. Factors which cannot readily be equated to money are called intangible or irreducible factors. Such factors are considered in conjunction with the monetary analysis when making the final decision on proposed courses of action.

CASH FLOW

A cash flow table shows the "money consequences" of a situation and its timing. For example, a simple problem might be to list the year-by-year consequences of purchasing and owning a used car:

Year	Cash Flow	
Beginning of first year 0	−$4500	Car purchased "now" for $4500 cash. The minus sign indicates a disbursement.
End of year 1	−350	
End of year 2	−350	
End of year 3	−350	Maintenance costs are $350 per year.
End of year 4	−350	
	+2000	This car is sold at the end of the fourth year for $2000. The plus sign represents the receipt of money.

This same cash flow may be represented graphically, as shown in Fig. A.1. The upward arrow represents a receipt of money, and the downward arrows represent disbursements. The horizontal axis represents the passage of time.

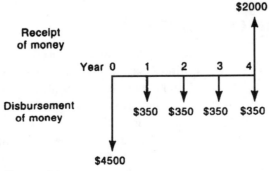

Figure A.1

<hr>

Example **A.1**

In January 1993 a firm purchased a used typewriter for $500. Repairs cost nothing in 1993 or 1994. Repairs are $85 in 1995, $130 in 1996, and $140 in 1997. The machine is sold in 1997 for $300. Complete the cash flow table.

Solution

Unless otherwise stated, the customary assumption is a beginning-of-year purchase, followed by end-of-year receipts or disbursements, and an end-of-year resale or salvage value. Thus the typewriter repairs and the typewriter sale are assumed to occur at the end of the year. Letting a minus sign represent a disbursement of money and a plus sign a receipt of money, we are able to set up the cash flow table:

Year	Cash Flow
Beginning of 1993	−$500
End of 1993	0
End of 1994	0
End of 1995	−85
End of 1996	−130
End of 1997	+160

Notice that at the end of 1997 the cash flow table shows +160, which is the net sum of −140 and +300. If we define year 0 as the beginning of 1993, the cash flow table becomes

Year	Cash Flow
0	−$500
1	0
2	0
3	−85
4	−130
5	+160

From this cash flow table, the definitions of year 0 and year 1 become clear. Year 0 is defined as the *beginning* of year 1. Year 1 is the *end* of year 1, and so forth.

TIME VALUE OF MONEY

When the money consequences of an alternative occur in a short period of time—say, less than one year—we might simply add up the various sums of money and obtain the net result. But we cannot treat money this way over longer periods of time. This is because money today does not have the same value as money at some future time.

Consider this question: Which would you prefer, $100 today or the assurance of receiving $100 a year from now? Clearly, you would prefer the $100 today. If you had the money today, rather than a year from now, you could use it for the year. And if you had no use for it, you could lend it to someone who would pay interest for the privilege of using your money for the year.

Simple Interest

Simple interest is interest that is computed on the original sum. Thus if one were to lend a present sum P to someone at a simple annual interest rate i, the future amount F due at the end of n years would be

$$F = P + Pin$$

Example A.2

How much will you receive back from a $500 loan to a friend for three years at 10 percent simple annual interest?

Solution

$$F = P + Pin = 500 + 500 \times 0.10 \times 3 = \$650$$

In Example A.2 one observes that the amount owed, based on 10 percent simple interest at the end of one year, is $500 + 500 \times 0.10 \times 1 = \$550$. But at simple interest there is no interest charged on the $50 interest, even though it is not paid until the end of the third year. Thus simple interest is not realistic and is seldom used. *Compound interest* charges interest on the principal owed plus the interest earned to date. This produces a charge of interest on interest, or compound interest. Engineering economics uses compound interest computations.

EQUIVALENCE

In the preceding section we saw that money at different points in time (for example, $100 today or $100 one year hence) may be equal in the sense that they both are $100, but $100 a year hence is *not* an acceptable substitute for $100 today. When we have acceptable substitutes, we say they are *equivalent* to each other. Thus at 8 percent interest, $108 a year hence is equivalent to $100 today.

Example **A.3**

At a 10 percent per year (compound) interest rate, $500 now is *equivalent* to how much three years hence?

Solution

A value of $500 now will increase by 10 percent in each of the three years.

$$Now = \$500.00$$
$$End\ of\ 1st\ year = 500 + 10\%(500) = 550.00$$
$$End\ of\ 2nd\ year = 550 + 10\%(550) = 605.00$$
$$End\ of\ 3rd\ year = 605 + 10\%(605) = 665.50$$

Thus $500 now is *equivalent* to $665.50 at the end of three years. Note that interest is charged each year on the original $500 plus the unpaid interest. This compound interest computation gives an answer that is $15.50 higher than the simple-interest computation in Example A.2.

Equivalence is an essential factor in engineering economics. Suppose we wish to select the better of two alternatives. First, we must compute their cash flows. For example,

	Alternative	
Year	*A*	*B*
0	−$2000	−$2800
1	+800	+1100
2	+800	+1100
3	+800	+1100

The larger investment in alternative *B* results in larger subsequent benefits, but we have no direct way of knowing whether it is better than alternative *A*. So we do not know which to select. To make a decision, we must resolve the alternatives into *equivalent* sums so that they may be compared accurately.

COMPOUND INTEREST

To facilitate equivalence computations, a series of compound interest factors will be derived here, and their use will be illustrated in examples.

Symbols and Functional Notation

i = effective interest rate per interest period. In equations, the interest rate is stated as a decimal (that is, 8 percent interest is 0.08).

n = number of interest periods. Usually the interest period is one year, but it could be something else.

P = a present sum of money.

F = a future sum of money. The future sum F is an amount n interest periods from the present that is equivalent to P at interest rate i.

A = an end-of-period cash receipt or disbursement in a uniform series continuing for n periods. The entire series is equivalent to P or F at interest rate i.

Table A.1 Periodic compounding: Functional notation and formulas

Factor	Given	To Find	Functional Notation	Formula
Single payment				
Compound amount factor	P	F	$(F/P, i\%, n)$	$F = P(1 + i)^n$
Present worth factor	F	P	$(P/F, i\%, n)$	$P = F(1 + i)^{-n}$
Uniform payment series				
Sinking fund factor	F	A	$(A/F, i\%, n)$	$A = F\left[\dfrac{i}{(1+i)^n - 1}\right]$
Capital recovery factor	P	A	$(A/P, i\%, n)$	$A = P\left[\dfrac{i(1+i)^n}{(1+i)^n - 1}\right]$
Compound amount factor	A	F	$(F/A, i\%, n)$	$F = A\left[\dfrac{(1+i)^n - 1}{i}\right]$
Present worth factor	A	P	$(P/A, i\%, n)$	$P = A\left[\dfrac{(1+i)^n - 1}{i(1+i)^n}\right]$
Uniform gradient				
Gradient present worth	G	P	$(P/G, i\%, n)$	$P = G\left[\dfrac{(1+i)^n - 1}{i^2(1+i)^n} - \dfrac{n}{i(1+i)^n}\right]$
Gradient future worth	G	F	$(F/G, i\%, n)$	$F = G\left[\dfrac{(1+i)^n - 1}{i^2} - \dfrac{n}{1}\right]$
Gradient uniform series	G	A	$(A/G, i\%, n)$	$A = G\left[\dfrac{1}{i} - \dfrac{n}{(1+i)^n - 1}\right]$

G = uniform period-by-period increase in cash flows; the uniform gradient.

r = nominal annual interest rate.

From Table A.1 we can see that the functional notation scheme is based on writing (to find/given, i, n). Thus, if we wished to find the future sum F, given a uniform series of receipts A, the proper compound interest factor to use would be $(F/A, i, n)$.

Single-Payment Formulas

Suppose a present sum of money P is invested for one year at interest rate i. At the end of the year, the initial investment P is received together with interest equal to Pi, or a total amount $P + Pi$. Factoring P, the sum at the end of one year is $P(1 + i)$. If the investment is allowed to remain for subsequent years, the progression is as follows:

Amount at Beginning of the Period	+	Interest for the Period	=	Amount at End of the Period
1st year, P	+	Pi	=	$P(1 + i)$
2nd year, $P(1 + i)$	+	$Pi(1 + i)$	=	$P(1 + i)^2$
3rd year, $P(1 + i)^2$	+	$Pi(1 + i)^2$	=	$P(1 + i)^3$
nth year, $P(1 + i)^{n-1}$	+	$Pi(1 + i)^{n-1}$	=	$P(1 + i)^n$

The present sum P increases in n periods to $P(1 + i)^n$. This gives a relation between a present sum P and its equivalent future sum F:

$$\text{Future sum} = (\text{present sum})(1 + i)^n$$
$$F = P(1 + i)^n$$

This is the *single-payment compound amount formula*. In functional notation it is written

$$F = P(F/P, i, n)$$

The relationship may be rewritten as

$$\text{Present sum} = (\text{Future sum}) (1 + i)^{-n}$$
$$P = F(1 + i)^{-n}$$

This is the *single-payment present worth formula*. It is written

$$P = F(P/F, i, n)$$

Example A.4

At a 10 percent per year interest rate, $500 now is *equivalent* to how much three years hence?

Solution

This problem was solved in Example A.3. Now it can be solved using a single-payment formula. $P = \$500$, $n = 3$ years, $i = 10$ percent, and $F = $ unknown:

$$F = P(1 + i)^n = 500(1 + 0.10)^3 = \$665.50.$$

This problem also may be solved using a compound interest table:

$$F = P(F/P, i, n) = 500(F/P, 10\%, 3)$$

From the 10 percent compound interest table, read $(F/P, 10\%, 3) = 1.331$.

$$F = 500(F/P, 10\%, 3) = 500(1.331) = \$665.50$$

Example A.5

To raise money for a new business, a man asks you to lend him some money. He offers to pay you $3000 at the end of four years. How much should you give him now if you want 12 percent interest per year?

Solution

$P = $ unknown, $F = \$3000$, $n = 4$ years, and $i = 12$ percent:

$$P = F(1 + i)^{-n} = 3000(1 + 0.12)^{-4} = \$1906.55$$

Alternative computation using a compound interest table:

$$P = F(P/F, i, n) = 3000(P/F, 12\%, 4) = 3000(0.6355) = \$1906.50$$

Note that the solution based on the compound interest table is slightly different from the exact solution using a hand-held calculator. In engineering economics the compound interest tables are always considered to be sufficiently accurate.

Uniform Payment Series Formulas

Consider the situation shown in Fig. A.2. Using the single-payment compound amount factor, we can write an equation for F in terms of A:

$$F = A + A(1 + i) + A(1 + i)^2 \qquad \text{(i)}$$

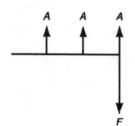

A = End-of-period cash receipt or disbursement in a uniform series continuing for n periods

F = A future sum of money

Figure A.2

In this situation, with $n = 3$, Eq. (i) may be written in a more general form:

$$F = A + A(1 + i) + A(1 + i)^{n-1} \qquad \text{(ii)}$$

Multiply Eq. (ii) by $(1 + i)$ $\quad (1 + i)F = A(1 + i) + A(1 + i)^{n-1} + A(1 + i)^n \qquad$ **(iii)**

Subtract Eq. (ii): $\qquad\qquad -F = A + A(1 + i) + A(1 + i)^{n-1} \qquad$ **(ii)**

$$iF = -A + A(1 + i)^n$$

This produces the *uniform series compound amount formula:*

$$F = A\left(\frac{(1+i)^n - 1}{i}\right)$$

Solving this equation for A produces the *uniform series sinking fund formula:*

$$A = F\left(\frac{i}{(1+i)^n - 1}\right)$$

Since $F = P(1 + i)^n$, we can substitute this expression for F in the equation and obtain the *uniform series capital recovery formula:*

$$A = P\left(\frac{i(1+i)^n}{(1+i)^n - 1}\right)$$

Solving the equation for P produces the *uniform series present worth formula:*

$$P = A\left(\frac{(1+i)^n - 1}{i(1+i)^n}\right)$$

In functional notation, the uniform series factors are

Compound amount $(F/A, i, n)$

Sinking fund $(A/F, i, n)$

Capital recovery $(A/P, i, n)$

Present worth $(P/A, i, n)$

Example **A.6**

If $100 is deposited at the end of each year in a savings account that pays 6 percent interest per year, how much will be in the account at the end of five years?

Solution

$A = \$100$, $F =$ unknown, $n = 5$ years, and $i = 6$ percent:

$$F = A(F/A, i, n) = 100(F/A, 6\%, 5) = 100(5.637) = \$563.70$$

Example **A.7**

A fund established to produce a desired amount at the end of a given period, by means of a series of payments throughout the period, is called a *sinking fund*. A sinking fund is to be established to accumulate money to replace a $10,000 machine. If the machine is to be replaced at the end of 12 years, how much should be deposited in the sinking fund each year? Assume the fund earns 10 percent annual interest.

Solution

Annual sinking fund deposit $A = 10,000(A/F, 10\%, 12)$

$$= 10,000(0.0468) = \$468$$

Example **A.8**

An individual is considering the purchase of a used automobile. The total price is $6200. With $1240 as a down payment, and the balance paid in 48 equal monthly payments with interest at 1 percent per month, compute the monthly payment. The payments are due at the end of each month.

Solution

The amount to be repaid by the 48 monthly payments is the cost of the automobile *minus* the $1240 downpayment.

$P = \$4960$, $A =$ unknown, $n = 48$ monthly payments, and $i = 1$ percent per month:

$$A = P(A/P, 1\%, 48) = 4960(0.0263) = \$130.45$$

Example **A.9**

A couple sell their home. In addition to cash, they take a mortgage on the house. The mortgage will be paid off by monthly payments of $450 for 50 months. The couple decides to sell the mortgage to a local bank. The bank will buy the mortgage, but it requires a 1 percent per month interest rate on its investment. How much will the bank pay for the mortgage?

Solution

$A = \$450$, $n = 50$ months, $i = 1$ percent per month, and $P =$ unknown:

$$P = A(P/A, i, n) = 450(P/A, 1\%, 50) = 450(39.196) = \$17,638.20$$

Uniform Gradient

At times one will encounter a situation where the cash flow series is not a constant amount A. Instead, it is an increasing series. The cash flow shown in Fig. A.3 may

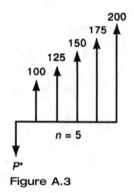

Figure A.3

be resolved into two components (Fig. A.4). We can compute the value of P^* as equal to P' plus P. And we already have the equation for P': $P' = A(P/A, i, n)$. The value for P in the right-hand diagram is

$$P = G\left[\frac{(1+i)^n - 1}{i^2(1+i)^n} - \frac{n}{i(1+i)^n}\right]$$

This is the *uniform gradient present worth formula*. In functional notation, the relationship is $P = G(P/G, i, n)$.

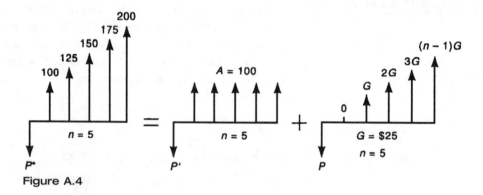

Figure A.4

The maintenance on a machine is expected to be $155 at the end of the first year, and it is expected to increase $35 each year for the following seven years (Exhibit 1). What sum of money should be set aside now to pay the maintenance for the eight-year period? Assume 6 percent interest.

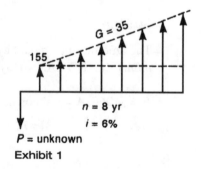

Exhibit 1

Solution

$$P = 155(P/A, 6\%, 8) + 35(P/G, 6\%, 8)$$
$$= 155(6.210) + 35(19.841) = \$1656.99$$

In the gradient series, if—instead of the present sum, P—an equivalent uniform series A is desired, the problem might appear as shown in Fig. A.5. The relationship between A' and G in the right-hand diagram is

$$A' = G\left[\frac{1}{i} - \frac{n}{(1+i)^n - 1}\right]$$

In functional notation, the uniform gradient (to) uniform series factor is: $A' = G(A/G, i, n)$.

The uniform gradient uniform series factor may be read from the compound interest tables directly, or computed as

$$(A/G, i, n) = \frac{1 - n(A/F, i, n)}{i}$$

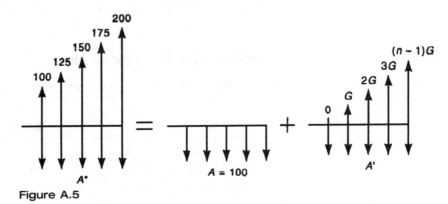

Figure A.5

Note carefully the diagrams for the uniform gradient factors. The first term in the uniform gradient is zero and the last term is $(n-1)G$. But we use n in the equations and function notation. The derivations (not shown here) were done on this basis, and the uniform gradient compound interest tables are computed this way.

Example **A.11**

For the situation in Example A.10, we wish now to know the uniform annual maintenance cost. Compute an equivalent A for the maintenance costs.

Solution

Refer to Exhibit 2 The equivalent uniform annual maintenance cost is

$$A = 155 + 35(A/G, 6\%, 8) = 155 + 35(3.195) = \$266.83$$

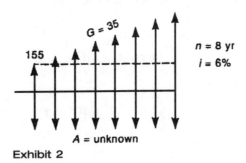

Exhibit 2

Standard compound interest tables give values for eight interest factors: two single payments, four uniform payment series, and two uniform gradients. The tables do *not* give the uniform gradient future worth factor, $(F/G, i, n)$. If it is needed, it may be computed from two tabulated factors:

$$(F/G, i, n) = (P/G, i, n)(F/P, i, n)$$

For example, if $i = 10$ percent and $n = 12$ years, then $(F/G, 10\%, 12) = (P/G, 10\%, 12)(F/P, 10\%, 12) = (29.901)(3.138) = 93.83$.

A second method of computing the uniform gradient future worth factor is

$$(F/G, i, n) = \frac{(F/A, i, n) - n}{i}$$

Using this equation for $i = 10$ percent and $n = 12$ years, $(F/G, 10\%, 12) = [(F/A, 10\%, 12) - 12]/0.10 = (21.384 - 12)/0.10 = 93.84$.

Continuous Compounding

Table A.2 Continuous compounding: Functional notation and formulas

Factor	Given	To Find	Functional Notation	Formula
Single payment				
Compound amount factor	P	F	$(F/P, r\%, n)$	$F = P[e^{rn}]$
Present worth factor	F	P	$(P/F, r\%, n)$	$P = F[e^{-rn}]$
Uniform payment series				
Sinking fund factor	F	A	$(A/F, r\%, n)$	$A = F\left[\frac{e^r - 1}{e^{rn} - 1}\right]$
Capital recovery factor	P	A	$(A/P, r\%, n)$	$A = P\left[\frac{e^r - 1}{1 - e^{-rn}}\right]$
Compound amount factor	A	F	$(F/A, r\%, n)$	$F = A\left[\frac{e^{rn} - 1}{e^r - 1}\right]$
Present worth factor	A	P	$(P/A, r\%, n)$	$P = A\left[\frac{1 - e^{-rn}}{e^r - 1}\right]$

r = nominal annual interest rate, n = number of years.

Example A.12

Five hundred dollars is deposited each year into a savings bank account that pays 5 percent nominal interest, compounded continuously. How much will be in the account at the end of five years?

Solution

$A = \$500$, $r = 0.05$, $n = 5$ years.

$$F = A(F/A, r\%, n) = A\left[\frac{e^{rn} - 1}{e^r - 1}\right] = 500\left[\frac{e^{0.05(5)} - 1}{e^{0.05} - 1}\right] = \$2769.84$$

NOMINAL AND EFFECTIVE INTEREST

Nominal interest is the annual interest rate without considering the effect of any compounding. *Effective interest* is the annual interest rate taking into account the effect of any compounding during the year.

Non-Annual Compounding

Frequently an interest rate is described as an annual rate, even though the interest period may be something other than one year. A bank may pay 1 percent interest on the amount in a savings account every three months. The *nominal* interest rate in this situation is $4 \times 1\% = 4\%$. But if you deposited $1000 in such an account, would you have $104\%(1000) = \$1040$ in the account at the end of one year? The answer is no, you would have more. The amount in the account would increase as follows:

Amount in Account

Beginning of year:	1000.00
End of three months:	$1000.00 + 1\%(1000.00) = 1010.00$
End of six months:	$1010.00 + 1\%(1010.00) = 1020.10$
End of nine months:	$1020.10 + 1\%(1020.10) = 1030.30$
End of one year:	$1030.30 + 1\%(1030.30) = 1040.60$

At the end of one year, the interest of $40.60, divided by the original $1000, gives a rate of 4.06 percent. This is the *effective* interest rate.

$$\text{Effective interest rate per year:} \quad i_{\text{eff}} = (1 + r/m)^m - 1$$

where r = nominal annual interest rate
m = number of compound periods per year
r/m = effective interest rate per period

Example A.13

A bank charges 1.5 percent interest per month on the unpaid balance for purchases made on its credit card. What nominal interest rate is it charging? What is the effective interest rate?

Solution

The nominal interest rate is simply the annual interest ignoring compounding, or $12(1.5\%) = 18\%$.

$$\text{Effective interest rate} = (1 + 0.015)^{12} - 1 = 0.1956 = 19.56\%$$

Continuous Compounding

When m, the number of compound periods per year, becomes very large and approaches infinity, the duration of the interest period decreases from Δt to dt. For this condition of *continuous compounding*, the effective interest rate per year is

$$i_{\text{eff}} = e^r - 1$$

where r = nominal annual interest rate.

Example A.14

If the bank in Example A.13 changes its policy and charges 1.5 percent per month, compounded continuously, what nominal and what effective interest rate is it charging?

Solution

Nominal annual interest rate, $r = 12 \times 1.5\% = 18\%$

Effective interest rate per year, $i_{\text{eff}} = e^{0.18} - 1 = 0.1972 = 19.72\%$

SOLVING ENGINEERING ECONOMICS PROBLEMS

The techniques presented so far illustrate how to convert single amounts of money, and uniform or gradient series of money, into some equivalent sum at another point in time. These compound interest computations are an essential part of engineering economics problems.

The typical situation is that we have a number of alternatives; the question is, which alternative should we select? The customary method of solution is to express each alternative in some common form and then choose the best, taking both the monetary and intangible factors into account. In most computations an interest rate must be used. It is often called the minimum attractive rate of return (MARR), to indicate that this is the smallest interest rate, or rate of return, at which one is willing to invest money.

Criteria

Engineering economics problems inevitably fall into one of three categories:

1. *Fixed input*. The amount of money or other input resources is fixed. *Example*: A project engineer has a budget of $450,000 to overhaul a plant.

2. *Fixed output*. There is a fixed task or other output to be accomplished. *Example*: A mechanical contractor has been awarded a fixed-price contract to air-condition a building.

3. *Neither input nor output fixed*. This is the general situation, where neither the amount of money (or other inputs) nor the amount of benefits (or other outputs) is fixed. *Example*: A consulting engineering firm has more work available than it can handle. It is considering paying the staff to work evenings to increase the amount of design work it can perform.

There are five major methods of comparing alternatives: present worth, future worth, annual cost, rate of return, and benefit-cost analysis. These are presented in the sections that follow.

PRESENT WORTH

Present worth analysis converts all of the money consequences of an alternative into an equivalent present sum. The criteria are

Category	Present Worth Criterion
Fixed input	Maximize the present worth of benefits or other outputs
Fixed output	Minimize the present worth of costs or other inputs
Neither input nor output fixed	Maximize present worth of benefits minus present worth of costs, or maximize net present worth

Appropriate Problems

Present worth analysis is most frequently used to determine the present value of future money receipts and disbursements. We might want to know, for example, the present worth of an income-producing property, such as an oil well. This should provide an estimate of the price at which the property could be bought or sold.

An important restriction in the use of present worth calculation is that there must be a common analysis period for comparing alternatives. It would be incorrect, for example, to compare the present worth (PW) of cost of pump *A*, expected to last 6 years, with the PW of cost of pump *B*, expected to last 12 years (Fig. A.6). In situations like this, the solution is either to use some other analysis technique (generally, the annual cost method is suitable in these situations) or to restructure the problem so that there is a common analysis period.

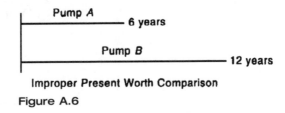

Improper Present Worth Comparison

Figure A.6

In this example, a customary assumption would be that a pump is needed for 12 years and that pump *A* will be replaced by an identical pump *A* at the end of 6 years. This gives a 12-year common analysis period (Fig. A.7). This approach is easy to use when the different lives of the alternatives have a practical least-common-multiple life. When this is not true (for example, the life of *J* equals 7 years and the life of *K* equals 11 years), some assumptions must be made to select a suitable common analysis period, or the present worth method should not be used.

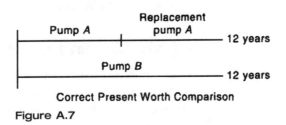

Correct Present Worth Comparison

Figure A.7

Example A.15

Machine *X* has an initial cost of $10,000, an annual maintenance cost of $500 per year, and no salvage value at the end of its 4-year useful life. Machine *Y* costs $20,000, and the first year there is no maintenance cost. Maintenance is $100 the second year, and it increases $100 per year thereafter. The machine has an anticipated $5000 salvage value at the end of its 12-year useful life. If the minimum attractive rate of return (MARR) is 8 percent, which machine should be selected?

Solution

The analysis period is not stated in the problem. Therefore, we select the least common multiple of the lives, or 12 years, as the analysis period.

Present worth of cost of 12 years of machine X:

$$PW = 10,000 + 10,000(P/F, 8\%, 4) + 10,000(P/F, 8\%, 8) + 500(P/A, 8\%, 12)$$
$$= 10,000 + 10,000(0.7350) + 10,000(0.5403) + 500(7.536) = \$26,521$$

Present worth of cost of 12 years of machine Y:

$$PW = 20,000 + 100(P/G, 8\%, 12) - 5000(P/F, 8\%, 12)$$
$$= 20,000 + 100(34.634) - 5000(0.3971) = \$21,478$$

Choose machine Y, with its smaller PW of cost.

Example A.16

Two alternatives have the following cash flows:

	Alternative	
Year	A	B
0	−$2000	−$2800
1	+800	+1100
2	+800	+1100
3	+800	+1100

At a 4 percent interest rate, which alternative should be selected?

Solution

The net present worth of each alternative is computed:

$$\text{Net present worth (NPW)} = \text{PW of benefit} - \text{PW of cost}$$
$$NPW_A = 800(P/A, 4\%, 3) - 2000 = 800(2.775) - 2000 = \$220.00$$
$$NPW_B = 1100(P/A, 4\%, 3) - 2800 = 1100(2.775) - 2800 = \$252.50$$

To maximize NPW, choose alternative B.

Infinite Life and Capitalized Cost

In the special situation where the analysis period is infinite ($n = \infty$), an analysis of the present worth of cost is called *capitalized cost*. There are a few public projects where the analysis period is infinity. Other examples are permanent endowments and cemetery perpetual care.

When n equals infinity, a present sum P will accrue interest of Pi for every future interest period. For the principal sum P to continue undiminished (an essential requirement for n equal to infinity), the end-of-period sum A that can be disbursed is Pi (Fig. A.8). When $n = \infty$, the fundamental relationship is

$$A = Pi$$

Some form of this equation is used whenever there is a problem involving an infinite analysis period.

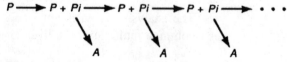

Figure A.8

In his will, a man wishes to establish a perpetual trust to provide for the maintenance of a small local park. If the annual maintenance is $7500 per year and the trust account can earn 5 percent interest, how much money must be set aside in the trust?

Solution

When $n = \infty$, $A = Pi$ or $P = A/i$. The capitalized cost is $P = A/i = \$7500/0.05 = \$150,000$.

FUTURE WORTH OR VALUE

In present worth analysis, the comparison is made in terms of the equivalent present costs and benefits. But the analysis need not be made in terms of the present—it can be made in terms of a past, present, or future time. Although the numerical calculations may look different, the decision is unaffected by the selected point in time. Often we do want to know what the future situation will be if we take some particular couse of action now. An analysis based on some future point in time is called *future worth analysis*.

Category	Future Worth Criterion
Fixed input	Maximize the future worth of benefits or other outputs
Fixed output	Minimize the future worth of costs or other inputs
Neither input nor output fixed	Maximize future worth of benefits minus future worth of costs, or maximize net future worth

Two alternatives have the following cash flows:

	Alternative	
Year	A	B
0	−$2000	−$2800
1	+800	+1100
2	+800	+1100
3	+800	+1100

At a 4 percent interest rate, which alternative should be selected?

Solution

In Example A.16, this problem was solved by present worth analysis at year 0. Here it will be solved by future worth analysis at the end of year 3.

Net future worth (NFW) = FW of benefits − FW of cost

$$NFW_A = 800(F/A, 4\%, 3) - 2000(F/P, 4\%, 3)$$
$$= 800(3.122) - 2000(1.125) = +\$247.60$$

$$NFW_B = 1100(F/A, 4\%, 3) - 2800(F/P, 4\%, 3)$$
$$= 1100(3.122) - 2800(1.125) = +\$284.20$$

To maximize NFW, choose alternative *B*.

ANNUAL COST

The annual cost method is more accurately described as the method of equivalent uniform annual cost (EUAC). Where the computation is of benefits, it is called the method of equivalent uniform annual benefits (EUAB).

Criteria

For each of the three possible categories of problems, there is an annual cost criterion for economic efficiency.

Category	Annual Cost Criterion
Fixed input	Maximize the equivalent uniform annual benefits (EUAB)
Fixed output	Minimize the equivalent uniform annual cost (EUAC)
Neither input nor output fixed	Maximize EUAB – EUAC

Application of Annual Cost Analysis

In the section on present worth, we pointed out that the present worth method requires a common analysis period for all alternatives. This restriction does not apply in all annual cost calculations, but it is important to understand the circumstances that justify comparing alternatives with different service lives.

Frequently, an analysis is done to provide for a more-or-less continuing requirement. For example, one might need to pump water from a well on a continuing basis. Regardless of whether each of two pumps has a useful service life of 6 years or 12 years, we would select the alternative whose annual cost is a minimum. And this still would be the case if the pumps' useful lives were the more troublesome 7 and 11 years. Thus, if we can assume a continuing need for an item, an annual cost comparison among alternatives of differing service lives is valid. The underlying assumption in these situations is that the shorter-lived alternative can be replaced with an identical item with identical costs, when it has reached the end of its useful life. This means that the EUAC of the initial alternative is equal to the EUAC for the continuing series of replacements.

On the other hand, if there is a specific requirement to pump water for 10 years, then each pump must be evaluated to see what costs will be incurred during the analysis period and what salvage value, if any, may be recovered at the end of the analysis period. The annual cost comparison needs to consider the actual circumstances of the situation.

Examination problems are often readily solved using the annual cost method. And the underlying "continuing requirement" is usually present, so an annual cost comparison of unequal-lived alternatives is an appropriate method of analysis.

Example A.19

Consider the following alternatives:

	A	B
First cost	$5000	$10,000
Annual maintenance	500	200
End-of-useful-life salvage value	600	1000
Useful life	5 years	15 years

Based on an 8 percent interest rate, which alternative should be selected?

Solution

Assuming both alternatives perform the same task and there is a continuing requirement, the goal is to minimize EUAC.

Alternative *A:*

$$EUAC = 5000(A/P, 8\%, 5) + 500 - 600(A/F, 8\%, 5)$$
$$= 5000(0.2505) + 500 - 600(0.1705) = \$1650$$

Alternative *B:*

$$EUAC = 10,000(A/P, 8\%, 15) + 200 - 1000(A/F, 8\%, 15)$$
$$= 10,000(0.1168) + 200 - 1000(0.0368) = \$1331$$

To minimize EUAC, select alternative *B*.

RATE OF RETURN ANALYSIS

A typical situation is a cash flow representing the costs and benefits. The rate of return may be defined as the interest rate where PW of cost = PW of benefits, EUAC = EUAB, or PW of cost – PW of benefits = 0.

Example A.20

Compute the rate of return for the investment represented by the following cash flow table.

Year:	0	1	2	3	4	5
Cash flow:	−$595	+250	+200	+150	+100	+50

Solution

This declining uniform gradient series may be separated into two cash flows (Exhibit 3) for which compound interest factors are available.

Note that the gradient series factors are based on an *increasing* gradient. Here the declining cash flow is solved by subtracting an increasing uniform gradient, as indicated in the figure.

PW of cost – PW of benefits = 0

$$595 - [250(P/A, i, 5) - 50(P/G, i, 5) = 0$$

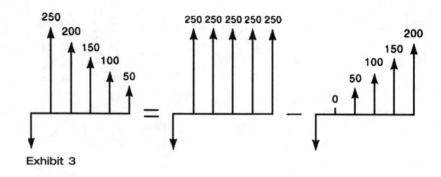

Exhibit 3

Try $i = 10\%$:

$$595 - [250(3.791) - 50(6.862)] = -9.65$$

Try $i = 12\%$:

$$595 - [250(3.605) - 50(6.397)] = +13.60$$

The rate of return is between 10 percent and 12 percent. It may be computed more accurately by linear interpolation:

$$\text{Rate of return} = 10\% + (2\%)\left(\frac{9.65 - 0}{13.60 + 9.65}\right) = 10.83\%.$$

Two Alternatives

Compute the incremental rate of return on the cash flow representing the difference between the two alternatives. Since we want to look at increments of *investment*, the cash flow for the difference between the alternatives is computed by taking the higher initial-cost alternative minus the lower initial-cost alternative. If the incremental rate of return is greater than or equal to the predetermined minimum attractive rate of return (MARR), choose the higher-cost alternative; otherwise, choose the lower-cost alternative.

Example A.21

Two alternatives have the following cash flows:

	Alternative	
Year	A	B
0	−$2000	−$2800
1	+800	+1100
2	+800	+1100
3	+800	+1100

If 4 percent is considered the minimum attractive rate of return (MARR), which alternative should be selected?

Solution

These two alternatives were previously examined in Examples A.16 and A.18 by present worth and future worth analysis. This time, the alternatives will be resolved using a rate-of-return analysis.

Note that the problem statement specifies a 4 percent MARR, whereas Examples A.16 and A.18 referred to a 4 percent interest rate. These are really two different ways of saying the same thing: The minimum acceptable time value of money is 4 percent.

First, tabulate the cash flow that represents the increment of investment between the alternatives. This is done by taking the higher initial-cost alternative minus the lower initial-cost alternative:

	Alternative		Difference Between Alternatives
Year	*A*	*B*	*B − A*
0	−$2000	−$2800	−$800
1	+800	+1100	+300
2	+800	+1100	+300
3	+800	+1100	+300

Then compute the rate of return on the increment of investment represented by the difference between the alternatives:

$$\text{PW of cost} = \text{PW of benefits}$$
$$800 = 300(P/A, i, 3)$$

$$(P/A, i, 3) = 800/300 = 2.67$$
$$i = 6.1\%$$

Since the incremental rate of return exceeds the 4 percent MARR, the increment of investment is desirable. Choose the higher-cost alternative *B*.

Before leaving this example, one should note something that relates to the rates of return on alternative *A* and on alternative *B*. These rates of return, if calculated, are

	Rate of Return
Alternative *A*	9.7%
Alternative *B*	8.7%

The correct answer to this problem has been shown to be alternative *B*, even though alternative *A* has a higher rate of return. The higher-cost alternative may be thought of as the lower-cost alternative plus the increment of investment between them. Viewed this way, the higher-cost alternative *B* is equal to the desirable lower-cost alternative *A* plus the difference between the alternatives.

The important conclusion is that computing the rate of return for each alternative does *not* provide the basis for choosing between alternatives. Instead, incremental analysis is required.

Example A.22

Consider the following:

	Alternative	
Year	A	B
0	−$200.0	−$131.0
1	+77.6	+48.1
2	+77.6	+48.1
3	+77.6	+48.1

If the MARR is 10 percent, which alternative should be selected?

Solution

To examine the increment of investment between the alternatives, we will examine the higher initial-cost alternative minus the lower initial-cost alternative, or $A - B$.

	Alternative		Increment
Year	A	B	A − B
0	−$200.0	−$131.0	−$69.0
1	+77.6	+48.1	+29.5
2	+77.6	+48.1	+29.5
3	+77.6	+48.1	+29.5

Solve for the incremental rate of return:

$$\text{PW of cost} = \text{PW of benefits}$$
$$69.0 = 29.5(P/A, i, 3)$$
$$(P/A, i, 3) = 69.0/29.5 = 2.339$$

From compound interest tables, the incremental rate of return is between 12 percent and 18 percent. This is a desirable increment of investment; hence we select the higher-initial-cost alternative *A*.

Three or More Alternatives

When there are three or more mutually exclusive alternatives, proceed with the same logic presented for two alternatives. The components of incremental analysis are listed below.

Step 1. Compute the rate of return for each alternative. Reject any alternative where the rate of return is less than the desired MARR. (This step is not essential, but helps to immediately identify unacceptable alternatives.)

Step 2. Rank the remaining alternatives in order of increasing initial cost.

Step 3. Examine the increment of investment between the two lowest-cost alternatives as described for the two-alternative problem. Select the better of the two alternatives and reject the other one.

Step 4. Take the preferred alternative from step 3. Consider the next higher initial-cost alternative and proceed with another two-alternative comparison.

Step 5. Continue until all alternatives have been examined and the best of the multiple alternatives has been identified.

Example **A.23**

Consider the following:

	Alternative	
Year	A	B
0	−$200.0	−$131.0
1	+77.6	+48.1
2	+77.6	+48.1
3	+77.6	+48.1

If the MARR is 10 percent, which alternative, if any, should be selected?

Solution

One should carefully note that this is a *three-alternative* problem, where the alternatives are A, B, and *Do nothing*. In this solution we will skip step 1. Reorganize the problem by placing the alternatives in order of increasing initial cost:

	Alternative		
Year	Do Nothing	B	A
0	0	−$131.0	−$200.0
1	0	+48.1	+77.6
2	0	+48.1	+77.6
3	0	+48.1	+77.6

Examine the B − *Do nothing* increment of investment:

Year	B − Do Nothing
0	−$131.0 − 0 = −$131.0
1	+48.1 − 0 = +48.1
2	+48.1 − 0 = +48.1
3	+48.1 − 0 = +48.1

Solve for the incremental rate of return:

$$PW \text{ of cost} = PW \text{ of benefits}$$
$$131.0 = 48.1(P/A, i, 3)$$
$$(P/A, i, 3) = 131.0/48.1 = 2.723$$

From compound interest tables, the incremental rate of return is about 5 percent. Since the incremental rate of return is less than 10 percent, the B − *Do nothing* increment is not desirable. Reject alternative B.

Year	A − Do Nothing
0	−$200.0 − 0 = −$200.0
1	+77.6 − 0 = +77.6
2	+77.6 − 0 = +77.6
3	+77.6 − 0 = +77.6

Next, consider the increment of investment between the two remaining alternatives. Solve for the incremental rate of return:

$$PW \text{ of cost} = PW \text{ of benefits}$$
$$200.0 = 77.6(P/A, i, 3)$$
$$(P/A, i, 3) = 200.0/77.6 = 2.577$$

The incremental rate of return is 8 percent, less than the desired 10 percent. Reject the increment and select the remaining alternative: *Do nothing*.

If you have not already done so, you should go back to Example A.22 and see how the slightly changed wording of the problem has radically altered it. Example A.22 required a choice between two undesirable alternatives. This example adds the *Do nothing* alternative, which is superior to *A* and *B*.

BENEFIT-COST ANALYSIS

Generally, in public works and governmental economic analyses, the dominant method of analysis is the *benefit-cost ratio*. It is simply the ratio of benefits divided by costs, taking into account the time value of money.

$$B/C = \frac{PW \text{ of benefits}}{PW \text{ of cost}} = \frac{\text{Equivalent uniform annual benefits}}{\text{Equivalent uniform annual cost}}$$

For a given interest rate, a B/C ratio ≥ 1 reflects an acceptable project. The B/C analysis method is parallel to rate-of-return analysis. The same kind of incremental analysis is required.

Example A.24

Solve Example A.22 by benefit-cost analysis.

Solution

	Alternative		Increment
Year	*A*	*B*	*A − B*
0	−$200.0	−$131.0	−$69.0
1	+77.6	+48.1	+29.5
2	+77.6	+48.1	+29.5
3	+77.6	+48.1	+29.5

The benefit-cost ratio for the *A − B* increment is

$$B/C = \frac{PW \text{ of benefits}}{PW \text{ of cost}} = \frac{29.5(P/A, 10\%, 3)}{69.0} = \frac{73.37}{69.0} = 1.06$$

Since the B/C ratio exceeds 1, the increment of investment is desirable. Select the higher-cost alternative *A*.

BREAKEVEN ANALYSIS

In business, "breakeven" is defined as the point where income just covers costs. In engineering economics, the breakeven point is defined as the point where two alternatives are equivalent.

Example A.25

A city is considering a new $50,000 snowplow. The new machine will operate at a savings of $600 per day compared with the present equipment. Assume that the MARR is 12 percent, and the machine's life is 10 years with zero resale value at that time. How many days per year must the machine be used to justify the investment?

Solution

This breakeven problem may be readily solved by annual cost computations. We will set the equivalent uniform annual cost (EUAC) of the snowplow equal to its annual benefit and solve for the required annual utilization. Let X = breakeven point = days of operation per year.

$$EUAC = EUAB$$
$$50,000(A/P, 12\%, 10) = 600X$$
$$X = 50,000(0.1770)/600 = 14.8 \text{ days/year}$$

OPTIMIZATION

Optimization is the determination of the best or most favorable situation.

Minima-Maxima

In problems where the situation can be represented by a function, the customary approach is to set the first derivative of the function to zero and solve for the root(s) of this equation. If the second derivative is *positive*, the function is a minimum for the critical value; if it is *negative*, the function is a maximum.

Example A.26

A consulting engineering firm estimates that their net profit is given by the equation

$$P(x) = -0.03x^3 + 36x + 500 \quad x \geq 0$$

where x = number of employees and $P(x)$ = net profit. What is the optimal number of employees?

Solution

$$P'(x) = -0.09x^2 + 36 = 0 \quad P''(x) = -0.18x$$
$$x^2 = 36/0.09 = 400$$
$$x = 20 \text{ employees.}$$
$$P''(20) = -0.18(20) = -3.6$$

Since $P''(20) < 0$, the net profit is maximized for 20 employees.

Economic Problem—Best Alternative

Since engineering economics problems seek to identify the best or most favorable situation, they are by definition optimization problems. Most use compound interest computations in their solution, but some do not. Consider the following example.

Example **A.27**

A firm must decide which of three alternatives to adopt to expand its capacity. It wants a minimum annual profit of 20 percent of the initial cost of each increment of investment. Any money not invested in capacity expansion can be invested elsewhere for an annual yield of 20 percent of the initial cost.

Alternative	Initial Cost	Annual Profit	Profit Rate
A	$100,000	$30,000	30%
B	300,000	66,00	22
C	500,000	80,000	16

Which alternative should be selected?

Solution

Since alternative C fails to produce the 20 percent minimum annual profit, it is rejected. To decide between alternatives A and B, examine the profit rate for the B – A increment.

Alternative	Initial Cost	Annual Profit	Incremental Cost	Incremental Profit	Incremental Profit Rate
A	$100,000	$30,000			
			$200,000	$36,000	18%
B	300,000	66,000			

The B – A incremental profit rate is less than the minimum 20 percent, so alternative B should be rejected. Thus the best investment of $300,000, for example, would be alternative A (annual profit = $30,000) plus $200,000 invested elsewhere at 20 percent (annual profit = $40,000). This combination would yield a $70,000 annual profit, which is better than the alternative B profit of $66,000. Select A.

Economic Order Quantity

One special case of optimization occurs when an item is used continuously and is periodically purchased. Thus the inventory of the item fluctuates from zero (just prior to the receipt of the purchased quantity) to the purchased quantity (just after receipt). The simplest model for the economic order quantity (EOQ) is

$$EOQ = \sqrt{\frac{2BD}{E}}$$

where
> B = ordering cost, \$/order
> D = demand per period, units
> E = inventory holding cost, \$/unit/period
> EOC = economic order quantity, units

| Example **A.28** | A company uses 8000 wheels per year in its manufacture of golf carts. The wheels cost \$15 each and are purchased from an outside supplier. The money invested in the inventory costs 10 percent per year, and the warehousing cost amounts to an additional 2 percent per year. It costs \$150 to process each purchase order. When an order is placed, how many wheels should be ordered? |

Solution

$$EOQ = \sqrt{\frac{2 \times \$150 \times 8000}{(10\% + 2\%)(15.00)}} = 1155 \text{ wheels}$$

VALUATION AND DEPRECIATION

Depreciation of capital equipment is an important component of many after-tax economic analyses. For this reason, one must understand the fundamentals of depreciation accounting.

Notation

> BV = book value
> C = cost of the property (basis)
> D_j = depreciation in year j
> S_n = salvage value in year n

Depreciation is the systematic allocation of the cost of a capital asset over its useful life. *Book value* is the original cost of an asset, minus the accumulated depreciation of the asset.

$$BV = C - \Sigma(D_j)$$

In computing a schedule of depreciation charges, four items are considered.

1. Cost of the property, C (called the *basis* in tax law).

2. Type of property. Property is classified as either *tangible* (such as machinery) or *intangible* (such as a franchise or a copyright), and as either *real property* (real estate) or *personal property* (everything that is not real property).

3. Depreciable life in years, n.

4. Salvage value of the property at the end of its depreciable (useful) life, S_n.

Straight-Line Depreciation

The depreciation charge in any year is

$$D_j = \frac{C - S_n}{n}$$

An alternative computation is

$$\text{Depreciation charge in any year, } D_j = \frac{C - \begin{array}{c}\text{depreciation taken to}\\ \text{beginning of year } j - S_n\end{array}}{\begin{array}{c}\text{Remaining useful life at}\\ \text{beginning of year } j\end{array}}$$

Sum-of-Years'-Digits Depreciation

$$\text{Depreciation charge in any year, } D_j = \frac{\begin{array}{c}\text{Remaining depreciable life at}\\ \text{beginning of year}\end{array}}{\begin{array}{c}\text{Sum of years' digits for}\\ \text{total useful life}\end{array}} \times (C - S_n)$$

Declining-Balance Depreciation

Double declining-balance depreciation charge in any year, $D_j = \dfrac{2C}{m}\left(1 - \dfrac{2}{n}\right)^{j-1}$

Total depreciation at the end of n years, $C = \left[1 - \left(1 - \dfrac{2}{n}\right)^n\right]$

Book value at the end of j years, $\text{BV}_j = C\left(1 - \dfrac{2}{n}\right)^j$

For 150 percent declining-balance depreciation, replace the 2 in the three equations above with 1.5.

Sinking-Fund Depreciation

Depreciation charge in any year, $D_j = (C - S_n)(A/F, i\%, n)(F/P, i\%, j - 1)$

Modified Accelerated Cost Recovery System Depreciation

The modified accelerated cost recovery system (MACRS) depreciation method generally applies to property placed in service after 1986. To compute the MACRS depreciation for an item, one must know

1. Cost (basis) of the item.

2. Property class. All tangible property is classified in one of six classes (3, 5, 7, 10, 15, and 20 years), which is the life over which it is depreciated (see Table A.3). Residential real estate and nonresidential real estate are in two separate real property classes of 27.5 years and 39 years, respectively.

3. Depreciation computation.

Table A.3 MACRS classes of depreciable property

Property Class	Personal Property (All Property Except Real Estate)
3-year property	Special handling devices for food and beverage manufacture Special tools for the manufacture of finished plastic products, fabricated metal products, and motor vehicles Property with an asset depreciation range (ADR) midpoint life of 4 years or less
5-year property	Automobiles* and trucks Aircraft (of non–air-transport companies) Equipment used in research and experimentation Computers Petroleum drilling equipment Property with an ADR midpoint life of more than 4 years and less than 10 years
7-year property	All other property not assigned to another class Office furniture, fixtures, and equipment Property with an ADR midpoint life of 10 years or more, and less than 16 years
10-year property	Assets used in petroleum refining and preparation of certain food products Vessels and water transportation equipment Property with an ADR midpoint life of 16 years or more, and less than 20 years
15-year property	Telephone distribution plants Municipal sewage treatment plants Property with an ADR midpoint life of 20 years or more, and less than 25 years
20-year property	Municipal sewers Property with an ADR midpoint life of 25 years or more

Property Class	Real Property (Real Estate)
27.5 years	Residential rental property (does not include hotels and motels)
39 years	Nonresidential real property

*The depreciation deduction for automobiles is limited to $2860 in the first tax year and is reduced in subsequent years.

- Use double-declining-balance depreciation for 3-, 5-, 7-, and 10-year property classes with conversion to straight-line depreciation in the year that increases the deduction.

- Use 150%-declining-balance depreciation for 15- and 20-year property classes with conversion to straight-line depreciation in the year that increases the deduction.

- In MACRS, the salvage value is assumed to be zero.

Half-Year Convention

Except for real property, a half-year convention is used. Under this convention all property is considered to be placed in service in the middle of the tax year, and a half-year of depreciation is allowed in the first year. For each of the remaining years, one is allowed a full year of depreciation. If the property is disposed of

Table A.4 MACRS* depreciation for personal property—half-year convention

If the Recovery Year Is	The Applicable Percentage for the Class of Property Is			
	3-Year Class	5-Year Class	7-Year Class	10-Year Class
1	33.33	20.00	14.29	10.00
2	44.45	32.00	24.49	18.00
3	14.81†	19.20	17.49	14.40
4	7.41	11.52†	12.49	11.52
5		11.52	8.93†	9.22
6		5.76	8.92	7.37
7			8.93	6.55†
8			4.46	6.55
9				6.56
10				6.55
11				3.28

*In the *Fundamentals of Engineering Reference Handbook*, this table is called "Modified ACRS Factors."

†Use straight-line depreciation for the year marked and all subsequent years.

prior to the end of the recovery period (property class life), a half-year of depreciation is allowed in that year. If the property is held for the entire recovery period, a half-year of depreciation is allowed for the year following the end of the recovery period (see Table A.4). Owing to the half-year convention, a general form of the double-declining-balance computation must be used to compute the year-by-year depreciation.

$$\text{DDB depreciation in any year, } D_j = \frac{2}{n}(C - \text{depreciation in years prior to } j)$$

Example A.29

A $5000 computer has an anticipated $500 salvage value at the end of its five-year depreciable life. Compute the depreciation schedule for the machinery by (a) sum-of-years'-digits depreciation and (b) MACRS depreciation. Do the MACRS computation by hand, and then compare the results with the values from Table A.4.

Solution

(a) Sum-of-years'-digits depreciation:

$$D_j = \frac{n-j+1}{\frac{n}{2}(n+1)}(C - S_n)$$

$$D_1 = \frac{5-1+1}{\frac{5}{2}(5+1)}(5000 - 500) = \$1500$$

$$D_2 = \frac{5-2+1}{\frac{5}{2}(5+1)}(5000-500) = \$1200$$

$$D_3 = \frac{5-3+1}{\frac{5}{2}(5+1)}(5000-500) = \quad 900$$

$$D_4 = \frac{5-4+1}{\frac{5}{2}(5+1)}(5000-500) = \quad 600$$

$$D_5 = \frac{5-5+1}{\frac{5}{2}(5+1)}(5000-500) = \quad 300$$

$$\overline{\$4500}$$

(b) MACRS depreciation. Double-declining-balance with conversion to straight-line. Five-year property class. Half-year convention. Salvage value S_n is assumed to be zero for MACRS. Using the general DDB computation,

Year

1 (half-year) $D_1 = \frac{1}{2} \times \frac{2}{5}(5000-0) \quad = \$1000$

2 $\qquad\qquad D_2 = \frac{2}{5}(5000-1000) \quad = \ 1600$

3 $\qquad\qquad D_3 = \frac{2}{5}(5000-2600) \quad = \quad 960$

4 $\qquad\qquad D_4 = \frac{2}{5}(5000-3560) \quad = \quad 576$

5 $\qquad\qquad D_5 = \frac{2}{5}(5000-4136) \quad = \quad 346$

6 (half-year) $D_6 = \frac{1}{2} \times \frac{2}{5}(5000-4482) \ = \quad 104$

$$\overline{\$4586}$$

The computation must now be modified to convert to straight-line depreciation at the point where the straight-line depreciation will be larger. Using the alternative straight-line computation,

$$D_5 = \frac{5000-4136-0}{1.5 \text{ years remaining}} = \$576$$

This is more than the \$346 computed using DDB, hence switch to straight-line for year 5 and beyond.

$$D_6 \text{ (half-year)} = \frac{1}{2}(576) = \$288$$

Answers:

	Depreciation	
Year	SOYD	MACRS
1	$1500	$1000
2	1200	1600
3	900	960
4	600	576
5	300	576
6	0	288
	$4500	$5000

The computed MACRS depreciation is identical to the result obtained from Table A.4.

TAX CONSEQUENCES

Income taxes represent another of the various kinds of disbursements encountered in an economic analysis. The starting point in an after-tax computation is the before-tax cash flow. Generally, the before-tax cash flow contains three types of entries:

1. Disbursements of money to purchase capital assets. These expenditures create no direct tax consequence, for they are the exchange of one asset (money) for another (capital equipment).

2. Periodic receipts and/or disbursements representing operating income and/or expenses. These increase or decrease the year-by-year tax liability of the firm.

3. Receipts of money from the sale of capital assets, usually in the form of a salvage value when the equipment is removed. The tax consequences depend on the relationship between the book value (cost − depreciation taken) of the asset and its salvage value.

Situation	Tax Consequence
Salvage value > Book value	Capital gain on differences
Salvage value = Book value	No tax consequence
Salvage value < Book value	Capital loss on difference

After determining the before-tax cash flow, compute the depreciation schedule for any capital assets. Next, compute taxable income, the taxable component of the before-tax cash flow minus the depreciation. The income tax is the taxable income times the appropriate tax rate. Finally, the after-tax cash flow is the before-tax cash flow adjusted for income taxes.

To organize these data, it is customary to arrange them in the form of a cash flow table, as follows:

Year	Before-Tax Cash Flow	Depreciation	Taxable Income	Income Taxes	After-Tax Cash Flow
0	•				•
1	•	•	•	•	•

Example A.30

A corporation expects to receive $32,000 each year for 15 years from the sale of a product. There will be an initial investment of $150,000. Manufacturing and sales expenses will be $8067 per year. Assume straight-line depreciation, a 15-year useful life, and no salvage value. Use a 46 percent income tax rate. Determine the projected after-tax rate of return.

Solution

Straight-line depreciation, $D_j = \dfrac{C - S_n}{n} = \dfrac{\$150,000 - 0}{15} = \$10,000$ per year

Year	Before-Tax Cash Flow	Depreciation	Taxable Income	Income Taxes	After-Tax Cash Flow
0	−150,000				−150,000
1	+23,933	10,000	13,933	−6,409	+17,524
2	+23,933	10,000	13,933	−6,409	+17,524
•	•	•	•	•	•
•	•	•	•	•	•
•	•	•	•	•	•
15	+23,933	10,000	13,933	−6,409	+17,524

Take the after-tax cash flow and compute the rate of return at which the PW of cost equals the PW of benefits.

$$150,000 = 17,524(P/A, i\%, 15)$$

$$(P/A, i\%, 15) = \frac{150,000}{17,524} = 8.559$$

From the compound interest tables, the after-tax rate of return is $i = 8\%$.

INFLATION

Inflation is characterized by rising prices for goods and services, whereas deflation produces a fall in prices. An inflationary trend makes future dollars have less purchasing power than present dollars. This helps long-term borrowers of money, for they may repay a loan of present dollars in the future with dollars of reduced buying power. The help to borrowers is at the expense of lenders. Deflation has the opposite effect. Money borrowed at one point in time, followed by a deflationary period, subjects the borrower to loan repayment with dollars of greater purchasing power than those borrowed. This is to the lenders' advantage at the expense of borrowers.

Price changes occur in a variety of ways. One method of stating a price change is as a uniform rate of price change per year.

f = General inflation rate per interest period
i = Effective interest rate per interest period

The following situation will illustrate the computations. A mortgage is to be repaid in three equal payments of $5000 at the end of years 1, 2, and 3. If the annual inflation rate, f, is 8% during this period, and a 12% annual interest rate (*i*) is desired, what is the maximum amount the investor would be willing to pay for the mortgage?

The computation is a two-step process. First, the three future payments must be converted to dollars with the same purchasing power as today's (year 0) dollars.

Year	Actual Cash Flow	Multiplied by			Cash Flow Adjusted to Today's (yr. 0) Dollars
0	—	—			—
1	+5000	×	$(1 + 0.08)^{-1}$	=	+4630
2	+5000	×	$(1 + 0.08)^{-2}$	=	+4286
3	+5000	×	$(1 + 0.08)^{-3}$	=	+3969

The general form of the adjusting multiplier is

$$(1 + f)^{-n} = (P/F, f, n)$$

Now that the problem has been converted to dollars of the same purchasing power (today's dollars, in this example), we can proceed to compute the present worth of the future payments.

Year	Adjusted Cash Flow	Multiplied by			Present Worth
0	—	—			—
1	+4630	×	$(1 + 0.12)^{-1}$	=	+4134
2	+4286	×	$(1 + 0.12)^{-2}$	=	+3417
3	+3969	×	$(1 + 0.12)^{-3}$	=	+2825
					$10,376

The general form of the discounting multiplier is

$$(1 + i)^{-n} = (P/F, i\%, n)$$

Alternative Solution

Instead of doing the inflation and interest rate computations separately, one can compute a combined equivalent interest rate, *d*.

$$d = (1 + f)(1 + i) - 1 = i + f + i(f)$$

For this cash flow, $d = 0.12 + 0.08 + 0.12(0.08) = 0.2096$. Since we do not have 20.96 percent interest tables, the problem has to be calculated using present worth equations.

$$PW = 5000(1 + 0.2096)^{-1} + 5000(1 + 0.2096)^{-2} + 5000(1 + 0.2096)^{-3}$$
$$= 4134 + 3417 + 2825 = \$10,376$$

Example **A.31**

One economist has predicted that there will be 7 percent per year inflation of prices during the next 10 years. If this proves to be correct, an item that presently sells for $10 would sell for what price 10 years hence?

Solution

$$f = 7\%, \ P = \$10$$
$$F = ?, \ n = 10 \text{ years}$$

Here the computation is to find the future worth F, rather than the present worth, P.

$$F = P(1 + f)^{10} = 10(1 + 0.07)^{10} = \$19.67$$

Effect of Inflation on Rate of Return

The effect of inflation on the computed rate of return for an investment depends on how future benefits respond to the inflation. If benefits produce constant dollars, which are not increased by inflation, the effect of inflation is to reduce the before-tax rate of return on the investment. If, on the other hand, the dollar benefits increase to keep up with the inflation, the before-tax rate of return will not be adversely affected by the inflation.

This is not true when an after-tax analysis is made. Even if the future benefits increase to match the inflation rate, the allowable depreciation schedule does not increase. The result will be increased taxable income and income tax payments. This reduces the available after-tax benefits and, therefore, the after-tax rate of return.

Example **A.32**

A man bought a 5 percent tax-free municipal bond. It cost $1000 and will pay $50 interest each year for 20 years. The bond will mature at the end of 20 years and return the original $1000. If there is 2% annual inflation during this period, what rate of return will the investor receive after considering the effect of inflation?

Solution

$$d = 0.05, \ i = \text{unknown}, \ j = 0.02$$
$$d = i + j + i(j)$$
$$0.05 = i + 0.02 + 0.02i$$
$$1.02i = 0.03, \ i = 0.294 = 2.94\%$$

RISK ANALYSIS

Probability

Probability can be considered to be the long-run relative frequency of occurrence of an outcome. There are two possible outcomes from flipping a coin (a head or a tail). If, for example, a coin is flipped over and over, we can expect in the long run that half the time heads will appear and half the time tails will appear. We would say the probability of flipping a head is 0.50 and of flipping a tail is 0.50. Since the probabilities are defined so that the sum of probabilities for all possible outcomes is 1, the situation is

$$\text{Probability of flipping a head} = 0.50$$
$$\text{Probability of flipping a tail} = 0.50$$
$$\text{Sum of all possible outcomes} = \overline{1.00}$$

Example A.33

If one were to roll one die (that is, one-half of a pair of dice), what is the probability that either a 1 or a 6 would result?

Solution

Since a die is a perfect six-sided cube, the probability of any side appearing is 1/6.

$$\text{Probability of rolling a } 1 = P(1) = 1/6$$
$$2 = P(2) = 1/6$$
$$3 = P(3) = 1/6$$
$$4 = P(4) = 1/6$$
$$5 = P(5) = 1/6$$
$$6 = P(6) = 1/6$$

Sum of all possible outcomes = 6/6 = 1. The probability of rolling a 1 or a 6 = 1/6 + 1/6 = 1/3.

In the preceding examples, the probability of each outcome was the same. This need not be the case.

Example A.34

In the game of blackjack, a perfect hand is a 10 or a face card plus an ace. What is the probability of being dealt a 10 or a face card from a newly shuffled deck of 52 cards? What is the probability of being dealt an ace in this same situation?

Solution

The three outcomes examined are to be dealt a 10 or a face card, an ace, or some other card. Every card in the deck represents one of these three possible outcomes. There are 4 aces; 16 10s, jacks, queens, and kings; and 32 other cards.

$$\text{Probability of being dealt a } 10 \text{ or a face card} = 16/52 = 0.31$$
$$\text{Probability of being dealt an ace} = 4/52 = 0.08$$
$$\text{Probability of being dealt some other card} = 32/52 = \underline{0.61}$$
$$1.00$$

Risk

The term *risk* has a special meaning in statistics. It is defined as a situation where there are two or more possible outcomes and the probability associated with each outcome is known. In each of the two previous examples there is a risk situation. We could not know in advance what playing card would be dealt or what number would be rolled by the die. However, since the various probabilities could be computed, our definition of risk has been satisfied. Probability and risk are not restricted to gambling games. For example, in a particular engineering course, a student has computed the probability for each of the letter grades he might receive as follows:

Grade	Grade Point	Probability P(Grade)
A	4.0	0.10
B	3.0	0.30
C	2.0	0.25
D	1.0	0.20
F	0	0.15
		1.00

From the table we see that the grade with the highest probability is a B. This, therefore, is the most likely grade. We also see that there is a substantial probability that some grade other than a B will be received. And the probabilities indicate that if a B is not received, the grade will probably be something less than a B. But in saying that the most likely grade is a B, other outcomes are ignored. In the next section we will show that a composite statistic may be computed using all the data.

Expected Value

In the last example the most likely grade of B in an engineering class had a probability of 0.30. That is not a very high probability. In some other course, say a math class, we might estimate a probability of 0.65 of obtaining a B, again making the B the most likely grade. While a B is most likely in both classes, it is more certain in the math class.

We can compute a weighted mean to give a better understanding of the total situation as represented by various possible outcomes. When the probabilities are used as the weighting factors, the result is called the *expected value* and is written

$$\text{Expected value} = \text{Outcome}_A \times P(A) + \text{Outcome}_B \times P(B) + \cdots$$

Example **A.35**

An engineer wishes to determine the risk of fire loss for her $200,000 home. From a fire rating bureau she obtains the following data:

Outcome	Probability
No fire loss	0.986 in any year
$10,000 fire loss	0.010
40,000 fire loss	0.003
200,000 fire loss	0.001

Compute the expected fire loss in any year.

Solution

$$\text{Expected fire loss} = 10,000(0.010) + 40,000(0.003) + 200,000(0.001) = \$420$$

REFERENCE

Newnan, Donald G. *Engineering Economic Analysis*, 5th ed. Engineering Press, San Jose, CA, 1995.

INTEREST TABLES

Compound interest factors

$\frac{1}{2}\%$ $\frac{1}{2}\%$

	Single Payment		Uniform Payment Series				Uniform Gradient		
	Compound Amount Factor	Present Worth Factor	Sinking Fund Factor	Capital Recovery Factor	Compound Amount Factor	Present Worth Factor	Gradient Uniform Series	Gradient Present Worth	
	Find F Given P	Find P Given F	Find A Given F	Find A Given P	Find F Given A	Find P Given A	Find A Given G	Find P Given G	
n	F/P	P/F	A/F	A/P	F/A	P/A	A/G	P/G	n
1	1.005	.9950	1.0000	1.0050	1.000	0.995	0	0	1
2	1.010	.9901	.4988	.5038	2.005	1.985	0.499	0.991	2
3	1.015	.9851	.3317	.3367	3.015	2.970	0.996	2.959	3
4	1.020	.9802	.2481	.2531	4.030	3.951	1.494	5.903	4
5	1.025	.9754	.1980	.2030	5.050	4.926	1.990	9.803	5
6	1.030	.9705	.1646	.1696	6.076	5.896	2.486	14.660	6
7	1.036	.9657	.1407	.1457	7.106	6.862	2.980	20.448	7
8	1.041	.9609	.1228	.1278	8.141	7.823	3.474	27.178	8
9	1.046	.9561	.1089	.1139	9.182	8.779	3.967	34.825	9
10	1.051	.9513	.0978	.1028	10.228	9.730	4.459	43.389	10
11	1.056	.9466	.0887	.0937	11.279	10.677	4.950	52.855	11
12	1.062	.9419	.0811	.0861	12.336	11.619	5.441	63.218	12
13	1.067	.9372	.0746	.0796	13.397	12.556	5.931	74.465	13
14	1.072	.9326	.0691	.0741	14.464	13.489	6.419	86.590	14
15	1.078	.9279	.0644	.0694	15.537	14.417	6.907	99.574	15
16	1.083	.9233	.0602	.0652	16.614	15.340	7.394	113.427	16
17	1.088	.9187	.0565	.0615	17.697	16.259	7.880	128.125	17
18	1.094	.9141	.0532	.0582	18.786	17.173	8.366	143.668	18
19	1.099	.9096	.0503	.0553	19.880	18.082	8.850	160.037	19
20	1.105	9051	.0477	.0527	20.979	18.987	9.334	177.237	20
21	1.110	.9006	.0453	.0503	22.084	19.888	9.817	195.245	21
22	1.116	.8961	.0431	.0481	23.194	20.784	10.300	214.070	22
23	1.122	.8916	.0411	.0461	24.310	21.676	10.781	233.680	23
24	1.127	.8872	.0393	.0443	25.432	22.563	11.261	254.088	24
25	1.133	.8828	.0377	.0427	26.559	23.446	11.741	275.273	25
26	1.138	.8784	.0361	.0411	27.692	24.324	12.220	297.233	26
27	1.144	.8740	.0347	.0397	28.830	25.198	12.698	319.955	27
28	1.150	.8697	.0334	.0384	29.975	26.068	13.175	343.439	28
29	1.156	.8653	.0321	.0371	31.124	26.933	13.651	367.672	29
30	1.161	.8610	.0310	.0360	32.280	27.794	14.127	392.640	30
36	1.197	.8356	.0254	.0304	39.336	32.871	16.962	557.564	36
40	1.221	.8191	.0226	.0276	44.159	36.172	18.836	681.341	40
48	1.270	.7871	.0185	.0235	54.098	42.580	22.544	959.928	48
50	1.283	.7793	.0177	.0227	56.645	44.143	23.463	1 035.70	50
52	1.296	.7716	.0169	.0219	59.218	45.690	24.378	1 113.82	52
60	1.349	.7414	.0143	.0193	69.770	51.726	28.007	1 448.65	60
70	1.418	.7053	.0120	.0170	83.566	58.939	32.468	1 913.65	70
72	1.432	.6983	.0116	.0166	86.409	60.340	33.351	2 012.35	72
80	1.490	.6710	.0102	.0152	98.068	65.802	36.848	2 424.65	80
84	1.520	.6577	.00961	.0146	104.074	68.453	38.576	2 640.67	84
90	1.567	.6383	.00883	.0138	113.311	72.331	41.145	2 976.08	90
96	1.614	.6195	.00814	.0131	122.829	76.095	43.685	3 324.19	96
100	1.647	.6073	.00773	.0127	129.334	78.543	45.361	3 562.80	100
104	1.680	.5953	.00735	.0124	135.970	80.942	47.025	3 806.29	104
120	1.819	.5496	.00610	.0111	163.880	90.074	53.551	4 823.52	120
240	3.310	.3021	.00216	.00716	462.041	139.581	96.113	13 415.56	240
360	6.023	.1660	.00100	.00600	1 004.5	166.792	128.324	21 403.32	360
480	10.957	.0913	.00050	.00550	1 991.5	181.748	151.795	27 588.37	480

Compound interest factors

1%									1%
	Single Payment		**Uniform Payment Series**				**Uniform Gradient**		
	Compound Amount Factor	Present Worth Factor	Sinking Fund Factor	Capital Recovery Factor	Compound Amount Factor	Present Worth Factor	Gradient Uniform Series	Gradient Present Worth	
	Find F Given P	Find P Given F	Find A Given F	Find A Given P	Find F Given A	Find P Given A	Find A Given G	Find P Given G	
n	F/P	P/F	A/F	A/P	F/A	P/A	A/G	P/G	n
1	1.010	.9901	1.0000	1.0100	1.000	0.990	0	0	1
2	1.020	.9803	.4975	.5075	2.010	1.970	0.498	0.980	2
3	1.030	.9706	.3300	.3400	3.030	2.941	0.993	2.921	3
4	1.041	.9610	.2463	.2563	4.060	3.902	1.488	5.804	4
5	1.051	.9515	.1960	.2060	5.101	4.853	1.980	9.610	5
6	1.062	.9420	.1625	.1725	6.152	5.795	2.471	14.320	6
7	1.072	.9327	.1386	.1486	7.214	6.728	2.960	19.917	7
8	1.083	.9235	.1207	.1307	8.286	7.652	3.448	26.381	8
9	1.094	.9143	.1067	.1167	9.369	8.566	3.934	33.695	9
10	1.105	.9053	.0956	.1056	10.462	9.471	4.418	41.843	10
11	1.116	.8963	.0865	.0965	11.567	10.368	4.900	50.806	11
12	1.127	.8874	.0788	.0888	12.682	11.255	5.381	60.568	12
13	1.138	.8787	.0724	.0824	13.809	12.134	5.861	71.112	13
14	1.149	.8700	.0669	.0769	14.947	13.004	6.338	82.422	14
15	1.161	.8613	.0621	.0721	16.097	13.865	6.814	94.481	15
16	1.173	.8528	.0579	.0679	17.258	14.718	7.289	107.273	16
17	1.184	.8444	.0543	.0643	18.430	15.562	7.761	120.783	17
18	1.196	.8360	.0510	.0610	19.615	16.398	8.232	134.995	18
19	1.208	.8277	.0481	.0581	20.811	17.226	8.702	149.895	19
20	1.220	.8195	.0454	.0554	22.019	18.046	9.169	165.465	20
21	1.232	.8114	.0430	.0530	23.239	18.857	9.635	181.694	21
22	1.245	.8034	.0409	.0509	24.472	19.660	10.100	198.565	22
23	1.257	.7954	.0389	.0489	25.716	20.456	10.563	216.065	23
24	1.270	.7876	.0371	.0471	26.973	21.243	11.024	234.179	24
25	1.282	.7798	.0354	.0454	28.243	22.023	11.483	252.892	25
26	1.295	.7720	0339	.0439	29.526	22.795	11.941	272.195	26
27	1.308	.7644	.0324	.0424	30.821	23.560	12.397	292.069	27
28	1.321	.7568	.0311	.0411	32.129	24.316	12.852	312.504	28
29	1.335	.7493	.0299	.0399	33.450	25.066	13.304	333.486	29
30	1.348	.7419	.0287	.0387	34.785	25.808	13.756	355.001	30
36	1.431	.6989	.0232	.0332	43.077	30.107	16.428	494.620	36
40	1.489	.6717	.0205	.0305	48.886	32.835	18.178	596.854	40
48	1.612	.6203	.0163	.0263	61.223	37.974	21.598	820.144	48
50	1.645	.6080	.0155	.0255	64.463	39.196	22.436	879.417	50
52	1.678	.5961	.0148	.0248	67.769	40.394	23.269	939.916	52
60	1.817	.5504	.0122	.0222	81.670	44.955	26.533	1 192.80	60
70	2.007	.4983	.00993	.0199	100.676	50.168	30.470	1 528.64	70
72	2.047	.4885	.00955	.0196	104.710	51.150	31.239	1 597.86	72
80	2.217	.4511	.00822	.0182	121.671	54.888	34.249	1 879.87	80
84	2.307	.4335	.00765	.0177	130.672	56.648	35.717	2 023.31	84
90	2.449	.4084	.00690	.0169	144.863	59.161	37.872	2 240.56	90
96	2.599	.3847	.00625	.0163	159.927	61.528	39.973	2 459.42	96
100	2.705	.3697	.00587	.0159	170.481	63.029	41.343	2 605.77	100
104	2.815	.3553	.00551	.0155	181.464	64.471	42.688	2 752.17	104
120	3.300	.3030	.00435	.0143	230.039	69.701	47.835	3 334.11	120
240	10.893	.0918	.00101	.0110	989.254	90.819	75.739	6 878.59	240
360	35.950	.0278	.00029	.0103	3 495.0	97.218	89.699	8 720.43	360
480	118.648	.00843	.00008	.0101	11 764.8	99.157	95.920	9 511.15	480

Compound interest factors

$1\frac{1}{2}\%$ $1\frac{1}{2}\%$

	Single Payment		Uniform Payment Series				Uniform Gradient		
	Compound Amount Factor	Present Worth Factor	Sinking Fund Factor	Capital Recovery Factor	Compound Amount Factor	Present Worth Factor	Gradient Uniform Series	Gradient Present Worth	
	Find F Given P	Find P Given F	Find A Given F	Find A Given P	Find F Given A	Find P Given A	Find A Given G	Find P Given G	
n	F/P	P/F	A/F	A/P	F/A	P/A	A/G	P/G	n
1	1.015	.9852	1.0000	1.0150	1.000	0.985	0	0	1
2	1.030	.9707	.4963	.5113	2.015	1.956	0.496	0.970	2
3	1.046	.9563	.3284	.3434	3.045	2.912	0.990	2.883	3
4	1.061	.9422	.2444	.2594	4.091	3.854	1.481	5.709	4
5	1.077	.9283	.1941	.2091	5.152	4.783	1.970	9.422	5
6	1.093	.9145	.1605	.1755	6.230	5.697	2.456	13.994	6
7	1.110	.9010	.1366	.1516	7.323	6.598	2.940	19.400	7
8	1.126	.8877	.1186	.1336	8.433	7.486	3.422	25.614	8
9	1.143	.8746	.1046	.1196	9.559	8.360	3.901	32.610	9
10	1.161	.8617	.0934	.1084	10.703	9.222	4.377	40.365	10
11	1.178	.8489	.0843	.0993	11.863	10.071	4.851	48.855	11
12	1.196	.8364	.0767	.0917	13.041	10.907	5.322	58.054	12
13	1.214	.8240	.0702	.0852	14.237	11.731	5.791	67.943	13
14	1.232	.8118	.0647	.0797	15.450	12.543	6.258	78.496	14
15	1.250	.7999	.0599	.0749	16.682	13.343	6.722	89.694	15
16	1.269	.7880	.0558	.0708	17.932	14.131	7.184	101.514	16
17	1.288	.7764	.0521	.0671	19.201	14.908	7.643	113.937	17
18	1.307	.7649	.0488	.0638	20.489	15.673	8.100	126.940	18
19	1.327	.7536	.0459	.0609	21.797	16.426	8.554	140.505	19
20	1.347	.7425	.0432	.0582	23.124	17.169	9.005	154.611	20
21	1.367	.7315	.0409	.0559	24.470	17.900	9.455	169.241	21
22	1.388	.7207	.0387	.0537	25.837	18.621	9.902	184.375	22
23	1.408	.7100	.0367	.0517	27.225	19.331	10.346	199.996	23
24	1.430	.6995	.0349	.0499	28.633	20.030	10.788	216.085	24
25	1.451	.6892	.0333	.0483	30.063	20.720	11.227	232.626	25
26	1.473	.6790	.0317	.0467	31.514	21.399	11.664	249.601	26
27	1.495	.6690	.0303	.0453	32.987	22.068	12.099	266.995	27
28	1.517	.6591	.0290	.0440	34.481	22.727	12.531	284.790	28
29	1.540	.6494	.0278	.0428	35.999	23.376	12.961	302.972	29
30	1.563	.6398	.0266	.0416	37.539	24.016	13.388	321.525	30
36	1.709	.5851	.0212	.0362	47.276	27.661	15.901	439.823	36
40	1.814	.5513	.0184	.0334	54.268	29.916	17.528	524.349	40
48	2.043	.4894	.0144	.0294	69.565	34.042	20.666	703.537	48
50	2.105	.4750	.0136	.0286	73.682	35.000	21.428	749.955	50
52	2.169	.4611	.0128	.0278	77.925	35.929	22.179	796.868	52
60	2.443	.4093	.0104	.0254	96.214	39.380	25.093	988.157	60
70	2.835	.3527	.00817	.0232	122.363	43.155	28.529	1 231.15	70
72	2.921	.3423	.00781	.0228	128.076	43.845	29.189	1 279.78	72
80	3.291	.3039	.00655	.0215	152.710	46.407	31.742	1 473.06	80
84	3.493	.2863	.00602	.0210	166.172	47.579	32.967	1 568.50	84
90	3.819	.2619	.00532	.0203	187.929	49.210	34.740	1 709.53	90
96	4.176	.2395	.00472	.0197	211.719	50.702	36.438	1 847.46	96
100	4.432	.2256	.00437	.0194	228.802	51.625	37.529	1 937.43	100
104	4.704	.2126	.00405	.0190	246.932	52.494	38.589	2 025.69	104
120	5.969	.1675	.00302	.0180	331.286	55.498	42.518	2 359.69	120
240	35.632	.0281	.00043	.0154	2 308.8	64.796	59.737	3 870.68	240
360	212.700	.00470	.00007	.0151	14 113.3	66.353	64.966	4 310.71	360
480	1 269.7	.00079	.00001	.0150	84 577.8	66.614	66.288	4 415.74	480

Compound interest factors

2%									2%
	Single Payment		**Uniform Payment Series**				**Uniform Gradient**		
	Compound Amount Factor	Present Worth Factor	Sinking Fund Factor	Capital Recovery Factor	Compound Amount Factor	Present Worth Factor	Gradient Uniform Series	Gradient Present Worth	
	Find F Given P	Find P Given F	Find A Given F	Find A Given P	Find F Given A	Find P Given A	Find A Given G	Find P Given G	
n	F/P	P/F	A/F	A/P	F/A	P/A	A/G	P/G	n
1	1.020	.9804	1.0000	1.0200	1.000	0.980	0	0	1
2	1.040	.9612	.4951	.5151	2.020	1.942	0.495	0.961	2
3	1.061	.9423	.3268	.3468	3.060	2.884	0.987	2.846	3
4	1.082	.9238	.2426	.2626	4.122	3.808	1.475	5.617	4
5	1.104	.9057	.1922	.2122	5.204	4.713	1.960	9.240	5
6	1.126	.8880	.1585	.1785	6.308	5.601	2.442	13.679	6
7	1.149	.8706	.1345	.1545	7.434	6.472	2.921	18.903	7
8	1.172	.8535	.1165	.1365	8.583	7.325	3.396	24.877	8
9	1.195	.8368	.1025	.1225	9.755	8.162	3.868	31.571	9
10	1.219	.8203	.0913	.1113	10.950	8.983	4.337	38.954	10
11	1.243	.8043	.0822	.1022	12.169	9.787	4.802	46.996	11
12	1.268	.7885	.0746	.0946	13.412	10.575	5.264	55.669	12
13	1.294	.7730	.0681	.0881	14.680	11.348	5.723	64.946	13
14	1.319	.7579	.0626	.0826	15.974	12.106	6.178	74.798	14
15	1.346	.7430	.0578	.0778	17.293	12.849	6.631	85.200	15
16	1.373	.7284	.0537	.0737	18.639	13.578	7.080	96.127	16
17	1.400	.7142	.0500	.0700	20.012	14.292	7.526	107.553	17
18	1.428	.7002	.0467	.0667	21.412	14.992	7.968	119.456	18
19	1.457	.6864	.0438	.0638	22.840	15.678	8.407	131.812	19
20	1.486	.6730	.0412	.0612	24.297	16.351	8.843	144.598	20
21	1.516	.6598	.0388	.0588	25.783	17.011	9.276	157.793	21
22	1.546	.6468	.0366	.0566	27.299	17.658	9.705	171.377	22
23	1.577	.6342	.0347	.0547	28.845	18.292	10.132	185.328	23
24	1.608	.6217	.0329	.0529	30.422	18.914	10.555	199.628	24
25	1.641	.6095	.0312	.0512	32.030	19.523	10.974	214.256	25
26	1.673	.5976	.0297	.0497	33.671	20.121	11.391	229.169	26
27	1.707	.5859	.0283	.0483	35.344	20.707	11.804	244.428	27
28	1.741	.5744	.0270	.0470	37.051	21.281	12.214	259.936	28
29	1.776	.5631	.0258	.0458	38.792	21.844	12.621	275.703	29
30	1.811	.5521	.0247	.0447	40.568	22.396	13.025	291.713	30
36	2.040	.4902	.0192	.0392	51.994	25.489	15.381	392.036	36
40	2.208	.4529	.0166	.0366	60.402	27.355	16.888	461.989	40
48	2.587	.3865	.0126	.0326	79.353	30.673	19.755	605.961	48
50	2.692	.3715	.0118	.0318	84.579	31.424	20.442	642.355	50
52	2.800	.3571	.0111	.0311	90.016	32.145	21.116	678.779	52
60	3.281	.3048	.00877	.0288	114.051	34.761	23.696	823.692	60
70	4.000	.2500	.00667	.0267	149.977	37.499	26.663	999.829	70
72	4.161	.2403	.00633	.0263	158.056	37.984	27.223	1 034.050	72
80	4.875	.2051	.00516	.0252	193.771	39.744	29.357	1 166.781	80
84	5.277	.1895	.00468	.0247	213.865	40.525	30.361	1 230.413	84
90	5.943	.1683	.00405	.0240	247.155	41.587	31.793	1 322.164	90
96	6.693	.1494	.00351	.0235	284.645	42.529	33.137	1 409.291	96
100	7.245	.1380	.00320	.0232	312.230	43.098	33.986	1 464.747	100
104	7.842	.1275	.00292	.0229	342.090	43.624	34.799	1 518.082	104
120	10.765	.0929	.00205	.0220	488.255	45.355	37.711	1 710.411	120
240	115.887	.00863	.00017	.0202	5 744.4	49.569	47.911	2 374.878	240
360	1 247.5	.00080	.00002	.0200	62 326.8	49.960	49.711	2 483.567	360
480	13 429.8	.00007		.0200	671 442.0	49.996	49.964	2 498.027	480

Compound interest factors

4%									4%
	Single Payment		**Uniform Payment Series**				**Uniform Gradient**		
	Compound Amount Factor	Present Worth Factor	Sinking Fund Factor	Capital Recovery Factor	Compound Amount Factor	Present Worth Factor	Gradient Uniform Series	Gradient Present Worth	
	Find F Given P	Find P Given F	Find A Given F	Find A Given P	Find F Given A	Find P Given A	Find A Given G	Find P Given G	
n	F/P	P/F	A/F	A/P	F/A	P/A	A/G	P/G	n
1	1.040	.9615	1.0000	1.0400	1.000	0.962	0	0	1
2	1.082	.9246	.4902	.5302	2.040	1.886	0.490	0.925	2
3	1.125	.8890	.3203	.3603	3.122	2.775	0.974	2.702	3
4	1.170	.8548	.2355	.2755	4.246	3.630	1.451	5.267	4
5	1.217	.8219	.1846	.2246	5.416	4.452	1.922	8.555	5
6	1.265	.7903	.1508	.1908	6.633	5.242	2.386	12.506	6
7	1.316	.7599	.1266	.1666	7.898	6.002	2.843	17.066	7
8	1.369	.7307	.1085	.1485	9.214	6.733	3.294	22.180	8
9	1.423	.7026	.0945	.1345	10.583	7.435	3.739	27.801	9
10	1.480	.6756	.0833	.1233	12.006	8.111	4.177	33.881	10
11	1.539	.6496	.0741	.1141	13.486	8.760	4.609	40.377	11
12	1.601	.6246	.0666	.1066	15.026	9.385	5.034	47.248	12
13	1.665	.6006	.0601	.1001	16.627	9.986	5.453	54.454	13
14	1.732	.5775	.0547	.0947	18.292	10.563	5.866	61.962	14
15	1.801	.5553	.0499	.0899	20.024	11.118	6.272	69.735	15
16	1.873	.5339	.0458	.0858	21.825	11.652	6.672	77.744	16
17	1.948	.5134	.0422	.0822	23.697	12.166	7.066	85.958	17
18	2.029	.4936	.0390	.0790	25.645	12.659	7.453	94.350	18
19	2.107	.4746	.0361	.0761	27.671	13.134	7.834	102.893	19
20	2.191	.4564	.0336	.0736	29.778	13.590	8.209	111.564	20
21	2.279	.4388	.0313	.0713	31.969	14.029	8.578	120.341	21
22	2.370	.4220	.0292	.0692	34.248	14.451	8.941	129.202	22
23	2.465	.4057	.0273	.0673	36.618	14.857	9.297	138.128	23
24	2.563	.3901	.0256	.0656	39.083	15.247	9.648	147.101	24
25	2.666	.3751	.0240	.0640	41.646	15.622	9.993	156.104	25
26	2.772	.3607	.0226	.0626	44.312	15.983	10.331	165.121	26
27	2.883	.3468	.0212	.0612	47.084	16.330	10.664	174.138	27
28	2.999	.3335	.0200	.0600	49.968	16.663	10.991	183.142	28
29	3.119	.3207	.0189	.0589	52.966	16.984	11.312	192.120	29
30	3.243	.3083	.0178	.0578	56.085	17.292	11.627	201.062	30
31	3.373	.2965	.0169	.0569	59.328	17.588	11.937	209.955	31
32	3.508	.2851	.0159	.0559	62.701	17.874	12.241	218.792	32
33	3.648	.2741	.0151	.0551	66.209	18.148	12.540	227.563	33
34	3.794	.2636	.0143	.0543	69.858	18.411	12.832	236.260	34
35	3.946	.2534	.0136	.0536	73.652	18.665	13.120	244.876	35
40	4.801	.2083	.0105	.0505	95.025	19.793	14.476	286.530	40
45	5.841	.1712	.00826	.0483	121.029	20.720	15.705	325.402	45
50	7.107	.1407	.00655	.0466	152.667	21.482	16.812	361.163	50
55	8.646	.1157	.00523	.0452	191.159	22.109	17.807	393.689	55
60	10.520	.0951	.00420	.0442	237.990	22.623	18.697	422.996	60
65	12.799	.0781	.00339	.0434	294.968	23.047	19.491	449.201	65
70	15.572	.0642	.00275	.0427	364.290	23.395	20.196	472.479	70
75	18.945	.0528	.00223	.0422	448.630	23.680	20.821	493.041	75
80	23.050	.0434	.00181	.0418	551.244	23.915	21.372	511.116	80
85	28.044	.0357	.00148	.0415	676.089	24.109	21.857	526.938	85
90	34.119	.0293	.00121	.0412	827.981	24.267	22.283	540.737	90
95	41.511	.0241	.00099	.0410	1 012.8	24.398	22.655	552.730	95
100	50.505	.0198	.00081	.0408	1 237.6	24.505	22.980	563.125	100

Compound interest factors

	Single Payment		Uniform Payment Series				Uniform Gradient		
	Compound Amount Factor	Present Worth Factor	Sinking Fund Factor	Capital Recovery Factor	Compound Amount Factor	Present Worth Factor	Gradient Uniform Series	Gradient Present Worth	
	Find F Given P F/P	Find P Given F P/F	Find A Given F A/F	Find A Given P A/P	Find F Given A F/A	Find P Given A P/A	Find A Given G A/G	Find P Given G P/G	
n									n
1	1.060	.943	1.0000	1.0600	1.000	0.943	0	0	1
2	1.124	.8900	.4854	.5454	2.060	1.833	0.485	0.890	2
3	1.191	.8396	.3141	.3741	3.184	2.673	0.961	2.569	3
4	1.262	.7921	.2286	.2886	4.375	3.465	1.427	4.945	4
5	1.338	.7473	.1774	.2374	5.637	4.212	1.884	7.934	5
6	1.419	.7050	.1434	.2034	6.975	4.917	2.330	11.459	6
7	1.504	.6651	.1191	.1791	8.394	5.582	2.768	15.450	7
8	1.594	.6274	.1010	.1610	9.897	6.210	3.195	19.841	8
9	1.689	.5919	.0870	.1470	11.491	6.802	3.613	24.577	9
10	1.791	.5584	.0759	.1359	13.181	7.360	4.022	29.602	10
11	1.898	.5268	.0668	.1268	14.972	7.887	4.421	34.870	11
12	2.012	.4970	.0593	.1193	16.870	8.384	4.811	40.337	12
13	2.133	.4688	.0530	.1130	18.882	8.853	5.192	45.963	13
14	2.261	.4423	.0476	.1076	21.015	9.295	5.564	51.713	14
15	2.397	.4173	.0430	.1030	23.276	9.712	5.926	57.554	15
16	2.540	.3936	.0390	.0990	25.672	10.106	6.279	63.459	16
17	2.693	.3714	.0354	.0954	28.213	10.477	6.624	69.401	17
18	2.854	.3503	.0324	.0924	30.906	10.828	6.960	75.357	18
19	3.026	.3305	.0296	.0896	33.760	11.158	7.287	81.306	19
20	3.207	.3118	.0272	.0872	36.786	11.470	7.605	87.230	20
21	3.400	.2942	.0250	.0850	39.993	11.764	7.915	93.113	21
22	3.604	.2775	.0230	.0830	43.392	12.042	8.217	98.941	22
23	3.820	.2618	.0213	.0813	46.996	12.303	8.510	104.700	23
24	4.049	.2470	.0197	.0797	50.815	12.550	8.795	110.381	24
25	4.292	.2330	.0182	.0782	54.864	12.783	9.072	115.973	25
26	4.549	.2198	.0169	.0769	59.156	13.003	9.341	121.468	26
27	4.822	.2074	.0157	.0757	63.706	13.211	9.603	126.860	27
28	5.112	.1956	.0146	.0746	68.528	13.406	9.857	132.142	28
29	5.418	.1846	.0136	.0736	73.640	13.591	10.103	137.309	29
30	5.743	.1741	.0126	.0726	79.058	13.765	10.342	142.359	30
31	6.088	.1643	.0118	.0718	84.801	13.929	10.574	147.286	31
32	6.453	.1550	.0110	.0710	90.890	14.084	10.799	152.090	32
33	6.841	.1462	.0103	.0703	97.343	14.230	11.017	156.768	33
34	7.251	.1379	.00960	.0696	104.184	14.368	11.228	161.319	34
35	7.686	.1301	.00897	.0690	111.435	11.498	11.432	165.743	35
40	10.286	.0972	.00646	.0665	154.762	15.046	12.359	185.957	40
45	13.765	.0727	.00470	.0647	212.743	15.456	13.141	203.109	45
50	18.420	.0543	.00344	.0634	290.335	15.762	13.796	217.457	50
55	24.650	.0406	.00254	.0625	394.171	15.991	14.341	229.322	55
60	32.988	.0303	.00188	.0619	533.126	16.161	14.791	239.043	60
65	44.145	.0227	.00139	.0614	719.080	16.289	15.160	246.945	65
70	59.076	.0169	.00103	.0610	967.928	16.385	15.461	253.327	70
75	79.057	.0126	.00077	.0608	1 300.9	16.456	15.706	258.453	75
80	105.796	.00945	.00057	.0606	1 746.6	16.509	15.903	262.549	80
85	141.578	.00706	.00043	.0604	2 343.0	16.549	16.062	265.810	85
90	189.464	.00528	.00032	.0603	3 141.1	16.579	16.189	268.395	90
95	253.545	.00394	.00024	.0602	4 209.1	16.601	16.290	270.437	95
100	339.300	.00295	.00018	.0602	5 638.3	16.618	16.371	272.047	100

Compound interest factors

	8%								**8%**
	Single Payment		**Uniform Payment Series**				**Uniform Gradient**		
	Compound Amount Factor	Present Worth Factor	Sinking Fund Factor	Capital Recovery Factor	Compound Amount Factor	Present Worth Factor	Gradient Uniform Series	Gradient Present Worth	
	Find F Given P	Find P Given F	Find A Given F	Find A Given P	Find F Given A	Find P Given A	Find A Given G	Find P Given G	
n	*F/P*	*P/F*	*A/F*	*A/P*	*F/A*	*P/A*	*A/G*	*P/G*	*n*
1	1.080	.9259	1.0000	1.0800	1.000	0.926	0	0	1
2	1.166	.8573	.4808	.5608	2.080	1.783	0.481	0.857	2
3	1.260	.7938	.3080	.3880	3.246	2.577	0.949	2.445	3
4	1.360	.7350	.2219	.3019	4.506	3.312	1.404	4.650	4
5	1.469	.6806	.1705	.2505	5.867	3.993	1.846	7.372	5
6	1.587	.6302	.1363	.2163	7.336	4.623	2.276	10.523	6
7	1.714	.5835	.1121	.1921	8.923	5.206	2.694	14.024	7
8	1.851	.5403	.0940	.1740	10.637	5.747	3.099	17.806	8
9	1.999	.5002	.0801	.1601	12.488	6.247	3.491	21.808	9
10	2.159	.4632	.0690	.1490	14.487	6.710	3.871	25.977	10
11	2.332	.4289	.0601	.1401	16.645	7.139	4.240	30.266	11
12	2.518	.3971	.0527	.1327	18.977	7.536	4.596	34.634	12
13	2.720	.3677	.0465	.1265	21.495	7.904	4.940	39.046	13
14	2.937	.3405	.0413	.1213	24.215	8.244	5.273	43.472	14
15	3.172	.3152	.0368	.1168	27.152	8.559	5.594	47.886	15
16	3.426	.2919	.0330	.1130	30.324	8.851	5.905	52.264	16
17	3.700	.2703	.0296	.1096	33.750	9.122	6.204	56.588	17
18	3.996	.2502	.0267	.1067	37.450	9.372	6.492	60.843	18
19	4.316	.2317	.0241	.1041	41.446	9.604	6.770	65.013	19
20	4.661	.2145	.0219	.1019	45.762	9.818	7.037	69.090	20
21	5.034	.1987	.0198	.0998	50.423	10.017	7.294	73.063	21
22	5.437	.1839	.0180	.0980	55.457	10.201	7.541	76.926	22
23	5.871	.1703	.0164	.0964	60.893	10.371	7.779	80.673	24
24	6.341	.1577	.0150	.0950	66.765	10.529	8.007	84.300	24
25	6.848	.1460	.0137	.0937	73.106	10.675	8.225	87.804	25
26	7.396	.1352	.0125	.0925	79.954	10.810	8.435	91.184	26
27	7.988	.1252	.0114	.0914	87.351	10.935	8.636	94.439	27
28	8.627	.1159	.0105	.0905	95.339	11.051	8.829	97.569	28
29	9.317	.1073	.00962	.0896	103.966	11.158	9.013	100.574	29
30	10.063	.0994	.00883	.0888	113.283	11.258	9.190	103.456	30
31	10.868	.0920	.00811	.0881	123.346	11.350	9.358	106.216	31
32	11.737	.0852	.00745	.0875	134.214	11.435	9.520	108.858	32
33	12.676	.0789	.00685	.0869	145.951	11.514	9.674	111.382	33
34	13.690	.0730	.00630	.0863	158.627	11.587	9.821	113.792	34
35	14.785	.0676	.00580	.0858	172.317	11.655	9.961	116.092	35
40	21.725	.0460	.00386	.0839	259.057	11.925	10.570	126.042	40
45	31.920	.0313	.00259	.0826	386.506	12.108	11.045	133.733	45
50	46.902	.0213	.00174	.0817	573.771	12.233	11.411	139.593	50
55	68.914	.0145	.00118	.0812	848.925	12.319	11.690	144.006	55
60	101.257	.00988	.00080	.0808	1 253.2	12.377	11.902	147.300	60
65	148.780	.00672	.00054	.0805	1 847.3	12.416	12.060	149.739	65
70	218.607	.00457	.00037	.0804	2 720.1	12.443	12.178	151.533	70
75	321.205	.00311	.00025	.0802	4 002.6	12.461	12.266	152.845	75
80	471.956	.00212	.00017	.0802	5 887.0	12.474	12.330	153.800	80
85	693.458	.00144	.00012	.0801	8 655.7	12.482	12.377	154.492	85
90	1 018.9	.00098	.00008	.0801	12 724.0	12.488	12.412	154.993	90
95	1 497.1	.00067	.00005	.0801	18 701.6	12.492	12.437	155.352	95
100	2 199.8	.00045	.00004	.0800	27 484.6	12.494	12.455	155.611	100

Compound interest factors

10%									10%
	Single Payment		**Uniform Payment Series**				**Uniform Gradient**		
	Compound Amount Factor	Present Worth Factor	Sinking Fund Factor	Capital Recovery Factor	Compound Amount Factor	Present Worth Factor	Gradient Uniform Series	Gradient Present Worth	
	Find F Given P	Find P Given F	Find A Given F	Find A Given P	Find F Given A	Find P Given A	Find A Given G	Find P Given G	
n	F/P	P/F	A/F	A/P	F/A	P/A	A/G	P/G	n
1	1.100	.9091	1.0000	1.1000	1.000	0.909	0	0	1
2	1.210	.8264	.4762	.5762	2.100	1.736	0.476	0.826	2
3	1.331	.7513	.3021	.4021	3.310	2.487	0.937	2.329	3
4	1.464	.6830	.2155	.3155	4.641	3.170	1.381	4.378	4
5	1.611	.6209	.1638	.2638	6.105	3.791	1.810	6.862	5
6	1.772	.5645	.1296	.2296	7.716	4.355	2.224	9.684	6
7	1.949	.5132	.1054	.2054	9.487	4.868	2.622	12.763	7
8	2.144	.4665	.0874	.1874	11.436	5.335	3.004	16.029	8
9	2.358	.4241	.0736	.1736	13.579	5.759	3.372	19.421	9
10	2.594	.3855	.0627	.1627	15.937	6.145	3.725	22.891	10
11	2.853	.3505	.0540	.1540	18.531	6.495	4.064	26.396	11
12	3.138	.3186	.0468	.1468	21.384	6.814	4.388	29.901	12
13	3.452	.2897	.0408	.1408	24.523	7.103	4.699	33.377	13
14	3.797	.2633	.0357	.1357	27.975	7.367	4.996	36.801	14
15	4.177	.2394	.0315	.1315	31.772	7.606	5.279	40.152	15
16	4.595	.2176	.0278	.1278	35.950	7.824	5.549	43.416	16
17	5.054	.1978	.0247	.1247	40.545	8.022	5.807	46.582	17
18	5.560	.1799	.0219	.1219	45.599	8.201	6.053	49.640	18
19	6.116	.1635	.0195	.1195	51.159	8.365	6.286	52.583	19
20	6.728	.1486	.0175	.1175	57.275	8.514	6.508	55.407	20
21	7.400	.1351	.0156	.1156	64.003	8.649	6.719	58.110	21
22	8.140	.1228	.0140	.1140	71.403	8.772	6.919	60.689	22
23	8.954	.1117	.0126	.1126	79.543	8.883	7.108	63.146	24
24	9.850	.1015	.0113	.1113	88.497	8.985	7.288	65.481	24
25	10.835	.0923	.0102	.1102	98.347	9.077	7.458	67.696	25
26	11.918	.0839	.00916	.1092	109.182	9.161	7.619	69.794	26
27	13.110	.0763	.00826	.1083	121.100	9.237	7.770	71.777	27
28	14.421	.0693	.00745	.1075	134.210	9.307	7.914	73.650	28
29	15.863	.0630	.00673	.1067	148.631	9.370	8.049	75.415	29
30	17.449	.0573	.00608	.1061	164.494	9.427	8.176	77.077	30
31	19.194	.0521	.00550	.1055	181.944	9.479	8.296	78.640	31
32	21.114	.0474	.00497	.1050	201.138	9.526	8.409	80.108	32
33	23.225	.0431	.00450	.1045	222.252	9.569	8.515	81.486	33
34	25.548	.0391	.00407	.1041	245.477	9.609	8.615	82.777	34
35	28.102	.0356	.00369	.1037	271.025	9.644	8.709	83.987	35
40	45.259	.0221	.00226	.1023	442.593	9.779	9.096	88.953	40
45	72.891	.0137	.00139	.1014	718.905	9.863	9.374	92.454	45
50	117.391	.00852	.00086	.1009	1 163.9	9.915	9.570	94.889	50
55	189.059	.00529	.00053	.1005	1 880.6	9.947	9.708	96.562	55
60	304.482	.00328	.00033	.1003	3 034.8	9.967	9.802	97.701	60
65	490.371	.00204	.00020	.1002	4 893.7	9.980	9.867	98.471	65
70	789.748	.00127	.00013	.1001	7 887.5	9.987	9.911	98.987	70
75	1 271.9	.00079	.00008	.1001	12 709.0	9.992	9.941	99.332	75
80	2 048.4	.00049	.00005	.1000	20 474.0	9.995	9.961	99.561	80
85	3 229.0	.00030	.00003	.1000	32 979.7	9.997	9.974	99.712	85
90	5 313.0	.00019	.00002	.1000	53 120.3	9.998	9.983	99.812	90
95	8 556.7	.00012	.00001	.1000	85 556.9	9.999	9.989	99.877	95
100	13 780.6	.00007	.00001	.1000	137 796.3	9.999	9.993	99.920	100

Compound interest factors

12%									12%
	Single Payment		Uniform Payment Series				Uniform Gradient		
	Compound Amount Factor	Present Worth Factor	Sinking Fund Factor	Capital Recovery Factor	Compound Amount Factor	Present Worth Factor	Gradient Uniform Series	Gradient Present Worth	
	Find F Given P	Find P Given F	Find A Given F	Find A Given P	Find F Given A	Find P Given A	Find A Given G	Find P Given G	
n	F/P	P/F	A/F	A/P	F/A	P/A	A/G	P/G	n
1	1.120	.8929	1.0000	1.1200	1.000	0.893	0	0	1
2	1.254	.7972	.4717	.5917	2.120	1.690	0.472	0.797	2
3	1.405	.7118	.2963	.4163	3.374	2.402	0.925	2.221	3
4	1.574	.6355	.2092	.3292	4.779	3.037	1.359	4.127	4
5	1.762	.5674	.1574	.2774	6.353	3.605	1.775	6.397	5
6	1.974	.5066	.1232	.2432	8.115	4.111	2.172	8.930	6
7	2.211	.4523	.0991	.2191	10.089	4.564	2.551	11.644	7
8	2.476	.4039	.0813	.2013	12.300	4.968	2.913	14.471	8
9	2.773	.3606	.0677	.1877	14.776	5.328	3.257	17.356	9
10	3.106	.3220	.0570	.1770	17.549	5.650	3.585	20.254	10
11	3.479	.2875	.0484	.1684	20.655	5.938	3.895	23.129	11
12	3.896	.2567	.0414	.1614	24.133	6.194	4.190	25.952	12
13	4.363	.2292	.0357	.1557	28.029	6.424	4.468	28.702	13
14	4.887	.2046	.0309	.1509	32.393	6.628	4.732	31.362	14
15	5.474	.1827	.0268	.1468	37.280	6.811	4.980	33.920	15
16	6.130	.1631	.0234	.1434	42.753	6.974	5.215	36.367	16
17	6.866	.1456	.0205	.1405	48.884	7.120	5.435	38.697	17
18	7.690	.1300	.0179	.1379	55.750	7.250	5.643	40.908	18
19	8.613	.1161	.0158	.1358	63.440	7.366	5.838	42.998	19
20	9.646	.1037	.0139	.1339	72.052	7.469	6.020	44.968	20
21	10.804	.0926	.0122	.1322	81.699	7.562	6.191	46.819	21
22	12.100	.0826	.0108	.1308	92.503	7.645	6.351	48.554	22
23	13.552	.0738	.00956	.1296	104.603	7.718	6.501	50.178	24
24	15.179	.0659	.00846	.1285	118.155	7.784	6.641	51.693	24
25	17.000	.0588	.00750	.1275	133.334	7.843	6.771	53.105	25
26	19.040	.0525	.00665	.1267	150.334	7.896	6.892	54.418	26
27	21.325	.0469	.00590	.1259	169.374	7.943	7.005	55.637	27
28	23.884	.0419	.00524	.1252	190.699	7.984	7.110	56.767	28
29	26.750	.0374	.00466	.1247	214.583	8.022	7.207	57.814	29
30	29.960	.0334	.00414	.1241	241.333	8.055	7.297	58.782	30
31	33.555	.0298	.00369	.1237	271.293	8.085	7.381	59.676	31
32	37.582	.0266	.00328	.1233	304.848	8.112	7.459	60.501	32
33	42.092	.0238	.00292	.1229	342.429	8.135	7.530	61.261	33
34	47.143	.0212	.00260	.1226	384.521	8.157	7.596	61.961	34
35	52.800	.0189	.00232	.1223	431.663	8.176	7.658	62.605	35
40	93.051	.0107	.00130	.1213	767.091	8.244	7.899	65.116	40
45	163.988	.00610	.00074	.1207	1 358.2	8.283	8.057	66.734	45
50	289.002	.00346	.00042	.1204	2 400.0	8.304	8.160	67.762	50
55	509.321	.00196	.00024	.1202	4 236.0	8.317	8.225	68.408	55
60	897.597	.00111	.00013	.1201	7 471.6	8.324	8.266	68.810	60
65	1 581.9	.00063	.00008	.1201	13 173.9	8.328	8.292	69.058	65
70	2 787.8	.00036	.00004	.1200	23 223.3	8.330	8.308	69.210	70
75	4 913.1	.00020	.00002	.1200	40 933.8	8.332	8.318	69.303	75
80	8 658.5	.00012	.00001	.1200	72 145.7	8.332	8.324	69.359	80
85	15 259.2	.00007	.00001	.1200	127 151.7	8.333	8.328	69.393	85
90	26 891.9	.00004		.1200	224 091.1	8.333	8.330	69.414	90
95	47 392.8	.00002		.1200	394 931.4	8.333	8.331	69.426	95
100	83 522.3	.00001		.1200	696 010.5	8.333	8.332	69.434	100

Compound interest factors

18%									18%
	Single Payment		Uniform Payment Series				Uniform Gradient		
	Compound Amount Factor	Present Worth Factor	Sinking Fund Factor	Capital Recovery Factor	Compound Amount Factor	Present Worth Factor	Gradient Uniform Series	Gradient Present Worth	
n	Find *F* Given *P* *F/P*	Find *P* Given *F* *P/F*	Find *A* Given *F* *A/F*	Find *A* Given *P* *A/P*	Find *F* Given *A* *F/A*	Find *P* Given *A* *P/A*	Find *A* Given *G* *A/G*	Find *P* Given *G* *P/G*	*n*
1	1.180	.8475	1.0000	1.1800	1.000	0.847	0	0	1
2	1.392	.7182	.4587	.6387	2.180	1.566	0.459	0.718	2
3	1.643	.6086	.2799	.4599	3.572	2.174	0.890	1.935	3
4	1.939	.5158	.1917	.3717	5.215	2.690	1.295	3.483	4
5	2.288	.4371	.1398	.3198	7.154	3.127	1.673	5.231	5
6	2.700	.3704	.1059	.2859	9.442	3.498	2.025	7.083	6
7	3.185	.3139	.0824	.2624	12.142	3.812	2.353	8.967	7
8	3.759	.2660	.0652	.2452	15.327	4.078	2.656	10.829	8
9	4.435	.2255	.0524	.2324	19.086	4.303	2.936	12.633	9
10	5.234	.1911	.0425	.2225	23.521	4.494	3.194	14.352	10
11	6.176	.1619	.0348	.2148	28.755	4.656	3.430	15.972	11
12	7.288	.1372	.0286	.2086	34.931	4.793	3.647	17.481	12
13	8.599	.1163	.0237	.2037	42.219	4.910	3.845	18.877	13
14	10.147	.0985	.0197	.1997	50.818	5.008	4.025	20.158	14
15	11.974	.0835	.0164	.1964	60.965	5.092	4.189	21.327	15
16	14.129	.0708	.0137	.1937	72.939	5.162	4.337	22.389	16
17	16.672	.0600	.0115	.1915	87.068	5.222	4.471	23.348	17
18	19.673	.0508	.00964	.1896	103.740	5.273	4.592	24.212	18
19	23.214	.0431	.00810	.1881	123.413	5.316	4.700	24.988	19
20	27.393	.0365	.00682	.1868	146.628	5.353	4.798	25.681	20
21	32.324	.0309	.00575	.1857	174.021	5.384	4.885	26.330	21
22	38.142	.0262	.00485	.1848	206.345	5.410	4.963	26.851	22
23	45.008	.0222	.00409	.1841	244.487	5.432	5.033	27.339	24
24	53.109	.0188	.00345	.1835	289.494	5.451	5.095	27.772	24
25	62.669	.0160	.00292	.1829	342.603	5.467	5.150	28.155	25
26	73.949	.0135	.00247	.1825	405.272	5.480	5.199	28.494	26
27	87.260	.0115	.00209	.1821	479.221	5.492	5.243	28.791	27
28	102.966	.00971	.00177	.1818	566.480	5.502	5.281	29.054	28
29	121.500	.00823	.00149	.1815	669.447	5.510	5.315	29.284	29
30	143.370	.00697	.00126	.1813	790.947	5.517	5.345	29.486	30
31	169.177	.00591	.00107	.1811	934.317	5.523	5.371	29.664	31
32	199.629	.00501	.00091	.1809	1 103.5	5.528	5.394	29.819	32
33	235.562	.00425	.00077	.1808	1 303.1	5.532	5.415	29.955	33
34	277.963	.00360	.00065	.1806	1 538.7	5.536	5.433	30.074	34
35	327.997	.00305	.00055	.1806	1 816.6	5.539	5.449	30.177	35
40	750.377	.00133	.00024	.1802	4 163.2	5.548	5.502	30.527	40
45	1 716.7	.00058	.00010	.1801	9 531.6	5.552	5.529	30.701	45
50	3 927.3	.00025	.00005	.1800	21 813.0	5.554	5.543	30.786	50
55	8 984.8	.00011	.00002	.1800	49 910.1	5.555	5.549	30.827	55
60	20 555.1	.00005	.00001	.1800	114 189.4	5.555	5.553	30.846	60
65	47 025.1	.00002		.1800	261 244.7	5.555	5.554	30.856	65
70	107 581.9	.00001		.1800	597 671.7	5.556	5.555	30.860	70
75	46 122.1				1 367 339.2	5.556	5.555	30.862	75
100	15 424 131.9				85 689 616.2	5.556	5.555	30.864	100

A

AASHTO
Geometric Design Guidelines, 448
PIEV time recommendations, 452
Guide for Design of Pavement
Structure, 540–545
Policy on Geometric Design
of Highways and Streets.
See Green Book, AASHTO
Acceleration coefficient, 131
Accident studies, 479–481
Activated carbon, in water treatment,
386–387
Activated sludge treatment, 402–405
processes, 403–404
settling problems, 404
Aeration, 378–380, 404–405
Aerators, types of, 379, 380
Aerobic digestion, 411
Aggregate content of concrete, 9–10
Air stripping, 379–380
Alkalinity, 375
Alternative hypothesis, 475
American Association of State Highway
and Transportation Officials.
See AASHTO
Anaerobic digestion, 410
Analysis procedures, seismic bridge
design, 137
Anchorage length. *See* Development
length
Anchorage of walls, 286–287
Anchored sheetpile retaining wall,
221–224
Anchor piles, 222
Aquifer, 360
confined, 360
piezometric head, 360–361
unconfined, 360
Asphalt Institute, 545
Atterberg limits, soil, 421
Average precipitation, determining, 344

B

Backwashing, 383
Band speed, 538
Base flow, 346
Base shear, 262–263, 273–274
Batch reactors, 395
Beams
composite, 62–64
concrete, 13–21

masonry, 100–101
steel, 49–56
wood, 84–89, 186
Bearing area factor, 83
Bearing capacity
of deep (pile) foundations, 440–443
of shallow foundations, 437–440
Bearing-type connections, 74
Bearing wall system, 259
Bernoulli equation, 322
Best Available Treatment (BAT),
wastewater, 395
Bicycles, 529
Biochemical oxygen demand (BOD),
375–376, 394
Biological denitrification, 407–408
Body waves, 236
Bolted connections, 74–78
Braced frame, 66–68, 285–286
reliability factor for, 275
Breakpoint chlorination, 412
Bridge structures
continuous composite structure, 180
during earthquakes, 137
highway loads, 108–130
prestressed concrete design,
149–173
and reinforced concrete design,
140–149
seismic design, 130–140
structural steel design, 173–185
timber structures, 185–187
Bubble aerators, 379
Buckets, 332
Building frame system, 259
Building types
classification of, 259–260
reliability factors for, 275
Bulking, 404
Buoyant force, 320

C

Caissons, 440
Cantilever retaining wall, 211–219
Cantilevered sheetpile wall, 220–221
Carbonate alkalinity, 375
Carmen-Kozeny equation, 383
Cascade aerators, 379
Cavitation, 331
Cement factor, 10
Centrifugal force, 124
Chemical oxygen demand (CODD), 394

Chlorination
by-products of, 387
wastewater, 412
water, 385–386
Civil engineering
laws regulating practice of, 2
professional examination for, 2, 4–8
Civil Engineering License Review,
contents of, 1
*Civil Engineering Problems and
Solutions*, contents of, 1
Civil Engineering Professional Engineer
Exam, 2
dates offered, 5
development of, 4
exam day preparations, 6
materials permitted in examination
room, 7–8
pre-preparation for, 5–6
procedure for taking, 5
structure of, 4–5
Cladding, 290
Clayey soils, consistency of, 420–421
Closed stirrups, 23
Coagulation, 381–382
Coarse aggregate, 9–10
Columns
concrete, 33–37
flexure and shear, locating, 189
masonry, 101
plastic hinging for, 139–140
timber, 187
wood, 89–93, 187
Combined compression and flexure, 183
Combined footing, 196–200
Compatibility torsion, 22
Complete-mixed reactors, 395
Components supported by structures,
289–293
Composite beams, 62–64
Composite bridges, 179
Composite construction, 164–169
Composite girders, 179–182
Compression members, 182–183
Compression sedimentation, 400
Compression wave, 236
Computer applications, 551
Concrete
mix proportions, 9–10
prestressed, 37–49
quality control, 10–11
yield, 10

Confidence bounds, 474–475
Confined aquifer, 360
Connections
  bolted, 74–78
  bridge structures, 184–185
  welded, 78–81
  in wood members, 94–98
Conservation laws
  of continuity, 322
  of energy, 322–327
  of momentum, 327–329
Conservation of mass, 322
Consolidation settlement
  calculation of, 428–429
  cause of, 427
  time rate of, 429–431
Constant acceleration, 453
Continuity, laws of, 322
Continuous composite structure, 180
Conversation laws, of energy,
    322–327
Cooper-Jacob method, 362
Creep, 158, 163
Crest vertical curve, 462
Critical damping, 245
Critical factored torsion, 23
Critical flow, 338
Curvature factor, 83

D

Damping. *See* Vibrations
Darcy's law, 359, 360, 422
Darcy-Weisbach equation, 323
Dead loads, 122
  seismic, 261
Dead-man anchor, 222
Decision rule, 476
Decision sight distance, 460
Density functions, 473
Denitrification. *See* Biological
    denitrification
Descriptive statistics, 470–471
Design category, seismic, 261
Design response spectra, 252–253
Design speed, 457
Design strength, 12–13, 140
Destabilization, 381
Development length, 27–33
De-watering, sludge, 411–412
Diaphragms, 93–94
  and collector elements, 281–283
  diaphragm load, 272
  seismic design of, 278
Diffuse aeration, 404
Dihaloacetonitriles (DHANs), 387
Direct storm runoff, 347
Discrete sedimentation, 397
Disinfection byproducts (DBPs), 387
Displacement, 110

Dissolved oxygen concentration
    in streams
  biochemical oxygen demand (BOD),
      375–376
  mixing, 377
  oxygen deficit, 376
  oxygen sag model, 377–378
  reoxygenation, 377
Dissolved solids, 393
Domestic wastewater flows, 391
Drag struts. *See* Collector elements
Drainage basin. *See* Watershed
Drinking water, treatment and testing
    of, 372–373
Driver performance, 452–453
Dual structural systems, 260
  reliability factors for, 277
Ductility, 258
Dynamic response of structures.
    See Structural dynamics
Dynamic wheel load effects, 120

E

Earthquakes, 236–242
  bridge structures during, 137
  effects of, 238–242
  intensity of, 237–238
  magnitude of, 236–237
Earthwork, 496–499
Eccentric footing, 205–209
Effective duration, 347
Effective stress, soil, 423–425
Efficient section, 337
Elastic seismic response coefficient,
    131–136
Elastic shortening, 162
Elastic theory, 125
Electroneutrality, 373
Energy, laws of, 322–327
Energy conservation, 322
Equilibrium relationships, 373–374
Equipment supported by structures,
    289–293
Equivalent pipe method of water
    distribution, 368
Equivalent single-axle load (ESAL) factor,
    539
Evapotranspiration, 344–345
Examinations, 2, 4–8
Exchange capacity, 385

F

Fatigue stress, 142
Federal-Aid Highway Act of
    1962, 449
Federal Water Pollution Control Act
    Amendments of 1972, 395
Filtration, 383, 384
Fine aggregate, 9–10

Finite element analysis, 122
Finite strip analysis, 122
Fire-retardant treatment of lumber, 83
Flat use factor, 82
Flexural compression, 182
Flocculant sedimentation, 398
Flocculation, 381–382
Flow net, 422–423
Fluoridation, water, 386
Footing design, 189–211
  combined footing, 196–200
  eccentric footing, 205–209
  footing with eccentric load, 209–211
  isolated column spread footing,
      189–196
  strap footing, 200–205
Form factor, 83
Foundations and retaining structures
    footing design, 189–211
  pile foundations, 224–225
  retaining wall, 211–224
  symbols and abbreviations, 236–237
Foundations
  deep (pile), 440–443
  shallow, bearing capacity of,
      437–440
  vertical stress under, 425–427
Francis turbines, 333
Free moisture content, 10
Fundamental period of structure,
    255–256
Fundamentals of Engineering
    (FE/EIT) Exam, 2

G

Gage pressure, 320
Geotechnical engineering
  clayey soils, consistency of, 420–421
  clayey soils, consolidation in,
      427–431
  deep (pile) foundations, 440–443
  effective stress, 423–425
  flow nets, 422–423
  lateral earth pressure, 432–437
  recommended references for further
      study, 443
  relative density, soils, 419–420
  shallow foundations, bearing
      capacity of, 437–440
  shear strength, soil, 432
  soil particle size, 416–417
  soil permeability, 421–422
  soil solids, specific gravity of, 417
  symbols and abbreviations, 444–445
  vertical stress under a foundation,
      425–427
  weight-volume relationship, soils,
      417–419
Girder distribution factor, 122

Girders
    composite, 179–182
    plate, 177–178
    rolled steel, 173–176
    splices, 184
Gradually varied flow, 339–341
Gravity retaining wall, 219–220
Green Book, AASHTO, 452
    at-grade intersections, 503–504
    collector roads, 500–501
    design vehicles, 453
    freeways, 502–503
    grade separations and interchanges, 504
    highway curves, 491
    horizontal alignment, 461
    local roads, 499–500
    overview, 499
    roadside design, 504–505
    rural arterials, 501
    sight distances, 460
    stopping distance, 455, 457
    traffic volume, 467
    urban arterials, 502
    vertical alignment, 463, 465
Grillage analysis, 123
Grit chambers, 397
Groundwater, 368, 378
Group load, 139

H

Haloacetic acids (HAAs), 387
Handbook of Statistical Methods for Engineers and Scientists, 470
Hankinson's formula, 94
Hardy Cross methodology, 368
Hazen-Williams formula, 324, 368
Head loss, 323, 383
Henry's Law, 373
Heterogeneous processes, wastewater treatment, 402
High-rate digestion, 411
Highway bridge loads
    distribution of re: bridge decks, 122–124
    impact allowance, 120–121
    influence lines, 109–120
    load combinations, 126–130
    methods for determining, 125–126
    special considerations, 124–125
    traffic lanes, 108–109
    vehicular loading, 108–109, 179
Highway Capacity Manual (HCM), 448
    basic concepts, 506
    basic freeway segments, 512–515
    bicycles, 529
    freeway facilities, 510–512
    multilane highways, 509–510, 511, 512

    overview, 505
    pedestrians, 528–529
    ramps and ramp functions, 519–522
    signalized intersections, 522–526
    traffic signal cycle lengths, 533–535
    two-lane highways, 506–509
    unsignalized intersections, 527–528
    urban streets, 522
    weaving areas, 516–519
Highway characteristics
    design speed, 457
    horizontal alignment, 461–462
    sight distance, 457–461
    traffic flow, 466–470
    vehicle characteristics, 453–456
    vertical alignment, 462–465
Highway curves, 485–495
Highway functions, 456–457
Highway route surveying, 484–519
    compound curves, 489–490
    concentric circular curves, 488
    deflection angles, 487
    earthwork, 496–499
    parabolic vertical curves, 490–493
    simple circular curves, 485–489
    slope staking, 495–496
    spiral curves, 493–495
    superelevation, 495
    tangent offsets, 487
Highway system characteristics
    driver performance, 452–453
    highway functions, classification of, 456–457
Homogeneous processes, wastewater treatment, 400–402
Horizontal alignment, highway, 461–462
Horton's infiltration equation, 345
HS20-44 truck, 113, 124
Hydraulic conductivity, 359
Hydraulic jump, 336–337
Hydraulics
    conservation laws, 322–329
    hydrostatics, 319–322
    open channel flow, 334–341
    pumps and turbines, 329–333
    of sewers, 392
    symbols and abbreviations, 342
Hydrograph, defined, 346
Hydrologic cycle, 343
Hydrologic routing
    Puls method of, 355–358
    purpose of, 355
    reservoir routing, 355–358
    river routing, 358–359
Hydrology
    defined, 343
    evapotranspiration, 344–345
    hydrologic routing, 355–359
    infiltration, 345–346

    peak discharge estimation, 352–355
    precipitation, 344
    watershed hydrographs, 346–351
    well hydraulics, 359–365
Hydrostatics, 319–322
Hypocenter of earthquake, 236
Hypothesis testing, 475–477

I

Impact allowance, 120–121
Importance classification, 136
Importance factor, seismic, 258
Impulse turbines, 332
Inclined piles, 227–231
Industrial wastewater flows, 392
Infiltration, 345–346
Infiltration rates, sewers, 392
Influence lines, 109–120
Institute of Transportation Engineers(ITE), 448
    Trip Generation, 482
Intensity-duration-frequency (IDF) plot, 352
Intensity factor, 352
Ion exchange process for water softening, 385
Isolated column footing, 189–196

L

Lagging method, 348
Lateral earth pressure
    active type, 434–435
    at-rest type, 432–434
    passive type, 435–437
Lateral load distribution, 122–124
Lateral-stability-of-beams factor, 81
Liquefaction of soil, 239–240
Liquid limit, soil, 421
Live loads, 109, 122
Load balancing, 47–49
Load combinations
    classifications, 128–129
    highway bridge loads, 126–130
    and seismic design, 139
Load duration factor, 82
Load factor design coefficient, 128
Load factor design method, 125–126
Loss coefficient, 325
Loss of prestress, 41–44
Low-rate digestion, 411
Love wave, 236

M

Manholes, 393
Manning equation, 324, 334–336
Manning roughness factor, 334, 335
Manual of Transportation Engineering Studies (ITE), 477
Manual on Uniform Traffic Control Devices, (MUTCD), 529–530

Masonry structures, 98–105
  beams, 100–101
  columns, 101
  quality control methods for, 98–99
  shear walls, 102–103
  stresses in, 99–100
  walls, 286–287
Mass functions, 473
Maximum bending moment, 226
Maxwell's reciprocal theorem, 109, 111, 120
Mean, 471
Measures of central tendency, 471
Mechanical aeration, 404
Mercalli intensity index, 237–238
Mix. *See* Concrete mix
Mixing
  in rivers and streams, 377
  for water treatment, 380–381
Modal (dynamic) analysis of structures, 248–252, 307–312
Mohr-Coulomb failure criteria, 432
Moment-resisting frames, 255, 259–260
  reliability factor for, 275–276
Momentum, laws of, 327–329
Müller-Breslau's principle, 109, 110, 113, 115
Multistory structures, 248–252, 264–273
Muskingum river routing method, 358

N

National Council of Examiners for Engineering and Surveying (NCEES)
  Fundamentals of Engineering (FE/EIT) Exam, 2
  Professional Engineer Exam, 2
  transportation engineering references, list of, 449
Natural period. *See* Fundamental period
Net positive suction head (NPSH), 330–331
Newton's second law of motion, 455
Nitrification, 394
Nitrogenous oxygen demand, 394
Nominal strength, 13
Nonbuilding structures, 291–292
Non-diffuse aeration, 404
Nonuniform acceleration, 454
Normal distribution, 472–473
Null hypothesis, 475

O

Occupancy categories (seismic use groups), 258
Open channel flow
  efficient section, 337
  gradually varied, 339–341
  hydraulic jump, 336–337
  Manning equation, 334–336
  specific energy, 337–339
  uniform flow, 334–336

Orthogonal seismic forces, 138
Orthotopic plate analysis, 122
Overdamping, 245–246
Overturning of structure, 267
Oxidation-reduction reactions, 373
Oxygen
  critical deficit, 378
  deficit, 376
  demand, wastewater, 394
  dissolved, 375–377
  sag model, 377–378
  saturation values, 376
  transfer, 404

P

P-Delta effects, 33, 70, 271
Parking, 548–549
Passing sight distance, 459
Pavement design, 538–548
  AASHTO design method, 540–545
  Asphalt Institute (AI) method, 545–547
  ESAL factor, 539
  flexible pavement, 542–543
Plate girders, 56–62
Portland Cement Association (PCA)
  method, 547–548
  rigid pavement, 544–545
  Pavement Design Methods, 448
Peak discharge estimation, 352–355
  rational method, 352
  SCS method, 352
Peak-hour factor (PHF), 467
Pedestrians, 528–529
Perennial streamflow, 346
Peripheral speed factor, 332
Phosphorus, removal of from wastewater, 408
PIEV (perception, identification, emotion, volition) time, 452
Piezometric head, 361
Pile cap, 231–232
  beam analogy method, 231
  truss analogy method, 231
Pile foundations
  pile cap design, 231–232
  pile group with inclined piles, 227–231
  pile group with vertical piles, 224–227
Plastic hinging, 139–140
Plastic limit, soil, 421
Plate girders, 56–62, 177–178
Plug-flow reactors, 396
Poisson distribution, 474
Policy on Geometric Design of Highways and Streets. See Green Book
Portland Cement Association, 547
Positive-displacement pumps, 329
Precipitation, 344
Precipitation gages, 344
Prestressed concrete, 37–49
  for bridges, 149–173
  composite construction, 164–169

continuous structures, 169–173
creep, 158, 163
elastic shortening, 162
load balancing, 47–49
loss of prestress, 41–44, 158–164
propped construction, 164, 166
relaxation, 158
serviceability limit stage, 38–39
serviceability limit state, 149–150
shear in, 46–47
shrinkage, 158, 163
transfer limit stage, 37
transfer limit state, 149
ultimate limit, 39
ultimate limit state in flexure, 150–152
ultimate limit state in shear, 152–157
unpropped construction, 164, 165
Prestressed continuous structures, 169–173
Prestressing force, application of, 169
Prestress, loss of, 158–164
Primary (P) wave, 236
Prism test method, 98
Probability and statistical methods, 471–474
Process analysis, wastewater treatment
  reaction types, 395
  reactor types, 395–397
  types of reactions, 395
Professional Engineer
  educational requirements for becoming, 2
  examinations required for, 2
  experience necessary to become, 2
Professional Engineer Exam, 2
Propeller turbines, 333
Puls method of hydrologic routing, 355–358
Pumps
  brake horsepower, 338
  efficiency, 329
  horsepower, 329
  net positive section head (NPSH), 330–331
  performance of, 330, 331–332
  similitude, 338
  specific speed, 330
  types of, 330

Q

Queueing models, 549–550
Quicksand, 424

R

Rankine active earth pressure coefficient, 434
Rankine passive earth pressure coefficient, 436
Rayleigh procedure, 255
Rayleigh wave, 236
Reaction turbines, 332

Reaeration coefficients, 377
Recommended references for further
    study
    geotechnical engineering, 443
    transportation engineering, 553
Reinforced concrete design
    for bridges, 140–149
    fatigue stress limits, 142
    serviceability requirements, 140–149
    strength design, principles of, 140
Reinforcement
    footing design and, 190
Relaxation, 158
Reliability factor, seismic, 275–277
Reoxygenation, 377
Repetitive member factor, 81
Reservoir routing, 355–358
Response modification coefficient,
    258–259
Response modification factors, 137–138
Response spectra. *See* Structural dynamics
Retaining walls
    anchored sheetpile retaining wall,
        221–224
    cantilevered sheetpile wall, 220–221
    cantilever retaining wall, 211–219
    gravity retaining wall, 219–220
    lateral earth pressure behind, 432–437
Reynolds number, 323
Richter magnitude scale, 236–237
Rising sludge, 404
River routing, 358–359
Rolled steel girders, 173–176
Rotating biological contactors, 405, 406
Runoff coefficients, table of, 353

S

Sag vertical curve, 462
Sanitary sewers, design flow, 393
S-curve method, 348
Secondary (S) wave, 236
Secondary treatment, 395
Sedimentation
    wastewater treatment, 397–400
    water treatment, 382–383
Seepage velocity, 360
Seismic concepts, 236–242
Seismic design
    acceleration coefficient, 131
    analysis procedures for, 137
    for bridges, 130–140
    column plastic hinges, 139–140
    design procedure, 130–131
    elastic seismic response coefficient,
        131–136
    importance classification, 136
    load combinations and, 139
    orthogonal forces, 138
    response modification factors,
        137–138

    seismic performance category, 136
    transverse seismic response, 134
Seismic isolation of structures, 312–315
Seismic load, 275
Seismic performance category, 136
Seismic response coefficient, 261–262
Selectivity, 385
Service load design coefficient, 127
Service load design method, 125
Serviceability, 149–150
Serviceability limit stage, 38–39
Sewers
    design flows, 393
    flow velocity, 393
    hydraulics of, 392
    infiltration rates for, 392
    manholes, 393
    velocities, minimum and maximum,
        393
Shear reinforcement of members,
    21–22, 24
    prestressed concrete, 46–47
Shear walls, 94
    masonry, 102–103
    reliability factors for, 276–277
    wood, 285
Shored construction, 63
Shrinkage, 158, 163
Shrinkage limit, soil, 421
Shuttering, 164, 167
Sight distance, 457–461
Sight triangles, 457
Simple harmonic motion, 243, 248
Size factor for lumber, 81
Slip-critical bolts, 74
Slope staking, 495–496
Sludge
    aerobic digestion, 411
    anaerobic digestion, 410
    concentrations, 409
    de-watering, 411–412
    high-rate digestion, 411
    low-rate digestion, 411
    stabilization, 410
    thickening, 410
    in wastewater treatment, 402–405,
        409–412
    in water treatment, 387–388
Snyder's method, 348
Soil anchor, 222
Soil liquefaction, 239–240
Soil particle size
    classification systems for, 416
    distribution of, 416–417
Soil profile, types, 131–132
Soils
    bearing capacity of shallow
        foundations, 437–440
    classification systems, 416
    consistency of, 420–421

    consolidation in, 427–431
    deep (pile) foundations, 440–442
    effective stress, 423–425
    flow nets, 422–423
    lateral earth pressure, 432–437
    liquid limit, 421
    liquid state, 420
    particle size, 416–417
    permeability, 421–422
    plasticity index, 421
    plastic limit, 421
    plastic state, 420
    relative density, 419–420
    shear strength, 432
    shrinkage limit, 421
    total stress, 423
    unconfined compression strength of,
        by consistency, 433
    vertical stress and, 425–427
    weight-volume relationships, 417–419
Soil solids, specific gravity of, 417
Solubility relationships, 375
Space mean speed, 467
Specific energy, 337–339
Speed of progression, 538
Speed studies, 479
Spray aerators, 379
Stabilization ponds, 405, 407
Standard error of the mean, 471
State boards of engineering, list of, 3–4
Static lateral force analysis, 303–307,
    313
Statistical methods
    confidence bounds, 474–475
    descriptive statistics, 470–471
    hypothesis testing, 475–477
    probability, 471–474
Steady flow, 360–361
Steel, structural
    beams, 49–56
    for bridges, 173–185
    composite girders in, 179–182
    connections in bridge structures,
        184–185
    compression members, 65–69, 182–183
    flexure and compression of, 69–73,
        182, 183
    girder splices, 184
    plate girders, 56–62, 177–178
    rolled steel girders in, 173–176
    shored construction, 63
    unshored construction, 63
Stiffeners, 178
Stokes' law, 382, 397
Stopping sight distance, 457
Storage constant, 361
Storm flow, 347
Storm return period, 393
Storm sewers, design flow, 393
Storm water flow, 392

Story drift, 267–268
Strap footing, 200–205
Strength design method. *See* Load factor design method Stress, 125
Structural dynamics
  code requirements, 253
  design response spectra, 252–253, 254–255
  fundamental period, 255–256
  modal analysis, 248–252, 307–312
  rigidity, 299–300
  site parameters, 253–254
  spectral response, 252
  stiffness, 301–302
  system parameters, 258–264
  torsion, 293–299
Structural systems. *See* Building types
Surface water, 368, 378
Surface waves, 236
Surveying, 484–499
Sway frame, 66–68
Symbols and abbreviations
  foundations and retaining structures, 236–237
  geotechnical engineering, 444–445
  hydraulics, 342
  for wastewater treatment, 413
  for water treatment, 388
Synthetic unitgraph, 348

T

Tension field action, 57–58
Theis equations, 362
Theoretical distributions
  Normal distribution, 472–473
  Poisson distribution, 474
Theoretical oxygen demand (ThOD), 394
Thickness Design: Asphalt Pavements for Streets and Highways, 545
Thickness Design for Concrete Highway and Street Pavement, 547
Thiessen average, 344
Timber structures. *See* Wood structures
  allowable stresses, 185–186
  beams, 186
  columns, 187
  glued laminated, 185
Time mean speed, 467
Title acts, 2
Torsion reinforcement of members, 22–24
Total alkalinity, 375
Total Kjeldahl nitrogen (TKN), 407
Total suspended solids (TSS), 395
Traffic control devices
  defined, 529
  Manual on Uniform Traffic Control Devices (MUTCD), 529–530
  traffic markings, 530

traffic signals, 532–538
traffic signs, 530–532
Traffic engineering. *See also* Transportation engineering
  defined, 448
Traffic engineering studies
  accident studies, 479–481
  speed studies, 479
  traffic impact studies, 482–484
  volume studies, 477–489
Traffic flow, 466–470
  density, 469
  headway, 468
  spacing, 468
  speed, 467
  volume, 466, 467
Traffic impact studies, 482–484
Traffic lanes, 108–109
Traffic signals
  change intervals, 535–537
  cycle lengths, 533–535
  signal coordination, 537–538
  timing, elements of, 532–533
  warrants for installation of, 532
Traffic signs
  categories of, 530
  guide signs, 531–532
  regulatory, 531
  warnings, 531
Transfer limit stage, 37
Transfer limit state, 149
Transmissibility, 361
Transmission line, 368
Transportation
  design, 449
  pavement design, 538–548
  planning process, 449, 450
  travel demand modeling, 451–452
Transportation alternatives, evaluating, 550–551
Transportation engineering
  AASHTO geometric design guidelines, 499–505
  bicycles, 529
  computer applications for, 551
  defined, 448
  earthwork, 496–499
  Highway Capacity Manual (HCM), 505–529
  highway characteristics and design control, 452–470
  highway surveying, 494–499
  parking, 548–549
  pavement design, 538–548
  pedestrians, 528–529
  planning process, 449–452
  queueing models, 549–550
  recommended references for further study, 553
  role of professional engineer in, 448

slope staking, 495–496
software, 551
statistical methods for, 470–477
traffic control devices, 532
traffic signals, 532–538
traffic studies related to, 477–494
transportation alternatives, evaluating, 550–551
Transportation planning process
  overview of, 449–451
  travel demand modeling phase, 451–452
Transportation system, activity system, 449
Transverse seismic response, 134
Travel demand modeling, 451–452
Trickling filters, 405, 406
Trihalomethanes (THMs), 387
Tsunami (tidal wave), 240
Turbines, 332–333
  specific speed, 332
Turbomachinery, similitude, 329–330
Turbomachinery, specific speed, 330

U

Ultimate BOD concentration, 376
Ultimate limit stage, 39
Ultimate limit state
  in flexure, prestressed concrete design, 150–152
  in shear, prestressed concrete design, 152–157
Unconfined aquifer, 360
Underdamping, 246–247
Unitgraph, 347
Unit hydrograph
  described, 347–348
  duration, change of, 348–351
Unit strength method, 99
Unshored construction, 63
Unsteady flow, 361–365
Use groups, seismic, 258

V

van't Hoff-Arrhenius relationship, 386
Vehicle characteristics, 453–456
  dynamic, 455–456
  kinematic, 453–454
  static, 453
Vehicular loading, 108–109
Vehicular loading, 179
Velocity gradient, 382
Vertical alignment, highway, 462–465
Vertical piles, 224–227
Vibrations
  damped, 245–248
  simple harmonic motion, 243
  undamped, 242–243
Volume factor for lumber, 81–82
Volume studies, 477–479

W

Walls, anchorage of, 286–287
Wastewater
  characteristics of, 393–394
  oxygen demand, 394
  typical composition of solids in, 393
Wastewater flows
  domestic flows, 391
  industrial flows, 392
  infiltration rates, 392
  peak daily and hourly rats of, 391
  storm water flow, 392
Wastewater treatment
  batch readers, 395
  biological processes, 400–409
  bulking, 404
  chlorination, 412
  complete-mix reactors, 395
  diffuse aerations, 404
  disinfection in, 411–412
  federal mandates for, 395
  heterogeneous reactions, 395
  homogeneous reactions, 395
  mechanical aeration, 404
  nitrification, 394
  non-diffuse aeration, 404
  oxygen demand, 394
  physical processes, 397–400
  plug-flow reactors, 396
  process analysis, 395–397
  rising sludge, 404
  rotating biological contactors, 405, 406
  sedimentation, 397–400
  sewer design, 392–393
  sludge de-watering, 411–412
  sludge treatment and disposal,
    402–405, 409–412
  stabilization ponds, 405, 407
  symbols and abbreviations for, 413
  trickling filters, 405, 406
  wastewater, characteristics of, 393–394
  wastewater flows, 391–392
Water distribution systems
  distribution network, 368–369
  fire flow, 371

pressure requirements, 368
pressure tests, 370–371
pumping requirements, 370
required flows, 368–369
transmission line, 368
water source, 367–368
water storage, 369–370
Water elevation, 367
Water filters, 383
Water pressure
  requirements for, 368
  tests of, 370–371
Water quality
  alkalinity, 375
  common elements and radicals, table of,
    371
  common inorganic chemicals for water
    treatment, 372
  determinants of, 368
  dissolved oxygen concentration in
    streams, 375–378
  fecal coliform contamination, 372
  ion balances and, 373
  microbiological measurements for,
    372–373
Water softening
  conversion factors for, 384
  ion exchange process for, 385
  with lime/soda ash, 383–385
Water source, 367–368
Water storage, 369–370
  fire requirements, 370
Water table, defined, 360
Water treatment
  activated carbon in, 386–387
  aeration, 378–380
  air stripping, 379–380
  backwashing, 383
  chlorination, 385–386
  chlorination by-products, 387
  coagulation, 381–382
  common half-reactions for, 374
  common inorganic chemicals
    for, 372
  common solubility products, 375

disinfection, 386
electroneutrality, 373
filter media, 383
filtration, 383, 384
flocculation, 381–382
fluoridation, 386
general chemistry concepts
  related to, 373–375
groundwater vs. surface water, 378
mixing, 380–381
oxidation, 380
power requirements, 381
recarbonation, 384
sedimentation, 382–383
sludge treatment, 387–388
softening, 383–385
symbols and abbreviations, 388
unit processes in, 378
Watershed hydrographs, 346–351
  unitgraph, 347–348
  unitgraph duration, change of, 348–351
Watershed, defined, 346
Webster's Method, traffic signal cycle
  lengths, 535
Welded connections, 78–81
Well hydraulics, 359–365
  Darcy's law, 359
  steady flow, 360–361
  unsteady flow, 360, 361–365
Westergaard's plate theory, 123
Wet service factor, 82
Wheel line load, 122
Wind loads, 124
Wood structures, 81–98
  adjustment factors for, 81–83
  allowable stresses, 185–186
  beams, 84–89, 186
  bridges, 185–187
  columns, 89–93, 187
  connections in, 94–98
  glued laminated, 185
  stresses in, 81–84

Z

Zone settling, 398–400